East Africa
a travel survival kit
Geoff Crowther
Hugh Finlay

East Africa - a travel survival kit
2nd edition

Published by
Lonely Planet Publications Pty Ltd (ACN 005 607 983)
PO Box 617, Hawthorn, Vic 3122, Australia
Lonely Planet Publications, Inc
PO Box 2001A, Berkeley, CA 94702, USA

Printed by
Colorcraft, Hong Kong

Photographs by
Rona Abbott (RA)
Steve Barnes (SB)
Geoff Crowther (GC)
Eliot Elifson (EE)
Greg Elms (GE)
Hugh Finlay (HF)
Greg Herriman (GH)
Phillip Pascoe (PP)
Tony Wheeler (TW)

Front Cover: Maasai Tribe (Guido Alberto Rossi), The Image Bank

Safari Guide illustrations by
Matt King

First Published
September 1987

This edition
June 1991

Although the author and publisher have tried to make the information as accurate as possible, they accept no responsibility for any loss, injury or inconvenience sustained by any person using this book.

National Library of Australia Cataloguing in Publication Data

Crowther, Geoff
East Africa, a travel survival kit.

2nd ed.
Includes index.
ISBN 0 86442 111 7.

1. Africa, East - Description and travel - 1981 -
Guide-books. I. Finlay, Hugh. II. Title.

916.7604

text © Geoff Crowther & Hugh Finlay 1991
maps © Lonely Planet 1991
photos © photographers as indicated 1991
illustrations © Lonely Planet 1991

Geoff Crowther

Hugh Finlay

Born in Yorkshire, England, Geoff took to his heels early on in the search for the miraculous. The lure of the unknown took him to Kabul, Kathmandu and Lamu in the days before the overland bus companies began digging up the dirt along the tracks of Africa. His experiences led him to join the now legendary but sadly defunct alternative information centre BIT in the late '60s.

In 1977, he wrote his first guide for Lonely Planet – *Africa on the cheap*. He has also written *South America on a shoestring*, travel survival kits to *Korea* and *East Africa* and has co-authored LP's guides to *India, Malaysia, Singapore & Brunei* and *Morocco, Algeria & Tunisia*.

Though they still travel extensively, Geoff and Hyung Pun have discovered the joys of working on over-drive with their two-year-old son, Ashley Choson. They recently moved out of a banana shed which had been home for 10 years into a new house that Geoff (et al) built in Korean/mediaeval English style in the Northern Rivers area of New South Wales. When not travelling or writing, Geoff devotes his time to landscaping, dreaming up impossible schemes, arguing with everyone in sight, pursuing noxious weeds and brewing Davidson's plum wine.

After deciding there must be more to life than a career in civil engineering, Hugh first took off around Australia in the mid '70s, working at everything from parking cars to prospecting for diamonds in the back blocks of South Australia, before heading further afield. He spent three years travelling and working in three continents, including a stint on an irrigation project in Saudi Arabia, before joining Lonely Planet in 1985.

Hugh has also written the Lonely Planet guide *Jordan & Syria – a travel survival kit*, co-authored *Morocco, Algeria & Tunisia – a travel survival kit*, and has contributed to others including *Africa on a shoestring* and *India – a travel survival kit*.

Hugh and Linda are now finding life considerably enlivened by their daughter, Ella. When not travelling and writing, Hugh spends a good deal of time striving for the perfect home-brew beer.

From the Authors

As with all LP guides, this book is partially the result of research undertaken by the authors and feedback from travellers carrying copies of *Africa on a shoestring* and/or *East Africa – a travel survival kit*. There's also been a significant amount of input from Kenyans in various parts of the country and expatriates who live and work there.

For this edition, Geoff and Hugh both

spent time in Kenya writing *Kenya - a travel survival kit*, which apperas in full in this edition of East Africa. Geoff also travelled extensively in Tanzania, updating that country, while Hugh tackled the loop out through Uganda, Rwanda, Burundi, eastern Zaire and western Tanzania.

Without listing them in any order of preference, Geoff would like to sincerely thank the following people for their help, encouragement, friendship, hospitality and constructive criticism:

George Pavlu of Brisbane, Australia, who accompanied me on the trip to Kenya, contributed to the research, maintained his usual highly explosive degree of humour, and amazed all and sundry by his prodigious consumption of Tusker lager. A professional photographer and film scriptwriter, George was particularly instrumental in introducing me to many facets of Kenya about which I might otherwise have remained ignorant.

Malcolm Gascoigne of Yare Safaris, Nairobi, Kenya, who enthusiastically allowed me to clutter up his office and rummage through his files, introduced me to a host of people in the safari business and never missed a recreational session at Buffalo Bill's or the Florida 2000. A good head and shoulders above anyone else I met in Kenya and twice the size of his girlfriend, Susan, Malcolm's humour was contagious, his consumption of Tusker lager at least the equal of George's, and his knowledge of East Africa extremely valuable. May your Maralal hostel, camel and gorilla safaris prosper!

Jeannette Wittermans, a computer graphics artist and painter of Den Haag, Holland, for her smile, her quiet good humour and resourcefulness on a somewhat disastrous safari to Lake Turkana and a much less problematical one to the Aberdares, Mt Kenya and Samburu.

Willem and Yoke Wittermans of Nairobi, Kenya, for their matchless hospitality on two separate occasions and for the loan of their camping equipment.

Rachel Newphry of Yelverton, UK, for putting us up on two seperate occasions and maintaining such a mellow atmosphere at her rented villa in Kilifi.

Lillian Nabude of Nairobi, Kenya, who rescued me from the intricacies of the Kenyan telephone system, introduced me to Buffalo Bill's, put me onto works of African literature I would never otherwise have encountered, saved me a small fortune through her command of several African languages, and expanded my consciousness with stories of growing up in Africa, being a refugee and an unmarried mother there, and for her laughter and determination in the face of adversity. I hope your son didn't wreck the bicycle too soon!

Mark Savage of Nairobi, Kenya, for the loan of his Land Rover, camping equipment, tools, and his irreplaceable large-scale maps of northern Kenya for a safari to Lake Turkana. Mark has been an enthusiastic member of the Mountain Club of Kenya for many years and is the co-author of the excellent *Mt Kenya Map & Guide* – the best available.

Sarah Zaituni Nakubulwa of Nairobi, Kenya, for her captivating smile and mellow friendship which made me think seriously about leaving.

Suh Ja-Lee (known to everyone as 'Sue'), the resolute and dedicated proprietor of Buffalo Bill's, Nairobi, for maintaining the best watering hole in Kenya. Hang in there, Sue!

Hugh would like to thank:

Peter Pickernell for his hospitality and introduction to the highs and lows of Nairobi's nightlife.

Tony Wheeler for additional information on Hyrax Hill, Rhino Rescue, Gedi and Lamu in Kenya.

Paul Weeks, a researcher at the Ruwenzori National Park in western Uganda, for the constant updates on the everchanging situation in the country, and valuable info on places we would otherwise have overlooked.

Sarah Hinde, a fellow traveller in western

Uganda who obligingly supplied me with update material for the Semliki Valley area of Uganda.

Andy Murphy and Julia McKelvey, friends from way back, who generously played host to both Geoff and myself in Dar es Salaam on separate occasions as we researched Tanzania.

Steve Barnes for supplying us with some excellent transparencies taken during his working stint in East Africa.

From the Publisher

This edition of East Africa was edited at the Lonely Planet office in Melbourne by Diana Saad and Gillian Cummings. Margaret Jung was responsible for design, cover design, illustrations, title pages and maps. Proofreading was done by Michelle de Kretser.

Special thanks to Matt King for the Safari Guide illustrations, and to Valerie Tellini for the Kenya maps, illustrations and Safari Guide design. Thanks also to Sharon Wertheim for compiling the index.

Warning & Request

Things change, prices go up, schedules change, good places go bad and bad ones go bankrupt – nothing stays the same. So, if you find things better or worse, recently opened or long since closed, please write and tell us about it.

Between editions, when it is possible, we'll publish the most interesting letters and important information in a Stop Press section at the back of the book.

All information is greatly appreciated, and the best letters will receive a free copy of the next edition or any Lonely Planet book of your choice.

Contents

TANZANIA

MAP LEGEND

BOUNDARIES

–·–·–·– ....International Boundaries
–··–··–··· ....Internal Boundaries
·–··–··–· ....National Parks, Reserves
– – – – – – ....The Equator
················· ....The Tropics

SYMBOLS

◉ NEW DELHI ....National Capital
● BOMBAY ....Provincial or State Capital
● Pune ....Major Town
• Barsi ....Minor Town
🏠 ....Post Office
✈ ....Airport
ℹ ....Tourist Information
◒ ....Bus Station, Terminal
66 ....Highway Route Number
☾ ☥ ☥ ....Mosque, Church, Cathedral
∴ ....Temple, Ruin or Archaeological Site
🏠 ....Hostel
✚ ....Hospital
☀ ....Lookout
⚑ ....Camping Areas
⌐ ....Picnic Areas
⌂ ....Hut or Chalet
▲ ....Mountain
┿┿┿ ....Railway Station
⟋⟋ ....Road Bridge
╫╫╫ ....Road Rail Bridge
⇉ ⇇
 ....Road Tunnel
↦) (↤ ....Railway Tunnel
↷↷↷ ....Escarpment or Cliff
⟋ ....Pass
~~~ ....Ancient or Historic Wall

ROUTES

——————— ....Major Roads and Highways
- - - - - - - - - ....Unsealed Major Roads
——————— ....Sealed Roads
- - - - - - - - - ....Unsealed Roads, Tracks
——————— ....City Streets
+++++++++++++ ....Railways
—●— ....Subways
················· ....Walking Tracks
- - - - - - - - - ....Ferry Routes
—++ —++ —++ ....Cable Car or Chair Lift

HYDROGRAPHIC FEATURES

〜〜〜 ....Rivers, Creeks
- - - - - - ....Intermittent Streams
▬ ⊂⊃ ....Lakes, Intermittent Lake
〜〜 ....Coast Line
∽ ....Spring
≱ ╫ ....Waterfall
⸽ ⸽ ....Swamps
▭ ....Salt Lakes, Reefs
▭ ....Glacier

OTHER FEATURES

▭ Parks, Gardens and National Parks
▭ ....Built Up Area
▭ Market Place and Pedestrian Mall
▭ ....Plaza and Town Square
▭ ....Cemetery

Note: Not all the symbols displayed above will necessarily appear in this book

Introduction

If your vision of Africa is of elephants crossing the plain below Kilimanjaro, an Arab dhow sailing into Zanzibar, a million pink flamingos, Maasai tribespeople guarding their cattle – East Africa is where this vision becomes reality.

This book covers a small group of countries of absorbing interest and diversity. Whatever your interests, East Africa has plenty to see, experience and consider.

Kenya and Tanzania are the heart of African safariland. Some of the most famous reserves are found here and in a trip to these countries you will probably see everything from rhinos to lions, hippos to baboons, wildebeest to flamingos. Safaris are an experience in themselves, but some of the reserves are also spectacular – such as the Ngorongoro park in Tanzania which is in the crater of a colossal extinct volcano or the Amboseli park in Kenya which has Mt Kilimanjaro as a spectacular backdrop.

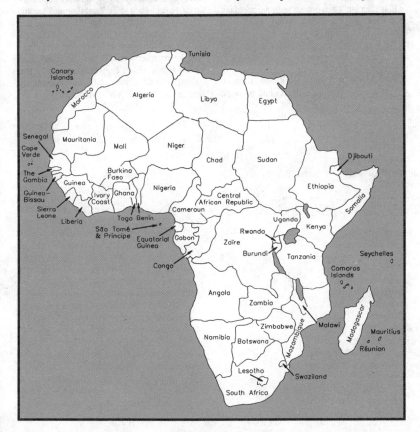

13

The reserves of Kenya and Tanzania are the region's best known natural attractions but far from the only ones. The superb Ruwenzori Mountains sprawl across the border between Uganda and Zaïre, further south are some of the most active volcanoes in Africa, particularly in the Parc National des Volcans in Rwanda. And Rwanda is, of course, famous for its scattered groups of mountain gorillas which you can also visit. Scuba divers will find plenty to interest them along the coast and around the offshore islands, while other visitors may find lazing on the beach and collecting a suntan quite enough exercise.

If lazing isn't a word in your vocabulary then East Africa offers some wonderful mountains to climb. If you're fit an assault on Mt Kenya or, best of all, snow capped Mt Kilimanjaro, the highest mountain in Africa, is within your reach.

East Africa isn't just wildlife and scenery – there are also people, cultures and politics.

Politically the region offers as wide a span of Africa's problems and aspirations as you could ask for. At one extreme there's Kenya where Africa really works and where stability and progress have been the norm – a situation very different from so many other African nations. Tanzania illustrates where the best of African intentions can go disastrously awry while Zaïre is one of the best examples of pure, untrammelled greed. Burundi is a painful example of the horrors of tribal animosity, and while Idi Amin may be gone Uganda has far from forgotten him.

The cultures and people of the region are equally interesting. Along the coast, and particularly on islands like Zanzibar and Lamu, you can observe the strong influence of the Arabs who came first as traders and later as slavers and remained in the region for centuries. Everywhere you'll see the many and varied tribes of the region, particularly the colourful and strong-minded Maasai of Kenya. Go there, it's a wonderful region.

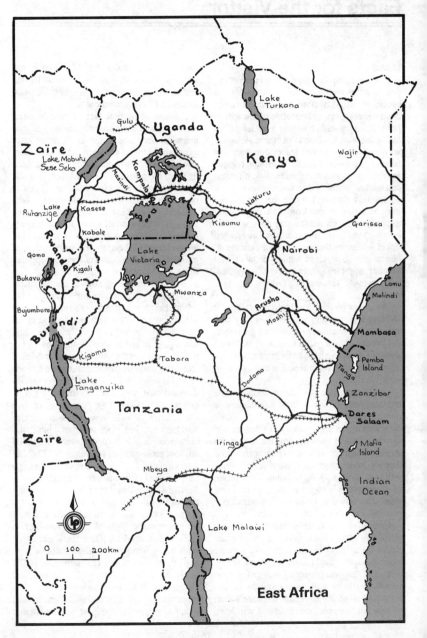

East Africa

Facts for the Visitor

VISAS

A visa is a stamp in your passport permitting you to enter a country and stay there for a specified period of time. Visas are obtained from the embassy or consulate of the appropriate country either before you set off or along the way. It's best to get them along the way, especially if your travel plans are not fixed, but keep your ear to the ground regarding the best places to get them. Two different consulates of the same country may have completely different requirements; the fee may be different, one consulate might want to see how much money you have whereas another won't, one might demand an onward ticket while another won't even mention it, one might issue visas while you wait, and another might insist on referring the application back to the capital (which can take weeks).

Whatever you do, don't turn up at a border without a visa unless you're absolutely sure visas aren't necessary or you can get one at the border. If you get this wrong you'll find yourself tramping back to the nearest consulate and, in some countries, this can be a long way.

You'll occasionally come across some tedious, petty-power freak at an embassy or consulate whose sole pleasure in life appears to be making as big a nuisance of themselves as possible and causing you the maximum amount of delay. If you bite the carrot and display your anger or frustration, the visa will take twice as long to issue. There's one of these creeps born every minute but if you want that visa don't display any emotion – pretend you have all day to waste.

Consular officials sometimes refuse point-blank to stamp a visa on anything other than a completely blank page, so make sure your passport has plenty of them. Zaïre demands that you produce a letter of recommendation from your own embassy before they will issue a visa. Embassies are aware of this bureaucratic nonsense and will have form letters available for the purpose, but you may have to pay for these – British embassies charge almost as much for these letters as the visa itself costs.

Another important fact to bear in mind about visas is their sheer cost. Very few of them are free and some are outrageously expensive. Unless you carry a passport from one of the Commonwealth or European Economic Community countries, you'll probably need quite a few visas, and if you're on a tight budget the cost of them can make a hole in your pocket. It's a good idea to make a rough calculation of what the visa fees are going to amount to before you set off, and allow for it. Make sure you have plenty of passport size photographs for visa applications – 24 should be sufficient.

Some countries, it seems, are so suspicious about your motives for wanting to pay a visit that they demand you have a ticket out of the country before they will let you in. So long as you intend to leave from the same place you arrived at, there is no problem, but if you want to enter at one point and leave from another, this can sometimes be a headache. Fortunately, few East African countries demand that you have an onward ticket, although I was asked for one when I applied for a Zaïre visa. If they do insist on you having one, but you want to spend the minimum possible (and have it refunded without problems) try buying an MCO (Miscellaneous Charges Order) from an international airline for, say, US$100.

An MCO is similar to having a deposit account with an airline and the beauty of it is that it looks like an airline ticket, but it isn't for any specific flight. It can be refunded in full or exchanged for a specific flight either with the airline you bought it from or with any other airline which is a member of IATA. Most consular and immigration officials accept an MCO as an onward ticket. The other way to get around having an onward ticket is to buy the cheapest ticket available out of the country and then get it refunded later on. If you do this, make sure you can get a refund without having to wait months. Don't forget to ask specifically where it can be refunded since some airlines will only refund tickets at the office where you bought them; some only at their head office.

Most East African countries take a strong line against South Africa to the point of refusing entry to nationals of that country. They are also not keen on people whose passports show that they have visited South Africa. If that's the case they may refuse to issue you with a visa or refuse entry when you get to the border. Tanzania is inordinately keen about this, so if your passport has South African stamps in it or even the stamps of border crossing points to or from Botswana, Zimbabwe, Lesotho or Swaziland, you'll have to get rid of it and have a new one issued.

PAPERWORK

The essential documents are a passport and an International Vaccination Card. If you already have a passport, make sure it's valid for a reasonably long period of time and has plenty of blank pages on which stamp-happy immigration officials can do their stuff. If it's half full and you're going to need a lot of visas, then get a new one before you set off. This way you won't have to waste time hanging around in a capital city somewhere while your embassy issues you with a new one. In some countries there is the option of getting a normal sized passport or a 'jumbo' passport. Get the larger one. US nationals can have extension pages stapled into otherwise full passports at any of their embassies.

Whoever supplies you with your vaccinations will provide you with an International Vaccination Card and the necessary stamps.

If you're taking your own transport or you're thinking of hiring a vehicle to tour certain national parks, get hold of an International Driving Permit before you set off. Any national motoring organisation will fix you up with this, provided you have a valid driving licence for your own country. The cost of these permits is generally about US$5.

An International Student Identity Card or the graduate equivalent is also very useful in many places and can save you a considerable amount of money. Some of the concessions available include airline tickets, train and riverboat fares and reduced entry charges to museums and archaeological sites. If you're not strictly entitled to a student card, it's often possible to get one if you book a flight with one of the 'bucket shop' ticket agencies that have proliferated in certain European and North American cities. The deal usually is that you buy an airline ticket and they'll provide you with a student card. Another possibility is to buy a fake card (average price around US$10). There always seems to be someone selling these wherever travellers collect in numbers, but examine them carefully before buying, as they vary a great deal in quality.

Another useful thing to have is a Youth Hostel Association (YHA) membership card, particularly for Kenya. Some of the hostels will allow you to stay without a card but others will insist you join up first. Concessions which are possible with an International Student Identity Card or a YHA membership card are mentioned in the appropriate chapters.

MONEY

It doesn't matter which currency you take if you only intend to use banks when you change it. If, however, you want to take advantage of the black market (usually cash only) then take a well-known currency – US dollars, UK pounds, French francs, German marks – otherwise no-one will know what the current exchange rate is or they'll offer you a very poor rate.

Travellers' Cheques & Cash

For maximum flexibility, take the larger slice of your money in travellers' cheques and the rest in cash – say up to US$500. American Express, Thomas Cook and Citibank cheques are the most widely used and their offices generally offer instant replacement in the event of loss or theft. Keep a record of the cheque numbers and the original bill of sale for the cheques in a safe place in case you lose them. Replacement is a whole lot quicker if you can produce this information. Even so, if you don't look clean and tidy, or they don't believe your story for some reason or another, replacement can take time since quite a few travellers have sold their cheques on the black market, or simply pretended to lose them, and then demanded a replacement set. This is particularly so with American Express cheques. You should avoid buying cheques from small banks which only have a few overseas branches, as you'll find them very difficult, if not impossible, to change in many places.

Make sure you buy a good range of denominations when you get the cheques – US$10, U$20, U$50 and US$100 – so you don't get stuck changing large denomination bills for short stays or for final expenses. Plenty of small cheques are essential for Tanzania if you don't want to end up with a mountain of local currency, since all accommodation over US$10 and all national park fees have to be paid in hard currency. This particularly thorny issue is discussed in greater detail in the Tanzania chapter and you're well advised to read it *before* you leave home.

Having a credit card and a personal chequebook is another excellent way of having funds to hand. With these you can generally withdraw up to US$150 in cash per day and up to US$1000 in travellers' cheques per week from any branch of the credit card company or participating banks. This virtually dispenses with the need to buy travellers' cheques in your home country though you should take some since you can only get that cash or travellers' cheques during banking hours.

With a VISA card, for example, any main branch of Barclays Bank will let you have the local equivalent of US$150 per day without contacting your bank. For any amount over US$150, they'll first telex your bank before giving you the money. You don't need a cheque account to do this. Similarly,

American Express offices will issue US dollar travellers' cheques up to virtually any amount against one of their cards and a personal cheque drawn on your bank. If you don't have a personal chequebook but you do have a credit card, there's usually no problem. Simply present your card and ask for a counter cheque. This is fine even if you don't have an actual cheque account but have, say, a deposit account. What will happen in that case is that the bank will bounce the cheque which you signed for American Express and American Express will send you a demand for the money or bill your American Express account. If you're on a long trip then you'll obviously have to arrange for someone back home to pay the monthly accounts.

National Westminster Eurocheque Cards are another possibility. With one of these and a personal cheque, you can withdraw up to UK£100 a day at selected banks in Kenya, Tanzania and Uganda. Nominated banks in Kenya are those of the Kenya Commercial Bank at both Kencom House and Kipande House in Nairobi, at Treasury Square in Mombasa, and in Kisumu and Nakuru; the National Bank of Kenya's main branches in Nairobi and Mombasa; and the Standard Chartered Bank's main branches in Nairobi and Mombasa. In Tanzania, it's the head office of the National Bank of Commerce in Dar es Salaam; and in Uganda it's either the head office of the Standard Chartered Bank or the Uganda Commercial Bank in Kampala.

Credit Cards

American Express, Diner's Club, Visa and MasterCard are all widely recognised credit cards which can be used to pay for accommodation, food, airline tickets, books, clothing and other services in most large towns, especially in Kenya (although less so in neighbouring countries). Even Kenyan Railways accepts VISA cards for railway tickets.

Credit cards also have their uses when 'sufficient funds' are demanded by immigration officials before they will allow you to enter a country. It's generally accepted that you have 'sufficient funds' if you have a credit card.

Money Transfers

If you run out of money while you're abroad and need more, ask your bank back home to send a draft to you (assuming you have money back home to send!). Make sure you specify the city and the bank branch. Transferred by cable or telex money should reach you within a few days. If you correspond by mail the process will take at least two weeks, often longer. Remember that some countries will only give you your money in local currency, and others will let you have it in US dollars or another hard currency. Find out what is possible before you request a transfer. You could lose a fair amount of money if there's an appreciable difference between the official and unofficial exchange rates (or be totally up shit creek in Tanzania). Kenya is probably the best place to transact this sort of business.

The Black Market

You cannot always change travellers' cheques in small places or, of course, when the banks are closed (though you don't need to in Tanzania when paying for accommodation costing over US$10 or national park entry fees as travellers' cheques are acceptable). This is one reason why you should bring some cash with you, but the major reason is that it allows you to take advantage of any street rate of exchange (black market). Sometimes you can change travellers' cheques on the black market but this isn't always the case.

There are some countries in East Africa where you can get considerably more for your hard currency on the streets than you can in the banks. In Uganda the difference is little short of spectacular; less so in Tanzania and Zaïre and, much of the time, hardly worth it in Kenya. Where the difference is large you are going to find life expensive if you change at the banks but relatively cheap otherwise.

The black market is a thorny issue. Some people regard it as morally reprehensible and a vocal minority as nothing short of economic sabotage. It's certainly predatory but some countries overvalue their currency to a degree that is totally Mickey Mouse. Several years ago, Tanzania was the biggest 'offender' in this respect with the black market rate some 10 times higher than the bank rate. Since then the IMF and World Bank have forced some common sense into their monetary policy so that now it's only half as much again. It has not been a popular decision (as articles in the national newspapers demonstrate) and has made life hard for a lot of people but it was necessary to rescue the economy from total bankruptcy and to secure urgent loans. Uganda, on the other hand, is still trying to pretend otherwise and Zaïre is heading much the same way.

You'll have to make up your own mind about which side of the moral fence you stand on but one thing is for sure – you won't meet many budget travellers who don't utilise the black market where there's a significant difference between the bank and street rates. And you'll meet plenty of officials – some of them in remarkable positions of authority and in full view of everyone around – who will make it plain that they're interested in swapping local currency for hard cash.

This doesn't mean that you should be blasé and incautious. Quite the opposite. There are draconian laws in most countries about changing money unofficially. Discretion is the name of the game. And the countries where there is a large disparity between the bank and street rates are not lacking in imagination either. Tanzania, for instance, demands that every tourist changes US$50 or the equivalent into Tanzanian shillings on entry and pays for all national park fees, any accommodation over US$10 and all domestic airline tickets in hard currency. Uganda demands that every tourist changes US$150 or the equivalent into Ugandan shillings on entry, though they are much slacker than Tanzania in enforcing this and there are multiple ways around the requirement.

If you're setting off from Europe, the

Crédit Suisse bank at the Zürich airport will change paper money from any country in the world at very reasonable rates and they will also issue paper money in all currencies. Their rates for some currencies are about the same as the black market rate.

When changing on the black market, have the exact amount you want to change available – avoid pulling out large wads of notes. Be very wary about sleight of hand and envelope tricks. Insist on personally counting out the notes that are handed to you. Don't let anyone do this for you and don't hand over your money until you're satisfied you have the exact amount agreed to. If at any point you hand the notes back to the dealer (because of some discrepancy, for example) count them out again when they're handed back to you, because if you don't you'll probably find that all but the smallest notes have been removed. Some operators are so sharp they'd have the shoes off your feet while you were tying up the laces. Don't allow yourself to be distracted by supposed alarms like 'police' and 'danger.' In many countries you won't have to take part in this sort of minidrama, as money is generally changed in certain shops or with merchants at a market, so it's a much more leisurely process. Indeed, in many places it's very unwise to change on the street as you may be set up by a police undercover agent.

Treat all the official and black market rates given in this book as a guide only. They are correct at the time the book goes to press, but coups, countries defaulting on their external debt repayments, devaluations and IMF strictures can alter the picture dramatically. You must check out all prices and exchange rates with your fellow travellers along the way. They are your best source of current information.

Currency Forms

Kenya, Tanzania and Uganda issue currency declaration forms on arrival. On these forms you must write down how much cash and travellers' cheques you are bringing into the country. Tanzania checks these very thoroughly when you leave at its southern borders with Zambia and Malawi and if there are any discrepancies you're in the soup. At the northern borders they apparently couldn't care less. Kenya certainly collects them when you leave but they are not scrutinised. When leaving Uganda your form will be collected and given no more than a cursory check. No currency declaration forms are issued when entering Zaïre, Rwanda or Burundi.

If you intend using the black market you must declare less than you are bringing in and hide the excess. More details about the forms can be found in the appropriate country chapters.

Money Safety

There is no 'safe' way to keep your money while you're travelling, but the best place is in contact with your skin where, hopefully, you'll be aware of an alien hand before your money disappears. One method is to wear a leather pouch hung around your neck and kept under a shirt or dress. If you do this, incorporate a length of old guitar string into the thong which goes around your neck (the D string should be thick enough). Many thieves carry scissors but few carry wire cutters.

Another method is to sew an invisible pocket inside the front of your trousers. Some travellers prefer a money belt. The trouble with money belts is that they're obvious and, if you're doing business, you have to open up the whole thing to get out cash unless you've stashed sufficient money elsewhere to pay for the transaction. Never assume no-one else is watching!

Ideally your passport should be in the same place that you keep your money, but this isn't always possible as some are either too thick or too stiff. Wherever you decide to put your money, it's a good idea to enclose it in a plastic bag. Under a hot sun that pouch or pocket will get soaked with sweat – repeatedly – and your cash or cheques will end up looking like they've been through the laundry.

And one last thought: Know where Nairobi taxi drivers keep their money? All over their body! Shoes, pockets, underpants – you name it.

COSTS

It's very difficult to predict what a trip to Africa is going to cost since so many factors are involved: how fast you want to travel, what degree of comfort you consider to be acceptable, how much sightseeing you want to do, whether you intend to hire a vehicle to explore a game park or rely on other tourists to give you a lift, whether you're travelling alone or in a group, whether you will be changing money on the street or in banks, and a host of other things.

There's only one thing which remains the same in Africa and that's the pace of change – it's fast. Inflation and devaluations can wreak havoc with your travel plans if you're on a very tight budget. You should budget for at least US$10 per day in the cheaper countries and US$20 per day in the more expensive ones. This should cover the cost of very basic accommodation, food in local cafés and the cheapest possible transport. It won't include the cost of getting to Africa, safaris in game parks or major purchases in markets. On the other hand, if you stay in one place for a while and cook your own food, you can reduce daily costs considerably since you won't be paying for transport and you'll get a better deal on the cost of accommodation.

Bargaining

Many purchases involve some degree of bargaining. This is always the case with things bought from a market, street stall or craft shop. Bargaining may also be necessary for hotels and transport in some places, although these are often fairly standard and you won't be paying any more than the local people. Food and drink bought at restaurants don't usually involve any bargaining. The prices will be written on the menu.

Where bargaining is the name of the game, commodities are looked on as being worth what their owners can get for them. The concept of a fixed price would invoke laughter. If you cop out and pay the first price

asked, you'll not only be considered a halfwit but you'll be doing your fellow travellers a disservice since this will create the impression that all travellers are equally stupid and are willing to pay outrageous prices. You are expected to bargain, it's part of the fun of going to Africa. All the same, no matter how good you are at it, you'll never get things as cheaply as local people do. To traders and hotel and café owners you represent wealth – whatever your appearance.

In most cases bargaining is conducted in a friendly, sometimes exaggeratingly extrovert manner, although there are occasions when it degenerates into a bleak exchange of numbers and leaden handshakes. Decide what you want to pay or what others have told you they've paid, and start off at a price at least 50% lower than this. The seller will inevitably start off at a higher price, sometimes up to 100% higher, than they are prepared to accept. This way you can both end up appearing to be generous. There will be times when you simply cannot get a shopkeeper to lower the prices to anywhere near what you know the product should be selling for. This probably means that a lot of tourists are passing through and if you don't pay those outrageous prices, some mug will. Don't lose your temper bargaining. There's no need to. You can always walk away and come back another day or go to a different shop. It's just theatre.

POST
Receiving Mail

When sending letters, try to use aerograms (air letters) rather than ordinary letters. If you send stamped letters it's sometimes necessary to ensure the stamps are franked in front of you. There's a chance that unfranked stamps will be steamed off, resold and the letter thrown away. Having said that, I've posted ordinary letters, parcels and postcards back home from all the countries which are covered in this book and all of them have arrived – and not all of them were franked in front of me.

There's little point in having any letter sent by Express Delivery (called Special

Delivery in the UK), as they won't get there any quicker, on average, than an air letter.

Receiving Mail

Have letters sent to you c/o Poste Restante, GPO, in whatever city or town you will be passing through. Alternatively, you can use the mail holding service operated by American Express offices and their agents if you have their cheques or one of their credit cards. Most embassies no longer hold mail and will forward it to the nearest poste restante. Plan ahead – it can take up to two weeks for a letter to arrive even in capital cities and it sometimes takes much longer in smaller places.

The majority of postes restantes are pretty reliable though there are exceptions. Mail is generally held for four weeks – sometimes more, sometimes less – after which it is returned to sender. The service is free in most places but in others, particularly ex-Belgian colonies, there is a small charge for each

letter collected. As a rule you need your passport as proof of identity. In large places where there's a lot of traffic the letters are generally sorted into alphabetical order, but in smaller places they may all be lumped together in the one box. Sometimes you're allowed to sort through them yourself; sometimes a post office employee will do the sorting for you.

If you're not receiving expected letters, ask them to check under every conceivable combination of your given name, surname, any other initials and even under 'M' (for Mr, Ms, Miss, Mrs). This sort of confusion isn't as widespread as many people believe, though most travellers have an improbable story to tell about it. If there is confusion, it's generally because of bad handwriting on the envelope or language difficulties. If you want to make absolutely sure that the fault won't be yours, have your friends address letters with your surname in block letters and underline it.

Avoid sending currency notes through the post. They'll often be stolen by post office employees no matter how cleverly you disguise the contents. There are all sorts of ways of finding out whether a letter is worth opening up. Still, some people do successfully get cash sent through the mail.

HEALTH

Travel health depends on your pre-departure preparations, your day-to-day health care while travelling and how you handle any medical problem or emergency that does develop. While the list of potential dangers can seem quite frightening, with a little luck, some basic precautions and adequate information few travellers experience more than upset stomachs.

Travel Health Guides

Two useful books are *The Traveller's Health Guide* by Dr A C Turner (Lascelles, London) and *Preservation of Personal Health in Warm Climates* published by the Ross Institute of Tropical Hygiene, Keppel St, London WC1. Another helpful book on health is David Werner's *Where There is No Doctor:*

a village health care handbook (Macmillan Press, London). *Travel with Children* by Maureen Wheeler (Lonely Planet Publications, Hawthorn) includes basic advice on travel health for younger children.

Pre-Departure Preparations
Medical Insurance Get some! You may never need it, but if you do you'll be very glad to have it. Medical treatment in East Africa is not free and public hospitals are often very crowded. Don't expect the same quality of medical treatment in an East African public hospital as you get back home either. There are many different travel insurance policies available and any travel agent will be able to recommend one.

Before you choose one collect several different policies and read through them for an hour or two, as the cost of a policy and the sort of cover offer can vary considerably. Many pitch themselves at the family package tour market and are not really appropriate for a long spell in Africa under your own steam. Usually medical insurance comes in a package which includes baggage insurance and life insurance, etc. You need to read through the baggage section carefully as many policies put a ceiling on how much they are prepared to pay for individual items which are lost or stolen. Check the small print:

1. Some policies specifically exclude 'dangerous activities' which can include scuba diving, motorcycling, even trekking. If such activities are on your agenda you don't want that sort of policy.
2. You may prefer a policy which pays doctors or hospitals direct rather than you having to pay on the spot and claim later. If you have to claim later make sure you keep all documentation. Some policies ask you to call back (reverse charges) to a centre in your home country where an immediate assessment of your problem is made.
3. Check if the policy covers ambulances or an emergency flight home. If you have to stretch out you will need two seats and somebody has to pay for them!

Medical Kit A small, straightforward medical kit is a wise thing to carry. A possible kit list includes:

1. Aspirin or Panadol – for pain or fever.
2. Antihistamine (such as Benadryl) – useful as a decongestant for colds, allergies, to ease the itch from insect bites or stings or to help prevent motion sickness.
3. Antibiotics – useful if you're travelling well off the beaten track, but they must be prescribed and you should carry the prescription with you.
4. Kaolin preparation (Pepto-Bismol), Imodium or Lomotil – for stomach upsets.
5. Rehydration mixture – for treatment of severe diarrhoea, this is particularly important if travelling with children.
6. Antiseptic, mercurochrome and antibiotic powder or similar 'dry' spray – for cuts and grazes.
7. Calamine lotion – to ease irritation from bites or stings.
8. Bandages and Band-aids – for minor injuries.
9. Scissors, tweezers and a thermometer (note that mercury thermometers are prohibited by airlines).
10. Insect repellent, sunscreen, suntan lotion, chap stick and water purification tablets.

Ideally antibiotics should be administered only under medical supervision and should never be taken indiscriminately. Overuse of antibiotics can weaken your body's ability to deal with infections naturally and can reduce the drug's efficacy on a future occasion. Take only the recommended dose at the prescribed intervals and continue using the antibiotic for the prescribed period, even if the illness seems to be cured earlier. Antibiotics are quite specific to the infections they can treat; stop immediately if there are any serious reactions and don't use it at all if you are unsure if you have the correct one.

In many countries if a medicine is available at all it will generally be available over the counter and the price will be much cheaper than in the West. However, be careful of buying drugs in developing countries, particularly where the expiry date may have passed or correct storage conditions may not have been followed. It's possible that drugs which are no longer recommended, or have even been banned, in the West are still being dispensed in many Third World countries.

Health Preparations Make sure you're healthy before you start travelling. If you are embarking on a long trip make sure your teeth are OK; dentists are few and far between in Africa and treatment is expensive.

If you wear glasses take a spare pair and your prescription. Losing your glasses can be a real problem, although in many places you can get new spectacles made up quickly, cheaply and competently.

If you require a particular medication take an adequate supply, as it may not be available locally. Take the prescription, with the generic rather than the brand name (which may not be locally available), as it will make getting replacements easier. It's a wise idea to have the prescription with you to show you legally use the medication – it's surprising how often over-the-counter drugs from one place are illegal without a prescription or even banned in another.

Immunisations Before you're allowed to enter most African countries you must have a valid International Vaccination Card as proof that you're not the carrier of some new and exotic plague. The essential vaccinations are cholera (valid for six months) and yellow fever (valid for 10 years). In addition, you're strongly advised to be vaccinated against typhoid (valid for one year), tetanus (valid for five to 10 years), tuberculosis (valid for life) and polio (valid for life). Gamma globulin shots are also available for protection against infectious hepatitis (Type A) but they are ineffective against serum hepatitis (Type B). Protection lasts three to six months. There is a vaccine available for Type B but it's only recommended for individuals at high risk. It's expensive, and the series of

three injections takes six months to complete.

You need to plan ahead for these vaccinations, as they cannot all be given at once and typhoid requires a second injection about two or three weeks after the first. Cholera and typhoid jabs usually leave you with a stiff and sore arm for two days afterwards if you've never had them before. The others generally don't have any effect. Tetanus requires a course of three injections.

If your vaccination card expires whilst you're away, there are a number of medical centres in African cities where you can be revaccinated. There's usually a small fee for these but sometimes they are free.

Avoid turning up at borders with expired vaccination cards, as officials may insist on you having the relevant injection before they will let you in and the same needle may be used on a whole host of people.

Your local physician will arrange a course of injections for you or in most large cities there are vaccination centres which you can find in the telephone book:

Belgium
    Ministère de la Santé Publique et de la Famille, Cité Administrative de l'État, Quartier de l'Esplanade, 1000 Brussels
    Centre Médical du Ministère des Affaires Etrangères, 9 Rue Brederode, 1000 Brussels
France
    Direction Départementale d'Action Sanitaire et Sociale, 57 Boulevard de Sevastopol, 75001 Paris (tel 4508 9690)
    Institut Pasteur, 25 Rue du Docteur Roux, 75015 Paris (tel 4566 5800)
Holland
    Any GGD office or the Academical Medical Centre, Amsterdam
Switzerland
    L'Institut d'Hygiène, 2 Quai du Cheval Blanc, 1200 Geneva (tel (022) 438075)

UK

Hospital for Tropical Diseases, 4 St Pancras Way, London, NW1 (tel (071) 387 4411). Injections here are free but they're often booked up about a month ahead.

West London Designated Vaccination Centre, 53 Great Cumberland Place, London W1 (tel (071) 262 6456). No appointment is necessary; the fees vary depending on the vaccine.

British Airways Immunisation Centre, Victoria Terminal, Buckingham Palace Rd, London, SW1 (tel (071) 834 2323). Try to book a few days in advance, or you might have to wait around for a few hours before they can fit you in.

British Airways Medical Centre, Speedbird House, Heathrow Airport, Hounslow, Middlesex (tel (081) 759 5511).

General Health

The main things which are likely to affect your general health while you're abroad are diet and climate. Stomach upsets are the most likely travel health problem but the majority of these upsets will be relatively minor. Don't become paranoid, trying the local food is part of the experience of travel after all.

Water Avoid drinking unboiled water anywhere it's not chlorinated, unless you're taking it from a mountain spring. Unboiled water is a major source of diarrhoea and hepatitis, as are salads that have been washed in contaminated water and unpeeled fruit that has been handled by someone with one of these infections.

Avoiding contaminated water is easier said than done, especially in the desert, and it may be that you'll have to drink water regardless of where it came from. This is part of travelling and there is no way you can eliminate all risks. Carrying a water bottle and a supply of water-purifying tablets is one way around this. Halazone, Potable Aqua and Sterotabs are all good for purifying water but they have little or no effect against amoebas or hepatitis virus. For this you need a 2% tincture of iodine – five drops per litre in clear water and 10 drops per litre in cloudy water. Wait 30 minutes and it's safe to drink.

Food & Nutrition Cheap food from cafés and street stands tends to be overcooked, very starchy (mainly maize and millet) and lacking in protein, vitamins and calcium. Supplement your diet with milk or yoghurt (where it's available and pasteurised) and fresh fruit or vitamin/mineral tablets. Avoid untreated milk and milk products – in many countries herds are not screened for brucellosis or tuberculosis. Peel all fruit. Read up on dietary requirements before you set off. And watch out for grit in rice and bread – a hard bite on the wrong thing can lead to a cracked tooth.

Climate In hot climates you sweat a great deal and lose a lot of water and salt. Make sure you drink sufficient liquid and have enough salt in your food to make good the losses (a teaspoon of salt per day is generally sufficient). If you don't make good the losses, you run the risk of suffering from heat exhaustion and cramps. Heat can also make you impatient and irritable. Try to take things at a slower pace. Hot, dry air will make your hair brittle, so oil it often with, say, refined coconut oil. Take great care of cuts, grazes and skin infections otherwise they tend to persist and get worse. Clean them well with antiseptic or mercurochrome. If they're weeping, bandage them up since open sores attract flies. Change bandages daily and use an antibiotic powder if necessary.

A temporary but troublesome skin condition from which many people from temperate climates suffer initially is prickly heat. Many tiny blisters form on one or more parts of your body – usually where the skin is thickest, such as your hands. They are sweat droplets which are trapped under your skin because your pores aren't large enough or haven't opened up sufficiently to cope with the greater volume of sweat. Anything which promotes sweating – exercise, tea, coffee, alcohol – makes it worse. Keep your skin aired and dry, reduce clothing to a loose-fitting minimum and keep out of direct sunlight. Calamine lotion or zinc oxide-based talcum powder helps to soothe the skin. Apart from that, there isn't much else you can do. The problem is one of acclimatisation and shouldn't persist more than a few days.

Adjustment to the outlook, habits and social customs of different people can take a lot out of you too. Many travellers suffer from some degree of culture shock. This is particularly true if you fly direct from your own country to an African city. Under these conditions, heat can aggravate petty irritations which would pass unnoticed in a more temperate climate. Exhausting all-night, all-day bus journeys over bad roads don't help if you're feeling this way. Make sure you get enough sleep.

Everyday Health A normal body temperature is 98.6°F or 37°C; more than 2°C higher is a 'high' fever. A normal adult pulse rate is 60 to 80 per minute (children 80 to 100, babies 100 to 140). You should know how to take a temperature and a pulse rate. As a general rule the pulse increases about 20 beats per minute for each °C rise in fever.

Respiration (breathing) rate is also an indicator of illness. Count the number of breaths per minute: between 12 and 20 is normal for adults and older children (up to 30 for younger children, 40 for babies). People with a high fever or serious respiratory illness (like pneumonia) breathe more quickly than normal. More than 40 shallow breaths a minute usually means pneumonia.

Many health problems can be avoided by taking care of yourself. Wash your hands frequently – it's quite easy to contaminate your own food. Clean your teeth with purified water rather than straight from the tap. Avoid climatic extremes: keep out of the sun when it's hot, dress warmly when it's cold. Avoid potential diseases by dressing sensibly. You can get worm infections through walking barefoot or dangerous coral cuts by walking over coral without shoes. You can avoid insect bites by covering bare skin when insects are around, by screening windows or beds or by using insect repellents. Seek local advice: if you're told the water is unsafe due to jellyfish, crocodiles or bilharzia, don't go in. In situations where

there is no information, discretion is the better part of valour.

Medical Problems & Treatment

Potential medical problems can be broken down into several areas. First there are the climatic and geographical considerations – problems caused by extremes of temperature, altitude or motion. Then there are diseases and illnesses caused by insanitation, insect bites or stings, and animal or human contact. Simple cuts, bites or scratches can also cause problems.

Self-diagnosis and treatment can be risky, so wherever possible seek qualified help. Although we do give treatment dosages in this section, they are for emergency use only. Medical advice should be sought before administering any drugs.

An embassy or consulate can usually recommend a good place to go for such advice. So can five-star hotels, although they often recommend doctors with five-star prices. (This is when that medical insurance really comes in useful!) In some places standards of medical attention are so low that for some ailments the best advice is to get on a plane and go somewhere else.

Climatic & Geographical Considerations
Heat Stroke This serious, sometimes fatal, condition can occur if the body's heat-regulating mechanism breaks down and the body temperature rises to dangerous levels. Long, continuous periods of exposure to high temperature can leave you vulnerable to heat stroke. You should avoid excessive alcohol or strenuous activity when you first arrive in a hot climate.

The symptoms are feeling unwell, not sweating very much or at all and a high body temperature (39°C to 41°C). Where sweating has ceased the skin becomes flushed and red. Severe, throbbing headaches and lack of coordination will also occur, and the sufferer may be confused or aggressive. Eventually the victim will become delirious or convulse. Hospitalisation is essential, but meanwhile get patients out of the sun, remove their clothing, cover them with a wet sheet or towel and then fan continually.

Fungal Infections Hot weather fungal infections are most likely to occur on the scalp, between the toes or fingers (athlete's foot), in the groin (jock itch or crotch rot) and on the body (ringworm). You get ringworm (which is a fungal infection, not a worm) from infected animals or by walking on damp areas, like shower floors.

To prevent fungal infections wear loose, comfortable clothes, avoid artificial fibres, wash frequently and dry carefully. If you do get an infection, wash the infected area daily with a disinfectant or medicated soap and water, and rinse and dry well. Apply an anti-fungal powder like the widely available Tinaderm. Try to expose the infected area to air or sunlight as much as possible and wash all towels and underwear in hot water as well as changing them often.

Tropical Ulcers These are sores which often start from some insignificant scratch or blister which doesn't seem to heal up. They often get worse and spread to other areas of the body and they can be quite painful. If you keep clean and look after any sores which you get on your arms and legs (from ill-fitting shoes, accidents to your feet, or from excessive scratching of insect bites) then it's unlikely you will be troubled by them. If you do develop sores which won't clear up then you need to hit the antibiotics quickly. Don't let them spread.

Altitude Sickness Acute Mountain Sickness or AMS occurs at high altitude and can be fatal. The lack of oxygen at high altitudes affects most people to some extent. Take it easy at first, increase your liquid intake and eat well. Even with acclimatisation you may still have trouble adjusting – headaches, nausea, dizziness, a dry cough, insomnia, breathlessness and loss of appetite are all signs to heed. If you reach a high altitude by trekking, acclimatisation takes place gradually and you are less likely to be affected than if you fly straight there.

Mild altitude problems will generally abate after a day or so but if the symptoms persist or become worse the only treatment is to descend – even 500 metres can help. Breathlessness, a dry, irritative cough (which may progress to the production of pink, frothy sputum), severe headache, loss of appetite, nausea, and sometimes vomiting are all danger signs. Increasing tiredness, confusion, and lack of coordination and balance are real danger signs. Any of these symptoms individually, even just a persistent headache, can be a warning.

There is no hard and fast rule as to how high is too high: AMS has been fatal at altitudes of 3000 metres, although 3500 to 4500 metres is the usual range. It is always wise to sleep at a lower altitude than the greatest height reached during the day.

Motion Sickness Eating lightly before and during a trip will reduce the chances of motion sickness. If you are prone to motion sickness try to find a place that minimises disturbance – near the wing on aircraft, close to midships on boats, near the centre on buses. Fresh air usually helps, reading or cigarette smoke doesn't. Commercial anti-motion-sickness preparations, which can cause drowsiness, have to be taken before the trip commences; when you're feeling sick it's too late. Ginger is a natural preventative and is available in capsule form.

Diseases of Insanitation

Diarrhoea Sooner or later most travellers get diarrhoea, so you may as well accept the inevitable. You can't really expect to travel halfway around the world without succumbing to diarrhoea at least once or twice, but it doesn't always mean that you've caught a bug. Depending on how much travelling you've done and what your guts are used to, it can be merely the result of a change of food. If you've spent all your life living out of sterilised, cellophane-wrapped packets and tins from the local supermarket, you're going to have a hard time until you adjust.

If and when you get a gut infection, avoid rushing off to the chemist and filling yourself with antibiotics. It's a harsh way to treat your system and you can build up a tolerance to them with overuse. Try to starve the bugs out first. Eat nothing and rest. Avoid travelling. Drink plenty of fluids. Have your tea with a little sugar and no milk. Diarrhoea will dehydrate you and may result in painful muscular cramps in your guts. The cramps are due to a bad salt balance in your blood, so take a small amount of salt with your tea. If you can find it, tincture of opium (known as 'paregoric' and often mixed with kaolin – a stronger version of Milk of Magnesia) will relieve the pain of cramps. Something else you may come across, called RD Sol, also helps to maintain a correct salt balance and so prevent cramps. It's a mixture of common salt, sodium bicarbonate, potassium chloride and dextrose. Two days of this regime should clear you out.

If you simply can't hack starving, keep to a *light* diet of curd, yoghurt, toast, dry biscuits, rice and tea. Stay away from butter, milk, sugar, cakes and fruit.

If starving doesn't work or you really have to move on and can't rest for a couple of days, try Pesulin (or Pesulin-O which is the same but with the addition of a tincture of opium). The dosage is two teaspoons four times daily for five days. Or try Lomotil – the dosage is two tablets three times daily for two days. Avoid overuse of Lomotil.

If you have no luck with either of these, change to antibiotics or see a doctor. There are many different varieties of antibiotics and you almost need to be a biochemist to know what the differences between them are. They include tetracycline, chlorostep, typhstrep, sulphatriad, streptomagma and thiazole. If possible, have a word with the chemist about their differences. Overuse will do you more harm than good but you must complete the course otherwise the infection may return and then you'll have even more difficulty getting rid of it.

Giardia Giardia is prevalent in tropical climates and is characterised by swelling of the stomach, pale-coloured faeces, diarrhoea and, after a while, depression and sometimes nausea. Many doctors recommend Flagyl – seven 250 mg doses over a three day period should clear up the symptoms, repeated a week later if not. Flagyl, however, has many side effects and some doctors prefer to treat giardia with Tinaba (tinadozole). Two grams taken all at once normally knocks it right out but if not you can repeat the dosage for up to three days.

Dysentery Dysentery is, unfortunately, quite prevalent in some places. It's characterised by diarrhoea containing blood and lots of mucus, and painful gut cramps. There are two types. Bacillary dysentery is short, sharp and nasty but rarely persistent – it's the most common variety. Amoebic dysentery is, as its name suggests, caused by amoebic parasites. This variety is much more difficult to treat and often persistent.

Bacillic dysentery comes on suddenly and lays you out with fever, nausea, painful cramps and diarrhoea but, because it's caused by bacteria, responds well to antibiotics. Amoebic dysentery builds up more slowly and is more dangerous. You cannot starve it out and if it's untreated it will get worse and permanently damage your intestines. If you see blood in your faeces persistently over two or three days, seek medical attention as soon as possible.

Flagyl (metronidazole) is the most commonly prescribed drug for amoebic dysentery. The dosage is six tablets per day for five to seven days. Flagyl is both an antibiotic and an antiparasitic as well. It is also used for the treatment of giardia and trichomoniasis. Flagyl should not be taken by pregnant women. If you get bacillic dysentery, the best thing for slowing down intestinal movements is codeine phosphate (30mg tablets – take two once every four hours). It's much more effective than Lomotil or Imodium and cheaper. Treatment for bacillic dysentery consists of a course of tetracycline or bactrim (antibiotics).

Hepatitis Hepatitis is a liver disease caused by a virus. There are basically two types – infectious hepatitis (known as Type A) and serum hepatitis (known as Type B). The one you're most likely to contract is Type A. It's very contagious and you pick it up by drinking water, eating food or using cutlery or crockery that's been contaminated by an infected person. Foods to avoid are salads (unless you know they have been washed thoroughly in purified water) and unpeeled fruit that may have been handled by someone with dirty hands. It's also possible to pick it up by sharing a towel or toothbrush with an infected person.

An estimated 10% of the population of the Third World are healthy carriers of Type B but the only ways you can contract this form are by having sex with an infected person or by being injected with a needle which has previously been used on an infected person.

Symptoms appear 15 to 50 days after infection (generally around 25 days) and consist of fever, loss of appetite, nausea, depression, complete lack of energy and pains around the base of your rib cage. Your skin will turn progressively yellow and the whites of your eyes yellow to orange. The easiest way to keep an eye on the situation is to watch the colour of your eyes and urine. If you have hepatitis, the colour of your urine will be deep orange no matter how much liquid you've drunk. If you haven't drunk much liquid and/or you're sweating a lot, don't jump to conclusions. Check it out by drinking a lot of liquid all at once. If the urine is still orange then you'd better start making plans to go somewhere you won't mind convalescing for a few weeks. Sometimes the disease lasts only a few weeks and you only get a few really bad days, but it can last for months. If it does get really bad, cash in that medical insurance you took out and fly back home.

There is no cure as such for hepatitis except rest and good food. Diets high in B vitamins are said to help. Fat-free diets have gone out of medical fashion, but you may find that grease and oil make you feel nauseous. Seeking medical attention is probably a waste of time and money although you are going to need a medical certificate for your insurance company if you decide to fly home. There's nothing doctors can do for you that you can't do for yourself other than run tests that will tell you how bad it is. Most people don't need telling; they can feel it! Wipe alcohol and cigarettes right off the slate. They'll not only make you feel much worse, but alcohol and nicotine can do permanent damage to a sick liver.

Think seriously about getting that gamma globulin vaccination.

Typhoid Typhoid fever is another gut infection that travels the faecal-oral route – ie, contaminated water and food are responsible. Typhoid is very infectious and vaccination against it is not totally effective. It is one of the most dangerous infections so medical help must be sought.

In its early stages typhoid resembles many other illnesses: sufferers may feel like they have a bad cold or flu on the way, as early symptoms are a headache, a sore throat, and a fever which rises a little each day until it is around 40°C or more. The victim's pulse is often slow relative to the degree of fever present and gets slower as the fever rises – unlike a normal fever where the pulse increases. There may also be vomiting, diarrhoea or constipation.

In the second week the high fever and slow pulse continue and a few pink spots may appear on the body; trembling, delirium, weakness, weight loss and dehydration are other symptoms. If there are no further complications, the fever and other symptoms will slowly go during the third week. However you must get medical help before this because pneumonia (acute infection of the lungs) or peritonitis (burst appendix) are common complications.

The fever should be treated by keeping the victim cool and dehydration should also be watched for. Chloramphenicol is the recommended antibiotic but there are fewer side affects with ampicillin. The adult dosage is two 250 mg capsules, four times a day. Children aged between eight and 12 years should have half the adult dose; younger children should have one-third the adult dose.

Patients who are allergic to penicillin should not be given ampicillin.

Worms These parasites are most common in rural, tropical areas and a stool test when you return home is not a bad idea. They can be present on unwashed vegetables or in undercooked meat and you can pick them up through your skin by walking in bare feet. Infestations may not show up for some time, and although they are generally not serious, if left untreated they can cause severe health problems. A stool test is necessary to pinpoint the problem and medication is often available over the counter.

Diseases Spread by People & Animals

Tetanus This potentially fatal disease is found in undeveloped tropical areas. It is difficult to treat but is preventable with immunisation. Tetanus occurs when a wound becomes infected by a germ which lives in the faeces of animals or people, so clean all cuts, punctures or animal bites. Tetanus is known as lockjaw, and the first symptom may be discomfort in swallowing, or stiffening of the jaw and neck; this is followed by painful convulsions of the jaw and body.

Rabies Rabies is found in many countries and is caused by a bite or scratch by an infected animal. Dogs are a noted carrier. Any bite, scratch or even lick from a mammal should be cleaned immediately and thoroughly. Scrub with soap and running water, and then clean with an alcohol solution. If there is any possibility that the animal is infected medical help should be sought immediately. Even if the animal is not rabid, all bites should be treated seriously as they can become infected or can result in tetanus. A rabies vaccination is now available and should be considered if you are in a high-risk category – eg, if you intend to explore caves (bat bites could be dangerous) or work with animals.

Meningococcal Meningitis Sub-Saharan Africa is considered the 'meningitis belt' and the meningitis season falls at the time most people would be attempting the overland trip across the Sahara – the northern winter before the rains come. Other areas which have recurring epidemics are Mongolia, Vietnam, Brazil, the Nile Valley and Nepal.

This very serious disease attacks the brain and can be fatal. A scattered, blotchy rash, fever, severe headache, sensitivity to light and neck stiffness which prevents forward bending of the head are the first symptoms. Death can occur within a few hours, so immediate treatment is important.

Treatment is large doses of penicillin given intravenously, or, if that is not possible, intramuscularly (ie, in the buttocks). Vaccination offers good protection for over a year, but you should also check for reports of current epidemics.

Tuberculosis Although this disease is widespread in many developing countries, it is not a serious risk to travellers. Young children are more susceptible than adults and vaccination is a sensible precaution for children under 12 travelling in endemic areas. TB is commonly spread by coughing or by unpasteurised dairy products from infected cows. Milk that has been boiled is safe to drink; the souring of milk to make yoghurt or cheese also kills the bacilli.

Bilharzia This is caused by blood flukes (minute worms) which live in the veins of the bladder or the large intestine. The eggs which the adult worms produce are discharged in urine or faeces. If they reach water, they hatch out and enter the bodies of a certain species of freshwater snails where they multiply for four or more weeks and are then discharged into the surrounding water. If they are to live, they must find and invade the body of a human being where they develop, mate and then make their way to the veins of their choice. Here they start to lay eggs and the cycle repeats itself. The snail favours shallow water near the shores of lakes and streams and they are more abundant in water which is polluted by human excrement. They particularly like reedy areas. Generally speaking, moving water contains less risk than stagnant water but you can never tell.

Bilharzia is quite a common disease in Africa so stay out of rivers and lakes. If you drink water from any of these places, boil it or sterilise it with chlorine tablets. The disease is painful and causes persistent and cumulative damage by repeated deposits of eggs. If you suspect you have it, seek medical advice as soon as possible – look for blood in your urine or faeces that isn't associated with diarrhoea. The only body of water in Africa which is largely free of bilharzia is Lake Malawi. Keep out of lakes Victoria, Tanganyika, Mobutu Sese Seko, Edward (Idi Amin) and Kivu and the River Nile. As the intermediate hosts (snails) live only in fresh water, there's no risk of catching bilharzia in the sea.

Sexually Transmitted Diseases Sexual contact with an infected sexual partner spreads these diseases. While abstinence is the only 100% preventative, using condoms is also effective. Gonorrhoea and syphilis are the most common of these diseases; sores, blisters or rashes around the genitals, discharges or pain when urinating are common symptoms. Symptoms may be less marked or not observed at all in women. Syphilis symptoms eventually disappear completely but the disease continues and can cause severe problems in later years. The treatment of gonorrhoea and syphilis is by antibiotics.

There are numerous other sexually transmitted diseases, for most of which effective treatment is available. However, there is no cure for herpes and there is also currently no cure for AIDS. AIDS, also known as 'Slim' in East Africa, is prevalent in Uganda, Rwanda, Burundi and Eastern Zaïre, although less so in Kenya and Tanzania. Most of those who have it are not aware of the fact, and hospitals (if they ever get to them) are likely to diagnose their symptoms as something more mundane. The obvious way to pick it up is to have sex with someone who has the disease. The obvious way to avoid it is to be celibate. Not everyone can do this so if you do have sex make sure you cut the risk as far as you can by using condoms. You are still a long way from 100% safe if you do this but the message has definitely got through and most sexually active Africans living in urban areas carry them.

There are two other ways you can pick it up. The first is if you need a blood transfusion. Blood donors in East Africa are rarely screened for AIDS and if you receive blood from an infected donor you will be exposed to the virus. Your options are probably limited if you get into the sort of strife which requires a transfusion. It is also possible to pick up the virus if you are injected with an unsterilised needle. If you do have an injection in Africa try to ensure the needle is either new or properly sterilised.

Insect-Borne Diseases
Malaria Malaria is caused by a blood parasite which is spread by certain species of night-flying mosquito (anopheles). Only the female insects spread the disease but you can contract it through a single bite from an insect carrying the parasite. Start on a course of antimalarial drugs before you set off and keep it up as you travel.

The drugs are fairly cheap in some places but horrendously expensive in others – the USA and Scandinavia in particular. There are basically two types: Proguanil (or Paludrine) which you take daily and Chloroquine which you take once or twice per week (depending on its strength). Both are marketed under various trade names. In some areas of Africa the parasite is beginning to acquire immunity to some of the drugs. This is particularly true in East and Central Africa. Here you will need to take Maloprim in addition to Chloroquine. You would be very unlucky to contract malaria if you are taking one or more of these drugs but they are not a 100% guarantee.

If you do develop malarial symptoms – high fever, severe headaches, shivering – and are not within reach of medical advice, the treatment is one single dose of four tablets (600 mg) of Chloroquine followed by two tablets (300 mg) six hours later and two tablets on each following day.

Other than the malaria hazard, mosquito bites can be troublesome and although it's probably useless to say this, *don't scratch the bites*. If you do, and they don't heal quickly, there's a chance of them becoming infected with something else. You'll come across people in Africa pockmarked with angry sores which started out as insignificant mosquito bites – the owners couldn't resist the urge to scratch them. Don't join them. Will-power works wonders, as does antihistamine cream. To keep the mosquitoes off at night, use an insect repellent or sleep under a fan. Mosquitoes don't like swift-moving currents of air and will stay on the walls of the room in these circumstances.

There is not yet a vaccination against malaria. Take those pills.

Trypanosomiasis (Sleeping Sickness)
This is another disease transmitted by biting insects, in this case by the tsetse fly. Like malaria, it's caused by minute parasites which live in the blood. The risk of infection is very small and confined to areas which are only a fraction of the total area inhabited by the tsetse fly. The flies are only found south of the Sahara but the disease is responsible for the absence of horses and cattle from large tracts of central Africa particularly central and eastern Tanzania.

The fly is about twice the size of a common housefly and recognisable from the scissorlike way it folds its wings while at rest. The disease is characterised by irregular fevers, abscesses, local oedema (puffy swellings caused by excess water retained in body tissues), inflammation of the glands and physical and mental lethargy. It responds well to treatment.

Yellow Fever Yellow fever is endemic in much of Africa. Get that vaccination before you set off and you won't have to worry about it.

Cuts, Bites & Stings
Cuts & Scratches Skin punctures can easily become infected in hot climates and may be difficult to heal. Treat any cut with an antiseptic solution and mercurochrome. Where possible avoid bandages and Band-aids, which can keep wounds wet. Coral cuts are notoriously slow to heal, as the coral injects a weak venom into the wound. Avoid coral cuts by wearing shoes when walking on reefs, and clean any cut thoroughly.

Bites & Stings Bee and wasp stings are usually painful rather than dangerous. Calamine lotion will give relief or ice packs will reduce the pain and swelling. There are some spiders with dangerous bites but antivenenes are usually available. Scorpion stings are notoriously painful and in Mexico can actually be fatal. Scorpions often shelter in shoes or clothing.

There are various fish and other sea creatures which can sting or bite dangerously or which are dangerous to eat. Again, local advice is the best suggestion.

Snakes To minimise your chances of being bitten always wear boots, socks and long trousers when walking through undergrowth where snakes may be present. Don't put your hands into holes and crevices, and be careful when collecting firewood.

Snake bites do not cause instantaneous death and antivenenes are usually available. Keep the victim calm and still, wrap the bitten limb tightly, as you would for a sprained ankle, and then attach a splint to immobilise it. Then seek medical help, if possible with the dead snake for identification. Don't attempt to catch the snake if there is even a remote possibility of being bitten again. Tourniquets and sucking out the poison are now comprehensively discredited.

Jellyfish Local advice is the best way of avoiding contact with these sea creatures with their stinging tentacles.

Fleas, Lice & Bedbugs Unwanted passengers you're likely to come across are fleas, lice and bedbugs. There isn't a lot you can do about fleas. They vary considerably in numbers from one season to another; some places have a lot, others none at all. The less money you pay for a bed or a meal, the more likely you are to encounter them.

You can generally avoid lice by washing yourself and your clothes frequently. You're most likely to pick them up in crowded places like buses and trains, but you might also get them by staying in very cheap hotels. You'll occasionally meet tribespeople whose hair is so matted and so unwashed that it's literally crawling with lice. However, it takes a while for lice to get stuck into you so you should get a companion to have a look through your hair about once a week to see if you've acquired any eggs. They are always laid near the base of the hairs. If you find any, you can either pick them out one by one (very laborious) or blitz them with insecticide shampoo like Lorexane or Suleo. We've had letters from people who have doused their hair in petrol or DDT. You're certainly guaranteed total wipeout this way but it does seem mildly hysterical!

With luck you won't come across bedbugs too often. These evil little bastards live in the crevices of walls and the framework of beds where they hide during the day. They look like lice but they move like greased lightning once you become aware of their presence and switch on the light to see what's happening. Look for telltale bloodstains on the walls near beds in budget hotels. If you see them, find another hotel.

Women's Health

Gynaecological Problems Poor diet, lowered resistance due to the use of antibiotics for stomach upsets and even contraceptive pills can lead to vaginal infections when travelling in hot climates. Keeping the genital area clean, and wearing skirts or loose-fitting trousers and cotton underwear will help to prevent infections.

Yeast infections, characterised by a rash, itch and discharge, can be treated with a vinegar or even lemon-juice douche or with yoghurt. Nystatin suppositories are the usual medical prescription. Trichomonas is a more serious infection; symptoms are a discharge and a burning sensation when urinating. Male sexual partners must also be treated, and if a vinegar-water douche is not effective medical attention should be sought. Flagyl is the prescribed drug.

Pregnancy Most miscarriages occur during the first three months of pregnancy, so this is the most risky time to travel. The last three months should also be spent within reasonable distance of good medical care, as quite serious problems can develop at this time. Pregnant women should avoid all unnecessary medication, but vaccinations and malarial prophylactics should still be taken where possible. Additional care should be taken to prevent illness and particular attention should be paid to diet and nutrition.

Don't Panic

The health section might seem long and off-putting. It isn't meant to be. Most travellers arrive healthy and leave even healthier. If you do pick up something, however, it's useful to know what to do about it.

ACCOMMODATION

Except in Burundi and Rwanda where options for cheap accommodation are very limited, you can usually find somewhere cheap to stay, even in the smallest towns. Options range from a wide choice of budget hotels, youth hostels (Kenya only), religious missions and Sikh temples, to camp sites. Some of these places (religious missions and Sikh temples) may be free but, if they are, please leave a donation otherwise it won't be long before they no longer welcome travellers – as has happened in other parts of Africa.

In budget hotels what you get depends largely on what you pay for although, in general, they're good value. You can certainly expect clean sheets and showers in all of them, but you don't always get a fan or mosquito net and, if you're paying rock-bottom prices, the showers will be cold. Pay a little more and you can expect hot showers. Very cheap hotels often double as brothels (or 'sperm palaces', as an American companion was fond of calling them) but so do many other more expensive hotels. Theft from hotel rooms generally isn't a problem, although only a fool would tempt fate by leaving money and other valuables lying around unattended for hours at a time. If a place looks safe, it generally is. Check the door locks and the design of keys. Many cheap hotels in Kenya also have a full-time doorman and even a locked grille and they won't let anyone in who is not staying there. Obviously, you need to take care in dormitory-type accommodation since you can't lock anything up (unless there are lockers). All in all, the chances of you being mugged in a dark alley at night in a dubious part of a city or along a deserted stretch of beach are far greater than having your gear stolen from a hotel room.

There are camp sites of a sort all over East Africa but they vary tremendously in what facilities they offer. Some are nothing more than a patch of dirt without even a tap. Others are purpose-built. Where there's nothing, religious missions will often allow you to camp in their compounds – usually for a small fee. Don't simply camp out in the bush or on a patch of wasteland in a town or city, however. You are asking for problems and if you leave your tent unattended, there'll be nothing left in it when you get back. In small villages off the beaten track, ask permission first from the village elder or chief.

BOOKS

You can walk into any decent bookshop in Europe, America or Australasia and find countless books on Western and Eastern history, culture, politics, economics, religion/philosophy, craft and anything else you care to name. Finding the same thing for Africa is somewhat more difficult except where it relates to European or American history. Things are improving, however, but so far only in the large format, hardback, photo-essay genre. What you will be hard-pressed to find is a good selection of novels, plays and biographies by contemporary African authors, many of them published by the African branches of major Western publishing houses. Heinemann's African Writers Series offers a major collection of such works but they're generally only available in large African cities. In East Africa, the bookshops of Nairobi carry an excellent selection but the choice is considerably more limited in Dar es Salaam and Arusha. In Western countries, they're to be found only in specialist bookshops.

General Books

There are some excellent but quite expensive photo-essay hardbacks which you may prefer to look for in a library. They include *Journey though Kenya* by Mohammed Amin, Duncan Willets & Brian Tetley (Bodley Head 1982). There is a companion volume entitled *Journey through Tanzania* by the same authors and publisher.

Other colourful books on the region include *Africa Adorned* by Angela Fisher (Collins, 1984), *Ivory Crisis* by Ian Parker & Mohammed Amin (Chatto & Windus 1983), *Isak Dinesen's Africa* by various authors (Bantam Books, 1985), *Africa: A History of a Continent* by Basil Davidson (Weidenfield & Nicolson, 1966) and *Through Open Doors: A View of Asian Cultures in Kenya* by Cynthia Salvadori (Kenway Publications, Nairobi, 1983).

History, Politics & Economics

There are numerous books on the history of Africa which include *The Penguin Atlas of African History* by Colin McEvedy (Penguin, 1980), *A Short History of Africa* by Roland Oliver & J D Fage (Penguin, 1962), and *The Story of Africa* by Basil Davidson (Mitchell Beazley/Channel Four, 1984). Also excellent reading is *The Africans – A Triple Heritage* by Ali A Mazrui (Guild Publishing 1986) which was published in conjunction with a BBC TV series of the same name.

For the origins and development of the

coastal Swahili culture and the effect on them of the arrival of the Portuguese in the Indian Ocean, the standard work is *The Portuguese Period in East Africa* by Justus Strandes (East African Literature Bureau, 1961). For a radical African viewpoint of the effects of colonialism in general, Walter Rodney's *How Europe Underdeveloped Africa* (Bogle L'Ouverture, 1976) is well worth a read.

Worthwhile contemporary accounts include the extremely readable but rather discouraging *The Africans* by David Lamb (Vintage Books/Random Books, 1984). Or there's *The Making of Contemporary Africa* by Bill Freund (Indiana, 1984) and *A Year in the Death of Africa* by Peter Gill (Paladin, 1986). On contemporary Kenyan politics, it's well worth reading Oginga Odinga's *Not Yet Uhuru* (Heinemann) and *Detained – A Prison Writer's Diary* by Ngugi wa Thiong'o (Heinemann, 1981) for a radically different view from that put out by the Kenyatta and Moi regimes.

The *Africa Review*, an annual production by World of Information (NTC Publishing Group, UK), offers an overview of the politics and economics of every African country as well as detailed facts and figures. It's well balanced and researched and makes no attempt to curry favours with any particular regime.

Travellers' & Other Accounts

Dian Fossey's research with the mountain gorillas of Rwanda is recounted in her book *Gorillas in the Mist* (Penguin, 1983). *The White Nile* by Alan Moorehead (Penguin, 1973) is a superbly evocative account of the exploration of the upper Nile and the rivalry between the European powers.

Journey to the Jade Sea by John Hillaby (Paladin, 1974) recounts this prolific travel writer's epic trek to Lake Turkana in northern Kenya in the days before the safari trucks began pounding up the dirt in this part of Kenya. Other books to look for include *Initiation* by J S Fontaine (Penguin, 1985), *A Bend in the River* by V S Naipaul (Penguin,

1979) and *Travels in the Congo* by André Gide (Penguin, 1927).

Two women's accounts of life in East Africa earlier this century have been recent best sellers. *Out of Africa* by Karen Blixen (Isak Dinesen) is published by Penguin books and has also been made into a hugely popular movie. *West with the Night* by Beryl Markham (North Point Press) has also been a major best seller.

African Fiction

Heinemann's African Writers Series probably has the greatest range of contemporary African authors. There's a list of their writers on the first page of each of their books. Two of Kenya's best authors are Ngugi wa Thiong'o and Meja Mwangi whose books are a good introduction to what's happening in East African literature at present. Ngugi is uncompromisingly radical and his harrowing criticism of the neocolonialist politics of the Kenyan establishment landed him in jail for a year, lost him his job at Nairobi University and forced him into exile. His books, on the other hand, are surprisingly not banned in Kenya even though he's considered a dangerously subversive thorn in the side of the government. Meja Mwangi sticks more to social issues and urban dislocation but has a brilliant sense of humour which threads its way right through his books.

Titles worth reading by Ngugi wa Thiong'o include *Petals of Blood* (1977), *A Grain of Wheat* (1967), *Devil on the Cross* and *Weep Not Child*. Titles by Meja Mwangi include *Going Down River Road, Kill me Quick* (1974) and *Carcass for Hounds* (1974). All these titles are published by Heinemann.

For a hilarious but at times poignant account of the higher education system and its relationship with the political system you probably can't beat *The People's Bachelor* by Austin Bukenya (East Africa Publishing House, Nairobi, 1972). Though set at Makerere University in Kampala, Uganda, shortly after independence, its theme is relevant to virtually all British ex-colonies. Another author whose books are well known even outside Africa is Chinua Achebe. Although Achebe is a Nigerian and his material is drawn from his experiences in that country, many of the themes and issues are relevant to contemporary East Africa. His most famous title is *Things Fall Apart* (Heinemann, 1958). Another well worth reading is *Ant Hills of the Savannah*, a much more recent publication. Another Nigerian author who writes about similar themes is Elechi Amadi. Try his *The Concubine* (Heinemann, 1968).

For writing by women in Africa try *Unwinding Threads* (Heinemann, 1983), a collection of short stories by many different authors from all over the continent.

Travel Guides

Africa on a shoestring by Geoff Crowther (Lonely Planet, 1989) covers more than 50 African countries, concentrating on practical information for budget travellers.

Insight Kenya, edited by Mohammed Amin & John Eames (APA Productions, 1985), is another of the popular APA guidebook series with many excellent photographs and a lively text. It concentrates more on the country's history, its peoples, cultures, sights and wildlife rather than on practical information and is a good book to read either before you go or whilst you're there.

Guide to Mt Kenya & Kilimanjaro, edited by Iain Allan (Mountain Club of Kenya, Nairobi, 1981), has been written and added to over the years by dedicated enthusiasts. It contains trail descriptions, maps, photographs, descriptions of fauna and flora, climate and geology, even mountain medicine. Unfortunately, it appears to be out of print at present but you may be able to find a copy at MCK's clubhouse at Wilson Airport in Nairobi.

More recent practical guides to East Africa which would be excellent companions for the one you are reading are those by David Else who spends a great deal of his time walking and trekking in various parts of Africa. The *Camping Guide to Kenya* (Bradt, 1990) covers every camp site in Kenya – the

cities, national parks and mountain areas – and contains information and advice for campers and backpackers venturing off the main routes into the more remote areas of Kenya. *Mountain Walking in Kenya* (Robertson-McCarta, 1990) covers a selection of walking routes through the mountain and highland regions of Kenya including everything from easy strolls around Lake Naivasha to expeditions on Mt Kenya. There's an equipment guide as well as accurate maps and colour wraps. *Mountain Walking in Tanzania, Malawi & Zimbabwe* (Robertson-McCarta, 1991) is a companion volume in the same style.

Field Guides

A Field Guide to the Larger Animals of Africa by Jean Dorst & Pierre Dandelot (Collins, 1970) together with *A Field Guide to the Birds of East Africa* by J G Williams & N Arlott (Collins, 1963) should suffice for most people's purposes in the national parks and wildlife reserves.

MAPS

Most travellers take the Michelin map *Southern Africa* (No 155) to East Africa. It's usually fairly accurate and certainly much better than the Bartholomew's map of the same area. Nevertheless, you shouldn't rely on it too much for detail in Eastern Zaïre or on the borders between Zaïre and Rwanda or Burundi.

There are other maps which some travellers say are better than the Michelin series. One which has often been recommended is the Freytag & Berndt *East Africa* map (1:2,000,000). It is published in four languages and includes rainfall averages and a distance chart. It's available throughout Europe and possibly in America. Another very good, detailed map, is the *East Africa/Ostafrika* (1:2,000,000) which is published by Ravenstein.

Reasonably good maps which you can buy in Kenya itself include the *Road Map of East Africa* (Text Book Centre Ltd) and *Kenya Tourist Map* (Macmillan Kenya). One of the best maps to Tanzania is *Tanzania – Land of Kilimanjaro* (Tanzania Tourist Corporation) but it's frequently out of print. The tourist office in Dar es Salaam is the most likely place to find it though I have seen it on sale in Nairobi bookshops.

WHAT TO BRING

Bring the minimum possible. An overweight bag will become a nightmare. A rucksack or backpack is preferable to an overnight bag since it will stand up to rougher treatment and is easier to carry. Choose a pack which will take some rough handling – overland travel destroys packs rapidly. Make sure the straps and buckles are well sewn on and strengthened if necessary before you set off. Whether you take a pack with or without a frame is up to you but there are some excellent packs on the market with internal frames (eg Berghaus). Probably the best stockists in Britain are the YHA Adventure Centre (tel (071) 836 8541), 14 Southampton St, London WC2. Take a strong plastic bag with you that will completely enclose the pack. Use it on dusty journeys whether your pack is in the luggage compartment of a bus or strapped onto the roof. If you don't, you'll be shaking dust out of your pack for the next week.

A sleeping bag is more or less essential. Deserts get very cold at night and, if you'll be visiting mountainous areas, you'll need

one there as well. You'll also be glad of it on long bus or train journeys as a supplement to the wooden seats or sacks of potatoes. A sheet sleeping bag – similar to the ones used in youth hostels – is also good when it is too hot to use a normal bag. It's cool and keeps the mosquitoes off your body. It also means you don't have to use hotel sheets if they look dubious.

Take clothes for both hot and cold climates, including at least one good sweater for use at night in the mountains and the desert. Gloves and a woolly hat are very useful if you are planning on climbing mountains. You needn't go overboard, however, and take everything in your wardrobe. Things like T-shirts, cotton shirts and sandals are very cheap in most places and it's usually more economical to buy these things along the way.

In some places, Tanzania for example, it's prohibited to wear clothes that reveal large areas of your body. This includes shorts, short skirts and see-through garments. The rules are relaxed at beach resorts of course. It's inadvisable for women to wear anything short or overly revealing in Muslim areas (the coastal areas of Kenya and Tanzania), otherwise they may well come in for a lot of hassling by local men or youths. Muslim women in these areas all wear the *bui bui* (the equivalent of the chador or burka in other Muslim countries) though, in East Africa, it doesn't cover the face and is worn with considerably more panache.

Some people take a small tent and a portable stove. These can be very useful and save you a small fortune, but they do add considerably to the weight of your pack. Camping equipment can be rented in several places in Kenya as well as in Arusha (Tanzania).

Don't forget the small essentials: a combination pocket knife or Swiss Army knife, needle and cotton and a small pair of scissors, pair of sunglasses, towel and toothbrushes, oral contraceptives, tampons and one or two good novels. Most toiletries – toilet paper, toothpaste, shaving cream, shampoo, suntan lotion, etc – are available in capital cities and large towns, except in Uganda where there's hardly anything. A water bottle (insulated) is very useful when it's hot or for walking in the mountains. It also enables you to give those dubious water holes a miss and so cut down your chances of getting hepatitis.

TRAVELLING COMPANIONS

Travelling overland is rarely a solo activity unless you want it that way. Even if you set off travelling alone you'll quickly meet other travellers who are heading in the same direction or who are returning. Crossroads where travellers congregate are good places to meet other people and team up with someone. The best are Arusha, Dar es Salaam, Lamu, Malindi, Mombasa, Nairobi and Zanzibar.

If you'd prefer to find someone before you set off, check the classified advertisements in national newspapers or the notice boards at colleges and universities before the summer holidays come up. If you're in London, England, the best publications to look for ads are *Time Out* and *TNT*. In New York, USA, try the New York Student Centre (tel (212) 695 0291), Hotel Empire, Broadway and 63rd St, or get hold of something like the *Village Voice*.

In some countries there are specific publications and organisations which cater for intending travellers looking for companions. In the UK, try *The Adventurers* which is published monthly by Adventurers International (tel (071) 480 6801), 12 Telford Yard, London E1 9BQ, and costs £1.75 per issue. At the back are two pages of advertisements from travellers seeking companions. There's no charge for inserting an advertisement. Otherwise try Travelmate, 6 Hayes Ave, Bournemouth BH7 7AD, or Odyssey International, 21 Cambridge Rd, Waterbeach, Cambridge CB5 9NJ, both of which gather and distribute intending travellers' details and plans to their members. Membership costs £15 to £25. These agencies are only as reliable as their members are willing to keep the agencies abreast of their plans as they evolve.

LANGUAGE

You will be able to get by in most of East Africa if you can speak English and French – English for Kenya, Tanzania and Uganda and French for Burundi, Rwanda and Eastern Zaïre.

It helps a lot, however, to have a working knowledge of KiSwahili (usually referred to as Swahili) which is rapidly becoming the *lingua franca* of much of Kenya and Tanzania and is also useful in the rest of the region. This is especially so in the rural areas where the local people may only have a smattering of education, if any, and are unlikely to be able to speak any English or French. Local people will always warm to any attempt to speak their language no matter how botched the effort.

There are scores of tribal languages spoken only in certain areas. Any particular one may be totally unintelligible even to a tribesperson from a neighbouring tribe. It's unlikely you will have time to pick up too much of these while you're travelling, but phrase books do exist if you are interested. The best place to find them is in the bookshops of Nairobi.

A *Swahili Phrasebook* by Robert Leonard is available in the Lonely Planet language survival kit series.

Pronunciation

KiSwahili vowels are pronounced as follows:

a	as the 'a' in 'father'
e	as the 'e' in 'better'
i	as the 'ee' sound in 'bee'
o	as the 'a' in 'law'
u	as the 'oo' in 'too'

Double vowels, or any two vowels together, are pronounced as two separate syllables. Thus *saa* (time/hour) is pronounced 'sa-a', and *yai* (egg) is pronounced 'ya-i'. There are no diphthongs as in English.

General Rules

KiSwahili relies heavily on prefixes; adjectives change prefix according to the number and class of the noun. Thus *mzuri, wazuri, vizuri* and *kizuri* are different forms of the word 'good'.

Verbs use a pronoun prefix:

I	*ni*
you	*u*
he/she	*a*
we	*tu*
you	*m*
they	*wa*

and a tense prefix:

present	*na*
past	*li*
future	*ta*
infinitive	*ku*

giving you:

We are going to Moshi.
   Tunakwenda Moshi.
Shall I take a picture?
   Nitapiga picha?
Juma spoke much.
   Juma alisema sana.

Some Useful Words & Phrases
hello*
   jambo or *salama*
welcome
   karibu
How are you?
   habari?
I'm fine, thanks
   mzuri
goodbye
   kwaheri

yes
   ndiyo
no
   hapana
thank you
   asante

thanks very much
   asante sana
What's your name?
   unaitwa nani?
It is...
   ninaitwa...

How was the journey?
   habari ya safari?
How much/how many?
   ngapi?
where?
   wapi?

money
   pesa
today
   leo
tomorrow
   kesho
guest house
   nyumba ya wageni
toilet
   choo
eat
   kula
sleep
   lala
want
   taka
come from
   toka
there is
   kuna
there isn't
   hakuna
White people
   wazungu

* There is also a respectful greeting used for elders: *shikamoo*. The reply is *marahaba*.

Food
food
   chakula
rice
   mchele or *wali*

bananas
  ndizi
bread
  mkate
vegetables
  mboga
salt
  chumvi

meat
  nyama
beef
  ng'ombe
goat
  mbuzi
chicken
  kuku
fish
  samaki
egg(s)
  (ma)yai

milk
  maziwa

water
  maji or *mai*

Numbers

½	*nusu*
1	*moja*
2	*mbili*
3	*tatu*
4	*nne*
5	*tano*
6	*sita*
7	*saba*
8	*nane*
9	*tisa*
10	*kumi*
11	*kumi na moja*
20	*ishirini*
30	*thelathini*
40	*arobaini*
50	*hamsini*
60	*sitini*
70	*sabini*
80	*themanini*
90	*tisini*
100	*mia*

Getting There

Many travellers get to East Africa overland as part of a much lengthier journey through the continent. Due to the civil war in Sudan, however, it is no longer possible to go overland down the Nile valley between Sudan and either Uganda or Kenya. The furthest you will get coming down from the north is Khartoum. From there to Kenya or Uganda you will have to fly. This means that there are only two overland routes open at present – the one from Zaïre into Burundi, Rwanda or Uganda and the one from Zambia or Malawi into Tanzania.

Flights from Cairo to Nairobi are not at all cheap: count on US$350 one way. This is not much more than a one-way London-Nairobi ticket bought in the UK with a possible stopover in Cairo (average price US$442)! A Khartoum-Nairobi ticket is nothing short of daylight robbery at US$375 one way! There's no advantage, either, in going first to Juba (the only major southern Sudanese city in government hands) since you'll have to both fly in and fly out again.

Trying to find a passage on a ship to Africa these days is virtually a waste of time. There are no regular passenger services and you won't get onto a freight ship without a merchant sailor's ticket. Don't believe any rumours that there are such ships. There are about four or five dhows which do the journey from Zanzibar and Mombasa to Karachi and Bombay each year via Somalia, South Yemen and Oman, but they are extremely difficult to locate and to get onto. The days of the dhows were numbered decades ago and those you find in Mombasa harbour will only be plying between Lamu, Mombasa, Pemba and Zanzibar.

AIR

Unless you are coming overland, flying is just about the only – and the most convenient – way of getting to Kenya. Nairobi is the main hub for flights and the route on which you are most likely to get a relatively cheap

ticket but it's worth checking out cheap charter flights to Mombasa from Europe too.

Buying an ordinary economy class ticket is not the most economical way to go, but it does give you maximum flexibility and the ticket is valid for 12 months.

Students and those under 26 can often get discounted tickets so it's worth checking first with a student travel bureau to see if there is anything on offer. Another option is an advanced purchase ticket which is usually between 30% and 40% cheaper than the full economy fare but has restrictions. You must purchase your ticket at least 21 days in advance (sometimes more) and you must stay away for a minimum period (usually 14 days) and return within 180 days (sometimes less). The main disadvantage is that stopovers are not allowed and if you have to change your dates of travel or destination then there will be extra charges to pay. Standby fares are another possibility. Some airlines will let you travel at the last minute if there are seats available just before departure. These tickets cost less than the economy fare but are usually not as cheap as the advance purchase fares.

Of all the options, however, the cheapest way to go is via the so-called 'bucket shops'. These are travel agents who sell discounted tickets. Airlines only sell a certain percentage of their tickets through bucket shops so the availability of seats can vary widely, particularly in the high season. You have to be flexible with these tickets although if the agents are sold out for one flight they can generally offer you something similar in the near future.

Most of the bucket shops are reputable organisations but be careful as there is always the occasional fly-by-night operator who sets up shop, takes your money for a bargain-basement ticket and then either disappears or issues you with an invalid or unusable ticket. Check carefully what you are buying before you hand over money although I've used bucket shops for years and been handed the most weird and wonderful tickets. For example, tickets issued in East Berlin but bought in London for a flight from London to Malaysia with stopovers in New Delhi, Bangkok and Kuala Lumpur. They've all been sweet.

Bucket shops generally advertise in newspapers and magazines and there's a lot of competition and different routes available so it's best to telephone first and then rush round if they have what you want. In Europe, the market for these sort of tickets to American and Asian destinations has been well developed over many years, but little has been available to African destinations south of the Sahara until fairly recently. Fares are becoming more flexible but the options are still limited. Luckily, Nairobi is one of the few destinations that does have plenty of options.

From North America
In the USA, the best way to find cheap flights is by checking the Sunday travel sections in the major newspapers such as the *Los Angeles Times* or *San Francisco Examiner-Chronicle* on the west coast and the *New York Times* on the east coast. The student travel bureaus are also worth trying – STA or Council Travel.

North America is a relative newcomer to the bucket shop traditions of Europe and Asia so ticket availability and the restrictions attached to them need to be weighed against what is on offer on the more normal advance purchase or full economy price tickets.

Return tickets to Nairobi from New York on Pan Am cost US$1785 in the low season (September 15 to November 30 and February 1 to May 14), and US$2745 in the high season (May 15 to September 14 and December 1 to January 31). Pan Am also has flights from Los Angeles for US$2939 in the low season and US$3139 in the high season.

To Dar es Salaam, a return Pan Am ticket from New York costs US$2107 in the low season and US$2938 in the high season. From Los Angeles the fares are US$2501 to US$3261 and US$3332 in the respective seasons.

Pan Am also has return fares from New York to Kigali for US$2340 in the low season and US$2938 in the high season, and from Los Angeles for US$2454 to US$3214 and US$3332 to US$4092 respectively.

From Canada, Lufthansa offers flights from Vancouver to Nairobi for US$2635 in the low season and US$3290 in the high season. To Dar es Salaam the fares are US$3032 and US$3499 and to Kigali they're US$2773 and US$3512 in the respective seasons. Lufthansa also has low season return fares from Toronto to Nairobi for US$2415, to Dar es Salaam for US$2802 and to Kigali for US$2553. The high season fares are US$3070 to Nairobi, US$3279 to Dar es Salaam and US$3292 to Kigali.

It may well be cheaper in the long run to fly first to London from the east coast of the USA using Virgin Atlantic (for around US$225 one way or US$560 return), or standby on the other airlines for a little more, and then buy a bucket shop ticket from there to Kenya with or without stopovers. But you must do your homework to be sure of this. All the main magazines which specialise in bucket shop advertisements in London will mail you copies so you can study current prices before you decide on a course of action.

From Europe
You can find bucket shops by the dozen in London, Paris, Amsterdam, Brussels, Frankfurt and a few other places too. In London, there are several newspapers with lots of bucket shop ads which will give you a good idea of current fares as well as specialist magazines catering entirely to the travel industry.

Trailfinder is a magazine put out three times a year by Trailfinders (tel (071) 938 3366), 42-50 Earls Court Rd, London W8 6EJ. It's free if you pick it up in London but if you want it mailed it costs £8 for three issues in the UK or Eire and £12 for the equivalent for three issues in Europe or elsewhere in the world (airmail). Trailfinders can fix you up with all your ticketing requirements for anywhere in the world as well as insurance, immunisation and books. They've been in business for years and can be highly recommended. All their staff are experienced travellers so they speak your language. Trailfinders is open Monday to Saturday from 9 am to 6 pm (7 pm on Thursday).

Africa Travel Now is a newspaper put out quarterly by Africa Travel Centre (tel (071) 387 1211), 4 Medway Court, Leigh St, London WC1H 9QX. It's free and, as its name indicates, it specialises entirely in travel to and around Africa. It contains an excellent rundown of discounted flight prices to most major cities in Africa as well as what safaris are available once you get there along with costs. You can book all your safaris in advance at this place in addition to getting your airline ticket if you care to do that. Office hours are Monday to Friday from 9.30 am to 5.30 pm and on Saturday from 10 am to 2 pm. As with Trailfinders, they're highly recommended.

Time Out (tel (071) 836 4411), Tower House, Southampton St, London WC2E 7HD, is London's weekly entertainment guide and it's available from all bookshops and newsagents. Subscription enquiries should be addressed to Time Out Subs, Unit 8 Grove Ash, Bletchley, Milton Keynes MK1 1BZ, UK.

The price of airline tickets from London to Nairobi advertised in the above magazines varies from £210 to £263 one way and from £370 to £390 return (the full fare is around £630). The airlines used are generally Aeroflot and other Eastern European and Middle Eastern airlines but this isn't always the case. Both Trailfinders and Africa Travel Centre can also fix you up with multistopover tickets such as Kenya, Madagascar, Réunion, Mauritius, Seychelles, Kenya for around £360 (valid 21 days) or £560 (valid for a year); London, Cairo, Nairobi, London for £447; London, Nairobi, Johannesburg, London for £655. There are also 'open jaws' tickets available (fly into one city/country and out of another) such as London-Kigali (Rwanda) plus Nairobi-London or vice versa for about £400. On these sort of tickets you make your own travel arrangements between where you arrive and where you leave from.

If you plan to head further east or to Australasia after Africa they can fix you up with this too. Nairobi, Delhi, Kathmandu, Bangkok, Singapore, Perth, for instance, costs around £620 while Nairobi-Delhi costs around £190 one way (comparable to anything you'll be offered at the bucket shops in Nairobi).

There is no advantage in buying a one-way ticket to Nairobi and then another one-way ticket back to Europe from there. You'll end up paying more than buying a return ticket in the first place. You may also run foul of immigration on arrival in Kenya without an onward ticket and be forced to buy one on the spot – an expensive exercise in lack of forethought.

There's not a lot of difference in the price of tickets from Europe to Dar es Salaam or Kilimanjaro (in Tanzania) than to Nairobi. A one-way ticket from London to Dar es Salaam or Kilimanjaro varies between £281 and £290 and a return ticket between £495 and £503. Tickets to Kigali, however, seem to be considerably cheaper for some reason or another. Here you're looking at around £210 one way and £390 return.

A Round the World (RTW) ticket is another economic option if that's what you want to do and have the time but only very few of these include African stopovers. Starting and finishing in London with stopovers in Delhi, Singapore, Sydney, Auckland, Honolulu, Los Angeles, Rio, Johannesburg, and Nairobi, you're looking at around £2000.

Don't take advertised fares as gospel truth. To comply with truth in advertising laws, UK companies must be able to offer *some* tickets at their cheapest quoted price but they might only have one or two of them each week. If you are not one of the lucky ones, you may find yourself looking at tickets which cost up to £50 more (one way or return). The best thing to do, therefore, is to start looking into tickets well before your intended departure date so you have a very good idea what is available.

Remember that discounted tickets cannot generally be paid for with a credit card. You must pay with cash or with a bank cheque.

To/From Asia

You may safely assume that flying is the only feasible way of getting between the Indian subcontinent and Kenya. There are plenty of flights between East Africa and Bombay due to the large Indian population in Kenya. There are bucket shops of a sort in New Delhi, Bombay and Calcutta and most of the discounted tickets will be with Air India. In New Delhi I'd recommend Tripsout Travel, 72/7 Tolstoy Lane behind the Government of India Tourist Office, Janpath.

Typical fares from Bombay to Nairobi are around US$440 return with either Ethiopian Airlines, Kenya Airways or PIA (via Karachi).

In Nairobi there are a lot of bucket shops offering tickets to Karachi, Islamabad, New Delhi, Bombay and Calcutta. Most of these will be with Air India or PIA.

From Australasia

There are no longer tight constraints on ticket discounting in Australia, but for Australians and New Zealanders there are simply very few route options to Africa. The only direct connection is the weekly Qantas flight from Perth to Harare (Zimbabwe) which costs about A$2230 (low season) and A$2560 (high season) return. Sydney-Harare costs around A$2600 (low season) and A$2990 (high season) return.

Sydney-Harare via Perth is the most expensive way to go, however. It's cheaper to go via Singapore and Bombay to Nairobi with Air India or a combination of Singapore Airlines and Air India. The published price for this is around A$2500 return but a good travel agent should be able to get it for you for around A$2300 return.

It obviously makes sense for Australasians to think in terms of a RTW ticket or an Australia/New Zealand-Europe round trip ticket with stopovers in Asia and Africa. It shouldn't be too much trouble for a travel agent to put together a ticket which includes various Asian stopovers plus a Nairobi stopover. Having Nairobi added to such a ticket bumps up the price a little and you may have to go through several travel agents before you get satisfaction as many of them know very little about deals via Africa.

It's probably best to start your search for a ticket by looking in the travel section of the Saturday issue of either the *Sydney Morning Herald* or the *Age* and by visiting a student travel bureau. It's also worth writing or telephoning for a copy of *Airfares Guide* from The Travel Specialists (tel (02) 262 3555), 62 Clarence St, Sydney, NSW 2000. They've been putting out this guide for a number of years now and it will give you a very good idea of what's available.

LEAVING EAST AFRICA

Nairobi is the best city in East Africa (and perhaps in the whole of Africa) to pick up cheap airline tickets for international flights. There is a lot of competition between travel agents so most of them lean over backwards to give you whatever discounts they can. They are the equivalent of bucket shops in Europe. Only a few of the airlines sell discounted tickets through these agents and none of them sell them directly from their own offices. The most common discounters are Aeroflot, Air India, EgyptAir, Olympic Airways, PIA and Sudan Airways and most of the cheap tickets available are for flights to Europe, although there are others to India, Pakistan and Singapore and sometimes to Madagascar, Mauritius and Réunion.

Tickets are paid for in local currency but to comply with government regulations it's usually necessary to produce your currency declaration form and bank receipts for the full amount you would pay if you bought the ticket direct from the airline concerned. It's important to bear this in mind if you are going to be leaving Kenya for a while and then returning later to buy your ticket, since your currency form will be collected at the border so you will lose the exchange credits recorded on it. The best thing to do in these circumstances is to buy your ticket just before you leave Kenya for the first time.

You can also pay for your ticket in foreign currency, travellers' cheques or with a credit card in which case you don't need bank receipts.

Tickets for international flights bought in either Tanzania or Uganda have to be paid for in hard currency, travellers' cheques or major credit cards (where accepted). You cannot pay for them in local currency and there are no cheap deals. Similarly, in Burundi and Rwanda, although you can pay in local currency, there are no cheap deals.

A Nairobi-London ticket on Aeroflot or Sudan Airways currently goes for KSh 6000 to KSh 7800 (about US$286 to US$371). The cheaper tickets typically involve flights which touch down in several places before reaching their final destination and, in some cases, may involve stopovers of up to three days before there's a connecting flight. You may or may not find this an interesting prospect. The more expensive tickets are usually for nonstop flights.

There may also be deals on Air Madagascar and Air Mauritius if you're looking for a ticket to take you to the Comoros Islands, Madagascar, Mauritius or Réunion.

Departure Tax
The airport departure tax for international flights from either Nairobi, Dar es Salaam or Kilimanjaro is US$20. You must pay this in foreign currency; local currency is not acceptable.

Getting Around

Most African countries offer a choice of railways, buses, minibuses (generally called *matatus*), taxis (whether shared or private) and trucks.

AIR

There's a good network of internal flights within Kenya and Tanzania but much less so in Uganda, Rwanda, Burundi and Zaïre. Most of these internal sectors are serviced by the respective national carrier but in Kenya there are also quite a few private companies which operate six to eight-seater twin propeller planes.

ROAD

The main roads of Kenya, Rwanda and Burundi are all sealed and generally in a good state of repair though you'll occasionally come across the odd rough patches. Likewise, the main road through southern Uganda from the Kenyan border to Kampala is also sealed and in good shape. The same cannot be said for the main roads of Tanzania (except for the Namanga-Arusha-Moshi section) which are often in an appalling state of repair. The situation is similar in Zaïre.

Roads in far-flung rural areas of all East African countries may well be in a bad state of repair, so breakdowns and getting stuck, especially in the wet season, are a regular feature of any journey. Desert roads in north and north-east Kenya may just be a set of tyre tracks left in the sand or dust by previous trucks. Don't pay too much attention to red lines drawn on maps in places like this. Many roads are impassable in the wet season and on some of them a convoy system may be in operation so it's only possible to travel at certain times of the day.

Bus, Matatu & Taxi

Buses are usually quicker than going by rail or truck. In Kenya, where there is a good network of sealed roads, you may have the choice of going by so-called 'luxury' bus or by ordinary bus over certain routes. The luxury buses cost more but are not always quicker than the ordinary buses. In Tanzania there's also a choice of 'luxury' and ordinary buses but only on the main routes: Arusha to Moshi and Dar es Salaam and Dar es Salaam to Mombasa. Uganda has ordinary buses only. There are very few full-size buses in Burundi and Rwanda – minibuses are the rule. In Zaïre, buses and minibuses are few and far between and you will be reliant on trucks for transport in most areas.

Most East African countries rely heavily on matatus for transport. They're generally more expensive than ordinary buses but quicker. In Kenya, Tanzania and Uganda you can expect them to be packed to bursting point. Due to overloading, excessive speed, poor maintenance and driver recklessness, matatus in Kenya and Uganda are not the safest way of getting around. In fact, they can be downright dangerous and newspaper reports of matatu pile-ups and crashes are a regular feature. In Rwanda and Burundi this isn't the case and travelling in minibuses is quite a civilised way of moving around.

Most countries also have shared taxis (which take up to five or six passengers and leave when they're full) and private taxis. You can forget about private taxis if you're on a budget, but shared taxis should definitely be considered. They can cost up to twice as much as the corresponding bus fare, but in some places they're only slightly more expensive than a matatu and they're certainly quicker and more comfortable. They're also considerably safer than matatus.

You may have to pay an additional fee for your baggage on some buses, matatus and shared taxis but this isn't usually the case.

Trucks

For many travellers, trucks are the favoured means of transport. They may be the *only* form of transport in some areas. They're not only the cheapest way of getting from A to B as a rule, but you also get an excellent view from the top of the load. Free lifts are the exception rather than the rule though it depends on the driver. You may well have to wait a long time until a free lift comes along and it's often not worth bothering. Hitching is a recognised form of public transport in much of Africa and local people expect to pay for it. So should you. Most of the time you will be on top of the load, though you can sometimes travel in the cab for about twice what it costs on top.

For most regular runs there will be a 'fare' which is more or less fixed and you'll be paying what the locals pay – but check this out before you agree to a price. Sometimes it's possible to get the truckie to lower the price if there's a group of you (form an impromptu group where possible). Trucks are generally cheaper than buses over the same distance but not always.

There are trucks on main routes to most places every day, but in the more remote areas they may only run once or twice a week. Many lifts are arranged the night before departure at the 'truck park' – a compound/dust patch that you'll find in almost every African town of any size. Just go there and ask around for a truck which is going the way you want to go. If the journey is going to take more than one night or one day, ask about food and drink.

TRAIN

Kenyan trains are excellent and are the preferred method of transport where they are available. Tanzanian trains are considerably slower but they are still the preferred means of transport since the roads are in such bad shape and going by bus is a generally uncomfortable experience. Ugandan trains are slower still and you probably wouldn't use them in the eastern part of the country, but they are the most convenient way of going west between Kampala and Kasese. Burundi, Rwanda and Eastern Zaïre have no railways.

Although the railway systems of Kenya, Uganda and Tanzania are interconnected, there are no international services.

Third class is usually very crowded and uncomfortable and you may have thieves to contend with so it's not generally recommended. Second class is preferable and will cost you about the same as a bus over the same distance. Travelling 1st class will cost you about double what a bus would cost but it does give you a considerable measure of privacy.

BOAT

There are quite a few possibilities for travelling by boat either on the lakes inland or along the coast. In particular, there are some amazingly venerable old steamships operating on the lakes. A trip on the MV *Liemba* on Lake Tanganyika is quite an experience. The only international lake connections are on Lake Tanganyika. There are no reliable international services on either Lake Victoria or Lake Kivu. Along the coast there are some regular shipping services including dhows – usually motorised but not always.

HITCHING

In Kenya, but less so in the other countries of East Africa, resident expatriates, international aid workers and the like who are driving their own vehicles seem to be reasonably generous about offering (free) lifts. It may be the only way of getting to some of the Ugandan national parks, for instance, since there's rarely any public transport right up to the entrance gates.

Remember that sticking out your thumb in many African countries is the equivalent of an obscene gesture, although allowances are generally made for foreigners. Wave your hand vertically up and down instead.

A word of warning about lifts in private cars. Smuggling across borders does go on, and if whatever is being smuggled is found, you may be arrested even though you knew nothing about it. Most travellers manage to convince police that they were merely hitching a ride and had nothing to do with the smuggler (passport stamps are a good indication of this), but the convincing can take days. Most of the time, however, it's simply a question of money changing hands between the driver and a customs official. In some places – especially Tanzanian borders – the 'contraband' is often unbelievably innocuous (detergent powder and cooking fat!) and the smuggling is done quite openly.

Kenya

Introduction

In past centuries the main visitors to Kenya were the Arab traders who plied their dhows along the eastern coast of Africa. These days it's tourists and adventurers who come to Kenya in large numbers – currently around one million annually – and little wonder as it has an amazing variety of attractions.

For many people Kenya means wildlife and in this field alone it is one of the best places in Africa. Millions of wildebeest on their annual migration, and equally large numbers of pink flamingos massing on the shores of the Rift Valley soda lakes are breathtaking sights. For sheer majesty it's hard to beat the sight of a herd of elephants crossing the flat plains with Africa's most famous mountain, the evocative snow-capped Kilimanjaro, rising in the background. Kenya is also the heart of safari country and a trip through a few of Kenya's spectacular reserves is a memorable experience.

If relaxation is on your mind then head for the coast. Mombasa is a town with a history and from here any of the superb picture-postcard beaches are easily accessible. But without doubt the highlight of the coast is the island of Lamu, where the Arab influence is evident and the pace of life definitely a few steps behind the rest of the country – the perfect place to unwind for a week, or two...

Those people seeking more energetic pursuits will find no shortage of challenges – Kenya has some excellent mountains to climb, especially the very popular Mt Kenya with its unusual alpine flora, and the much less visited Mt Elgon in the west on the Ugandan border. Organised camel treks through the semidesert north of the country also attract a steady stream of hardy souls.

The heart of this relatively prosperous country is the bustling capital, Nairobi, a friendly, modern and efficient city where things work and business can be taken care of in a snap – a far cry from so many other African countries where even simple things like a telephone call can be a major exercise. Added to this is the fact that Kenya has excellent air connections with Europe, Asia and elsewhere in Africa, making it the ideal place for a short visit, or the starting or finishing point for a longer sojourn in Africa. Either way it's a great place – don't miss it.

Facts about the Country

HISTORY
The Birthplace of Humanity

The Rift Valley, which runs through the centre of Kenya, has been established as the 'cradle of mankind' as a result of the now famous digs of the Leakey family in Olduvai Gorge (Tanzania) and around Lake Turkana (Kenya). Their discoveries of several hominoid skulls, one of which is estimated to be 2½ million years old, have radically altered the accepted theories on the origin of humans.

Before the East African digs, the generally accepted theory was that there were two different species of the ancestors of modern humans: the apelike *Australopithecus africanus* and the *Australopithecus robustus*. It was believed one of these died out while the other gave rise to *Homo sapiens*. The Leakey discoveries suggested that there was a third contemporary species, *Homo habilis*, and that it was this one which gave rise to modern humans while both the Australopithecus species died out, leaving no descendants.

The Tribes

This area of Africa has a large diversity of peoples – Kenya is home to almost every major language stock in Africa. Even Khoisan, the 'click' language spoken by the Bushmen and Hottentots in southern Africa, has its representatives, although these days they are only a tiny community close to the Tana River near the coast. This diversity is clear evidence that Kenya has been a major migratory pathway over the centuries.

The first wave of immigrants were the tall, nomadic, Cushitic speaking people from Ethiopia who began to move south around 2000 BC. They were pastoralists and depended on good grazing land for their cattle and goats, so when the climate began to change and the area around Lake Turkana became more arid, they were forced to resume their migration south. They were to reach as far as central Tanzania. A second group of pastoralists, the Eastern Cushitics, followed them around 1000 BC and occupied much of central Kenya. The rest of the ancestors of the country's medley of tribes arrived from all over Africa between 500 BC and 500 AD though there was still much movement and rivalry for land right up to the beginning of the 20th century. Even today it hasn't ended completely. The Bantu speaking people (such as the Gusii, Kikuyu, Akamba and Meru) arrived from West Africa while the Nilotic speakers (such as the Maasai, Luo, Samburu and Turkana) came from the Nile Valley in southern Sudan.

The Arabs

While migrations were going on in the interior, Muslims from the Arabian Peninsula and Shirazis from Persia (now Iran) began to visit the East African coast from the 8th century AD onwards. They came to trade, convert and settle, rather than conquer as they had done in North Africa and Spain. Their dhows would head down on the northeast monsoon bringing glassware, ironware, textiles, wheat and wine and return with ivory, slaves, tortoiseshell and rhino horn.

This trade soon extended right across the Indian Ocean to India and beyond. Even China entered the fray at one point early in the 15th century, with a fleet of 62 ships and an escort of some 37,000 men, after the king of Malindi had sent the Chinese emperor a gift of a giraffe! Many of the traders stayed to settle and intermarry with the Africans. As a result, a string of relatively affluent and Islamic-influenced coastal towns sprang up along the East African coast from Somalia to Mozambique, acting as entrepôts for the cross-Indian Ocean trade. Though there was naturally rivalry between these towns from time to time, up until the 16th century life was relatively peaceful. All this was to be rudely shattered with the arrival of the Portuguese.

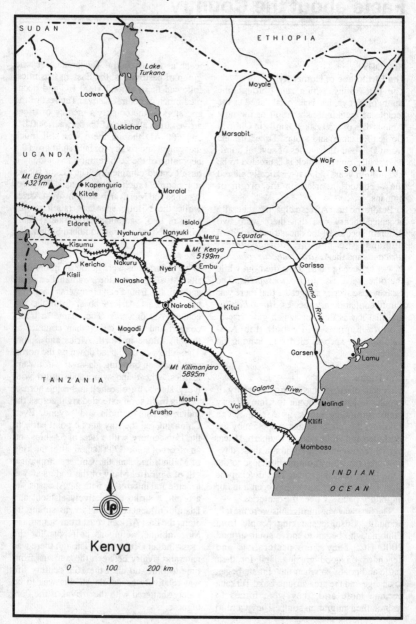

Kenya

0   100   200 km

The Portuguese

While the Spanish Crown was busy backing expeditions to the Americas, the Portuguese were determined to circumvent the Ottoman Turks' grip on trade with the Far East, particularly the trade in spices which were worth more than their weight in gold in Europe. Throughout the 15th century, the Portuguese had been exploring further and further down the western coast of Africa until, in 1498, they finally rounded the Cape of Good Hope and headed up the eastern coast under the command of Vasco da Gama.

They were given a hostile reception both at Sofala on the Mozambique coast and at Mombasa but were lucky to find a friendly sultan at Malindi who provided them with a pilot who knew the route to India. Da Gama was back again with another expedition in 1502, after selling the first expedition's cargo of spices in Portugal and earning a small fortune.

The main Portuguese onslaught began with Dom Francisco de Almeida's armada of 23 ships and some 1500 men in 1505. Sofala was burned to the ground and looted, Kilwa was occupied and garrisoned, and Mombasa was taken after a naval bombardment and fierce street fighting. Mombasa was sacked again by Nuña da Cunha in 1528. The Arab monopoly of Indian Ocean trade had been broken. Though the Ottoman Turks attempted to wrest it back from the Portuguese in 1585 and again in 1589, they were unsuccessful.

After the original onslaught, there followed two centuries of harsh colonial rule. Tribute was demanded and levies were imposed on all non-Portuguese ships visiting the coastal towns. Severe retribution was the reward for the slightest offence. Economic exploitation came hand in hand with a drive to convert the local population to Catholicism but they never had much success at this and, whenever they abandoned an outpost, those who had been 'converted' reverted back to Islam. Mombasa came to be their principle outpost following the construction of Fort Jesus there in 1593.

The Portuguese task was made easier since they were able to play one sultan off against another, but their grip over the East African coast was always tenuous since their outposts had to be supplied from Goa in India, where the Viceroy had his headquarters. Delays were inevitable. The colonial bureaucracy also became moribund because of the sale of offices to the highest bidder. And, in the final analysis, Portugal was too small a country with insufficient resources to effectively hold onto a worldwide empire.

The beginning of the end came in 1698 when Fort Jesus fell to the Arabs after a siege lasting 33 months and, by 1720, the Portuguese had packed up and left the Kenyan coast for good.

The Omani Dynasties

The Arabs were to remain in control of the East African coast until the coming of the British and Germans in the late 19th century. The depredations of the Portuguese period, however, had exacted a heavy price and the constant quarrelling among the Arab governors who succeeded them led to a decline in the trade and prosperity which the East African coast had once enjoyed. Political and economic recovery had to wait until the beginning of the 19th century.

Throughout the 18th century, Omani dynasties from the Persian Gulf entrenched themselves along the East African coast. They were nominally under the control of the Sultan of Oman but this control was largely ineffective until Seyyid Said came to the Omani throne in 1805. The Omanis had gradually built up a relatively powerful navy during the latter part of the 18th century and Seyyid Said decided to use this to bring the East African dynasties into line. In 1822 he sent an army to subdue Mombasa, Paté and Pemba, which were then ruled by the Mazrui clan.

The Mazruis appealed to Britain for help, which it provided the following year in the form of two warships on a survey mission. The commander of one of these ships, Captain Owen, decided to act first and ask questions later, so the British flag was raised over Fort Jesus and a protectorate was declared. A small garrison was left in charge, but three years later the British government repudiated the protectorate and the flag was hauled down. Seyyid Said reasserted his control the following year, garrisoned Fort Jesus and began to lay out clove plantations on Zanzibar. In 1832, he moved his court to Zanzibar.

19th Century Colonialism

By the mid-19th century, several European nations were showing an interest in the East African coast, including the British and the Germans. The British were interested in the suppression of the slave trade and when Seyyid Said moved to Zanzibar they set up a consulate at his court. Later an agreement was reached between the British and the Germans as to their spheres of interest in East Africa. Part of the deal was that the Sultan of Zanzibar would be allowed to retain a 16 km-wide strip of the Kenyan coastline under a British Protectorate. It remained as such right up until independence when the last Sultan of Zanzibar, Seyyid Khalifa, ceded the territory to the new government.

Since it was occupied by the Maasai pastoralists, the Kenyan interior, particularly the Rift Valley and the Aberdare highlands, remained impregnable to outsiders until the 1880s. Their reputation as a proud warrior tribe had been sufficient to deter Arab slavers and traders and European missionaries and explorers up to that date. But with the rest of Africa being combed by European explorers, Kenya's turn was soon to follow.

Notable early explorers who lived to tell the tale were Gustav Fischer (a German whose party was virtually annihilated by Maasai at Hell's Gate on Lake Naivasha in 1882), Joseph Thomson (a Scot who reached Lake Victoria via the Rift Valley lakes and the Aberdares in 1883), and Count Teleki von Szek (an Austrian who explored the Lake Turkana region and Mt Kenya in 1887). James Hannington, an Anglican bishop who set out in 1885 to set up a diocese in Uganda, wasn't quite so fortunate. Though he discovered Lake Bogoria (known as Lake Hannington during colonial days) he was killed when he reached the Nile.

By the late 19th century, the Maasai were considerably weakened and their numbers reduced by years of civil war between two opposing factions, the Ilmaasai and the Iloikop. The dispute was about which of the two were the true descendants of Olmasinta, the legendary founder of the tribe. Rinderpest (a cattle disease), cholera, smallpox and famine had also taken their toll between 1880 and 1892. Because of this, the British were able to negotiate a treaty with Olonana (these days known as Lenana), the *laibon* (chief, or spiritual leader of the Maasai). Armed with this treaty, the British were able to construct the Mombasa-Uganda railway through the heart of the Maasai grazing lands. The approximate halfway point of this railway is where Nairobi stands today.

White Settlement

With the railway completed and the headquarters of the colonial administration moved from Mombasa to Nairobi, White settlers began to move into the fertile highlands north of Nairobi in search of farming lands. Their interests naturally clashed with those of the Maasai, prompting the colonial authorities to pressure Olonana into restricting the Maasai to two reserves, one on either side of the new railway. Though this was a blow to Maasai independence, worse was to follow since the White settlers soon wanted the northern reserve as well. In 1910-11 those Maasai who lived there were forced to trek south, despite Olonana's objections.

Though it's probably true that it was the Maasai who had the greatest amount of land taken from them by the White settlers, the Kikuyu, a Bantu agricultural tribe which occupied the highlands around the western side of Mt Kenya, also suffered. The Kikuyu came to nurse a particular grievance about the alienation of land by White settlers later on in the 20th century. Many of the numerically larger tribes such as the Luo and Luyha and the tribes of the north-east were hardly affected, if at all.

White settlement in the early years of the

20th century was led by Lord Delamere, a pugnacious gentleman farmer from Cheshire, England. Since he was not familiar with the land, its pests and its wildlife, his first ventures – into sheep farming and, later, wheat growing – were disastrous failures. By 1912, however, following the move to the highlands, Delamere and his followers had put the colony onto a more realistic economic footing by establishing mixed agricultural farms. Other European settlers established coffee plantations about the same time, including Karen von Blixen and her hunter husband, Bror. Her memoirs are to be found in the book *Out of Africa*, which has also been made into a very successful film.

WW I interrupted settlement of Kenya for four years during which time some two-thirds of the 3000 White settlers formed impromptu cavalry units and went off in search of Germans in neighbouring Tanganyika, leaving their wives behind to manage the farms. They were not entirely successful but they did eventually manage to drive the German forces into Central Africa with assistance from Jan Smut's South African units. However, Vorbeck's intrepid unit of 155 Germans and 3000 Africans remained undefeated when the armistice was signed in November 1918. Under the Treaty of Versailles, Germany lost Tanganyika and the British were given a mandate by the League of Nations to control the territory.

Settlement of Kenya resumed after the war under a scheme where veterans of the European campaign were offered land in the highlands, either at rock-bottom prices or on long-term loans. The effect of this was to raise the White settler population to around 9000 by 1920. By the 1950s it had reached 80,000.

African Nationalism

While all this was going on, more and more Kikuyu were migrating to Nairobi or being drawn into the colonial economy in one way or another. They weren't at all happy about the alienation of their land and this led to the

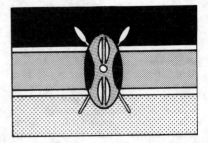

formation of a number of associations whose principle concern was the return of land to the Kikuyu.

One of the early leaders of the Kikuyu political associations was Harry Thuku. Shortly after he was arrested for his activities by the colonial authorities in March 1922, a crowd of Africans gathered outside the Nairobi Central Police Station where he was being held. Reports differ as to what happened next but by the time the police had stopped shooting, between 21 and 100 people had been killed. Thuku was eventually exiled to Kisimayo and was only finally released from jail in 1930 after he had agreed to cooperate with the colonial authorities. His cooperation cost him his leadership of the Kikuyu movement since he was thenceforth regarded as something of a collaborator. This early Sharpeville led to the politicisation of the Kikuyu and was the start of a sustained campaign for political, social and economic rights.

While Harry Thuku's star was on the wane, that of another member of the tribe was on the rise. His name was Johnstone Kamau, later changed to Jomo Kenyatta, who was to become independent Kenya's first president. Kenyatta was born in 1892 in the highlands north of Nairobi, the son of a peasant farmer. He spent the early years of his life as a shepherd tending his father's flocks. When he was in his teens he ran away to a nearby Church of Scotland mission school where he picked up an education.

At the age of 29 he moved to Nairobi. He worked there as a court interpreter and water-meter reader but his real skills lay elsewhere

– as an orator. He soon became the propaganda secretary of the East Africa Association which had been set up to campaign for land reform, better wages, education and medical facilities for Africans. At this time, Africans were barred from hotels and restaurants and were only considered for the most menial jobs within the colonial administration. Although it was official British government policy to favour African interests over those of the settlers in the event of conflicts, this was often ignored in practice because of the dominance of Lord Delamere's lobby in the Whites-only Legislative Council which had been formed after the protectorate became a colony. Recognising this, Kenyatta soon moved to the more outspoken Kikuyu Central Association as its secretary-general.

Shortly afterwards, in 1929, with money supplied by Indians with communist connections, he sailed for London to plead the Kikuyu case with the British colonial secretary. Though the colonial secretary declined to meet him, Kenyatta teamed up with a group called the League Against Imperialism which took him to Moscow and Berlin and then back again to Nairobi. He returned to London the following year and remained there for the next 15 years. He spent his time perfecting his oratory with Trafalgar Square crowds, studying revolutionary tactics in Moscow, visiting cooperative farms in Scandinavia and building up the Pan-African Federation with Hastings Banda (who later became the president of Malawi) and Kwame Nkrumah (who later became the president of Ghana). By the time he returned to Kenya in 1946, he was the recognised leader of the Kenyan liberation movement.

During WW II, the Belgian, British, French and Italian governments all recruited African troops to fight. The overall effect on Africans (as well as soldiers from other colonised peoples) was a realisation that the Europeans were not omnipotent. They could be defeated or, at the least, forced to come to terms with African aspirations for the same benefits and opportunities as their European overlords. Africans had also been trained in the use of arms. When the war ended, therefore, the returning soldiers were in no mood to accept the status quo and began to actively campaign for changes.

The main African political organisation involved in the confrontation with the colonial authorities was the Kenya African Union (KAU), first headed by Harry Thuku and then by James Gichuru who himself stood down in favour of Kenyatta on the latter's return from Britain. The Kikuyu Central Association had been banned in 1940 along with many other similar organisations.

The Mau Mau Rebellion

As the demands of the KAU became more and more strident and the colonial authorities less and less willing to make concessions, oath-taking ceremonies began to spread among various tribes like the Kikuyu, Maasai and Luo. Some of these secret oaths bound the participants to kill Europeans and their African collaborators.

The first blow was struck early in 1953 with the killing of a White farmer's entire herd of cattle. This was followed, a few weeks later, by the massacre of 21 Kikuyu loyal to the colonial government. The Mau Mau rebellion had started. The government declared an emergency and began to herd the tribespeople into 'protected villages' surrounded by barbed wire and booby-trapped trenches which they were forbidden to leave during the hours of darkness. Some 20,000 Kikuyu 'Home Guards' were recruited to assist British army units brought in to put down the rebellion and to help police the 'protected villages'. By the time it came to an end in 1956 with the defeat of the Mau Mau, the death toll stood at over 13,500 Africans – Mau Mau guerrillas, civilians and troops – and just over 100 Europeans, only 37 of which were settlers. In the process an additional 20,000 Kikuyus had been thrown into detention camps.

Only a month after the rebellion started, Kenyatta and several other KAU leaders were arrested and put on trial for allegedly being the leaders of the Mau Mau. It's very doubtful that Kenyatta had any influence over the Mau Mau commanders, let alone that he was one of their leaders, but he was, nevertheless, sentenced to seven years jail in the remote Turkana region after a trial lasting five months. He was released in 1959 but was immediately sent to Lodwar under house arrest.

The rebellion shook the settlers to the roots and gave rise to a number of White political parties with opposing demands, ranging from partition of the country between Blacks and Whites to the transfer of power to a democratically elected African government. It should have been obvious to anyone with eyes to see that the latter view would have to prevail in the end, but it wasn't adopted as official policy until the Lancaster House Conference in London in 1960. The rebellion did lead, however, to an exodus of White settlers who packed their bags and headed off to Rhodesia, South Africa and Australia. At the conference, independence was scheduled for December 1963 and the British government agreed to provide the new Kenyan government with US$100 million in grants and loans so that it would be able to buy out European farmers in the highlands and restore the land to the tribes from whom it had been taken.

In the meantime a division occurred in the ranks of KAU between those who wanted a unitary form of government with firm centralised control in Nairobi and the others who favoured a federal setup in order to avoid Kikuyu domination. The former renamed their party the Kenya African National Union (KANU) and the latter split off under the leadership of Ronald Ngala to become the Kenya African Democratic Union (KADU). Many of the White settlers, who had come to accept the inevitable, supported KADU.

Kenyatta was released from house arrest in mid-1961 and assumed the presidency of KANU. Despite his long period of incarceration by the colonial authorities, he appeared to harbour no resentment against the Whites and indeed set out to reassure the settlers that they would have a future in the country when independence came. At a packed meeting of settlers in Nakuru Town Hall in August 1963, he asked them to stay, saying that the country needed experience and that he didn't care where it came from. He assured them of the encouragement and protection of the new government and appealed for harmony, saying that he wanted to show the rest of the world that different racial groups were capable of living and working together. It did the trick. Kenyatta's speech transformed him, in the eyes of the settlers, from the feared and reviled spiritual leader of the Mau Mau into the venerable *mzee* (respected elder) of the post-independence years.

Most of the White settler farms have been bought out by the government over the years and the land divided up into small subsistence plots which support 15 to 20 people. This may well have appeased the pressure for land redistribution in a country with the world's highest birth rate but it has led to a serious decline in agricultural production (and therefore a diminishing tax base for the government) and has threatened to damage the region's delicate ecology. By 1980, Kenya was forced to import half its grain needs whereas in 1975 it was self-sufficient in these. The government is keen to halt the break-up of the 100-odd settler farms which remain but the prospects of being able to do this in a land-hungry nation are not good.

Independent Kenya

The two parties, KANU and KADU, formed a coalition government in 1962, but KANU and Kenyatta came to power in May 1963 following elections. Independence came on 12 December 1963 with Kenyatta as the first president. He was to rule Kenya until his death in 1978. Under Kenyatta's presidency, Kenya developed into one of Africa's most stable and prosperous nations. Unlike many other newly independent countries, there was no long string of coups and counter-coups, military holocausts, power-crazy dictators and secessionist movements. It wasn't all plain sailing but he left the country in a much better state than he found it and, although there were excesses, they were minor by African standards. By the time he died, there were enough Kenyans with a stake in their country's continued progress to ensure a relatively smooth succession to the presidency. Violence and instability would have benefited few people. Kenyatta's main failings were that he was excessively biased in favour of his own tribe and that he often regarded honest criticism as tantamount to treason.

Control of the government and large sectors of the economy still remain in the hands of the Kikuyu, to the social and financial detriment of other ethnic groups. Corruption in high places remains a problem and once prompted J M Kariuki, a former Mau Mau fighter and later an assistant minister in the government, to remark that Kenya had become a nation of '10 millionaires and 10 million beggars'. There are indeed great disparities in wealth. Many destitute squatters and unemployed people, especially in Nairobi, have little hope of ever finding employment – but this is hardly a problem peculiar to Kenya.

In 1964, Kenya effectively became a one-party state following the voluntary dissolution, of the opposition KADU party. With it died the party's policy of regionalism and the two-chamber Legislature became a single chamber, the National Assembly. However, when Oginga Odinga, a Luo, was purged from the KANU hierarchy in 1966 over allegations that he was plotting against the government, he resigned from the vice-presidency and formed his own opposition party, the Kenya People's Union. The party was later banned and Odinga was jailed. He was released when he agreed to rejoin KANU, but was imprisoned again in 1969 on spurious charges. After his release in 1971 he was banned from running for public office until 1977.

Similarly, Tom Mboya, an intelligent young Luo who was widely regarded as future presidential material, was murdered by a Kikuyu gunman in 1969. The ambitious Mboya was feared by influential Kikuyu who felt that he might have designs on succeeding Kenyatta as president. J M Kariuki, a very popular Kikuyu who spoke out stridently and often about the new Black elite and their corrupt practices, met a similar fate. He was assassinated in 1975. Other politicians who opposed Kenyatta – however mildly – found themselves arrested and held for long periods, often without trial.

Kenyatta was succeeded by Daniel arap Moi, a member of the Tugen tribe and regarded by Kikuyu power brokers as a suitable front man for their interests. Lacking the charisma of Kenyatta and the cult following which he enjoyed, Moi was even less willing to brook criticism of his regime and his early years were marked by the arrest of dissidents, the disbanding of tribal societies and the frequent closure of the universities. There were allegations of conspiracies to overthrow the government whose details were often so labyrinthine they could have come straight out of a modern spy novel. Whether these conspiracies were real or just a convenient facade to justify Moi's consol-

Jomo Kenyatta

idation of power is hard to tell since rarely were any names or details released.

What certainly was real was the attempted coup by the Kenyan Air Force in August 1982. It was put down by forces loyal to the government but, by the time it was over, about 120 people had been killed and there was widespread looting of the major shopping areas. Twelve ringleaders were subsequently sentenced to death and 900 others received jail sentences. The entire Kenyan Air Force was disbanded and replaced by a new unit. Since then, other alleged conspiracies have come to light but, again, rarely are the details made known. The most publicised of these clandestine opposition groups was Mwakenya which supposedly centred around a number of lecturers at Nairobi University along with the exiled novelist and playwright, Ngugi wa Thiong'o. Certainly Ngugi has made his opposition to the Kenyan government quite plain but there's little evidence to support the claim that he was a leading light behind the movement.

President Moi was re-elected in March 1987 in an election which was most notable for the controversial voting system used. Candidates could only run in the secret ballot election after gaining a set percentage of the vote in a preliminary election whereby voters queued behind the candidate of their choice. If the candidate gained more than 70% of the queue vote, they were automatically elected and did not have to take part in the secret ballot election. The outcome was that at least 45 constituencies had no secret ballot as the candidate who had received over 70% of the turnout in the queue vote was automatically elected (it didn't matter that in one case the turnout was less than 9% of registered voters). In other constituencies, the number of candidates was significantly reduced because the nominees failed to win sufficient support at the preliminary election.

After the election Moi considerably expanded his cabinet to 33 ministers – many on the basis of political patronage – and, as a result, the government's (and therefore Moi's) position seems totally secure. With the fall of a couple of outspoken politicians in the 1987 elections (amid allegations of vote rigging) it is unlikely that parliamentary opposition to Moi on major issues in the immediate future will be anything more than a whisper. Perhaps more significantly, changes to the constitution were rushed through parliament unopposed in late 1987 which gave Moi increased powers as President, including the right to dismiss senior judges and public servants without redress. The independence of the judiciary had been a much admired cornerstone of the Kenyan political system ever since independence and the changes were viewed with alarm by many sections of society.

In view of the above changes, there is now no effective political opposition within the parliamentary system and the party has further strengthened its hold by augmenting the ranks of the KANU Youth Brigade who essentially serve as pro-government vigilantes. They are frequently unleashed to disrupt demonstrations, harass opposition figures and maintain a climate of intimidation amongst those who might have similar thoughts.

These days, opposition comes only from groups in the civil field, notably the leaders of various Christian sects and especially the bishops of the Anglican Church. Many have come in for virulent public condemnation for their attacks on the government by various ministers and Moi himself, and there have been demands for their removal and even arrest on charges of sedition. So far, this hasn't happened but it may only be a question of time.

That the government feels under threat from these various civil opposition groups and Western opinion is all too obvious. In late 1989, a programme of screening all residents of Somali origin was announced. The intention behind it was to 'flush out' those who were in Kenya illegally – and there were certainly quite a lot including many who, though they'd never admit it, were involved in the slaughter of rhino and elephant. It's possible that the screening was insensitively handled and it certainly led to the flight of many to neighbouring Uganda and Tanzania, but what enraged the Kenyan government most was a press report in a Canadian newspaper which was highly critical of the exercise. The issue blew up into a full-scale diplomatic row which came close to the recall of ambassadors by both countries. Kenya regarded it as interference in its internal affairs while Canada upheld the freedom of the press. Tempers have since cooled but Western journalists are now viewed with suspicion by immigration officials on arrival.

Apart from political opposition, the government's main worry is the economy. The budget deficit stands at over US$600 million and is unlikely to improve in the foreseeable future. The main reason for this is the continuing population expansion of around 4% per annum (one of the highest in the world) which is going to see Kenya's population grow from 22-23 million at present to 37-38 million by the end of the century. This is already putting considerable strain on health and educational facilities and is likely to result in increasing social, economic and political turmoil. Of the estimated 400,000 school leavers who come onto the job market each year, only around 30,000 manage to find formal jobs. Or, put another way, of the labour pool of some seven million, there are only about one million formal wage-paying jobs. By the end of the century, it's estimated that the labour pool will double.

Other causes for the budget deficit include heavy maize purchases during 1986-87, increased university intake, the hosting of the All Africa Games in 1987, the 1988 elections, and the Nyayo and Silver Jubilee celebrations of 1988. If it goes ahead – as seems likely – the huge Times Media Complex in Uhuru Park, Nairobi, will further add to national indebtedness. The cost of this project has been set at over US$200 million, most of it coming from overseas banks in the form of a 10 year loan.

It's fair to say beyond the doom and gloom, on the other hand, that Kenya enjoys a healthier economic outlook than any of its neighbours. Tourism is booming, the tea and coffee sectors are relatively efficiently handled (though sales are restricted by international quotas) and the country is now self-sufficient in maize (the national staple food). The country has never had to experience lunatic dictators like Idi Amin followed by multiple civil wars (as in Uganda) or rigid 'socialist' dogmatism coupled with economic mismanagement (as in Tanzania). And it's still relatively stable despite political repression.

GEOGRAPHY

Kenya straddles the equator and covers an area of some 583,000 sq km which includes around 13,600 sq km of inland water in the form of part of Lake Victoria. It's bounded in the north by the arid bushlands and deserts of Ethiopia and Sudan, to the east by Somalia and the Indian Ocean, to the west by Uganda and Lake Victoria, and to the south by Tanzania.

The country can be roughly divided into four main zones: the Coastal Belt, the Rift Valley & Central Highlands, Western Kenya and the North & East of Kenya.

The Coastal Belt

This area covers some 480 km of Indian Ocean littoral including coral reefs and beaches, the Lamu archipelago, the Tana River estuary (Kenya's principal river) and a narrow, low lying and relatively fertile strip suitable for agriculture. Beyond this, the land rises fairly steeply towards the central plateau and gives way to bushland and scrub desert.

The Rift Valley & Central Highlands

These regions form the backbone of the country and it's here that Kenya is at its most spectacular scenically. The lake studded Rift Valley runs the whole length of the country from Lake Turkana to Lake Magadi and is peppered with the cones of extinct volcanos. It's bounded on the eastern side by the thickly forested slopes of the Aberdare mountains and, further to the east, by the massif of Mt Kenya – Africa's second highest mountain at 5199 metres. This is the most fertile area of the country and the lower slopes of the mountains are intensively cultivated. Nairobi, the capital, sits at the southern end of the central highlands.

Western Kenya

The west of the country consists of an undulating plateau stretching from the Sudanese border to Tanzania in the south. The northern part, particularly around the shores of Lake Victoria, is fertile, well watered and intensively cultivated and it's here that Mt Elgon is situated – Kenya's second highest mountain at 4321 metres. Further south the land gradually merges into scrub and savannah and is suitable only for cattle grazing but it's here that Kenya's largest and most popular wildlife sanctuaries are situated – Masai Mara, Amboseli and Tsavo. To the south of Amboseli rises the spectacular massif of Mt Kilimanjaro – Africa's highest mountain.

The North & East of Kenya

These two regions cover a vast mountainous area of bushland, scrub and desert where rainfall is sparse and where the land is suitable only for cattle grazing. It's this area, however, where Kenya is at its wildest and most untouched by the modern world.

CLIMATE

Because of Kenya's diverse geography, temperature, rainfall and humidity vary widely but there are effectively four zones about which generalisations can be made.

The undulating plateau of western Kenya is generally hot and fairly humid with rainfall spread throughout the year though most of it falls in the evenings. The highest falls are usually during April when a maximum of 200 mm may be recorded whilst the lowest falls are during June with an average of 60 mm. Temperatures range from a maximum of 30-34°C to a minimum of 14-18°C.

The central highlands and Rift Valley enjoy perhaps the most agreeable climate in the country though there's quite a variation between the hot and relatively dry floor of the central Rift Valley and the snow-covered peaks of Mt Kenya. Rainfall varies from a minimum of 20 mm in July to 200 mm in April and falls essentially in two seasons – March to May (the 'long rains') and October to December (the 'short rains'). The Aberdares and Mt Kenya are the country's main water catchment areas and falls of up to 3000 mm per year are often recorded. Average temperatures vary from a maximum of 22-26°C to a minimum of 10-14°C.

The vast semiarid bushlands, deserts and lava flows of northern and eastern Kenya are where the most extreme variations of temperature are to be found, ranging from up to 40°C during the day in the deserts down to 20°C or less at night. Rainfall in this area is sparse and when it does fall it often comes in the form of violent storms. July is generally the driest month and November the wettest. The average annual fall varies between 250 mm and 500 mm.

The fourth climatic zone is the coastal belt which is hot and humid all year round though tempered by sea breezes on the coast itself. Rainfall varies between a maximum of 240 mm in May to a minimum of 20 mm in February. The average annual fall is between 1000 mm and 1250 mm. Average temperatures vary little throughout the year ranging from a maximum of 30°C to a minimum of 22°C.

FLORA & FAUNA

Flora

With its range of geographical types, Kenya has a corresponding diversity in its flora. The vast plains of the south are characterised by the distinctive flat-topped acacia trees, and interspersed with these are the equally distinctive bottle-shaped baobab trees and thornbushes.

On the slopes of Mt Elgon and Mt Kenya the flora changes with altitude. Above about 1000 metres it is thick evergreen temperate forest which continues to around 2000 metres and then gives way to a belt of bamboo forest to about 3000 metres. Above this height is mountain moorland which is characterised by the amazing groundsel tree (*dendrosencio*) with its huge cabbagelike flowers, and giant lobelias with long spikes.

In the semidesert plains of the north and north-east the vegetation cover is unremarkable – scruffy thornbushes seem to go on forever. In the northern coastal areas mangroves are prolific and the trees are cut for export, mainly to the Middle East for use as scaffolding; mangrove wood is termite resistant and is in high demand.

Fauna
Kenya has such a dazzling array of wildlife that game viewing in the national parks is one of the main attractions of a visit to this country. All of the 'Big Five' (lion, buffalo, elephant, leopard and rhino) can be seen in at least two of the major parks, and there's a huge variety of other less famous but no less impressive animals.

To aid identification of animals while you're game spotting on safari, refer to the Safari Guide at the back of the book. For a full treatment of Kenya's animals, *A Field Guide to the Mammals of Africa* (Collins, 1988) has excellent colour plates to aid identification as does the smaller *A Field Guide to the Larger Mammals of Africa* (Collins, 1986). The main trouble with both these books is the relatively poor index (which lists many animals only by their Latin names) and the dispersion of the colour plates which are often far from the actual description of the animals in question. *Animals of East Africa* (Hodder & Stoughton, 1960) has good descriptive notes of the animals' habits and appearance, but the sketches are not the greatest and the notes on distribution are out of date.

The birdlife is equally varied and includes ostriches, vultures and a variety of eagles, waterbirds such as flamingos, storks, pelicans, herons, ibis and cormorants, and others such as the yellow weaver birds which you'll see everywhere. The best reference source for twitchers is *A Field Guide to the Birds of East Africa* by John G Williams. It is widely available in Kenya.

National Parks & Game Reserves
Kenya's national parks and game reserves rate among the best in Africa. Obviously the tremendous variety of birds and animals are the main attractions, and the more popular parks such as Masai Mara Game Reserve and Amboseli National Park see huge numbers of visitors – from the budget campers to the hundreds of dollars a day Hilton hoppers. In the peak season (January-February) on a game drive, you can observe at close quarters the daily habits of the prolific Nissan Urvan. Other smaller parks, such as Saiwa Swamp National Park, near Kitale in the country's western highlands, would be lucky to see a handful of visitors a day at any time of year.

As well as the wildlife to be seen, some parks have been gazetted to preserve the landscape itself, and these too can be exciting and rewarding places to visit – places such as Mt Kenya, Mt Elgon, Hell's Gate, Mt Longonot and the Kakamega Forest are all worth investigating. Marine life is also in abundance and the marine national parks of Malindi and Watamu off the central coast both offer excellent diving prospects.

What probably helps to make Kenyan parks such a draw card for the budget traveller is that the competition among safari companies for the traveller's dollar is so fierce that a safari of at least a few days is within the reach of the vast majority of travellers. For those at the other end of the scale the competition is equally brisk and there are lodges and tented camps within the major parks which have superb facilities and are a real experience – if you can afford them.

As Kenya relies so heavily on tourism for income, and because it's the animals which people have chiefly come to see, the government has placed a high priority on the conservation of the wildlife and the eradication of poaching. To this end it has appointed Richard Leakey, grandson of Louis Leakey, head of the Ministry of Wildlife, and he has not been afraid to stick his neck out and get things done. Poaching patrols are now much more efficient, extremely stiff penalties for poaching are now in effect, and the estimated 500 of the ministry's Land Rovers which had been left to rot due to lack of maintenance are gradually being refurbished and pressed into service. It was Leakey who recommended that President Moi should take a high profile stance on Kenya's anti-ivory policy and burn the stockpile of confiscated ivory in 1989. This action got good press coverage abroad but was widely criticised at home by people who thought that the ivory should have been sold and the money (estimated at around three million dollars) put to good use.

It's a moot point since although the tourist industry brings in some US$400 million a year, the budget for the national parks was, until very recently, only a tiny fraction of this amount and depended heavily for its anti-poaching measures on gifts from Western governments and environmental groups.

Yet, despite the risks, poaching still goes on and the war (for that is virtually what it is) between the Kenyan government and the poachers has escalated with the poachers turning to robbing tourists when denied elephants and rhino. It's easy to see why. There is big money in ivory and rhino horn and as long as the Taiwanese government and various Arab governments – notably the two Yemens, Oman and Kuwait – refuse to ban their importation, the slaughter of Kenya's wildlife is likely to continue. A kg of ivory is worth about US$300 wholesale and rhino horn is US$2000 a kg (or up to US$30,000 for a single horn). In the Middle East, rhino horn is prized for dagger handles whilst in China and Korea, in powdered form, it's a supposed aphrodisiac.

Although poaching has been going on for many years, it took on a new dimension in 1972 as a result of the drought in North-East Africa which rendered some 250,000 Somali pastoralists destitute as their sheep, goats and camels died by the million. Many drifted south armed with weapons ranging from bows and arrows to WW II guns and found poaching to be a suitable antidote to poverty. Meanwhile, corruption in the Kenyan wildlife department deepened with officials taking cutbacks in return for turning a blind eye to the poachers' activities. By 1976, it

was plain that the number of elephants being slaughtered by poachers far exceeded those dying as a result of the drought and the deforestation and it was estimated that there were over 1300 poachers operating within Tsavo National Park alone.

Worst was yet to come. In 1978, waves of Somalis hungry for ivory and rhino horn and encouraged by official corruption swept across the border and into the national parks, only this time they came with modern automatic weapons issued to them by the Somali government during the 1977 war with Ethiopia. They killed everything in their path including any Kenyan tribal poachers who they came across. By the end of the decade, some 104,000 elephants (about 62% of the total) and virtually the entire rhino population had been slaughtered.

There was little improvement during the early '80s despite the setting up of anti-poaching patrols armed with modern weapons, high speed vehicles and orders to shoot on sight. Part of the reason was the patrols' reluctance to engage the Somalis who have a reputation for toughness and uncompromising violence. By 1989, however, following George Adamson's murder by poachers in the Kora National Reserve and attacks on tourists in other national parks, the Kenyan government signalled its determination to seriously address the problem. Following Leakey's appointment, corrupt wildlife officials were sacked and the antipoaching units beefed up, even to the extent that 200 US-trained paramilitary personnel were deployed in 1990 on shoot-to-kill patrols.

The measures have had a large degree of success though it appears that some poachers, denied ivory, are turning to robbing tourists. A few tourists have actually been shot dead and others seriously injured but the numbers are very small – less than 10 so far. Put in the context of around 800,000 to one million tourists who visit Kenya each year, that's still a pretty good safety record and it's only fair to add that some areas are worse than others. Masai Mara, Amboseli and Samburu are considered safe, for example, whereas parts of Tsavo East and Meru are more dubious.

Entry Fees The entry fees to all national parks and to Masai Mara Game Reserve is KSh 220 per person per day plus KSh 50 for a car or KSh 60 for a truck. Camping costs KSh 50 per person per night. Entry fees to game reserves other than Masai Mara vary because they are administered by local county councils but to be on the safe side it's best to assume they are the same as for national parks. If you find them less, consider it a bonus.

Maps If you are driving your own vehicle it's a good idea to equip yourself with maps of the parks before you set out. The best are all published by the Survey of Kenya and obtainable either from the Public Map Office or bookshops in Nairobi. The ones you will need are SK 87 *Amboseli National Park*, SK 86 *Masai Mara Game Reserve*, SK 82 *Tsavo East National Park* and SK 78 *Tsavo West National Park*.

Getting to the National Parks Since you are not allowed to walk in the national parks (with the exception of Hell's Gate, Saiwa Swamp and certain designated areas within Nakuru) you will have to hitch a ride with other tourists, hire a vehicle or join an organised tour.

Hitching is really only feasible if the people you get a ride with are going to be camping. Since this requires some considerable preparation in terms of food, drink and equipment, people with their own cars are naturally reluctant to pick up hitchhikers. If they are going to be staying at the lodges then you have the problem of how to get from the lodge to the camp site at the end of the day. Lodges and camp sites are often a long way apart and driving in the parks is not allowed between 7 pm and dawn. You'll then have to face the problem of transport the following day for game drives and again when you want to leave. All in all, it can be very problematical and it's probably not worth the effort.

Most travellers opt to go on organised safaris. There are scores of different companies offering safaris and they cater for all pockets and tastes. The cheaper ones involve camping and a degree of self-help (erect your own tent, help with the catering, etc) and are for people who don't expect much in the way of comfort but do want an authentic experience in the African bush.

For a full description of safari possibilities, costs and company addresses, etc see the section on organised safaris in the Getting Around chapter.

The alternative to an organised safari is to get a group together and rent a vehicle. If you're looking for other people to join you on a safari using a rented vehicle then check out the notice boards at the Youth Hostel, Mrs Roche's or the Hotel Pigale in Nairobi. As with safaris, a full description of costs and conditions for vehicle hire can be found in the Getting Around chapter.

Accommodation Camping out in the bush is, of course, the authentic way of going about a safari. There's nothing quite like having just a sheet of canvas between you and what you would normally see only on the residents' side of a zoo. Full-on contact with the bush, its potential dangers and rewards is surely what you are looking for. Anything more luxurious than this is going to dilute the experience and remove the immediacy of it all.

It's true there are some beautifully conceived and constructed game lodges and, if you have the money, it's probably worth spending a night or two at one or another of them though it's probably true to say they are mainly for those who prefer to keep the bush at arm's length and a glass of ice-cold beer within arm's reach. Or for those who are simply on a package tour or short holiday and prefer creature comforts and predictability to the rigours of camping. Certainly the way in which some game lodges attract wildlife to their door is somewhat contrived. Hanging up shanks of meat in a tree which a 'resident' leopard comes to feed off 10 minutes later – despite the spotlights – is

Top: Nairobi, Kenya (TW)
Bottom: Children on Nairobi-Naivasha railway, Kenya (PP)

Top: Nairobi, Kenya (RA)
Left: Malindi market, Kenya (TW)
Right: Malindi market, Kenya (TW)]

hardly the essence of Africa. You might as well feed your domestic cat at home and smoke a joint. It's only fair to add, on the other hand, that not all game lodges go in for this sort of circus.

Animal Spotting In the parks and reserves you'll be spending a lot of time craning necks and keeping watchful eyes out for the animals and birds you've come so far to see. There are few telltale signs, as well as a few things you can do to maximise your chances. Most of them are just common sense but it's amazing the number of people who go belting around noisily expecting everything to come to them:

Drive slowly and, where possible, quietly, keeping eyes trained not only on the ground ahead but also to the side and in the branches above.

Go in search in the early morning or the late afternoon, although in the more popular parks such as Amboseli and Masai Mara the animals are actually changing their normal hunting habits to fit in with the tourists, so at midday, when most people are safely back in their lodges stuffing their faces, the carnivores are out hunting in the hope that they may be able to do the same thing – in peace.

Vultures circling are not necessarily an indication of a kill below, but if they are gathering in trees and seem to be waiting you can reasonably assume they are waiting their turn on the carcass.

In wooded country, agitated and noisy monkeys or baboons are often a sign that there's a big cat (probably a leopard) around.

Do's & Don'ts In their quest for the perfect photo opportunity some drivers do some crazy things to that end. Again, a healthy dose of common sense goes a long way, but too many drivers seem to lack one.

Never get too close to the animals and back off if they are getting edgy or nervous. On the safari I was on a female cheetah (with cub) became extremely agitated when she was totally surrounded and hemmed in by a dozen minibuses, all full of excited visitors trying to get their 'shot'. She reacted by dropping the cub and bolting.

Never get out of your vehicle, except at designated points where this is permitted. The animals may look tame and harmless enough but this is not a zoo – the animals are wild and you should treat them as such.

Animals always have the right of way. Don't follow predators as they move off – you try stalking something when you've got half a dozen minibuses in tow.

Keep to the tracks. One of the biggest dangers in the parks today is land degradation from too many vehicles crisscrossing the countryside. Amboseli's choking dust is largely a result of this, and although Masai Mara is less fragile, it too needs to be treated with care.

Don't light fires, and dispose of cigarettes thoughtfully.

Don't litter the parks and camp sites. Unfortunately the worst offenders are often the safari drivers and cooks who toss everything and anything out the window with gay abandon, and leave camp sites littered with all manner of crap. It won't do any harm to point out to them the consequences of what they're doing, or clean it up yourself.

GOVERNMENT

Kenya is a one-party state with the Kenya African National Union (KANO) being the only legal political party. The government consists of the president, who holds executive power, and a legislative assembly of 188 members, 176 of whom are elected. There's a high degree of political patronage (Kikuyu being the major beneficiaries) and, following the 1988 elections, it's probably true to say that the executive's hold on power is unassailable. Opposition within the party and government does exist but there are definite limits to which it is tolerated and accusations of treason against those who oppose executive policy are not uncommon.

The judiciary were, until 1987, independent of government pressure and free to interpret both the constitution and the laws passed by the legislative assembly. In that year, however, parliament rushed through a bill giving the president the right to dismiss judges without recourse to a tribunal, thus effectively silencing them as a source of opposition. The measure was viewed with dismay by many sectors of Kenyan society, but it's now generally accepted that if you have anything negative to say about the government and its policies then you'd better not do it in public. Detention without trial is a common result of indiscretion. Indeed, it would not be inappropriate to slightly mis-quote Louis XIV's classic statement:

L'état?

C'est Moi!

ECONOMY

The cornerstone of Kenya's capitalist economy is agriculture which employs around 80% of the population, contributes some 31% to the GDP, and accounts for over 50% of the country's export earnings. The principal food crops are maize, sorghum, cassava, beans and fruit while the main cash crops are coffee, tea, cotton, sisal, pyrethrum and tobacco. The bulk of the food crops are grown by subsistence farmers on small plots of land whereas most of the cash crops originate from large, privately owned plantations employing contract labour though there's a significant input from smaller growers. Coffee and tea are the largest of the agricultural export earners with annual production being around 120,000 tonnes and 160,000 tonnes respectively.

While such figures might be a healthy sign for the country's balance of payments (tea fetches between US$2.70 and US$4 per kg on the world market), there's a great deal of discontent among the small farmers and labourers who are paid just US$0.10 per kg (for tea). In 1989-90, the country witnessed riots over this paltry sum. The dispute was handled badly by the Kenya Tea Development Authority (KTDA) and, although several heads have rolled and price increases were promised, there's still a long way to go before a settlement is reached. The situation is similar in the coffee sector and exacerbated by quotas imposed by the international cartel controlling this product which limits Kenya's ability to dispose of its stockpile. Coffee exports amounted to about 40% of export earnings in 1987.

On the other hand, tourism has replaced coffee as the country's largest export earner with arrivals up from 665,000 in 1987 to around one million in 1990. It seems likely that this growth will continue although there are concerns that the continued depletion of the wildlife in Kenya's game parks through poaching may lead to a fall-off, with Tanzania becoming the preferred destination. This issue is now being addressed and strict conservation measures are being implemented.

In addition to agriculture and tourism, Kenya has a relatively well developed industrial base which accounts for some 15% of GDP though the bulk of this is concentrated around Nairobi and Mombasa. The principal manufactures include processed food, vehicles and accessories, construction materials, engineering, textiles, glass and chemicals. Initially, this sector of the economy was developed with import substitution in mind but the bias has now changed in favour of joint-venture, export-oriented industries as a result of increasing deficit in the balance of payments and IMF loan conditions. Kenya's external debt of around US$4 billion is still considered to be low but the most worrying thing is the proportion of the country's foreign exchange earnings which goes into servicing foreign debt – currently around 35%.

Mining is a relatively small contributor to GNP and centred around the extraction of soda and fluorspar for export. There are other minerals, which include silver, gold, lead and limestone, but these have yet to be developed commercially.

Kenya's major export trading partners are the UK (17%), Germany (11.5%), Uganda (about 9%), the USA (about 7%) and the Netherlands (6.5%).

Some 75% of domestic energy requirements are imported, mainly in the form of oil from Saudi Arabia, but geothermal projects are being developed and there are four hydroelectric plants in operation along the Tana River. These will soon be joined by a huge new hydroelectric plant built in the Turkwel Gorge which is due to come on line in 1990.

Kenya's major sources of imports are Saudi Arabia (18.5%), the UK (about 14%), Japan (10%), Germany (8%) and the USA (5.5%).

POPULATION & PEOPLE

Kenya's population stands at around 23

million and is made up almost entirely of Africans with small (although influential) minorities of Asians (about 80,000), Arabs (about 40,000) and Europeans (about 40,000). The population growth rate of 3.8% is one of the highest in the world and is putting great strain on the country's ability to expand economically, provide reasonable educational facilities and other urban services. It has also resulted in tremendous pressure to increase the area of land under cultivation or for grazing with its associated environmental problems.

There are more than 70 tribal groups among the Africans, although the distinctions between many of them are already blurred and are becoming more so as Western cultural values become more ingrained. Traditional values are disintegrating as more and more people move to the larger towns, family and tribal groups become scattered and the tribal elders gradually die off.

Yet even though the average African may have outwardly drifted away from tribal traditions, tribe is still the single most important part of a person's identity. When two Africans meet and introduce themselves they will almost always say right at the outset what tribe they are each from. Although nominally

Christian for the most part, a surprising number of people still practice traditional customs. Some of the more inhumane customs, such as cliterodectomy (female circumcision), were outlawed by the British, usually with the aid of the local missionaries, but circumcision still remains the principal rite of passage from childhood to adulthood for boys.

The most important distinguishing feature between the tribes is language. The majority of Kenya's Africans fall into one of two major groups: the Bantu speakers and the Nilotic speakers. The Bantu people arrived in East Africa in waves from West Africa over a period of time from around 500 BC. Among the Bantu the largest tribal groups are the Kikuyu, Meru, Gusii, Embu, Akamba, Luyha and Mijikenda. The Nilotic speakers migrated to the area from the Nile Valley some time earlier but then had to make room for the migrations of Bantu speaking people. Nilotic speaking groups include the Maasai, Turkana, Samburu, Pokot and Kalenjin. All these tribal groups account for something over 90% of the total African population in Kenya. The Kikuyu and the Luo are by far the most numerous groups, and between them hold practically all the positions of power and influence in the country.

Maasai warrior

A third language grouping, and in fact the first migrants into the country, are the Cushitic speakers who occupy the north-east of the country and include such tribes as the El-Molo, Somali, Rendille and the Galla.

On the coast the Swahili is the name given to the local people who, while having various tribal ancestries, have in common the fact that they have been mixing, trading and intermarrying both among themselves and with overseas immigrants for hundreds of years.

Bantu Speakers

Kikuyu The Kikuyu number more than three million and their heartland is the area around Mt Kenya. The original Kikuyu are thought to have migrated to the area from the east and north-east of Africa over a period of two hundred years from the 16th century, and were actually part of the group known as Meru. They overran the original occupants of the area such as the Athi and the Gumba, although intermarriage and trading did take place.

The Kikuyu's new land was bordered by the Maasai and, although there were periods of calm between the two groups, there were also times when raids were carried out against each other's property and cattle. Both groups placed a high value on cattle. Intermarriage was not uncommon between them and there are a number of similarities – particularly in dress, weaponry, and dancing – shared by both as a result of their intermingling.

The administration of the clans (*mwaki*), made up of many family groups (*nyumba*), was originally taken care of by a council of elders, with a good deal of importance being placed on the role of the witch doctor, medicine man and the blacksmith. Traditionally the Kikuyu God (*Ngai*) is believed to reside on Mt Kenya (*kirinyaga* – variously 'mountain of brightness', 'mountain of whiteness' and even 'the black and white peak spotted like ostrich feathers') which accounts for the practice of orientating Kikuyu homes with the door facing Mt Kenya.

Initiation rites for both boys and girls are important ceremonies and consist of circumcision in boys and clitoridectomy in girls (the latter now rarely practiced), accompanied by elaborate preparations and rituals. Each group of youths of the same age belong to an age-set (*riika*) and pass through the various stages of life (with associated rituals) together.

Subgroups of the Kikuyu include the Embu, Ndia and Mbeere.

Akamba The traditional homeland of the Akamba people (*Ukumbani*) is the region east of Nairobi towards Tsavo National Park. They migrated here from the south several centuries ago in search of food, mainly the fruit of the baobab tree which was accorded great nutritional value.

The Akamba were great traders and ranged all the way from the coast to Lake Victoria and up to Lake Turkana. Ivory was one of the main barter items but locally made products such as beer, honey, iron weapons and ornaments were also traded. They used to obtain food stocks from the neighbouring Maasai and Kikuyu, as their own low altitude land was relatively poor and couldn't sustain the increasing population which followed their arrival in the area.

In colonial times, the Akamba were highly regarded by the British for their intelligence and fighting ability, and were drafted in large numbers into the British Army. Thousands lost their lives in WW I. When it came to land, however, the British were not quite as respectful and tried to limit the number of cattle the Akamba could own (by confiscating them) and also settle more Europeans in Ukumbani. The Akamba response was the formation of the Ukamba Members Association, whose members marched en masse to Nairobi and squatted peacefully at Kariokor market in protest. After three weeks, the administration gave way and the cattle were eventually returned to the people.

All Akamba adolescents go through initiation rites to adulthood at around the age of 12, and have the same age-set groups common to many of Kenya's tribes. The various age-set rituals involve the men, and the women to a lesser extent, gaining seniority as they get older. Young parents were known as 'junior elders' *(mwanake* for men, *mwiitu* for women) and were responsible for the maintenance and upkeep of the village. Once his children were old enough to become junior elders themselves, the mwanake went through a ceremony to become a 'medium elder' *(nthele)*, and later in life a 'full elder' *(atumia ma kivalo)* with the responsibility for death ceremonies and administering the law. The last stage of a person's life is that of 'senior elder' *(atumia ma kisuka)* who is responsible for the holy places.

Akamba subgroups include the Kitui, Masaku and Mumoni.

Gusii The Gusii number around one million and inhabit an area in the western highlands east of Lake Victoria. The area is dominated by Nilotic speaking groups with just this pocket of the Bantu speaking Gusii. Being a relatively small group, the Gusii were always on the move following influxes of other groups into their lands. After migrating to the Mt Elgon area sometime before the 15th century, the Gusii were gradually pushed south by the advancing Luo, and over the next couple of centuries came into conflict with the Maasai and the Kipsigis. They finally settled in the hills east of Lake Victoria as the high ridges were easier to defend. Having fought hard for their autonomy, the Gusii were unwilling to give it up to the British and suffered heavy losses in conflicts early this century. Following these conflicts the men were conscripted in large numbers into the British Army.

The Gusii family typically consists of a man, his wives and their married sons, all living together in a single compound. Large families served two purposes: with high infant mortality rates the survival of the family was assured, and the large numbers facilitated defence of the family enclosure. Initiation ceremonies are performed for both boys and girls, and rituals accompany all important events. Death is considered not to be natural but the work of 'witchcraft'. The

Gusii were primarily cattle keepers but also practiced some crop cultivation and millet beer was often an important ingredient at big occasions.

As is the case with many of Kenya's ethnic groups, medicine men *(abanyamorigo)* had a highly privileged and respected position. Their duty was to maintain the physical and mental wellbeing of the group – doctor and social worker combined. One of the more bizarre practices was (and still is) the removal of sections of the skull or spine to aid maladies such as backache or concussion.

Meru The Meru arrived in the area north-east of Mt Kenya from the coast sometime around the 14th century following invasions of that area by Somalis from the north. The group was led by a chief known as the *mogwe* up until 1974 when the incumbent converted to Christianity and denied his son inheriting the role. A group of tribal elders *(njuuri)* were all powerful, and along with the mogwe and witch doctor would administer justice as they saw fit – which often consisted of giving poison-laced beer to an accused person.

Other curious practices included holding a newly born child to face Mt Kenya and then blessing it by spitting on it, and witch doctors who might eliminate one of their rival's sons by putting poison on the circumcision blade.

Subgroups of the Meru include the Chuka, Igembe, Igoji, Tharaka, Muthambi, Tigania and Imenti.

Swahili Although the people of the coast do not have a common heritage, they do have a linguistic link which unites them – KiSwahili (commonly referred to as Swahili), a Bantu-based language which evolved as a means of communication between Africans and foreign traders such as Arabs, Persians and the Portuguese. As might be expected with such diverse inputs, the Swahili language borrows words from Arabic, Hindi, Portuguese and even English. The word *swahili* is a derivative of the Arabic word for coast – *sahel*.

Arab traders first started plying the coast

in their sailing dhows sometime before the 7th century, arriving with the north-east monsoon and sailing home on the south-west monsoon. The main exports were ivory, tortoiseshell and leopard skins, while items such as glass beads from India and porcelain from as far afield as China found their way here.

After the 7th century Islam became a strong influence as traders began settling along the coast. Today the majority of the coastal people are Muslims, although it's a world away from the stricter forms of Islam which prevail in some places in the Middle East.

Swahili subgroups include Bajun, Siyu, Pate, Mvita, Fundi, Shela, Ozi, Vumba and Amu (residents of Lamu).

Nilotic Speakers

Maasai It is the Maasai more than anyone who have become the symbol of 'tribal' Kenya. With an (often exaggerated) reputation as fierce warriors and a supercilious demeanour, the Maasai have largely managed to stay outside the mainstream of development in Kenya and still maintain their cattle herds in the area south of Nairobi straddling the Tanzanian border.

They first came to the region from the Sudan and eventually came to dominate a large area of central Kenya until, in the late 19th century, they were decimated by famine and disease, and their cattle herds routed by rindepest. Up until the Masai Mara Game Reserve was created in the early 1960s, the Maasai had plenty of space for cattle grazing, but at a stroke much of this land was put off limits. As their population increased (both the cattle and the Maasai) pressure for land became intense and conflict with the authorities constant. Settlement programmes have only been reluctantly accepted as Maasai traditions scorn agriculture and land ownership is a foreign concept to them.

Another consequence of the competition for land is that many of the ceremonial traditions can no longer be fulfilled. Part of the ceremony where a man becomes a warrior (*moran*) involves a group of young men

Maasai woman

around the age of 14 going out and building a village (*manyatta*) after their circumcision ceremony. Here they spend as long as eight years alone, and while the tradition and will survives, the land is just not available.

Tourism provides an income to some, either through selling everyday items (gourds, necklaces, clubs and spears), dancing or simply posing for photographs. However, while a few can make a lot of money from tourism the benefits are not widespread.

Luo The Luo people live in the west of the country on the shores of Lake Victoria. Along with the Maasai, they migrated south from the Nile region of Sudan around the 15th century. Although they clashed heavily with the existing Bantu speaking people of the area, intermarriage and cultural mixing readily took place.

The Luo are unusual amongst Kenya's ethnic groups in that circumcision is not performed on either sex. This practice was instead replaced by something that one can imagine being almost as painful – the extraction of four or six teeth from the bottom jaw. Although it is not done that much these days, you still see many middle-aged and older people of the region who are minus a few bottom pegs.

Although originally cattle herders, the Luo have adopted fishing and subsistence agriculture. The family group consists of the man, his wife (or wives) and their sons and daughters-in-law. The house compound is enclosed by a fence, and includes separate huts for the man and for each wife and son. (There is a good reconstruction of a Luo village in the grounds of the Kisumu Museum.)

The family group is member of a larger grouping of families *(dhoot)*, several of which in turn make up a group of geographically related people *(ogandi)*, each led by a chief *(ruoth)*. Collectively the ogandi constitute the Luo tribe. As is the case with many tribes, great importance is placed on the role of the medicine man and the spirits.

Turkana The Turkana are another of Kenya's more colourful (and warlike) people. Originally from the Karamajong district of north-eastern Uganda, the Turkana number around 250,000 and live in the virtual desert country of Kenya's north-west. Due to their isolation, the Turkana are probably the least affected by the 20th century of all Kenya's people.

Like the Samburu and the Maasai (with whom they are linguistically linked), the Turkana are cattle herders first, and more recently they have taken up fishing the waters of Lake Turkana and even growing the occasional crops, weather permitting. But unlike the other two tribes, the Turkana have discontinued the practice of circumcision.

The traditional dress of the Turkana people is amazing, as is the number of people who still wear it – catching a bus up in the north-west is a real eye-opener for a first-time visitor. The men cover part of their hair with mud which is then painted blue and decorated with ostrich and other feathers. The main garment they wear, despite the blast-furnace heat of the region, is a woollen blanket (usually a garish modern checked one) which is worn around one shoulder.

Traditional accessories include a small wooden stool carved out of a single piece of wood (used either as a pillow or a stool), a wooden stick with a distinctive shape, and a wrist knife. Both the men and the women wear with great flourish the lip plug through the lower lip which looks a bit gruesome to tourists. The women wear a variety of beaded and metal adornment, much of it indicating to the trained eye events in the woman's life. A half skirt of animal skins and a piece of black cloth are the only garments worn, although these days pieces of colourful cloth are not uncommon for use as baby slings.

Tattooing is also surprisingly common and usually has special meaning. Men are tattooed on the shoulders and upper arm each time they kill an enemy – the right shoulder for killing a man, the left for a woman; it's surprising the number of men you still see with these markings. Witch doctors and prophets are held in high regard and tattooing on someone's lower stomach is usually a sign of witch doctors' attempts to cast out an undesirable spirit rather than any sort of decoration.

Samburu Closely related to the Maasai, and in fact speaking the same language, the Samburu occupy an arid area directly north of Mt Kenya. It seems that when the Maasai migrated to the area from Sudan, some headed east (and became the Samburu) while the bulk of them continued south to the area they occupy today.

As is often the case, age-sets are an integral part of the society and the men pass through various stages before becoming a powerful elder at the top of the ladder. Circumcision is practiced in both sexes; with the girls it is only done on the day of marriage, which is usually when she is around 16 years old. Men are often in their thirties by the time they pass out of warriorhood and become elders qualified to marry.

Kalenjin Kalenjin, which means 'I say to

you' in Nandi, is a name formulated in the 1950s to describe the group of peoples previously called the Nandi by the British. The Nandi tag was erroneous as, although the people were all Nandi speakers (one of many dialects), they were not all Nandis; the other groups included the Kipsigis, Marakwet, Pokot and Tugen (arap Moi's people).

Kalenjin in traditional dress

The Kalenjin people occupy the western edge of the central Rift Valley area which includes Kericho, Eldoret, Kitale, Baringo and the Mt Elgon area. They first migrated to the area west of Lake Turkana from southern Sudan around 2000 years ago and gradually moved south as the climate changed and the forests dwindled.

Although originally pastoralists, most Kalenjin groups took up agriculture. Some of them, however, such as the Okiek, stuck to the forests and to a hunter-gatherer existence. Beekeeping was a common practice and the honey was used not only in trade but also for brewing beer. As with most tribes, Kalenjin have age-sets into which a man is initiated after circumcision and remains for the rest of his life. Polygamy was widely practiced. Administration of the law is carried out at the *kok* – an informal gathering of the clan's elders and other interested parties in the dispute. Unusually, the doctors were mostly women and they used herbal remedies in their work. Other specialist doctors practiced trepanning (taking out pieces of the skull to cure certain ailments), which is also practiced by the Bantu speaking Gusii of the Kisii district.

The Asians

The economically important Asian minority is made up largely of people of Indian descent whose ancestors originated from the western state of Gujarat and from the Punjab. Unlike the situation in Uganda, sensibility prevailed and the Asians here were not thrown into exile, largely because their influence was too great. Uganda is still trying to get its economy back on track.

India's connections with East Africa go back centuries to the days when hundreds of dhows used to make the trip between the west coast of India or the Persian Gulf and the coastal towns of East Africa every year. In those days, however, the Indians came as traders and only a very few stayed to settle. This all changed with the building of the Mombasa-Uganda railway at the turn of the century. In order to construct it, the British colonial authorities brought in some 32,000 indentured labourers from Gujarat and Punjab. When their contracts expired many of them decided to stay and set up businesses. Their numbers were augmented after WW II with the encouragement of the British.

Since they were an industrious and economically aggressive community they quickly ended up controlling large parts of the economies of Kenya, Tanzania and Uganda as merchants, artisans and financiers. Not only that, but they kept very much to themselves, regarding the Africans as culturally inferior and lazy. Few gave their active support to the Black nationalist movements in the run-up to independence despite being urged to do so by Nehru, the Prime Minister of India. And when independence came, like many of the White settlers, they were very hesitant to accept local citizenship, preferring to wait and see what would happen. To the Africans, therefore, it seemed they were not willing to throw their lot in with the newly independent nations and were there simply as exploiters.

As is well known, Idi Amin used this suspicion and resentment as a convenient ruse to enrich himself and his cronies. Uganda's economy collapsed shortly afterwards since Amin's henchmen were incapable of running the industries and businesses which the Asians had been forced to leave. Asians have fared somewhat better in Tanzania though nationalisation of many of their concerns has considerably reduced their control over the economy. It is in Kenya that they have fared best of all. Here they have a virtual stranglehold over the service sector (the smaller hotels, restaurants and bars, road transport and the tourist trade), the textile trade, book publishing and bookshops, and they are very important in the construction business.

For a time in the 1970s it seemed that there was little future for them in Africa. Governments were under heavy pressure to 'Africanise' their economies and job markets. Even in Kenya thousands of shops owned by Asians who had not taken out Kenyan nationality were confiscated in the early 1970s and they were forbidden to trade in the rural areas. Those days appear to have passed and African attitudes towards them have mellowed. What seemed like a widespread demand that they should go 'home' has been quietly dropped and the Asians are there to stay. The lesson of what happened to the economy of Uganda when the Asians were thrown out is one reason for this.

The Dispossessed

Kenya, being a relatively stable country with opportunities to make a living or at least working the tourists for hand-outs, is a natural magnet for refugees from strife-torn neighbouring countries. Nairobi and Mombasa and, to a lesser degree, the coastal resort towns, are the favoured destinations. You'll come across plenty of these people on your travels and it's relatively easy to remain anonymous if you can make enough money to stay off the streets.

There's nothing remarkable about this as such – it happens all over the world. What is remarkable in Kenya are the number of unattached teenage mothers – many of them Kenyan but also quite a lot from Uganda, Sudan, Ethiopia and even Rwanda. With the break-up of many traditional communities as a result of colonial policies that were designed to bring people into the money economy, and the continuation of this system under post-colonial regimes, there has been large-scale movement of people to urban areas. Most arrive with nothing and are forced to live in overcrowded shantytowns (some 60% of Nairobi's population live in these places) with little hope of anything resembling a steady job with reasonable pay. As a result, all the facets of urban alienation can be found in these places with drunkenness, theft and rape (particularly of schoolgirls) being fairly commonplace. But this isn't confined to the major urban areas. It appears to be fairly widespread everywhere outside of tribal areas that are still traditional.

As far as the girls are concerned, once they become pregnant they're expelled from school (in other words, it's the end of their educational prospects) and, as likely as not, rejected by their families, too. In 1986, the number of young girls who found themselves in this position (according to official figures) was 11,000 and it's been rising steadily ever since. The options for those to whom this happens are extremely limited. A few shelters do exist (usually run by Christian organisations) but it's only the lucky few who get in. For the rest, it's very poorly paid domestic work or the flesh market.

Laws regarding the responsibilities of paternity in Kenya either don't exist or are hardly ever enforced – it's definitely a man's world – and establishment Kenyan society remains tight-lipped about the problem. What it remains even more tight-lipped about is the practice of well-to-do Kenyan families recruiting little girls from the bush as domestic servants. Those recruited are even more circumspect.

Though clothed and fed and, if lucky, paid a pittance which varies between US$1 and US$16 a month, these children work on average 15 to 17 hours a day with no days off. Some get no pay at all with just food and clothing provided in lieu of salary. The reason their parents push them into this, apart from the wages which they expect to recoup, is the hope that their children will acquire a training and education of sorts. The reality is often quite different. These girls are often raped by either the man of the house or his sons and thrown out when they become pregnant. Like their more fortunate counterparts who did actually go to school before being expelled, these girls, as likely as not, join the flesh market.

Whatever you may think of prostitution, it's a hard life in Kenya. Minimal rentals, even in rough areas of Nairobi, are around KSh 2000 (about US$95) a month. In better areas it's frequently KSh 4000 to KSh 5000 (US$190 to US$240) a month. Add on decent clothes and footwear and medical attention when necessary, that's a lot of money to be made even to make ends meet – let alone save anything. It's not surprising, therefore, that those who do manage to get their heads above water head for the bars and discos frequented by expatriate workers and tourists since it's more lucrative and there is the vague possibility of marriage or, at least, a long-term friendship. Even so, it's not that easy. Ever since the advent of AIDS, there's been a profound reluctance to tempt fate and prostitutes now carry condoms out of economic necessity as well as to protect themselves from infection.

It isn't just pregnant young girls who find themselves dispossessed of course. The conditions under which young boys have to work in the coffee, sisal and rice plantations are equally onerous and many find their way onto the streets of Nairobi and Mombasa along with other jobless adult males.

Blaming the government for this state of affairs is all too easy for those from rich Western countries but is, to a large degree, unfair. Because of Kenya's high birth rate and the limited amount of funds available, the government is already flat out keeping pace with the demand for schools, hospitals and other social services, the transport infrastructure, and paying interest on its foreign loans. Given this, it's unlikely that much can be done in the foreseeable future for those who fall under the category of the dispossessed.

RELIGION

It's probably true to say that most Kenyans outside of the coastal and eastern provinces are Christians of one sort or another whilst most of those on the coast and in the eastern part of the country are Muslim. Muslims make up some 30% of the population. In the more remote tribal areas you'll find a mixture of Muslims, Christians and those who follow their ancestral tribal beliefs.

As a result of intense missionary activity from colonial times to the present, just about every Christian sect is represented in Kenya, from Lutherans to Catholics to Seventh Day Adventists and Weslyans. The success which all these weird and wonderful sects have enjoyed would be quite mind boggling if it were not for the fact that they have always judiciously combined Jesus with education and medicine – two commodities in short supply until recently in Kenya. Indeed, there are still many remote areas of Kenya where the only place you can get an education or medical help is at a mission station and there's no doubt that those who volunteer to staff them are dedicated people.

On the other hand, the situation is often not as simple as it might at first appear. As with Catholicism in Central and South America which found it necessary to incorporate native deities and saints into the Roman Catholic pantheon in order to placate local sensibilities, African Christianity is frequently syncretic. This is especially so where a tribe has strong ancestral beliefs. There are also many pure home-grown African Christian sects which owe no allegiance to any of the major Western cults. The only thing they have in common is the Bible though their interpretation of it is often radically different. It's worth checking out a few churches whilst you're in Kenya if only to get an understanding of where the religion is headed and even if you can't understand the language which is being used, you'll certainly be captivated by what

only Africans can do with such beauty and precision – unaccompanied choral singing.

The upsurge of home-grown Christian sects has much to do with cultural resurgence, the continuing struggle against neocolonialism, and the alienation brought about by migration to urban centres far from tribal homelands in search of work. Some of these sects are distinctly radical and viewed with alarm by the government. The Tent of the Living God, for instance, was denounced by the President as being anti-Christ and three of its leaders were arrested at a gathering in Eastleigh, Nairobi, in late January 1990. The charges against them were thrown out of court the following week and the men released but the government's action was perhaps an indicator of how it intends to deal with such perceived threats to the status quo in the future.

It isn't just the radical sects which worry the government, however. In the absence of any effective political opposition within the party, even mainstream church leaders have taken to criticising the government

Jamia Mosque - Nairobi

from the relative safety of their pulpits. They have likewise been denounced and accused of treason though none have yet been arrested.

As far as Islam is concerned, most Muslims belong to the Sunni branch of the faith and, as a result, the Sunni communities have been able to attract substantial Saudi Arabian funding for schools and hospitals along the coast and elsewhere.

Only a small minority belong to the Shia branch of Islam and most are to be found among the Asian community. On the other hand, Shiites have been coming to East Africa from all over the Eastern Islamic world for centuries, partially to escape persecution but mainly for trading purposes. They didn't come here to convert souls and there was a high degree of cooperation between the schismatic sects and the Sunnis which is why there's a total absence of Shiite customs in Swahili culture today.

Among the Asian community, there are representatives of virtually all Shiite sects but the most influential are the Ismailis – followers of the Aga Khan. As with all Ismailis, they represent a very liberal version of Islam and are perhaps the only branch of the faith which is strongly committed to the education of women at all levels and their participation in commerce and business. It's obvious that the sect has prospered well in Kenya, going by all the schools and hospitals dedicated to the Aga Khan which you will come across in most urban centres.

Hinduism, as is the case in India, remains a self-contained religion which concerns only those born into it. You'll come across a considerable number of temples in the larger urban areas where most of those of Indian origin live. There are literally scores of different sects of Hinduism to be found in Kenya which are too numerous to mention here but many are economically quite influential.

For a superb and very detailed account of each and every Asian-derived sect of both Islam and Hinduism see *Through Open Doors – A View of Asian Cultures in Kenya*, by Cynthia Salvadori (Kenway Publications, Nairobi, 1989). This is a large-format, hardback book with many illustrations on sale in most of Nairobi's bookshops. It's one of the best researched and readable books I've ever come across.

HOLIDAYS & FESTIVALS

January
  New Year's Day (1st)
March-April
  Good Friday
  Easter Monday
  Id-ul-Fitr (end of Ramadan, 1991-93)
May
  Labour Day (1st)
June
  Madaraka Day (1st)
October
  Kenyatta Day (20th)
December
  Independence Day (12th)
  Christmas Day (25th)
  Boxing Day (26th)

LANGUAGE

English and KiSwahili are the official languages and are taught in schools throughout Kenya, but there are many other major tribal languages which include Kikuyu, Luo and Kikamba as well as a plethora of minor tribal languages. Most urban Kenyans and even tribal people involved in the tourist industry speak English so you shouldn't experience too many problems making yourself understood. Italian and German are also spoken by many Kenyans but usually only among those associated with the tourist trade on the coast.

It's extremely useful, however, to have a working knowledge of KiSwahili, especially outside of urban areas and in remote parts of the country since this will open doors and enable you to communicate with people who don't speak English. It's also the most common language which speakers of different tribal languages use to communicate with each other. Even tribespeople who haven't been to school will be able to speak *some* KiSwahili as a rule. Not only that, but if you're planning on visiting Tanzania then you'll find it extremely useful as it's essentially become the official language there (though English is still used extensively).

Facts for the Visitor

VISAS

Visas are required by all except nationals of Commonwealth countries (excluding nationals of Australia and Sri Lanka and British passport holders of Indian, Pakistani and Bangladeshi origin), Denmark, Ethiopia, Germany, the Irish Republic, Italy, Norway, Spain, Sweden, Turkey and Uruguay. Those who don't need visas are issued on entry with a Visitor's Pass valid for a stay of up to six months. Three months is the average but it depends what you ask for.

If you enter Kenya through a land border no-one will ever ask you for an onward ticket or 'sufficient funds'. This isn't always the case if you enter by air. A lot depends on what you look like, whether you're male or female, what you write on your immigration card and which immigration officer you deal with. If it's fairly obvious that you aren't intending to stay and work then you'll generally be given the benefit of the doubt. Put yourself in a strong position before you arrive: look smart and write the name of an expensive hotel on your immigration card in the appropriate section.

Single women have been told at times that 'sufficient funds' in the absence of an onward ticket were suspect 'because women lose money easily'! Perhaps the appropriate rejoinder should be that 'men spend money faster'. To balance these experiences, it should be said that we've never heard of anyone being refused entry to Kenya even if, as a last resort, they've had to buy a refundable onward ticket.

So long as your visa remains valid you can visit either Tanzania or Uganda and return without having to apply for another visa. This does not apply to visiting any other countries. There is, however, a charge at the border for doing this – usually about US$4.

Embassies

Visas can be obtained from the following Kenyan diplomatic representatives in:

Australia
  33 Ainslie Ave, Canberra (tel 474788)
Belgium
  1-5 Avenue de la Joyeuse, 1040 Brussels (tel 2303065)
Canada
  Ottawa, Ontario (tel 5631773)
Egypt
  20 Boulos Hanna St, PO Box 362, Dokki, Cairo (tel 704455)
Ethiopia
  Fikre Miriam Rd, Hiher Kebelle 01, PO Box 3301, Addis Ababa (tel 610033)
France
  3 Rue Cimaros, 75116 Paris (tel 4553 3500)
Germany
  5300 Bonn-Bad Godesburg 2, Micael Plaza, Villichgasse 17, Bonn (tel 356042)
India
  E-66 Vasant Marg, 110057 New Delhi (tel 672280)
Italy
  Icilio No 14, 00153 Rome (tel 5781192)
Japan
  24-20 Nishi-Azobu 3-Chome, Minato-Ku, Tokyo (tel 7234006)
Nigeria
  52 Queens Drive, Ikoyi, PO Box 6464, Lagos (tel 682768)
Pakistan
  Sector G-6/3, House 8, St 88, PO Box 2097, Islamabad (tel 811243)
Rwanda
  Boulevard de Nyabugogo just off the Place de l'Unité Nationale, PO Box 1215, Kigali (tel 72774)
Somalia
  Km 4 Via Mecca, PO Box 618, Mogadishu (tel 80857)
Sudan
  Street 3 Amarat, PO Box 8242, Khartoum (tel 40386)
Sweden
  Birger Jarlsgatan 37, 2tr, 10395 Stockholm (tel 218300)
Tanzania
  NIC Investment House, Samora Ave, PO Box 5231, Dar es Salaam (tel 31526)
Uganda
  Plot No 60, Kira Rd, PO Box 5220, Kampala (tel 231861)
UK
  45 Portland Place, London W1N 4AS (tel 6377861)

USA
  2249 R St NW, Washington DC 20008 (tel 3876101)
Zaïre
  5002 Ave de l'Onganda, BP 9667, Gombe, Kinshasa (tel 30117)
Zambia
  Harambee House, 5207 United Nations Ave, Lusaka (tel 227938)
Zimbabwe
  95 Park Lane, PO Box 4069, Harare (tel 790847)

Where there is no Kenyan embassy or high commission, visas can be obtained from the British embassy or high commission.

The cost of visas generally increases with the distance from Kenya and so do the hassles of getting them. We've had cliff-hanger stories from Australia where the high commission took 1½ months to issue a visa. All this time they hung on to the person's passport who only got it back (with a visa) *one* day before the departure date. This is not at all typical but it does indicate that you should apply well in advance if you're flying direct.

In New York visas cost US$10, and you must have two photographs and an onward ticket or a letter from your bank saying you have at least US$2000 in your account. They're issued in 24 hours and are valid for a stay of six months. In London they cost £5, you do not need photographs or onward tickets, and they are issued in 15 minutes. In Australia they cost A$17, require three photos and are *usually* issued within 10 days if you send your passport from another city. Visas are also available on arrival at Jomo Kenyatta International Airport in Nairobi for US$10.

Closer to Kenya things are generally simpler and less time consuming:

Rwanda The embassy is on the Boulevard de Nyabugogo just off the Place de l'Unité Nationale next to the Panafrique Hotel and is open Monday to Friday from 8.30 am to noon and 2 to 4.30 pm. Visas cost RFr 700, require two photographs and are issued the same day if you apply before 11.30 am. No onward tickets or minimum funds are asked for.

Tanzania The embassy is on the 14th floor, NIC Investment House, Samora Ave at the junction with Mirambo St, Dar es Salaam. Visas cost TSh 700, require two photographs and take 24 hours to issue. The embassy is open Monday to Friday from 9 am to noon.

Uganda The high commission (tel 31861) is at Plot No 60, Kira Rd near the Uganda Museum. It's open Monday to Friday from 8.30 am to 12.30 pm and 2 to 4.30 pm. Visas cost US$3, are issued in 24 hours and two photos are required. If you make your application before noon the visa can usually be issued the same day.

Zambia In Lusaka they cost Kw 15, require two photographs and are issued in 24 hours. No onward ticket is required.

Visa Extensions

Visas can be renewed in Nairobi at Immigration (tel 332110), Nyayo House (ground floor), on the corner of Kenyatta Ave and Uhuru Highway or at the office in Mombasa (tel 311745) during normal office hours.

A single re-entry permit costs US$8 and a multiple-entry permit US$40. You must pay in foreign currency. No onward tickets or 'sufficient funds' are demanded. Remember that you don't need a re-entry permit if you're only going to visit Tanzania or Uganda *so long as your visa remains valid*. The staff here are friendly and helpful.

Other African Visas

Since Nairobi is a common gateway city to East Africa and the city centre is easy to get around, many travellers spend some time here picking up visas for other countries which they intend to visit. If you are going to do this you need to plan ahead because some embassies only accept visa applications in the mornings, others only on certain days of the week. Some take 24 hours to issue, others 48 hours. Some visas (Sudan, for instance) may have to be referred to the country's capital city but this is rare.

If you're heading for Zaïre get the visa here, where it costs around US$8, rather than in Uganda, Rwanda or Tanzania where you'll pay at least US$70!

Burundi The embassy is on the 14th floor, Development House, Moi Ave (tel 728340). Visas cost KSh 200, require two photographs and take 24 hours. The visa is good for a visit from one to 60 days, depending what you put on the form, and is valid for three months from the date of issue. You can only apply on Mondays and Wednesdays, and collect on Tuesday and Thursday at 4 pm. The embassy is open Monday to Thursday from 8.30 am to 12.30 pm and 2 to 5 pm.

Egypt The embassy is at Chai House, Koinange St (tel 25991). It's open Monday to Friday from 9 am to noon. One month, single-entry visas cost KSh 380, require two photos, an onward ticket and vaccination certificate for yellow fever and cholera. They take 48 hours to issue and you can collect them in the afternoons only from 2 to 3.30 pm.

Ethiopia The embassy is on State House Ave (tel 723035). It's open Monday to Friday from 8.30 am to 12.30 pm and 2.30 to 5 pm. Tourist and transit visas all cost KSh 90, require one photo and take between 24 and 48 hours to issue. Entry and exit is by air only and you must have an onward ticket.

Madagascar There is no Malagasy embassy/consulate as such in Nairobi but visa applications are processed at the Air Madagascar office in the Hilton Hotel block (City Hall Way). Visas cost KSh 170, require four photographs and an onward ticket and are issued in 24 hours.

Rwanda The embassy (tel 334341) is on the 12th floor, International House, Mama Ngina St, Nairobi. It's open Monday to Friday from 8.30 am to 12.30 pm and 2 to 5 pm. One month visas cost KSh 200, require two photos and take 24 hours to issue. On the application form it will ask you the date when you want to enter Rwanda. Think carefully about this as the visa will run from then.

Somalia The embassy is at International House, Mama Ngina St (tel 24301). Visa applications are only accepted on Monday and Tuesday mornings. One month visas cost KSh 300, require two photographs and are issued in 24 hours. You must have a letter from your embassy stating your profession and a valid reason for visiting Somalia. It's then up to the embassy staff to decide if you qualify for an entry visa – it's by no means assured.

Sudan The embassy is on the 7th floor, Minet ICDC House, Mamlaka Rd (tel 720853). A one month visa costs KSh 200, requires two photographs and takes around one month to issue as all applications have to be forwarded to Khartoum. An onward ticket is necessary.

Tanzania The high commission is on the 4th floor, Continental House, on the corner of Harambee Ave and Uhuru Highway (tel 331056/7). It's open Monday to Friday from 9 am to 5 pm. Visas cost from KSh 100 to KSh 600 (depending on your nationality), require two photographs and take 48 hours to issue.

Uganda The visa section of the high commission is on the 4th floor, Baring Arcade, Phoenix House, Kenyatta Ave. It's not a good place to get a visa as they cost US$20 which must be paid in cash dollars or by travellers' cheque! The office is open from 9.30 am to 12.30 pm and 2.30 to 4 pm. The two week visas take 24 hours to issue and require one photo.

Zaïre The embassy is in Electricity House, Harambee Ave (tel 29771). A one month visa costs KSh 160, a two month visa costs KSh 280 and a three month visa is KSh 350. There is no extra charge for multiple entry; just request it on your visa application form. Four photographs and a letter of introduction from your own embassy are required, and the visas take 24 hours to issue. The staff are pleasant and the embassy is open Monday to Friday from 9 am to noon.

Zambia The high commission is on Nyerere Rd next door to the YWCA (tel 724796). It's open only on Mondays and Fridays from 8.30 am to 12.30 pm and 2 to 4.30 pm, and on Wednesdays from 8.30 am to 12.30 pm. One month, single-entry visas cost KSh 200, require three photographs and take 48 hours to issue. Double entry visas cost KSh 400, multiple entry KSh 600.

Francophone Countries The French Embassy (Embassy House, Harambee Ave; tel 339783) issues visas for French speaking countries which don't have embassies in Nairobi, such as Chad and Central African Republic, for instance. See the Tourist Information section later in this chapter for a full list of foreign diplomatic missions in Kenya.

Working in Kenya

Foreigners will find that jobs are hard to find and working permits are even harder to obtain. Basically the rule of thumb is that if an African can do the job there's no need to hire a *mzungu* (White person). The only real possibilities are teaching jobs and working for one of the international aid agencies. All this sort of work has to be arranged, and permits obtained, before you arrive in Kenya.

MONEY

The unit of currency is the Kenyan shilling (KSh), which is made up of 100 cents. Notes in circulation are KSh 500, 200, 100, 50, 20 and 10; coins are KSh 5 (seven-sided) and KSh 1, and 50, 10 and 5 cents.

The official bank rates fluctuate according to the international currency markets but not by a great deal. The Kenyan shilling is virtually a hard currency, especially in surrounding countries.

US$1	=	KSh 22.00
UK£1	=	KSh 35.30
A$1	=	KSh 17.00
Y100	=	KSh 15.66
C$1	=	KSh 18.60

Import and export of local currency is allowed up to KSh 100 and, when you leave the country, customs officials will ask you if you are carrying any. If you say you are not that's generally the end of the matter. If you're only leaving the country for a short while and intend to return via the same border and don't want to convert all your Kenyan shillings into another currency, you can leave any excess at a border post against a receipt and pick it up again when you get back.

When leaving via Nairobi airport it's possible to reconvert any amount of Kenya shillings to hard currency as long as you have the bank receipts to cover the amount. This is only possible at the airport, and not only is the exchange rate a little low but they charge KSh 100 commission! This facility is obviously meant for those who are leaving the country and have excess shillings (which you can't legally export) but they don't ask to see your air ticket at the time so presumably anyone could do this.

It used to be possible, and still may be, to cash US dollar travellers' cheques at banks in Kenya and get US dollars cash for them, but it's becoming harder. At most banks you'll be met with a flat 'No' but some people are successful. Certainly you have to prove that you are leaving the country within 48 hours (air ticket, dated visa) and you generally need a convincing story about why you need cash dollars.

You can get cash dollars with no problems if you make a withdrawal against your home account using a Visa card at Barclays Bank. So long as you don't want more than US$150 to US$200 per day it takes about 20 minutes. One traveller reported that she was able to get US$1000 in cash though that required a telex to the bank in her home country. Asked why she wanted that amount, she told them she was going to Tanzania where hotel bills and national park entry fees had to be paid in hard currency. Several other travellers have used the same explanation with success. Another traveller reported that it's possible to change your travellers' cheques to gambling chips at the casino in Nairobi, then after a while go back to the cashier and change the chips back to cash dollars.

Bank Charges
Travellers' cheques attract a 1% commission at some banks but none at all at others (at Barclays there's generally no commission). Barclays is probably the best bank to change cheques at since there's hardly any red tape and the transaction takes just a few minutes. Banking hours are Monday to Friday from 8 or 9 am to 2 pm and on the first and last Saturdays of the month from 9 to 11 am.

The Black Market
There is a black market for hard currency in Nairobi but as you only get a few shillings over the bank rate, it's only worth it if you are on a real shoestring budget. You will no doubt be approached by people (mainly in Nairobi) who offer to buy US dollars and UK pounds from you at a rate which you almost can't refuse (KSh 30 for the US dollar). It's more than likely you are being set up for a rip-off. There is no way *anyone* is going to give you KSh 30 to the US dollar.

If you do want to change money on the black market then it obviously has to be with money which is not declared on your currency form (see below). Keep away from the street hustlers and deal direct with shopkeepers. The travellers' grapevine is the best source of info as to who is currently offering the best rates.

Currency Declaration Forms
Currency declaration forms are usually issued on arrival although you may have to ask for one at the Namanga border between Kenya and Tanzania. These are collected when you leave, but not scrutinised. You cannot change travellers' cheques without a currency form so it's to your advantage to make sure you obtain one.

If for any reason you don't get one, or lose yours, they can be obtained from the Central Bank of Kenya, 9th floor, Ukulima House, Haile Selassie Ave, Nairobi, without any fuss (it takes about 10 minutes). Before you report to the bank you must first get a declaration from the police station on the corner of Harry Thuku Rd and University Way near the university stating that you have lost your original form. There is no fuss about this, just tell them your story.

Currency declaration forms can also be obtained from the Customs desk in the main post office in the larger towns (such as Kisumu, Eldoret and Mombasa).

Currency forms and bank receipts have to be produced when buying international flight tickets in Kenya. If you are intending to do this plan ahead because if you leave the country and then return you will no longer have your original currency form and you will have lost credit for the money which you changed on your first visit. See the Getting There chapter for further details on how this affects you.

Transferring Money

Kenya is a good place to have funds transferred to. It generally takes only a few days. You can collect your money entirely in US dollars travellers' cheques but the money is transferred first into Kenyan shillings then back into dollars. If you are going to spend all the money in Kenya it's worth getting Kenya shillings travellers' cheques and saving yourself a few percentage points commission.

Travellers' cheques issued in Kenya are sometimes stamped 'Non-negotiable in the Republic of South Africa'. If you intend to go there, this is going to cause problems. It is, after all, your money and not the bank's. Some travellers regard this sort of interference as totally unacceptable and have spent the best part of a day arguing with bank officials. Some have been successful. Barclays Bank does this, which is nonsense since they have scores of branches in South Africa.

It's also possible to get cash (dollars or shillings) with a Visa card at Barclays Bank.

At the Bank of Kenya's Bureau de Change at Jomo Kenyatta International Airport, Nairobi, you can exchange shillings for cash dollars up to any amount so long as you have bank receipts to cover the transaction.

COSTS

The cost of budget accommodation in Kenya is very reasonable so long as you're happy with communal showers and toilets. Clean sheets are invariably provided and sometimes you'll also get soap and a towel. For this you're looking at US$3 a single and US$5 a double and up. It can be slightly cheaper on the coast, especially at Lamu. If you want your own bathroom costs rise to around US$5 a single and US$7 a double and up. Again, it can be slightly cheaper on the coast but more expensive in Nairobi.

There are plenty of small cafés in every town, usually in a certain area. They cater to local people and you can get a traditional meal for about US$1. Often the food isn't up to much but sometimes it can be excellent. For a little more the Indian restaurants are great value. Some offer all-you-can-eat lunches for around US$2. They're not only tasty but you won't need to eat for the rest of the day either. A splurge at a better class restaurant is going to set you back between US$5 and US$10.

The price of beer and soft drinks is regulated by the government. At any place other than a tourist hotel (officially known as a Class D establishment), soft drinks are up to KSh 3, and the excellent local beer (Tusker, White Cap and Pilsner) is around KSh 15. At a Class D place you'll pay up to KSh 8 and KSh 30 respectively.

Public transport is very reasonable and the trains are excellent value. To travel from one end of Kenya to the other (Mombasa to Malaba) on the train in 2nd class is going to cost you about US$18. In 3rd class it's less than half of that. Buses are priced about halfway between the 3rd and 2nd class train fares.

The thing that is going to cost you most in Kenya is safaris. A safari for three nights and four days, for instance, by companies which cater for budget travellers is priced around US$130; seven days costs around US$200. This includes transport, food, hire of tents, national park entry fees, camping fees and the wages of the guides and cooks. In other words, more or less everything except a few drinks and tips.

Car hire is even more expensive and is probably out of reach of most budget travellers. A 4WD Suzuki costs around US$500 per week with unlimited mileage; petrol is extra. If you don't want 4WD then a small car, such as a Nissan Sunny, costs around US$400 per week.

TIPPING

With such an active tourist industry, Kenya is a country where tipping is expected. Obviously there's no need to tip in the very basic African eateries or hotels, in *matatus* (local minibuses) or when using other public transport. In better restaurants 5% to 10% of the bill is the usual amount. Porters at hotels and railway stations get around KSh 5 per bag.

If you take a safari then it's also expected that you tip your driver, guide and cook, or at least give them a useful gift of some description. In money terms, KSh 30 per day for the driver, less for cooks and assistants, is about the right amount. This is the cost per person and how much you give obviously depends on whether they have worked well to make your safari enjoyable.

TOURIST INFORMATION

Considering the extent to which the country relies on tourism, there is very little in the way of printed information available, and it's incredible to think that there's not even a tourist office in Nairobi! There are a couple of free weekly pamphlets which go some way towards filling the gap, but they are by no means comprehensive. The best of them is the *Tourist's Kenya*, and it is available at the larger hotels and travel agents in Nairobi. It lists major hotels and airlines and gives schedules for trains, Kenya Airways and the Lake Victoria ferries. It also has a non-exhaustive list of car hire and safari operators. Another one is the monthly *Tourist Index*.

Local Tourist Offices

The only tourist offices in the country are the ones in Mombasa on Moi Ave (tel 311231) and in Malindi on Lamu Rd.

Overseas Reps

The Ministry of Tourism maintains several overseas offices:

France
    Kenya Tourist Office, 5 Rue Volney, Paris 75002
Germany
    Kenya Tourist Office, Hochstrasse 53, 7 Frankfurt
Sweden
    Kenya Tourist Office, Birger Jarlsgatan, S 102 95 Stockholm
Switzerland
    Kenya Tourist Office, Bleicherweg 30, CH-8039 Zurich
UK
    Kenya Tourist Office, 13 New Burlington St, London WIX IFF
USA
    Kenya Tourist Office, 9100 Wilshire Blvd, Doheney Plaza Suite 111, Beverly Hills CA 90121
    Kenya Tourist Office, 60 East 56th St, New York NY 10022

Foreign Embassies

Countries which have diplomatic representation in Kenya (all in Nairobi) include:

Algeria
    Matungulu House, Mamlaka Rd, PO Box 53902 (tel 724634)
Australia
    New Chancery, Riverside Drive, PO Box 30360 (tel 749955)
Belgium
    Silopark House, Mama Ngina St, PO Box 30461 (tel 20501)
Burundi
    Development House, Moi Ave, PO Box 44439 (tel 728430)
Canada
    Comcraft House, Haile Selassie Ave, PO Box 30481 (tel 334033)
Denmark
    HFCK Building, Koinange St, PO Box 40412 (tel 331088)
Egypt
    Chai House, Koinange St, PO Box 30285 (tel 25991)

Ethiopia
State House Ave, PO Box 45198 (tel 723035)
France
Embassy House, Harambee Ave, PO Box 41784 (tel 339783)
Germany
Embassy House, Harambee Ave, PO Box 30180 (tel 26661)
Ghana
Muthaiga Rd, PO Box 48534 (tel 65417)
India
Jeevan Bharati Building, Harambee Ave, PO Box 30074 (tel 22566)
Japan
ICEA Building, Kenyatta Ave, PO Box 60202 (tel 332955)
Libya
Jamahiriya House, Loita St, PO Box 60149 (tel 337493)
Malawi
Bruce House, Standard St, PO Box 30453 (tel 21174)
Nigeria
Lenana Rd, Hurlingham, PO Box 30516 (tel 564116)
Pakistan
St Michael's Rd, Westlands, PO Box 30045 (tel 61666)
Rwanda
International House, Mama Ngina St, PO Box 48579 (tel 334341)
Somalia
International House, Mama Ngina St, PO Box 30769 (tel 24301)
Sudan
Minet ICDC House, Mamlaka Rd, PO Box 48784 (tel 720853)
Tanzania
Continental House, Harambee Ave, PO Box 47790 (tel 331056)
Uganda
Phoenix House, Baring Arcade, Kenyatta Ave
UK
Bruce House, Standard St, PO Box 30465 (tel 335944)
USA
Embassy Building, corner Haile Selassie Ave and Moi Ave, PO Box 30137 (tel 334141)
USSR
Lenana Rd, PO Box 30049 (tel 722462)
Zaïre
Electricity House, Harambee Ave, PO Box 48106 (tel 29771)
Zambia
Nyerere Rd, off Central Park, PO Box 48741 (tel 724796)
Zimbabwe
Minet ICDC Building, Mamlaka Rd, PO Box 30806 (tel 721071)

GENERAL INFORMATION
Post

The Kenyan postal system is very reliable. Letters sent from Kenya rarely go astray but do take up to two weeks to reach Australia or the USA. Incoming letters to Kenya take around a week to reach Nairobi.

Parcels or books sent by surface mail take up to 4½ months to arrive – but they do get there. I can vouch for this – I've sent plenty of stuff this way!

Postal Rates The airmail rates in KSh for items posted from Kenya are:

Item	Africa	Europe	USA & Australia
letter	4.40	5.50	7.70
postcard	2.80	3.90	5.50
aerogramme	3.40	3.40	3.40

The surface mail rates in KSh for parcels posted in Kenya are:

Weight	Europe	USA	Australia
5 kg	160	183	135
10 kg	211	326	168
15 kg	274	469	207
20 kg	328	608	246

Parcel Post Kenya is a good place to send home parcels of goodies, or excess gear. In the main post office in Nairobi you'll always see at least a couple of people busily taping and wrapping boxes to send home. You have to take the parcel *unwrapped* to be inspected by customs at the post office not later than 3.30 pm. You then wrap and send it. The whole process is very simple and, apart from wrapping the parcel, takes only a few minutes.

Right outside the post office in Nairobi there's usually a guy selling all the things you'll need to safely wrap a parcel. When he's there, he hangs out right at the foot of the steps to the bridge across Haile Selassie Ave. Trouble is, he's not always there so it's best to bring along your own cardboard, paper, tape and string. The cheapest place to get this stuff is the supermarket on Koinange St between Kenyatta Ave and Standard St in Nairobi. Otherwise go to Biba on Kenyatta Ave at the junction with Muindi Mbingu St.

Receiving Mail Letters can be sent care of poste restante in any town. Virtually every traveller uses Nairobi as a mail drop and so the amount of mail in poste restante here is amazing. The vast majority of it finds its way into the correct pigeon holes though there's naturally the occasional mistake. Most of the mistakes are entirely the fault of the letter writer. Make sure you write the addressee's name in block capitals and underline it! I can only admire the ingenuity of the postal staff in sorting out poste restante letters into the correct pile after seeing the way that some people address letters. You'd think some people had never been to school! Don't blame the Nairobi postal staff – blame your friends. Nevertheless, if you're not getting expected letters, try looking under all possible initials including 'M' (for M, Mr, Mrs, Ms, if you're an English or French speaker), 'S' (for Señor, Señora, etc, if you're a Spanish or Portuguese speaker), etc.

Some travellers use the American Express Clients Mail Service and this can be a useful alternative to poste restante. Officially you are supposed to have an Amex card or be using their travellers' cheques to avail yourself of this service but no check of this is made at the office in Nairobi. The postal addresses in Nairobi and Mombasa are:

American Express Clients Mail Service
Express Kenya Ltd
PO Box 40433
Nairobi

Express Mombasa
PO Box 90631
Mombasa

The Nairobi office is in Bruce House on Standard St (tel 334722), while the Mombasa office is on Nkrumah Rd (tel 312461).

Telephones
As you might expect, the phone system also works well.

International Calls International calls are easy to make from Nairobi, Mombasa and Kisumu where you can either go through the operator or dial it yourself using a phone-card. These are available from the post office counter in denominations of KSh 200, 400 and 1000. A KSh 200 card gives you around three minutes to Australia or the USA, slightly more to Europe and the UK.

In Nairobi there is one card phone at the main post office and another in the Extelcoms office in Haile Selassie Ave. There are also two in the lobby of the Kenyatta Conference Centre and these are by far the best to use as there's little background noise here. In Mombasa and Kisumu there's one phone at the main post office.

Operator connected calls are also easy to make. The Extelcoms office in Nairobi is open from 8 am to midnight. Again, the Kenyatta Conference Centre is the best place to ring from as there's an international call office in the lobby and this is much quieter and less frantic than the Extelcoms office. It is only open until 6 pm, however.

In other towns calls can be made from the post office, although there may be some delay in getting through to the international operator in Nairobi.

Internal Calls Local and trunk calls are also quite straightforward. There are public phone boxes in every town and these all seem to work. The only problem is that there aren't enough of them, especially in Nairobi where you'll find a queue of four or five people at each box. Local calls cost KSh 1, while STD (long-distance) rates vary depending on the distance. Call boxes accept only KSh 1 and KSh 5 coins. When making an internal call, make sure you put a KSh 1 coin into the machine first (regardless of what you insert after that). If you don't, you may have problems.

Calls to Tanzania are only STD calls, not international.

Electricity
Kenya uses the 240 volt system. The power supply is reliable and uninterrupted in most places.

Time
Time in Kenya is GMT plus three hours all year round.

One thing that must be borne in mind is that Swahili time is six hours out of whack with the way we tell the time, so that midday and midnight are 6 o'clock (*saa sitta*) Swahili time, and 7 am and 7 pm are 1 o'clock (*saa moja*). Just add or subtract six hours from the time you are told and hopefully from the context you'll be able to work out whether it's am or pm the person is talking about! You don't come across this all that often unless you speak Swahili but you still need to be prepared for it – I met one person who missed the one daily bus from a particular town on two consecutive days because he was at the station six hours late.

Business Hours
Government Offices & Businesses These offices are open Monday to Friday from 8 or 8.30 am to 1 pm, and 2 to 5pm. Some private businesses are also open on Saturday mornings from around 8.30 am to 12.30 pm.

Banks Banking hours are Monday to Friday from 9 am to 2 pm. Banks are also open on the first and last Saturday of the month from 9 to 11 am.

In Nairobi and Mombasa there are branches of Barclays Bank which stay open until 4.30 or 5 pm Monday to Saturday. The branch of Barclays Bank at Nairobi airport is open 24 hours.

Outside normal banking hours you may be able to change at one of the five-star tourist hotels, although many are reluctant to help unless you're a guest.

MEDIA
Newspapers & Magazines
Tabloid newspapers are printed in both English and Swahili. Of the three English language papers, the best is probably the *Daily Nation*, which has a surprising amount of both local and overseas coverage. The others are the *Kenya Times* (the KANU party rag) and the *Standard*.

If your Swahili is up to it there's the *Kenya Leo)* (the Swahili version of the *Kenya Times*) and the *Taifa Leo* (the Swahili version of the *Daily Nation*).

There is also a surprising range of locally produced magazines in both English and Swahili. Principal among them is the *Weekly Review* (KSh 20) which is the Kenyan equivalent of *Time/Newsweek*. Radicals berate this magazine as being a tool of government propaganda but it does, nevertheless, discuss issues in much greater detail than any of the daily newspapers and it's well worth a read. There are plenty of other weekly magazines but they're largely titillative and cater to the lowest common denominator (much like the *News of the World* in the UK or *The Sun* in Australia).

Foreign newspapers (up to a week old) in English, French and German are readily available in Nairobi and Mombasa (but expensive!), as are current affairs magazines such as *Time*, *Newsweek* and the like (at the usual price you'd pay at home).

Radio & TV
The Voice of Kenya radio has transmissions

in English, Swahili and more specialised languages such as Hindi and African languages.

The BBC World Service transmits to East Africa on short wave around 12 hours a day and has programmes in English and Swahili.

TV is widespread and most programmes are imported from Europe and the USA.

HEALTH

Kenya is a fairly healthy country to visit. Malaria is endemic and you need to take precautions against chloroquine-resistant strains. Chloroquine-based malaria tablets are available over the counter even in tiny stores out in the country.

Tap water throughout the country is safe to drink but treat with suspicion water obtained from other sources, especially wells and bores.

For a full rundown of health considerations for travelling in East Africa, see the Health section in the introductory Facts for the Visitor chapter.

DANGERS & ANNOYANCES
Theft

Travelling in Kenya is basically trouble free but you definitely do need to keep your wits about you. The time when you face the biggest risk is within the first couple of days of arriving in the country. The people who make a living by relieving people of their possessions can often spot new arrivals by their uncertain movements and general unfamiliarity with the place. This is particularly true in Nairobi, and in fact the number of people who get their passports and money knocked off on the No 34 public bus in from the airport is amazing. The thieves use the 'instant crowd' technique, you'll find yourself jostled and before you know it your bag or money-belt strap has been slashed. Personally, I wouldn't use this bus for quids but, instead, take the Kenya Airways minibus, or even a taxi and get into Nairobi with your valuables intact.

Never leave your gear unattended anywhere as chances are it won't be there when you get back, no matter how short a time you are away. In hotel rooms your gear is generally safe but use your common sense and never leave valuables such as passport, other documents, money and preferably camera equipment in any hotel room. In some places (particularly the real cheapies/brothels) the door locks are purely cosmetic.

The place to carry your passport, money and other precious documents is in a pouch against your skin, either around your waist or your neck. Neither method is foolproof but both give a good measure of security and make it much harder to lose things. Leather pouches are far more comfortable to have against your skin than synthetic ones, and the moisture from perspiration is far less likely to turn your precious documents into a soggy pulp.

If you are the victim of a snatch theft, think twice before yelling 'thief' and trying to catch the guy. Once caught, brutal and often lethal punishment is often meted out on the spot by angry crowds, so either be prepared to defend your assailant or give up your possessions as lost.

Confidence Tricks

In Nairobi the chances are you'll come across people who play on the emotions and gullibility of foreigners. People with tales about being 'refugees', usually from Uganda or South Africa, can sound very convincing as they draw you into their net but they all end up asking for money. If you do give any, expect to be 'arrested' by plainclothes 'police', complete with fake ID cards, who then extract a 'fine' from you on the basis that 'it's illegal to give money to foreigners'. It's actually only illegal to give them foreign currency. Stories such as this abound and the number of travellers who get taken in is legend. The best policy is to ignore all such requests for money even though by doing this you'll occasionally be turning down what is a genuine request for help.

Another trick in Nairobi is the envelope full of money which gets dropped on the footpath in front of you. The idea is that, as you are reaching to pick it up, someone else (the accomplice of the person who dropped it) grabs it and then suggests to you that as you both found it you should go somewhere and share your 'good luck'. If you go along the only thing that will be shared is your money in a side alley somewhere.

Another tried and tested con trick is what appears to be a school student who approaches you with a photostated sponsorship form headed by the name of a school. He tells you his school needs funds to buy equipment and can you give a donation? Look at the form and you'll find the names of two or three wonderfully philanthropic people (usually from the USA, Germany or the UK) who have apparently donated KSh 700 or even KSh 900 to this worthy cause. If you fall for this then you need your head examined. If the person proves persistent, just ask him to go along with you to a telephone so you can confirm that the request is genuine and that the person is a registered student at the school in question.

In Nakuru they don't lack ingenuity either. A trick that has been popular for years involves tourists with cars. Locals splash oil on your wheels, then tell you that your wheel bearings, differential or something else had failed, and then direct you to a nearby garage where their friends would 'fix' the problem – for a substantial fee. We've even had reports of oil being splashed on the back wheels and then the driver being told that the rear differential had failed even though the car was front wheel drive!

Mugging

Foreigners do occasionally get mugged but if you're sensible the chances of it happening to you are extremely small. There are certain places in Nairobi and on the coast where it's not recommended to walk at night, but other than that it's just a matter of common sense: don't go out boozing in the nightclubs carrying your valuables and then go rolling home down the street; don't wear your wealth, or you become a very tempting target. Leave valuable jewellery at home, keep cameras out of sight and don't pull out wads of money to pay for something. Always have enough small change for everyday transactions

handy and keep the rest concealed. Take a cue from the taxi drivers of Nairobi who stash their money in at least half a dozen places on their body and in various articles of clothing.

Lastly, be wary on crowded matatus. It's not the ragamuffins you should watch but those who appear to be well dressed and on their way home from work. Plenty of these people work the matatus and you, as a tourist, are just one of their targets. Kenyans get hit, too.

WOMEN TRAVELLERS

Sexual harassment of women is far less prevalent in Kenya than in many countries though essentially this relates only to White women. If you're Black and walking the streets alone after 7 pm, there's a very good chance you'll be arrested, accused of being a whore and pressured into bribing your way out. KSh 200 is the usual amount. Refuse to pay and you could well spend the night in a cell at the central police station, taken to court the following morning and fined KSh 1000. From the people I've met whom this has happened to, you break no ice protesting your innocence even if you're married and your husband happens to be back at a hotel room or elsewhere. It can even happen if you're a Black woman in the company of a White man. The obvious way around this is to take taxis at night if you're going anywhere.

White women come under the category of 'tourists' and enjoy a somewhat dubious though privileged status. If you're one of these, you may get the occasional hassle but it's rarely persistent if treated with the cold shoulder. There are certain areas in Nairobi where you wouldn't want to walk alone at night, but that applies equally to men, though usually for different reasons.

FILM & PHOTOGRAPHY
Film

Film is widely available in Nairobi and the price is fairly competitive with what you'd pay at home. You'll need plenty of it – Kenya has heaps to photograph, and anyone with a camera inevitably gets very shutter-happy in the game parks looking for that 'perfect' shot.

It's wise to take with you films of varying ASAs. If you're using a zoom or long focal length camera (recommended) you're going to need film of at least 200 ASA to give you enough light, especially as the best photo opportunities are early and late in the day when the light is not as bright as the middle daylight hours. Higher speed film also makes it possible to take photos with a higher shutter speed, which is important when you're trying to photograph moving animals while at the same time you're being bumped around inside a minibus.

Some of the lodges have salt licks which the animals are attracted to at night, so with 800 or 1600 ASA or higher film non-flash photos are a possibility.

You'll find 64, 100, 200 and 400 ASA slide film readily available in Nairobi and Mombasa but 800 ASA hard to find and 1600 ASA almost impossible to find. The same is true for colour negative film. As an indication of price, slide film in Nairobi costs KSh 322 for Kodachrome 64 (36 exposures, processing included). Colour negative film costs KSh 177 for Ektachrome 200 (36) and KSh 140 for Fujichrome 100 (36).

Cameras & Lenses

Wildlife Photography For serious wildlife photography a SLR (single lens reflex) camera which can take long focal length lenses is necessary. If all you have is a little generic 'snapomatic' you may as well leave it behind. Although they are becoming more sophisticated these days, the maximum focal length is around 70 mm – still too small for getting decent shots.

Zoom lenses are probably the best for wildlife photography as you can frame your shot easily to get the best composition. This is important as the animals are constantly and often quickly on the move. The 70 mm to 210 mm zoom lenses are popular and the 200 mm is really the minimum you need to get good close-up shots. The only problem with zoom lenses is that with all the glass (lenses) inside

them they absorb about 1½ 'f' stops of light, which is where the 200 and 400 ASA film starts to become useful.

Telephoto (fixed focal length) lenses give better results than zoom lenses but you're limited by having to carry a separate lens for every focal length. A 400 mm or 500 mm lens brings the action right up close, but again you need the 200 or 400 ASA film to make the most of them. You certainly need a 400 mm or 500 mm lens if you're keen on photographing birdlife.

Another option is to carry a 2x teleconverter, which is a small adaptor which fits between the lens and the camera body, and doubles the focal length of your lens, so a 200 mm lens becomes 400 mm. These are a good cheap way of getting the long focal length without having to buy expensive lenses. They do, however, have a couple of disadvantages. The first is that, like the larger lenses themselves, a teleconverter uses about 1½ 'f' stops of light. Another disadvantage is that, depending on the camera and lens, teleconverters can make it extremely difficult to focus quickly and precisely, which is an important consideration when both you and the animals are on the move.

When using long lenses a tripod can be extremely useful, and with anything greater than about 300 mm it's a necessity. The problem here is that in the confined space of the hatch of a minibus (assuming you'll be taking an organised safari) it is impossible to set up the tripod, especially when you are sharing the confined space with at least three or four other people. Miniature tripods are available and these are useful for setting up on the roof of the van, although you can also rest the lens itself on the roof, provided that the van engine is switched off to kill any vibration.

Whatever combination of camera, lenses and accessories you decide to carry, make sure they are kept in a decent bag which will protect them from the elements, the dust, and the knocks they are bound to receive. It's also vital to make sure that your travel insurance policy includes your camera gear if it gets stolen.

Camera Hire

If you don't have the inclination or the resources to buy expensive equipment but still want some decent pictures of your safari, it is possible to hire SLR cameras and lenses in Nairobi. You're looking at around KSh 100 per day for the camera, and as much again for a 70 mm to 210 mm zoom lens. Places to try include Elite Camera House on Kimathi St, or Expo Cameras and Camera Experts on Mama Ngina St.

Selling Cameras

With the high duty placed on imported goods, you may be surprised to find that your old used camera is worth quite a bit in Kenya. Obviously the better the condition of the camera, the more it will be worth. There are a few camera shops in Nairobi which deal in second-hand equipment, so check them out. One place to try is Expo Cameras on Mama Ngina St. If you do sell your camera chances are they'll pay you in Kenyan shillings, so if it's at the end of your stay you'll need to have enough bank exchange certificates to reconvert the shillings to hard currency at the airport.

Film Processing

There are plenty of one hour film processing labs in Nairobi, and at least one in all other major towns. They handle colour print film only and can process any film speeds. The cost is reasonable and the results just as good as what you'd get back home. One good place is the lab next to the Coffee House on Mama Ngina St. This place also has a wide variety of film for sale. Developing and mounting of slides costs around KSh 95 for 36 exposures.

Photographing People

As is the case in any country where you are a tourist, this is a subject which has to be approached with some sensitivity. The colourful people in Kenya, such as the Maasai and the Samburu, have had so many rubbernecks pointing cameras at them for so many years that they are utterly sick to death of it – with good reason. There are even signs up in Namanga and Amboseli that it is prohibited to take photos of the Maasai. This doesn't mean that you can't, but just that you'll have to pay for it. Much as you may find this abhorrent, it is nevertheless an aspect of the tourism industry you'll just have to accept – put yourself in their position and try to think what you'd do.

It is of course possible to take pictures of people with zoom lenses but, most of the time, what's the point? By paying or giving some sort of gift, you can not only get a better picture by using a smaller lenses but you have some interaction with your subject. You might even get an invitation to see the family (and possibly photograph them).

ACCOMMODATION

Kenya has a good range of accommodation from the very basic US$3 a night budget hotels up to luxury tented camps in the national parks for up to $500 a night!

Hotels

Real bottom of the range hotels (known everywhere as Boardings & Lodgings; 'hotels' are often only restaurants) are generally brothels first and hotels second. This in itself is not a problem as long as you don't mind the noise, disruption and general atmosphere. Most places don't mind renting out rooms all night, although in some you get distinctly strange looks when they discover that not only do you want the room for the whole night, but that you want to spend it alone! These places are also not all that clean – you'll have to ask for clean sheets, the rooms are often claustrophobic cells, the common facilities smell and the whole place exudes a seedy air. On the other hand, you do occasionally come across cheap places which are clean and pleasant places to stay, so don't dismiss them totally; there's usually at least one cheap Boarding & Lodging in each town. On the plus side, they are cheap. Expect to pay around KSh 50/85 for a single/double room.

Things improve dramatically if you have a few shillings more to spend, although there are always exceptions. For example, for around KSh 95/145 a single/double, you will get a clean room with private bath and soap and towel supplied. These places often have a restaurant and bar (usually noisy). They really have no advantage over the really cheap places except perhaps that you get your own bathroom.

Those who prefer a mid-range hotel are well catered for. If you're willing to spend US$10 to US$25 a night then you can expect all the basic comforts and sometimes even a touch of luxury including clean sheets and beds, your own shower and toilet with hot water, towels, soap and toilet paper, a table and chair and often a telephone and room service.

At the top end of the market you have all the usual international chain hotels with prices to match. These start at around KSh 600/800 for a single/double and head up from there. Some of these places are old colonial buildings with bags of atmosphere, but most are modern and somewhat characterless. The resort hotels on the coast and the lodges in the game parks also fall into this category, although some of the latter are superb places to stay if you can afford it – having animals come to drink at the salt lick in front of your lodge as you sit on the verandah sipping a cool drink is just great, but pleasures such as this set you back around KSh 2000/2500 for full board.

Youth Hostels

The only youth hostels affiliated with the IYHA are in Nairobi and Malindi though the one operated by Yare Safaris in Maralal is a member of the national network. If you like youth hostels, they are fine. At KSh 60 for a dorm bed they are not that cheap but, as usual, they are good places to meet people.

Camping

There are enough opportunities for camping that it is worth considering bringing a tent. It is also possible to hire camping equipment in Nairobi and elsewhere but it's not the sort of lightweight gear you could carry without a vehicle.

There are camp sites in just about every national park and game reserve and these are usually very basic. There'll be a toilet block with a couple of long-drops, usually a water tap but very little else. Private sites are few and far between but where they do exist they offer more in the way of facilities. Often it's possible to camp in the grounds of a hotel but this is obviously not an option in the bigger towns where space is limited.

Camping out in the bush is also possible though you would be advised to ask permission first. On the coast this is not advisable and sleeping on the beaches would be just asking for trouble.

Just in case you thought that the tented camps in the game parks might be a cheap option – forget it. They are luxury camps with all the facilities laid on, and high prices. The 'tents' barely justify the name – they usually just have canvas or mosquito netting for walls, but otherwise have a roof and bathroom.

FOOD

For the main part Kenyan cuisine consists largely of stodge filler and is really just survival food for the locals – maximum filling-up potential at minimum cost. It is still possible to eat cheaply and well although the lack of variety becomes tedious after a while. People with carnivorous habits are far better served by the local tucker than vegetarians.

The most basic local eateries (often known as *hotelis*) hardly warrant being called restaurants. These places usually have a limited menu and are open only for lunch – the main meal of the day. If you're on a tight budget you'll find yourself eating in these places most of the time. However, if you have the resources, even in the smaller towns it's usually possible to find a restaurant that offers more variety and better food at a higher price. Often these places are connected with the mid-range and top-end hotels.

Putting together your own food is a viable option if you are camping and carrying cooking gear. Every town has a market and there's usually an excellent range of fresh produce available.

Fast food has taken off in a big way and virtually every town has a place that serves food that rates high in grease and low in price. Fried chips with lashings of lurid tomato sauce are a basic filler, but sausages, eggs, fish and chicken are also popular. In Nairobi there are literally dozens of these places, and they can be handy places to pick up a snack.

The only place where any sort of distinctive cuisine has developed is on the coast where the Swahili dishes reflect the history of contact with the Arabs and other Indian Ocean traders – coconut and spices are used heavily and the results are generally excellent.

As might be expected with the large number of Asians in Kenya, there are also Indian restaurants, although these are mainly confined to Nairobi and Mombasa.

Vegetarians are not well catered for. Away from the two main cities there are virtually no vegetarian dishes to accompany the starch. Beans are going to figure prominently in any vegetarian's culinary encounters in Kenya! Buying fresh vegetables in the market can help relieve the tedium – and perhaps the constipation – which no doubt results.

Snacks

Sambusas are probably the most common snack and are obvious descendants of the Indian samosa. They are deep-fried pastry triangles stuffed with spiced mince meat. Occasionally you come across sambusas with vegetarian filling, but this is usually only in the Indian restaurants. If you can find them freshly made and still warm, sambusas can be excellent. However, more often by the time you get them they are at least several hours old, are cold and have gone limp and greasy from the oil saturation...

Another item that fits into the pure starch category is that curious beast known as the *mandazi*. It's a semisweet, flat doughnut and, once again, when they're fresh they can be very good. They are usually cooked and eaten at breakfast time and as often as not are dunked in tea. Should you decide to eat one later in the day, chances are it will be stale and hard.

Something that you don't come across that often but which makes an excellent snack meal is *mkate mayai* (literally bread-eggs). This was originally an Arab dish and is now found in countries as far ranging as Kenya and Singapore. Basically it's a wheat dough which is spread into a thin pancake, is filled with minced meat and raw egg and is then folded into a neat parcel and fried on a hotplate. The Iqbal Hotel in Nairobi is a good place to try this snack.

Seemingly on every second street corner you come across someone trying to make a few bob selling corn cobs roasted on a wire grille over a bed of hot coals. You pay only a couple of shillings for these. Another street-corner snack is deep-fried yams, eaten hot with a squeeze of lemon juice and a sprinkling of chilli powder.

Main Dishes

Basically it's meat, meat and more meat, accompanied by starch of some sort. The meat is usually in a stew with perhaps some potato or other vegetables thrown in, and is often as tough as an old boot. Beef, goat and mutton are the most commonly eaten.

The starch comes in three major forms: potatoes, rice and *ugali*, the last of these is maize meal which is cooked up into a thick porridge until it sets hard. It's then served up in flat bricks. It's incredibly stodgy, almost totally devoid of any flavour and tends to sit on the stomach like a royal corgi, but most Kenyans swear it's the bees' knees. It's certainly the equivalent of mashed potato for the Pommies or sticky rice for the Chinese and Koreans but it certainly isn't a culinary orgasm. Freshly cooked it's palatable; when stale, just about inedible. Naturally, you must try it at least once and some travellers actually get to like it, but don't hold your breath! The only thing it has going for it is that it's cheap.

Cooked red kidney beans are always an

alternative to meat and are widely available in local eateries.

Roast chicken and steak are popular dishes in the more upmarket restaurants of the bigger towns. Food in this sort of place differs little from what you might get at home.

Fruit

This is where Kenya really excels. Because of the ranges in climate found in the country, there's an excellent array of fruits. The tropical ones are especially good. Depending on the place and the season you can buy mangoes, papaya, pineapple, oranges, guavas, custard apples, bananas (many varieties) and coconuts. Prices are cheap and the quality very high.

Menus

Menus, where they exist in the cheaper places, are usually just a chalked list on a board on the wall. In better restaurants they are usually just in English.

The list which follows gives the main words you are likely to come across when trying to decipher Swahili menus.

food	chakula
raw	mbichi
ripe	mbivu
sweet	tamu
cup	kikombe
fork	uma
glass	glasi
knife	kisu
napkin	kitambaa
plate	sahani
table	mesa
teaspoon	kijiko
aubergine	biringani
cabbage	kabichi
capsicum	pilipili baridi
carrots	karoti
cassava	muhogo
garlic	vitunguu saumu
kidney beans	maharagwe

lettuce	salad
onions	vitunguu
plantains	ndizi
potatoes	viazi
spinach	sukuma wiki
tomatoes	nyanya
vegetables	mboga
beef	nyama ya ngombe
meat	nyama
mutton, goat	nyama ya mbuzi
pork	nyama ya nguruwe
steak	steki
crab	kaa
fish	samaki
lobster	kamba
squid	ngisi
bananas	ndizi
coconut (green)	dafu
coconut (ripe)	nazi
custard apples	stafeli
dates	tende
fruit	matunda
grapefruits	madanzi
guava	pera
limes	ndimu
mangoes	maembe
oranges	machungwa
papayas	paipai
passionfruit	pasheni
pineapples	mananasi
sugar cane	miwa
watermelon	tikiti
boiled spinach	sukuma wiki
curry	mchuzi
kebabs	mushkaki
maize meal porridge	ugali
mashed plantains	
& maize	matoke
meat stew	karanga
rice	wali
soup	supu
vegetable stew	mboga
boiled	chemka
fried	kaanga
roast	choma

hot/cold	*moto/baridi*
hot (spicy)	*hoho*
bread	*mkate*
butter	*siagi*
egg(s)	*yai(mayai)*
Indian bread	*chapati*
pepper	*pilipili*
salt	*chumvi*
sauce	*mchuzi*
sugar	*sukari*
yoghurt	*maziwalala*

DRINKS
Tea & Coffee
Despite the fact that Kenya grows some of the finest tea and coffee in the world, getting a decent cup of either can be difficult.

Tea *(chai)* is the national obsession and is drunk in large quantities. It bears little resemblance to what you might be used to but as long as you look on it as just a different hot drink and not actually tea it can be quite good. Be warned that it is generally very milky and horrendously sweet. Chai is made the same way in Kenya as it is in India: all the ingredients (tea, milk and masses of sugar) are put into cold water and the whole lot is brought to the boil and stewed. Finding a good honest cup of tea is virtually impossible outside the fancy restaurants. For tea without milk ask for *chai kavu*.

Coffee is similarly disappointing. Instant coffee is what is generally used, and in small quantities, so, once again, you're looking at a sweet milky concoction which is not quite what you might be expecting. However, as each cup is individually made it's somewhat easier to order one tailored to your own liking.

Beer
Kenya has a thriving local brewing industry and formidable quantities of beer are consumed. It's probably true to say that beer is the most widely available manufactured product in the country. Go to just a tiny group of *dukas* (local stores) by the side of the road somewhere and chances are one of them will either be a bar, or it will stock beer. Sure, it won't be cold, but then even in the most upmarket places beer is available both chilled and warm. Why warm you might ask as your face wrinkles in horror?! The answer is because most Africans appear to prefer it that way. I've certainly never seen them drink cold White Cap though you'll occasionally see an African drinking cold Pilsener or Premium. My co-author, Hugh, who's a true-blue Aussie, reckons the Poms love it warm but that's a barrel of bullshit. Kenyan beer bears no resemblance to that fine brew produced in the British Isles which, to be at its best, has to be served at a specific temperature – neither too cold nor too warm and preferably pumped from the barrel. Kenyan beers are essentially lagers and they're all bottled.

Their names are White Cap, Tusker and Pilsner and they're sold in 500 ml bottles. Like Australian commercial beers they are basically the same product with different

labels (though there is a discernible difference in taste) but most people end up sticking to just one brand. White Cap and Tusker also have 300 ml upmarket beers – Export and Premium respectively – and these are slightly stronger and more expensive. Guinness is also available but tastes and looks nothing like the genuine Irish article (or even the bastardised English variety outside of Kilburn High Road).

Until early November 1989, beer prices were strictly controlled by the government and there was only a very slight price difference between a beer in a spit-and-sawdust shack and a five-star hotel. That all changed with deregulation but, because of the competition for the nation's beer money, prices have once again stabilised after a short period of greed and opportunism.

They are cheapest bought from a supermarket where a 500 ml bottle will cost you around KSh 12. Bought from a normal bar, you are looking at KSh 14 to KSh 15. Even in the tourist hotels the top whack seems to be about KSh 35 on the coast, KSh 25 in Nairobi, so it's still affordable, though you will occasionally come across a place which wants KSh 40 a bottle.

Wine

Kenya also has a fledgeling wine industry and the Lake Naivasha Colombard wines are said to be quite good. This is something that cannot be said about the most commonly encountered Kenyan wine – papaya wine. It tastes foul and even the smell is unbearable.

On the other hand, you can get cheap imported European wine by the glass for around KSh 40 in Nairobi restaurants. This is expensive when compared to the price of beer but is actually not too bad.

Local Brews

Although it is strictly illegal to brew or distil liquor this doesn't stop it going on. Pombe is the local beer and is usually a fermented brew made with bananas or millet and sugar. You may get the chance to sample it here and there and it shouldn't do you any harm. The same cannot be said for the distilled drinks,

known locally as *changa*, as these are often very effective poisons – inefficient/amateur distilling techniques ensure various percentages of methyl alcohol creep into the brew. They'll blind you if you're lucky; kill you if you're not. Leave it alone!

Soft Drinks

All the old favourites are here – Coke, Pepsi, Fanta, etc – and they go under the generic term of soda. As with the beer, prices have been deregulated so they vary depending on where you buy. In most places you pay around KSh 3.50 per bottle but in the more exclusive places you can pay up to KSh 10 though a more usual price would be KSh 8. There are no such predictable prices for freshly squeezed fruit juices which range from KSh 10 to KSh 30 per glass.

MAPS

Largely as a result of the prosperous tourism industry, there's a wide range of maps available, although many are just made to look pretty and have very little practical use.

One of the best maps of the region is the Hallwag map of *Kenya & Tanzania* which also covers Uganda, Rwanda, Burundi and the very eastern part of Zaïre. Covering a similar area, but not as well, is the Hildebrand's travel map of *East Africa*. The Michelin maps are usually pretty reliable but their only one which covers this area (No 155, Southern Africa) really covers too wide an area to give enough detail.

The *Tourist Map of Kenya*, printed and published in Kenya, gives good detail and there are a few similar ones.

Macmillan publish a series of maps to the game parks and these are not bad value at KSh 75.

At the Public Map Office next to the Kenyatta Conference Centre in Nairobi they have a stock of government survey maps covering the whole country. The most popular ones (Mt Kenya, Mt Elgon and those covering the game parks) are often out of stock but it's worth getting hold of these maps if possible. The only trouble with maps published by the Survey of Kenya other than those available in the bookshops is that they're not available to the general public without official authorisation. This is hard to get and takes time so, if you're a tourist with limited time, you can forget it. Even people with credentials, such as Kenyan residents of the Mountain Club of Kenya (MCK), have great difficulty or find it simply impossible to get hold of detailed maps of the country.

ACTIVITIES
Diving & Snorkelling
Malindi and Watamu are the spots for scuba diving, the latter being the preferred of the two. At Watamu, diving is from a boat not far offshore. A typical anchor dive is made at 12 to 15 metres depth. Visibility is often only fair and in fact Kenyan diving visibility has a poor reputation due to the plankton in the water. There is, however, usually plenty of fish in the water even if the coral is not that spectacular. A typical dive costs KSh 400, plus KSh 50 extra for transport if the dive is from Watamu. For more information contact the Dive Shop, Driftwood Club, Malindi.

Windsurfing
Most of the resort hotels south and north of Mombasa have windsurfers for hire, and the conditions are ideal – the waters are protected by the offshore reefs and the winds are usually reasonably strong and constant. The going rate at most places seems to be about KSh 80 per hour, more if you need instruction.

Beaches
One of the great attractions of Kenya is the superb beaches which line the coast. Many travellers find themselves staying much longer than they anticipated. This is real picture postcard stuff – coconut palms, dazzling white sand and clear blue water. The only problem is that for the most part the resort hotels have a virtual monopoly on accommodation, although there are a couple of budget options both south and north of Mombasa.

The beach at Diani is one of the best although it's dotted fairly solidly with resorts. Tiwi Beach, between Diani and Mombasa, is much lower key and you can camp right on the beach at the Twiga Lodge. There are similar possibilities north of Mombasa.

Caving
For information on this bizarre activity contact the Cave Exploration Group of East Africa, PO Box 47583, Nairobi.

Desert Grandeur
There's the opportunity to experience this on either side of Lake Turkana and for a considerable distance south of there on the eastern side of the lake. For most travellers, this is one of the highlights of their trip to Kenya.

On the western side access to the lake is easy with a bitumen road all the way from Kitale, and there's at least one bus and often a matatu or two every day in each direction. If you're heading up this way then don't miss the opportunity of exploring the Cherangani Hills east of the Kitale-Lodwar road using the Marich Pass Field Centre as your base.

The eastern side is perhaps more challenging since the mountains and the desert begin much further south but public transport is much more limited. The Turkana, Samburu and Rendille tribespeople are also fascinating and, like the Maasai, have hung on to their traditional ways. It's certainly an area which you shouldn't miss at any cost.

Climbing & Walking
Mt Kenya is the obvious one, but other promising and relatively unexplored territory includes Mt Elgon on the Uganda border, the Cherangani Hills north of Eldoret and even the Ngong Hills close to Nairobi. For more information refer to the relevant chapter or contact the MCK at their clubhouse at Wilson Airport (meetings every Tuesday at 8.30 pm – visitors welcome), or at their Nairobi address (tel 501747, PO Box 45741).

Gliding
The Gliding Club of Kenya has its headquarters in Mweiga near Nyeri in the

Aberdares, and there are flights every day except during July and August. For more information contact the Gliding Club of Kenya (tel Nyeri 2969), PO Box 926, Nyeri.

Ballooning

Balloon safaris in the game parks are an absolutely superb way of seeing the savannah plains and of course the animals, but without the intrusion of vehicles and dozens of other tourists doing the same thing. The most popular of these trips is the one in the Masai Mara Game Reserve. The hot-air balloons depart daily from Keekorok Lodge just after dawn and return around mid-morning. The flight includes a champagne-style breakfast on the plains. The cost is KSh 4000 (about US$190). Bookings can be made through Block Hotels (tel 335807), PO Box 47557, Nairobi, or at Keekorok Lodge.

There's another outfit which offers balloon trips in Taita Hills Game Reserve. Bookings for this can be made through the Hilton International (tel 334000), PO Box 30624, Nairobi.

Fishing

The Kenya Fisheries Department operates a number of fishing camps in various parts of the country. They are really only an option if you have your own transport as the sites are off the main roads. Before you head off you need to get a fishing licence from the Fisheries Department. Advance bookings are not taken so it's just a matter of turning up at the site. For full details of the exact locations of the camps, see the Fisheries Department in Nairobi; the office is near the National Museum.

White-Water Rafting

Rafting is still in its infancy in Kenya, perhaps because of the limited possibilities – there are only two major rivers in Kenya, the Athi/Galana and Tana. The Tana flows through relatively flat country so it's sluggish and unsuitable for rafting. The Athi/Galana, on the other hand, has substantial rapids, chutes and waterfalls. The only outfit which can fix you up with a trip down

this river is operated by Mark Savage (tel 521590), PO Box 44827, Nairobi. He has two units of the Avon Ranger 3 river rafts.

A day trip from Nairobi consists of putting in just above Sagana on the Athi River and finishing about four km above the Masinga dam. The trip starts with about two km of mild rapids followed by six km of smooth water and then two km of Grade 4-plus rapids without a breather and another two km of the same grade but with a few calm stretches for bailing out. This is followed by porterage around a waterfall and a further 13 km of smooth water to the takeout point.

There's also an exciting three day trip available from Yatta Gap on the Athi down to Tsavo Safari Camp (74 km) and, if permission can be obtained from the National Parks Authority, trips all the way down to Malindi may be available in 1991.

THINGS TO BUY

Kenya is an excellent place for souvenirs, although much of the cheap stuff available is just pure junk mass produced by hand for the tourist trade. Look carefully at what's available before parting with your money.

Nairobi and Mombasa are the main centres but much of the stuff comes from the various regions, so it's often possible to pick up the same at source, although you then have the problem of transporting it.

Woodcarving

There's plenty of scope here. The best pieces, and also the most expensive, are the *makonde* carvings, made from ebony, a very black and very heavy wood. This genre of carving had its origins in the highlands on both sides of the Ruvuma River in southern Tanzania but, because of its popularity, has been copied by other carvers all over East Africa. Done with inspiration, attention to detail, and an appreciation of the life force which motivates its imagery, it's a unique art form. Unfortunately, too many imitators create inferior products. Much of what is passed off as ebony is lighter (and cheaper) wood blackened with Kiwi boot polish and the quality of the carving is often slap-dash.

A quality piece of makonde carving is always superbly finished.

Maybe you don't care too much about this. Perhaps you like what you imagine to be the slightly rough quality of 'ethnic art'. But, if you do, you're not buying makonde, you're buying repro rubbish.

Before you buy any of this type of carving, do the rounds of the expensive craft shops in Nairobi and see what it ought to look like. Better still, buy it in Tanzania where it's much cheaper anyway. And, when you've seen the real thing, don't get too fetishistic about ebony. There are some excellent Kenyan carvers even if they do it on local hardwoods and employ Kiwi boot polish as the finish.

Basically, there are two forms of this art – the traditional and the modern – and they're instantly distinguishable. The modern stuff is pure Modigliani, though the carvers have doubtless never heard of the man or seen any of his works.

The best pieces, available from the expensive craft shops, are probably made in Tanzania, but you shouldn't pass up the opportunity of having a good look at what is hawked around the bars of Nairobi. Some of it is good; most of it is rubbish. If you're interested, heavy bargaining is the name of the game.

Sisal Baskets

Sisal baskets, or *kiondos*, are probably the most distinctive Kenyan souvenir and are now popular and widely available in the West. They are still an excellent buy here and the range is staggering – take a look in the market in Nairobi (although buying here is expensive). They come in a variety of sizes, colours and configurations with many different straps and closures. Expect to pay around KSh 60 for a basic one up to around KSh 250 for a large one with a leather 'neck'. Some of the finer ones have the bark of the baobab tree woven into them and this bumps up the price considerably.

Jewellery & Tribal Souvenirs

Most of the jewellery on sale is of tribal origin, although very little of it is the genuine article. The colourful Maasai beaded jewellery is the most striking and the most popular, and items include long earrings and the sets of three 'collars', all made with brightly coloured beads.

Other Maasai items include the decorated *calabash* – dried gourds used to store a mixture of blood and milk which is then left to ferment for a few days before it is drunk. Before the mixture is placed in the gourd, specific grasses are burnt inside it, and the soot deposit imparts a certain flavour and aids in fermentation. As you might imagine, these gourds often smell a bit, but are quite strikingly decorated with Maasai beads. Spears and shields are also popular although these are all made specifically for the tourist trade these days.

One of the best places to pick up Maasai souvenirs is at Namanga on the Tanzanian border. This is where all the minibuses headed for Amboseli pass through and stop for a few minutes, so prices are outrageous. However, with some persistent bargaining you can reduce the prices to realistic levels. They know as well as you that the prices they ask are ridiculous, but there are plenty of well-heeled tourists passing through here who have more money than sense. For instance, the starting price for earrings is KSh 100 per pair, but they are quite happy to sell them for KSh 10; similarly I expressed

Silver armlet and hinged anklet

an interest in a calabash and was quoted KSh 500 – and eventually paid KSh 35!

All this stuff is bought cheaper out in the bush away from the tourist circuits but buying still demands judicious haggling.

Batiks

Batiks are another good buy and there's a tremendous range, although the good ones are not cheap. The cheapest ones are printed on cotton and you can expect to pay around KSh 300 for one measuring about one metre by one metre, although the price also varies depending on the artist.

Batiks printed on silk are of superior quality and the prices are generally in the thousands rather than the hundreds of shillings.

Fabrics

Kangas and *kikois* are the local sarongs and they serve many useful purposes.

Kangas are colourful prints on thin cotton. Each bears a Swahili proverb and they are always sold in pairs – one to wrap around your waist and one to carry your baby with on your back – though you can buy just one if you prefer. Biashara St in Mombasa is the kanga centre in Kenya, and here you'll pay upwards of KSh 150 for a pair, depending on the quality.

Kikois are made of a thicker cotton and just have stripes. They are originally from Lamu and this is still the best place to buy them, although the kanga shops in Mombasa also stock them. These days they are also made into travellers' clothes in Lamu.

Stone

Soapstone carvings come from Kisii in the west of Kenya. The soft, lightly coloured soapstone is carved into dozens of different shapes – from ashtrays to elephants. The best place for buying Kisii soapstone carvings is not in Kisii, as you might expect, but in Kisumu on Lake Victoria. The only problem is that it's extremely heavy and a kg or two of dead weight in your rucksack is not something to be taken lightly.

Elephant Hair Bracelets

On the streets of Nairobi you'll undoubtedly be approached by hawkers trying to flog you 'elephant hair' bracelets. Despite all the protestations to the contrary, these bracelets are made either from reed grass, which is then covered in boot polish, or from slivers of cow horn. You can safely assume that none of them are the real McCoy.

WHAT TO BRING

Bring the minimum. One thing that many travellers in Kenya find once they actually get there is that they have far too much gear. This is not only an uncomfortable inconvenience, it also means that instead of taking back some special reminders of Kenya you'll be taking back the same extra pullover and jeans that you set off with. Unless it's absolutely essential, *leave it at home!*

A rucksack is far more practical than an overnight bag, and is essential if you plan to climb Mt Kenya or do any amount of walking. It is worth buying a good quality bag right at the start – African travel soon sorts out the good stuff from the junk, and if it's the latter you've opted for you'll be cursing it the whole way.

What type of pack you buy is largely a matter of personal preference. I find that the travel packs with the straps which zip into a compartment in the back are excellent. Although expensive, they are a compromise solution to a number of different problems; they are not really suited for specialised activities such as climbing or serious walking. Of the other types of packs, internal frame ones seem to be the best as they have less protuberances and straps to catch on things.

A day pack is a worthwhile item, if only for keeping your camera dry and out of the incredible dust which seems to permeate every crack and crevice when you're on safari, especially at Amboseli. For those reasons and for security, it needs to be one which zips shut. Quite a few travellers use the local kiondos which are fine if they suit your purpose.

A sleeping bag is more or less essential if you are travelling overland beyond Kenya, but in the country itself there are enough hotels for you not to need one. On the other hand, carrying a sleeping bag and closed-cell foam mat does give you a greater degree of flexibility and means that if you take a safari you know you'll have adequate gear. Sleeping bags are the one thing which all camping safari companies require you to provide.

There's always much discussion about the pros and cons of carrying a tent, and basically it boils down to what sort of travelling you want to do, and how much weight you're prepared to carry. As with a sleeping bag, a tent is far from essential if you're just travelling from town to town, but carrying your own portable shelter opens up a whole stack of exciting possibilities. The same applies to carrying a stove and cooking gear, so give some careful thought as to what you want to do, and how. On the other hand, the full range of camping equipment can be hired from various places in Nairobi (principally Atul's on Biashara St) and from certain hotels elsewhere in the country (principally the Naro Moru River Lodge on the northern side of Mt Kenya).

Quite a few travellers carry a mosquito net, and with the risk of malaria, there is no doubt that this is not a bad idea. Personally I found that with judicious use of insect repellent and mosquito coils, I was never unduly discomfited. On the topic of insect repellent, bring a good supply and make sure that whatever you bring has as the active ingredient NN-diethyl-m-toluamide, commonly known more sensibly as DEET. This has been found to be the most effective against mosquitoes. Brands which have this include Mijex and Rid. Mosquito coils are what the locals use (when they use anything at all, that is) to keep the mozzies at bay, and local brands such as Doom (!) are available in even the smallest stores.

Clothes need to be both practical and take into account local sensibilities. Although Kenya straddles the equator, the large variations in altitude lead to equally large variations in climate. The coast is hot and steamy year-round, while Nairobi and the western highlands get decidedly cool in the evenings in July and August, so you need to carry one decent warm pullover as well as warm weather gear. A windproof and waterproof jacket also comes in handy, particularly during the rainy season. Most travellers seem to get around in T-shirts and shorts which is fine in most areas, but you should be a little more circumspect on the Muslim-dominated coast, particularly in Lamu. Here women should wear tops that keep the shoulders covered and skirts or pants which reach at least to the knees. Shorts on men are likewise not particularly appreciated.

Overlooked by many people but absolutely indispensable is a good pair of sunglasses. The amount of glare you experience in the bright tropical light is not only uncomfortable but can damage your eyes. A hat which shades your face and neck is also well worth considering. A water bottle is well worth any slight inconvenience it may cause. It needs to be unbreakable, have a good seal, and hold at least one litre.

Also important are little things which can make life just that little bit more comfortable: a Swiss Army knife, a small sewing kit (including a few metres of fishing line and a large needle for emergency rucksack surgery), a 10 metre length of light nylon cord for a washing line, and a half tennis ball makes a good fits-all washbasin plug.

Most toiletries – soap, shampoo, toothpaste, toilet paper, tampons – are available throughout the country.

The one thing that you're really going to appreciate in Kenya is a pair of binoculars, whether they be pocket ones or larger field binoculars. When out in the game parks you can put them to constant use and they are essential for identifying the dozens of species and animals and birds that you'll come across. If you don't plan on going to the game parks they are less essential, but are still handy just for the scenery, or perhaps for trying to spot that potential lift coming over the horizon when you're stuck out in the north somewhere...

Getting There

As Kenya is the main gateway to East Africa, for flights from North America, Europe, Asia and Australasia see the introductory Getting There chapter.

TO/FROM SOMALIA
Overland
With the current state of internal strife in Somalia it is not considered safe to travel overland between the two countries, although that has not stopped a few intrepid (crazy?) travellers in the past. There is also the problem of well-armed *shifta* (bandits) to contend with who are getting more desperate and mean by the week as a result of the Kenyan government's determined crackdown on Somali poachers. Buses and other vehicles along this route have become fair game and although they travel with an army escort, don't assume the soldiers are going to use the guns which they carry.

Kisimayo to Garissa There is usually one daily bus between Kisimayo and the tiny Somali border settlement of Liboi. There is a small adobe guest house here as well as a couple of basic eateries and a small market. The Kenyan bus arrives in Somali Liboi at around 9 am on Wednesday, Friday and Sunday for the seven hour journey to Garissa. Obviously you need to clear Somali customs and immigration before getting on the bus. It stops on the Kenyan side for customs formalities which take half an hour or so.

In Kenyan Liboi there is the *Cairo Hotel* which has basic rooms and meals.

TO/FROM SUDAN
Air
Kenya Airways and Sudan Airways operate direct flights between Khartoum and Nairobi.

Overland
As is the case with Somalia, the internal strife within Sudan has put the overland route through the south of that country off limits to travellers.

TO/FROM TANZANIA
Air
The cheapest options to fly between Tanzania and Kenya are the flights between Dar es Salaam and Nairobi (about US$50) and Zanzibar and Mombasa (about US$28), though you must add the US$20 departure tax to these prices. The Zanzibar-Mombasa flight by Kenya Airways is very popular so there's heavy demand for tickets. You need to book at least two weeks ahead if you want to be sure of getting a seat.

Overland
Dar es Salaam to Mombasa There are a number of bus companies (such as Coast, Cat and Tawfiq) which do the run from Dar es Salaam to Mombasa via Tanga and vice versa though usually only once per week in either direction. The trip takes anything from 16 to 24 hours or eight to 12 hours from Tanga. The border at Lunga Lunga-Horohoro is quite straightforward but it takes as much as four hours to clear all 50 or so people through both posts. The fare from Dar es Salaam to Mombasa is TSh 2500. The Cat bus office in Dar es Salaam is on Msimbazi St close to the Kariakoo Market and the Caltex station.

If you're going to take one of these buses it's worth considering doing the journey partly by train. It's much more comfortable, and costs only about TSh 300 more, to take the overnight train 1st class from Dar es Salaam to Tanga. From Tanga, pick up one of the buses running between Dar es Salaam and Mombasa at around 8 am. The trip from Tanga to Mombasa costs TSh 700.

You can also do the journey the hard way. From Tanga to the Tanzanian border post at Horohoro there are a couple of buses per day along the rough single-lane dirt road which cost TSh 300. From Horohoro it's a six km walk to the Kenyan border post at Lunga Lunga and there's very little traffic so hitching is difficult. Once through the Kenyan border post, however, there are frequent matatus for the one hour journey to Mombasa.

Arusha & Moshi to Nairobi Kilimanjaro Bus Service operate a regular luxury bus between Arusha/Moshi and Nairobi. The bus departs Arusha at 9 am on Monday, Thursday and Saturday and arrives in Nairobi at 3.30 pm. There's also another service which departs Moshi at 7 am on Monday, Thursday and Saturday, arrives in Arusha at 9 am and Nairobi at 2.30 pm. In the opposite direction the bus departs Nairobi at 9 am on Tuesday, Friday and Sunday arriving in Arusha at 3.30 pm. The fares are KSh 150/TSh 1250 (Nairobi-Moshi) and KSh 140/TSh 1150 (Nairobi-Arusha). You need to book in advance for these buses as there's heavy demand for tickets. The booking office in Nairobi is at Goldline (tel 25279), Cross Rd. In Arusha and Moshi the bus office is at the bus station.

It's just as easy to do this journey in stages and since the Kenyan and Tanzanian border posts are next to each other at Namanga, there's no long walk involved. There are frequent matatus and shared taxis from Arusha to Namanga every day which go when full and cost TSh 500/1000 to TSh 1300 (negotiable) respectively. The taxis normally take about 1½ hours though there are a number of kamikaze drivers who are totally crazy and will get you there in just one hour. From the Kenyan side of the border there are frequent matatus and shared taxis which go when full and cost KSh 80 and KSh 120 respectively. The journey by taxi takes about two hours and by matatu about three hours. Both have their depot outside the petrol station on Ronald Ngala St close to the junction with River Rd.

Moshi to Voi & Musoma to Kisii The crossing between Moshi and Voi via Taveta is also reliable as far as transport goes (buses, matatus and shared taxis) but between Musoma and Kisii in the north there's very little traffic and you'll have to rely on hitching a ride or doing a lot of walking especially in the border area.

Boat
It used to be possible to get from Pemba, Zanzibar or Dar es Salaam to Mombasa by the *Virgin Butterfly* hydrofoil but the service has been suspended. There are now only occasional dhows between these places. In Dar es Salaam you'll have to make enquiries down at the Malindi dhow dock but it could take you several days to find one. The fare should be around TSh 3000 and the journey will take anything from 24 to 36 hours depending on the currents.

Between Zanzibar and Mombasa it's much easier. There are motorised dhows and other boats usually once or twice per week in either direction. To find out when they go and make a booking you need to go to the Institute of Marine Science workshop on Mizingani Rd – there's a small sign at the gate here (which is flanked by the Tanzanian and Zanzibari flags) which says, 'Tickets for Dar, Pemba, Mombasa'. The fare is TSh 2000 or US$11 and the journey takes about 12 hours but can take quite a bit longer depending on the currents.

Bring adequate supplies of food and drink with you if you take any of these boats.

There are no steamers on Lake Victoria which connect Kenya with Tanzania.

TO/FROM UGANDA
Overland
The two main border posts which most overland travellers use are Malaba and Busia with Malaba being by far the most commonly used.

Kampala to Nairobi via Malaba Between Jinja (USh 1500, two hours) or Kampala (USh 2200, three hours) and Malaba there are frequent matatus until the late afternoon. There are also frequent matatus in either direction between Tororo and Malaba (Uganda) which cost USh 200 and take less than one hour. The road has recently been resurfaced and is excellent, although it does mean that the drivers can get up to terrifying speeds, especially between Jinja and Kampala. There's also a train from Tororo to Kampala but it only runs three times a week and is diabolically slow.

The Ugandan and Kenyan border posts are about one km from each other at Malaba and you will have to walk. When leaving Uganda you will probably be asked for your currency declaration form, which isn't checked, and whether you have any Ugandan shillings in your possession (it's officially illegal to export them) but otherwise there's no fuss or baggage searches. Entering Kenya you have to fill in a currency form but there's no searches or other inconvenience. On the Kenyan side there are hordes of money-changers who will greet you, both while on your way through neutral territory to the Kenyan post and after you clear Kenyan immigration. The rate is not too bad.

There are trains from Malaba to Nairobi via Eldoret and Nakuru on Wednesday, Saturday and Sunday at 4 pm, arriving in Nairobi the next day at 9.30 am. The fares are KSh 440 in 1st class, KSh 207 in 2nd class and KSh 107 in 3rd class. The trains do not connect with the Ugandan system.

If you don't want to take the train, there are daily buses by different companies between Malaba and Nairobi which depart at around 7.30 pm arriving at about 5.30 am the next day. The fare is KSh 160. If you prefer to travel by day there are plenty of matatus between Bungoma and Malaba which cost KSh 20 and take about 45 minutes. If you stay in Bungoma overnight there are plenty of cheap hotels to choose from. From Bungoma there are several daily buses to Nairobi which leave at about 8 am and arrive about 5 pm the same day.

The other main entry point into Kenya from Uganda is via Busia further south. There are frequent matatus between Jinja and Busia and between Busia and Kisumu.

LEAVING KENYA
Departure Tax
The airport departure tax for international flights is US$20. You must pay this in foreign currency; Kenyan shillings are not accepted. It is possible to change US$ travellers' cheques to US$ cash in Nairobi but there are certain limitations which are discussed in the Money section in the Facts for the Visitor chapter.

Getting Around

AIR

Kenya Airways

Kenya Airways, the national carrier, connects the main cities of Nairobi, Mombasa, Kisumu and Malindi. It's advisable to book in advance and essential to reconfirm 48 hours before departure if you're coming from either Malindi or Kisumu and have to connect with an international flight from either Nairobi or Mombasa airports. Otherwise you may well find that your seat has been reallocated. The flight schedules can be found in the respective city chapters.

Private Airlines

There are also a number of private airlines which connect the main cities with smaller towns and certain national parks. From Nairobi's Wilson Airport, the main one is Kenya Aviation which connects Nairobi with Amboseli National Park, Masai Mara Game Reserve, Eldoret, Lamu, Lodwar, Loyangalani, Nanyuki and Nyeri. The flight schedule can be found in the Nairobi chapter.

Other private airlines connect Mombasa with Malindi and Lamu. They are Eagle Aviation, Prestige Air Services, Skyways Airlines and Equator Airlines. Their flight schedules can be found in the Mombasa, Malindi and Lamu chapters.

BUS

Kenya has a network of regular buses, matatus (normally minibuses), shared taxis and normal private taxis. The cheapest form of transport is buses, next matatus and lastly private taxis (expensive). There's not a lot to choose in terms of journey times between normal buses and matatus but there is a lot in terms of safety.

Regular Bus

Bus fares are generally about halfway between what you would pay on the railways in 2nd class but journey times are quicker.

Unlike the trains, which usually travel at night, many buses travel during the day so you may prefer to take a bus if you want to see the countryside. All the bus companies are privately owned but some of them run better buses than others. Coastline Safari, Goldline, Tana River Bus Company, Malindi Bus and Garissa Express are about the best of the bunch. Mawingo Bus Service and Akamba Bus Service are somewhat cheaper but their buses are older. It's worth paying that little extra for a good bus on a long journey.

Some Kenyan towns have what you might call a 'bus station', although this is often nothing more than a dirt patch. In others each bus company will have its own terminus though these are often close to each other. There are exceptions and these are indicated on the street maps. Matatu and shared taxi ranks sometimes share the same stations as buses but this isn't always the case, especially in Nairobi.

Matatu

Most matatu drivers are under a lot of pressure from their owners to maximise profits so they tend to drive recklessly and overload their vehicles. They also put in long working days. Stories about matatu smashes and overturnings in which a few people are killed and many injured can be found almost daily in the newspapers. There has been a determined police crackdown on such practices but bribery continues to undermine the success of it. Of course, many travellers use them and, in some cases, there is no alternative, but if there is (such as a bus or train) then take that in preference. The Mombasa-Nairobi road is notorious for smashes.

Overcrowding, on the other hand, isn't confined to matatus. I once counted 136 people getting off a Malindi-Mombasa bus at Kilifi excluding the driver and his mate.

As in most East African countries, you can always find a matatu which is going to the next town or further afield so long as it's not too late in the day. Simply ask around among the drivers at the park. Sometimes it's shared with the bus station. Matatus leave when full and the fares are fixed. It's unlikely you will be asked for more money than what other passengers are paying.

TRAIN
Kenyan Railways are excellent; they're a very popular way of travelling, generally run on time and they're considerably safer than travelling by bus or matatu. The main railway line runs from Mombasa to Malaba on the Kenya-Uganda border via Voi, Nairobi, Nakuru and Eldoret with branch lines from Nakuru to Kisumu, Nairobi to Nanyuki, Voi to Taveta and Eldoret to Kitale. There are no passenger services on the Nairobi-Nanyuki or Eldoret-Kitale branches. Although the Kenyan tracks are continuous with both the Tanzanian and Ugandan systems, there are no international services at present.

Classes
First class consists of two-berth compartments with a washbasin, drinking water, a wardrobe and a drinks service. There's a lockable door between one compartment and the adjacent one so, if there are four of you travelling together, you can make one compartment out of two, if you wish. They're usually very clean.

Second class consists of four-berth compartments with a washbasin and drinking water supply. Third class is seats only. All the compartments have fans. Sexes are separated in 1st and 2nd class unless you book the whole compartment. Third class can get a little wearing on the nerves on long journeys especially if they are overnight (which most are). Second class is more than adequate in this respect and 1st class is definitely a touch of luxury as far as budget travel goes.

There is a dining car on most trains offering dinner and breakfast (two sittings). Dinner on the Nairobi-Mombasa or Mombasa-Nairobi runs is an East African experience you should not miss at any price,

but try to go to the second sitting as you can hang around afterwards and continue your conversation. The food is excellent and plentiful. You are served four courses on starched white linen with silver-plated cutlery by usually immaculately dressed waiters, though some of the uniforms are getting decidedly tatty at the edges. Dinner costs KSh 120 and breakfast is KSh 80. Smaller portions are available for children at KSh 60 and KSh 40 respectively.

Reservations
You must book in advance for both 1st and 2nd class – two to three days is usually sufficient – otherwise you'll probably find that there are no berths available and will have to go 3rd class. If you're in Malindi and planning on taking the Mombasa-Nairobi train, bookings can be made with agents in Malindi. Compartment and berth numbers are posted up about 30 minutes prior to departure. Bedding (sheets, pillow and blanket) is available for KSh 25 if you don't have a sleeping bag and mattresses can be hired for KSh 15. Attendants will come round to ask you if you want bedding before the train departs.

BOAT
Lake Victoria Ferries
Ferries connect Kisumu with Kendu Bay, Kuwur, Homa Bay, Mfangano and Mbita but there are no international services connecting these Kenyan ports with those of Tanzania or Uganda.

Dhows
Sailing on a dhow along the East African coast is one of Kenya's most worthwhile and memorable experiences. There's nothing quite like drifting along the ocean in the middle of the night with the moon up high, the only sounds the lapping of the waves against the side of the boat and subdued conversation. It's enjoyable at any time of day, however, even when the breeze drops and the boat virtually comes to a standstill.

There are no creature comforts aboard these dhows so when night comes you simply bed down wherever there is space. You'll probably get off these boats smelling of fish since fish oil is used to condition the timbers of the boat – nothing that a shower won't remove! Take drinking water and food with you although fish is often caught on the way and cooked up on deck over charcoal. Dhows can be picked up in Mombasa, Malindi and Lamu.

Many of the smaller dhows these days have been fitted with outboard motors so that progress can be made when there's no wind. The larger dhows are all motorised and most of them don't even have sails.

Large, motorised dhows connect Mombasa with the Tanzanian islands of Pemba and Zanzibar and with Dar es Salaam though there's usually only one per week.

DRIVING

If you are bringing your own vehicle to Kenya you should get a free three month permit at the border on entry, so long as you have a valid carnet de passage for it. If you don't have a carnet you should be able to get a free one week permit at the border on entry after which you must get an 'Authorisation permit for a foreign private vehicle' which costs KSh 3900 (about US$244). Before you do this, however, get in touch with the Automobile Association in Nairobi.

When you are driving your own vehicle there are certain routes in north-east Kenya where you must obtain police permission before setting out. This is just a formality but there will be a roadblock to enforce this. The main stretch where this applies is between Isiolo and Marsabit where all transport must travel in convoy at a particular time of day unless you're turning off to go somewhere else.

Road Safety

Kenyan roads in the south-western part of the country – west of a line drawn through Malindi, Isiolo and Kitale – are excellent. In fact they're some of the best in Africa. North and north-east of this line and in the national

parks they are all gravel roads, usually in a reasonable state of repair though there are long sections of corrugated gravel in some parts. Driving on these, at the necessary speed to avoid wrecking a vehicle, can be agony on your kidneys after several hours, especially if you're on a bus which has had a double set of unyielding springs fitted to it. Naturally, there are washouts on some of these gravel roads during the rainy seasons and, under these circumstances, journey times can be considerably longer.

Right up in the north on the eastern side of Lake Turkana, especially in the Kaisut and Chalbi deserts, you can make good headway in the dry season and the roads (which would be better described as tracks) are often surprisingly smooth and in good condition. This is certainly true of the road from Wamba to North Horr via Parsaloi, Baragoi, South Horr and Loyangalani. After rain, however, it's another story, particularly on the flat parts of the deserts. They turn into treacherous seas of mud, often as much as a metre deep in places. Only a complete fool would attempt to drive in these circumstances without 4WD, sand ladders, adequate jacking equipment, shovels, a tow rope or wire, drinking water and spare metal jerrycans of fuel. This is particularly true of the stretches of track between North Horr and Maikona and on any of the tracks leading off the Marsabit-Isiolo road to South Horr.

To get out of the mud, if you're really stuck, you're going to be entirely dependent on the small number of vehicles which *may* pass by and *may* stop and help (they won't want to get stuck either), or on a passing herd of camels. It's going to cost you money either way. Not only that but you can sometimes drive for hours only to find that it's impossible to cross a river, which may not even exist in the dry season, and have to drive all the way back again. Fuel is very difficult to find in this region and is usually only available at mission stations at up to three times what you would pay for it in Nairobi – and they'll only sell you a limited amount. Make adequate preparations if you are driving your own vehicle.

Vehicle Hire

Hiring a vehicle to tour Kenya (or at least the national parks) is a relatively expensive way of seeing the country but it does give you freedom of movement and is sometimes the only way of getting to the more remote parts of the country. On the other hand, if you're sharing costs, it's quite a feasible option.

There are a number of factors to take into consideration before deciding what type of vehicle to take and which company to go through, and there's no real substitute for sitting down with pen and paper and working out as near as possible what the total cost will be. To do this you'll need as many hire charge leaflets as you can get hold of and a distances table.

The other major consideration is what type of vehicle is going to be suitable to enable you to get where you want to go. Outside of the rainy season, a 2WD vehicle may be perfectly adequate in some parts of the country including Masai Mara Game Reserve and Amboseli and Tsavo national parks, but it won't get you to Lake Turkana and would restrict your movements in the Aberdare and Meru national parks and the Buffalo Springs and Samburu game reserves. Most companies also have a policy of insisting that you take a 4WD vehicle if you're going upcountry and off the beaten track.

Hire Charges This is something of a mine-field since the daily/weekly base rates vary quite a lot as do the km (mileage) charges. What initially looks cheap often works out just as expensive as anything else. No company offers unlimited free km on a daily basis; to get this you must hire on a weekly basis. Again, some of the so-called 'unlimited' km rates are not quite that. Most have a ceiling of 1200 km to 1400 km per week free after which you pay the excess at the normal km rate. Some companies also offer the option of 500 km or 1200 km to 1400 km per week free of charge with corresponding lower or higher base rates. If you're not planning on going too far then it may be more economical to opt for the lower

free km rate. Also, some companies include insurance in the weekly rates; others don't.

To give you some idea of average costs, the base rates for a 2WD saloon car are between KSh 300 and KSh 500 per day plus mileage or KSh 2750 and KSh 4000 per week plus mileage. 'Unlimited' km weekly rates for this type of car vary between KSh 6200 and KSh 6600.

In the next category, an average small 4WD vehicle such as a Suzuki Sierra costs between KSh 500 and KSh 600 per day plus mileage or KSh 3200 and KSh 7500 per week plus mileage. 'Unlimited' km rates are between KSh 8600 and KSh 15,000.

In the highest category – a 4WD Isuzu Trooper, for instance – daily rates vary between KSh 900 and KSh 1350 plus mileage or KSh 8100 and KSh 16,250 per week plus mileage. The 'unlimited' km rates are between KSh 12,000 and KSh 29,000.

If you're not hiring on the basis of 'unlimited' mileage then average rates are KSh 4 (2WD saloon cars), KSh 5.50 (4WD Suzuki Sierra) and KSh 9 (Isuzu Trooper) per km.

Minimum Mileage Conditions Where you're paying a km charge, some companies stipulate 50 km per day for saloon cars, 65 km per day for station wagons and 100 km per day for 4WD and camping vehicles. Other companies make no such conditions.

Insurance Third party insurance is compulsory but this does not cover you for damage to the vehicle or damage to anyone else's property. That being the case, you could be in big trouble financially if you have an accident and particularly if your vehicle is a write-off. The only way around this is to take out additional Collision Damage Waiver (CDW) insurance which usually absolves you of any financial responsibility except for the first KSh 1000 (or less – depends on the insurance company) in the event of an accident. Most companies strongly recommend that you cover yourself in this way. CDW usually doesn't cover tyres or tools nor does it usually cover windscreens.

Average daily rates for CDW cover are KSh 280 for saloon cars and KSh 400 for 4WD vehicles.

Deposits There's a wide variation in the deposits charged on hired vehicles. It's usually the estimated total hire charges (base rate plus km) plus KSh 4000 to KSh 5000. If you don't take out CDW cover then the KSh 4000 to KSh 5000 may be increased to the full replacement value of the vehicle. On the other hand, if you do take out CDW cover then the KSh 4000 to KSh 5000 excess is usually waived. No deposit is necessary if you are paying by credit card.

Driving Licences & Driver's Age An international driving licence or your own national driving licence is standard. Some companies stipulate a minimum age of 23 but with others it is 25. There are occasionally stipulations about endorsements on licences (clean licences preferred) and that you must have been driving for at least two years.

Quality of Maintenance Although it's not always the case, it's probably true to say that the more you pay for a vehicle, the better condition it will be in. It's worth paying attention to this especially if you're planning on going a long way. It doesn't necessarily mean that the cheaper companies neglect maintenance but, in some cases, they certainly do as our feedback mail indicates.

The other factor related to maintenance is what the company will do for you, if anything, in the event of a major breakdown. The major companies *may* deliver you a replacement vehicle and make arrangements for recovery of the other but with most you'll be entirely responsible for getting it fixed and back on the road. Only when you return the vehicle will you be refunded and you'll need receipts to prove what you spent.

Equipment Some companies provide you with adequate tools to tackle breakdowns, others with just sufficient to change a tyre. If you have mechanical skills, it's worth enquiring about what tools are provided. The

only company which includes a full complement of camping equipment including tents in their hire charges on 4WD vehicles is Habib's. With other companies you'll have to hire this separately.

One-Way Rates If you want to hire a vehicle in one place and drop it in another there will be additional charges to pay. These vary depending on the vehicle and the company but range from KSh 1000 to KSh 3000.

Taking a Hired Vehicle to Tanzania Only the larger (and more expensive) companies cater for this and there are additional charges. Briefly, these are KSh 1000 for insurance and KSh 2500 for documentation (both payable to the hire company) plus US$100 for Tanzanian road tax (payable to the Tanzanian customs on entry).

Which Company? At the top end of the market are two companies:

Hertz
  PO Box 42196, Nairobi, tel (331960, 331973/4)
  PO Box 84782, Mombasa (tel 316333/4, 315079)
  PO Box 365, Malindi (tel 20069, 20040)
Avis
  Kenyatta Ave, Nairobi (tel 336703/4)
  Moi Ave, Mombasa (tel 23048)
  Sitawi House, Malindi (tel 20513)

Both these companies have branch offices at Jomo Kenyatta International Airport (Nairobi), Moi Airport (Mombasa) and at many of the beach resort hotels both north and south of Mombasa and at Malindi.

In much the same league but considerably less expensive on weekly rates is Europcar (tel 334722/3/4/5/6), PO Box 40433, Nairobi, and PO Box 90631, Mombasa (tel 312461). They also have a branch office at Jomo Kenyatta International Airport .

Similar, but for no discernible reason since their vehicles are not new and, in some cases, quite tatty, is Glory (tel 24428, 22910), PO Box 66969, Nairobi; PO Box 85527, Mombasa (tel 21159, 313561); and PO Box 994, Malindi (tel 20065).

Budget also slot into this category but, if their Australian operations are anything to go by, they may be in receivership. If not, they're at PO Box 59767, Nairobi (tel 23304, 24081), and Moi Ave, Mombasa (tel 24600, 24065).

Beneath the above there's an excellent choice of good, reliable companies with well-maintained vehicles and they all have approximately the same rates. What they don't have is large fleets of vehicles so it's important to book in advance if you want to be sure of getting what you want – particularly a 4WD vehicle. Typical daily rates would be KSh 1200 (2WD saloon), KSh 1650 (4WD Suzuki Sierra) and KSh 3000 (4WD Isuzu Trooper). Corresponding weekly rates without 'unlimited' mileage would be KSh 7000, KSh 10,500 and KSh 20,500. Remember to add CDW charges to the above rates. Companies which we can recommend in this category include:

Habib's
    PO Box 48095, Agip House, Haile Selassie Ave, Nairobi (tel 20463, 23816, 20985)
Central Rent-a-Car
    PO Box 49439, Fedha Towers, Standard St, Nairobi (tel 22888, 332296)
    PO Box 99753, Moi Ave, Mombasa (tel 20171, 312070)
Let's Go Travel
    PO Box 60342, Caxton House, Standard St, Nairobi (tel 29539/40, 340331)
Market Car Hire
    PO Box 49713, Market Service Station, Koinange & Banda streets, Nairobi (tel 25797, 335735)
Payless
    PO Box 49713, Olympic House, Koinange St, Nairobi (tel 338400)
Nutty Car Hire, Tours & Travel
    PO Box 45833, Puri Building, Muindi Mbingu St, Nairobi (tel 542605, 542696)
Galu Safaris Ltd
    PO Box 56707, Standard St, Nairobi (tel 20365, 336570)
    PO Box 99143, Ambalal House, Nkrumah Rd, Mombasa (tel 314174, 314226)

HITCHING

Hitching is usually good on the main roads and may well be preferable to travelling by matatu, but if you are picked up by an African driver and are expecting a free lift then make this clear from the outset. Most will expect a contribution at least. Hitching to the national parks, on the other hand, can be very difficult since most people either go on a tour or hire their own vehicle. Apart from that, once you get to the park lodges or camping areas, you will be entirely dependent on persuading other tourists with their own vehicles to take you out with them to view game since walking in the parks is forbidden.

Safaris

ORGANISED SAFARIS

There are essentially two types of organised safaris available – those where you camp at night and those where you stay in game lodges or luxury tented camps at night. Whichever you go on, they typically start and end in either Nairobi or Mombasa though there are a number of exceptions to this. Apart from transfer to and from Nairobi or Mombasa and driving from one park to another, once you're in a park you'll be taken on a number of game drives – usually two and sometimes three per day. Each drive typically lasts two to 2½ hours and the best (in terms of sighting animals) are those in the early morning and late afternoon when the animals are at their most active. The vehicles used for these drives are six to eight seater minibuses with roof hatches, Land Rovers or open-sided trucks.

As a general rule, you'll be left to your own devices between late morning and around 3 pm other than for lunch though, if you're on a camping safari, you may well be taken to a lodge in the early afternoon to relax over a cold beer or have a swim in the pool (if permitted – at some lodges the pool is for guests only). You may also be taken to a lodge after the late afternoon game drive for the same thing before returning to camp for dinner.

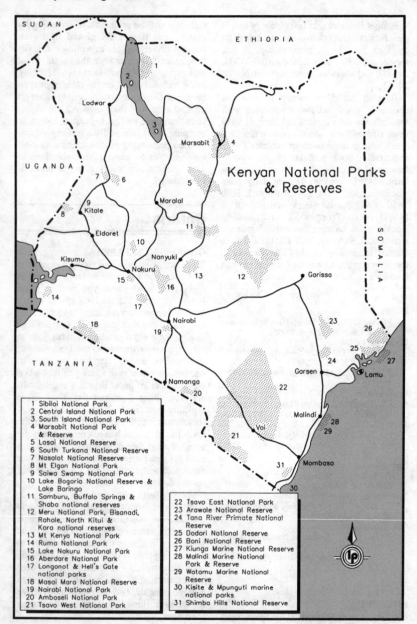

Kenyan National Parks & Reserves

1 Sibiloi National Park
2 Central Island National Park
3 South Island National Park
4 Marsabit National Park & Reserve
5 Losai National Reserve
6 South Turkana National Reserve
7 Nasolot National Reserve
8 Mt Elgon National Park
9 Saiwa Swamp National Park
10 Lake Bogoria National Reserve & Lake Baringo
11 Samburu, Buffalo Springs & Shaba national reserves
12 Meru National Park, Bisanadi, Rahole, North Kitui & Kora national reserves
13 Mt Kenya National Park
14 Ruma National Park
15 Lake Nakuru National Park
16 Aberdare National Park
17 Longonot & Hell's Gate national parks
18 Masai Mara National Reserve
19 Nairobi National Park
20 Amboseli National Park
21 Tsavo West National Park
22 Tsavo East National Park
23 Arawale National Reserve
24 Tana River Primate National Reserve
25 Dodori National Reserve
26 Boni National Reserve
27 Kiunga Marine National Reserve
28 Malindi Marine National Park & Reserve
29 Watamu Marine National Reserve
30 Kisite & Mpunguti marine national parks
31 Shimba Hills National Reserve

Camping Safaris

Camping safaris cater for budget travellers, for the young (or young at heart) and for those who are prepared to put up with discomfort. They are no-frills safaris, there are none of life's little luxuries such as flush toilets, running water or iced drinks, they can be quite demanding depending on where you go, and you'll be expected to lend a hand. You'll end up sweaty and dusty and there may well be no showers available – even cold ones. On the other hand, you're in for an authentic adventure in the African bush with nothing between you and the animals at night except a sheet of canvas and the embers of a dying fire. It's not at all unusual for elephants or hippos to trundle through the camp at night, or even the occasional lion. No-one has so far been eaten or trampled on.

Another plus for these safaris is that you'll probably find yourself with travellers from the four corners of the earth. Those safaris which use trucks frequently have as many as half a dozen different nationalities on board.

The price of your safari will include three meals a day cooked by the camp's cook(s) though on some safaris you'll be expected to lend a hand in the preparation and cleanup. Food is of the 'plain but plenty' variety.

The price will also include all the necessary camping gear except a sleeping bag which you must provide or hire locally. The tents provided sleep two people as a rule and you'll be expected to erect and dismantle it yourself though there are some safaris where the camp is taken on ahead of you and the tents erected by the staff. Tents are invariably of the type which sleep two people and, if you're a single traveller, you'll be expected to share with someone else. If you don't want to do that then you'll be up for a 'single supplement' of between 15% to 20% on the price of the safari which will allow you to have a tent of your own. Mosquito nets are generally not provided so you'll have to hire one yourself or bring along insect repellent either in the form of coils or a skin cream.

You'll need to bring all your own clothing and footwear sufficient to cover you for hot days and cold nights but the amount of baggage which you'll be allowed to bring with you is limited. Excess gear can usually be stored at the safari company's offices. Don't forget to bring along a torch (flashlight) and penknife – the company will provide kerosene lanterns for the camp but they won't be left on all night.

There are also a number of somewhat more expensive camping safaris available which utilise permanent camp sites with pre-erected tents fitted with mosquito nets, beds and sheets and which have showers (though there's sometimes not enough water for everyone to have a shower).

Remember that at the end of one of these safaris your driver/guide and the cooks will expect a reasonable tip. This is only fair since wages are low and these people will have made a lot of effort to make your trip a memorable one. Be generous here. Other travellers are going to follow you and the last thing anyone wants to find themselves closeted with is a disgruntled driver/guide who couldn't care less whether you see game or not.

Lodge Safaris

The other type of safari is for those who want luxury at night and in between game drives. On these the accommodation is in game lodges or luxury tented camps. There are plenty of beautifully conceived and superbly sited lodges in the main national parks where you can expect a fully self-contained room or cottage, cuisine of an international standard, a terrace bar with ice-cold drinks, a swimming pool and videos and plenty of staff to cater for all your requirements. Many of these lodges overlook a watering hole or salt lick so you can sit on the viewing terrace and watch the animals from there. The watering hole or salt lick will usually be floodlit at night. Some of the lodges put out bait or salt to encourage certain animals to visit the spot and while this is often very contrived, it usually guarantees you a sighting of animals which you'd be very lucky to see otherwise.

There's obviously a considerable difference in price for these safaris as opposed to camping and most of the people who go on them are package tourists with expectations and attitudes of mind quite dissimilar to those who opt for a camping safari. Essentially for them, it's a holiday rather than in-depth involvement in Africa, its people and wildlife. It's the African bush at arm's length. On the other hand, if you have the money, it's worth staying at the occasional lodge just for the contrast.

Lodge safaris will cost you at least four times what a camping safari costs – and often considerably more. Luxury tented camps are no less expensive than lodges and the more exclusive ones cost up to four times the price of a lodge. They're for people to whom money is no object and who want to experience what it must have been like in the days of the big-game hunters except that it's cameras rather than guns which they tote these days.

Safari Options

There's a whole plethora of options available whether you take a camping safari or a lodge safari ranging from two days to 15 days and sometimes 25 days. If possible, it's best to go on a safari which lasts at least five days and preferably longer since otherwise a good deal of your time will be taken up driving to and from the national parks and Nairobi. You'll also see a great deal more on a longer safari and have a much better chance of catching sight of all the major animals. Remember that sightings of any particular animal cannot be guaranteed but the longer you spend looking, the better your chances are. A longer safari will also give you the opportunity of having some involvement with the local tribespeople.

A three day safari typically takes you either to Amboseli or Masai Mara. A four day safari would take you to Amboseli and Tsavo, to Masai Mara or to Samburu and Buffalo Springs. A five day safari would take you to Amboseli and Tsavo or to Masai Mara and Lake Nakuru whereas a six day safari would take you to lakes Nakuru, Bogoria and Baringo plus Masai Mara or to Lake Nakuru, Masai Mara and Amboseli. Going onto a seven day safari, you could expect to visit at least two of the Rift Valley lakes plus Masai Mara and Amboseli whereas on an 11 day safari you would take in one or more of the Rift Valley lakes plus Masai Mara, Amboseli and Tsavo or Mt Kenya, Samburu and Buffalo Springs, Meru, Lake Nakuru and Masai Mara.

Most of the safari companies cover the above standard routes but some also specialise in different routings designed to take you off the beaten track. There are, for instance, safaris which take in Masai Mara, Lake Victoria, Mt Elgon, Saiwa Swamp and Nakuru and others which take in Mt Kenya, Samburu and Buffalo Springs, Nyahururu, Lake Nakuru and Masai Mara. Other safaris visit Shaba, rather than Samburu and Buffalo Springs, where you'll hardly see another vehicle.

Most companies also offer safaris to Lake Turkana which range from seven days to 12 days. The shorter trips take one or other of the standard routes – Nairobi, Nakuru, Nyahururu, Maralal, Baragoi, South Horr and Loyangalani or Nairobi, Isiolo, Maralal, Baragoi, South Horr and Loyangalani. The longer trips detour from this route and take you to either or both of the Mathew's Range and the Ndoto Mountains. A full description of the options available can be found in the East of Turkana section in the Northern Kenya chapter.

Safari Costs

There's a lot of competition for the tourist dollar among the safari companies and prices for the same tour are very similar. Generally, the longer you go for, the less it costs per day.

For camping safaris you are looking at around KSh 1000 (US$48 to US$50) per day for three days, KSh 900 to KSh 920 (US$43 to US$45) per day for four days, KSh 860 to KSh 870 (US$40 to US$42) per day for five days, and KSh 775 (US$37) per day for seven or more days. The price per day for safaris over 11 days tends to rise somewhat since there's a lot more organisation involved and you'll be going to remote areas where there are no services available so everything has to be trucked in.

The prices for safaris which involve staying in lodges or tented camps will be at least four times the above daily rate.

Remember that if you're a single traveller and want a tent or room to yourself you'll have to multiply the above figures by a factor of 15% to 20%.

Prices include camping equipment or accommodation at a lodge, transport (including game drives), camp site and park entry fees and three cooked meals a day.

Frequency of Departures

This varies a lot from company to company and depends on the season. In the high season, many companies have daily or every second day departures to the most popular game parks – Amboseli, Masai Mara and Tsavo – since there's high demand. To the less frequented parks such as Samburu and Buffalo Springs, Shaba and Meru, they generally leave only once or twice per week. Safaris to Lake Turkana are usually only once weekly. In addition, most companies will leave for any of the most popular game parks at any time so long as you have a minimum number of people wanting to go – sometimes four, sometimes six. In the low season, there are fewer departures.

It obviously makes a lot of sense to either book ahead or to get a group together rather than just turn up and expect to leave the very next morning. Advance booking is essential for the Lake Turkana safaris since they're heavily subscribed. It's also essential for any of the 'Exotic Options' described below.

Which Safari Company?

There is no doubt that some safari companies are better than others. The main factors which make for the difference are the quality and type of vehicles used, the standard of the food and the skills and knowledge of the drivers/guides. It's equally true that any particular company can take a bunch of people on safari one week and bring them back fully satisfied and yet the following week take a different set of people on the same safari and end up with a virtual mutiny. That's an extreme example, but whether a company gets praised or condemned can hinge on something as simple as a puncture which takes half a day to fix and for which there are no tools on board. Or a broken spring which involves having to wait around for most of the day whilst a replacement vehicle is sent out from Nairobi. There's obviously a lot which companies can do to head off breakdowns but a broken spring, for example, isn't reasonably one of them on a short safari though you would expect such spares to be on board for longer journeys and certainly on a safari to Lake Turkana.

The other major factor to take into consideration before you decide to go with any particular company is whether they actually operate their own safaris with their own vehicles or whether they are just agents for other safari companies. If they're just agents then obviously part of what you pay is their commission but the most important thing here is, if anything goes wrong or the itinerary is changed without your agreement, you have very little comeback and you'll be pushing shit uphill to get a refund. We get letters about this *all* the time from travellers to whom this happened.

Unfortunately, the situation isn't that easy to avoid. It's a minefield working out which are genuine safari companies and which are just agents. Go into any office in Nairobi and, naturally, they all have their own vehicles and, of course, they'll compensate you at the end of the safari if anything went seriously wrong. Not so if they're just agents. They will already have paid the lion's share of what you gave them to the company which actually provided the vehicles and staff so that gives them very little room for manoeuvre. Likewise, there's no way that the actual safari company is going to provide the agent with a refund.

It's perfectly obvious that quite a few so-called safari companies are merely agents. Simply pick up half a dozen leaflets from various companies and compare the wording on them. You'll find that quite a few are identical!

Another aspect of the safari business in Kenya is that there's a good deal of swapping of clients when one company's vehicle(s) are full for any particular safari and another's are not. This isn't philanthropy; it's pure business. In other words, you may find yourself on a certain company's safari which is not the one you booked through. The reputable companies won't do this without informing you but the agents certainly will.

Despite the pitfalls mentioned here, there are a number of reliable companies offering camping safaris which have their own vehicles and an excellent track record. Most of the people who run them paid their dues driving overland trucks around Africa for years so you can be sure they know the business back to front. They are:

Yare Safaris Ltd

1st floor, Union Towers, Mama Ngina St, PO Box 63006, Nairobi (tel 559313). This company specialises in safaris to Samburu Game Reserve (four days), Lake Turkana (eight days), Masai Mara and Nakuru (six days) and the gorilla sanctuaries/volcanos of Zaïre and the Serengeti (Tanzania) (25 days), plus they also offer the only genuine camel safari available in Kenya (five days).

In addition, they operate an excellent hostel/camp site at Maralal and, for those who intend to stay there or go on one of their safaris, there's a free transfer vehicle to and from Nairobi once a week. They're also willing to advise you even if you don't go on one of their safaris and they offer 8% discounts to IYHF members on the prices of all safaris booked either through their own offices or at the Youth Hostel in Nairobi.

Safari-Camp Services

Corner Koinange and Moktar Daddah streets, PO Box 44801, Nairobi (tel 330130, 28936). This company has been operating for years and has an excellent reputation. It offers both standard economy camping safaris plus what it calls 'lodge equivalent' camping safaris for those who prefer somewhat better facilities.

Its most popular safari is probably the Turkana Bus (seven days) but they also offer the Wildlife Bus (Samburu, Mt Kenya, Nyahururu, Lake Nakuru and Masai Mara – seven days), the Coast Bus (Nairobi-Mombasa via Amboseli and Tsavo – four days), the Hemingway (a 'lodge equivalent' safari to Samburu, Nyahururu, Lake Nakuru and Masai Mara – seven or 10 days) and Vanishing Africa (a 'lodge equivalent' safari to Masai Mara, lakes Nakuru, Bogoria and Baringo, Maralal, Lake Turkana, the Mathew's Range and Samburu – 14 days).

Gametrackers Camping Safaris

Finance House, Banda St between Koinange and Loita streets, PO Box 62042, Nairobi (tel 338927, 22703). This company offers safaris to Lake Turkana (eight days), Amboseli, Lake Nakuru and Masai Mara (seven days), Masai Mara and the Rift Valley lakes (six days), Amboseli (three days), and Lake Turkana plus a camel walk in Rendille country (10 days). They're highly recommended.

Special Camping Safaris Ltd

Gilfillan House, Kenyatta Ave, PO Box 51512, Nairobi (tel 338325, 20072). This is a small company operated by two people and their Kenyan staff and they pride themselves on personal service. They offer Lake Turkana, Samburu and Mt Kenya (10 days), Masai Mara (four days), Mt Kenya, Meru, Samburu, Maralal, lakes Baringo, Nakuru and Naivasha and Masai Mara (10 days), Amboseli, Tsavo and the coast (10 days) plus walking safaris in the Loita Hills (seven days) and horse-riding safaris on the Rift Valley escarpment (three days).

Bushbuck Adventures

3rd floor, Gilfillan House, Kenyatta Ave, PO Box 67449, Nairobi (tel 728737). To quote the company's leaflet, 'We do not offer safaris for those requiring all the comforts of home, nor do we offer rock bottom prices and comparable facilities. We specialise in safaris for (those) who want reasonable comfort while still feeling close to nature'. As a result, they're relatively expensive.

They offer Masai Mara (five days – US$710), Amboseli, Tsavo, Chyulu Hills (six days – US$845), Shaba, Mathew's Range, Ndoto Mountains, Lake Turkana, Maralal, Lake Bogoria (12 days – US$1550), Mt Kenya, Shaba and Meru (six days – US$845) and Masai Mara, Lake Victoria, Mt Elgon, Saiwa Swamp and Lake Nakuru (12 days – US$1550). Again, highly recommended.

Best Camping Tours

2nd floor, Nanak House, corner Kimathi and Banda streets, PO Box 40223, Nairobi (tel 29667, 29675). This is another company which offers budget camping safaris on all the main routes ranging from Amboseli and Tsavo (four days) right through to Masai Mara, Lake Nakuru, Amboseli and Tsavo (15 days).

This company has had a variable press over the last few years judging from the feedback which we've received – some abuse it virulently; others praise it. What seems to be happening is that they push their drivers too hard for too long (sometimes 20 days with no time off) so they get tired and bad tempered. There have also been complaints that the groups are too large and the food gets scarce towards the end of the trip. It's probably no worse than any other company in this respect.

Exotic Safaris
1st floor, South Wing, Uniafric House, Koinange St, PO Box 54483, Nairobi (tel 338811). We've had good reports of this company which offers a full range of safaris along the standard routes from Amboseli (three days) through lakes Nakuru, Bogoria and Baringo and Masai Mara (six days) to Mt Kenya, Samburu and Masai Mara (eight days) and Lake Turkana (eight days).

Centrex Tours & Travel
1st floor, Hughes Building, Muindi Mbingu St, PO Box 41830, Nairobi (tel 332267, 330539).

Farways Safaricentre Ltd
Opposite Castle Hotel, Moi Ave, PO Box 87815, Mombasa (tel 23307/9). This is a reputable company with its own vehicles and has a branch in Nairobi.

Safari Seekers
5th floor, Jubilee Insurance Exchange Building, Kaunda St, PO Box 23247, Nairobi (tel 26206).

Savuka Tours & Safaris
3rd floor, Pan Africa House, Kenyatta Ave, PO Box 20433, Nairobi (tel 725907, 25108).

Sunwise Travel Ltd
4th floor, Nanak House, corner Kimathi and Banda streets, PO Box 39073, Nairobi (tel 336777, 338715). Mainly luxury safaris.

Tete Travel Services Ltd
Corner Koinange and Moktar Daddah streets (above Goldstar Restaurant), PO Box 30729, Nairobi (tel 729461).

This is by no means an exhaustive list of companies which offer budget camping safaris nor is there necessarily any implication that others are unreliable (though some are). It's obvious, too, that if everyone who reads this book uses the companies listed above then they may get oversubscribed. On the other hand, we do get hundreds of letters from travellers every year describing their experiences with various safari companies. Some get consistently good reports and others get variable reports but there are some which get consistently bad reports. Regarding the latter category, we suggest you avoid:

Ebra Tours & Camping Safaris Ltd
4th floor, Standard Building, Standard St, PO Box 43457, Nairobi (tel 334937, 331494)

Massay Bush Safaris
3rd floor, Chester House, Koinange St, PO Box 74521, Nairobi (tel 727317)

Nutty Safaris
1st floor, Puri Building, Muindi Mbingu St, Nairobi (tel 21032, 26213)

There are also some lesser known safari companies which you should give a wide berth. They include Kiwa Safaris ('...a rip-off merchant well known to the police and the Ministry of Tourism...'), and Parrot Tours & Travels (tel 723796), Cambian Building, Moi Ave, PO Box 62951, Nairobi. Parrot Tours isn't even licensed and the owners are frequently in trouble with the authorities.

We've also had some bad reports and some very good reports about Nana Safaris (tel 21396), Chester House, PO Box 59603, Nairobi. On one of their safaris to Masai Mara and Lake Nakuru, the clients had to return to Nairobi by public bus from Nakuru and were only taken on three of the promised six game drives. On another, the group set off without a single tent! There was subsequently no compensation and a lot of aggro from the manager.

Similarly, Through the Lens Safaris, Jubilee House, Nairobi, came in for both good and bad reports. The complaints stemmed from lack of compensation and aggro from the management after a safari went seriously wrong (one group had been abandoned by their drunk driver in Tsavo!).

While many of these complaints are undoubtedly justified, it's only fair to say that some of the people who were caught out had been in too much of a hurry to go on a safari, hadn't done their homework, and had unrealistic expectations. Also, in some cases, it was just pure bad luck.

If you don't want to camp but prefer to stay in a lodge each night then check out:

African Tours & Hotels
Utalii House, Uhuru Highway, PO Box 30471, Nairobi (tel 336858)
Moi Ave, PO Box 90604, Mombasa (tel 23509)

Crossways Car Hire Tours & Travel
Banda St, Nairobi (tel 23949)

United Touring Company
International House, Mama Ngina St, PO Box 42196, Nairobi (tel 331960, 24847/8)
Moi Ave, PO Box 84782, Mombasa (tel 316333/4)

It's recommended that in this category you avoid Birds Paradise Tours & Travel (tel 22596, 722219), Standard St, PO Box 22121, Nairobi.

EXOTIC OPTIONS
Camel Safaris
There are only three companies which offer camel safaris at present and only one which is exclusively that. The other two are part of longer safaris to Lake Turkana by vehicle.

The first is that operated by Yare Safaris Ltd (tel 559313), 1st floor, Union Towers, Mama Ngina St, PO Box 63006, Nairobi, from their Maralal hostel. This is a five day trek along the Ewaso Nyiro River (which flows through Samburu and Buffalo Springs game reserves) and it leaves every Sunday.

On the first day you are transferred by vehicle to the camel base camp at Barsalinga bridge and from here you have the choice of riding the camels or walking alongside them for the next five days (it's up to you as the camels are not used for transporting food or equipment). You'll be accompanied the whole way by Samburu *morani* (warriors) and there's plenty of game to see in this unspoilt area. Your excess baggage and the camp is moved on ahead of you each day by support vehicle. The camps are equipped with two-person tents, mattresses and showers. The safari ends back at the Maralal hostel on Thursday. The cost is KSh 5500 (about US$262) which includes all transport, food, camping equipment (except sleeping bags) and transfer from Nairobi to Maralal and vice versa. There's an 8% discount on the cost of this safari for all IYHF members.

Gametrackers Camping Safaris (tel 338927), Finance House, Banda St (between Koinange and Loita streets), PO Box 62042, Nairobi, offer a partial four day walking/camel trek through the Ndoto Mountains, south-east of Lake Turkana, which is part of a 10 day safari to Lake Turkana but here the camels transport your food, water and equipment. You walk alongside them accompanied by Rendille guides. The cost of the safari is KSh 7000 (about US$333) which includes all transport, meals,

park entry fees, camp site fees and camping equipment (except sleeping bags). Departures depend on demand.

Bushbuck Adventures (tel 728737), 3rd floor, Gilfillan House, Kenyatta Ave, PO Box 67449, Nairobi, offer a 10 day camel trek once a year (in late October) which takes you to the Ndoto Mountains and Milgis Lugger or the Amaya River and Mt Silali depending on prevailing conditions. The camels are used for transportation of food and equipment – you walk. This trek costs US$1850.

The same company also offers a partial walking/camel trek through the Mathew's Range and the Ndoto Mountains which is part of a 12 day safari which also takes in Shaba National Reserve, Lake Turkana, Maralal and Lake Bogoria. Again, the camels are used for transporting food, water and equipment. The cost of this safari is US$1550 which includes all transport, food, camping equipment (except sleeping bags), park entry and camp site fees. Departures depend on demand.

Walking Safaris
Special Camping Safaris Ltd (tel 338325), Gilfillan House, Kenyatta Ave, PO Box 51512, Nairobi, offer a seven day walking safari in the Loita Hills including transfer to and from Nairobi. This trek takes you down the Nkuruman Escarpment into the Rift Valley accompanied by an experienced Maasai guide. You cover about 10 km (approximately five to six hours walk) per day and you're expected to carry food. At night you sleep in the open on groundsheets. As the company says, 'It's not suitable for vegetarians as a goat will be slaughtered for the farewell feast'. The trek costs KSh 5200 (about US$248). Departures depend on demand.

Horse-Riding Safaris
Special Camping Safaris Ltd (address above) also offer three day horse-riding safaris through the Ngong Hills and the Kitengela Reserve where you'll get beautiful views over the Rift Valley. Accommodation

overnight is in tents and the cost of the safari is KSh 8100 (about US$386) which includes the horses, food, camping equipment (except sleeping bag) and other transport.

Flying Safaris

These safaris essentially cater only for the rich and those interested in big-game fishing. They centre around Rusinga Island in Lake Victoria. A light aircraft collects you from your nearest airstrip in the early morning and returns you in time for lunch or an afternoon game drive. In the meantime a motorboat takes you out on Lake Victoria where you can feed and photograph fish eagles and fish for Nile perch – the largest freshwater fish in the world. Angling gear is provided. Bookings can be made through Lonrho Hotels Kenya (tel 723776), PO Box 58581, Nairobi.

Balloon Safaris

For those with the money to spare, here is a unique experience to view the wildlife of Masai Mara Game Reserve from the air. These hot-air balloons depart daily from Keekorok Lodge just after dawn and return around mid-morning. The flight includes a champagne-style breakfast on the plains. The cost is KSh 4000 (about US$190). Bookings can be made through Block Hotels (tel 335807), PO Box 47557, Nairobi, or at Keekorok Lodge.

Further Afield

A few companies in Nairobi offer safaris to the Tanzanian game parks of Lake Manyara, Ngorongoro Crater and Serengeti but most of them are just agents for Tanzanian safari companies based in Arusha so you might as well go there yourself and organise things from there. It would certainly cost less doing it that way.

There is one outfit, however, which offers a superb 25 day safari from Nairobi all the way to Zaïre and back which takes in Uganda, Rwanda, the gorillas of Kahuzi Biega National Park (Zaïre), Lake Kivu (Zaïre), a chimpanzee sanctuary (Zaïre), Nyiragongo volcano (Zaïre), northern Tanzania, Serengeti National Park (Tanzania) and Masai Mara Game Reserve (Kenya). For those with less time available, there's the option of joining the vehicle in Kigali (Rwanda) for 12 or 20 days of the Zaïre section only.

The people who operate this safari are all thoroughly experienced African overland hands and the company has its own well-maintained 4WD trucks. It's a part camping and part budget hotel safari and it's excellent value at KSh 10,780 (about US$513) plus national park entry fees and budget hotel accommodation (US$100 for the gorillas, US$40 for the chimpanzees, US$30 for Nyiragongo (optional), US$42 for Serengeti) and US$45 for the food kitty. The food kitty is operated by the clients which allows greater flexibility in the choice of meals which are cooked by the camp's cook. Those joining this safari for only 12 or 20 days pay only US$25 or US$40 to the food kitty respectively. The price includes transport, camping equipment (except sleeping bags) and a camp cook. There's an 8% discount on these prices for all IYHF members.

For more details contact Yare Safaris Ltd (tel 559313), 1st floor, Union Towers, Mama Ngina St, PO Box 63006, Nairobi. Departures are usually once a month.

DO-IT-YOURSELF SAFARIS

This is a viable proposition in Kenya if you can get a group together to share the costs since you will have to rent a vehicle and camping equipment. The costs of renting a suitable vehicle can be found under 'Vehicle Hire' earlier on in this chapter.

Doing it yourself has several advantages over organised safaris. The main one is flexibility – you can go where you want, stop whenever you like and stay as long as you like. You don't have to follow the standard tourist routes. Another is that you can choose your travelling companions.

The main disadvantage is the extra effort you have to put in to organise the safari – hiring equipment, buying food and drink, cooking and agreeing among yourselves where you want to go and which route to take. It can also be a worry if none of you have mechanical skills and/or no tools and the vehicle breaks down. There's also the security of the vehicle and contents to think about if you want to leave it somewhere and go off walking. If you do this then you'll have to pay someone to guard it. Lastly, there's the question of maps especially if you intend to get right off the beaten track. Reasonably good large-scale maps are readily available in Kenya but the detailed ones are unavailable without going through a great deal of red tape. This means you could find yourself out in the middle of nowhere with not a clue where you're going and have to backtrack.

As far as costs go, it's probably true to say that organising your own safari is going to cost at least as much and usually more than going on a company organised safari. By how much more depends on a lot of factors but mainly the cost of hiring a vehicle and buying fuel. You'll have to sit down and work this out yourself.

Nairobi

Mark Knopfler could almost have been singing about Nairobi when he wrote *Telegraph Road*. Until the late 1800s there was nothing there. It was just a watering hole for the Maasai. Then came the Mombasa-Uganda railway, with its 32,000 indentured Indian labourers from Gujarat and Punjab, along with their British colonial overlords intent on beating the German colonial push for the Ugandan heartland. Being approximately halfway between Mombasa and Uganda and a convenient place to pause before the arduous climb into the highlands, it quickly became tent city.

Much of the area was still a foul-smelling swamp at this time and game roamed freely over the adjoining plains, yet by 1900 it had become a town of substantial buildings and five years later succeeded Mombasa as the capital of the British East Africa Protectorate. Since then it has gone from strength to strength and is now the largest city between Cairo and Johannesburg. The tower blocks of Nairobi can be seen for miles as you crest the hills which surround the plain on which it sits. Yet, in terms of the world's largest cities, Nairobi is still small with a population of about one million. You can walk from one end of the central business district to the other in 20 minutes. And where else in the world would you be able to see lion, cheetah, rhino and giraffe roaming free with the tower blocks of a city as a backdrop?

It's a very cosmopolitan place, lively, interesting, pleasantly landscaped and a good place to get essential business and bureaucratic matters sewn up. This is no Third World capital city though there are some very overcrowded shantytowns on the outskirts and even across the other side of the Nairobi River from Kirinyaga Rd. The latter are periodically bulldozed away and burnt down by the City Council's *askaris* (police) in the interests of hygiene but it takes only days for them to regenerate!

Like most cities, Nairobi has its crowded market and trading areas, its middle class/office workers' suburbs and its spacious mansions and beautiful flower-decked gardens for the rich and powerful. The first is an area full of local colour, energy, aspirations and opportunism where manual workers, exhausted matatu drivers, the unemployed, the devious, the down-and-out and the disoriented mingle with budget travellers, whores, shopkeepers, high school students, food stall vendors, drowsy security guards and those with life's little illicit goodies for sale. It's called River Rd – though, of course, it spans more than just this road itself. One of the funniest yet most poignant yarns I have ever read about an area such as this is to be found in a novel by Kenyan author Meja Mwangi called *Going Down River Road* (Heinemann: African Writers Series). I'd recommend this book to anyone and especially travellers passing through Nairobi. Even if you are not staying in this area you should make a point of getting down there one evening just to see how the other half lives on the wrong side of Tom Mboya St.

Elsewhere in Nairobi there are all the sort of things that you won't have seen for months if you've been hacking your way across the Central African Republic and Zaïre from West Africa or making do with the shortages in Zambia and Tanzania. Things like the latest films on big screens, bookshops, restaurants, cafés and bars full of travellers from all over the world, offices where you can get things done with the minimum of fuss, banks where you can change travellers' cheques in less than five minutes and a poste restante where you sort out your own letters from the pile so you don't end up with that feeling that letters have been put in the wrong pigeon hole. It's a great place to stay for a few days but if you stay too long it gets expensive because almost everyone you meet wants to do the same as you did when you first arrived –

splurge at the restaurants and drink your fill in the bars.

Orientation

The compact city centre is in the area bounded by Uhuru Highway, Haile Selassie Ave, Tom Mboya St and University Way. The main bus and train stations are within a few minutes walk of this area, while the main travellers' accommodation area is centred around Latema Rd, just east of Tom Mboya St on the fringe of the bustling and somewhat sleazy River Rd area.

To the west of the centre is one of the more enlightened bits of Nairobi town planning – Uhuru Park, although it will soon be over-shadowed in the not too distant future by President Moi's shot at immortality – the 60-odd storey Times Media complex. The building of such a totally over-the-top sky-scraper is Moi's bit of one-upmanship over Kenyatta (who has the conference centre) and over the rest of the continent – if it goes ahead it will be the tallest building in Africa. It's been a controversial project since the planning stages, but the only person with the courage to oppose it publicly, Professor Mathaai, found her attempted court injunction against the project unceremoniously tossed out on its ear along with an unbeliev-able amount of personal abuse and public harassment. It seems there's little room for legitimate opposition in Kenya – especially from a woman.

The park itself is a much needed lung for this increasingly crowded city and quite apart from the fact that a good quarter of it is going to disappear with the construction of the Times Media complex, the resulting traffic congestion is going to be horrendous. It's bad enough already at rush hours.

Directly west of Uhuru Park, and still within walking distance of the centre (although it's not advisable to try it at night), are some of the city's better mid and top-range hotels, the popular Youth Hostel, a number of government ministries and the hospitals. Beyond here are the sprawling upper middle class suburbs of Ngong and Hurlingham with their large detached houses

and carefully tended gardens surrounded by high fences, and guarded by askaris along with prominent signs warning that the prem-ises are patrolled by 'Ultimate Security', 'Total Security', 'Securicor' and the like. These signs are surely one of the most endur-ing impressions of suburban Nairobi!

North of the centre is the University, the National Museum, the International Casino and one of Nairobi's original colonial hotels, the Norfolk. Beyond here is Westlands, another of Nairobi's upper middle class suburbs. North-east of the centre is Parklands, a slightly less desirable suburb which is home to many of Nairobi's Asian minority and where the Aga Khan Hospital is to be found. Close to the hospital is the popular Mrs Roche's guest house. Going east, there is the bustling and predominantly African suburb of Eastleigh along with the country bus station.

South of the city is Nairobi National Park, and to the park's north-east is Jomo Kenyatta International Airport which is connected to the city by an excellent dual carriageway.

Information

Tourist Office In a city the size of Nairobi, and in a country which relies so heavily on tourism, it seems inconceivable that there is no tourist office, but there isn't.

There is an 80 page leaflet called *Tourist's Kenya* (tel 337169, PO Box 40025) which is published every two weeks. It is free of charge and available from most large hotels – the Thorn Tree Café in the New Stanley Hotel is the most convenient place to find it. It contains most of what you'll need to know – hotels, restaurants, airlines, embassies, tour and safari operators – but it doesn't bend over backwards to keep its factual informa-tion up to date or even comprehensive.

Other similar free publications which you can pick up from hotels and bookstores are *What's On* (tel 728290/7, PO Box 49010), published by Nation Printers & Publishers, and *Tourist Index* (tel 26206, PO Box 9165). Both of these are published monthly.

Post The main post office is on Haile

Selassie Ave and is open Monday to Friday from 8 am to 5 pm and Saturday from 9 am to noon. The poste restante is well organised and they'll let you look through as many piles as you like plus there's no charge for letters collected. The only trouble is that the counter which deals with it is also one of the few which sells stamps, so the queues are often long.

With the huge volume of poste restante mail here it's not surprising that some letters get misfiled but, surprisingly, it doesn't happen too often. As a favour to other travellers you should pull out any letters you come across which are misfiled so the clerk can get them into the right pile.

This post office is also the best one from which to post parcels. The contents of all parcels sent overseas have to be inspected by the post office staff before being sealed so don't arrive with a sealed parcel or you'll have to pull it apart again. Bring all packing materials with you as there are none for sale at the post office. One of the cheapest places to buy good packing materials is at the supermarket on Posta Rd opposite where the old GPO used to stand (now demolished). Otherwise, try Biba on Kenyatta Ave at Muindi Mbingu St.

Telephone The Extelcoms office is on Haile Selassie Ave, almost opposite the post office. It is open from 8 am to midnight and you can make direct-dial calls yourself from here with a phonecard or go through the operator. They also have telex and fax facilities here.

The best place to make a call during normal business hours if you have to go through the operator is at the telephone exchange on the ground floor of the Kenyatta Conference Centre. If there is no conference in progress this office is much quieter than the Extelcoms office, and there are also two card phones here.

Banks At Jomo Kenyatta International Airport the branch of Barclays Bank is open 24 hours a day, seven days a week. In Nairobi, the bank's branch on the corner of

Kenyatta Ave and Wabera St is open Monday to Saturday from 9 am to 4.30 pm.

Foreign Embassies For a list of embassies in Nairobi, see the Visas section in the Facts for the Visitor chapter.

Airlines Airlines with offices in Nairobi include:

Aeroflot
    Corner House, Mama Ngina St (tel 20746)
Air Botswana
    Hilton Hotel (tel 338309)
Air France
    Hilton Hotel (tel 728910)
Air India
    Jeevan Bharati Building, Harambee Ave (tel 334788)
Air Madagascar
    Hilton Hotel (tel 25286)
Air Rwanda
    Mama Ngina St (tel 332225)
Air Mauritius
    Union Towers, Moi Ave (tel 29166)
Air Malawi
    680 Hotel, Muindi Mbingu St (tel 340212)
Air Zaïre
    Shretta House, Kimathi St (tel 25625)
Air Zimbabwe
    Chester House, Koinange St (tel 339522)
Alitalia
    Hilton Hotel (tel 24361)
British Airways
    International Life House, Mama Ngina St (tel 334362)
Cameroon Airlines
    HFCK Building, Kenyatta Ave (tel 337788)
EgyptAir
    Hilton Arcade (tel 26821)
Ethiopian Airlines
    Bruce House, Muindi Mbingu St (tel 330837)
Kenya Airways
    Koinange St (tel 29291)
KLM
    Fedha Towers, Muindi Mbingu St (tel 332673)
Pakistan International Airlines (PIA)
    ICEA Building, Banda St (tel 333900)
Pan Am
    Hilton Hotel (tel 23581)
Sabena
    International Life House, Mama Ngina St (tel 333284)
Somali Airlines
    Bruce House, Mama Ngina St (tel 335409)

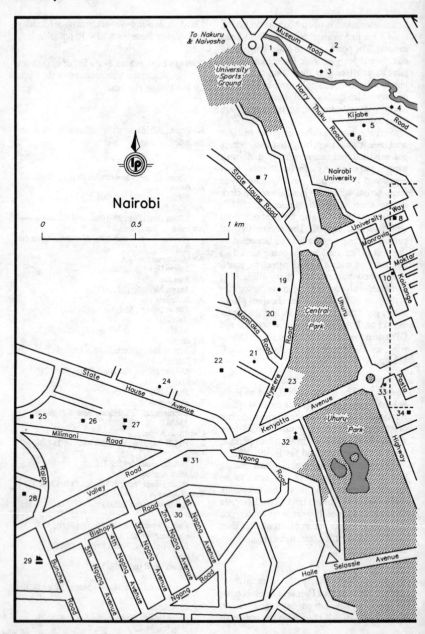

Nairobi

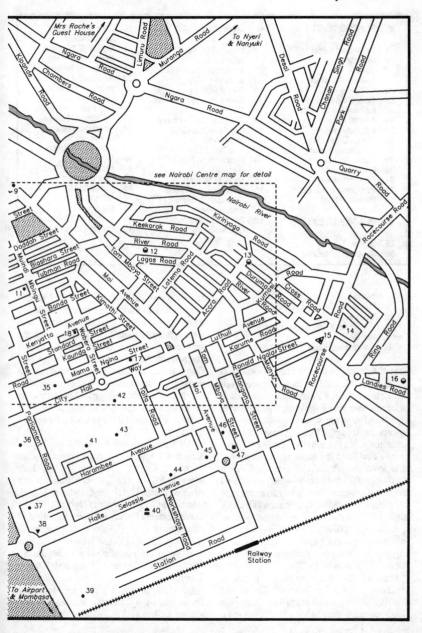

■ PLACES TO STAY

1	Boulevard Hotel
6	Norfolk Hotel
7	YMCA
8	Nairobi Safari Club
20	YWCA
22	Green View Lodge
23	Nairobi Serena Hotel
25	Sagret Hotel
26	Milimani Hotel
27	Heron Court Hotel
28	Grosvenor Hotel
29	Youth Hostel
30	Fairview Hotel
31	Panafric Hotel
34	Intercontinental Hotel
47	Hermes Hotel

▼ PLACES TO EAT

27 Buffalo Bill's
38 Caboose Restaurant

● OTHER

2	National Museum
3	Snake Park
4	Text Book Centre
5	Spinners Web
9	Police Station
10	Kenya Airways Termnal
11	City Market
12	Akamba Bus Terminal
13	Goldline/Coastline/ Mawingo Bus Terminals
14	East African Road Services
15	Taxis to Namanga
16	Country Bus Station
17	Rwandan & Somali Embassies
18	Barclays Bank, Ugandan High Commission
19	Zambian High Commission
21	Sudan & Zimbabwe Embassies
24	Ethiopian Embassy
32	All Saints Cathedral
33	Immigration (Nyayo House)
35	City Hall
36	Parliament House
37	Tanzanian High Commission
39	Railway Museum
40	GPO
41	Public Map Office
42	Law Courts
43	Kenyatta Conference Centre
44	Extelcoms
45	American Embassy
46	Burundi Embassy

Sudan Airways
    UTC Building, General Kago St (tel 21326)
Uganda Airlines
    Uganda House, Kenyatta Ave (tel 21354)
Zambia Airways
    Hamilton House, Kaunda St (tel 29908)

Travel Agents To get the best possible deal on an airline ticket, first make the rounds of the airline offices to ascertain the standard price and then make the rounds of the travel agents. Always get several quotes from the agents as things change constantly. It's sometimes, but not usually, possible to get as good a deal from the actual airline offices as it is from the agents. European and Asian destinations are the ones to which you'll find the best discounts. This is less so in the case of North American destinations and virtually impossible for Australasian destinations.

Most of the heavily discounted tickets will involve stopovers between connections – EgyptAir, Ethiopian Airlines and Sudan Airways, for example.

One of the most popular agents is Hanzuwan-el-Kindly Tours & Travel (tel 26810, 338729), Rajab Manzil Building (4th floor, room 3), Tom Mboya St. It used to be run by a man called Fehed A S H el-Kindly though he was known to everyone as Eddie. These days it's run by his brother Salim, and although most travellers speak well of the services provided, some recent reports suggest that he might be letting things slip. One traveller who had been assured that his bookings were confirmed later discovered he was No 146 on the waiting list! It's advisable to be cautious and not to hand over your money or passport until you actually see the ticket.

Also recommended are Prince Travel, Kenyatta Conference Centre (especially for flights to Cairo); Crocodile Travel, Tom Mboya St, in the same block as the Ambassadeur Hotel; and Falcon Travel, International House, Mama Ngina St. Banko Travel, Latema Rd, are also very friendly and offer similar deals. Others which are worth checking out are Let's Go Travel on Standard St close to the junction with Koinange St, Appel Travel, Tamana Tours and Kambo Travel.

Local expats speak highly of Molo Bay Tours, run by a Canadian woman and her Maasai husband.

Cultural Centres All the foreign cultural organisations have libraries which are open to the public and are free of charge except for the American Cultural Centre which is for members only. Both the French and German cultural centres welcome travellers. The addresses are:

Alliance Française
    ICEA Building, ground floor, Kenyatta Ave (tel 340054). Open Monday to Friday from 10 am to 1 pm and 2 to 5.15 pm and on Saturday from 9.30 am to noon. There is a good French restaurant here, too, which is open in the evenings.
American Cultural Centre
    National Bank Building, Harambee Ave (tel 337877). Open Monday to Friday from 10 am to 5 pm and on Saturday from 10 am to 1 pm.
British Council
    ICEA Building, mezzanine floor, Kenyatta Ave (tel 334855). Open Monday to Friday from 10 am to 5 pm and on Saturday from 9 am to noon.
French Cultural Centre
    Maison Française, corner Monrovia and Loita streets (tel 336263). Open Monday to Friday from 10 am to 5 pm and on Saturday from 10 am to 1 pm.
Goethe-Institut
    Maendeleo House, corner Monrovia and Loita streets (tel 24640). Open Monday to Friday from 10 am to 6 pm.
Italian Cultural Institute
    Prudential Building, Wabera St (tel 21615). Open Monday to Friday from 8.30 am to 1 pm and 2.30 to 5 pm.
Japan Information Centre
    Matungulu House, Mamlaka Rd (tel 331196). Open Monday to Friday from 10 am to noon and 2.10 to 4.30 pm.

Bookshops The best selection of bookshops are along Kimathi St (Nation Bookshop – next to the New Stanley Hotel) and Mama Ngina St (Prestige Books – next to 20th Century Cinema). There are others but they don't carry the same range. The Text Book Centre on Kijabe Rd is not right in the centre and so the prices are a little lower.

For both new and second-hand books there are pavement bookstalls scattered throughout Tom Mboya St and Latema Rd.

Maps There are many maps of Nairobi available in the bookshops but probably the best is the *City of Nairobi: Map & Guide* in English, French and German published by the Survey of Kenya in a red front cover with partially coloured photographs on the back cover. It covers the suburbs as well as having a detailed map of the central area. If you're going to be staying for a long time, however, the *A to Z: Guide to Nairobi* by D T Dobie (Kenway Publications) is worth buying.

Photography For passport-size photographs, the cheapest place to go is the machine under the yellow and black sign 'Photo Me', a few doors up Kenyatta Ave from the Nation Bookshop on the corner of Kimathi St. It costs KSh 25 for four prints and takes about three minutes. There's another machine on the corner of Tom Mboya St and Accra Rd. You can also get them from the photography shop in Kimathi House opposite the New Stanley Hotel but here they cost KSh 35 for three prints.

For camera repairs or equipment rental the Camera Maintenance Centre (tel 26920) in the Hilton Arcade is definitely not cheap. Make sure you get a quote beforehand as quite a few people have felt they've been ripped off here. Alternatively try Camera Experts (tel 337750) or Expo Cameras, both on Mama Ngina St.

Emergency If you need medical treatment try Dr Sheth on the 3rd floor of Bruce House on Standard St. This doctor has his own pathology laboratory if you need blood or stool tests. He charges KSh 300 per consultation plus laboratory fees. There is also a dentist on the same floor.

Otherwise go to the Nairobi Hospital which has the same scale of charges as Dr Seth. Avoid like the plague Kenyatta Hospital since, although it's free, treatment here is possibly worse than the ailment, according to local residents. The Aga Khan Hospital in Parklands opposite Mrs Roche's is also not a bad place.

Vaccinations You can get these at City Hall Clinic, Mama Ngina St. It is open for jabs from 8.30 to 11.30 am Monday to Friday.

Yellow fever shots cost KSh 250, cholera KSh 100, meningitis KSh 100, typhoid KSh 250 and tetanus KSh 100.

If you want a gamma globulin shot (for hepatitis) go to Dr Sheth, 3rd floor, Bruce House, Standard St.

Safety You may hear rumours about Nairobi being a dangerous city at night as far as robberies go. We've certainly had enough letters from people whom this has happened to but never once on any occasion that I've been to Nairobi have I felt uneasy or threatened walking back to my hotel. Perhaps I just look like I know where I'm going or pull out my wallet when someone asks me for a few shillings down a dark alley. And I don't walk across Uhuru Park at night.

The best thing that can be said is to be vigilant. It's no worse than many other cities around the world and there are plenty worse. You should definitely not walk from the centre to the Youth Hostel or through Uhuru Park or along Uhuru Highway/Waiyaki Way anywhere between Westlands and the round-about with Haile Selassie Ave at night. You are asking for trouble. That taxi home may cost you KSh 60 but could save you a lot of money.

While we're on this subject, don't forget to read the stories in the Dangers & Annoyances section of the Facts for the Visitor chapter.

Left Luggage Many of the cheaper hotels, such as the Iqbal, the New Kenya Lodge and Mrs Roche's will store baggage for you, usually for a small daily charge. You're advised not to leave anything valuable with left luggage.

Nairobi railway station also has a left luggage office which is open daily from 8 am to noon and 1 to 6.30 pm. It costs KSh 12 per item.

Car Rental All the major companies, and many smaller ones have offices in the city centre, and the bigger ones such as Avis and Hertz have desks at the airport. A com-

prehensive description of car hire can be found in the Getting Around chapter.

Camping Equipment Hire If you want to hire anything from a sleeping bag to a folding toilet seat, tent or mosquito net, the best place to go to is Atul's (tel 25935, 28064), Biashara St. They have the lot and are open Monday to Friday from 8.30 am to 12.30 pm and 2 to 5.30 pm and on Saturday from 8.30 am to 12.30 pm and 2.30 to 4.30 pm. Hire charges have to be paid in full before commencement of hire as well as a deposit for each item. The deposits are refunded when hired items are returned in good condition. Identification is required (eg passport).

The items which they have for hire are far too numerous to mention here but they print a list which you can pick up for KSh 10. Advance booking is highly recommended and saves a lot of time. If you'd like a list before going to Kenya, write to PO Box 43202, Nairobi.

National Museum
The National Museum is on Museum Rd off Museum Hill which itself is off Uhuru Highway. The museum has a good exhibition on prehistoric people, an incredible collection of native birds, mammals and tribal crafts and a new section on the culture, history and crafts of the coastal Swahili people. It's just unfortunate that many of the displays are moth-eaten and tatty these days.

Opening hours are 9.30 am to 6 pm daily and admission is KSh 50.

National Museums of Kenya
CONTRIBUTION
50·00
We are grateful for your contribution towards the cost of running the organisation. Thank you.
N° 94065

Snake Park

Opposite the museum the Snake Park has living examples of most of the snake species found in East Africa – some of them are in glass cages, others in open pits. There are also tortoises and crocodiles. Hours and entry charges are the same as for the museum.

National Archives

Right opposite the Hilton Hotel on Moi Ave are the National Archives. They're regarded by many as better value than the National Museum and entry is free. They don't just contain the sort of documents that you would expect in such a building but photographs of Mzee Kenyatta and Moi visiting different countries and exhibitions of handicrafts and paintings.

Railway Museum

The Railway Museum is on Station Rd – follow the railway tracks until you are almost at the bridge under Uhuru Highway or walk across the small piece of waste ground just next to the Uhuru Highway/Haile Selassie Ave roundabout.

In addition to old steam engines and rolling stock it will give you a good idea of Kenya's history since the beginning of the colonial period. There's also a scale model of the venerable MV *Liemba* which plies the waters of Lake Tanganyika between Mpulungu (Zambia) and Bujumbura (Burundi).

It's open daily from 8 am to 4.45 pm; entry is KSh 10, or KSh 5 for students.

Parliament House

Like to take a look at how democracy works in Kenya? If so, you can get a permit for a seat in the public gallery at Parliament House on Parliament Rd or, if Parliament is out of session, you can tour the buildings by arrangement with the Sergeant-at-Arms.

Art Galleries

There's not much in Nairobi in the way of art galleries. The only one is the Gallery Watatu in the ground floor of Bruce House on Standard St. This place usually has some interesting works by local artists and is worth a quick look.

Kenyatta Conference Centre

There is a viewing level on the 28th floor of the centre but the revolving restaurant no longer operates. If you'd like to go up there, you must request a guide at the information desk on the ground floor. He'll expect a tip but otherwise it's free. You're allowed to take photographs from the viewing level. Access is sometimes restricted when there's a conference in progress.

Places to Stay – bottom end

There is a very good selection of budget hotels in Nairobi and the majority of them, except for two very popular places outside of the city centre, are between Tom Mboya St and River Rd so if you find that one is full it's only a short walk to another.

In the Centre The *New Kenya Lodge* (tel 22202), River Rd at the junction with Latema Rd, is a legend among budget travellers and still one of the cheapest. There's always a wild and interesting bunch of people from all over the world staying here. Accommodation is basic but clean and there's hot water in the evenings. Rooms with shared bathroom facilities cost KSh 95/120/140 for singles/doubles/triples.

The same people who own this have also opened the *New Kenya Lodge Annex* just around the corner on Duruma Rd. Prices here are KSh 45 for a dorm bed plus KSh 95/120 for singles/doubles but there's cold water only and many travellers comment that the annexe doesn't have the same atmosphere as the old place and that some of the rooms don't even have windows! All the same, it's very popular, the staff are friendly, baggage is safe, and the notice board makes interesting reading. Baggage storage costs KSh 50 per week.

Sharing the legend is the *Iqbal Hotel* (tel 20914), Latema Rd, which has been popular for years. It is still very pleasant although recent price hikes mean it's not the bargain it once was. This place is so popular that it's unlikely you'll get a bed or room here after 9 am. The best plan is to turn up at 8 am and put your name on the waiting list. Checkout time is 10 am and the free beds are allocated then. Ali, the manager, is a friendly bloke who keeps a sense of humour in conditions which are sometimes trying. There's supposedly hot water available in the morning but you have to be up early to get it. Beds in three-bed rooms go for KSh 90, while double/triple rooms cost KSh 180/270, all with common facilities. Baggage is safe here and there's a store room where you can leave excess gear (KSh 5 per day) if you are going away for a while. The Iqbal's notice board is always a good place to look for just about anything.

If the above two are full there are three others on Dubois Rd, just off Latema Rd. The *Bujumbura Lodge* (tel 28078) is very basic but clean and quiet and very secure. The toilets and showers are clean and there is erratic hot water. It's not that friendly a place and we've had two complaints that some of the ceilings leak but it's OK for a short stay. Prices are KSh 85 a single (only two of these) and KSh 110/125 for doubles/triples. The *New Safe Life Lodging* is very similar and the staff are cheerful. The single rooms are overpriced at KSh 120 but the doubles for KSh 165 are not bad value. The *Nyandarwa Lodging* is very clean, quiet and comfortable and you can get a large double room for KSh 145. They also have single rooms but they're just glorified cupboards and not such good value for money at KSh 95.

Back on Latema Rd, the *Sunrise Hotel* is clean, secure and friendly and there's usually hot water in the mornings and evenings. Rooms here cost KSh 145/190 for singles/doubles with shared bathroom facilities. The front two rooms overlooking the street are the largest and have a balcony but they are right next door to the Modern 24-Hour Green Bar which rages 24 hours a day, 365 days a year, so if you want a quiet room take one of those at the back of the hotel. If you're looking for material for a novel, on the other hand, then take one of these rooms.

Right at the bottom of the scale is the *Al Mansura Hotel* on Munyu Rd. It's basic and the rooms are clean enough but it's really only good for a night if you can't get in elsewhere. Women are likely to feel uncomfortable in this place. A bed in a shared room costs KSh 50; doubles are KSh 100.

Outside the Centre There are two very popular places away from the city centre. *Mrs Roche's*, 3rd Parklands Ave opposite the Aga Khan Hospital, is, like the New Kenya and the Iqbal, a legend. Mrs Roche has been making travellers welcome for almost 20 years and it's a favourite with campers and those with their own vehicle as well as those who don't particularly want a room in the city centre. There's always an amazing band of people here and the whole place has the general atmosphere of a gypsy camp – there's never a dull moment. It's situated in a very pleasant area amongst trees and flowering shrubs and is a very mellow place to stay. It's just a pity that some travellers with vehicles seem to disembowel them here and leave the discarded parts lying around for other travellers to camp amongst. Camping costs KSh 35 per night while a bed in a shared room costs KSh 60. Because it's so popular you may have to sleep on the floor for the first night until a bed is available.

This is another place with a good notice board. You can leave baggage for KSh 20. To get to Mrs Roche's, take a matatu (KSh 3) from the junction of Latema Rd and Tom Mboya St right outside the Odeon Cinema. They will have 'Aga Khan' in the front windscreen. Tell the driver you're heading for Mrs Roche's guest house. It's well known.

There are several places to eat cheaply in the immediate vicinity and the nearest bar (which also has an excellent barbecue) is the Everest Hotel just up the road. It's a lively place and I've met Mrs Roche there on several occasions!

The other very popular place is the *Youth Hostel* (tel 21789), Ralph Bunche Rd between Valley Rd and Ngong Rd. It's often very crowded here so it's a good place to meet other travellers. It's very clean, well run, stays open all day and there's always hot water in the showers. The wardens here are very friendly and will lock up gear safely for you for up to two weeks for KSh 10, then it's KSh 15 per day after that. On a day-to-day basis there are lockers to keep your gear in when you go out, but you must supply your own lock. The notice board here (for messages, things for sale, etc) is one of the best in Africa. A bed in a shared room costs KSh 70 but you must have a YHA membership card to stay. If not, you'll have to pay a temporary membership fee of KSh 30 per night or join the association for KSh 170 for a year.

Any matatu or bus which goes down either Valley Rd or Ngong Rd will drop you at Ralph Bunche Rd. The No 8 matatu which goes down Ngong Rd is probably the most convenient. You can pick it up either outside the Hilton Hotel or on Kenyatta Ave on the corner with Uhuru Highway. If you're returning to the Youth Hostel after dark don't be tempted to walk back from the centre of the city. Many people have been robbed. Always take a matatu or taxi.

The Ys There is both a *YMCA* (tel 337468) and *YWCA* (tel 338689) in Nairobi. The former is on State House Rd and the latter on Mamlaka Rd off Nyerere Rd. The YMCA costs KSh 180 per person for full board in a dormitory, KSh 210 per person in a shared room and KSh 230/420 for single/double rooms, all with communal facilities. Rooms with private bath are more expensive at around KSh 335/530. This place seems to have a semipermanent population of local students so could be an interesting place to stay.

The YWCA is reluctant to take short-term visitors. It prefers to take people who are going to stay at least one month and the room rates are geared towards this. It does, however, take couples as well as single women.

Camping Mrs Roche's is the only place to go if you want to camp. In the high season the limited garden space gets pretty cramped, not only with tents but also with vehicles. It costs KSh 35 per person to put up your tent.

Places to Stay – middle
In the Centre There are several mid-range hotels in the same area as the bulk of the budget hotels. One of the cheapest is the *Gloria Hotel* (tel 28916), Ronald Ngala St almost on the corner with Tom Mboya St. Rooms here are good value at KSh 190/215/360 for a single/double/triple. All rooms are with bath and hot water, and the price includes breakfast. The only problem here is that the rooms cop the noise from the street below. Just a couple of doors along is the *Terrace Hotel* (tel 21636) which has rooms with bath and hot water for KSh 180/215 including breakfast. It doesn't win any prizes for friendliness and some of the rooms are noisy, but overall it's not a bad place.

One of the best places in this category is the *Dolat Hotel* (tel 22797), Mfangano St, which is very quiet and friendly and costs KSh 172/253 for singles/doubles with bath and hot water. The sheets are changed daily and the rooms kept spotless. It's a good secure place and quite a few travellers stay here.

More expensive is the *Salama Hotel* (tel 25899), on the corner of Tom Mboya St and Luthuli Ave. It's a little on the pricey side at KSh 370/410/625 for a single/double/triple including breakfast and it's hard to see what the advantage is over places like the Gloria and the Terrace for around half the price, especially as the extra money doesn't buy you relief from the street noise. Similarly overpriced is the *Solace Hotel* (tel 331277), Tom Mboya St, more or less opposite the Salama Hotel. Rooms here cost KSh 300/430 for singles/doubles including breakfast.

The *Sirikwa Lodge* (tel 26089) is another at the top of this bracket and is on the corner of Munyu and Accra roads. For KSh 314/374/575 you get a clean room with bath and hot water, breakfast is included and each room has a phone. Accra Rd is somewhat

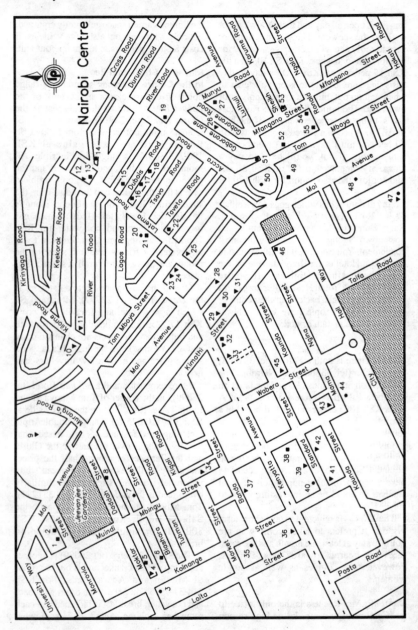

Nairobi Centre

■ PLACES TO STAY	▼ PLACES TO EAT	42 Dragon Pearl Restaurant
1 New Garden Hotel	4 Goldstar	43 The Coffee Bar
2 Parkside Hotel	Restaurant	45 Trattoria Restaurant
5 Terminal Hotel	9 Khyber Restaurant	47 Tamarind
6 Embassy Hotel	10 Dhaba Restaurant	Restaurant
8 Hotel Pigale	11 Mayur Restaurant,	
13 New Kenya Lodge	Supreme	● OTHER
14 New Kenya Lodge	Restaurant	
Annexe	12 Bull Café	3 Kenya Airways
15 New Safe Life	23 Panda Restaurant	Terminal
Lodging	24 Growers Café	7 Atul's Camping
16 Nyandarwa Lodging	25 Nairobi Burgers	Equipment Hire
17 Africana Hotel	26 Malindi Dishes	16 DPS & Wepesi
18 Bujumbura Lodge	Restaurant	taxis
19 Sirikwa Lodge	28 The Honey Pot	20 Modern Green
21 Sunrise Hotel	29 Supermac	24-Hour Bar
22 Iqbal Hotel	31 Jax Restaurant	29 Elite Camera
27 Al Mansura Hotel	32 Thorn Tree Café	House
30 Oakwood Hotel	33 Jacaranda Café	35 New Florida
32 New Stanley Hotel	34 Blukat Restaurant	Nightclub
38 Sixeighty Hotel	36 Harvest Restaurant	40 Let's Go Travel
46 Hilton Hotel	37 African Heritage	44 City Hall
49 Ambassadeur Hotel	Café	47 American Cultural
51 Salama Hotel	39 Akasaka Japanese	Centre
52 Solace Hotel	Restaurant,	48 Florida 2000
53 Dolat Hotel	The Pub	Nightclub
54 Terrace Hotel	41 Beneva Coffee	50 National Archives
55 Gloria Hotel	House	

quieter than Tom Mboya St so this place is not a bad bet. Another quiet place is the *Africana Hotel* (tel 20654) on Dubois Rd between Accra and Latema roads. The rates are KSh 330/420/600 for rooms with bath, hot water and breakfast. It's good value and secure.

Further away from this area at the junction of Tom Mboya St and Haile Selassie Ave is the *Hermes Hotel* which has self-contained double rooms with breakfast for KSh 480. The quietest rooms are at the back. The hotel has its own restaurant including an all-you-can-eat lunch. The food is good and the staff friendly.

Personally, I feel that the mid-range hotels in the vicinity of Jeevanjee Gardens and the central market are better value than those on the River Rd side of Moi Ave if only for the noise factor and the vehicle fumes but not everyone agrees.

Very popular (especially with US Peace Corps volunteers who get a 25% discount) is the *Hotel Pigale* (tel 331403), Moktar Daddah St facing Jeevanjee Gardens. Singles/doubles/triples here with bathroom, hot water, soap and towel cost KSh 210/265/380 including taxes. There are only 21 rooms so you need to get there early. There's a good notice board in the reception area which is worth checking out if you're looking for something.

Across the other side of Jeevanjee Gardens are two other somewhat more expensive hotels, the *New Garden Hotel* and the *Parkside Hotel*. The New Garden is excellent value at KSh 265/310/470 for singles/doubles/triples with bathroom, hot water and breakfast. They also have doubles without shower for KSh 265. The Parkside has singles/doubles for KSh 277/385 with bathroom, hot water and breakfast. The staff are very friendly and the hotel has its own restaurant.

Opposite the Kenya Airways terminal is the *Terminal Hotel* (tel 28817), Moktar Daddah St, which is also popular with travellers. It offers rooms with bath, hot water, soap and towel and clean sheets for KSh 290/430/575 including taxes but without breakfast. Some of the rooms are getting a little tatty these days but the staff are friendly and honest and valuables left in the rooms are safe. There's a same-day laundry service on weekdays (but not at weekends).

Close by is the *Embassy Hotel* (tel 24087), Biashara St between Koinange St and Muindi Mbingu St. Rooms here, all with bathroom, hot water, soap and towel, cost KSh 360/515 for singles/doubles including taxes. They also have a number of smaller singles for KSh 300.

Outside the Centre Across the other side of Central Park, up a gravel track off Nyerere Rd at the back of the Minet ICDC House, is the *Green View Lodge* (tel 720908). It consists of several blocks of wooden huts in leafy surroundings with its own bar and restaurant. The rooms are reminiscent of a country cottage and are good value at KSh 145/240 for singles/doubles with shared bathroom facilities and KSh 478 for a double with private bathroom. All prices include breakfast.

Most of the other mid-range hotels are along Milimani Rd, Ralph Bunche Rd and Bishops Rd.

Very popular indeed with travellers and expatriates on contract work is the *Heron Court Hotel* (tel 720740, PO Box 41848), Milimani Rd. It's a large place and excellent value at KSh 420/540 for singles/doubles with bathroom, hot water, soap and towels. They also have self-contained apartments with a double bedroom, separate lounge with balcony, bathroom and fully equipped kitchen for KSh 470/590 a single/double. Breakfast is not included in the room rates. The sheets and towels are changed daily in both types of room and the hotel facilities include a swimming pool, sauna, massage, guarded car park, shop and 24 hour laundry service. The staff here are friendly and

helpful and security is excellent. At the front of the hotel is one of Nairobi's most popular bar/restaurants, Buffalo Bill's, which is open from early morning until around 11 pm daily.

Right at the top of Milimani Rd at the junction with Ralph Bunche Rd is the *Sagret Hotel* (tel 720933, PO Box 18324) which is of a somewhat higher standard than the Heron Court and offers singles/doubles with bathroom for KSh 520/835 including breakfast. The hotel has its own bar and restaurant.

Turning left up Ralph Bunche Rd brings you to the *Grosvenor Hotel* (tel 722080, Box 41038) which offers singles/doubles for KSh 460/595 including breakfast and all taxes. The hotel is divided up into several main buildings and cottages spread out over extensive wooded lawns and gardens and dates from the colonial era. It's getting a little tatty at the edges these days but has managed to preserve its olde-worlde charm and is popular with working expatriates and families since children can play in safety on the lawns and there are swings provided for them. There's also a swimming pool, bar and grill, an Ethiopian restaurant (which is excellent) and a Japanese restaurant.

On Bishops Rd at the back of the Panafric Hotel is the *Fairview Hotel* (tel 723211, PO Box 40842). Billed as 'the country hotel in the city' with some justification due to its pleasant garden and quiet location, it offers singles for KSh 430 to KSh 600, doubles for KSh 695 to KSh 900 and family units for KSh 900 to KSh 1440, all with bathroom, telephone, TV and video service, and including breakfast. Other meals average around KSh 120 but the food is said to be only average. The staff are friendly and helpful and it's a very popular place to stay for expatriates on contract work in Nairobi. Guests are entitled to use the swimming pool at the Panafric Hotel.

At the top end of this section is the *Oakwood Hotel* (tel 20592, PO Box 40683), Kimathi St, right opposite the New Stanley Hotel. This is a very pleasant place to stay and there are 23 self-contained rooms costing KSh 570/960/1170 a single/double/triple including breakfast and all taxes.

There's constant hot water, a telephone and TV with in-house movies in every room and an overnight laundry service. Other hotel facilities include a private bar, restaurant and roof terrace.

Places to Stay – top end

In a city the size of Nairobi there are naturally many top-range hotels, some of them in the city centre and others outside this immediate area. If you are planning on staying in one it is worth booking through one of the travel agents in town instead of paying the so-called 'rack rates' as they can often get you a considerable discount. At the Serena, for example, it's possible to get a discount of nearly 40% by booking through UTC.

The *Ambassadeur Hotel* (tel 336803, PO Box 30399) on Moi Ave is right in the city centre and costs KSh 755/960/1250 for singles/doubles/triples. As with all hotels in this range, rooms are with bath and hot water. Somewhat more expensive but again right in the centre of town, on Muindi Mbingu St between Standard St and Kenyatta Ave, is the *Sixeighty Hotel* (tel 332680, PO Box 43436). This is a large modern hotel and good value at KSh 865/1320/1680 for singles/doubles/triples without breakfast. Even better value and less expensive is the *Boulevard Hotel* (tel 27567, PO Box 42831), Harry Thuku Rd, which offers rooms with bathroom, balcony, telephone and radio for KSh 720/900/1020 a single/double/triple including taxes but excluding breakfast. The hotel facilities include swimming pool, tennis court, restaurant, barbecue, bar and beer garden.

Similar in price to the above but up on Milimani Rd is the *Milimani Hotel* (tel 720760, PO Box 30715). This is a huge, rambling place popular with expatriates on contract and charges KSh 1080/1440/2015 for singles/doubles/triples including breakfast and taxes.

The *New Stanley Hotel* (tel 333233, PO Box 30680) on the corner of Kimathi St and Kenyatta Ave was built in 1907 and despite numerous subsequent renovations still has that old colonial charm. On the other hand, it's just about due for renovation again as it's definitely tatty around the edges these days and the staff can be decidedly unhelpful at times. Singles/doubles/triples here including taxes cost KSh 1680/2040/2650. The Thorn Tree Café at street level is a popular attraction here though the food is mediocre and service can be agonisingly slow.

The *Norfolk Hotel* (tel 3355422, PO Box 40064), Harry Thuku Rd, is even older than the New Stanley – it was built in 1904 – and was *the* place to stay in the old days. It's still extremely popular among those with the money to spend and a taste for nostalgia and is set in beautiful gardens. Singles and doubles in the main block range between KSh 2160 and KSh 2800 plus there are studio suites at KSh 3480 and luxury cottages from KSh 5040 to KSh 7200. The hotel has a popular terrace bar and restaurant.

Back in the city centre, the *Hilton Hotel* (tel 334000, PO Box 30624), Mama Ngina St at Moi Ave, has all the usual Hilton facilities including a rooftop swimming pool yet, despite the relatively high price, some of the rooms are surprisingly gloomy and tatty. Singles here go for KSh 1475 to KSh 1920, doubles for KSh 1850 to KSh 2400 and suites for KSh 3960 to KSh 9840. The *Intercontinental Hotel* (tel 335550, PO Box 30353), City Hall Way, is somewhat impersonal and a little frayed at the edges but certainly much more pleasant than the Hilton. Singles here cost KSh 1615 to KSh 1965, doubles KSh 1975 to KSh 2480 and suites KSh 3422 to KSh 6824.

Just outside the city centre, in the corner of Central Park between Kenyatta Ave and Nyerere Rd, is the *Nairobi Serena Hotel* (tel 725111, PO Box 46302) which has to be one of the city's most pleasant hotels. Even Jimmy Carter stays here! It underwent a complete refit fairly recently and rooms now cost KSh 2220/2820/3480 for singles/doubles/triples without breakfast but including taxes. There are also suites for KSh 3480 a single, KSh 4200 a double and a 'state suite' for KSh 6000.

A little further up Kenyatta Ave where it turns into Valley Rd is the *Panafric Hotel* (tel 720822, PO Box 30486), a huge, multistorey modern hotel with all the facilities you'd expect. Rooms here cost KSh 1620/2160/3025 for singles/doubles/triples including breakfast and all taxes plus they have suites going for KSh 3600/3960 a single/double.

The most expensive hotel in Nairobi is the new *Nairobi Safari Club* (tel 330621, PO Box 43564), University Way at Koinange St. The cheapest rooms are KSh 3205/3565 for singles/doubles in 'executive suites', followed by 'panorama suites' at KSh 3815/4175 and 'penthouse luxury suites' at KSh 9815/13,550. To these prices you also have to add the cost of temporary membership.

Places to Eat

For most people with limited means, lunch is the main meal of the day and this is what the cheaper restaurants cater for. That doesn't mean that they're all closed in the evening (though quite a few are). It does mean, however, that what is available in the early evening is often what is left over from lunch time and the choice is limited. If you want a full meal in the evening it generally involves a splurge or eating from a barbecue attached to a bar.

Nairobi is replete with restaurants offering cuisines from all over the world – Italian, Spanish, Japanese, Chinese, Korean, Indian, Thai, Lebanese, steak houses, seafood specialists, etc – and at many the prices are surprisingly reasonable. For around US$8 per person you could eat well at quite a few of them. For US$10 to US$15 per person you could eat very well at almost all of them and if you spent that much at some of them you'd hardly need to eat anything the next day.

Places to Eat – cheap

There are a lot of very cheap cafés and restaurants in the Latema Rd/River Rd area and at the top end of Tom Mboya St where you can pick up a very cheap, traditional African breakfast of mandazi and tea or coffee. Most of these places would also be able to fix you up with eggs and the like. Since many of them are Indian run, they also have traditional Indian breakfast foods like samosa and idli (rice dumplings) with a sauce.

For good local food the restaurant in the *Iqbal Hotel* is very popular and is something of a meeting place for travellers. The mkate mayai at KSh 21 here is excellent, although it does come served with a curious side plate of shredded lettuce with tomato sauce! One gets the feeling that the animals and birds used in the stews here died of plain old age, but the cabbage and potato stew is very good.

The *Malindi Dishes* restaurant in Gaborone Rd is well worth trying at least once. As the name suggests, the food here has the Swahili influence of the coast, and so coconut and spices are used to rev up what is otherwise pretty ordinary cuisine. Main dishes are in the KSh 40 to KSh 70 range, and they have excellent fruit shakes for KSh 18 as well as all the usual snacks and burgers.

For a good solid meal of a mixture of Western and local food, such as steak and matoke (mashed plantains and maize) or maharagwe (kidney beans), try the *Coffee Bar* on Mama Ngina St opposite City Hall. It's only open at lunch time and is popular with business people. Meals are priced at around KSh 40 to KSh 50 and are excellent value. Another place up at this end of town is the *Beneva Coffee House* on the corner of Standard and Koinange streets.

Another ultra-cheap café which is fairly popular is the *Bull Café* round the corner from the New Kenya Lodge on Ngariama Rd.

If staying at Mrs Roche's up in Parklands, the *Stop 'n Eat* offers ugali, ngombe (beef), etc for KSh 10 to KSh 18.

Very popular with the lunch time business crowd and said to be one of the cheapest in Nairobi for the quality of food it offers is the *Jacaranda Café* in the Phoenix House Arcade between Kenyatta Ave and Standard St. Hamburger, chips and salad cost just KSh 24! Similar are the row of ramshackle wooden eateries between the Railway Museum and Haile Selassie Ave which are jammed with local office workers in three-piece suits at lunch time. It's quite a sight!

Fast Food That well-known English staple, fish & chips, has caught on in a big way in Nairobi and there are scores of places offering it. They're all cheap but the quality varies from grease ad nauseam to excellent.

My own recommendation for a lunch of fish & chips is *Supermac* on Kimathi St, directly opposite the Thorn Tree Café on the mezzanine floor of the shopping centre there. It's very popular at lunch time and deservedly so. They not only do some of the best fish & chips in Nairobi but also offer sausages, salads and fruit juices. Get there early if you don't want to queue.

Also recommended for this type of fast food is the *Prestige Restaurant*, Tsavo Lane off Latema Rd, which offers large servings of sausage, chips and salad for KSh 18. It's popular with local people.

The hamburger is all-conquering in Nairobi too, though, surprisingly, none of the American chains have got a foothold in Kenya yet. Too much Indian entrepreneurship perhaps? What has got a solid foothold is the *Wimpy* chain which has branches on Kenyatta Ave, Tom Mboya St and Mondolane St. They have the usual range of snacks and meals (burgers, sausages, eggs, fish, chicken, milkshakes, etc) costing up to KSh 60 and are open from 7.30 am to 9.30 pm. Another good café for a meal of burgers, fish or chicken with a mountain of chips and salad for around KSh 40 is *Nairobi Burgers* on Tom Mboya St right opposite the end of Latema Rd. They also serve sweets, soups and ice cream – it's a very popular place.

Good Breakfasts The *Growers Café* on Tom Mboya St is deservedly popular with both local people and travellers and the prices are reasonable. They have such things as eggs (boiled or fried), sausages and other hot foods, fruit salads with or without yoghurt and good coffee. Another popular breakfast place is the *Honey Pot* on Moi Ave. Here a breakfast of eggs, sausages, juice, toast, jam and tea or coffee is KSh 34.

If you're staying over in the Koinange St area, the *Goldstar Restaurant* on the corner of Koinange and Moktar Daddah streets is a good place for breakfast. For KSh 40 you get juice, cornflakes, eggs, toast, jam and tea or coffee. For a little extra, they'll add on bacon and a sausage.

Big Lunches Kenya is the home of all-you-can-eat lunches at a set price and Nairobi has a wide choice of them, most offering Indian food. One of the best is the *Supreme Restaurant* on River Rd, which offers excellent Indian vegetarian food for KSh 65 to KSh 80 depending on whether you want the ordinary or the 'delux' lunch and whether you want dessert. It also has superb fruit juices.

Similar is the *Blukat Restaurant*, Muindi Mbingu St between Banda St and Kigali Rd. It offers both vegetarian and meat set lunches for around KSh 60. The day's specials are chalked up on a blackboard outside the restaurant. You'll see quite a few travellers eating here.

In the Harambee Plaza Building on the corner of Uhuru Highway and Haile Selassie Ave, the *Caboose Restaurant* does an 'African buffet' on Wednesdays from 12.30 to 3 pm for KSh 110, while on other weekdays the usual 'businessman's buffet' costs KSh 90.

The *African Heritage Café*, which you reach through the African Heritage shop on Kenyatta Ave or through a separate entrance on Banda St, is also highly recommended for lunch. There are actually two parts to the restaurant – the main room adjoining Banda St which tends to be somewhat gloomy and is more expensive and the much lighter barbecue grill in the centre of the building. The food in the barbecue section is excellent and there's a choice of meat, fish or chicken which comes complete with chips and salad for KSh 65 to KSh 80 depending on what you have. Get here early if you don't want to wait for a table as it's a popular place to eat.

The restaurant at *The Pub* underneath the Sixeighty Hotel, on Standard St between Muindi Mbingu St and Koinange St, offers similar barbecued fare to that of the African Heritage Café and the prices are much the same though some dishes cost up to KSh 100. The only trouble with this place is the variability of the meat dishes – sometimes the meat is beautiful and tender; other times it's tough as old boots. Lunch is served from noon to 2 pm and dinner from 6 to 11 pm.

Another good place to go for lunch and well-cooked, straightforward food is the *Harvest* on Kenyatta Ave between Koinange St and Loita St. It's a very pleasant spot to eat.

Jax Restaurant on the 1st floor of the Old Mutual Building, Kimathi St, is a very popular place for lunch. It offers a wide selection of beautifully prepared hot meals, a salad buffet and Goan specialities in various different dining areas, including open-air dining. There's a licensed bar and you can eat well for KSh 80 and up. It's open from 8 am to 5 pm Monday to Friday, 8 am to 5 pm on Saturday but closed on Sundays and public holidays.

Quite a few people eat at *Buffalo Bill's* in front of the Heron Court Hotel, Milimani Rd, and while the food is quite good it works out relatively expensive because of the hefty 15% service charges and tax which is added to the bill.

Out of the centre in Rhapta Rd, Westlands, is the *Kenya Continental Hotel*. The outdoor restaurant here serves mainly meat, and you order it by the kg! Chicken is KSh 115 a kg, meat KSh 65 and extras such as salads and chips are KSh 12 each. The atmosphere is lively and the jukebox loud – a good place but you'll probably have to get a taxi there as it's hard to find.

Places to Eat – more expensive

The choice here is legion and spans just about every cuisine in the world. If you're going to be spending any amount of time in Nairobi and want to explore the full range of possibilities then it's worth buying a copy of *Nairobi Eating Out Guide* by Alan Graham which lists more than 200 of these establishments. This booklet, which is sold by most bookshops in Nairobi, is actually an extract from the *Kenya Travel Handbook* by the same author (PO Box 11285, Nairobi).

Most of these restaurants are licensed and offer beer, wine and spirits but the major exceptions are the Indian vegetarian restaurants which usually offer only fruit juices and tea or coffee.

Virtually all these restaurants accept international credit cards but they don't all take the full range of them.

Good Breakfasts For a breakfast splurge, try one of the buffets at one of the major hotels. The *Illiki Café* on the ground floor of the Ambassadeur Hotel on Moi Ave is excellent value. Here you can make a total pig of yourself for KSh 100. They offer the works – a variety of juices, milk, yoghurt, cereals, porridge, eggs, bacon, beans, sausages, toast, fruits, cakes, you name it.

Most of the other top-end hotels also do buffet breakfasts, although all charge around KSh 120 to KSh 155. Those at the *Hilton* and the *Norfolk* are superb, the *Nairobi Serena* pretty good, the *Intercontinental* fair and the *New Stanley* extremely poor.

Indian Food By far the best place in Nairobi for North Indian tucker is the *Dhaba Restaurant* (tel 334862) up at the top end of Tom Mboya St. A lot of work and thought has gone into the decor here with some fine watercolour murals of Punjabi rural life and ceilings made of mangrove poles and plaster. It's very popular among Indian families which is a good indication of the quality of the food. The house speciality is the 'takataka' meat dishes, which take their name from the noise which comes from the tandoori kitchen as the chef prepares the meat with huge cleavers. Main dishes are in the range of KSh 83 to KSh 95, so expect a full meal to come to around KSh 145 per person with drinks.

The *Mayur Restaurant* (tel 331586), above the Supreme Restaurant (mentioned previously under 'Big Lunches') has been famous for superb Indian vegetarian food for years. It's not bad value at KSh 110 but the hushed atmosphere is a bit daunting. This place seems to have lost out badly to the newer and more gregarious Dhaba.

Also excellent is the *Minar Restaurant* (tel 29999), Banda St, which specialises in

Mughlai dishes and offers buffet lunches and à la carte dinners. Expect to pay around KSh 180 for a three-course dinner including coffee. The restaurant is licensed, the service friendly and the restaurant is open from noon to 2 pm and 7 to 10.30 pm daily.

At the Meridien Court Hotel on Murang'a Rd up near the top end of Moi Ave, the *Khyber Restaurant* (tel 25595) also specialises in Mughlai dishes and offers a buffet lunch. Dinner choices include tandoori chicken, lamb or fish (KSh 80 to KSh 100), other special lamb or chicken dishes (KSh 90 to KSh 140), seafood (KSh 115 to KSh 275), vegetarian dishes (KSh 35 to KSh 85) and the usual range of Indian breads and sweets. It's licensed and open from 12.30 to 2.30 pm and 7 to 10.30 pm daily including holidays.

If you're staying at the Milimani Rd/Ralph Bunche Rd end of town then you can't beat a meal at *The Golden Candle* (tel 720480), Ralph Bunche Rd, close to the Grosvenor Hotel. The food here really is good and some travellers rate it as the best Indian food in Nairobi. They specialise in North Indian and Mughlai dishes (KSh 55 to KSh 200) but also offer charcoal-grilled steaks and chops (KSh 90 to KSh 115), seafood (KSh 95 to KSh 240) and Indian vegetarian dishes (KSh 50 to KSh 80). It's licensed and open from 12.30 to 3 pm and 6.30 to 11 pm Tuesday to Sunday; closed Mondays.

Chinese Food Nairobi has a reasonable selection of Chinese restaurants although none of them are cheap. One of the best is the *Panda Restaurant* on the corner of Tom Mboya and Cabral streets where the speciality is dishes from the Szechuan region of China. Similar is the *China Plate* (tel 20900), on the corner of Accra and Taveta roads, which also has Szechuan dishes in the range of KSh 90 to KSh 160. It's open daily from 12.30 to 2.30 pm and 7 to 10.30 pm.

Other places include: the *Dragon Pearl* (tel 340451), Bruce House, Standard St; the *Rickshaw Restaurant* (tel 23604) in Fedha Towers, Muindi Mbingu St at Kaunda St,

which offers Mandarin, Cantonese and Szechuan dishes from KSh 180 and up; and the *Hong Kong Restaurant* (tel 28612) on Koinange St, which offers Cantonese dishes for KSh 145 to KSh 325. Most of the main dishes at the above Chinese restaurants are available in full or half portions.

Thai Food Nairobi's first Thai restaurant is in the Westlands shopping centre, just a few minutes north of the city centre along Uhuru Highway. The *Bangkok Restaurant* (tel 751311) has a good reputation and is in the Rank Xerox Building.

Italian Food For Italian food there is really only one place to go and that is the very popular *Trattoria* (tel 340855) on the corner of Wabera and Kaunda streets. It is open daily from 8.30 am to 11.30 pm and both the atmosphere and the food here are excellent. There's a wide choice on the menu but the attitude of the waiters can be decidedly supercilious and when the change comes you'd better take possession of it in a big hurry otherwise it will be snatched up at the speed of lightning regardless of the amount! A soup, main course, salad, dessert and a carafe or two of house chianti will relieve you of between US$10 to US$15. As you might expect, the ice cream here is superb.

Also good is the *Marino Restaurant* (tel 336210) on the 1st floor of the National Housing Corporation Building, Aga Khan Walk, just off Haile Selassie Ave. It has a spacious interior dining area as well as an open-air patio and is open from 9 am to 2 pm and 7 to 10 pm Monday to Saturday; closed on Sunday. There's a wide range of Italian and continental dishes with main courses priced from KSh 80 to KSh 155.

Outside of the city centre are two other Italian restaurants – the *Toona Tree* and *La Galleria* (tel 742600), both of them in the International Casino, Westlands Rd across from the National Museum. They offer a range of pizzas, seafood and charcoal-grilled meats from KSh 50 to KSh 195 and the Toona Tree has live bands on Tuesday, Thursday and Saturday evenings. The Toona

Tree is open from 12.30 to 2 pm and 7.30 to 11 pm Tuesday to Saturday and 12.30 to 3 pm and 7.30 to 11 pm on Sunday but is closed on Monday. La Galleria is open from noon to 2.30 pm Monday to Friday and 7 to 10.30 pm Monday to Saturday.

Japanese Food There's one Japanese restaurant in the city centre, the *Akasaka*, which you'll find next to The Pub on Standard St between Koinange and Muindi Mbingu streets. As you might expect, it's done out in traditional Japanese style and there's even a tatami room which you can reserve in advance though mostly it's table and chairs. They offer the full range of Japanese cuisine including tempura, teriyaki, sukiyaki, shabushabu and yosenabe as well as a full range of soups and appetisers. A full meal will cost KSh 100 to KSh 240 per person. It's licensed and open daily from 6 to 9 pm plus they're open for box lunches from 12.30 to 2 pm.

The only other Japanese restaurant in town is the *Shogun* (tel 720563) at the Grosvenor Hotel on Ralph Bunche Rd. It offers the same range of dishes as the Akasaka but there's a choice of eating at the sushi bar, at tables and chairs or cross-legged at low tables in tatami rooms. It's licensed and open daily but there's only a limited range of dishes available at lunch time.

Korean Food The only Korean restaurant in Nairobi is the *Restaurant Koreana* (tel 335544) on the 1st floor of Kenindia House, Loita St. Soups cost KSh 30 to KSh 60, starters KSh 60 to KSh 85, side dishes from KSh 18, seafood KSh 85 to KSh 90 and main dishes KSh 60 to KSh 120. It's licensed and open from 11.45 am to 2.30 pm and 6.30 to 10.30 pm Monday to Saturday and closed Sunday.

Other Cuisines The only Spanish restaurant in town is *El Patio* (tel 340114) on the mezzanine floor of the Reinsurance Plaza Building, Taifa Rd at the junction with Aga Khan Walk. A meal here costs between KSh 95 and KSh 275 and the restaurant is open from 9.30 am to 10 pm Monday to Friday and 7 to 10 pm Saturday. It's closed on Sunday.

There's an excellent Ethiopian restaurant at the *Grosvenor Hotel*, Ralph Bunche Rd, which is well worth trying if you're staying in the area. Otherwise Ethiopian specialities are included in the dinner time menu at the African Heritage Café for around KSh 120.

Seafood & Steak The best seafood restaurant in Nairobi is the *Tamarind* (tel 338959) in the National Bank Building, Aga Khan Walk between Harambee Ave and Haile Selassie Ave. They offer a wide selection of exotic seafood dishes and culinary influences range from European to Asian to coastal Swahili. The cuisine is superb as are the surroundings which are decorated in a sumptuous Arabic-Moorish style. Eating here is definitely a major night out as most main courses are priced well over KSh 180 with crab and prawn dishes up to KSh 350 and lobster at KSh 60 per 100 g. There's also a special vegetarian menu. It's open for lunch Monday to Saturday from 12.30 to 1.45 pm and daily for dinner from 6.30 to 9.45 pm.

For steak eaters who haven't seen a decent doorstep since they left Argentina, Australia, Uruguay or America and are looking for a gut-busting extravaganza then there's no better place than the *Carnivore*, out at Langata just past Wilson Airport (bus Nos 14, 24 and 124). Tell the conductor where you are going and it's a one km signposted walk from where you are dropped off. It's easy to hitch back into the centre when you're ready to go. Otherwise, negotiate for a taxi. Whether it's lunch or dinner you take there's always beef, pork, lamb, ham, chicken, sausages and at least one game meat (often wildebeest or zebra). The roasts are barbecued on Maasai spears and the waiters carve off hunks onto your plate until you tell them it's enough. Prices include salads, bread, desserts and coffee. Meals here can be surprisingly cheap given the amount you receive and you're looking at KSh 180 and up which is great value.

Entertainment

Cinema Nairobi is a good place to take in a few films and at a price substantially lower than what you'd pay back home, but if you don't want scratched films then go to one of the better cinemas such as *The Nairobi* (behind The Kenya) and *20th Century*, Mama Ngina St. The cheaper ones (KSh 10 downstairs, KSh 15 in the upper circle) are on Latema Rd and include the *Odeon* and *Embassy*. There are also two good drive-ins if you have the transport, both have snack bars and bars. Nairobi is also a good place to see an Indian film. If you've never seen one of these then treat yourself one evening. If you have seen them before, you won't need persuading! Check with local papers to see what's on.

Theatre At the *Phoenix Theatre*, Parliament Rd, the auditorium is small and the acting professionally competent but it's quite expensive (around KSh 120). Check with local papers to see what's on.

Discos There's a good selection of discos in the centre of Nairobi. Single men may or may not find the attention of the many unattached women found in most of them to be exactly what they're looking for but there's never any pressure other than the occasional request for a drink. Perhaps the most popular in the centre of town is the *Florida 2000* on Moi Ave near City Hall Way. Entry costs KSh 100 for men and KSh 50 for women and it's open until 6 am. Also very popular is the *New Florida* (known to resident expatriates as the 'Mad House') on the corner of Koinange and Banda streets which is a most unusually shaped building with a petrol station underneath it! Entry charges are the same as the Florida 2000 and it stays open until 5 am. There are floor shows at about 1 am at both discos but they're pretty kitsch and the dancers are obviously bored to tears.

Another popular disco in the centre is *Visions* on Kimathi St which is open daily except Monday from 9 pm.

Less popular but probably just as good is the *Hollywood* on Moktar Daddah St between Koinange and Muindi Mbingu streets where the entry charges are the same as the above.

Beer in all these places is reasonably priced but other drinks, especially imported liquors, are more expensive. Snacks are available at all of them.

There don't appear to be any rigid dress regulations at any of these discos. Joggers and jeans are quite acceptable as are clean T-shirts though it's probably true to say that most men wear open-necked shirts and a pair of slacks and the local women are always well turned out.

Further out of town is *Bubbles* alongside the International Casino, Westlands Rd, which costs KSh 100 for men and KSh 50 for women.

There's a live band/disco every night at the *Carnivore* in Langata but entry will cost you KSh 50 per person. There's usually a good crowd and it makes a refreshing change from the more enclosed and crowded space of the New Florida or the Florida 2000 in town.

Live Music The *African Heritage Café* on Banda St is a popular place to hear live bands every Saturday and Sunday afternoon between 2 and 5 pm. There's a cover charge of KSh 20.

Much further out of town, just below the roundabout at Dagoretti Corner on Ngong Rd, is the *Bombax Club* which has live bands every Thursday, Friday, Saturday and Sunday. Unlike many of the other discos and bars mentioned in this section, this one is frequented mainly by local Kenyans with only a sprinkling of Whites but the atmosphere is very friendly and convivial. There's a cover charge of KSh 20. To get there, take a minibus or matatu to Dagoretti Corner from Kenyatta Ave outside Nyayo House or share a taxi (KSh 95).

There are plenty of other bars which lay on live music but many of them are in Eastleigh and to find them you're going to need an African friend to show you where they are.

Bars The *Thorn Tree Café* in the New Stanley Hotel on the corner of Kimathi St and Kenyatta Ave is a bit passé these days but is still the place to be seen and is still something of a meeting place with travellers. The service is generally supercilious and lousy and a beer takes forever to arrive. Perhaps this is just a ploy by the management to discourage 'shabby' travellers who might lower the tone of the place. Whatever the case, if you sit down between 11 am and 2 pm and 5 and 7 pm you'll have to order something to eat as well. The best thing about the Thorn Tree is the notice board where you can leave personal messages (but not advertisements of any kind, such as things for sale, looking for people to join a safari, etc).

Another popular bar (where you don't have to buy a meal in order to have a beer) is *The Pub* on Standard St between Koinange and Muindi Mbingu streets. It's designed to resemble an English pub (in which it fails miserably) and is open daily from 11 am to 11 pm. It attracts a remarkable cross section of the population and is a good place to go if you're a single man looking for some action. It does vary from night to night but there are usually plenty of girls in this place but that doesn't mean it's solely a pick-up joint. The Pub is part of the Sixeighty Hotel which has another open-air bar, the *Terrace Bar*, on the 1st floor above the entrance lobby.

The liveliest bar in Nairobi by far, however, is *Buffalo Bill's* at the Heron Court Hotel, Milimani Rd, which even got a three paragraph mention in the National Geographic magazine in May 1990 in an article describing the Rift Valley. Decked out with mock covered wagons (in denim!) complete with 'County Jail' surrounding a central bar and run by a resilient Korean woman, it's extremely popular with a wide variety of resident expatriates, tourists and local, unattached African women. It's *the* place to go if you're a single man but equally as much fun if you're a couple. While it's open all day, everyday, until around 11 pm, it only runs full-bore from about 5.30 pm onwards. Most of the women you see here migrate to the Florida 2000 once the bar closes. Meals and snacks are available throughout the day up until around 10.30 pm.

For an unparalleled spit-and-sawdust binge put aside a whole evening to join the beer swilling, garrulous hordes at the *Modern 24-Hour Green Bar*, Latema Rd next to the Sunrise Lodge. This place rages 24 hours a day, 365 days a year and the front door has never been closed since 1968 – except for one day in 1989 during a national census! All human life is here – teenage girls chewing *miraa* (stimulating leafy twigs and shoots), hustlers, whores, dope dealers and what one traveller once described as 'lowlife Whites'. The jukebox is always on full blast with screaming Indian vocalists or African reggae and the bar is completely encased in heavy duty wire mesh with a tiny hole through which money goes first and beer comes out afterwards. It's a great night out if you have the stamina but is definitely not for the squeamish.

Those looking for more genteel surroundings in which to sip their beer should try either the *Grosvenor Hotel*, Ralph Bunche Rd at the junction with Lenana Rd and close to the Youth Hostel, or the lawn of the *Fairview Hotel*, Bishops Rd close to 3rd Ngong Ave. For fading touches of the colonial era, try the terrace bar at the *Norfolk Hotel* which is open at lunch time and in the evening from 5 to 11 pm. Friday nights is when the young White population of Nairobi descends on this bar to drink itself legless. If you have transport, local residents also recommend the intimate atmosphere of the *Hurlingham Hotel*, Argwings Kodhek Rd about three km from the centre of town. They also offer very good, very cheap pub meals. You can eat lunch out in the garden.

Activities
Clubs & Societies For something with more intellectual and less alcoholic content there are a lot of specialist clubs and societies in Nairobi, many of which welcome visitors. Most of the foreign cultural organisations have film and lecture evenings (usually free of charge) at least once or twice a week. Give

them a ring and see what they have organised. In addition to these, some local clubs you may be interested in contacting include:

Mountain Club of Kenya (MCK)
PO Box 45741, Nairobi (tel 501747). The club meets every Tuesday at 8 pm at the clubhouse at Wilson Airport. Members frequently organise climbing weekends at various sites around the country. Information on climbing Mt Kenya and Kilimanjaro is available on the same evening.

East African Wildlife Society
Nairobi Hilton, PO Box 20110, Nairobi (tel 27047). This society is in the forefront of conservation efforts in East Africa and it publishes an interesting monthly magazine. Membership costs KSh 190 but entitles you to certain reductions in the national parks.

Nairobi Chess Club
PO Box 50443, Nairobi (tel 25007). The club meets every Thursday after 5.30 pm at the French Cultural Centre, on the corner of Monrovia and Loita streets.

Nairobi Photographic Society
PO Box 49879, Nairobi (tel 891075). Members meet at 8.30 pm on the first and third Thursdays of each month at St John Ambulance Headquarters behind the Donovan Maule Theatre.

Sports For sporting facilities, contact one or other of the following: Impala Club (tel 568684), Ngong Rd; Nairobi Club (tel 725726), Ngong Rd; Nairobi Gymkhana (tel 742804), on corner of Rwathia and Forest roads; Parklands Sports Club (tel 742938), Ojijo Rd. They all offer facilities for tennis, squash, cricket and some of them also play football and hockey.

Swimming Pools Most of the international tourist hotels have swimming pools which can be used by nonresidents for a daily fee of KSh 40. The YMCA on State House Rd also has a large pool with spring board which you can use for KSh 20.

Things to Buy
Nairobi is a good place to pick up souvenirs although you do need to shop around. The City Market on Muindi Mbingu St has a good range of stuff, particularly kiondo baskets, and there's a whole gaggle of stalls in Kigali St behind the Jamia Mosque. It's all a bit of a tourist trap and you need to bargain fiercely.

Even though they originated in Tanzania (and they're still much cheaper there), makonde wood carvings have caught on in a big way in Nairobi and the shops are full of them. At the cheaper end of the market, however, it's worth looking at the examples which hawkers bring around to the bars where tourists congregate. Buffalo Bill's at the Heron Court Hotel is one of the best places. The quality of the carving varies a lot but if you're not in a hurry then you can find some really fine examples at bargain basement prices. Expect to pay around a half to two-thirds of the price first asked.

If you're not into bargaining or want top quality stuff, there are plenty of 'fixed price' souvenir shops around, although even at these they'll usually give you a 'special price' if you are obviously not a Hilton hopper. Two of the better ones are the one on the corner of Kaunda and Wabera streets, and another on Tubman Rd near the corner of Muindi Mbingu St.

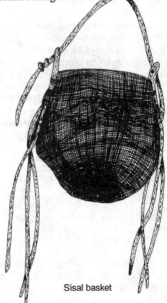

Sisal basket

If you want to get kitted out in the latest in designer 'White hunter' safari gear there are literally dozens of shops selling all the requisite stuff at outrageous prices.

The Spinners Web describes itself as a 'consignment handicraft shop' which sells goods made in workshops and by self-help groups around the country. They have some superb stuff, including hand-knitted jumpers, all sorts of fabrics and the huge Turkana baskets. The shop is on Kijabe Rd, around the corner from the Norfolk Hotel.

For a much less touristed atmosphere try the Kariokor Market east of the centre on Racecourse Rd in Eastleigh. It's a few minutes by bus.

Getting There & Away
Air Kenya Airways is the main domestic carrier and has the following internal flights from Nairobi's Jomo Kenyatta International Airport:

To	Frequency
Kisumu	13 flights weekly
Malindi	10 flights weekly
Mombasa	4 flights daily

Make sure you reconfirm flights 48 hours before departure and remember that delays are frequent on Kenya Airways.

Air Kenya Aviation is one of many small operators and runs the following flights from Wilson Airport (prices quoted are one way; return fares are slightly less than double). As is the case with most of the smaller operators, baggage allowance is only 15 kg, and excess is charged at the rate of KSh 15 per kg.

To	Frequency	Fare
Nyeri	daily	KSh 1200
Nanyuki	daily	KSh 1200
Eldoret	2 weekly	KSh 1500
Masai Mara	2 daily	KSh 1585
Lamu	daily	KSh 2700
Amboseli	daily	KSh 1250
Lodwar	3 weekly	KSh 2880
Loyangalani	3 weekly	KSh 3360

Bus In Nairobi most long-distance bus offices are along Accra Rd near the junction with River Rd. For Mombasa there are numerous companies (such as Coast, Akamba, Mawingo, Goldline and Malaika) doing the run, both by day and night. The cost varies from KSh 165 (Mawingo) to KSh 190 (Coast) and the trip takes around eight hours with a meal break on the way.

The main country bus station is just off Landies Rd, about 15 minutes walk from the budget hotel area around Latema Rd. It's a huge but reasonably well-organised place, and all the buses have their destinations displayed in the window so it's just a matter of wandering around and finding the one you want. There is at least one daily departure and often more to virtually every main town in the country, and the buses leave when full.

There is one daily direct bus to Garissa with Garissa Express (except when flooding cuts the road) which leaves from outside the Munawar Hotel opposite the Kenya Bus Depot in Eastleigh. The fare is KSh 115 and the journey takes about eight hours. The depot is a 10 minute matatu ride from Ronald Ngala St (Route No 9).

Share-Taxi This is a good alternative to that dangerous and heart-stopping mode of transport – the matatu. Share-taxis are usually Peugeot 504 station wagons which take seven passengers and leave when full. They are much quicker than the matatus as they go point to point without stopping, and of course are more expensive. Again, most of the companies have their offices around the Accra Rd and River Rd area. DPS and Wepesi, in the same office on Dubois Rd, have daily Peugeots to Kisumu (KSh 215, four hours), Kakamega (KSh 250), Busia (KSh 300), Nakuru (KSh 205, two hours) and Kericho (KSh 205). These departures are only in the mornings so you need to be at the office by around 7 am.

For the Tanzanian border at Namanga the taxis leave from the top side of the service station on the corner of Ronald Ngala St and River Rd. They run throughout the day, take about two hours and cost KSh 120. Minibuses also run to Namanga from the same place, cost KSh 95 and take up to three hours.

Train Trains run from Nairobi to Mombasa every day in both directions at 5 and 7 pm and the journey takes about 13 hours. The fares are: KSh 420 in 1st class, KSh 197 in 2nd class and KSh 99 in 3rd class. This is a popular run so book your tickets as far in advance as possible, although you shouldn't have any trouble a day or two before. The fare to Voi is KSh 293/138/69 in 1st/2nd/3rd class.

To the Ugandan border at Malaba there are trains on Tuesday, Friday and Saturday at 3 pm arriving at 8.30 am the next day. In the opposite direction they depart Malaba on Wednesday, Saturday and Sunday at 4 pm and arrive at 9.30 am the next day. The fares are KSh 440 in 1st class, KSh 207 in 2nd class and KSh 103 in 3rd class. En route to Malaba these trains go through Naivasha (KSh 92/43/22), Nakuru (KSh 147/69/35), Eldoret (KSh 305/143/72) and Bungoma (KSh 400/188/94).

The Nairobi-Kisumu trains depart daily at 6 pm arriving at Kisumu at 8 am the next day. In the opposite direction they depart daily at 6.30 pm arriving at Nairobi at 7.35 am the next day. Depending on demand there is usually an additional train ('express') at 5.30 pm from Nairobi daily for the first week of every month (and sometimes for the second week too) which arrives at Kisumu at 6.40 am the next day. The fares are KSh 317 in 1st class, KSh 149 in 2nd class and KSh 75 in 3rd class. This is also a popular route and the train is often booked out weeks in advance. If that's the case you may have to rely on the extra coach which is added on the day of departure if demand warrants (it usually does). Many of the carriages used on the Kisumu run are older than those used on the Nairobi-Mombasa run and are not such good value.

Hitching For Mombasa, take bus Nos 13 or 109 as far as the airport turn-off and hitch from there. For Nakuru and Kisumu, take bus No 23 from the Hilton to the end of its route and hitch from there. Otherwise start from the junction of Waiyaki Rd and Chiromo Rd (the extension of Uhuru Highway) in Westlands. For Nanyuki and Nyeri take bus Nos 45 or No 145 from the central bus station up Thika Rd to the entrance to Kenyatta College and hitch from there. Make sure you get off the bus at the college entrance not the exit. It's very difficult to hitch from the latter. Otherwise, start from the roundabout where Thika Rd meets Forest Rd and Muranga Rd.

Getting Around

Airport Transport The Jomo Kenyatta International Airport is 15 km out of town off the road to Mombasa. The cheapest way of getting into town is on the city bus No 34 *but* (and this is a big but) *you must keep your wits about you!* The number of people who get ripped off on this bus doesn't bear thinking about. The usual story is that an 'instant crowd' forms, you are jostled and before you know it your bag or money pouch has been slashed or ripped off. It's not much of an introduction to Kenya to lose your valuables on the first day so take the airline bus if you are at all hesitant. There is generally no problem when catching the bus from the city to the airport. The fare is KSh 6 and the trip takes about 45 minutes, more in peak periods.

A safer and far more pleasant way of getting into town is the Kenya Airways minibus. This leaves the airline's city terminus on Koinange St at 7, 8, 9, 10 and 11.30 am, and 2.30, 4.45, 6.30 and 8 pm. The trip takes about 30 minutes and costs KSh 70. When coming in from the airport this bus will drop you at any of the hotels in the centre, which is great if you're jetlagged.

The third way to or from the airport is by taxi, and this is really the only option if you have a dawn or late-night flight. The standard fare is KSh 300. If you want to share a taxi to the airport check out the notice boards at the Iqbal, the New Kenya Lodge and the Pigale.

To Wilson Airport (for small aircraft to Malindi, Lamu, etc) take bus Nos 14, 24 or 124 from in front of Development House, Moi Ave, and elsewhere. The fare is KSh 2.50 off-peak.

Bus Buses are the cheapest way of getting around Nairobi, but there is no great need to use them. The only ones you are likely to need are the No 34 to the airport and those mentioned in the Around Nairobi section. Forget about them in rush hours if you have a backpack – you'll never get on and if by some Herculean feat you manage to do that, you'll never get off!

Taxi Taxis cannot usually be hailed on the street (because they don't cruise for passengers) but there are taxi ranks at the railway station, the museum and outside most of the main hotels. The cabs are not metered but the fares charged are remarkably standard and few cabbies attempt to overcharge. KSh 60 gets you just about anywhere within the city centre. The same would be true from Ralph Bunche Rd or Milimani Rd to the main post office though they sometimes ask for KSh 70 as it involves backtracking down the other side of Haile Selassie Ave.

Outside this immediate area, the fare generally goes up to KSh 95.

In addition to the usual saloon car taxis, there are now quite a lot of brand new London taxis which are rumoured to belong to a very prominent politician. These cost more – KSh 70 around the centre, KSh 120 outside it.

Around Nairobi

NAIROBI NATIONAL PARK

This park is the most accessible of all Kenya's game parks, being only a few km from the city centre. You should set aside a morning or an afternoon to see it. As in all the game parks, you must visit it in a vehicle; walking is prohibited. This means you will either have to arrange a lift at the entrance gate with other tourists, go on a tour, or hire a car. Entry to the park costs KSh 220 per person (Kenya residents KSh 50), plus KSh 50 for a vehicle.

Nairobi National Park is the oldest park in the country, having been gazetted in 1946.

For a park so close to the city centre you can see an amazing variety of animals – with a backdrop of jumbo jets coming in to land at Jomo Kenyatta International Airport which is adjacent to the park! Gazelle, oryx, lion, zebra, giraffe, buffalo, cheetah and leopard are all seen regularly. Elephants are not found in this park as the habitat is unsuitable. However, it is in this park that you have one of the best chances for spotting a rhino – they are doing quite well here as the poachers prefer more remote areas.

The concentrations of game are higher in the dry season when water sources outside the park have dried up. Water is more plentiful inside the park as small dams have been built on the Mbagathi River which forms the southern boundary of the park.

The 'Animal Orphanage' by the main gate has a sign inside the gate which reads 'this is not a zoo' – it is. From time to time they do have young abandoned animals which are nursed through to good health and then released, but basically it is just a zoo, although it's been much improved by recent renovation and rebuilding of enclosures.

Getting There & Away

If you want to hitch a ride through the park from the main gate, city bus No 24 from Moi Ave goes right by it.

There are many companies offering tours of Nairobi National Park and there's probably not much to choose between them. They usually depart twice a day at 9.30 am and 2 pm for a four hour tour and cost from KSh 200. If you hang around in front of the Hilton Hotel at around 2 pm it is often possible to get a discounted seat on a tour at the last minute as they try to fill the van.

Most of the tour companies also offer a daylong combined tour of the national park with a visit to the Bomas of Kenya and including a gargantuan lunch at The Carnivore for KSh 600.

LANGATA GIRAFFE CENTRE

The Langata Giraffe Centre is on Gogo Falls Rd near the Hardy Estate Shopping Centre in Langata, about 18 km from Nairobi centre.

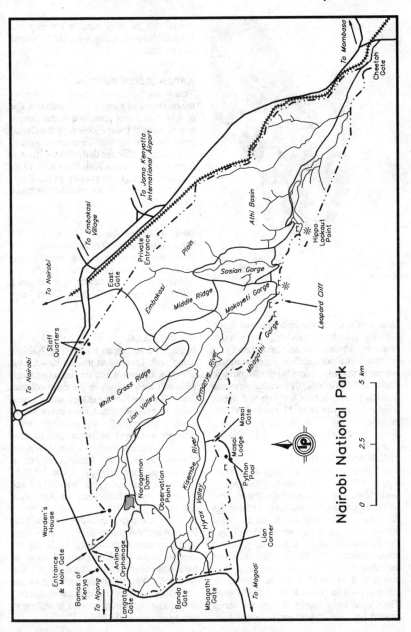

Nairobi National Park

Here you can observe and handfeed Roth-schild giraffes from a raised circular wooden structure which also houses a display of information about giraffes. It's open during school terms from 4 to 5.30 pm Monday to Friday and 10 am to 5.30 pm on Saturday and Sunday. During school holidays and public holidays it's open from 11 am to 5.30 pm. Admission costs KSh 30 (free to children). To get there from the centre take bus No 24.

THE BOMAS OF KENYA

The Bomas of Kenya at Langata – a short way past the entrance to the national park on the right-hand side – is a cultural centre. Here you can see traditional dances and hear songs from the country's 16 ethnic groups amid authentically recreated surroundings though the dances are all done by one group of professionals rather than representatives of the tribes themselves. There is a daily performance at 2.30 pm (3.30 pm at weekends). Entry costs KSh 100 or KSh 50 for students. There's the usual clutter of souvenir shops around the site. If you are not on a tour,

matatu No 24 from outside Development House, Moi Ave, will get you there in about half an hour.

KAREN BLIXEN MUSEUM

This is the farmhouse which was formerly the residence of Karen Blixen, author of *Out of Africa*, and was presented to the Kenyan government at independence by the Danish government along with the adjacent agricultural college. It's open daily from 9.30 am to 6 pm and entry costs KSh 50 or KSh 10 for students. It's right next door to the Karen College on Karen Rd between the residential areas of Karen and Langata.

Getting There & Away

Take public bus No 27 from Kenyatta Ave or from the corner of Ralph Bunche and Ngong roads, or No 24 from Moi Ave. Bus No 111 will also get you most of the way but you'll have to change to No 24 at the Karen Shopping Centre.

NGONG HILLS

Ngong and Karen, to the west of Nairobi, along with Limuru, to the north, were the sites where many White settlers set up farms and built their houses in the early colonial days. The transformation they wrought was quite remarkable so that, even today, as you catch a glimpse of a half-timbered house through woodland or landscaped gardens full of flowering trees, you could imagine yourself to be in the Home Counties of England or some other European location. And, yes, the eucalypts which you see growing everywhere were an Australian import.

There are some excellent views over Nairobi and down into the Rift Valley from various points in the Ngong Hills, but it's unwise to go wandering around alone as people have been mugged here, especially at weekends. What you really need to get a feel for in these areas is your own car or, alternatively, that of a resident who is willing to drive you around the place.

LIMURU

Limuru is possibly even more 'European' in the feeling it leaves you than the Ngong Hills except that there are vast coffee and tea estates blanketing the rolling hills in between swathes of conifer and eucalypt forest. It's up here that you'll find *The Kentmere Club* (tel (0154) 41053, PO Box 39508, Nairobi), Limuru Rd, Tigoni. This is the quintessential White settlers' club – even more so than the Norfolk Hotel in Nairobi. It consists of a series of low, intimate wooden cottages with shingle roofs connected to each other by quaint walkways and bridges and a main block built in the same style which houses a restaurant and a superb re-creation of an English country pub with low ceilings, exposed beams and log-burning fireplaces. You wouldn't know the difference between this place and the Spaniard's Inn on Hampstead Heath if it weren't for the Tusker and White Cap instead of bar pumps and real ale.

The restaurant here is probably the best in Kenya. Certainly the spreads which I saw being laid out on Christmas Eve were absolutely superb. It would have to be *the* place to go for a Christmas banquet though it's naturally not cheap – KSh 600 for Christmas Eve or New Year's Eve dinner and KSh 360 for Christmas Day lunch. Advance booking is essential.

If you'd like to rent a cottage here then make enquiries over the phone. It's very peaceful.

Not far from the Kentmere Club is the *Waterfalls Inn* (tel (0154) 40672) with its picnic site, waterfalls, viewing point, restaurant and disco. Admission here costs KSh 95 per car including up to six passengers plus there's pony, horse and camel riding available at KSh 25 to KSh 60. To get there, turn off right from the Limuru Rd when you see the sign for Limuru Girls' School. The Waterfalls Inn (signposted) is 2½ km down the dirt road from the turn-off.

Another thing you can do at Limuru is to visit a tea farm. If you've never done this before then it's worth a day out. Visits are organised by Mitchell's Kiambethu Tea Farm (tel (0154) 40756) at Tigoni, about 35 km north-east of Nairobi. Here you'll be shown the whole process of tea production as well as taken on an accompanied walk into the forest to see the Colobus monkeys. Visits here come in a package which includes pre-lunch drinks and a three-course lunch, all for KSh 300 per person. Groups are preferred and visits are by prior arrangement only.

Getting There & Away

Public bus No 116 will take you fairly close to the farm. If you have your own transport then take the C62 Limuru Rd past City Park and turn left at Muthaiga roundabout. Seven km further on you reach Ruaka village where you turn right by the signpost for Nazareth Hospital and onto the D407 Limuru Rd (otherwise known as Banana Rd). Some 14½ km down this road you'll see a signpost for Limuru Girls' School where you turn right. Go down past the school and take the entrance on the left-hand side signposted 'L G Mitchell'.

The Coast

This cannot be less than natural beauty, the endless sand, the reefs, the lot, are completely unmatched in the world.

Ernst Hemingway

The coast of Kenya is one of the country's main attractions. It offers a combination of historical sites, trading ports with a strong Arab-Muslim influence, superb beaches and diving opportunities – an area not to be missed.

Mombasa is the coast capital, if you like, and is the first port of call for most people after leaving Nairobi. It is an old trading port with a history going back at least to the 12th century, and the old city here shows heavy influence of the town's previous rulers – the mosques and the Portuguese fort in particular. It has a steamy humid climate but is a pleasant place nonetheless. Unfortunately many people are in such a rush to get to the beach that they really only transit Mombasa, which is a pity as the city, particularly the old part, is well worth exploring.

South of Mombasa it's basically beaches all the way to the Tanzanian border at Lunga Lunga. Apart from the resort development at Diani Beach everything is pretty low-key and it's easy to while away a few days (or weeks) here.

To the north it's much the same story, with Malindi being the big coastal resort centre, but there's a couple of interesting attractions here as well – the historical site of Gedi just a short bus ride to the south, and the excellent diving on the coral reef in the offshore Malindi and Watamu marine national parks.

Head further north and you come to the island of Lamu – a beautiful Arab-influenced town which has been something of a travellers' Mecca for years and still draws visitors by the thousands. Despite that it retains the very distinctive personality which attracted people to it in the first place – an easy-going unhurried pace, traditional architecture and a unique culture which owes a

great deal to its Muslim roots but has evolved over the centuries.

The people of the coast are the Swahili, and it's here that KiSwahili – the lingua franca of the modern nation – evolved as a means of communication between the local inhabitants and the Arab traders who first began plying their dhows up and down this coast sometime before the 7th century. Other influences also shaped the language and there is a smattering of not only Arabic but also Portuguese, Hindi and English words.

History

The first traders here appear to have been Arabs from the Persian Gulf who sailed south along the coast during the north-east monsoon, sailing home north with the south-west monsoon. By the 12th century some substantial settlements had developed, mainly on islands, such as Lamu, Mandu, Pemba and Zanzibar, as these provided greater security than the coast itself. The main export trade in this early part was in ivory, tortoiseshell and leopard skins, while items such as glass beads from India and porcelain from as far afield as China were finding their way here.

From the 12th to the 15th centuries settlements grew and a dynasty was established at Kilwa (in present day Tanzania), and so by the end of this period Mombasa, Malindi and Paté (in the Lamu archipelago) were all substantial towns. The inhabitants were largely Arab but there was also substantial numbers of African labourers. Intermarriage was common and the settlements were far closer connected culturally with the Islamic Persian Gulf than they were with inland Kenya. Although all these city-states had this common heritage and cultural link, they were all virtually independent and were often vying for power against each other.

So preoccupied were they with their own internal struggles that the coastal centres were quite unprepared for the arrival of the

Kenyan South Coast

0   25   50 km

Portuguese in 1498. Before long they were paying tribute to the Portuguese and by 1506 the Portuguese had sacked and gained control of the entire coast. In the century which followed the Portuguese had raided Mombasa on two further occasions and built the beautiful defensive Fort Jesus in that city.

Trade was the main interest of the Portuguese and they concentrated their activities in that area. They did not exercise direct control over the administration of the coastal cities – just kept them in line and dependent.

Not all the locals were happy with this arrangement and the troubles started for the Portuguese with local uprisings in the 17th century. They were mainly inspired by the disaffected Sheikh Yusuf of Mombasa, who spent most of his time in conflict with the Portuguese, and in fact occupied Fort Jesus in Mombasa after murdering the Portuguese commandant there in 1631. With the help of the sultans of Oman, the Portuguese were defeated and Fort Jesus occupied by 1698.

The Omani dynasties flourished and Mombasa and Paté became the pre-eminent spots on the coast, although both were defeated by Lamu in 1810. The internecine struggles of the various Omani factions led to Zanzibar coming into ascendancy, which led the rulers of Mombasa to seek British assistance. The British, however, were reluctant to intervene and jeopardise their alliance with Seyyid Said, the Omani ruler, as their route to India passed close to Muscat. Before long the whole coast was under the control of the Omani ruler.

It was in this period of Omani rule that the slave trade flourished. Up until this time it had been carried out only on a small scale, but soon the newly established clove plantations on Zanzibar required labourers, and from there slaves were shipped to the Persian Gulf and beyond. It was also this increase in economic activity that brought the first Indian and European traders into the area. Trade agreements were made with the Americans (1833), the British (1839) and the French (1844), and exports to India also flourished – ivory, cloves, hides and coconut oil were all-important. This increase in trade

led Seyyid Said to transfer his capital from Muscat to Zanzibar in 1840, and decreased his reliance on the slave trade for revenue. He was thus able to sign a treaty banning the export of slaves to the Middle East.

Despite the fact that the British East Africa Company took over administration of the interior of the country, a 10-mile-wide coastal strip was recognised as the sultan's patch and it was leased from him in 1887, first for a 50 year period and then permanently. In 1920 the coastal strip became the British protectorate, the rest of the country having become a fully fledged British colony.

Mombasa

Mombasa is the largest port on the coast of East Africa. It has a population of nearly half a million of which about 70% are African, the rest being mainly Asian with a small minority of Europeans. Its docks not only serve Kenya, but also Uganda, Rwanda and Burundi. The bulk of the town sprawls over Mombasa Island which is connected to the mainland by an artificial causeway which carries the rail and road links. In recent years Mombasa has spread onto the mainland both north and south of the island.

Large Mombasa may be but, like Dar es Salaam to the south, it has retained its low-level traditional character and there are few high-rise buildings. The old town between the massive, Portuguese-built Fort Jesus and the old dhow careening dock remains much the same as it was in the mid-19th century, asphalt streets and craft shops apart. It's a hot and steamy town, as you might expect being so close to the equator, but an interesting place to visit.

History
Mombasa's history goes back to at least the 12th century when it was described by Arab chroniclers as being a small town and the residence of the King of the Zenj – Arabic for black Africans. It later became an import-

ant settlement for the Shirazis and remained so until the arrival of the Portuguese in the early 16th century. Determined to destroy the Arab monopoly over maritime trade in the Indian Ocean, especially with regard to spices, the Portuguese, under Dom Francisco de Almeida, attacked Mombasa with a fleet of 16 ships in 1505. After a day and a half it was all over and the town was burnt to the ground. So great was the quantity of loot that much of it had to be left behind, for fear of overloading the ships, when the fleet sailed for India.

The town was quickly rebuilt and it wasn't long before it regained its commanding position over trade in the area, but peace didn't last long. In 1528, another Portuguese fleet under Nuña da Cunha arrived on the East African coast too late to catch the south-western monsoon which would take them to India, so they were forced to look around for temporary quarters. Naturally, Mombasa was in no mood to welcome them but, unfortunately, Mombasa was at that time engaged in bitter disputes with the kings of Malindi, Pemba and Zanzibar. An alliance was patched together and the Portuguese were again able to take Mombasa, but sickness and constant skirmishing over many months eventually decided the outcome. The city was again burnt to the ground and the Portuguese sailed for India.

The Portuguese finally made a bid for permanency in 1593 when the construction of Fort Jesus was begun, but in 1631 they were massacred to the last person in an uprising by the townspeople. The following year a Portuguese fleet was sent from Goa and Muscat to avenge the killings but was unable to retake the town. By this time, however, the Mombasan ruler had decided that further resistance was useless and, having reduced the town to rubble and cut down all the fruit trees and palms, he withdrew to the mainland. It was reoccupied without a fight by the Portuguese the following year.

Portuguese hegemony of the Indian Ocean was on the wane by this time, not only because of corruption and nepotism within their own ranks, but because of Dutch,

French and English activity in India and South-East Asia. The 17th century also saw the rise of Oman as a naval power and it was the Omanis who, in 1698, were the next to drive the Portuguese from Mombasa, after a 33 month siege in which all the defenders were slaughtered. Even this disaster wasn't enough to convince the Portuguese that their days were over. Mombasa was reoccupied yet again but the end finally came in 1729 following an invasion by an Arab fleet, a general uprising of the population in which Portuguese settlers were slaughtered and an abortive counteroffensive which involved the entire military resources of the Viceroyalty of Goa.

In 1832 the Sultan of Oman moved his capital from Muscat to Zanzibar and from then until Kenya's independence in 1963 the red flag of Zanzibar fluttered over Fort Jesus. Meanwhile, the British became active along the East African coast. In their attempts to suppress the slave trade, they interfered increasingly in the affairs of Zanzibar until, in 1895, the British East Africa Protectorate was set up with Mombasa as the capital (until it was moved to Nairobi) and the Sultan of Oman's possessions were administered as a part of it. When independence came, the Sultan's coastal possessions were attached to the new republic.

During the protectorate years the British confirmed Mombasa's status as East Africa's most important port by constructing a railway from Mombasa to Uganda. It was completed in 1901, using indentured labourers from Gujarat and Punjab in India – hence the origin of Kenya's (and Uganda's and Tanzania's) Asian population.

Information & Orientation
Tourist Office The regional tourist office (tel 311231) is just past the famous tusks on Moi Ave and is open Monday to Friday from 8 am to noon and 2 to 4.30 pm, and on Saturdays from 8 am to noon. They have a good map of Mombasa for sale but otherwise they're geared to high spenders – mainly those who want to stay at a beach resort hotel – so they're of little help to budget travellers.

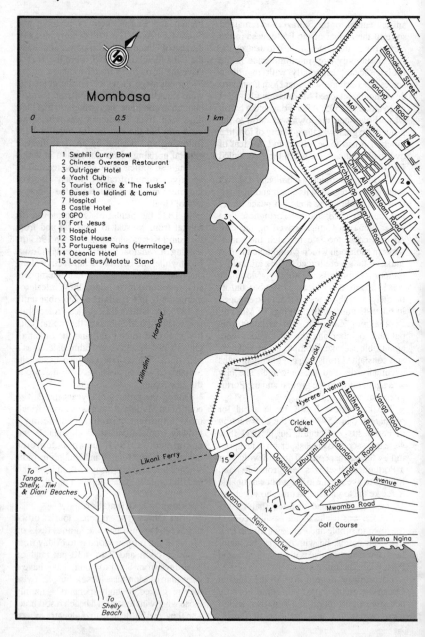

Mombasa

0   0.5   1 km

1 Swahili Curry Bowl
2 Chinese Overseas Restaurant
3 Outrigger Hotel
4 Yacht Club
5 Tourist Office & 'The Tusks'
6 Buses to Malindi & Lamu
7 Hospital
8 Castle Hotel
9 GPO
10 Fort Jesus
11 Hospital
12 State House
13 Portuguese Ruins (Hermitage)
14 Oceanic Hotel
15 Local Bus/Matatu Stand

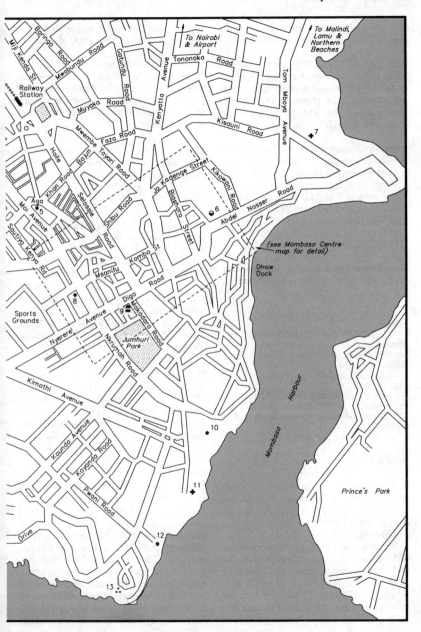

You can also buy the local guide books to Fort Jesus and Mombasa Old Town here.

Post The GPO is on Digo Rd and is open Monday to Friday from 8 am to 4.30 pm and on Saturday from 8 am to noon. There is one international card phone in the bank of phones outside the post office, or you can make calls through the operator.

Bank The branch of Barclays Bank on Moi Ave, just up the road from the Castle Hotel, is open Monday to Friday from 8.30 am to 4.30 pm, and on Saturday from 8.30 am to 12.30 pm and 2 to 4.30 pm. Outside these hours you can change travellers' cheques at the Castle Hotel, or at any of the beach resort hotels north and south of Mombasa, although a commission may be charged.

Consulates The following countries have diplomatic representation in Mombasa:

Austria
  Raili House, Nyerere Ave (tel 313386)
Belgium
  Mitchell Cotts Building, Moi Ave (tel 20231)
Denmark
  Liwatoni Bay (tel 311826)
France
  Southern House, Moi Ave (tel 20501)
India
  Bank of India Building, Nkrumah Rd (tel 24433)
Netherlands
  ABN Bank Building, Nkrumah Rd (tel 311043)
Sweden
  Southern House, Moi Ave (tel 20501)

Books If you'd like more details about Mombasa's stirring history, the best account is to be found in *The Portuguese Period in East Africa* by Justus Strandes (East African Literature Bureau, 1971) which can be bought in most good bookshops in Nairobi and Mombasa.

Before you set off on a tour of the old town of Mombasa get a copy of the booklet *The Old Town Mombasa: A Historical Guide* by Judy Aldrick & Rosemary Macdonald, published by the Friends of Fort Jesus. It can be bought from either the tourist office or at Fort Jesus for KSh 50. This excellent guide is an essential companion for an exploration of this part of town and has photographs, drawings and a map.

Also well worth buying is *Fort Jesus* by James Kirkman, which gives a detailed account of the history of the Fort, as well as pointing out the salient features. It is available from the fort (KSh 20) or the tourist office (KSh 30).

Maps The best map you can buy of Mombasa is the Survey of Kenya's *Mombasa Island & Environs*, last published in 1977. Many of the street names have changed, but little else.

Left Luggage The left luggage service at the railway station costs KSh 12 per item per day. It is open from 8 am to noon and 2 to 6.30 pm Monday to Saturday, and from 7.30 to 10 am and 2 to 6.30 pm on Sunday.

Car Rental All the major companies and many of the smaller outfits have offices here as well as in Nairobi. Details can be found under Vehicle Hire in the Getting Around chapter.

Motoring Organisations The Automobile Association of Kenya (tel 26778) has its office just north of the tourist office on the road which connects Aga Khan Rd with the railway station. They have a few road maps and may be of use if you have specific questions about roads or traffic conditions.

Fort Jesus
The old town's biggest attraction dominates the harbour entrance. Begun in 1593 by the Portuguese, it changed hands nine times between 1631 and 1875. These days it's a museum and is open daily from 8.30 am to 6 pm. Entry costs KSh 50 (KSh 5 for Kenyan residents). There are no student reductions. It's well worth a visit and it's easy to pass a couple of hours here. Early morning is the best time as the air is still cool and the rest of the tourists are still in bed. The guidebook, *Fort Jesus*, by James Kirkman is useful for

a full description of the history and finer points of the fort.

The fort was designed by an Italian architect, Joao Batista Cairato, who had done a lot of work for the Portuguese in Goa. He incorporated some ingenious elements into the design, such as the angular configuration of the walls, making it impossible for would-be invaders to lay siege to one wall without being sitting ducks for soldiers in one of the other walls.

The most interesting features today include the Omani house in the San Felipe bastion in the north-west corner of the fort. Built in the late 18th century it has served different purposes as the purpose of the fort changed – it was the Chief Warder's House when the fort was a prison in the early 20th century. The view of the old town from the roof here is excellent.

The museum along the southern wall is built over what was the barracks rooms for the garrison. The exhibits are mostly ceramics but include other interesting odds and ends and have either been donated from private collections or dug up from various sites along the coast. The origins of many of the pieces are a reflection of the variety of cultures which have influenced the coastal culture – Chinese, Indian, Portuguese and Persian. Also displayed in the museum are finds from the Portuguese frigate *Santo António de Tanná* which sank off the Fort during the siege in 1697.

The western (seaward) wall of the fort is probably the most interesting and includes an Omani audience hall (now covered by a second storey but still complete with official inscriptions – and unofficial graffiti) and the Passage of the Arches – a passage cut through the coral giving access to the outer part of the fort, although it was later blocked off.

The Old Town

The old town isn't as immediately interesting as the Fort, but it's still a fascinating area to wander around in. Early morning or late afternoon is the best time to walk around; there's more activity then, and it's very quiet in the middle of the day.

Though its history goes back centuries, most of the houses in the old town are no more than 100 years old but you'll come across the occasional one which dates back to the first half of the 19th century. They represent a combination of styles and traditions which include the long-established coastal Swahili architecture commonly found in Lamu, various late 19th century Indian styles and British colonial architecture with its broad, shady verandahs and glazed and shuttered windows.

There are very few houses constructed entirely of coral rag, however. Most are of wattle and daub though they may include coral here and there. Most of the old palm thatch or tile roofing has been replaced with corrugated iron as well. What does remain are many examples of the massive, intricately carved doors and door frames characteristic of Swahili houses in Lamu and Zanzibar. It seems that when anyone of importance moved from these towns to Mombasa they brought their doors with them or had them newly made up to reflect their financial status. Of course, they're not as numerous as they used to be, either because of the ravages of time, or because they have been bought by collectors and shipped abroad. There is now a preservation order on those remaining so further losses should hopefully be prevented.

It's not just carved doors that you should look out for, though. Almost as much effort was put into the construction of balconies, their support brackets and enclosures. Fine fret work and lattice work are a feature of the enclosures, reflecting the Muslim need for women's privacy. Sadly, quite a few of these were damaged or destroyed along Mbarak Hinawy Rd in the days when oversized trucks used the road for access to the old port.

By 1900, most of the houses in the main streets were owned by Indian business people and traders whilst Mbarak Hinawy Rd (previously called Vasco da Gama St) and Government Square had become the centre for colonial government offices, banks, con-

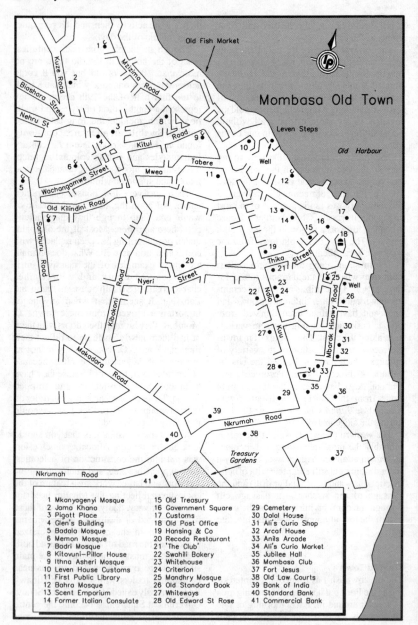

Mombasa Old Town

Old Fish Market

Old Harbour

Leven Steps

Well

Old Fish Market

Kuze Road

Mzizima Road

Biashara Street

Nehru St

Kitui Road

Wachangomwe Street

Old Kilindini Road

Samburu Road

Tabere

Mwea

Kibokoni Road

Nyeri Street

Mokadara Road

Thika Street

Ndia Kuu

Mbarak Hinawy Road

Well

Nkrumah Road

Treasury Gardens

Nkrumah Road

1 Mkanyagenyi Mosque
2 Jama Khana
3 Pigott Place
4 Glen's Building
5 Badala Mosque
6 Memon Mosque
7 Badri Mosque
8 Kitovuni–Pillar House
9 Ithna Asheri Mosque
10 Leven House Customs
11 First Public Library
12 Bahra Mosque
13 Scent Emporium
14 Former Italian Consulate

15 Old Treasury
16 Government Square
17 Customs
18 Old Post Office
19 Hansing & Co
20 Recodo Restaurant
21 'The Club'
22 Swahili Bakery
23 Whitehouse
24 Criterion
25 Mandhry Mosque
26 Old Standard Book
27 Whiteways
28 Old Edward St Rose

29 Cemetery
30 Dalal House
31 Ali's Curio Shop
32 Arcaf House
33 Anils Arcade
34 Ali's Curio Market
35 Jubilee Hall
36 Mombasa Club
37 Fort Jesus
38 Old Law Courts
39 Bank of India
40 Standard Bank
41 Commercial Bank

sulates and business or living quarters for colonial officials. Ndia Kuu housed immigrant entrepreneurs from India, Goa and Europe. The colonial headquarters at this time were situated in Leven House on the waterfront overlooking the old harbour, but shortly afterwards they were moved to Government Square and, in 1910, moved again up the hill to Treasury Square above Fort Jesus.

In later years as Mombasa expanded along what are today the main roads, many of the businesses which had shops and offices in the old town gradually moved out, leaving behind ornate signs, etched glass windows and other relics of former times. Their exact location is described in *The Old Town Mombasa: A Historical Guide*.

You can start your exploration of the old town anywhere you like but the main points of interest are marked on the street map. There is a notice in Government Square saying that photography of the old harbour area (but not the buildings) is prohibited. I don't know how serious the authorities are about this since I can't imagine what is so sensitive about the place, but if you want pictures of it there are plenty of narrow streets leading off to the waterfront between the square and the Leven Steps where no-one will bother you.

Places to Stay

There's a lot of choice for budget travellers and for those who want something slightly better, both in the centre of the city and on the mainland to the north and south. Accommodation up and down the coast from Mombasa Island itself is dealt with separately.

Places to Stay – bottom end

One of the best value for money places in this category is the *Mvita Hotel*, on the corner of Hospital and Turkana streets. The entrance is on the first alley on the left-hand side on Turkana St or through the bar on the ground floor on Hospital St. It's Indian run, very clean and quiet, secure, friendly, all the rooms have fans and a hand basin and the beds are comfortable. Even toilet paper is provided. The showers and toilets are scrubbed out daily. It costs KSh 145/180 for double/triple rooms but is often full as it's only a small place. There's a lively bar downstairs (which you can't hear in the rooms upstairs) and at lunch and dinner times barbecued meat and other snacks are available in the back yard.

Equally good value and popular with travellers is the *Cosy Guest House* (tel 313064), Haile Selassie Rd, which costs KSh 90 a single, KSh 120 a double and KSh 180 a triple, all with common facilities. All the rooms have fans but due to chronic water problems the toilets can stink. It will most likely be full if you get there late in the day. On the opposite side of the road from the Cozy Guest House is the *Midnight Guest House* (tel 26725) which is not all that friendly but would do if you're stuck. It costs KSh 90 a single and KSh 145 a double with common showers and toilets.

Just around the corner on Shibu Rd is the friendly *New Al Jazira Hotel* which has double/triple rooms with balcony and common bath and toilets for KSh 95/145. As is the case with many Mombasa hotels, there are no single rooms.

If all these places are full then you could try the *Balgis Hotel* (tel 313358), Digo Rd, which is very friendly. It's about the cheapest in Mombasa with dorm beds for KSh 40 and single/double rooms for 85/110 with common bath. The rooms only have internal windows which makes them pretty hot, except the dorm which has windows overlooking the noisy Digo Rd. Another real cheapie which is habitable is the *Down Town Lodge* on Hospital St for KSh 85/110, but the rooms here don't have fans.

Heading towards the northern end of town, the *Al Nasser Lodging* (tel 313032) on Abdel Nasser Rd is good value at KSh 70/145 for single/double rooms with shower.

Another budget hotel in this area, and one which has been popular for years, is the *New People's Hotel* (tel 312831), Abdel Nasser

Rd right next to where the buses leave for Malindi and Lamu. Some travellers rate this place very highly and it certainly compares very well in price with the others but it is a little tatty and the rooms which face onto the main road are very noisy and the air stinks of diesel fumes. This is mainly because of the bus drivers who seem to have a fetish about revving their engines for anything up to an hour before they actually leave. The management are friendly and gear left in the rooms is safe. It costs KSh 70/120/140 a single/double/triple for a room with common showers and toilets, and KSh 100/205/310 with bathroom. All the rooms have fans, the sheets are clean and the water in the showers is generally lukewarm. It's a large place and is rarely full. There's a good, cheap restaurant downstairs.

Another place which has been a popular budget hotel for years is the *Hydro Hotel* (tel 23784), on Digo Rd at the junction with Kenyatta Ave. It's a bit shabby these days but is undeniably cheap at KSh 50 for a dorm bed, and KSh 85/165 for slightly cramped single/double rooms with fan. There is also one room with four beds for KSh 190. The restaurant on the 1st floor is not bad and serves some Swahili dishes.

The *New Britania Boarding & Lodging* on Gusii St is yet another popular place. The hotel entrance is through the downstairs bar and then up the stairs. The bar itself is a lively and friendly place. The rooms are clean and good value at KSh 120, and if the place is full you can sleep an extra person or two on the floor.

Up the scale a bit is the *ABC Lodge* near the Glory Guest House on Shibu Rd. The rooms are a good size and have their own bath and fan. At KSh 110/210 they're not bad value.

Somewhat more expensive than the above (but not necessarily better value) is the *Hotel Fortuna*, Haile Selassie Rd, which costs KSh 180 a single and KSh 240 a double, both with private showers and toilets. The *Hotel Fortuna Annex* across the road shares the same reception but is cheaper at KSh 120/155 for rooms with common bath.

Places to Stay – middle

One of the best in this range is the friendly *Hotel Relax* (tel 311346), Meru Rd, which is clean and good value at KSh 335 a double including shower, toilet and breakfast. Soap and towels are also provided, all the rooms have fans and are cleaned daily. There are also a couple of rooms with common facilities and these are excellent value at KSh 185 including breakfast. It's also possible to store luggage here if you're heading up or down the coast; there's no charge for this.

On the next block is the *Hotel Splendid* (tel 20967), a huge place which is rarely full. It is much more expensive at KSh 455 for a double with bathroom and breakfast. It's a very clean and modern place and there's a popular rooftop restaurant which gets sea breezes in the evenings. The hotel has an annexe on Meru Rd between Digo Rd and Msanifu Kombo St and rooms here go for KSh 305 for a double with breakfast.

Better value perhaps is the *Continental Guest House* (tel 315916) on Haile Selassie Rd near the Hotel Fortuna. Double rooms (no singles) go for KSh 240 with bath and breakfast. This is a new place which usually fills up early. Close by is the *Visitor's Inn* on the corner of Shibu Rd. It's not a bad place at KSh 130/210 with bath and breakfast although some of the rooms overlook Haile Selassie Rd and so cop the noise. The entrance is on Shibu Rd and is easy to miss.

Another new place is the *Glory Guest House* (tel 314557) on Shibu Rd. The rooms are a bit on the small side but are spotlessly clean and well maintained. The charge is KSh 270/380 for singles/doubles with bath and hot water. Air-con doubles cost KSh 450.

The best place to stay in this range is the beautiful *New Palm Tree Hotel* (tel 312167), Nkrumah Rd, which I'd rate as being very similar in quality to the much more expensive Castle Hotel. A very comfortable room here costs KSh 290 a single and KSh 430 a double with a shower and toilet and including breakfast. The hotel has its own bar and restaurant.

The most expensive place in this category is the *Hotel Hermes* (tel 313599) on Msanifu

Kombo St near the Sheik Jundoni Mosque. You could hardly call it a friendly place but the rooms are pleasant, if a little dingy, and the tariff of KSh 385/480 includes bath and breakfast.

Places to Stay – top end

In the centre of town is the very popular *Castle Hotel* (tel 21683), Moi Ave, costs KSh 870 a single and KSh 1380 a double, including breakfast. The hotel has a coffee shop and a good restaurant, and the terrace bar is the Mombasa equivalent of the Thorn Tree Café in Nairobi. You'll find all the comforts and facilities you would expect of a top-end place.

The older, colonial style *Manor Hotel* (tel 31643), Nyerere Ave, with a wide verandah and surrounding garden, is cheaper at KSh 540 to KSh 660 a single and KSh 840 to KSh 960 a double with bath and breakfast. It's a very pleasant place with a bar and restaurant.

At Ras Liwatoni, the *New Outrigger Hotel* (tel 20822) is at the very top of the range. It's a Belgian-managed resort type place right on the beach, but also has a swimming pool if you can't stagger that far. All rooms are air-conditioned, have a private bath and a balcony facing the sea. The tariff is KSh 835/1075 for a single/double with breakfast.

Places to Eat

Mombasa has a good range of restaurants. If you are putting your own food together, or want to stock up with goodies to take down the coast, the Fort Supermarket on Nyerere Ave is well stocked, and there's a wide variety of fruit and vegies in the market on Digo Rd next to the Hydro Hotel.

Places to Eat – cheap

If you are just looking for fish or chicken with chips try the *Blue Fin Restaurant*, on the corner of Meru Rd and Msanifu Kombo St. There's very little variety but it's not a bad place. There's a better choice at the *Blue Room Restaurant* on Haile Selassie Rd. They have excellent burgers for KSh 20 to KSh 35, depending on what you have with it, and the

fish & chips and Indian snacks are also worth a try.

The *Pan Coffee House* near the GPO on Digo Rd is another place doing standard food which is worth trying. The *Masumin Restaurant*, opposite the GPO on Digo Rd, does a good full breakfast for KSh 35, and at other times has various curries with rice for KSh 30, as well as steaks and cheap juices.

The *Kenya Coffee House* on Moi Ave is a good place for fresh coffee and snacks, and you can also buy coffee beans here.

Indian Food Since many of the restaurants in Mombasa are Indian owned you can find excellent curries and thalis and at lunch time (12.30 to around 3 pm) there is often a cheap, substantial set meal available. One which you'll hear nothing but praise for is the *Geetanjalee*, Msanifu Kombo St, which offers a 'deluxe' thali for KSh 55. Both the food and service are excellent.

Similar is the *New Chetna Restaurant*, Haile Selassie Rd directly under the Cosy Guest House. Here it's South Indian vegetarian food (masala dosa, idli, etc) and sweets, plus they offer an all-you-can-eat set vegetarian lunch for KSh 55. It's a very popular restaurant.

Excellent tandoori specialities can be found at the very popular *Splendid View Restaurant*, opposite, but not part of, the Hotel Splendid. They have things like chicken, lamb, fruit juices and lassis and you can eat well here for around KSh 60. There are tables outside and inside.

Swahili Food For coastal Swahili dishes made with coconut and coconut milk, the *Swahili Curry Bowl*, Tangana Rd off Moi Ave, is recommended. Prices are reasonable. It's also one of *the* places for coffee and ice cream. Don't bother trekking out here on a Sunday as it's closed then.

Another excellent place, and one you should try at least once, is the *Recoda Restaurant* on Nyeri St in the old town. It's a hugely popular place amongst the locals and the tables are set up along the footpath. The atmosphere is great and the waiters are keen

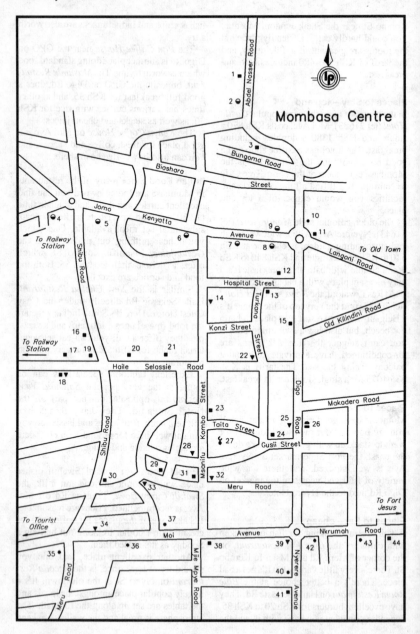

Mombasa Centre

■ PLACES TO STAY

1   New People's Hotel
3   Al Nasser Lodging
11 Hydro Hotel
12 Down Town Lodge
13 Mvita Hotel
15 Balgis Hotel
16 New Al Jazira Hotel
17 Midnight Guest House
18 Cosy Guest House
19 Visitor's Inn
20 Continental Guest House
21 Hotel Fortuna
23 Hotel Hermes
24 New Britania Boarding & Lodging
29 Hotel Relax
30 Glory Guest House
31 Hotel Splendid
38 Castle Hotel
41 Manor Hotel
44 New Palm Tree Hotel

▼ PLACES TO EAT

14 Geetanjalee Restaurant
18 New Chetna Restaurant
22 Blue Room Restaurant
25 Masumin Restaurant
28 Splendid View Restaurant
32 Blue Fin Restaurant
33 Pistacchio Ice Cream & Coffee Bar
34 Kenya Coffee House
39 Fontanella Restaurant

● OTHER

2   Buses to Malindi & Lamu
4   Coast Bus
5   Bus Station
6   Cat Bus
7   Mawingo Buses
8   Akamba Bus
9   Malindi Taxi Bus
10 Market
26 GPO
27 Sheik Jundoni Mosque
35 Rainbow House Night Club
36 Barclays Bank
37 Istanbul Bar
40 Fort Supermarket
42 Executive Air Services
43 American Express

to explain what is available that day – usually dishes such as beans in coconut, grilled fish (KSh 50), meat, superb chapatis and salad. You may well find yourself coming back here each night (it's not open at lunch time).

The restaurant in the *Hydro Hotel* also has some Swahili dishes but certainly lacks the atmosphere of the Recoda.

Places to Eat – more expensive

Going up in price, the rooftop restaurant in the *Hotel Splendid* catches the breeze in the evenings and has surprisingly moderate prices, although the food is only mediocre; KSh 40 to KSh 70 for a main meal, KSh 55 for steak with chips and vegetables. Don't come here with any ideas of having a quick meal, as the service is hardly lightning fast.

The *Pistacchio Ice Cream & Coffee Bar* is a small café near the Hotel Splendid. Not only does it have excellent ice cream, but the fruit shakes (expensive at KSh 19) are great. The buffet lunch or dinner for KSh 80 is not bad value although the selection is limited. They also serve à la carte dishes such as spaghetti.

For Chinese tucker you could try the *Chinese Overseas Restaurant* on Moi Ave, just north of the tusks. It's not cheap, however, as dishes are priced in the range of KSh 80 to KSh 150.

The *Fontanella Restaurant* is in a shady courtyard on the corner of Digo Rd and Moi Ave. The extensive menu runs the whole gamut from fish & chips (KSh 40) through steaks (KSh 90) to lobster thermidor (KSh 300) – great for a splurge or just a quiet beer or snack.

Entertainment

For an ice-cold beer in the heat of the day many people go to the terrace of the *Castle Hotel* which overlooks Moi Ave. It's the nearest thing you'll find to the Thorn Tree Café in Nairobi but the comparison isn't really valid. If you prefer more local colour and a livelier place then try the *Istanbul Bar* also on Moi Ave, on the opposite side of the road from the Castle Hotel towards the tusks. It's primarily a pick-up joint but attractively set under *makuti* (plaited palm leaf) roofs and has an atmosphere not unlike that of the Modern 24-Hour Green Bar in Nairobi.

For a night out the *Rainbow House Night Club*, on the corner of Meru Rd and Moi Ave, is perhaps a little less daunting than some of the others and is a popular disco and African reggae club. It's always filled with local ragers, sailors, whores and travellers. There are plenty of other excellent reggae clubs in the suburbs which are very cheap and good fun – ask around.

Things to Buy

Mombasa isn't the craft entrepôt you might expect it to be, but it's not too bad either. The trouble is that there are a lot of tourists and sailors who pass through this port with lots of dollars to shed in a hurry. Bargains, therefore, can take a long time to negotiate. There are a lot of craft stalls along Msanifu Kombo St near the junction with Moi Ave; along Moi Ave itself from the Castle Hotel down to the roundabout with Nyerere Ave; along Jomo Kenyatta Ave close to the junction with Digo Rd; and a few in the old town close to Fort Jesus.

Have a look around – you might find something. Makonde wood carvings, stone chess sets and animal or human figurines, basketwork, drums and other musical instruments and paintings are the sorts of things that are sold.

Biashara St west of Digo Rd is the centre for fabrics and *kangas,* those colourful, beautifully patterned, wraparound skirts complete with Swahili proverbs, which most East African women wear (other than Hindus) even if they wear it under a *bui bui* (black wraparound skirt). You may need to bargain a little over the price (but not too much). What you get is generally what you pay for and, as a rule, they cost around KSh 150 a pair (they are not sold singly). Assuming you are willing to bargain, the price you pay for one will reflect the quality of the cloth. Buy them in Mombasa if possible. You can sometimes get them as cheaply in Nairobi but elsewhere prices escalate rapidly.

Getting There & Away

Air Four companies operate flights from Mombasa to Malindi and Lamu. They are Eagle Aviation Ltd (tel 316054), Prestige Air Services Ltd (tel 21443), Skyways Airlines (tel 432167) and Equator Airlines.

They all have two flights per day in either direction between Mombasa, Malindi and Lamu. Flights from Mombasa depart at 8.30 am and 2.15 pm and arrive Malindi 30 minutes later. The fare to Malindi is KSh 900 one way and KSh 1800 return. Children over two years old pay full fare. Check-in time is 30 minutes before departure and the baggage allowance is 10 kg per person. Most of the time they don't hassle if your baggage is over 10 kg but, even if they do, excess charges are minimal. The airport departure tax is KSh 50 at Malindi and Mombasa but there's no charge at Lamu.

Kenya Airways also flies Mombasa-Malindi-Nairobi in either direction once daily except on Saturday, using F50 propeller planes. If you're relying on these flights to get back to Nairobi to connect with an international flight, then make absolutely sure you have a confirmed booking or, preferably, go back a day before. Don't join the legion of people who are left on the tarmac tearing out their hair because they didn't reconfirm and the flight was full.

There is a KSh 50 departure tax payable on all flights out of Mombasa.

Bus & Matatu In Mombasa bus offices are mainly along Jomo Kenyatta Ave. For Nairobi buses there are many departures daily in either direction (mostly in the early morning and late evening) by, among others, Coast, Cat, Mawingo, Malaika and Akamba. The fare ranges from KSh 165 to KSh 190 and the trip takes seven to eight hours including a meal break about halfway.

To Malindi there are also many departures daily in either direction from early morning until late afternoon by several bus companies and matatus. Buses take up to three hours; matatus about two hours. In Mombasa they all depart from outside the New People's Hotel, Abdel Nasser Rd. See the Malindi section for more details and for the alternative of hiring a share-taxi.

It's possible to go straight through from Mombasa to Lamu but most travellers stop en route at Malindi.

For Tanga and Dar es Salaam in Tanzania, Cat Bus has departures on Monday, Wednesday and Friday at 4 pm. The journey to Tanga takes about eight hours (KSh 145) and all the way to Dar es Salaam about 20 hours (KSh 360).

For buses and matatus to the south of Mombasa you first need to get off the island via the Likoni ferry (see below).

Train Trains to or from Nairobi operate in either direction at 5 and 7 pm, arriving at 8 and 8.30 am respectively. There's nothing to choose between the two trains, except that on the 5 pm train you get to see a bit more of the countryside before it gets dark. The fares in KSh are:

Destination	1st class	2nd class	3rd class
Voi	155	74	35
Tsavo	205	95	50
Nairobi	505	236	118

You should make a reservation as far in advance as possible as demand sometimes exceeds supply. The booking office at the station in Mombasa is open daily from 8 am to noon and 2 to 6.30 pm.

Boat Depending on the season, it's possible to get a ride on a dhow to Pemba, Zanzibar or Dar es Salaam in Tanzania. It's hard to pin them down as to what day they are likely to depart, let alone what time, so you need to be persistent. Hang around at the dhow dock in the old town and ask a lot of questions. Once you find a boat, make sure you are well stocked as the trip takes anything up to 36 hours to Dar es Salaam (if it goes via Zanzibar) and you get zilch in the way of food or facilities. The toilet is a long-drop perched out over the back of the boat. Expect to pay around KSh 240 to Dar es Salaam.

If you're interested in yachts or boats to India or the Seychelles it's worth getting out

to Kilibi Creek. Most of the people with yachts moor at Kilibi Creek because mooring berths at the Mombasa Yacht Club are very expensive. If you want to make enquiries you can get to Kilibi by going to Tom's Beach, about 1½ km out of Mombasa centre, near the Seahorse Hotel.

Getting Around
Airport Transport There's a regular public bus which goes to the airport and costs KSh 3.50. Any 'Port Reitz' matatu will take you past the airport turn-off (ask to be dropped off) from where it's about a 10 minute walk. The standard taxi fare is KSh 190.

Likoni Ferry This ferry connects Mombasa Island with the southern mainland and runs at frequent intervals throughout the night and day. There's a crossing every 20 minutes on average between 5 and 12.30 am; less frequently between 12.30 and 5 am. It's free to pedestrians. To get to the ferry from the centre of town take a Likoni matatu from outside the GPO on Digo Rd.

Taxi Mombasa's superbly beaten up old taxis are not metered so make sure you agree on a fare before stepping in.

Harbour Cruises Cruises around the old harbour and Kilindini Harbour – the modern harbour where container ships and the like dock – are available through the Castle Hotel, Moi Ave. There is a four hour lunch cruise at 10.30 am which includes lunch, live music and swimming but it's not cheap at KSh 840. The evening cruise departs at 6.30 pm and costs KSh 1080. For information or bookings phone 315569. It may well be possible to find cheaper cruises if you ask around.

South of Mombasa

The real attractions of the coast south of Mombasa are the beaches, and although it is basically all resort hotels, there are a few options for the budget traveller – at Tiwi and Diani beaches.

All the beaches are white coral sand and are protected by a coral reef so there is no danger from sharks when you go swimming. Tiwi is probably the best beach – at Diani all the sand has washed away in places leaving just a coral bed.

SHELLY BEACH

Shelly Beach is the closest beach to Mombasa and as such, is not a bad place to swim if you just want to day-trip from Mombasa. There is no budget accommodation available here, nor any restaurants, so forget it for a long stay unless you want an expensive resort.

Places to Stay

The only place here is the *Shelly Beach Hotel* (tel 451001), about three km from the Likoni ferry. As far as resort hotels go it's not a bad place, and seems to be popular with British tour groups. Most people seem to prefer swimming in the pool than in the sea just a few metres away. Half board rates are KSh 710/1080 for single/double rooms, or KSh 920/1680 with air-con. In the off season it may be possible to get a reduction on these rates, but don't expect too much.

Getting There & Away

From the Likoni ferry, take the first turn to the left after the bus stand. From here it's a 30 minute walk and there are occasional matatus and enough traffic to make hitching possible.

TIWI BEACH

Next along the coast is Tiwi Beach, and it too is about three km off the main coast road, along a dirt track which winds its way through the coastal scrub. This is the best beach to head for if you have your own camping gear, and it's also probably the least developed of all the beaches so you need to be fairly self-sufficient.

The beach itself is a lot wider than at Shelly Beach.

Places to Stay & Eat

The only relatively cheap place is the very popular *Twiga Lodge* (tel (0127) 4061). It is certainly *the* place to camp along the coast as you can pitch your tent just a few metres from the water, there's plenty of shade and if you have a vehicle there's room for it too. The cost is KSh 35 per person to camp, and KSh 35 to rent a tent, although they only have a couple of these so don't rely on one being available. Single/double rooms go for KSh 240/430 with breakfast, while the cheapest *bandas* (circular, grass-thatched traditional-style houses) cost KSh 430 for four people. The restaurant does good meals for around KSh 60 to KSh 95, and also serves snacks and drinks. It's a good place to stay as there's usually an interesting mix of people here.

Right next door to the Twiga Lodge are the *Coral Cove Sea Cottages* (tel (0127) 4164). The bandas here range in price and facilities from KSh 110 for a basic double with no facilities to KSh 190 for a double with bath and cooking gear. It's a very pleasant place to stay and popular with young expatriate workers.

If you are putting your own food together the Twiga Lodge has a basic provision store which has a limited range of tinned and fresh foods. About 500 metres back along the track towards the main road there's a small fruit and vegie stall which also has limited stocks of varying quality.

Getting There & Away

The buses and matatus drop you at the start of the dirt access road, from where it's a three km or 45 minute walk. This road used to be notorious for muggings but these days there are plainclothes police 'patrolling' (read: sitting under a tree) the road and it is supposedly safe. Certainly if there are a few (or more) of you it should be no problem, but solo travellers are still better off waiting for a lift. There's a few trucks and cars going in and out so you shouldn't have to wait long.

DIANI BEACH

Diani is *the* typical 'tropical paradise' beach:

coconut palms, dazzling white sand and clear blue water. It's also the most developed – virtually the whole beach front is taken up with resorts ranging from expensive upwards, although it must be said that most of these resorts are not too intrusive as they have low lines and local materials are often incorporated.

The Diani Beach road runs parallel to the coast about 100 metres inland, so the resorts are well shielded from the outside world.

Information & Orientation

Just south of the T-junction where the road from the main Mombasa-Tanzania highway joins the smaller beach road is a shopping centre which seems to expand by the month to cash in on the package tourists with bulging wallets. Not only are there a couple of expensive souvenir shops and boutiques, but more usefully there is a couple of fairly well-stocked supermarkets where you can stock up with goodies, two banks, a petrol station and a couple of car hire places. The branch of Barclays Bank is open Monday to Friday from 10 am to 3 pm.

Also here is the rather unusual South Coast Fitness Centre where you can hire go-karts to zip around the track they have there. You can also rent bicycles but these are such dreadful old clunkers that it's hard to imagine going any distance on one. They cost KSh 40 for half a day or KSh 80 for a full day, and there's a KSh 200 deposit.

Back up on the main road is the village of Ukunda, and it's here that you find the nearest post office and basic lodges to Diani. It's a few km and it's advisable not to walk – this road is also notorious for people getting mugged. It's not a problem as there are plenty of matatus (and KBS buses) running backwards and forwards all day on their way to or from Likoni.

Places to Stay – bottom end

The only cheap place is *Dan Trench's*, behind the Trade Winds Hotel. It's not well signposted but is the place on the right, directly behind the Trade Winds. Unfortunately, this place, like Dan himself, is on the

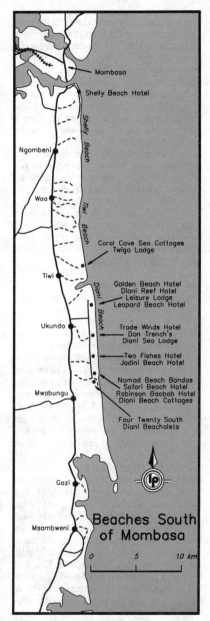

Beaches South of Mombasa

Mombasa
Shelly Beach Hotel
Ngombeni
Shelly Beach
Waa
Tiwi Beach
Coral Cove Sea Cottages
Twiga Lodge
Tiwi
Diani Beach
Golden Beach Hotel
Diani Reef Hotel
Leisure Lodge
Leopard Beach Hotel
Ukunda
Trade Winds Hotel
Dan Trench's
Diani Sea Lodge
Two Fishes Hotel
Jadini Beach Hotel
Nomad Beach Bandas
Safari Beach Hotel
Robinson Baobab Hotel
Diani Beach Cottages
Mwabungu
Four Twenty South
Diani Beachalets
Gazi
Msambweni
0   5   10 km

way down which is a real shame as it's been a travellers' haven for years. The camping is the best bet at KSh 35 per person but the site is not all that wonderful and as it's not securely fenced, theft is a real problem. The small dorm here has just four beds at KSh 60 each. There's just one very small double banda, the thatch roof of which would be an entomologist's delight. If you're staying here you can use the beach and bar at the Trade Winds Hotel.

It's also possible to camp at the *Diani Beachalets* (see below) for KSh 50 per person, with use of the communal cooking facilities included. It's far safer than at Dan's as there is an askari on duty at night.

In Ukunda, the village up on the main road, the *Sunset Lodge* charges KSh 60 for a double but as the whole idea of coming to Diani is to stay at the beach there seems little point in staying at Ukunda.

Places to Stay – middle

There's only one place in this category, and that's the *Diani Beachalets* (tel (01261) 2180) at the southern end of the beach, a couple of hundred metres past the end of the bitumen, where the buses and matatus stop and turn around. The site itself is quite pleasant, the only problem being that at this end of the beach there's no sand – it's just a flat coral bed. This may just be a seasonal phenomenon but certainly didn't look like it. Unlike the up-market resorts, there's no pool, restaurant or bar, although there is a tennis court which you can use for a small fee.

There is a range of bandas available; the cheapest ones have their own fridge but communal cooking and washing facilities. For KSh 180 for two they are pretty good value, although you need to bring all your own food or be prepared to go to the Diani shopping centre as nothing is sold on site. The more expensive rooms and cottages are fully self-contained and range in price from KSh 235 for a double room up to KSh 565 for a six bed cottage. These rates increase by 50% in the high seasons (July to September, December to February).

The next cheapest option are the *Four Twenty South* beach cottages, right at the southern end of the bitumen road. These are fully self-contained, sleep four people and cost from KSh 505 to KSh 790 depending on the season. You need to supply your own bed linen and food.

Places to Stay – top end

The other hotels along this beach cost from KSh 540 per person per day including breakfast in the off season up to around KSh 2400 for a double with full board in the high season. They all offer much the same – air-con rooms, swimming pool, bars, restaurant and have water sports equipment for hire. The better ones, such as the Trade Winds, have been designed with the environment in mind and are fairly unobtrusive; others, such as the Golden Beach, are something of an eyesore.

From north to south along the strip the hotels are:

Golden Beach Hotel, from KSh 560 per person with breakfast

Diani Reef Hotel (tel (01261) 2175), KSh 2160/2400 a single/double with breakfast, up to KSh 2400/2880 for full board

Leisure Lodge (tel (01261) 2011), KSh 1620/2160 for full board

Leopard Beach Hotel (tel (01261) 2111), KSh 805/1265 for half board

Trade Winds Hotel (tel (01261) 2016), KSh 1500/1980 for full board

Diani Sea Lodge (tel (01261) 2114), KSh 1390/1860 for full board

Two Fishes Hotel (tel (01261) 2101), KSh 1680/2280 for full board

Jadini Beach Hotel (tel (01261) 2021), KSh 1740/2665 with breakfast

Nomad Beach Bandas (tel (01261) 2155), KSh 1105/2185 with breakfast

Safari Beach Hotel (tel (01261) 2088), KSh 1980/2940 with breakfast

Robinson Baobab Hotel (tel (01261) 2026), KSh 2160/3120 for full board

Diani Beach Cottages, KSh 1080/2160 for half board

Places to Eat

If you are staying at Dan Trench's or Diani Beachalets and want to put your own food together the supermarkets at the Diani shopping centre are pretty well stocked. For fresh fruit and seafood buy from the hawkers who come around to these places on a bicycle with baskets laden.

For a regular meal, the restaurant in the *South Coast Fitness Centre* does a reasonable fish, chips and salad for KSh 80. Also in the shopping centre is the *Cheers* restaurant but it is more expensive.

If you feel like lashing out, the *Trade Winds Hotel* has a huge buffet lunch for KSh 155 or dinner for KSh 180. The other resorts no doubt have similar deals.

Ali Barbour's is an expensive seafood restaurant set in a coral cave between the Trade Winds Hotel and the Diani Sea Lodge. Don't expect to have any change out of KSh 720 for two people. Opposite the Two Fishes Hotel is the *Bush Baby Restaurant*, an open-air restaurant and night club and not a bad place for a bop.

Entertainment

Apart from the hotel bars and fairly sterile and contrived discos, there's not much to do at night. There is a troupe of local dancers who do the rounds of the resorts to give the resort guests their dash of local colour but that's about the limit of it.

Getting There & Away

Diani is the most accessible beach if you are dependent on public transport. From the Likoni ferry there are KBS buses (No 32) every 20 minutes or so from early morning until around 7 pm. The fare is KSh 9.50 and the trip takes about 30 minutes.

There are also plenty of matatus doing the Likoni-Diani trip. They do the journey slightly faster and cost KSh 8.50.

When the buses and matatus get to Diani they first head north along the Diani road then turn around and go to the southern end of the bitumen where they turn again and head for Likoni. Just tell the driver where you want to get off.

SHIMONI

Shimoni is right out at the end of a small peninsula 76 km south of Likoni, and not far from the Tanzanian border. Apart from a

couple of expensive lodges catering to game fishers, there's very little in Shimoni apart from a couple of coral caves which are worth exploring.

Offshore lies Wasini Island which is well worth a visit.

Places to Stay

The *Pemba Channel Fishing Club* (tel Msambweni 5Y2) and the *Shimoni Reef Fishing Club* (tel Msambweni 5Y9) both charge around KSh 1320/1920 for full board.

If you have your own gear it should be possible to camp on Wasini Island.

Getting There & Away

There are a couple of direct buses and matatus daily to and from Likoni.

WASINI ISLAND

Wasini is a small unspoilt island off the Shimoni peninsula. The peace and quiet found here is very soothing – there are no cars, roads, running water and the only electricity comes from generators. It's a great place to relax, experience the undiluted Swahili culture and organise a visit to the Kisiti/Mpungutu Marine National Park.

On a wander around you can come across Muslim ruins, local women weaving mats, men preparing for fishing by mending nets and making fish traps, the coral garden with its odd-shaped stands of old coral that you can walk through and beautiful pools.

Snorkelling

Masood Abdullah, who runs the Mpunguti Restaurant, can arrange trips to the marine park to see some of the best fish and coral in Kenya. His dhow will take you for KSh 250 per person to the park, plus KSh 20 per person for snorkel and mask. It's also possible to hire a dugout canoe and do it yourself for KSh 100.

Places to Stay & Eat

The *Mpunguti Restaurant* has the only accommodation on the island. Camping is possible on the grass for KSh 35 per person, or else you can pay KSh 360 for a small cottage including three excellent meals a day. If you are camping bring supplies from Mombasa; there's fish, coconuts, maize flour and rice for sale on the island but very little else.

Getting There & Away

From Likoni take a taxi to Shimoni for KSh 480, or one of the few KBS buses for KSh 35. You could also take a Lunga Lunga matatu but would then have to hitch the 14 km from the main road to Shimoni.

Once at Shimoni take a matatu boat for the 10 minute ride to Wasini for KSh 40 return. Alternatively, the dhow from the Mpunguti Restaurant on the island runs if there are five or more people (KSh 50 per person).

SHIMBA HILLS NATIONAL RESERVE

This national reserve is in the hills behind the coast south of Mombasa, directly inland from Diani Beach. The forest setting is beautiful but the game is not prolific. There is a baited water hole at the Shimba Hills Lodge, and so it's possible you'll see leopards and plenty of elephants but not much else. Other animals which frequent the reserve include the rare sable antelope – a tall and compact animal with beautifully curved horns on both the male and female. The adult bull is a dark brown on the upper body and white below, while the female is a lighter brown. The animals are, unfortunately, often killed by poachers for meat, and this is the only park or reserve where they are found.

Places to Stay

The *camp site* has a superb location on the edge of the range with views right down to Diani Beach. It's about three km from the main gate, which itself is about three km from the village of Kwale.

The only alternative to camping is the *Shimba Hills Lodge* (tel Nairobi 335807) where single/double rooms cost KSh 1535/4200 with half board. For some curious reason children under seven years old are not admitted to this lodge. The water hole here is baited to attract a few animals and is floodlit at night.

Getting There & Away

There are KBS buses to Kwale, from where it shouldn't be too difficult to hitch to the park entrance. Once there, however, you may have a long wait for a vehicle. The road from Kwale to Kinango, the next inland town, actually passes through the northern part of the park and there's a chance of seeing animals from the KBS buses. The No 34 bus goes from Likoni to Kwale.

North of Mombasa

MOMBASA TO KILIFI

Like the coast south of Mombasa, the north coast has been well developed almost two-thirds of the way up to Kilifi with resort complexes which take up much of the beach frontage. Most of them cater to package tourists on two to three week holidays from Europe but there is scope for individual initiative here and there although only the 'youth hostel' at Kanamai and Jauss Farm at Vipingo genuinely fall into the budget accommodation bracket.

As with Shelly and much of Tiwi beaches south of Mombasa, the northern beaches are plagued with seaweed which clogs them and makes swimming an often unpleasant experience. Only at the expensive resort hotels are people employed to minimise this inconvenience by raking it into piles and either burning it or burying it. Elsewhere you literally have to jump into the soup.

Going north from Mombasa the names of the beaches are Nyali, Bamburi, Shanzu, Kikambala and Vipingo.

Mamba Village

Mamba Village (tel 472709) is north of Mombasa on the mainland opposite Nyali Golf Club in the Nyali Estate. It's a crocodile farm set amongst streams, waterfalls and wooden bridges. If you've never seen a crocodile farm with reptiles ranging from the newly born to the full grown, here's your chance. Personally, I've seen a lot of these farms in the past and I don't find them that interesting. They're often just a collection of concrete and wire-mesh cages with thousands of young crocodiles up to five years old and a few token, full grown adults to pull in the punters. You pay through the nose to see them, too, even though the owners of the farms are making megabucks selling skins to Gucci and the like.

Bamburi Quarry Nature Trail

Further up the coast this nature trail (tel 485729) has been created on reclaimed and reforested areas damaged by cement production activities which ceased in 1971. Once the forest was established, the area was restocked with plants and animals in an attempt to create a mini replica of the wildlife parks of Kenya. At present, animal species represented include eland, oryx, waterbuck, buffalo, wart hog, bush pig, various monkeys and many different varieties of birds. There's also what the owners claim to be an 'orphan' hippo which was introduced as a baby from Naivasha and which has remained bottle-fed ever since. A likely story!

The complex also includes a fish farm, crocodile farm, reptile pit and plant nursery. The centre is open daily from 2 to 5.30 pm. Feeding time is at 4 pm. To get there take a public bus to Bamburi Quarry Nature Trail stop (signposted) on the main Mombasa-Malindi road.

Places to Stay – bottom end

There are very few cheap places to stay on the beaches north of Mombasa. Even places way back from the beach with nothing special going for them can be remarkably expensive.

One of the few genuine cheapies is the *Kanamai Conference Centre* (tel Kikambala 46, PO Box 46) at Kikambala Beach which was previously a youth hostel but is no longer affiliated to the IYHF. Here they have dormitory beds for KSh 40 to KSh 50 (depending on the number of bunks per room) and one, two and three bedroom self-contained cottages which cost KSh 360/470/660 in the low season and KSh 420/550/780

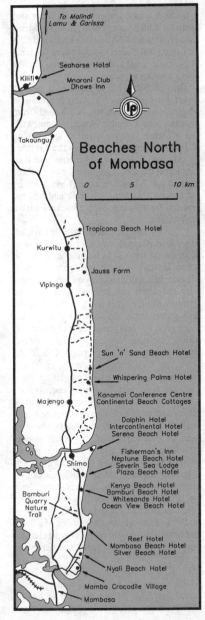

To Malindi Lamu & Garissa

Seahorse Hotel
Kilifi
Mnarani Club
Dhows Inn

Takaungu

Beaches North of Mombasa

0   5   10 km

Tropicana Beach Hotel
Kurwitu
Jauss Farm
Vipingo

Sun 'n' Sand Beach Hotel

Whispering Palms Hotel

Kanamai Conference Centre
Continental Beach Cottages
Majengo

Dolphin Hotel
Intercontinental Hotel
Serena Beach Hotel

Fisherman's Inn
Neptune Beach Hotel
Severin Sea Lodge
Plaza Beach Hotel
Shimo

Kenya Beach Hotel
Bamburi Beach Hotel
Whitesands Hotel
Ocean View Beach Hotel
Bamburi
Quarry
Nature
Trail

Reef Hotel
Mombasa Beach Hotel
Silver Beach Hotel

Nyali Beach Hotel

Mamba Crocodile Village
Mombasa

in the high season respectively. You can also camp for KSh 35 per person per night. Meals are available for KSh 50 (breakfast) and KSh 70 (lunch and dinner) – expensive for what is basically ugali and chicken stew. There's also a laundry service.

The trouble with this place is getting there! First you have to take a matatu to Majengo on the Mombasa-Kilifi road (from near the New People's Hotel in Mombasa). Get off when you see a yellow sign saying 'Camping Kanamai'. Go down the dirt track by this sign for about 300 metres and then turn left at the fork. Continue for about three km and you'll find it on the left-hand side by the beach. It's a long, hot walk and lifts are few and far between. With a backpack it's a major effort.

Close by are the *Continental Beach Cottages* which are described by people who have stayed there as 'a bargain' at KSh 480 for a bungalow with bedroom, lounge, kitchen, bathroom and air-con but which are very run-down and infested with ants and termites. On the other hand, you may be the only guests there and there's a good swimming pool, bar and restaurant and a pleasant beach. Cheap meals (omelette and chips and curries) are available for around KSh 50. As with the Conference Centre, the only problem about this place is getting there from the main road. Taxis are expensive.

If you're staying at either of the above places and want a change of scene or a cold beer, the Whispering Palms Hotel is about 15 minutes walk north along the beach. Breakfasts here cost KSh 50 and you can use their swimming pool for KSh 60 per day.

Further up the coast at Vipingo, about 40 km north of Mombasa, there is *Jauss Farm* (tel (01251) 2218) which consists of a camp site, a number of budget chalets as well as luxury farm houses on 85 hectares of a dairy and tropical fruit farm with its own quiet and unspoiled silver sand beach. The camp site is equipped with showers and toilets and costs KSh 60 per person per night. Tents, which sleep two to three people, can be rented for KSh 90 per night. The budget chalets are fairly basic twin rooms with clean

beds and mattresses, and toilets and showers have to be shared with those occupying the camp site. The chalets are lockable and cost KSh 120 per person per night.

The luxury farm houses are fully furnished and include the use of lounge, verandah, bathroom, shower and fully equipped kitchen. They cost KSh 1020 for one with a double bedroom and KSh 1800 for one with four double bedrooms.

Breakfasts can be ordered for KSh 60 and evening meals for KSh 120 plus there's an on-site shop which sells meat, fruit and vegetables as well as canned goods. Other facilities include a swimming pool, full workshop facilities including the services of an expert mechanic, a video lounge, snorkel and scuba gear rental and 24 hour Masai security staff.

Bookings can be made by telephoning the above number but you are welcome to simply turn up and take pot luck. The place is managed by British-based Into Africa Safaris (tel (0883) 347784), 143 Stafford Rd, Caterham CR3 6JH, UK. They can arrange budget camping safaris from Jauss Farm and many tours leave from the camp site.

There are interesting Arab ruins and slave trading caves nearby.

It's much easier to get to Jauss Farm than to the Kanamai 'youth hostel' since it's only one km from the main Mombasa-Malindi road. To get there, take a bus or matatu from Mombasa and get off two km north of Vipingo where there's a sign for Jauss Farm. It's about 15 minutes walk from there towards the beach to the farm (again signposted). Alternatively, get off in Vipingo village and telephone the farm from the post office. They'll come and collect you free of charge most of the time.

Places to Stay – top end

Virtually all the other hotels along this stretch of the East African coast before you arrive at Kilifi are resort complexes and cater largely for package tourists from Europe. Most of them are so self-contained that many of those staying there hardly ever see anything of Africa other than Mombasa airport, the inside of minibuses, the hotel itself and Black Kenyan waiters. As at the hotels south of Mombasa and at Malindi, many cater almost exclusively for one specific European nationality whether they be British, German or Italian (French people don't feature prominently in East African tourism). There's precious little intermingling.

All the hotels compete furiously with each other to provide the utmost in creature comforts, mellow surroundings, day trips and sports facilities and there's little to choose between them though it's generally true to say that the further you get from Mombasa, the cheaper and less ritzy they become.

Down at Nyali Beach – the closest to Mombasa – even places which don't face the sea and are in no way hotel resorts, and which you might imagine should be fairly cheap given the facilities they offer, can be surprisingly expensive. The *Bamburi Chalets*, for example, which offers self-contained cottages with two bunk beds, two normal beds, shower, cooking facilities, gas stove and refrigerator and use of swimming pool cost between KSh 1440 and KSh 3000 per night depending on the season. Likewise, the *Fishermen's Inn*, further up the coast, charges KSh 720/960 for singles/doubles with breakfast in the low season and KSh 960/1200 in the high season. Meals at the Fishermen's will cost you between KSh 180 and KSh 300.

It's unlikely that if you intend to stay at any of the genuine resort complexes that you'll be reading this book since you'd have reserved your hotel via an agent and your air fares would be included in a package deal. Should you wish to make your own arrangements for staying at any of the resort complexes, however, here's a selection of the hotels.

Nyali Beach The following resorts are at Nyali Beach:

Mombasa Beach Hotel (five star) PO Box 90414, Mombasa (tel 471861). Singles/doubles/triples for KSh 1620/2160/3025 with breakfast

Nyali Beach Hotel (five star) PO Box 90414,

Mombasa. Singles/doubles for KSh 2580/3360 with breakfast and KSh 2750/3695 for full board

Reef Hotel (four star) PO Box 82234, Mombasa (tel 471771). Singles/doubles/triples for KSh 2480/3455/4735 with breakfast and KSh 2670/3840/5310 for full board

Silver Beach Hotel (four star) PO Box 81443, Mombasa. Singles/doubles for KSh 1105/1680 with full board

Kenyatta-Bamburi Beach Further north are the following hotels:

Bamburi Beach Hotel (three star) PO Box 83966, Mombasa (tel 485611). Singles/doubles/triples for KSh 1045/1370/1720 with breakfast and KSh 1080/1440/1830 for half board

Kenya Beach Hotel (three star) PO Box 95748, Mombasa. Singles/doubles for KSh 1315/1980 for full board

Neptune Beach Hotel (three star) PO Box 83125, Mombasa (tel 485701). Singles/doubles/ for KSh 1250/1765 with breakfast and KSh 1320/1910 for full board

Ocean View Beach Hotel (four star) PO Box 81127, Mombasa. Singles/doubles for KSh 1105/1470 for full board

Plaza Beach Hotel (four star) PO Box 88299, Mombasa. Singles/doubles for KSh 1200/1705 with breakfast and KSh 1550/2630 for full board

Severin Sea Lodge (five star) PO Box 82169, Mombasa (tel 485001). Singles/doubles/triples for KSh 1550/1775/3325 with breakfast and KSh 1740/2160/3900 for full board

Whitesands Hotel (four star) PO Box 90173, Mombasa (tel 485926). Singles/doubles/triples for KSh 1705/2330/2990 with breakfast and KSh 1800/2520/3275 for full board

Shanzu Beach At Shanzu Beach there are the following resorts:

Dolphin Hotel (five star) PO Box 81443, Mombasa. Singles/doubles for KSh 1140/1740 for full board

Intercontinental Hotel (five star) PO Box 83492, Mombasa (tel 485811). Singles/doubles/triples for KSh 2285/2900/3560 with breakfast and KSh 2635/3655/4735 for full board

Serena Beach Hotel (five star) PO Box 90352, Mombasa (tel 485721). Singles/doubles at KSh 2640/3360 for half board plus KSh 145 supplement per person for full board

Kikambala Beach Finally, Kikambala Beach offers the following:

Whispering Palms Hotel (three star) PO Box 5,

Kikambala (tel Kikambala 3, 4, 5, 6). Singles/doubles/triples for KSh 1380/1860/2605 for full board

Sun 'n' Sand Beach Hotel (four star) PO Box 2, Kikambala (tel Kikambala 8). Singles/doubles for KSh 1645/2195 with breakfast and KSh 1740/2390 for full board

Takaungu

Right up at the top end of this long line of beaches close to Kilifi is the village of Takaungu. It's supposedly the oldest slave port on the Kenyan coast – Zanzibar is the oldest. It's worth a visit if you have the time. The local people are very superstitious and no-one goes down to the beach at night except the fishers. If you can speak Swahili you'll hear many weird stories going around which date back to the slaving days. It's an interesting place right off the beaten track where you won't meet any other travellers.

Places to Stay Rooms can be rented in private houses in Takaungu for around KSh 35 per night. Ask around in the tea shops.

KILIFI

Other than Mtwapa Creek, just north of Mombasa, Kilifi is the first major break in the coastline between Mombasa and Malindi and there is still no bridge across the creek, though this will soon change with the completion of the Japanese-funded suspension bridge. Once this happens, the ferries which transport all vehicles from one side to the other will be made redundant and a colourful era of Kenyan coastal history will come to an end. So too, perhaps, will the livelihoods of those who presently sell packets of roasted cashew nuts (the cheapest in Kenya) and fruit juices to travellers waiting for the arrival of the ferries on either side of the creek.

Kilifi has been a backwater for many years, ignored by developers yet coveted by discerning White Kenyans, artists, writers and adventurers from various parts of the world who have gradually bought up most of the land overlooking the wide creek and the ocean and built, in many cases, some quite stunning and imaginative houses. They form a sort of society within a society and keep largely to themselves. Without an introduction, it's unlikely you'll meet them though sailing a yacht into the creek would probably secure you an invitation! Kilifi Creek is a popular anchorage spot for yachties in this part of the world and you can meet them in the evening at the Seahorse Hotel off to the left of the main road on the northern side of the creek.

So why stop off in Kilifi? The answer to this is mainly for the contrast it offers to Mombasa and Malindi and for the Mnarani Ruins on a bluff overlooking the creek on the Mombasa side. Very few travellers ever see these ruins yet they're well preserved and just as interesting as those at Gedi though not as extensive. The beach, too, on either side of the creek is very pleasant and doesn't suffer from the seaweed problem which plagues the beaches further south. The only problem is access which is mostly through private property though you can walk along it from the ferry landing at low tide.

The present district centre of Kilifi is on the northern bank of the creek.

Information

Kilifi consists of the small village of Mnarani (or Manarani) on the southern bank of the creek and Kilifi itself on the northern bank. It's a small town which you can walk around within minutes.

There's a good variety of shops (including a small bookshop), a lively open-air market and an enclosed fruit and vegetable market, a post office, a number of basic hotels and two banks.

Barclays Bank is open Monday to Friday from 8.30 am to 1 pm and on Saturday from 8.30 to 11 am. The Kenya Commercial Bank keeps the same hours.

Azzura Tours (tel 2385, PO Box 2, Kilifi) on Kilifi's main street can organise car rental, boat trips and safaris and is an agent for Garissa Express buses.

Mnarani Ruins

Mnarani, on the southern bank of Kilifi Creek overlooking the ferry landing, was once one of the string of Swahili city-states

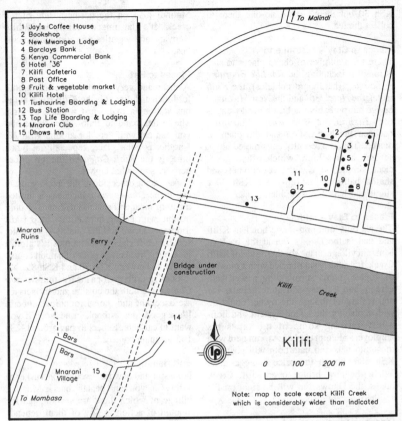

1 Jay's Coffee House
2 Bookshop
3 New Mwangea Lodge
4 Barclays Bank
5 Kenya Commercial Bank
6 Hotel '36'
7 Kilifi Cafeteria
8 Post Office
9 Fruit & vegetable market
10 Kilifi Hotel
11 Tushaurine Boarding & Lodging
12 Bus Station
13 Top Life Boarding & Lodging
14 Mnarani Club
15 Dhows Inn

To Malindi

Mnarani
Ruins

Ferry

Bridge under
construction

Kilifi Creek

Bars

Bars

Mnarani
Village

To Mombasa

Kilifi

0   100   200 m

Note: map to scale except Kilifi Creek
which is considerably wider than indicated

which dotted the East African coast. Excavations carried out in 1954 showed that the site was occupied from the end of the 14th century to around the first half of the 17th century after which it was destroyed by marauding Galla tribespeople. The principal ruins here include the Great Mosque with its finely carved inscription around the mihrab (niche in mosque showing direction of Mecca), a group of tombs to the north (including one pillar tomb), a small mosque dating from the 16th century, and parts of the town wall and a gate. There's also a large and forbiddingly deep well whose shaft must go down at least as far as the low tide level of the creek.

Mnarani was associated with Kioni, at the mouth of Kilifi Creek on the same side, and with Kitoka, about 3½ km south of here on the northern bank of Takaungu Creek. A carved stone with an interlaced ornament, probably from a mihrab, was found at Kioni on the cliff above the creek and is presently in the Fort Jesus museum at Mombasa. The ruins at Kitoka include a mosque similar to the small mosque at Mnarani along with a few houses. All these settlements were subject to Mombasa.

The Mnarani ruins are just above the southern ferry landing stage and the path to them (about 300 metres) is prominently signposted on the main road. Entry costs

KSh 30 but there's often no-one there to collect the fee.

Places to Stay – bottom end

There are a number of cheap places to stay at in Kilifi including the *Top Life Boarding & Lodging* (hardboard cubicles), the *Kilifi Hotel*, the *Hotel '36'* and the *New Mwangea Lodge* but probably the best place to stay is the *Tushaurine Boarding & Lodging* between the bus station and the open-air market. This is a recently constructed hotel, several storeys high, which offers good, clean, simple rooms with mosquito nets and shared bathroom facilities for KSh 70 a single and KSh 145 a double.

Places to Stay – middle

There's only one mid-range hotel in Kilifi and that is the *Dhows Inn* at the back of Mnarani village on the southern side of Kilifi Creek. It's a fairly small place with a number of double rooms surrounding a well-kept garden, and a lively and quite popular bar and restaurant though the owner could do with replacing the sound system and definitely retiring some of the tapes his employees attempt to play. A room here with mosquito nets and bathroom will cost you KSh 300 though the price is negotiable. When the new bridge over Kilifi Creek opens, the Dhows Inn will be right on the southern access road.

Places to Stay – top end

The large resort complex at Kilifi is the somewhat exclusive *Mnarani Club* on the southern side of Kilifi Creek and quite close to the Dhows Inn. It caters largely to package tourists from Germany and Switzerland and it's these people who keep the craft shop owners of Mnarani village smiling. Despite its size, the Mnarani Club is hardly visible from the main road or even from a boat on the creek since it's constructed of local materials including some enormous makuti roofs and surrounded by beautifully landscaped gardens full of flowering trees.

The other top-range hotel is the *Seahorse Hotel* off to the left of the main Mombasa-Malindi road on the northern side of the creek. It's patronised mainly by White Kenyans and yachties of various nationalities.

Places to Eat

A cheap and very popular place to eat both for lunch and dinner is the *Kilifi Hotel* at the bus station (actually just a patch of dirt). They offer standard Indo-African fare and you can eat well here for around KSh 30. Another popular place, especially at lunch time, is the *Kilifi Cafeteria* though prices here are somewhat higher.

Across the other side of the creek, you can eat at the *Dhows Inn* which has a limited menu of meat and seafood dishes. The only trouble with eating here is that food takes forever to arrive and the quality is variable: sometimes it's good, sometimes it's almost inedible. The average price of a main course would be between KSh 70 and KSh 85.

For a splurge, go for a meal at the *Mnarani Club* where both the cuisine and the service are excellent and the surroundings superb. It's a good idea to book in advance if you want to eat here. Expect to pay around KSh 145 for main courses.

Entertainment

For a spit-and-sawdust evening on Tusker or White Cap you can't beat the bars in Mnarani village of which there are several, but the amount of action in any of them depends largely on how many tourists brave the 200 metres or so of dirt road between the Mnarani Club and the village. Don't expect cold beers at any of these places.

The bar at the *Dhows Inn* is usually pretty lively and you can be assured of cold beer – ice-cold if you get there early.

The *Mnarani Club* has a nightly floor show – usually of tribal dancing – followed by a live African band which plays till late. The residents can be quite shy about dancing so don't expect too much action. On the other hand, this means you have the floor to yourself. Entry to the show and dance costs KSh 100 unless you ate dinner there or the manager takes a liking to you. Nonresidents can rent windsurfing equipment from this hotel during the day for KSh 100 per hour.

Other travellers have recommended the far more informal *Kilifi Club* directly opposite the Mnarani Club on the northern side of the creek.

Getting There & Away
All the buses and matatus which ply between Mombasa and Malindi stop at Kilifi but getting on a bus at Kilifi to go to either Mombasa or Malindi can be problematical since they're often full. Matatus are a much better bet.

The Tara Bus company also run buses between Kilifi and Nairobi twice daily. They depart Kilifi at 7.40 am and 7.40 pm and arrive in Nairobi at 4.30 pm and 4.30 am respectively.

MALINDI
Malindi was an important Swahili settlement as far back as the 14th century and often rivalled Mombasa and Paté for control of this part of the East African coast. It was also one of the very few places where the early Portuguese mariners found a sympathetic welcome, and today you can still see the cross which Vasco da Gama erected as a navigational aid.

These days, on account of its excellent beaches, it has experienced a tourist boom similar to that north and south of Mombasa and resort hotels are strung out all the way along the coast. On the other hand, it still retains a recognisable African centre where commerce, business and everyday activities, which aren't necessarily connected with the tourist trade, continue. Cotton growing and processing, sisal production and fishing are still major income earners. It isn't, however, a Lamu or Zanzibar. The streets here are relatively wide and straight and there are few buildings more than a century old.

It's a popular port of call for travellers heading north from Mombasa or south from Lamu, and the beaches here have one major advantage over those close to Mombasa and that is the absence of seaweed. There's a break in the coral reef at this point along the

coast and this prevents the build up of seaweed which often chokes the beaches around Mombasa and makes swimming unpleasant. It also means that the surf is able to make it right through to the shore. Sharks are no problem either. The only drawback to Malindi is the brown silt which flows down the Galana River at the northern end of the bay during the rainy season which makes the sea very muddy. For the rest of the year it's perfect and even during the rainy season you can largely avoid the muddy waters by going to the beaches south of town.

Information
Tourist Office There is a tourist office next door to Kenya Airways opposite the shopping centre on the Lamu road. The staff are helpful and enthusiastic and they have a lot of information about the area, particularly accommodation.

Bank Barclays Bank is open Monday to Friday from 8.30 am to 1 pm and 2.30 to 5 pm and on Saturday from 8.30 am to noon. In the low season it's often closed on Saturdays. The Standard Chartered Bank has much the same hours of opening.

Immigration There is an office next to the Juma Mosque and pillar tombs on the waterfront (see street map for location).

Railway Bookings Travel agents in Malindi can make you bookings on the Mombasa-Nairobi railway but will charge you KSh 50 for the service. Save money and make your own booking by making a KSh 5 telephone call to (011) 312221.

A Warning
Don't walk back to your hotel along the beach at night. Many people have been mugged at knife point. Go back along the main road (which has street lighting) or take a taxi. You also need to exercise caution if returning from the Baobab Café to the Youth Hostel late at night – people have even been mugged along that short stretch of road,

although you're probably safe if you're part of a group.

Malindi Town

Malindi has a pedigree going back to the 12th century and was one of the ports visited by the Chinese junks of Cheng Ho between 1417 and 1419, before the emperor of China prohibited further overseas voyages. It was one of the few places on the coast to offer a friendly welcome to the early Portuguese mariners and to this day the pillar erected by Vasco da Gama as a navigational aid still stands on the promontory at the southern end of the bay. The cross which surmounts this pillar is of Lisbon stone (and therefore original) but the supporting pillar is of local coral.

There's also the partial remains of a Portuguese church, which is undoubtedly the one which St Francis Xavier visited on his way to India. A painting of the crucifixion is still faintly visible. Not far to the north are a number of pillar tombs and the remains of a mosque and a palace. Other than this, however, little remains of the old town. The nearest substantial ruins from pre-Portuguese days are at Gedi, south of Malindi.

Siva instrument

Malindi Marine National Park

The most popular excursion from Malindi is to the Marine National Park to the south of town past Silver Sands. Here you can rent a glass-bottomed boat to take you out to the coral reef. Snorkelling gear is provided though there generally aren't enough sets for everyone at the same time. The variety and colours of the coral and the fish are simply amazing and you'll be surprised how close you can get to the fish without alarming them. On the other hand, the area is getting a little overused and there's been quite a lot of damage to the coral. Shell collectors have also degraded the area.

The best time to go is at low tide and, preferably, on a calm day when the water will be clear. It's advisable to wear a pair of canvas shoes or thongs for wading across the coral to where the boats are moored in case you step on a sea urchin or a stone fish. These fish are extremely well camouflaged and can inflict a very painful sting. The boat trips generally last an hour.

You can arrange these trips in Malindi – people come round the hotels to ask if you are interested in going. The usual price is KSh 145 per person which includes a taxi to take you to and from your hotel, hire of the boat and the park entry fee. You may be able to get it for less if you bargain hard but you won't be able to knock too much off this price.

Scuba Diving

If you'd like to go scuba diving you can do this from the Driftwood Club at Silver Sands. A dive costs KSh 400 (KSh 450 if they do it at Watamu including the cost of transport). They also have a diving school here for those who wish to learn but it's not cheap at KSh 2500.

Places to Stay – bottom end

There are a number of cheap, basic lodges in the centre of town, but they're usually fairly noisy at night and you don't get the benefit of sea breezes or instant access to the beach.

Most travellers prefer to stay in one of the hotels on the beach.

In Town If you do want to stay in the centre of town there are several places where you can get a single room for around KSh 55 and a double for KSh 70 to KSh 95 with shared bathroom facilities. They include the *New Safari Hotel* (KSh 40 for a dormitory bed and KSh 95 for a double room), the *Malindi Rest House* (KSh 95 a double) and the *Lamu Hotel.* Also here is the *Tana Hotel* which has been thoroughly renovated, is very clean and comfortable and costs KSh 120/180 for singles/doubles with shared bathroom or KSh 240 for a self-contained double.

Closer to the beach is *La Fortuna Hotel,* which changes its name to the 'Lucky Lodge' according to the particular tourist season. It is fairly basic but provides mosquito nets and costs KSh 95 a double with shared bathroom.

Right over the other side of town and not far from the beach is the very clean *Youth Hostel* (tel 20531) which is popular with those who are quite happy with a dormitory bed. There's a fridge for use by residents but mosquito nets are not provided. Each room has six beds at a cost of KSh 40 per person. No membership card is required to stay here.

On the Beach The main area for budget hotels in this position is close to the fishing jetty. Probably the best value for money is the *Travellers' Inn* which is very pleasant and clean, has excellent showers and mosquito netting on the windows. It costs KSh 145/180/240 for singles/doubles/triples between September and April and a little less during the rest of the year. The staff are very friendly and soft drinks and food are available. It's very popular so you may find it's full during the high season.

Also quite popular is the *Metro Hotel,* although it's hard to see why since all but one of the rooms (a triple at KSh 212 which overlooks the ocean and gets the sea breezes) are dingy, hardboard-partitioned cells. The other rooms cost KSh 70 a single and KSh 140 a double with mosquito coils and towels provided. The showers are hopeless and the water supply is totally inadequate. It's run by Mary Wanini who's very friendly and helpful. The beer garden at the front of the property, which used to be a very lively place, is currently closed but may reopen.

The other similarly priced place to stay here is *Gilani's Hotel* next door to the Metro, but many travellers who have stayed here have described the place as 'a dump'.

About 1½ km south of the above hotels along the coast road is the very popular *Silver Sands Camp Site* (tel 236), which is used by long-distance overland safari trucks whenever they come through. It costs KSh 50 per person to camp here (less in the low season) and there are good toilets and saltwater showers as well as freshwater taps but very little shade. Those without tents can rent one for KSh 90. There are also two types of banda for rent. The so-called 'green' bandas, of which there are three, are actually tents under a makuti roof and cost KSh 160/300/450 for singles/doubles/triples (less in the low season) and have mosquito nets, own shower and toilet and electric lights. The 'white' bandas are actually huts and have two single beds, mosquito nets, screened windows, electric lights and lockable doors but common shower and toilet facilities. They cost KSh 205/385/540 for singles/doubles/triples (less in the low season). Bicycles can be rented for KSh 45 per day.

The beach here is excellent and is protected by a coral reef. At the far end of the camp site there's a snack bar with a large shady terrace which offers cold drinks and snacks such as hamburgers and a shop selling everything from suntan lotion to biscuits. They also offer breakfast for KSh 40 and dinners from KSh 40 and up.

The only other cheap place to stay is the *Lutheran Guest House* (tel 21098) at the opposite end of town off the Lamu road. This place is excellent value and very popular. It offers singles/doubles without bathroom for KSh 95/180 and self-contained singles/doubles at KSh 130/240. They also have a bungalow which is fully equipped and which has two bedrooms for KSh 360 per night, KSh 1200 per week or KSh 4200 per month.

Places to Stay – middle

There are few places to stay in this price range and their tariffs vary considerably from one month to another. The cheapest is *Ozi's Bed & Breakfast* (tel 20218, PO Box 60, Malindi), overlooking the beach near the fishing jetty. Singles/doubles/triples cost KSh 180/265/395 with breakfast in the low season (May to July) and KSh 240/480/720 in the high season (16 December to 9 January). For the rest of the year it is KSh 190/300/450 (4 September to 10 November and 10 January to 30 April) and KSh 215/395/595 (29 July to 3 September and 11 November to 15 December).

Half-board rates are available for KSh 90/180/270 extra for singles/doubles/triples. All prices are inclusive of government taxes. Checkout time is 10 am and children between the ages of three and 10 are given a 50% discount.

More expensive are *Malindi Cottages/Robinson Island* (tel 20304, 21071; PO Box 992, Malindi), out on the Lamu road and close to the Eden Roc Hotel. This place consists of several fully furnished and self-contained cottages surrounding a swimming pool each with two bedrooms, a sitting room, kitchen and verandah. Facilities include a refrigerator, gas cooker, mosquito nets and fans. Each cottage sleeps up to five adults and costs KSh 480 during May and June, KSh 720 during August. For the rest of the year they cost KSh 575.

The owners of this place also run the *Sultan's Cottages* further up the Lamu road where they have one self-contained cottage which sleeps two people for KSh 360 per day. Reservations can also be made in Nairobi (tel 743414/5, PO Box 14960) and Mombasa (Farways Safari Centre Ltd, tel 23307/9, PO Box 87815).

More expensive still are the *African Dream Cottages* (tel 21296, PO Box 939, Malindi), on the Lamu road. All the units here are self-contained (though a cooker costs an extra KSh 120 per day) and have

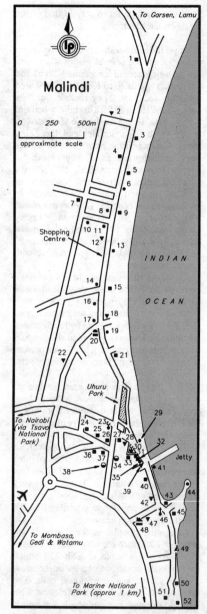

■ PLACES TO STAY		
	43 Sailfish Club	10 Snake Park &
	45 Scorpio Villas	Falconry
1 Sultan's Cottages &	48 Youth Hostel	11 Stardust Club
Mango Inn	49 Silver Sands Camp	13 Tourist Office &
3 Sea View Lodges	Site	Kenya Airways
4 Malindi Cottages/	50 Driftwood Club	14 Barclays Bank
Robinson Island	51 Coconut Village	16 Slot Machines
5 Eden Roc Hotel	52 The Tropical Village	17 Police
7 Lutheran Guest		19 Standard Chartered
House	▼ PLACES TO EAT	Bank & Prestige
9 African Dream		Air Services
Cottages	2 Eddie's Restaurant	20 Post Office
15 Blue Marlin Hotel	12 Beer Garden	23 Mosque
21 Lawford's Hotel	18 Palm Garden	29 Craft Market
24 Lamu Hotel	22 Urafiki Bar &	30 Juma Mosque &
25 Malindi Rest House	Restaurant	Pillar Tombs
26 New Safari Hotel	28 Bahari Restaurant	34 Tana River Buses
27 Lucky Lodge/	39 I Love Pizza	35 Malindi Fishing Club
La Fortuna	42 Baobab Café- Pint	38 Malindi Bus Service
31 Gilani's Hotel	Pot	41 Fish Market
32 Metro Hotel	47 Travellers Café	44 Vasco da Gama
33 Ozi's Bed &		Cross
Breakfast	● OTHER	46 Portuguese Church
36 Salama Lodge		
37 Tana Hotel	6 Tropicana Club 28	
40 Travellers' Inn	8 Shopping Centre	

four beds. There's a swimming pool and private beach. In the low season (30 April to 16 July and 27 August to 8 October) the units cost KSh 540 per day, KSh 2880 a week or KSh 4800 a fortnight. In the high season (1 January to 26 February and 30 July to 27 August) they cost KSh 1080 per day, KSh 6000 a week or KSh 10,800 a fortnight. Intermediate prices prevail for the rest of the year. A bar and restaurant are in the planning stages.

Just beyond the Eden Roc Hotel on the Lamu road are *Sea View Lodges* which consist of a number of round makuti-roofed cottages divided in half to form two double rooms each with its own shower and toilet. The prices here are much the same as at African Dream Cottages but the place is considerably run-down, breakfasts take forever to arrive, the swimming pool resembles an algal broth and the bar is moribund. A substantial discount on the posted tariff can be expected if you look like you're about to go elsewhere.

Places to Stay – top end

Malindi's top-range hotels are strung out along the beach front both north and south of the town centre and more are being built each year. Some are very imaginatively designed and consist of clusters of makuti-roofed cottages in beautifully landscaped gardens full of flowering trees. Others are fairly standard beach hotels. All of them have swimming pools and other sporting facilities and many have a discotheque. They cater mostly, but not exclusively, to package tourists from Europe on two to three week holidays and they all seem to pitch their business at a specific nationality – British, German or Italian. Very little intermingling seems to take place and you can definitely feel you've come to the wrong spot in some hotels if you don't belong to the dominant nationality. It's a common trait with package tourism anywhere in the world.

Most of the hotels impose a supplement over the Christmas and New Year periods which can be quite considerable (KSh 360, for example), so bear this in mind if you intend to stay at this time of the year.

Closest to town on the Lamu road are *Lawford's Hotel* (tel 20440/1, PO Box 20, Malindi), and *Blue Marlin Hotel* (tel 20440/1, PO Box 54, Malindi). Both cater largely to German tourists and there's even a German consulate in the Blue Marlin Hotel! Lawford's is the cheaper of the two and in the low season it offers bungalows for KSh 600 and KSh 720 for singles and KSh 840 and KSh 960 for doubles. Rooms in the main building are KSh 840/1080/1510 for singles/doubles/triples. For the rest of the year the bungalows are KSh 840 to KSh 960 for singles and KSh 1130 to KSh 1270 a double. Rooms in the main building at this time are KSh 1055/1405/1970 for singles/doubles/triples. All prices are for half board and include taxes.

The Blue Marlin offers a somewhat higher class of accommodation with superb facilities and costs KSh 810/1080/1510 for singles/doubles/triples in the low season and KSh 950/1250/1765 in the high season. There are also rooms with four beds for KSh 1945/2270 in the low/high seasons. All prices are for half board and include taxes. Full board costs an extra KSh 70 per person per day.

Both Lawford's and the Blue Marlin offer discounts to Kenyan residents.

Further up the Lamu road is the *Eden Roc Hotel* (tel 20480/1/2, PO Box 350, Malindi), one of the few hotels which seems to have a mixed clientele. It's also one of the few places with tennis courts though these are not open to nonresidents. The hotel has three seasons: 1 December to 15 April (high), 16 April to 30 June (shoulder) and 1 July to 30 November (low). Standard rooms (fan, shower, toilet and balcony) cost KSh 490/575/685 for breakfast/half board/full board per person in the high season and KSh 295/380/480 in the low season. Deluxe rooms (air-con, shower, toilet and balcony) cost KSh 530/610/730 per person in the high season and KSh 330/420/530 in the low season. There's also a somewhat cheaper bungalow with shower, fan and toilet as well

as more expensive double suites. All prices include taxes and service charge. The hotel has a swimming pool and a popular discotheque which goes until dawn every night.

South of town, the top-range hotels stretch all the way from the path leading to the Vasco da Gama monument down to Casuarina Beach and the Malindi Marine National Park.

First is the *Sailfish Club* (tel 20016, PO Box 243), which is a very intimate hotel with only nine rooms all of them self-contained and air-conditioned. It's essentially for those interested in big-game fishing and caters largely for charters.

Opposite is *Scorpio Villas* (tel 20194, 20892; PO Box 368, Malindi) which has 17 cottages spread over some 1½ hectares of beautiful tropical gardens with three swimming pools and just 50 metres from Silver Sands beach. All the cottages are fully furnished in Lamu style and come complete with your own cook/house steward. There's an excellent restaurant and bar within the complex. It's Italian owned and Italians form the bulk of the clientele. B&B charges are KSh 840 for a double cottage, KSh 1560 for a cottage with four beds and KSh 2160 for a cottage with six beds. Half board costs a further KSh 300 per person per day and full board KSh 480 per person per day.

Further down the beach beyond the Silver Sands Camp Site is the *Driftwood Club* (tel 20155, PO Box 63, Malindi). This was one of the first beach resorts to be built at Malindi and it's different from the other hotels as it's used more by individual travellers rather than package groups. Although it gets more of a mixture of nationalities, the clientele is mainly British and White Kenyan. The club offers a variety of rooms from just KSh 550/755 for singles/doubles with shared bathroom facilities to luxury cottages with two bedrooms, two bathrooms, living room, verandah, air-con and use of private swimming pool for KSh 4800. Singles/doubles/triples in the main building cost KSh 790/1055/1475 with fan and bathroom and KSh 1030/1295/1715 with air-con and bathroom. There are also more expensive rooms with air-con and bath for KSh 1270/1535/ 1955. These prices include breakfast and all taxes and service charge. The bar, restaurant and other facilities are open to nonresidents on payment of a temporary membership fee of KSh 10 per day.

Next down the beach is *Coconut Village* (tel 20928, 20252; PO Box 868, Malindi), where the clientele is mainly Italian. Double rooms with full board here cost between KSh 720 and KSh 1920 per person per day depending on the time of year (and there are no less than eight 'seasons'!). Single occupancy rates are plus 50% of the above prices. Children under two years old are free of charge and those under 12 years old pay 50% of the above rates. Half board prices are KSh 100 less per day and with breakfast only they're KSh 200 less per day. All prices include taxes and service charge. The hotel has a popular open-air, makuti-roofed disco-theque which overlooks the beach.

Next door is the *Tropical Village* (tel 20256) where, again, the clientele is mainly Italian. Rooms here in the high season cost KSh 1320 to KSh 2040 a single for half board and KSh 1440 to KSh 2280 a double for full board.

Next on down is the *African Dream Village* (tel 20442/3/4) which is owned by the same people who run the African Dream Cottages on the Lamu road. Unlike the cottages, this is a fully fledged beach resort which has double rooms with shower, toilet, verandah, air-con and telephone, and a range of facilities which include swimming pool, sports centre, bars and restaurant. Full board rates in the high season are KSh 2250/3000/3240 for singles/doubles/triples and KSh 1140/1680/1620 in the low season. There are two shoulder periods where the rates are intermediate.

Beyond the above is the *Silver Sands Villas* (tel 20842, PO Box 91, Malindi) which consists of a main building with single and double rooms and a number of two and four person self-contained villas. Half board in the main building costs KSh 2510/3815 for singles/doubles in the high season and KSh 1465/2225 in the low season. A two

person villa in the high season costs KSh 4610 and KSh 2690 in the low season. Four person villas cost KSh 7630 to KSh 8700 in the high season and KSh 2690 to KSh 5075 in the low season. All prices include taxes and service charges.

Further down the beach still are three other resort hotels – the *White Elephant, Jambo Club* and *Kivolini Hotel.*

Places to Eat – cheap

There's not a lot of choice in this range as many of the cafés which travellers used to use in the past have closed down. Two which have survived the tourist boom and which remain popular are the *Travellers' Café* and the *Baobab Café – Pint Pot,* both very close to each other near the Portuguese Church. The Travellers' Café offers Western and African-style meals for between KSh 30 and KSh 55. The Baobab is a full-on Western-style restaurant with a good selection of dishes, including seafood, ranging from KSh 50 to KSh 65, fruit juices from KSh 14 to KSh 18 and breakfasts from KSh 18 and up. Part of the premises is a bar where you can get ice-cold beers at normal prices.

Other cheap meals can be found in the restaurants at the hotels in the centre of town. The fare is standard Indo-African. The *Bahari Restaurant* offers much the same sort of thing plus seafood and very good milk shakes. Also worth visiting for its excellent milk shakes and fruit juices is the *Malindi Fruit Juice Garden* in the market. Further afield, it's worth trying the *Urafiki Bar & Restaurant* on Kenyatta Rd which offers ugali and meat stew for around KSh 30. The bar here gets very lively later on in the evening and the jukebox knows no other setting than full bore.

Slightly more expensive but excellent value is the *Palm Garden* on Lamu road opposite the petrol station. They do very tasty food here at prices similar to those at the Baobab Café. The menu is mainly sea-foods and curries. Make sure you eat in the main part of the restaurant under the makuti-roofed shelters at the back rather than in the part which fronts onto the street as here they only do snacks, fruit juices and the like.

Ozi's Bed & Breakfast is also worth checking out for reasonably priced curries (around KSh 70) though they do have more expensive seafood dishes such as prawns and lobster.

It's also possible to eat German-style food relatively cheaply at the *Beer Garden* on the Lamu road if you choose the simple dishes such as wurst and potato salad or something similar but most of the dishes here will be at least KSh 120.

Places to Eat – more expensive

For a splurge it's worth trying the *Driftwood Club* where you have to pay KSh 10 per day for temporary membership. This entitles you to the use of the swimming pool, hot showers, bar and restaurant. The prices are very reasonable – lunch for KSh 65, dinner for KSh 80, good snacks for KSh 21 and up (smoked sailfish and prawn sandwiches, etc), and à la carte seafood main dishes for KSh 40 to KSh 80. It's especially convenient if you are staying at the Silver Sands Camp Site.

At the *Eden Roc Hotel*, simply brave the *haute couture* and the Ambre Soleil and have one of their set meals in the dining room. It's open to nonresidents. For KSh 85 you get soup, avocado vinaigrette and a self-service buffet consisting of a choice of some 10 different salads, pepper steak, vegetables and three sweets plus coffee.

I Love Pizza in front of the fishing jetty and close to the Metro Hotel is a popular place for a splurge. As you might expect, it serves Italian food (pizzas and pastas for around KSh 80) but also such things as chicken casserole and seafood dishes though these will cost you KSh 145 and up. It's open from 11 am to 11 pm daily.

Recently opened and an excellent place to while away a long lunch hour or a whole evening is *Eddie's* (tel 20283) which is probably one of the best seafood restaurants in Malindi as well as having a tastefully intimate atmosphere. It's open from noon to 2.30 pm and 7.30 to 10.30 pm and there's a swimming pool which you can cool off in before eating your meal. Expect to pay KSh 120 and up.

Entertainment

Because Malindi is a holiday resort there are a lot of lively bars and discos to visit in the evening, some of which rock away until dawn. The most famous of them is the *Stardust Club* which generally doesn't get started until late (10 or 11 pm) and costs KSh 50 entry. You can also get a meal here. The *Tropicana Club 28* is similar but can get very hot and sweaty as it's quite a small place and is often packed out. Entry costs KSh 100.

There's also a disco at least once a week – usually on Wednesdays – at *Coconut Village* past the Driftwood Club and, if you get there early enough, you won't have to pay the entry charge. It's a pleasant place to dance away the evening and you won't drown in perspiration as it's open-air under makuti roofs right on the beach. The bar is incredible and is worth a visit just to see it. It's built around a living tree with one of the branches as the bar top!

Another place which is worth checking out if you want to catch a film is the *Malindi Fishing Club*, right next to the Metro Hotel. It's a very attractive, traditionally constructed building with a makuti roof. There's a bar and snacks are available. The clientele, mainly British, are friendly, although some of the videos they show are decidedly daggy.

The two liveliest tourist bars are the *Beer Garden* and the *Baobab Café* though the tape collection at the Beer Garden is positively antediluvian. Bring your own. The beers are ice-cold at both of them. One of the liveliest African bars is the *Urafiki Bar & Restaurant* with its deafening jukebox that seems to play Franco nonstop. It closes by 11.30 pm and the beers are often lukewarm but, somehow, you don't notice the Arctic fetish of ice-cold beer.

Things to Buy

A few years ago there were many craft shops lining both sides of the road between Uhuru Park and the post office but major drainage works forced them to relocate onto the beach below Gilani's Hotel and the Metro. This has made it much more of a sellers' market since why else would you go there. All the same, prices are reasonable (though you must, of course, bargain) and the quality is high. They offer makonde carvings, wooden animal carvings, soapstone and wooden chess sets, basketware and the like. If you have unwanted or excess gear (T-shirts, jeans, cameras) you can often do a part-exchange deal with these people.

Getting There & Away

Air Four companies operate flights to Malindi from Mombasa and Lamu. They are Eagle Aviation Ltd (tel Malindi 21258, Mombasa 316054, Lamu 3119), Prestige Air Services Ltd (tel Malindi 20860/1, Mombasa 21443), Skyways Airlines (tel Malindi 21260, Mombasa 432167, Lamu 3226), and Equator Airlines (tel Malindi 2053). All these companies have their offices on the Lamu road in Malindi though they are more spread out in Mombasa.

They all have two flights per day in either direction between Mombasa and Malindi and between Lamu and Malindi. Flights from Mombasa depart at 8.30 am and 2.15 pm and arrive in Malindi 30 minutes later. From Lamu they depart at either 10 or 11 am and 4 pm and arrive in Malindi 40 minutes later. The fare from Lamu to Malindi is KSh 900 one way and KSh 1800 return. Children over two years old pay full fare. Check-in time is 30 minutes before departure and the baggage allowance is 10 kg per person. Most of time they don't hassle if your baggage is over 10 kg but, even if they do, excess charges are minimal. The airport departure tax is KSh 50 at Malindi and Mombasa but there's no charge at Lamu.

Kenya Airways also flies Nairobi-Malindi-Mombasa in either direction once daily except on Saturday using F50 propeller planes. If you're relying on these flights to get back to Mombasa or Nairobi to connect with an international flight then make absolutely sure you have a confirmed booking or, preferably, go back a day before.

Bus & Matatu Three bus companies operate between Mombasa, Malindi and Lamu on a daily basis. They are Malindi Bus Service, Tana River Bus Service and Garissa Express and they all have offices in Mombasa, Malindi and Lamu. There are several departures daily in either direction between Mombasa and Malindi which take about 2½ hours and cost KSh 55. There are also matatus which do this run taking about two hours and costing KSh 70. There's no need to book in advance from Mombasa if you turn up early enough in the morning. In Mombasa the buses leave from outside the New People's Hotel early in the morning. Matatus leave from the same place all day until late afternoon and go when full.

Both the buses and matatus literally *fly* up and down this coast road as though they were being pursued by a marauding army of *shifta* (bandits) in high-speed Land Cruisers, and they pack in as many punters as they possibly can. I counted 138 people on one such bus and that didn't include the driver and his mate!

At present, there's a ferry crossing between Mombasa and Malindi over Kilifi Creek (about halfway) but a Japanese company is busy building a huge suspension bridge and approach roads and, when finished, this will cut the journey time between Mombasa and Malindi by about half an hour. In the meantime, on arrival at Kilifi, you have to get off your bus or matatu, walk onto the ferry, and reboard on the other side.

Buses from Lamu to Malindi leave from the mainland between 7 and 7.30 am. The fare from Lamu to Malindi is KSh 120 and the journey takes about five hours. You must book tickets in advance for this journey as there's heavy demand for tickets.

Share-Taxi It's also possible to find Peugeot 504 station wagons which do the journey between Mombasa and Malindi. They go when full (seven passengers) and cost KSh 60 per person. You'll find them at the bus station in Malindi but only in the mornings. Commissioning a normal taxi to take you between Mombasa and Malindi will cost you far more.

Train You can make advance reservations for Kenyan Railways at most of the large hotels in Malindi but they'll charge you KSh 50 for the service. All they do for this is make a telephone call to Mombasa railway station. You can do it yourself for a fraction of the cost.

Getting Around
Bicycle Rental You can rent bicycles from the Silver Sands Camp Site and from outside the Tropicana Club 28 at KSh 45 per day. This is probably the best way to get around town unless you prefer to walk.

Dhow Trips Dhow trips around the area can be arranged at Nelson Safaris which have a small office on the beach front between Gilani's Hotel and the Metro Hotel. The average cost would be KSh 300 per person per day including food.

WATAMU
About 24 km south of Malindi, Watamu is a smaller beach resort development with its own marine national park – part of the Marine National Reserve which stretches south from Malindi. The coral reef here is even more spectacular than at Malindi since it has been much less exploited and poached by shell hunters. In addition, underwater visibility is not affected by silt brought down into the sea by the Galana River.

The coast at Watamu is broken up into three separate coves divided by craggy and eroded headlands and there are a number of similarly eroded islands just offshore. The coral sand is a dazzling white and although there is some shade from coconut palms, you'll probably have to retreat to the cooler confines of a hotel bar or restaurant in the middle of the day. The most southerly cove is fronted entirely by extensive beach resorts and exclusive private houses as is much of the central cove, though less so. The northern cove and part of the headland is covered by the rambling Watamu Beach Hotel at the back of which is the actual village of Watamu.

Before tourist development got underway here, Watamu was a mellow little fishing village of makuti-roofed cottages nestled beneath coconut palms and it still retains much of that atmosphere despite the intrusion of souvenir shops, bars, restaurants and night clubs catering for the tourist hordes. A lot of development has taken place on the outskirts of the village and seems destined to continue.

Information
There is a branch of Barclays Bank in the village of Watamu which is open from 9 am to noon on Monday, Wednesday and Friday.

Watamu Marine National Park
The actual coral reef lies between one and

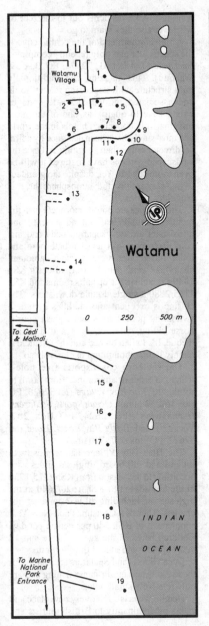

1	Watamu Beach Hotel
2	Nyambene Lodge
3	Blue Lodge
4	Bicycle Hire
5	La Bamba Country Lodge & American Bar
6	Watamu Paradise Restaurant & Cottages
7	Come Back Club/Mustafa's Restaurant
8	Villa Veronica, Mwikali Lodge
9	Barclays Bank
10	Happy Night Bar & Restaurant
11	Hotel Dante Bar & Restaurant
12	Barracuda Inn
13	Seventh Day Adventist Youth Camp
14	Watamu Cottages
15	Blue Bay Village
16	Ocean Sports
17	Seafarers
18	Hemmingways
19	Turtle Bay Beach Hotel

two km offshore and to get to it you'll have to hire a glass-bottomed boat. These can be arranged at any of the large hotels or, alternatively, at the marine park entrance which is at the end of the peninsula just south of the Turtle Bay Beach Hotel. Expect to pay KSh 220 per person. It's worth every cent!

There are also boat trips to a group of caves at the entrance to Mida Creek which are home to a school of giant rock cod many of which are up to two metres long. Diving equipment is usually necessary to get down to their level since, most of the time, they remain stationary on the bottom.

Places to Stay – bottom end

Budget accommodation has always been something of a problem in Watamu but the choice is getting better. The best deals are probably to be found by asking around among the local people for a room in a private house. Most of the people who offer such rooms specifically request not to be included in a guide book so it's fair to respect their wishes. Until you find a private room, the cheapest places to stay are the *Nyambene Lodge* and the *Blue Lodge* in the village. They're both basic lodges with simple rooms and shared bathroom facilities.

Better is the *Villa Veronica Mwikali Lodge*

(PO Box 57, Watamu), opposite the Hotel Dante Bar & Restaurant. This is a very friendly and secure place which offers spotlessly clean rooms with fan, mosquito nets, shower and toilet for KSh 300 a double including breakfast. Close by is the *Iritoni Hotel* which costs KSh 180 a double without breakfast but has only two rooms.

On the main road leaving the village is the *Watamu Paradise Restaurant & Cottages* (tel 32062, PO Box 249, Watamu) which has a number of cottages each containing three double bedrooms with fan, mosquito nets and bathroom. A double here costs KSh 300. It's a very pleasant place to stay and there's a swimming pool in the complex.

Considerably further out of the village, not far from the junction of the road to Gedi, are the *Watamu Cottages*. While they're one of the best deals in Watamu at KSh 145 per person with breakfast, they're often full for obvious reasons but worth trying to get into. There's a swimming pool in the compound.

It may occasionally be possible to get a cheap room at the *Seventh Day Adventist Youth Camp* if there's no group there but don't count on it. You can also camp here if you have your own tent but the facilities are minimal though there is a gas cooker which you can use.

Places to Stay – top end

Top-end hotels take up much of the beach frontage along each of the three coves. As at Malindi, they're mostly resort-type hotels which cater to package tourists' every need and are quite specific as to the European nationality which they appeal to – German, British or Italian.

At the northern end and next to Watamu village is the rambling *Watamu Beach Hotel* (tel 32001, 32010), where most of the German tourists stay. Full board here costs KSh 1175/1650/2295 for singles/doubles/triples and KSh 1245/1790/2435 with air-con. It has all the usual facilities including a swimming pool, open-air and covered bars, a huge restaurant and a plethora of boats

waiting to take residents out to the reef or wherever else they want to go.

At the northern end of the central cove is the spectacular and only recently completed *Barracuda Inn* (tel 61, 70, 74; PO Box 59, Watamu). This amazing and traditionally built structure with its soaring makuti roofs and associated individual rustic cottages would have to qualify as one of the most imaginatively conceived hotels in the world and must surely have been designed by a film set director rather than an architect. Once the landscaped gardens have matured it will be even more superb. Yet, despite the grandeur of its conception, the atmosphere here is languidly informal.

The cottages are double storeyed: upstairs there's a double bed but no air-con, and downstairs are two separate beds and air-con. Each room has its own bathroom and toilet, refrigerator, stereo system, table and chairs and verandah. Full board costs KSh 1440 a double in the upstairs rooms and KSh 1165/2880 a single/double downstairs. The cuisine is excellent and facilities include a swimming pool, tennis and squash courts, horse riding, boating, bars and a discotheque. It's Italian owned and the clientele is mainly Italian though not exclusively so.

The southern cove sports five hotels which, in order of appearance from north to south, are *Blue Bay Village* (tel 32626, PO Box 162, Watamu), *Ocean Sports, Seafarers, Hemingways* (tel 32624, PO Box 267, Watamu), and *Turtle Bay Beach Hotel* (tel 32622, PO Box 457, Watamu).

The Blue Bay Village caters mostly to Italians and full board singles/doubles vary according to the season from KSh 1115/1750 in the low season to KSh 1620/2640 in the high season, including all taxes and service charges. There's a Christmas and New Year supplement of KSh 540 per person per day. Children between the ages of three and 12 years are charged at half the adult rate.

Ocean Sports and Seafarers are mainly for those interested in big-game fishing and are only relatively small hotels.

Hemingways is a relatively new place and caters predominantly to British tourists and

White Kenyans. High season half board rates are KSh 2575/3960 for singles/doubles (KSh 1920/2880 for Kenyan residents) and low season rates are KSh 1190 per person. The full board supplement is KSh 180 per person at any time of year plus there is an additional supplement of KSh 360 per person per day between 20 December and 1 January. All prices include taxes and service charges. Malindi airport transfers are available for KSh 180 each way. The hotel has its own deep-sea fishing boats.

At the far end of the cove is the Turtle Bay Beach Hotel which caters to a mixture of nationalities – mainly British and German. Like the Watamu Beach Hotel, it's a huge, rambling place with all the usual facilities and water sports equipment. Prices vary according to the season and the standard of room. In the low season, full board in a standard twin room costs KSh 630/1250 for singles/doubles and, in the high season, KSh 1185/1580. 'Superior' twin rooms in the low season cost KSh 810/1440 and, in the high season, KSh 1365/1760. Deluxe twin rooms in the low season cost KSh 990/1620 and, in the high season, KSh 1545/1940. All 'superior' and deluxe twin rooms have air-con and a sea view.

Places to Eat

Budget eating facilities are at a premium in Watamu though it is possible to get simple meals at one or other of the local bars in the village.

More expensive but excellent value are the meals at the *Watamu Paradise Restaurant & Cottages* which offers both meat and seafood dishes. The food here is very tasty and pleasantly presented and you can eat well for around KSh 70 so long as you don't go for such things as lobster. The menu, on the other hand, requires a high degree of imaginative interpretation since it sports such bizarre concoctions as 'Onion omqiiate', 'Thaliathel', 'Paper steak', 'Loabster, and 'Crubs'! Not far away and very similar in quality is the *Come Back Club/Mustafa's Restaurant*. It is open all night and has loud music.

Diagonally opposite Mustafa's is the *Hotel Dante Bar & Restaurant* (tel 32243) which offers good Italian fare. The *Happy Night Bar & Restaurant* has ice-cold beers and European-style food, all at Kenyan (rather than lodge) prices. It often has live music or disco nights.

Apart from the places which are just restaurants as such, you can use the facilities at any of the large hotels even if you're not a resident – most of them have a bar, restaurant, swimming pool and disco. It's also possible to utilise their water sport facilities though there will be a charge for this. Scuba diving at the Seafarer Hotel is quite expensive. It's wise to book in advance if you want a meal at any of these hotels.

In addition to the restaurants and hotels at Watamu, there's the *La Bamba Country Lodge, Coco Grill Bar & Restaurant* and the *American Bar* opposite the main entrance to the Watamu Beach Hotel which are worth checking out.

Getting There & Away

There are plenty of matatus from the bus station in Malindi to Watamu throughout the day. They cost KSh 12 and take about 30 minutes. Most of these first go down to the Turtle Bay Beach Hotel after which they turn around and go to Watamu village. On the return journey they generally go direct from Watamu village to Malindi without first going down to the Turtle Bay Beach Hotel.

Getting Around

Bicycles can be hired for KSh 20 per hour or KSh 100 per day from a place next door to the Nyambene Lodge in Watamu village.

GEDI

Some three to four km from Watamu, just off the main Malindi-Mombasa road, are the famous Gedi ruins, one of the principal historical monuments on the coast. Though the ruins are extensive, this Arab-Swahili town is something of a mystery since it's not mentioned in any of the Portuguese or Arab chronicles of the time.

Excavations, which have uncovered such things as Ming Chinese porcelain and glass and glazed earthenware from Persia, have indicated the 13th century as the time of its foundation, but it was inexplicably abandoned in the 17th or 18th century, possibly because the sea receded and left the town high and dry, or because of marauding Galla tribespeople from the north. The forest took over and the site was not rediscovered until the 1920s. Even if you only have a passing interest in archaeology it's worth a visit.

Entry costs KSh 50 (KSh 20 for student card holders). A good guidebook with map is for sale at the entrance.

The site is surprisingly large and surrounded by two walls, the inner one of which was possibly built to enclose a smaller area after the city was temporarily abandoned in the 15th to 16th centuries. In places it actually incorporates earlier houses into its structure. The site is lush and green with numerous baobab trees. Monkeys chatter in the tree tops, lizards rustle in the undergrowth and large, colourful butterflies flutter among the ruins.

The buildings were constructed of coral rag, coral lime and earth and some have pictures incised into the plaster finish of their walls, though many of these have deteriorated in recent years. The toilet facilities in the houses are particularly impressive, generally in a double-cubicle style with a squat toilet in one and a wash stand in the other where a bowl would have been used. Fancier versions even have double 'washbasins' with a bidet between them.

The other notable feature of the site is the great number of wells, many of them of remarkable depth!

Most of the interesting excavated buildings are concentrated in a dense cluster near the entrance gate. There are several other scattered around the site within the inner wall and even between the inner and outer walls. Outside the site, by the car park, there's a small museum with some items found on the site. Other items are exhibited in Fort Jesus in Mombasa.

The Tombs

On your right as you enter the site is the Dated Tomb, so called because the Muslim date corresponding to 1399 has been deciphered. This tomb has provided a reference point for dating other buildings within the complex. Next to it is the Tomb of the Fluted Pillar which is characteristic of such pillar designs found up and down the East African coast. There's another good example of this kind of pillar in Lamu.

The Great Mosque

The Great Mosque originally dates from the mid-15th century but was rebuilt a century later, possibly as a result of damage sustained at the time of Gedi's first abandonment. The mosque is of typical East African design with a mihrab facing towards Mecca. You can see where porcelain bowls were once mounted in the walls flanking the mihrab.

The Palace

Behind the mosque are the ruins of the extensive palace which is entered through an arched door. Once through the doorway, you enter a reception court and then a large audience hall while to the left of this are numerous smaller rooms. Look for the many 'bathrooms' and the room flanking the audience hall with its square niches in the walls intended for lamps. Behind that room is another one with no doorway at all which would probably have been used to store valuables. Entry was by ladder through a small hatch high up in the wall. Beyond this is a kitchen area with a small but still very deep well.

The palace also has a particularly fine pillar tomb while to the right is the Annexe with four individual apartments, each with its own courtyard.

The Houses

In all, 14 houses have been excavated at Gedi, 10 of which are in a compact group beside the Great Mosque and the Palace. They're named after particular features of their design or after objects found in them by archaeologists. They include the House of the Cowrie, House of the Cistern and House of the Porcelain Bowl.

Other Buildings

Follow the signposted path from the Tomb of the Fluted Pillar to the adjoining House of the Dhow and House of the Double Court with a nearby tomb. There are pictures in the wall plaster in these houses. A path follows close to the inner city wall from here to the Mosque of the Three Aisles where you will also find the largest well in Gedi. Beside it is the inner wall of the East Gate from where a path leads to the Mosque Between the Walls; a path cuts back to the car park from here.

Alternatively, from the East Gate you can follow another path right around the inner circuit of the inner wall or divert to the Mosque on the Wall at the southern extremity of the outer wall. The House on the West Wall actually comprises several adjoining houses of typical design while at the northern end of the town there is the more complex North Gate.

Getting There & Away

Take the same matatu as you would to go to Watamu but get off at Gedi village, where the matatu turns off from the main Malindi-Mombasa road. From there it's about a one km signposted walk to the monument along a gravel road.

It's also possible to get a taxi to take you on a round trip from Malindi for about KSh 360 with an hour or more to look around the site. Could be worth it if your time is limited and there's a small group to share costs.

Lamu

In the early 1970s Lamu acquired a reputation as the Kathmandu of Africa – a place of fantasy and other-worldliness wrapped in a cloak of mediaeval romance. It drew all self-respecting seekers of the miraculous, globetrotters, and that much maligned bunch of people called hippies. The attraction was obvious. Both Kathmandu and Lamu were remote, unique and fascinating self-contained societies which had somehow escaped the depredations of the 20th century with their culture, their centuries-old way of life and their architecture intact.

Though Kathmandu is now overrun with well-heeled tourists and the hippies have retired to their rural communes or into business as purveyors of the world's handicrafts, Lamu remains much the same as it has always been – to a degree.

With an almost exclusively Muslim population, it is Kenya's oldest living town and has changed little in appearance or character over the centuries. Access is still exclusively by diesel-powered launch from the mainland (though there's an airstrip on Manda Island) and the only motor-powered vehicle on the island is that owned by the District Commissioner. The streets are far too narrow and winding to accommodate anything other than pedestrians or donkeys. Men still wear the full length white robes known as *khanzus* and the *kofia* caps, and women cover themselves with the black wraparound bui bui as they do in other Islamic cultures, although here it's a liberalised version which often hugs their bodies, falls short of the ankles and dispenses completely with the dehumanising veil in front of the face.

There are probably more dhows to be seen here than anywhere else along the East African coast and local festivals still take place with complete disregard for camera-toting tourists. The beach at Shela is still magnificent and uncluttered and nothing happens in a hurry. It's one of the most relaxing places you'll ever have the pleasure to visit.

At least, that was the story until the late 1980s. Since then a number of pressures have been threatening to undermine the fabric of this unique Swahili settlement. The most important is tourism. In the high season several hundred tourists visit Lamu every day, either by air or overland by bus and launch, and Kenyan Airways is reportedly planning to introduce a DC-9 jet on the route. One of the spin-offs of this influx is that many of the houses at Shela have been bought up by foreigners. As a result, local newspapers (particularly *Mvita*, published in Mombasa) have begun running scare articles with headlines such as 'Lamu Under Siege', and suggesting that tourism is gradually destroying the culture and even physical fabric of Lamu. It's a moot point but neither entirely right or wrong.

The other major pressure is population increase. It's expected that the town's current population of some 12,000 will increase to 30,000 by the end of the century. To accommodate and provide services for all those extra people is going to take some very sensitive planning.

Tourism certainly distorts centuries-old cultural values and economic patterns and can even destroy them but Lamu urgently needs an injection of cash for preservation, restoration, creation of employment, schools and for a cleanup – particularly of the open drainage system. Tourism could be the source of that cash and, to a large extent, is already. And it's hardly fair to blame tourism for corrugated iron replacing traditional wall and roofing materials. Most tourists would much prefer to see traditional materials used.

There was also a spate of overzealousness by the police where local young men seen in the company of *wazungu* (White people) were arrested and accused of illegal currency dealings, selling drugs or some other trumped-up charge. Appeals on their behalf apparently fell on deaf ears and cast a shadow over relationships between residents and visitors. This sort of harassment appears now to have stopped.

What perhaps poses the biggest threat to Lamu – if the rumour is true (and officials are very tight-lipped about this) – is the construction of a US military base on neighbouring Manda Island. Dredgers were already at work in late 1989 in the channel separating the two islands but it wasn't for the benefit of Lamu's tiny harbour since the dredgers were far too close to Manda. Let's all hope it is just a rumour and the dredging was for some other purpose.

History

The 20th century may have brought Lamu a measure of peace and tranquillity but it has not always been that way. The town was only of minor importance in the string of Swahili settlements which stretched from Somalia to Mozambique. Although it was a thriving port by the early 1500s, it surrendered without a fight to the early Portuguese mariners and was generally politically dependent on the more important Sultanate of Paté which, at the time, was the most important island port in the archipelago. It did manage to avoid, until the late 1700s, the frequent wars between the sultanates of Paté, Mombasa and Malindi following the decline of Portuguese influence in the area.

After that there followed many years of internecine strife between the various island city-states of Lamu, Paté, Faza and Siyu, which only ended in 1813 when Lamu defeated the forces of Paté in a battle at Shela. Shortly afterwards Lamu became subject to the Sultanate of Zanzibar which nominally controlled the whole of the coastal strip from Kilwa to the Somali border (under a British Protectorate from 1890) until Kenya became independent in 1963.

In common with all the other Swahili coastal city-states, Lamu had a slave-based economy until the turn of the 20th century when the British forced the Sultan of Zanzibar to sign an antislaving agreement and subsequently intercepted dhows carrying slaves north from that island. All that cheap labour fuelled a period of economic growth for Lamu and traders grew rich by exporting ivory, cowries, tortoiseshell, mangrove poles, oil seeds and grains, and importing oriental linen, silks, spices and porcelain. When it came to an end in 1907 with the abolition of slavery, the economy of the island rapidly went into decline and stayed that way until very recently when increased receipts from tourism gave it a new lease of life. That decline, and its strong sense of tradition, is what has preserved the Lamu you see today. No other Swahili town, other than Zanzibar, can offer you such a cultural feast and an undisturbed traditional style of architecture.

Information & Orientation

Tourist Office The office is on the waterfront next to the Standard Chartered Bank and staffed by enthusiastic people but it's of limited use. They don't even know the schedules of the ferries to the outlying islands. The office also purports to offer a railway and air ticket booking service for KSh 30 and KSh 40 respectively but save your money because there'll be no ticket waiting for you on arrival. I learnt this from personal experience at Mombasa railway station.

Bank The Standard Chartered Bank on the harbour front is the only bank in Lamu. It's open Monday to Friday from 8.30 am to 1 pm and Saturday from 8.30 to 11 am. In the low season, cashing a cheque can take as little as half an hour but in the high season it can take considerably longer. Get there early.

Books There are some excellent books about Lamu and the Swahili civilisation if you are interested in digging deeper into this fascinating period of East African history and culture. The best general account is *The Portuguese Period in East Africa* by Justus Strandes (East African Literature Bureau, Nairobi, 1971). This is a translation of a book originally published in German in 1899 with up-to-date notes and appendices detailing recent archaeological findings, some of which contradict Strandes' opinions. It's very readable.

Lamu: A Study of the Swahili Town by Usam Ghaidan (East African Literature Bureau, Nairobi, 1975), is a very detailed study of Lamu by an Iraqi who was formerly a Lecturer in Architecture at the University of Nairobi and has since devoted his time to research into the Swahili architecture of the north Kenyan coast. You can find both of the above books in most good bookshops in Nairobi or Mombasa and the latter at the museum in Lamu.

If you're going to stay long in Lamu the leaflet-map *Lamu: Map & Guide to the Archipelago, the Island & the Town* is worth buying at the museum bookshop.

Bookshops Apart from the museum, the Lamu Book Centre, next door to the Garissa Express office, has a small but reasonable selection of English-language novels and other books. It's also the only place where you can buy local newspapers and international news magazines (*Time, Newsweek,* etc). It's open from 6.30 am to 12.30 pm and 2.30 to 9 pm.

Dhow Trips See the Islands Around Lamu section later in this chapter for details about dhow trips.

Lamu Town

The town dates back to at least the late 14th century when the Pwani Mosque was built. Most buildings date from the 18th century, but the lower parts and basements are often considerably older. The streets are narrow, cool and quiet and there are many small courtyards and intimate spaces enclosed by high walls. Traditionally, buildings were constructed entirely out of local materials – faced coral-rag blocks for the walls, wooden floors supported by mangrove poles, makuti roofs and intricately carved shutters for windows. This is changing gradually with the increasing use of imported materials and is one of the factors of great concern to conservationists.

One of the most outstanding features of the houses here, as in old Zanzibar, is the intricately carved doors and lintels which have kept generations of carpenters busy. Sadly, many of them have disappeared in recent years but the skill has not been lost. Walk down to the far end of the harbour front in the opposite direction to Shela and you'll see them being made.

Only a few of the mosques have minarets

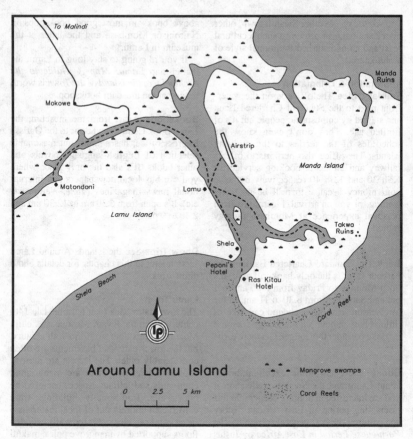

Around Lamu Island

```
To Malindi
Manda Ruins
Mokowe
Airstrip
Manda Island
Matondoni          Lamu
Lamu Island
Takwa Ruins
Shela
Peponi's Hotel
Shela Beach        Ras Kitau Hotel
                   Coral Reef
```

0   2.5   5 km

Mangrove swamps

Coral Reefs

and even these are small affairs. This, combined with the fact that there's little outward decoration and few doors and windows opening onto the street, make them hard to distinguish from domestic buildings.

There is pressure from private developers for permission to build modern hotels on the island but, so far, this has been blocked by the National Museums of Kenya. Nevertheless, you will come across the occasional modern building on the outskirts of town which sticks out like a sore thumb.

Lamu Museum

A couple of hours spent in the Lamu Museum, on the waterfront next to Petley's Inn, is an excellent introduction to the culture and history of Lamu. It's one of the most interesting small museums in Kenya. There's a reconstruction of a traditional Swahili house, charts, maps, ethnological displays, models of the various types of dhow and two examples of the remarkable and ornately carved ivory *siwa* – a wind instrument peculiar to the coastal region which is often used as a fanfare at weddings. There's a good slide show available at the museum – ask to see it.

Top: At work, Lamu, Kenya (GC)
Bottom: Lamu, Kenya (GC)

Top: Giraffe and calves, Masai Mara National Park, Kenya (GH)
Left: Camel trekking in Ndoto Mountains near Milgis River, Kenya (SB)
Right: Zebra at Amboseli National Park, Kenya (SB)

Entry costs KSh 30 (KSh 10 for residents) and the museum is open daily from 8 am to 6 pm.

The museum has a good bookshop specialising in books on Lamu and the Swahili culture.

Swahili House Museum

If the museum stokes your interest in Swahili culture then you should also visit this museum tucked away off to the side of Yumbe House (a hotel). It's a beautifully restored traditional house with furniture and other house wares as well as a pleasant courtyard. Entry costs KSh 30 (KSh 10 for residents) and it's open at the same times as the main museum.

Swahili house

Lamu Fort

The building of this massive structure was begun by the Sultan Paté in 1810 and completed in 1823. From 1910 right up to 1984 it was used as a prison. There are now ambitious plans to convert it into an aquarium, maritime history and natural history museum with a restaurant and other amenities. Progress has been slow but is going ahead. At the time of writing it was closed to the public.

Dhow Building & Repairing

You'll see many dhows anchored in the harbour at the southern end of town but if you want to see them being built or repaired you can do this at Shela or Matondoni villages. The latter is perhaps the best place to see this and you have a choice of walking there (about two hours), hiring a donkey, or hiring a dhow and sailing there. If you choose the dhow it will cost about KSh 240

for the boat (so you need a small group together to share the cost) but it usually includes a barbecued fish lunch.

To walk there, leave the main street of Lamu up the alleyway by the side of Kenya Cold Drinks and continue in as straight a line as possible to the back end of town. From here a well-defined track leads out into the country. You pass a football pitch on the right-hand side after 100 metres. Follow the touch line of the pitch and continue in the same direction past the paddock/garden on the left-hand side and then turn left onto another track. This is the one to Matondoni. The football pitch has telephone wires running above it. These go to Matondoni and they're almost always visible from the track so if you follow them you can't go wrong. If you don't cut across the football pitch you'll head off into the middle of nowhere and probably get lost – although this can be interesting (old houses, wells, goats, etc).

Set off early if you are walking. It gets very hot later on in the day. There's a small café in the village where you can get fish and rice for around KSh 18 as well as fruit juice. There are no guest houses in the village but a bed or floor space can usually be arranged in a private house if you ask around. An impromptu group of travellers generally collects later in the afternoon so you can all share a ride in a dhow back to Lamu.

One traveller also recommended a visit to Kipongani village where local people make straw mats, baskets and hats. It's a friendly place and tea and snacks can be arranged plus there's a beautiful empty beach nearby with waves.

Donkey Sanctuary

One of the most unexpected sights on Lamu is the Donkey Sanctuary which is run by the International Donkey Protection Trust of Sidmouth, Devon, UK. Injured, sick or worn-out donkeys are brought here to find rest and protection. As in most societies where they're used as beasts of burden, donkeys are regularly abused or get injured so it's good to see something positive being done for their welfare. The sanctuary is right on the waterfront.

Shela Village & The Beach

The most popular beach is just past Shela village, a 40 minute walk from Lamu. To get there, follow the harbour-front road till it ends and then follow the shore line. You will pass the new hospital built by the Saudi Arabian government and a ginning factory before you get to Shela. If the tide is out, you can walk along the beach most of the way. When it's in, you may well have to do a considerable amount of wading up to your thighs and deeper. If that doesn't appeal, there is a track all the way from Lamu to Shela but there are many turn-offs so stay with the ones which run closest to the shore (you may find yourself in a few cul-de-sacs doing this as a number of turn-offs to the left run to private houses and end there).

A popular alternative to walking there is to take a dhow. This should cost KSh 12 per person. There's also a motor boat operated by Peponi's Hotel which costs KSh 70 shared between however many of you there are.

The best part of the beach if you want waves is well past Peponi's Hotel – there's no surf at Peponi's because you're still in the channel between Lamu and Manda islands. There was a spate of robberies and a couple of rapes way out along this beach several years ago but there's been no repeat of that following a big police crackdown at the time, so it's probably safe to go as far along the beach as you like. It's possible to hire wind surfing equipment at Peponi's.

Shela itself is a very pleasant little village and well worth a wander around. The ancestors of the people here came from Takwa when that settlement was abandoned in the late 17th century and they still speak a dialect of Swahili which is distinct from that of Lamu. Many have migrated to Malindi in recent years. Don't miss the famous mosque with its characteristic minaret at the back of Peponi's. Many of the houses in this village have been bought up and restored by foreigners in the last few years so it has a surprising air of affluence about it yet the languorous

atmosphere remains unspoiled. Quite a few travellers prefer to stay in Shela rather than in Lamu town.

Places to Stay – bottom end

Lamu has been catering for budget travellers for well over a decade but, in the last few years, budget hotels have mushroomed to cater for the hordes of travellers who come to stay here. As a result, there's a bewildering choice of simple, rustic lodges, rooftops and whole houses to rent. Don't believe a word anyone tells you about there being running water 24 hours a day at any of these places. There often isn't. Water is not an abundant commodity on Lamu and restrictions are in force most of the year. It's usually only available early in the morning and early in the evening which, in most cases, means bucket showers only and somewhat smelly toilets.

Prices are remarkably consistent because there's a lot of competition though you obviously get what you pay for both in terms of facilities and position. A dormitory bed or space on the floor of a rooftop would be around KSh 60, a single room between KSh 95 and KSh 120, and a double room KSh 120 to KSh 240. Almost all of these would involve sharing bathroom facilities but some of the higher priced doubles might have their own bathroom. Prices rise in the high season (August-September) by a factor of up to 50%.

If a lodge is full when you arrive but you like it a lot and want to be first in line for a room, they'll usually let you sleep on the roof or elsewhere until the following morning.

Where you stay initially will probably depend largely on what sort of room you are offered, what's available and who meets you getting off the ferry from the mainland. Most of the young men who meet the ferries have no connection with any of the lodges other than the hope of a tip (from travellers) or a small commission (from the hotel management). Some of them can be very insistent. Those who board the ferry from the airstrip on Manda Island for the trip across the channel are very insistent indeed and incredibly difficult to shake off.

If you plan on staying in Lamu for a while it's worth making enquiries about renting a house, so long as there's a group of you to share the cost. On a daily basis it won't be much cheaper (if at all) than staying at a lodge but on a monthly basis you're looking at a considerable saving. You can share them with as many people as you feel comfortable with or have space for and prices usually include a houseboy. Some of the simpler houses can be very cheap indeed and include a refrigerator and cooking facilities. They're available in Lamu town itself but also at Shela and between Lamu and Shela. Some of them can be excellent value and very spacious. You need to ask around and see what is available. It's possible to find some remarkably luxurious places especially around Shela.

Lamu Town It's virtually impossible to arrange budget hotels in any order of preference since there are so many and conditions and facilities vary so much. This selection has been done on the basis of the cheapest available beds or rooms but implies no preference – hotel owners please note!

On the waterfront, close to the jetty, is the *New Shamuty Lodge* which is friendly, relaxed and has a large rooftop with mattresses and chairs. Doubles cost KSh 50 with shared bathroom facilities. Also on the waterfront at the far end of town is the *Kisiwani Lodge* which has singles/doubles for KSh 60/95 in the low season and KSh 120/145 in the high season, all with shared bathroom facilities. It's very basic, there's no toilet paper and the sheets have been described as 'near rags' but it's a popular place to stay. High season prices are a rip-off. Attached to the lodge is the Lick 'n Smile Restaurant which is equally basic and has a very limited range of food. We have had many complaints from travellers who have stayed at this hotel about theft and the lack of cooperation from the owner, Ali Banana.

On the first street parallel to the waterfront is the *Kenya Lodge* which is equally basic and costs KSh 50 a single. It's fairly clean and has mosquito nets and cold bucket

showers. Next to the fort is the *New Castle Lodge* which overlooks the main square and picks up sea breezes since it's fairly high up. It has a rooftop dormitory for KSh 50 per bed and doubles at KSh 180 with shared bathroom facilities. There's an amusing notice in the reception which lets you know that 'Drugs and spirits are prohibited. Prostitutes, beach boys and homosexuals are not allowed in your rooms. Hotel nakedness and public exposure of yourselves is not permitted on the roof terrace. Love and fun affairs with the staff of this hotel is not allowed'!

Also in this range is the *Saiga Lodge* which is very basic but friendly and has rooms for KSh 60 on the roof, and the *Rainbow Guest House* at the back of the Dhow Lodge which has doubles for KSh 95.

Kadara's Lodge, at the Shela end of town, is airy and pleasant with a courtyard and has doubles with shared bathroom facilities for KSh 85. Doubles with private bathroom and sea views cost KSh 120. Close to the post office is the *Dhow Lodge* which only has a few rooms, some of them scruffy, others reasonable. The rooms are high and airy with string beds and thin mattresses. Doubles/triples with shared bathroom cost KSh 120/180. The lodge has its own well.

The *Salama Guest House* at the other end of town is very popular and well run and, as a result, often full. The downstairs rooms cost KSh 120/180 for doubles/triples with shared bathroom and the upstairs rooms cost KSh 85/180/240 for singles/doubles/triples with own bathroom. There are also rooms with four beds for KSh 300. Discounts of 20% are available if you stay more than just a few days. It's worth trying to get in here.

Behind this area is the equally popular *Jambo Guest House* though it only has four double rooms at KSh 240 (negotiable if you stay for a week) including breakfast. Fans and mosquito nets are provided and there's use of a refrigerator and gas stove. There's also a large rooftop area. The *Lala Salama Guest House* is similar and has doubles with shared bathroom for KSh 180. Right opposite the Jambo Guest House is the similarly priced *Karibuni Guest House*.

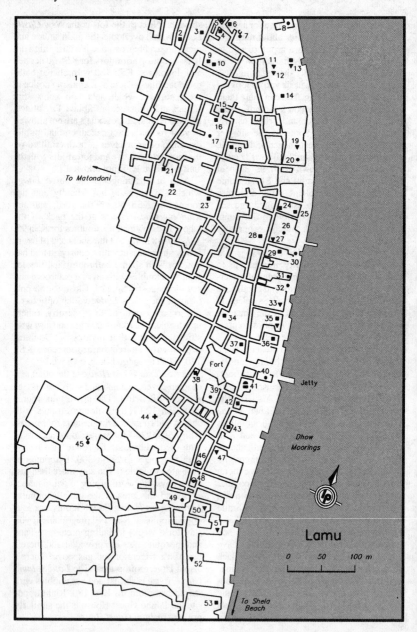

To Matondoni

Fort

Jetty

Dhow
Moorings

Lamu

0   50   100 m

To Shela
Beach

■ PLACES TO STAY

1	Peace Guest House
2	Jannat House
3	Sanctuary Guest House
4	Karibuni Guest House
5	Jambo Guest House
6	Saiga Lodge
9	Pole Pole Guest House
10	Suli Suli House
13	Kisiwani Lodge
14	Salama Guest House
15	Yumbe House
16	Pool House
18	Shuweri Guest House
21	Hal-Udy Guest House
22	Darini Guest House
23	Lala Salama Guest House, Sanaa Guest House
24	Kenya Lodge
25	Casuarina Rest House
28	Lamu Guest House, Samaki Guest House
29	Petley's Inn
34	Bahati Lodge
35	Full Moon Guest House
36	New Shamuty Lodge
37	New Mahrus Hotel
38	New Castle Lodge
42	Dhow Lodge
43	Rainbow Guest House
53	Kadara's Lodge

▼ PLACES TO EAT

11	Jambo Café
12	Yoghurt Inn
13	Lick 'n Smile Restaurant
19	Ghai's Restaurant
27	Kenya Cold Drinks
33	Bush Gardens Restaurant
35	Hapahapa Restaurant
47	New Star Restaurant
50	Equator Restaurant
51	Sindbad Restaurant
52	Sabrina Restaurant

● OTHER

7	Jamaa Mosque
8	Door Carvers
17	Swahili House Museum
20	Donkey Sanctuary
26	Lamu Museum
30	Prestige Air Services
31	Standard Chartered Bank
32	Tourist Information Bureau & Equator Airlines
39	Market
40	Customs
41	Post Office
44	Hospital
45	Riyadha Mosque
46	Malindi Bus
48	Tana River Bus
49	Garissa Express & Lamu Book Centre

The *Sanaa Guest House* is a very pleasant little place which offers doubles with bathroom for KSh 240 and a choice of double beds or two single beds. They're not keen on alcoholic beverages here as the notice, 'No Beer', implies.

Very good value, clean and simple, is the *Lamu Guest House* at the back of the Lamu Museum. There's a choice of different rooms here but the best are probably those on the top floor which cost KSh 180 for a double and a bathroom shared with one other room. There are no fans but the sea breezes and sea views adequately compensate for this. Lower down there are doubles with bathroom and fan for KSh 360 and smaller doubles with the same facilities for KSh 240. All the rooms can be occupied singly for about two-thirds of the above prices.

Back on the waterfront and close to the jetty is the popular *Full Moon Guest House* which is very friendly and has an excellent 1st floor balcony but only has four rooms. It costs KSh 215 for either a double or a single with shared bathroom facilities. It does have a lot of charm but the doubles are perhaps not worth the price whereas the triple room is. If you're staying for a week or more then the price is KSh 155.

Right out at the back of town (10 minutes walk) is the *Peace Guest House* which is clean, provides mosquito nets and morning tea and costs KSh 85 for a dormitory bed and KSh 180 to KSh 360 for a double. It's a wooden building surrounded by gardens. You can also camp here for KSh 50. Facilities include two showers and access to the kitchen. This place has been highly recommended by everyone who has stayed there. If you're heading there, enquire first at the

Jambo Café close to the Yoghurt Inn on the street parallel to the waterfront.

Another place well worth considering if there's a group of you is the *Shuweri Guest House* just below the Swahili House Museum. You may need to ask where it is as it only has a tiny sign. You're looking at a whole house here, albeit small, with six beds in one large room (partially divided into two), an upstairs, open-air, makuti-roofed 'lounge', refrigerator, cooking facilities and a very helpful houseboy. It's a bargain at KSh 360 if staying long term.

The *Bahati Lodge*, off to the right of the fort as you face it, has an excellent position with the top rooms overlooking the harbour and catching the sea breezes but it's very primitive. That doesn't seem to stop people staying here if they can get one of the bedrooms on the top floor but the rooms on the ground floor are Dickensian and a rip-off. Singles/doubles/triples cost KSh 90/145/215 with shared bathroom facilities. Mosquito nets are provided.

More expensive but right on the waterfront is the *Casuarina Rest House* which was formerly the police headquarters. It offers large, airy rooms with good views and it's clean, well maintained and scrubbed down daily. It's excellent value at KSh 300 to KSh 360 a double depending on how long you intend to stay. There's access to a large flat roof area.

The Kisiwani Lodge also appears to be moving into the whole-house rental business. They're setting up the *Sanctuary Guest House* which will cost KSh 2400 per day for a house with three self-contained suites, two other suites with one double room each and a further suite with two double bedrooms. Facilities include a garden, refrigerator, kitchen and rooftop area. That's a good deal if you're a large group.

Similar is *Suli Suli House* next to the Pole Pole Guest House. Those who have stayed there describe this place as 'an amazing eight bedroom house with courtyard'. It's very clean and the caretaker, Tabu, is an excellent cook. Rates vary from KSh 360 to KSh 720 depending on how long you intend to stay.

My good friend and fellow globetrotter, Tony Wheeler, who spent some time in Lamu during 1989 along with his wife Maureen and their two kids, recommended the *Mlangilangi House*, behind the fort. It's a very pleasant old house and has rooms for KSh 240 plus use of kitchen facilities. He also recommended the *Pool House* near the Swahili House Museum – so called because it has a swimming pool – which has four double rooms around the pool all with bathrooms and mosquito nets for KSh 300 (less if staying a few nights).

Finally, but also top of the range in this section, are the *Mtamwini Guest House*, which offers singles/doubles for KSh 240/360 with bathroom, and *Dudu's Guest House*, up behind the fort, which is a beautiful old house with terrace offering large rooms with fan, mosquito nets, bathrooms and use of kitchen for KSh 360.

Shela Quite a few travellers, especially beach lovers, prefer to stay at Shela village rather than in Lamu itself.

If you're going to stay here for a while – and it seems most of the people who stay here do – then it's best to ask around for a house to rent and have a small group together to share the cost. Many of the houses here are owned by expatriate foreigners (especially Italians) who have poured vast amounts of money into them but only live here for part of the year. Most of them have been very sensitively upgraded and some are stunning. Quite a lot of them can be rented out so talk to the caretakers.

In the meantime, stay at the *Samahane Guest House* (tel 3100) which has double rooms with twin beds, table and chair and shared bathrooms for KSh 240. It's simple, clean and catches the sea breezes.

Cheap, simple rooms with no frills and shared bathroom facilities can also be found at the *Stop Over Restaurant* right on the beach.

The other former guest house – the *Shela Rest House* – was being converted into self-contained apartments at the end of 1989 and is destined to become a mid to top-end hotel.

Other places worth trying here are *Akasimani House*, close to the Samahane, and *Giovanna's House*. The latter costs KSh 1200 per night but sleeps four people on two floors and has a garden, kitchen and pergola. Ask for Omari, the caretaker, if you want to rent it.

Places to Stay – middle

The most beautiful place by far to stay in this range is *Yumbe House* (tel (0121) 3101, PO Box 81, Lamu), adjacent to the Swahili House Museum. If any hotel exposes the lie about 'tourism eating into the fabric of Lamu' this is it! Here is a four storey traditional house surrounding a central courtyard which has been superbly and sensitively converted into a hotel with airy terraces and makuti roofs. All rooms are self-contained, it's spotlessly clean, towels and soap are provided and there are mosquito nets. It's excellent value at KSh 430/650 for singles/doubles including breakfast. It's simply the best!

Also very good but nowhere near as attractive is *Hal-Udy Guest House* which has four self-contained suites (bedroom and sitting room plus terrace) with refrigerators and cooking facilities for KSh 300/480 a single/double in the low season and KSh 480/720 in the high season (less if you stay for a week or longer). Mosquito nets are provided and there's a houseboy. It's very popular with slightly older couples with children who prefer to do their own cooking (or, at least, some of it).

Far less attractive than the above two and nowhere near the same value is the *New Mahrus Hotel* (tel 3001, PO Box 25, Lamu), adjacent to the square in front of the fort. This hotel has been going for years and is long overdue for a complete rehabilitation – many of the rooms are no better than anything you'd find at a third of the price. It would also benefit if half the staff were sacked tomorrow and replaced by new blood. The level of indifference here is staggering. I can't recommend it but die-hards do stay

here. The worst rooms ('3rd class') cost KSh 205/360 a single/double. Better rooms ('2nd class') cost KSh 300/480 and the best rooms ('1st class') cost KSh 480/600. All prices include breakfast.

Other mid-range hotels which are worth checking out if the Yumbe and Hal-Udy are full are the *Darini Guest House* (KSh 480 for an apartment including breakfast) and *Jannat House* (KSh 480 per room – five rooms in total).

Places to Stay – top end

Lamu Town The only top-range hotel in Lamu itself is *Petley's Inn* (tel 48, PO Box 4, Lamu) right on the harbour front next to the Lamu Museum. It was originally set up in the late 19th century by Percy Petley – a somewhat eccentric English colonist who ran plantations on the mainland at Witu until he retired to Lamu. It has been renovated since then, of course, but in traditional style with the addition of a swimming pool, (occasional) disco and two restaurants (neither of which are anything special). It also has the only hotel bar in Lamu (there are two other non-hotel bars).

Full board at Petley's is KSh 2040/2760 for singles/doubles or KSh 2280/3000 for a sea-facing room with private shower and balcony. Half board rates are KSh 1800/2400 for singles/doubles or KSh 1920/2640 for a sea-facing room. Children between the ages of three and 12 pay 50%.

Shela At the far end of Shela village and right on the beach is *Peponi's Hotel* (tel 29, PO Box 24, Lamu) which is *the* place to stay if you want a top-range hotel on Lamu. It consists of self-contained, whitewashed cottages with their own verandahs facing the channel between Lamu and Manda islands and is reckoned to be one of the best hotels in the world, both in terms of its position and the quality of the cuisine. It's run by young Danish people and up-market informality is the name of the game here. The rates for full board are KSh 3460/4655 a single/double. Children sharing the same accommodation are charged KSh 530 (one to three years), KSh 1060 (four to 10 years) and KSh 1875 (over 10 years). The hotel has its own restaurant (residents only) plus a grill and bar which are open to both residents and non-residents. There's a full range of water sports facilities. Advance booking is essential and the hotel is closed during May and June.

Diagonally opposite Peponi's, across the channel on Manda Island, is another top-range hotel, the *Ras Kitau Hotel* – or at least it used to be top range. Recent reports indicate that it has gone downhill rapidly and that there are management disputes which have yet to be resolved. It's been impossible to ascertain current rates.

Places to Eat – cheap

One of the cheapest places to eat in Lamu is the *New Star Restaurant*. You certainly won't beat the prices and some people recommend it highly, but others visit once and never return. Service is certainly slow (depending on what you order and the time of day) and the menu is often an unbridled act of creativity. I thought the food was average but nothing special. They also have good yoghurt. Similar in price is the *Sabrina Restaurant* which serves mainly Indian food for main courses and Western breakfasts but they do offer very reasonably priced lobster, prawn and crab dishes. Again, the food is only average. For standard African fare, the *Jambo Café* just before the Yoghurt Inn has become popular of late. It's used a lot by local people so guaranteed to be cheap.

For consistently reliable good food at a reasonable price there are four very popular restaurants. The first is the *Sindbad Restaurant* on the waterfront overlooking the dhow moorings. Here you can get pancakes with various fillings, grilled fish and salad for KSh 30 or a full lunch or dinner of soup, main course and fruit juice for KSh 55.

The *Yoghurt Inn* has also been popular for years and has an attractive garden with individual outside tables each with a grass roof. It offers banana pancakes with honey for just KSh 12, grilled fish for KSh 45, crab for KSh

50, yoghurt for KSh 5.50 and lassi for KSh 16. There are also daily 'specials' such as crab with avocado salad for KSh 85. The food is generally very good and well presented but they brew up foul tea. It's open daily from 7 am to 9.30 pm except on Fridays when it's open from 7 am to noon and 4 to 9.30 pm.

Somewhat more expensive but very popular is *Bush Gardens* on the waterfront, next door to the Hapahapa Restaurant. It's run by the very personable and energetic 'Bush Baby' who personally supervises the cooking which sometimes makes for slow service but guarantees you an excellent meal. Fish dishes (barracuda, tuna, snapper or shark) cost KSh 50 to KSh 60, crab KSh 95, prawns KSh 115 and lobster KSh 130, all served with chips or coconut rice and salad. Fruit juices are also available. While it stays open all day, you can only get a meal here at lunch time or dinner time as, in the afternoon, 'Bush Baby' is out catching the fish. It's arguably the best seafood restaurant in Lamu.

Next door is the *Hapahapa Restaurant* which is also very good and offers a similar range of dishes, including seafood and possibly the best fruit juices and milkshakes in town (KSh 12 for half a pint and KSh 18 for a full pint). Prices are similar to those at Bush Gardens.

Most travellers come across a man popularly called 'Ali Hippy' who, for several years now, has been offering travellers meals at his house for between KSh 95 and KSh 120. The meal usually includes lobster, crab, fish, coconut rice and vegetable stew and the whole family entertains you while you eat. Most people come away quite satisfied (it's definitely an unusual evening out) but others have complained that KSh 120 is a lot to pay for heaps of rice and very little fish or that the meal is rushed and there's no time to relax, so it appears that what he lays on varies a lot.

At Shela, the *Stop Over Restaurant* right on the beach is a popular place to eat or drink and prices are very reasonable though they only offer simple meals.

Places to Eat – more expensive

For a splurge there are several places you can try. Probably the best for a night out is the *Equator Restaurant* which is open from noon to 2 pm and 6 to 9 pm. The atmosphere here is very relaxing (classical music and oldies) and many people rate it as the best restaurant in Lamu though they tend to over-cook the lobster. At the bottom of the range you can get a meal for KSh 65 to KSh 80 plus they have crab (very popular) for KSh 95, a three-course dinner with pineapple steak for KSh 110 and lobster for KSh 155. It's a good place but it's *very* popular so book a table in advance if possible. It can be more expensive than Ghai's but it's well worth the little extra.

Equally popular is *Ghai's*, on the water-front next to the donkey sanctuary. Ghai may be somewhat eccentric but he considers himself to be the best seafood cook on the island. This is usually the case but not always – a friend who ate there recently described the meal he got in these terms: 'fish curry and grilled whole fish both mediocre, fish tough and flavourless, rice blah, salad poor'. Prices are almost identical to those at the Equator.

A meal at *Petley's Inn* – either in the restaurant itself or in the adjacent barbecue garden – also used to be a popular splurge but these days the food is only mediocre and you'll see very few people eating here. Most meals are priced between KSh 180 and KSh 210 and there's nothing under KSh 120. The ice cream, on the other hand, is very good.

The rooftop restaurant at the *New Mahrus Hotel* touts itself as a classy restaurant but the food is only average and the hygiene suspect.

For a splurge at Shela the *Barbecue Grill* at Peponi's offers delicious food and is open to nonresidents. There's a choice of both barbecued fish and meat and a superb range of salads. Expect to pay around KSh 80 to KSh 90 for a meal.

Places to Drink

Fruit Juices Two of the best places for fruit juices are the *Sindbad Restaurant*, on the waterfront, and the *Hapahapa Restaurant*.

Kenya Cold Drinks used to be another very popular place for fruit juices but a lot of travellers have complained recently of watered-down juices and the fact that they're often out of most of the things on the menu. There were certainly not many people in there every time I passed it.

Beer & Spirits There are three places where you can get a beer in Lamu itself but only one which has cold beers. This is the bar at *Petley's Inn* which is an English-style pub, the entrance to which is in the alley between the hotel and the barbecue garden opposite. It's the most popular watering hole on the island and is open to nonresidents. The only trouble with this bar is that the beer is always 'running out' – usually by 8 pm but some-times even earlier – and after that they'll only sell you spirits. The beer doesn't actually 'run out' at all – it's just the hotel's way of making it plain that you're not staying there. The bar is open at lunch times from noon to around 2 pm and in the evening from 5 pm to around 9.30 pm (though it often closes earlier).

One bar which never 'runs out' of beer is that at the *Police Club* but they are always warm so you have to be slightly desperate to drink here. It's open in the evenings until fairly late and you don't have to be in the police to get in. Ask directions when you get to the Garissa Express bus office.

There's another bar at the *Civil Servants' Club* which has a disco on Friday and Satur-day nights. Entry costs KSh 20 and it's a good night out.

Out at Shela, *Peponi's* is a mandatory watering hole and the beers here are always ice-cold and never 'run out'. The bar is on the verandah overlooking the channel and beach. It's open all day until late at night.

Getting There & Away

Air Four companies operate flights to Lamu from Mombasa and Malindi. They are Eagle Aviation Ltd (tel Mombasa 316054, Malindi 21258, Lamu 3119), Prestige Air Services Ltd (tel Mombasa 21443, Malindi 20860/1), Skyways Airlines (tel Mombasa 432167,

Malindi 21260, Lamu 3226) and Equator Airlines (tel Malindi 2053).

They all have two flights per day in either direction between Mombasa and Lamu and Malindi and Lamu. Flights from Mombasa depart at 8.30 am and 2.15 pm and arrive in Lamu an hour and 10 minutes later. From Malindi they depart at 9 am and 3 pm and arrive 40 minutes later. In the opposite direction, they depart Lamu at 10 am and 4 pm for both Mombasa and Malindi. The fares are KSh 1680 (Mombasa-Lamu) and KSh 1020 (Malindi-Lamu) one way. Return fares are double. Children over two years old pay full fare. Check-in time is 30 minutes before departure and the baggage allowance is 10 kg per person. Most of the time they don't hassle if your baggage is over 10 kg but, even if they do, excess charges are minimal. The airport departure tax is KSh 50 at Malindi but there's no charge at Lamu.

The airport at Lamu is on Manda Island and the ferry across the channel to Lamu costs KSh 12. Hotel touts will be waiting for you at the airport and will pursue you all the way. They're very persistent and hard to shake off.

Bus Three bus companies operate between Mombasa, Malindi and Lamu on a daily basis. They are Malindi Bus Service, Tana River Bus Service and Garissa Express and they all have offices in Mombasa, Malindi and Lamu. The fare from Malindi to Lamu is KSh 120 and the journey takes about five hours. Buses leave in either direction at 7 or 8 am depending on the company. The buses from Mombasa to Lamu arrive in Malindi around 8.30 am and leave around 9.30 am so there's a choice of departure times from Malindi if seats are available. It's wise to book in advance as there's heavy demand for tickets. Garissa Express also operate a daily service between Garissa and Lamu which costs KSh 180 and takes eight to 10 hours.

The buses terminate at the ferry jetty on the mainland not far from Mokowe. From here you take a motorised ferry to Lamu which costs KSh 12.

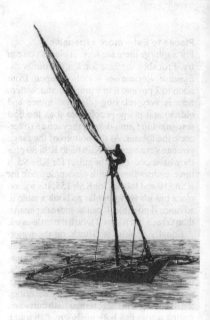

Dhow Other than trips around the Lamu archipelago, you can also find dhows sailing to Mombasa. The journey takes two days on average and prices are negotiable. Before you set off you need to get permission from the District Commissioner. His office is on the harbour front close to the post office and opposite the main quay. It's best if you can persuade the captain of the dhow to take you along here and guide you through the formalities. It shouldn't take more than 1½ hours in that case. Usually they will do this without charging you money but be prepared to pay if the captain is unwilling.

Getting Around

There are frequent ferries between Lamu and the bus terminus on the mainland (near Mokowe). The fare is KSh 6. Ferries between the airstrip on Manda Island and Lamu cost KSh 12.

There are also regular ferries between Lamu and Paté Island – see below for details.

Islands Around Lamu

A popular activity while you're in Lamu is to take a dhow trip to one of the neighbouring islands. You need a small group (six to eight people) to share costs if you're going to do this but it's very easy to put a group like that together in Lamu. Just ask around in the restaurants or the budget hotels.

Since taking tourists around the archipelago is one of the easiest ways of making money for dhow owners in Lamu, there's a lot of competition and you'll be asked constantly by different people if you want to go on a trip. You'll also see many notices advertising trips in the restaurants. Negotiation over the price and what is included in it is essential both to avoid misunderstandings and being overcharged. The price of day trips is usually settled quickly because a lot of travellers will have been on them and the cost will be well known.

Dhow trips are usually superb whoever you go with so it's unfair to recommend any particular dhow or captain but, if you're going on a long trip – say, three days – then it's a very good idea to check out both the dhow and the crew before committing yourself. Don't hand over any money until the day of departure except, perhaps, a float for food for a long trip. Also, on long trips, it's probably best to organise your own beer and soft drink supplies. And remember that the person who touts for your business is often not the captain of the boat but an intermediary who takes a commission for finding you.

Dhows without an outboard motor are naturally entirely dependent on wind to get them anywhere though poling – or even pushing – the boat is fairly common along narrow creeks and channels. If you have to pole the boat or you get becalmed out in the channels between the islands, there's no point in remonstrating with the captain. He's not God and there's nothing he can do about it yet it's surprising how many people imagine otherwise. With that in mind, never go on a long trip if you have a deadline to meet. A three day trip can occasionally turn into five, though not usually.

Likewise, dhows are dependent on the tides. You can't sail up creeks if the tide is out and there's not enough depth of water to float the boat. This will be the main factor determining departure and return times.

To give you some idea of what a longer dhow trip involves, a brief description of the one which I took with five others at the end of 1989 follows:

After discussions with three different middlemen in Lamu about trips to Kiwayu we made our choice and arranged to meet outside the Kisiwani Lodge at 6 am the next morning. The price was fixed at KSh 4000 for a three day trip or around KSh 180 to KSh 200 per person per day including food. Meanwhile we purchased beers and soft drinks from the Kenya Breweries depot and dropped them off at the Kisiwani (the crews will generally do this for you but it will cost more).

Next morning the dhow finally turned up at 7.30 am along with a crew of four and we set off in the direction of the channel between Manda Island and the mainland. Since the wind wasn't in the right direction, the dhow had to tack all the way to the channel by which time it was low tide. There was sufficient water in the channel to keep the boat afloat – but only just – but the wind had dropped completely. There was no alternative but to pole and push the dhow all the way to the end of the channel and naturally we all lent a hand. It took hours.

Once out in the open sea again, the wind picked up and we were able to get close to Paté Island but then again the wind dropped and the clouds burst. It looked very much like we and all our gear were about to get a soaking so it was with considerable relief that we discovered the crew had brought along an enormous sheet of plastic.

After the storm, the wind picked up again and we reached Mtangawanda by about 3.30 pm where we got off the boat and had a late lunch cooked by the crew. Despite only having one charcoal burner, they did an excellent job of this and the food was delicious.

We set off again about 4.30 pm and headed for Faza with a stiff side wind which enabled us to make good progress for the next two hours. After that it died completely and darkness fell. By 10 pm, it was obvious we were going nowhere that night so the anchor was dropped and a meal prepared (by torch light!). By now we were all getting to know each other very well and there was a good rapport between crew and passengers. The tranquillity and beauty of a becalmed night at sea added immensely to this. After the meal, we all bedded down as best we could for a night of 14th century discomfort.

By first light we discovered that seepage through the hull of the boat had brought the water level to well above the toe-boards so it was all hands on deck and bail out with anything to hand. Shortly after this, the wind picked up and we sped our way across the channel between Paté Island and Kiwayu, arriving about 11 am off the tip of the island. At this point, all the passengers and one of the crew got off the dhow and went snorkelling among the reefs on the eastern side. The dhow, meanwhile, sailed on to Kiwayu village.

We caught up with the dhow again around 3 pm after walking along the beach and climbing over the ridge. Lunch was prepared by the crew (again delicious) and we settled down to an afternoon and evening of relaxation – sunbathing, fishing and exploring the village. Those with tents camped on the beach and the others took a banda at the camp site.

Next morning brought heavy rain but by 11 am we were on our way back to Lamu with a strong tail wind and making excellent progress. Just off Faza, however, the wind died again and the captain (rightly) predicted there'd be no more that day so it was Faza for the night at his family's house. But it wasn't that simple getting off the boat! The tide was out and we couldn't sail up the creek to the town. It didn't look like a particularly feasible idea from the relative 'comfort' of the boat but, after some persuasion, we all jumped overboard with our packs on our heads and headed for the shore in thigh-deep water. There were no mishaps but a lot of jokes and laughter. Half an hour later we reached Faza.

The dhow was brought up at high tide and we were given three bedrooms to share at the family house. That evening a superb meal was prepared for us by the captain's family which we ate in the company of what must have been a good proportion of the town's younger children, all fascinated by this strange collection of wazungu that had turned up in town. Though we did offer, the family refused to take any money for the meal and the accommodation.

After the meal, the captain gave us his prediction about the winds next day – pretty pessimistic – and advised us to take the motor launch back to Lamu. The food was at an end, the last beers had been consumed with the meal that night and so, in the end, we all opted for the motor launch rather than another possible two days and a night back to Lamu. He did, on the other hand, firmly offer to take any or all of us back to Lamu on the dhow if that's what we preferred at no further cost.

All things considered, an excellent trip, superb value, great company, quite an adventure and I'd do it again.

In addition to dhows there are a number of regular motorised ferries which connect Lamu with various towns on the islands.

MANDA ISLAND

This is the easiest of the islands to get to since it's just across the channel from Lamu and almost everyone takes a half-day trip to the Takwa ruins at the head of the creek which almost bisects the island. The average cost of a dhow to this place is around KSh 360 shared by however many people you can put together. Sometimes this includes a barbecued fresh fish lunch but not always so settle this issue before you leave.

The extensive Takwa ruins are what remains of an old Swahili city which flourished between the 15th and 17th centuries and which attained a peak population of some 2500. It was abandoned for reasons unknown when the townspeople moved to Shela. The ruins consist of the remains of about 100 limestone and coral houses, all aligned towards Mecca as well as a mosque and tomb dated 1683 (1094 by the Islamic calendar). The settlement is surrounded by the remains of a wall and huge baobab trees dot the site. It's maintained by the National Museums of Kenya and entry costs KSh 30.

There's a *camp site* adjacent to the ruins for those who wish to stay overnight.

Just off the north-east coast of Manda is Manda Toto Island which offers some of the best snorkelling possibilities in the archipelago. The reefs here are excellent and there are also good beaches. The only way to get here is by dhow.

Getting There & Away

The trip across to Manda takes about 1½ hours and can only be done at high tide as it's reached by a long mangrove-fringed inlet which is too shallow at low tide. You may well have to wade up the final stretch so wear shorts. Since you have to catch the outgoing tide, your time at the site will probably not be more than 45 minutes.

It's possible to walk to the Takwa ruins from either the airstrip or Ras Kitau but it's quite a long way and the paths are not too clear.

PATÉ ISLAND

There are a number of historical sites on Paté

Lamu Archipelago

INDIAN OCEAN

0   7.5   15 km

Coral Reefs

Island including Paté the town, Siyu, Mtangawanda and Faza. All are still inhabited – mainly by fishers and mangrove pole cutters – but very little effort has been put into preserving or clearing the remains of the once powerful Swahili city-states and that's not likely to happen until tourist receipts warrant the expense. Indeed, the only foreigners who come to this island are those on dhow trips and the occasional archaeologist so you can expect to be a novelty and treated with friendly curiosity especially by the children.

Accommodation and food on the island is easy to arrange with local families. The cost is negotiable but very reasonable. There are no guest houses as such except at Faza but there's generally one or two simple restaurants which offer basic meals like bean or meat stews and tea.

Partly because the island is so low lying, mosquitos are a real pest and you're going to need insect repellent. Mosquito coils are for sale in the island's shops.

Paté

The origins of Paté are disputed. There are

claims that it was founded in the 8th century by immigrants from Arabia, but recent excavations have produced nothing earlier than the 13th century when another group of Arabs, the Nabahani, arrived and gradually came to exert considerable influence over the other semiautonomous settlements along the coast.

By the time the Portuguese arrived in the early 16th century, Paté's fortunes were on the decline but were given a shot in the arm by the European mariners' interest in the silk cloth for which the town was famous and the introduction by the Portuguese of gunpowder. A number of Portuguese merchants reputedly settled here but their welcome was relatively short-lived and by the mid-17th century their descendants had withdrawn to Mombasa following a series of uprisings by the Patéans against taxes imposed by the Portuguese authorities.

For the next half century or so, Paté regained some of its former importance and successfully fought off attempts by the Omani Arabs to take it over. Paté's harbour, however, had long been silting up and the city-state was eventually forced into using that of Lamu. The dependency created frequent tensions particularly as Paté claimed sovereignty over Lamu and the two were frequently at war. The final crunch came in 1812 when a Patéan army was soundly defeated at Shela. Thereafter, Paté faded into insignificance and lost all importance after the ruling family were driven out by Seyyid Majid in 1865 and were forced to set up the short-lived Sultanate of Witu on the mainland.

Today, Paté resembles a down-at-heel Lamu. The narrow, winding streets and high-walled houses are there but the streets are earthen and the coral rag walls unplastered. Its one redeeming feature is the Nabahani ruins just outside of town. These are quite extensive and include walls, tombs, mosques and houses. They're worth exploring but they've never been seriously excavated or cleared so it can be difficult to get around because of the tangle of vegetation. In addition, local farmers plant their tobacco crops among the ruins and have demolished substantial sections of the walls.

Getting There & Away There is a motor launch which leaves Lamu for Mtangawanda (about two hours) and Faza (about four hours) three times a week on Monday, Wednesday and Friday (Tuesday, Thursday and Saturday in the opposite direction). The fare is KSh 30.

From Mtangawanda it's about an hour's walk to Paté town along a narrow footpath through thick bush and across tidal flats but you're unlikely to get lost as the path is easy to follow and you'll probably be walking it together with local people who get off the launch.

The launch doesn't always call at Mtangawanda on the return trip from Faza to Lamu, so it's best to walk across to Faza and take it from there, paying a visit to Siyu on the way.

Siyu

Founded in the 15th century, Siyu was famous not for commerce or military opportunism but as a centre of Islamic scholarship and crafts, particularly between the 17th and 19th centuries. In its heyday it boasted some 30,000 inhabitants and was the largest settlement on the island though, today, less than 4000 people live here and there are few signs of its former cultural and religious influence.

Though one of the last upholders of coastal independence, Siyu's demise came in 1847 when it was occupied by the Sultan of Zanzibar's troops. The huge fort outside town dates from this period and is one of the largest buildings on the island. It's well worth a visit to this fort which, unlike many other Swahili relics, has undergone considerable renovation.

The modern village displays little of Siyu's former glory and consists essentially of a sprawl of simple mud-walled and makuti-roofed houses.

Getting There & Away The mangrove-lined channel leading up to Siyu is too shallow and silted up to allow the passage of anything but the smallest boats and so cannot be reached directly from the sea by dhow or motor launch. The only feasible access is on foot either from Paté or Faza.

From Paté it's about eight km to Siyu along an earth track through the bush. The first part is tricky since there are turn-offs which are easy to miss so it's a good idea to take a guide with you as far as the tidal inlet. From here on it's easy as the path bears left and then continues straight through to Siyu. This last leg should take you about one hour.

Faza

Faza has had a chequered history. It was destroyed by Paté in the 13th century and refounded in the 16th century only to be destroyed again by the Portuguese in 1586 as a result of its collaboration with the Turkish fleet of Amir Ali Bey. It was subsequently rebuilt and switched its allegiances to the Portuguese during their attempts to subdue Paté in the 17th century but declined into insignificance during the 18th and 19th centuries. These days it has regained some of its former importance as a result of being chosen as the district headquarters for Paté Island which includes part of the Kenya mainland to the north.

Faza has very little to offer in the way of interesting ruins. About the only thing there is in the town itself are the remains of the Kunjanja Mosque right on the creek front next to the district headquarters where the ferries anchor. Even so, most of it is just a roofless pile of rubble though there's a beautifully carved mihrab and some fine Arabic inscriptions above the doorway. Outside town is the tomb of Amir Hamad, commander of the Sultan of Zanzibar's forces, who was killed here in 1844 whilst campaigning against Siyu and Paté.

The modern town is quite extensive and includes a post office, telephone exchange, the district headquarters, a simple restaurant, two general stores (including one owned by Bwana Mzee Saad) and two guest houses – *Lamu House* and *Shela House*. These two houses are essentially family residences but they're more than willing to turn over one or more bedrooms for your use and cook you a delicious evening meal if you need somewhere to stay. The price is negotiable but the family is very friendly. The simple *restaurant* mentioned above offers bean stews, tea and mandazi for just a few cents and is a popular meeting place for the men of the town. It's an interesting place to wander around and easy to strike up conversations with just about anyone – men, women or children. Most of the houses here are mud-walled or coral-rag walled with makuti roofs though concrete and corrugated iron have made their appearance too.

Getting There & Away The inlet leading up to Faza from the main channel is deep enough at high tide to allow the passage of dhows and motor launches (though at low tide you'll have to walk in over the mud and sand banks from the main channel).

There's a regular motor launch which connects Lamu with Faza via Mtangawanda three times a week on Monday, Wednesday and Friday (Tuesday, Thursday and Saturday in the opposite direction). The fare is KSh 30 and the journey takes four hours. From Faza to Lamu, the launch leaves at about 6 am but you need to be down by the district headquarters about half an hour before that as you have to ferried out to the launch in small boats (costs KSh 1.50).

Getting to Siyu from Faza involves a two hour walk through shambas and thick bush along an earth track. The first hour's walk as far as the disused airstrip involves no problems and there are generally people to ask direction of if you're unsure. The second half is more confusing and you may need a guide so it might be best in the long run to take a guide with you all the way from Faza.

KIWAYU ISLAND

Kiwayu Island is at the far north-east of the Lamu archipelago and is included in the Kiunga Marine National Reserve. It acquired a reputation some years ago as an exclusive hideaway for rock stars and various other members of the glitterati, both local and foreign. It's unlikely you'll be rubbing shoulders with these people. The main reason for coming here is to explore the coral reefs off the eastern side of the island which the tourist literature rates as some of the best along the Kenyan coast. Personally, I think it's somewhat overrated (Watamu was better) but the dhow trip there was definitely one of the highlights of my last trip to Lamu and I can highly recommend it.

The village on the western side of the island where the dhows drop anchor is quite small but it does have a general store with a limited range of basics. The place to stay here is the *Kiwayu Camping Site* run by a friendly man named Kasim. There are several beautifully conceived bandas to stay in, all constructed out of wooden poles and makuti including one on stilts and another built over a tree. The cost varies between KSh 240 and KSh 360 depending on which one you take, but they'll all sleep up to three people. Clean sheets, pillows and mattresses are provided as well as a kerosene lantern and mosquito coil. There are good toilet and shower facilities. Campers can erect their tents here for KSh 30 including use of showers and toilets. You'll pay the same charge even if you camp on the beach below the site since this is also apparently owned by Kasim. There's a

covered dining and cooking area for the use of both campers and banda dwellers.

Way up above the village on the crest of the hill are a series of much larger, white-washed bandas and a partly stone-built dining hall and bar. They're apparently owned by a Nakuru man who keeps them solely for his own use and those of his friends but they look partly derelict and there was no caretaker to be seen anywhere.

Further up the coast across from Kiwayu on the mainland is the *Mkokoni* luxury lodge which is where the glitterati stay. The cost of a night here is KSh 6240 with full board. There's a speed launch to it from Lamu which takes less than an hour or charter flights by African Express Airways (Lamu) in six-seater planes for KSh 8400 return. You can forget about going up there for a cold beer if you're staying at the camp site as there's no transport across the channel between the island and the mainland.

Getting There & Away

Virtually the only way to get to Kiwayu is by dhow and, for most people, this would be part of a longer trip from Lamu with stop-overs elsewhere. If there's sufficient wind, the return trip to Kiwayu from Lamu takes three days and two nights.

The Rift Valley

In Kenya the Rift Valley comes down through Lake Turkana, the Cherangani Hills, lakes Baringo, Bogoria, Nakuru and Naivasha then exits south through the plains to Tanzania. Together these areas make up some of Kenya's most interesting places to visit. Lake Turkana (dealt with in the Northern Kenya chapter) is a huge lake in the semidesert north, home to nomadic pastoralists and a world away from the tourist minibuses and fancy hotels of the south. The Cherangani Hills provide some excellent walking opportunities and brilliant scenery – and hair-raising roads. More accessible are the central lakes which attract literally hundreds of species of birds and many animals alike – they're a naturalist's dream and a visit to at least one of them is a must.

Volcanic activity is usually an accompaniment to rift valleys, and Kenya has Mt Longonot – accessible, easy to climb and certainly the most dominant feature of the landscape as you enter the Rift Valley from Nairobi, and Mt Kenya – at 5200 metres it's a challenging climb, although Point Lenana at 4985 metres can be reached without specialist equipment. Further south of course you have the vast plains, home of the Maasai,

and also home to a profusion of wildlife that you're not likely to come across anywhere else in the world – not to be missed.

What is the Rift Valley?

What is known as the Rift Valley in Kenya is in fact part of the Afro-Arabian rift system which stretches some 6000 km from the Dead Sea in the Middle East, south through the Red Sea, Ethiopia, Kenya, Tanzania and Malawi to Mozambique. There's a western branch of the system which forms the string of lakes in the centre of the African continent – Mobutu Sese Seko (formerly Albert) and Rutanzige (formerly Edward) forming part of the Uganda-Zaïre border, Kivu on the Zaïre-Rwanda border and Tanganyika on the Tanzania-Zaire border. This western arm joins up with the main system at the northern tip of Lake Malawi.

The Rift Valley system consists of a series of troughs and areas of uplift known as swells. The troughs, generally 40 km to 55 km wide, are along parallel fault lines and are formed by blocks dropping down in relation to the rest of the land. They account for most of the lakes and escarpments in East Africa. The swells are the land on either side

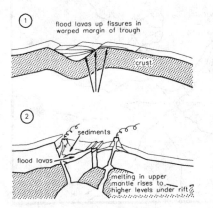

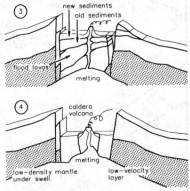

of the troughs, and it's on these that you find two of Africa's mightiest peaks, Kilimanjaro (5895 metres) and Mt Kenya (5199 metres), and lesser peaks such as Mt Elgon (4321 metres) – all extinct volcanoes. The floor of the Rift Valley is still dropping, although at the rate of a few mm per year you are hardly likely to notice anything!

The Rift Valley is certainly not one long well-formed valley with huge escarpments either side, although this does occur in places (the Rift Valley Province is one such place). Sometimes there is just a single scarp on one side (such as the Nkuruman Escarpment east of Masai Mara) or just a series of small

scarps. In some cases uplift has occurred between parallel fault lines and this has led to the formation of often spectacular mountain ranges, such as the Ruwenzoris on the Uganda-Zaïre border.

Soda Lakes

Because the shoulders of the rift slope directly away from the valley, the drainage system in the valley is generally poor, and this has resulted in the shallow lakes along the valley floor in Kenya, some of which have no outlet. Due to high evaporation, the waters have become extremely concentrated and the high alkalinity from the volcanic

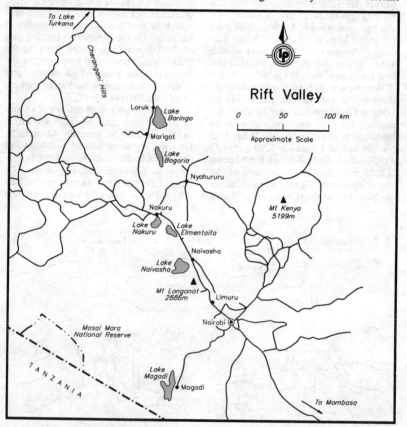

Rift Valley

0   50   100 km

Approximate Scale

deposits around makes the perfect environment for microscopic blue-green algae and diatoms, which in turn provide food for tiny crustaceans and insect larvae. These in turn are eaten by certain species of soda-resistant fish.

The water of these soda lakes (Nakuru, Bogoria and Magadi in Kenya, Lake Natron in Tanzania) may feel a little strange to the touch (it's soapy) and often doesn't smell too pleasant (though this is mostly due to the bird shit). What's all this about soapy water and bird shit got to do with me, you might ask. Well, the fact is it's simply heaven to many species of water bird and they flock here in their millions – it's a twitcher's paradise!

Foremost among the birds is the deep pink lesser flamingo (*Phoeniconaias minor*), which feeds on the blue-green algae, and the pale pink greater flamingo (*Phoenicopterus ruber*), which feeds on the tiny crustaceans and insect larvae. Also numerous are various species of duck, pelican, cormorant and stork. The highest concentrations of these birds are found where food is most abundant and this can vary from year to year and lake to lake. Another curious feature of the uplifting of the valley shoulders is the effect it has had on existing drainage patterns, although this of course happened in the last couple of millions years. In Uganda it caused the White Nile to form a pond (Lake Nyoga) after it left Lake Victoria, flow up what was previously a tributary, and into the northern end of Lake Albert via a circuitous route. Prior to the uplift the river had flowed direct from Lake Victoria into the southern end of Lake Albert.

Views

The best place to view the escarpments of the Rift Valley is from the viewpoints along the Nairobi-Naivasha road, just past Limuru. Here the road descends into the valley and the views are stunning. Mt Longonot is directly in front while the plains of the Maasai sweep away to the south. Predictably there are souvenir stalls at the viewpoints (signposted) but the stuff for sale is some of the worst I saw in the whole country.

The old road to Naivasha also descends into the rift in this area, and it's the route to take if you are heading for Mt Longonot or Masai Mara, as the new road runs direct to Naivasha. It's also the road used by the heavy vehicles and is in a diabolical state. This road was originally built by Italian POWs in WW II, and there is a chapel at the bottom of the scarp.

Getting There & Around

Lakes Naivasha, Nakuru, Elmenteita and, to a lesser extent, Baringo are readily accessible to independent travellers without their own vehicle. There are plenty of buses and matatus and a rail link between Nairobi, Naivasha and Nakuru and less frequent buses and matatus between Nakuru and Marigat (for Lake Baringo). The other lakes, however, are more remote and there's no public transport. Hitching is very difficult and can be impossible. There's also the problem that both lakes Nakuru and Bogoria are in national parks, which you are not allowed to walk in – you must tour them in a vehicle.

Renting a vehicle may be expensive for budget travellers but it would certainly work out cheaper for four people to hire a vehicle to visit Naivasha, Nakuru, Bogoria and Baringo than for them all to pay individually for safari company tours. A one day tour of Lake Nakuru starting from Nairobi goes for around US$40. A two day tour of lakes Nakuru, Bogoria and Baringo costs about US$150 per person. A car hired for several days and shared between four people would cost considerably less than the total cost of a two day tour for four people.

MT LONGONOT NATIONAL PARK

Hill climbers and view seekers should not miss the opportunity of climbing to the rim of dormant Longonot (2886 metres), a fairly young volcano which still retains the typical shape of these mountains, although it's far from being a perfect conical shape.

As this is gazetted a national park there is an entrance fee of KSh 220. The scramble up to the rim takes about 45 minutes from the parking area, and to do the circuit of the rim a further 2½ to three hours is needed. If you're feeling game there's a track leading down inside the crater to the bottom. If you want to do this it's worth hiring a local guide before you set off.

Places to Stay

There's no accommodation in the park or immediate vicinity, but it is possible to camp at the *ranger's station* at the foot of the mountain. If you are just on a day trip you can leave your gear at the Longonot railway or police station.

Getting There & Away

If you don't have your own transport it's a long walk from Longonot railway station on the old road to Naivasha. It's about seven km into the track head, and even if you have your own car it's wise to pay someone to keep an eye on it, or leave it at the Longonot railway station.

LAKE ELMENTEITA

Like Lake Nakuru, Elmenteita is a shallow, soda lake with a similar ecology. Flamingos live here too, but in nowhere near the same numbers as at Nakuru. It does have the advantage, though, that it's not a national park so you can walk around it and you don't have to pay to get in. The easiest way to get there is to take a matatu along the Naivasha-Nakuru road and get off at one of the viewpoints (signposted) on the escarpment above the lake. Walk down from there or hitch a ride if there's anything going.

NAIVASHA

There's very little of interest in the town of Naivasha itself. It's just a small service centre for the surrounding agricultural district. Most travellers just pass through here on the way to or from Mt Longonot, Lake Naivasha, Hells' Gate National Park and Nakuru. The main road actually skirts the town so if you're just going direct from Nairobi to Nakuru you don't actually pass through Naivasha. It's a good place to stock up with supplies if you're planning a sojourn

by the lake as there are very limited stocks in the dukas dotted along the lake shore road.

The area around Naivasha was actually one of the first settled by wazungu and the Delamere Estates, originally owned by Lord Delamere, surround the town and stretch away to the west towards Nakuru. Many of the plots around Naivasha are still European owned – hardly surprising as this was one of the stamping grounds of the Happy Valley set of the 1930s.

The town is basically just a couple of streets, and everything is within walking distance.

Places to Stay – bottom end

If you need to stay overnight in Naivasha there's a good range of budget hotels. The *Naivasha Super Lodge* has no doubles but the single beds are large enough for a couple. At KSh 60 it's not bad value. For something a little less cosy try the *Olenkipai Boarding & Lodging* or the *Heshima Bar Boarding & Lodging*, both of which are adequate and charge around KSh 70 for a double.

There are plenty of other cheap places along Kariuki Chotara Rd.

Places to Stay – middle

For more salubrious lodgings the *Naivasha Silver Hotel* on Kenyatta Ave is a new place with clean rooms complete with bath, hot water and telephone for KSh 180/240 a single/double. It seems a trifle out of place in this small rural town.

More upmarket still is the *La Belle Inn* (tel (0311) 20116) on Moi Ave, which has a certain faded charm. Rooms cost KSh 205/385 including a light breakfast.

Places to Eat

For a breakfast lash-out you can't beat the *La Belle Inn*. For KSh 95 you get fresh juice, croissant with butter and home-made jam, toast, eggs, bacon, sausage, tomato and tea or coffee – worth its weight in cholesterol! The outdoor terrace is also a pleasant place to have a beer or a light meal, and is a popular watering hole with people on their way through town; it is closed on Tuesdays.

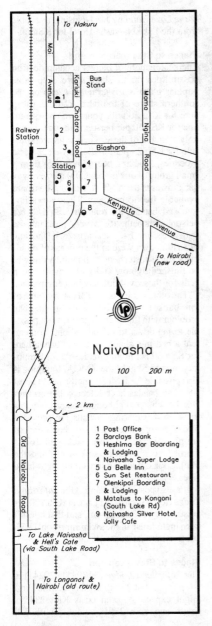

Naivasha

0   100   200 m

~ 2 km

To Nakuru

Moi Avenue

Kariuki Chotara Road

Bus Stand

Mama Ngina Road

Railway Station

Biashara

Station

Kenyatta Avenue

To Nairobi (new road)

To Lake Naivasha & Hell's Gate (via South Lake Road)

Old Nairobi Road

To Longonot & Nairobi (old route)

1 Post Office
2 Barclays Bank
3 Heshima Bar Boarding & Lodging
4 Naivasha Super Lodge
5 La Belle Inn
6 Sun Set Restaurant
7 Olenkipai Boarding & Lodging
8 Matatus to Kongoni (South Lake Rd)
9 Naivasha Silver Hotel, Jolly Cafe

The *Jolly Cafe* next to the Silver Hotel on Kenyatta Ave is slightly less extravagant and has decent food. For good old no-frills African stodge try the *Sun Set Restaurant* on the corner of Kenyatta Ave and Kariuki Chotara Rd.

Getting There & Away
Bus & Matatu The bus and matatu station is on Kariuki Chotara Rd. There are frequent buses and matatus to Nairobi, Nakuru and all points further west. There are also departures for Nyahururu and Narok.

Train Travel from Naivasha to Nairobi by train is inconvenient as all the trains pass through in the early hours of the morning. The trains to Kisumu and Malaba pass through in the late afternoon. Unless you are prepared to travel 3rd class, make a booking in Nairobi before arriving in Naivasha.

Hitching It's useless trying to hitch out of Naivasha town to Nairobi without first getting onto the main (new) road. The accepted point for hitching, and where the main road passes closest to the town, is about 500 metres east of the bus station. It's about one km to the main road in either the Nakuru or Nairobi direction.

LAKE NAIVASHA
Naivasha is one of the Rift Valley's freshwater lakes and its ecology is quite different from that of the soda lakes. It's home to an incredible variety of bird species and one of the main focuses of conservation efforts in Kenya. Not everyone supports these efforts, however, and the ecology of the lake has been interfered with on a number of occasions, the most notable introductions being sport fish, commercial fish, the North American red swamp crayfish, the South American coypu or nutria (an escapee from a fur farm) and various aquatic plants including *salvinia* which is a menace on Lake Kariba in southern Africa.

The lake has ebbed and flowed over the years as half-submerged fencing posts indicate. Early in the 1890s it dried up almost completely but then it rose a phenomenal 15 metres and inundated a far larger area than it presently occupies. It has receded since then and currently covers about 170 sq km.

Since it's a freshwater lake which can be used for irrigation purposes, the surrounding countryside is a major production area of fresh fruit and vegetables as well as beef cattle both for domestic consumption and export. There's even a fledgeling vineyard on the eastern shore.

On the western side of Lake Naivasha, past the village of Kongoni, there is a crater lake with lush vegetation at the bottom of a beautiful but small volcanic crater. If you have transport it's worth visiting. You have to cross private land for about 500 metres in order to get there, so close all gates behind you or ask permission if necessary. South of the lake is the Hell's Gate National Park which is well worth exploring.

Almost opposite Hippo Point, a couple of km past Fisherman's Camp, is Elsamere, the former home of the late Joy Adamson of *Born Free* fame. She bought the house in 1967 with the view that she and her husband, George might retire there. She did much of her writing from Elsamere right up until her murder in 1980. It seems George never spent much time there. It is now a small museum and for KSh 50 someone will show you around, and you get an excellent afternoon tea with mountains of home-made cakes and biscuits! It's open daily between 3 and 5 pm.

Between 1937 and 1950 Lake Naivasha was Nairobi's airport! Imperial Airways and then BOAC flew Empire and Solent flying boats here on the four day journey from Southampton. Passengers came ashore at the Lake Naivasha Hotel where buses would be waiting to shuttle them to Nairobi. The lake also featured strongly with the decadent Happy Valley settler crowd in the '30s. The mansion known as Oserian (or the Djinn Palace) which features in the book (and the dreadful movie) *White Mischief* is on the southern shore of the lake. It's privately owned and is not open to the public. For a full account of the history of European activity in the area, get hold of a copy of *Naivasha & the Lake Hotel* by Jan Hemsing, available from the Lake Naivasha Hotel for KSh 60.

Places to Stay – bottom end

There's a couple of budget accommodation possibilities on the lake shore. The most popular place is *Fisherman's Camp* on the southern shore of the lake. You can camp here for KSh 50 with your own tent or rent one for KSh 50 per person, although there's only a couple of these. There's firewood for sale for KSh 20 per bundle, as well as basic groceries, food and beer (of course) from a small group of dukas about 500 metres away back towards the YMCA. Rowing boats are available free to campers. There are a few four-bed bandas for rent for KSh 180 per person with bath. It's a very pleasant site with grass and shady acacia trees. At the time of writing they were in the process of building a youth hostel here, so hopefully this will be finished by now and will provide cheap beds for those without camping equipment.

The other choice is the *YMCA*, a couple of km back towards Naivasha town. The problem with this place is that it's not possible to get down to the lake shore. You can rent a bed in a shabby concrete banda here for KSh 80 per night plus KSh 5 for temporary membership of the YMCA. Camping is also possible for KSh 50 but it's not the best site. The bandas have kitchens but no firewood or charcoal although you can buy this for KSh 4. Cooking utensils are provided free of charge. The office here has a limited supply of canned and packaged foods (corned beef, biscuits, soft drinks and the like). Look out for the sign on the right-hand side.

It's also possible to camp at the *Safariland Lodge* (tel (0311) 20241), but at KSh 120 per person it's a blatant rip-off, and that doesn't even include use of the swimming pool (KSh 30, free to other guests)!

Places to Stay – top end

The *Safariland Lodge* (tel (0311) 20241) is a top-range hotel with all the facilities you might expect. A room costs KSh 2345 a single and KSh 2795 a double with full

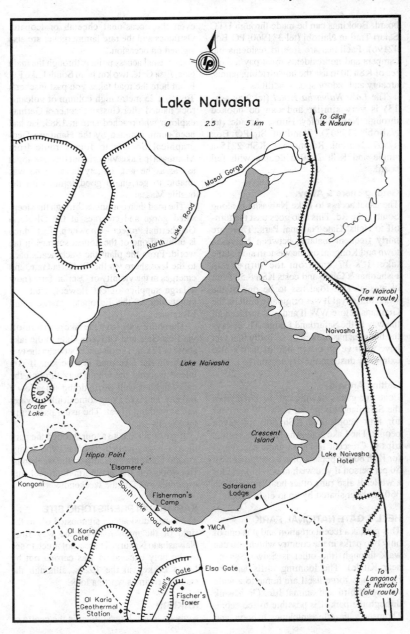

Lake Naivasha

0   2.5   5 km

To Gilgil
& Nakuru

Masai Gorge

North Lake Road

To Nairobi
(new route)

Naivasha

Lake Naivasha

Crater
Lake

Crescent
Island

Hippo Point

Lake Naivasha
Hotel

'Elsamere'

Kongoni

South Lake Road

Fisherman's
Camp

dukas

Safariland
Lodge

YMCA

Ol Karia
Gate

Elsa Gate

Hell's
Gate

Fischer's
Tower

To
Langonot
& Nairobi
(old route)

Ol Karia
Geothermal
Station

board. Bookings can be made through UTC Safari Trail in Nairobi (tel 331960, PO Box 42196). Facilities are free to residents but campers and nonresidents must pay a daily fee of KSh 30 to use the horse-riding, tennis, archery and indoor sports facilities.

The *Lake Naivasha Hotel* (tel Naivasha 13) is very similar and can be booked through New Stanley House Arcade (tel Nairobi 335807), Standard St, PO Box 47557, Nairobi. Rooms cost KSh 2215 a single and KSh 2940 a double with full board.

Getting There & Away

The usual access to Lake Naivasha is along South Lake Rd. This also goes past the turn-off to Hells' Gate National Park. There are fairly frequent matatus between Naivasha town and Kongoni on the western side of the lake. It's 17 km from the turn-off to Fisherman's Camp and costs KSh 8.50 from Naivasha. This road has to be one of the worst in Kenya! It was originally built by the Germans before WW II and was surfaced all the way to the Safariland Lodge. These days the bitumen has broken up so badly that you have to drive on either side of it. It's also extremely dusty in the dry season.

Getting Around

Boats for game viewing can be hired from the Safariland Lodge for KSh 320 per hour for four people and KSh 560 for seven people. The Lake Naivasha Hotel also offers trips to Crescent Island (a game sanctuary) for KSh 80 per person, plus a charge of KSh 50 per person if you wish to get off there for a while. It also runs other boat trips at KSh 350 per hour shared by up to eight people.

HELL'S GATE NATIONAL PARK

This park is a recent creation and it is one of only two parks in the country which you can walk through (the other is Saiwa Swamp near Kitale). The looming cliffs and the Hell's Gate gorge itself are home to a wide variety of bird and animal life. On a walk through the park it is possible to see zebra, Thomson's gazelle, antelope, baboon and even the occasional cheetah or leopard. Ostriches and the rare lammergeyer are also sighted on occasion.

The usual access point is through the main gate, Elsa Gate, two km from South Lake Rd. From here the road takes you past Fischer's Tower, a 25 metre high column of volcanic rock named after Gustav Fischer, a German explorer who reached here in 1883. He had been commissioned by the Hamburg Geographical Society to find a route from Mombasa to Lake Victoria but this was about as far as he got, largely because he was unable to get on to good terms with the hostile Maasai.

The road then continues through the steep-sided gorge and emerges at the Ol Karia Geothermal Project – a power project which is utilising one of the hottest sources in the world. From the plant the track heads back to the lake shore via the Ol Karia Gate, and emerges in the vicinity of Oserian farm (now a large supplier of cut flowers, fruit and vegetables to the European market) and Elsamere.

The entire walk from the lake road turn-off via Elsa Gate and Ol Karia Gate to the lake shore is 22 km. The distance between the two gates via the lake road is nine km. If you intend walking the whole way through the park (and it is well worth doing so), allow a full day, and take along some drinking water and something to eat. The usual park entry fees apply.

If you want to take a tour through the park there's a guy called Thomas who hangs around Fisherman's Camp on the weekends. He works on the geothermal project and organises tours on the weekends.

KARIANDUSI PREHISTORIC SITE

The Kariandusi site is signposted off to the right of the main road on the way from Naivasha to Nakuru. There's not much to see as the only excavation was carried out by Louis Leakey in the 1920s, although the small museum is worth a look.

NAKURU

Kenya's fourth largest town is the centre of

a rich farming area about halfway between Nairobi and Kisumu on the main road and railway line to Uganda. It's here that the railway forks, one branch going to Kisumu on Lake Victoria and the other to Malaba on the Ugandan border.

It's a pleasant town with a population of 75,000 but it's of interest mainly to those who work and farm in the area. The big draw for travellers is the nearby Lake Nakuru National Park with its prolific birdlife. The Menengai Crater and Hyrax Hill Prehistoric Site in the immediate area are both worth a visit (see later in this chapter).

Places to Stay – bottom end

The *Amigos Guest House* on Gusil Rd is a friendly place to stay and is the best value in Nakuru. Rooms cost KSh 70/120/180 a single/double/triple with common bath. Don't confuse this place with the other Amigos at the junction of Kenyatta Ave and Bondoni Rd. The other one isn't anywhere near as good and can be very noisy because of the upstairs bar.

Another good place is the *Tropical Lodge* on Moi Rd. It's clean and friendly and charges KSh 85/120 for singles/doubles.

Places to Stay – middle

Going up in price, the *Mukoh Hotel* on the corner of Mosque and Gusil roads is very clean, quiet and comfortable. It costs KSh 95/145 a single/double without bathroom and KSh 120/190 with bathroom. Soap and towels are provided and there is erratic hot water.

A new place in the centre of the town is the *Shik Parkview Hotel* (tel 45330) on the corner of Kenyatta Ave and Bondoni Rd. It's not that chic and at KSh 120/215 with common bath and breakfast is somewhat overpriced. A single with bathroom and breakfast is KSh 180. The rooms overlooking Kenyatta Ave are noisy. The best thing about this place is its proximity to the bus and railway stations.

The *Shiriksho High Life Hotel* on Mosque Rd is conveniently close to the bus and matatu stand but otherwise is not a great bargain. Rooms with common bath go for KSh 120/215.

Places to Stay – top end

There's a choice of two top-end places in Nakuru. The old-established *Midland Hotel* (tel 43954) on Kamati Rd is a rambling old place with rooms for KSh 335/605 with bath, hot water and breakfast. A very pleasant alternative is the newly constructed *Waterbuck Hotel* (tel 40081, 44122) on the corner of Kenyatta Ave and West Rd, which offers very pleasantly decorated, self-contained rooms all with balcony for KSh 420 a single and KSh 600 a double including a substantial breakfast. The hotel has its own bar, restaurant and barbecue bar and the staff are very friendly. Vehicles can be parked safely in the hotel compound which is guarded 24 hours a day.

Places to Eat

For the price and quality of food, the best place to eat is the *Tipsy Restaurant* on Gusil Rd. It's very popular with local people especially at lunch time. They offer Indian curries, Western food and lake fish. It's very tasty food.

The restaurant on the ground floor of the *Mukoh Hotel* is a good place for breakfast and also serves good meals and snacks. For just a coffee and a snack try the *Kenya Coffee House* on the corner of Moi Rd and Kenyatta Ave. You can also buy roasted coffee beans here.

The town's flashiest restaurant is probably the *Oyster Shell Restaurant*, upstairs on Kenyatta Ave near the corner of Club Rd. The menu is extensive and the focus is on Western food, but expect to spend around KSh 120 per person on a meal here.

You could also try the restaurant in the *Midland Hotel*. It's large and not that popular so you may feel a little lost in the cavernous room. Main dishes are in the KSh 60 to KSh 120 range, and they also do a KSh 130 four-course curry set meal.

If you like eating alfresco then head off to the barbecue bar at the *Hotel Waterbuck* (at the back of the hotel) where there's an excel-

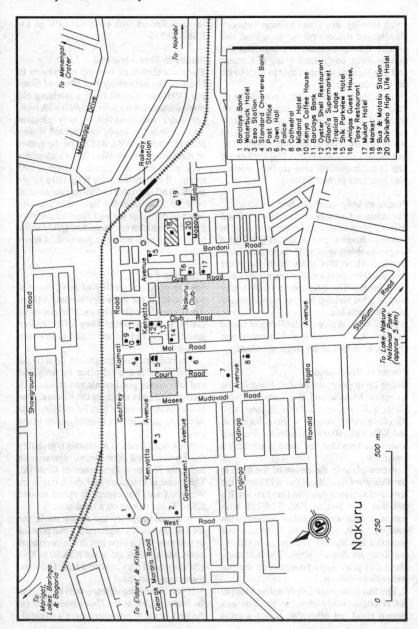

To Menengai Crater

To Nairobi

Menengai Drive

Railway Station

1	Barclays Bank
2	Waterbuck Hotel
3	Esso Station
4	Standard Chartered Bank
5	Post Office
6	Town Hall
7	Police
8	Cathedral
9	Midland Hotel
10	Kenyo Coffee House
11	Barclays Bank
12	Oyster Shell Restaurant
13	Gilani's Supermarket
14	Tropical Lodge
15	Shik Parkview Hotel
16	Amigos Guest House,
	Tipsy Restaurant
17	Mukoh Hotel
18	Market
19	Bus & Matatu Station
20	Shiriksho High Life Hotel

Mosque

Bondoni Road

Gusil Road

Nakuru Club

Avenue

Kenyatta Road

Kamati Road

Club Road

Moi Road

Court

Moses Road

Mudavadi Road

Ngala Road

Stadium Road

To Lake Nakuru National Park (approx 5 km)

Geoffrey Avenue

Kenyatta Avenue

Government Avenue

Odinga Avenue

Ronald Avenue

Oginga Avenue

West Road

George Morara Road

To Eldoret & Kitale

To Marigat, Lakes Baringo & Bogoria

Showground Road

Nakuru

500 m

250

0

lent range of delicious food priced from KSh 40 to KSh 70 and where you can eat under makuti-roofed gazebos by candlelight. If you like a game of darts, this is the place! The local players are very keen and very hard to beat. Get there early if you want to eat.

Getting There & Away

Road The bus and matatu station is right in the thick of things at the eastern edge of town, near the railway line. It's a pretty chaotic place although generally it doesn't take too long to locate the bus, matatu or Peugeot you want. There are regular departures for Naivasha, Nairobi, Nyahururu and all points west.

Train As is the case with Naivasha, trains often come through here in the middle of the night so you're better off going by road. The Kisumu and Nairobi trains come through daily (nightly?) at 12.30 am and 2.25 am respectively, while the Malaba trains are on Tuesday, Friday and Saturday at 8.45 pm. Also like Naivasha, you need to make an advance reservation in Nairobi if you're heading west and want to travel in 1st or 2nd class. The fares in KSh are:

Destination	1st class	2nd class	3rd class
Nairobi	176	83	40
Kisumu	210	98	49
Eldoret	195	92	45
Malaba	356	165	85

LAKE NAKURU NATIONAL PARK

Created in 1961, the park has since been considerably increased in size and now covers an area of some 200 sq km. Like most of the other Rift Valley lakes, it is a shallow soda lake. Some years ago the level of the lake rose and this resulted in a mass migration of the flamingos to other Rift Valley lakes, principally Bogoria, Magadi and Natron. What had been dubbed 'the world's greatest ornithological spectacle' suddenly wasn't anywhere near as spectacular. Since then the lake has receded and the flamingos have returned. Once again you have the opportunity of seeing up to two million flamingos along with tens of thousands of other birds. It's an ornithologists' paradise and one of the world's most magnificent sights. Those of you who have seen the film, *Out of Africa*, and remember the footage of the flight over the vast flocks of flamingos, are in for a very similar treat. Simply go up to the lookout on the top of Baboon Cliffs on the western side of the lake and feast your eyes on the endless pink masses which fringe the lake.

Don't blame us, though, if the birds are not there in such profusion or even if the lake dries up! The flamingos migrate from time to time if food gets scarce and there's a better supply elsewhere – usually to Lake Bogoria further north or to lakes Magadi and Natron further south.

The lake is very shallow and fluctuates by up to four metres annually. When the water is low the soda crystallises out along the shoreline as a blinding white band of powder which is going to severely test your skills as a photographer. Lake Nakuru last dried up in the late 1950s and, at that time, soda dust storms and dust devils whipped up by high winds made life unbearable for people in the town and surrounding area. In the dry season you'll see these dust devils (like tiny tornadoes) whipping up soda into the air as they course along the shoreline.

Since the park also has areas of grassland, bush, forest and rocky cliffs there are many other animals to be seen apart from birds. One species you'll see plenty of are wart hogs with their amusing way of running with their tails erect. Right by the water you'll come across waterbuck and buffalo, while further into the bush are Thomson's gazelle and reedbuck – there's even the occasional leopard. Around the cliffs you may catch sight of hyrax and birds of prey. There's even a small herd of hippos which generally lives along the northern shore of the lake.

The national park entrance is about six km from the centre of Nakuru. Entry costs KSh 220 per person plus KSh 50 per vehicle. As in most national parks, you must be in a vehicle. Walking is not permitted so you will either have to hitch a ride with other tourists, rent your own vehicle or go on a tour.

You can get out of your vehicle on the lake shore and at certain viewpoints – but only there. It's a memorable experience being in the proximity of several hundred thousand flamingos feeding, preening, grunting and honking and even more memorable when several thousand of them decide that you're a little too close for comfort and they take off to find a more congenial spot. Don't drive too close to the water's edge, the mud is very soft! Take your cue from the tracks of other vehicles.

Rhino Rescue

Many of Africa's animals are threatened by the loss of their habitat due to human over-population or by poachers, and it's the poor rhino which is in the greatest danger. The rhino's horn, its trademark cause the problem – plenty of people covet them and this only serves to push the price up as they become increasingly rare.

The stark statistics are horrific. In 1970, it is estimated that Kenya had about 20,000 black rhinos. By 1985, that number had dwindled to just 425 and rhinos were so few and so scattered that it was becoming increasingly difficult for a lady rhino to meet a compatible gentleman rhino, object baby rhinos. With this huge fall in the numbers, the price of rhino horn on the black market had soared from US$35 per kg to over US$30,000 per kg – and is still rising. Elsewhere in Africa, the fall in rhino numbers has been equally dramatic.

Rhino horn is a popular ingredient in many Chinese traditional medicines and we all know of the supposed effects of rhino horn on one's libido. But the major market for rhino horn is, of all places, North Yemen, where Djambia daggers with rhino horn handles are worth over US$15,000. These fantastic prices are inspiring ruthless tactics from poachers who tote modern weapons and are as likely to shoot as run when con-fronted by rangers. In 1990, their brazenness reached new heights when they shot not only

Kenya's only five white rhinos (in Meru National Park), but also shot the armed guards first in order to do so!

The only solution is felt to be small parks where rhinos can be carefully watched and protected. Funded by Rhino Rescue, an organisation set up in 1986 specifically to save the rhino, the Nakuru National Park was selected as the first manageable rhino sanc-tuary. The park is now protected by a 74 km electric fence with manned guard posts every 15 km. The construction involved over 11,000 fence posts and 880 km of high tensile wire. An initial group of 19 rhino was established and there are plans to increase this number, possibly to as many as 60.

Additional sanctuaries are planned but saving the rhino isn't going to come cheap. Donations can be sent to:

Rhino Rescue,
PO Box 1
Saxmundham
Suffolk, IP17 3JT
UK

Places to Stay – bottom end

There is a good camping site, known as the *Backpackers' Campsite* just inside the park gate which costs KSh 60 per person per night. Fresh water is available and there's a couple of long-drop toilets but you need to bring all your own food. Make sure tents are securely zipped up when you're away from them otherwise the vervet monkeys will steal everything inside them. If you are backpack-ing and trying to hitch a ride, the rangers at the gate will let you camp here without paying the park entry until you are success-ful.

If you have no camping equipment there's the very basic *Florida Day & Night Club* about half a km before the entrance gate.

A km or so further into the park is the *Njoro Campsite* and this is the one to head for if you have a vehicle. It's a beautiful grassy site under acacia trees, there's fire-wood around, water on tap and the usual long-drop toilets.

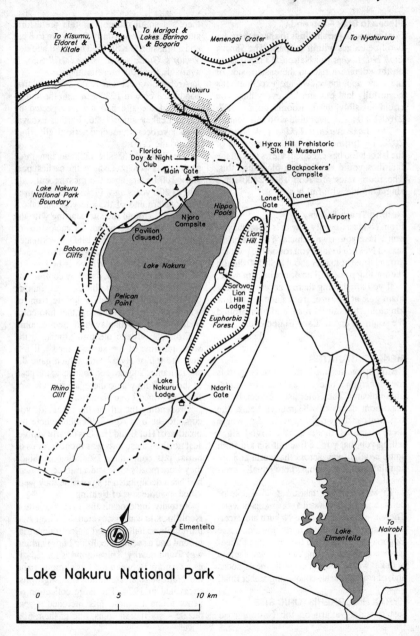

Lake Nakuru National Park

To Kisumu, Eldoret & Kitale

To Marigat & Lakes Baringo & Bogoria

Menengai Crater

To Nyahururu

Nakuru

Hyrax Hill Prehistoric Site & Museum

Florida Day & Night Club

Main Gate

Backpackers' Campsite

Lanet Gate

Lanet

Lake Nakuru National Park Boundary

Hippo Pools

Airport

Njoro Campsite

Pavilion (disused)

Lion Hill

Baboon Cliffs

Lake Nakuru

Sarova Lion Hill Lodge

Pelican Point

Euphorbia Forest

Rhino Cliff

Lake Nakuru Lodge

Ndarit Gate

Elmenteita

Lake Elmenteita

To Nairobi

0   5   10 km

Places to Stay – top end

For those with the shillings to spend there are two fine lodges within the park. The *Sarova Lion Hill Lodge* (tel Nairobi 333233) is up on the edge of a rise on the eastern side of the park and the views are excellent. It's beautifully laid out and has everything you could possibly need. Rooms go for KSh 2160/2580 a single/double with full board.

The *Lake Nakuru Lodge* (tel Nairobi 20225) is further south on the same side of the lake. It too has excellent views and all the facilities you'd expect in a place like this. The room rates are KSh 1800/2400 for a single/double with full board.

Getting There & Away

From Nakuru the only way in is by taxi if you don't have your own vehicle. You can hire a taxi in Nakuru to take you round the park for around three hours for about KSh 540 though the starting price will no doubt be a lot more.

If you are driving there's access from the main gate at Nakuru, from Lanet just a few km along the Nairobi road, and from around the southern end of Lake Elmenteita.

MENENGAI CRATER

Rising up on the northern side of Nakuru is the Menengai Crater, an extinct 2490 metre high volcano. The crater itself descends to a maximum depth of 483 metres below the rim. You can drive right up to the edge, where there's one of those totally trivial signs telling you that you're five million km from some city halfway across the world and six squillion km from somewhere equally irrelevant.

To walk up there takes a solid couple of hours, and it's *up*, but still a very pleasant walk. The views back over Lake Nakuru are excellent, as are the views north towards Lake Bogoria once you reach the top. About three-quarters of the way along there is a small group of dukas where you can get basic meals, sodas and, of course, the all-conquering amber fluid.

HYRAX HILL PREHISTORIC SITE

Just outside Nakuru on the Nairobi road

there's a small museum at this prehistoric site. The site is open daily from 9 am to 6 pm and admission is KSh 15. The small booklet, *Visitor's Guide to the Hyrax Hill Site*, is available from the museum there.

Archaeological excavations were first conducted here in 1937 although the significance of the site had been suspected by Louis Leakey since 1926. Further excavations have been conducted periodically, right up into the 1980s.

The finds at the site indicate that three settlements were made here, the earliest possibly 3000 years ago, the most recent only 200 to 300 years ago. From the museum at the northern end of the site you can take a short stroll around the site, starting with the North-East Village where 13 enclosures or pits were excavated. Only Pit D, investigated in 1865, is still open; the others have grown over. The North-East Village is believed to be about 400 years old, dated by comparison with the nearby Lanet site. A great number of potsherds were found on the site, some of which have been pieced together into complete jars and are displayed in the museum.

From the village the trail climbs to the scant remains of the stone-walled hill fort near the top of Hyrax Hill, which gave the site its name. You can continue up to the peak of the hill from where there is a fine view of flamingo-lined Lake Nakuru.

Descending the hill on the other side you come to the Iron Age Settlement where the position of Hut B and Hut C is clearly visible. Just north of these huts was found a series of burial pits containing 19 skeletons. Since they were mostly male and a number of them had been decapitated it's possible they were killed in some sort of fighting.

Virtually underneath the Iron Age site a Neolithic site was discovered. The Iron Age burial pits actually topped a Neolithic burial mound and a second Neolithic burial mound was found nearby. This mound is fenced off as a display. Between the burial mound and the Nairobi road are more Iron Age pits, excavated in 1974. The large collection of items found in these pits included a real puzzle – six Indian coins, one of them 500 years old, two of them dating from 1918 and 1919!

Finally, following the path back to the museum, there's a *bau* board in a large rock. This popular game is played throughout East Africa.

LAKE BOGORIA

The two completely dissimilar lakes Bogoria and Baringo are north of Nakuru off the B4 highway to Marigat and Lodwar. Lake Bogoria is a shallow soda lake while Lake Baringo is a deeper freshwater lake. They're connected to Nakuru by the B4 road which is a superb, sealed highway the whole way. Bogoria is a national park so there's an entry fee of KSh 220 per person plus KSh 50 per vehicle.

Most of the birdlife on Bogoria has migrated to the (presently) richer pastures of Lake Nakuru but the stalwarts (of all species) remain. It's a very peaceful area but it doesn't currently compare with the ornithological spectacle of Nakuru. There are, however, the hot springs and geysers about three-quarters of the way down the lake going south. They're not comparable with those at Rotorua in New Zealand but if you've never seen geysers before then this is the place. The springs are boiling hot so don't put your bare foot or hand into them unless you want to nurse scalds for the next week.

The land to the west of the lake is a hot and relatively barren wilderness of rocks and scrub, and animals are rare though you may be lucky to catch sight of a greater kudu, impala and klipspringer. The eastern side of the lake is dominated by the sheer face of the northern extremities of the Aberdares.

Places to Stay

There are two camp sites at the southern end of the lake – *Acacia* and *Riverside* – but there are no facilities whatsoever and the lake water is totally unpalatable. Bring all water and food with you if you are intending to stay at either site. Otherwise, the camp sites are shady and very pleasant.

There's another *camp site* just outside the northern entrance gate (Loboi). Drinking water is available here and there's a small shop nearby which sells basic supplies (canned food, jam, biscuits, washing powder, soft drinks, etc). A top-range lodge has also been built near the entrance but few people seem to stay there.

Getting There & Away

There are two entrance gates to Lake Bogoria – one from the south (Mogotio) and another from the north (Loboi). You'll see the signpost for the southern entrance on the B4 about 38 km past Nakuru heading north but, if you take it, you'll probably regret it! Most of this road is good smooth dust or gravel but there is about five km of it which leads down to the southern park entrance which will certainly rip apart any tyres and destroy any vehicle driven at more than a few km per hour. Without 4WD you'd be wasting your time. These razor-sharp lava beds don't end once you reach the park gate but continue for at least as far on the other side. In addition, signposting along the route from the turn-off is almost nonexistent.

A far better entry to the park is from the Loboi Gate just a few km before you reach Marigat on the B4. It's also signposted. From the turn-off, it's a good 15 km to the actual park entry gate but the road is now sealed the whole way.

Whichever gate you enter through, you're going to need your own vehicle since hitching is well-nigh impossible. Very few people visit Bogoria and those who do are usually in tourist minibuses so they won't pick you up unless you're booked with them. It *may* be possible to walk into the park since there are no large predators living here (with the possible exception of the occasional leopard) but don't count on it. Officially, you're supposed to tour the park in a vehicle.

LAKE BARINGO

Some 15 km north of the town of Marigat you come to the village of Kampi-ya-Samaki which is the centre for exploring Lake Baringo. This lake, like Naivasha, is a freshwater lake with a very different ecology from Lake Bogoria. It supports many different species of aquatic and birdlife as well as crocodiles and herds of hippos which invade the grassy shore every evening to browse on the vegetation. You'll hear their characteristic grunt as you walk back to your tent or banda after dark or settle down for the night. They might even decide to crop the grass right next to your tent. If they do, stay where you are. They're not aggressive animals – they don't need to be with a bulk and jaws like that! – but if you frighten them or annoy them they might go for you. And, despite all appearances, they can *move*!

Crocodiles and hippos apart, Lake Baringo's main attraction is the birdlife and the lake is the bird-watching centre of Kenya. People come here to engage in this activity from all over the world. Kenya has over 1200 different species of birds and over 450 of them have been sighted at Lake Baringo. Some bird-watchers are so keen they're known as 'twitchers' since their primary concern seems to be to rack up sightings of as many different bird species as possible. It's a serious business and the Lake Baringo Club even has a 'resident ornithologist' who leads bird-watching walks and gives advice to guests. A few years ago he set a world record for the number of species seen in one 24 hour period – over 300!

There's a constant twittering, chirping and cooing of birds in the trees around the lake, in the rushes on the lake and even on the steep face of the nearby escarpment. Even if you've had no previous interest in bird watching, it's hard to resist setting off on the dawn bird walk and the highlight of the morning is likely to be a sighting of hornbills or the magnificent eagles which live almost exclusively on rock hyrax.

Places to Stay – bottom end

There's a superb place to stay just before the village called *Robert's Camp* (tel Kampi-ya-Samaki 3 – through the operator) where you can camp for KSh 60 per person per night with bundles of firewood for KSh 25. Facilities include clean showers and toilets. There are also three double bandas available with

use of cooking facilities for KSh 120 per person plus 18% tax. I'd strongly recommend the bandas if there is one available but demand is heavy and it would be wise to book one in advance (through David Roberts Wildlife, PO Box 1051, Nakuru). They are beautiful, circular, grass-thatched traditionally styled houses which are clean as a new pin and furnished with comfortable beds, table and chairs and mosquito netting at the windows. Showers and toilets are separate and cooking facilities are available for a small extra charge. They are superb value. The people here are very friendly and there's a huge land tortoise which ambles around the grounds and appears to be used to the attention it receives.

If you're camping here then you need to exercise some common sense regarding the hippos. Although hippos may graze within just a metre of your tent at night, you should not approach nearer than 20 metres to them. It's dangerous to go nearer especially if they have young ones. Don't frighten them in any way with headlights, torches (flashlights) or loud noises and don't use flash photography. No-one's ever been hurt by a hippo in over 10 years but they are wild animals and should be treated with respect.

If this place is full or you have no camping equipment then try the *Bahari Lodge* in Kampi-ya-Samaki which costs KSh 35 a single and KSh 60 a double. It's basic. This village is also the only place you will find beer apart from the lodge next door to the Robert's and the bar on the main road above the Robert's site. There's a lively bar at the end of the road facing you as you enter the village. The beer is cheap but lukewarm and the clientele isn't used to seeing wazungu but it's a good crowd. It's also one of the few places with electric lights.

You can also check out some of the other similarly priced hotels in Kampi-ya-Samaki.

There are also places to stay in Marigat if you prefer though it's quite a way from the lake shore and it's not the world's most interesting place. At the crossroads of the B4 and the village is the *Wananchi Lodge* which costs KSh 60 a double and is basic but pro-

Top: Lion, Masai Mara National Park, Kenya (SB)
Bottom: Oryx, Samburu, Kenya (SB)

Top: Vulture in flight, Masai Mara National Park, Kenya (SB)
Bottom: Balloons, Masai Mara National Park, Kenya (HF)

vides towels, soap and mosquito nets. More expensive is the *Marigat Inn* about 1½ km from the main road turn-off (where there's a sign for it). It costs KSh 85 a double and is very pleasant with its own bar and restaurant.

Places to Stay – top end

Right next door to the Robert's Camp is the *Lake Baringo Club*, one of the Block Hotels chain (reservations through Nairobi, tel 335807 or telex 22146; PO Box 47557). Singles/doubles here cost KSh 1855/2275 for half board and KSh 1950/2465 for full board. There's a considerable discount in the low season (1 April to 30 June) when the rates are KSh 870 per person for half board and KSh 965 per person for full board. Children under 12 years old sharing a room with adults are free apart from being charged 50% of the adult meal prices. Facilities at the Club include a swimming pool, darts, table tennis, badminton, a library and a whole range of local excursions including boat trips and bird-watching trips accompanied by an expert.

Scheduled one hour boat trips cost KSh 180 per person (minimum three people), other boat trips KSh 600 per boat per hour (minimum eight people), bird walks KSh 60 per person (or KSh 90 including transport) and camel rides KSh 40 per half-hour. They also offer trips to Lake Bogoria for KSh 530 per person (minimum three people) and to a nearby Njemps village for KSh 75 per person (minimum three people). The Njemps are the local tribespeople who live in villages around the lake shore and practice a mixture of pastoralism and fishing. The club has an arrangement with the headman of the village which they take you to so you're allowed to walk around freely and to take photographs though you'll probably be hassled to buy some of the handicrafts which they produce.

The club also offers trips to what it calls a 'snake park' but you'd be wasting your time since there are no snakes there any longer.

The facilities at the club are open to non-residents on payment of KSh 50 per person per day temporary membership unless you're eating either lunch or dinner there in which case it's free. Use of the swimming pool costs KSh 50 per person per day regardless of whether you eat meals here. If you drive in, on the other hand, you probably won't be asked for the fee.

The other top-end hotel is *Island Camp* which is also part of the Block Hotels chain. This is a luxury tented lodge which is rated highly by those who have stayed there but is even more expensive. There are 25 double tents each with their own shower and toilet, two bars, a swimming pool and water sports facilities. Singles/doubles cost KSh 2305/2930 for half board and KSh 2400/3120 for full board. In the low season (1 April to 30 June) the charges are KSh 1045 per person for half board and KSh 1140 per person for full board.

The prices of various activities here include water-skiing (KSh 1300 per hour), windsurfing (KSh 175 per hour), boat trips (KSh 600 per hour), bird walks on the island (KSh 30 per person) and a Njemps dancing performance (KSh 550 shared between those who watch).

Boat transfers from the mainland to the island cost KSh 210 return and car transfers from the airstrip on the mainland to the boat jetty are KSh 210 each way.

Places to Eat

If you're camping at Robert's Camp and want to keep costs down then you'll have to bring your own food with you as well as cooking facilities and equipment (unless you want to cook over a wood fire). Only very basic foodstuffs are available in the village of Kampi-ya-Samaki, and a slightly better choice in Marigat, so bring what you will need from Nakuru.

Travellers have reported that in Kampi-ya-Samaki, Moses at the Lake View Hotel will provide meals on request for KSh 50. Some hotels also serve fried fish for just KSh 4 to KSh 5.

Those who want to splurge can eat at the *Lake Baringo Club*. As you might expect, the meals here are very good but will cost you KSh 130 for breakfast and KSh 240 for either lunch or dinner. The club is also the only place where you will be able to find a cold beer as well as the only place where you can buy petrol and diesel between Marigat and Maralal.

Getting There & Away

There are frequent matatus between Nakuru and Marigat but they don't all continue on to Kampi-ya-Samaki, so you may have to hitch from Marigat or take another of the infrequent matatus which go to the village. In the opposite direction, there's a minibus from Kampi-ya-Samaki at about 7 am which goes to Nakuru and another which comes through later from Loruk at the top end of the lake.

It's an interesting journey between Nakuru and Baringo since the country remains relatively lush and green until you pass the equator where it almost immediately becomes drier and dustier and continues to get more barren and forbidding the further north you go. As you near Marigat there are spectacular mountains, ridges and escarpments.

A gravel track connects Loruk at the top end of the lake with the Nyahururu-Maralal road. It's in good shape if you have your own transport and are contemplating doing the trip. There's no public transport along this road and hitching is extremely difficult.

LAKE MAGADI

Lake Magadi is the most southerly of the Rift Valley lakes in Kenya and is very rarely visited by tourists because of its remoteness. Like most of the Rift Valley lakes, it is a soda lake and supports many flamingos and other water birds. It also has a soda extraction factory, hence the railway line here. A few years ago it was the site of a major rescue operation of young flamingos when drought threatened hundreds of thousands of them because of soda encrustation on their feathers – this doesn't affect the adults.

Magadi is quite different from the lakes to the north as it lies in semidesert. Temperatures hover around the 38°C mark during the day and much of the lake is a semisolid sludge of water and soda salts. There is a series of hot springs around the periphery of the lake.

Getting There & Away

There is a rail link to the lake shore which branches off from the main Nairobi-Mombasa line but there are no passenger services along it. There's also a minor road from Nairobi (the C58) but there's no public transport along it so you will either have to hitch or have your own vehicle.

The Central Highlands

The Kenyan central highlands comprise the Aberdares, which begin around Limuru just north-west of Nairobi and continue on up to Maralal, plus the massif of Mt Kenya itself. They form the eastern wall of the Rift Valley and are the heartland of the Kikuyu people. Within the main area are two national parks, Aberdare and Mt Kenya.

It's a very fertile region, well watered, intensively cultivated and thickly forested. The climate, likewise, is excellent. Given these qualities, it's not surprising that the land was coveted by the White settlers who began arriving in ever increasing numbers once the Mombasa-Uganda railway was completed. Here they could grow anything year-round and particularly cash crops in demand in Europe. It's also not surprising

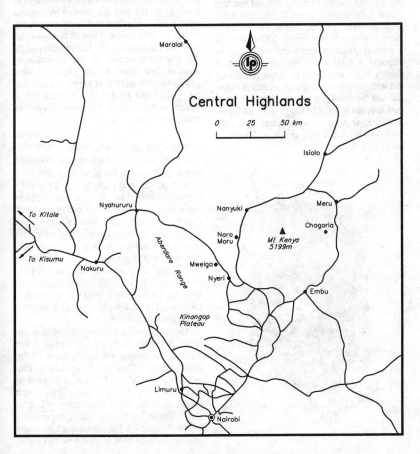

Central Highlands

0   25   50 km

that the Kikuyu eventually became so disenchanted with the alienation of their best land that war erupted between the two groups in the form of the Mau Mau Rebellion. Probably no other event was of more importance than this in forcing the British colonial authorities to reassess their position and ultimately to grant independence to the country.

While White Kenyan farmers still exist in considerable numbers in the area, their holdings have been reduced and much of the land parcelled out among the Kikuyu but it's anyone's guess how much longer this subdivision and further encroachment on the forest can continue, given the current level of population growth, before the environment is seriously threatened. Soil erosion is a serious problem and plots too small to support a family are common. It's true there's still a great deal of forest remaining but with pressure on it for construction material and firewood (the most common form of fuel for cooking and heating) there are limits to the expansion of agricultural land. It's wise to remember that much of Kenya is scrub and desert.

Kikuyu man

The Aberdares

Known to the Kikuyu as *nyandarua*, 'drying hide', the Aberdares were named after the president of the Royal Geographical Society by the explorer Thomson in 1884. With peaks of up to 4000 metres and covered in dense forests and bamboo thickets, the lower eastern slopes were long cultivated by the Kikuyu while the higher regions were left to the leopard, buffalo, lion and elephant. The arrival of the Europeans saw the establishment of coffee and tea plantations on the eastern side and wheat and pyrethrum farms on the western slopes. Most of this land has now been returned to the Kikuyu. Not all of the higher reaches of the Aberdares, however, are dense forest. There are also extensive areas of mist-covered moors along the ridges and a good swathe of forest out of which the Aberdare National Park was created in 1950.

ABERDARE NATIONAL PARK

This park essentially encloses the moorland and high forest of the Kinangop plateau – around 60 km long – along with an eastern salient reaching down to the lower slopes in the vicinity of Nyeri. Only rarely does this park feature in the itineraries of safari companies and it's even less visited by individual travellers. There are various reasons for this. The main one is perhaps the weather. As on Mt Kenya, rain can be expected at any time and when it arrives, it's heavy. Roads turn into mud slides and 4WD is absolutely essential. The park is often closed during the wet season as a result.

Another drawback (though the wild game would no doubt describe it as a plus) is the difficulty of seeing animals because of the dense forest. This is not savannah like Amboseli and Masai Mara so you have to take your time and stay a few nights which brings us to the third drawback – where to stay? There are indeed three camp sites within the park but facilities are minimal and you're going to need a good tent and warm sleeping gear. Add to that the fact that there's no public transport whatsoever, hitching is virtually impossible and that, as elsewhere, walking isn't permitted without special permission. That essentially puts them out of reach for anyone without their own transport. The only other accommodation possibilities are the two very expensive lodges – The Ark and Treetops – which you are not allowed to drive to in your own vehicle. You must make advance reservations for both and be driven there in the lodges' transport.

In the dry season it may be possible to walk over the high moorland between the four main peaks if the weather is favourable but you can't do this without the express permission of the game warden at Mweiga north of Nyeri (tel Mweiga 24). If this is what you want to do then it's best to first contact the Kenya Mountain Club in Nairobi before setting out. They may be planning such a trip.

These sorts of difficulties and/or the expense involved put off most independent travellers but if you're determined to go then the rewards can well justify the effort.

The park does offer a variety of fauna, flora and scenery which you won't find elsewhere except, perhaps, on Mt Kenya. There's also the dramatic Gura Waterfall which drops a full 300 metres, thick forest, alpine moorland and a good chance of seeing the elusive bongo, a black leopard, elephants, hundreds of species of birds and even a rhino. The major plus about this park is that you'll never feel part of the safari bus gravy train as you can often do in Masai Mara, Amboseli or Nairobi national parks.

Places to Stay

If you wish to camp in the park, reservations have to be made at the Park Headquarters at Mweiga (tel Mweiga 24), about 12 km north of Nyeri. The charges are standard.

Both of the lodges are built beside water holes and animals – especially elephant and buffalo – are lured to them by salt which is spread below the viewing platforms each day. This is obviously a contrived way of getting the animals to turn up but it pulls in the well-heeled punters and they, in turn, keep Lonrho, Block Hotels, Kodak and Nikon in business. What it doesn't do is anything positive to the immediate environment. Elephants eat a prodigious amount of herbage each day and trample down even more. Buffaloes aren't exactly light on the hoof either. The two combined make sure that the area in front of the viewing platforms resembles a matatu stand which, in turn, makes the smaller and more timid animals reluctant to approach because of lack of cover. I suppose if you pay big bucks the video has to be good even if it's thin on authenticity.

On the other hand, *Treetops* isn't exactly a 'luxury' lodge with its trestle tables, creaking floorboards, shoe-box sized rooms and shared bathroom facilities, though it does have that yuppie appeal of knowing that you've stayed under the same roof as various crowned heads of Europe and presidents of state – there are even faded mug-shots of the *nomenclatura* on the walls.

Full board including transfer from Nyeri but excluding park entry fees at Treetops costs KSh 2010 (ordinary room) and KSh 3150 (suite) per person between 1 July and 31 March, and KSh 1075 per person the rest of the year. Children under seven years old are not admitted. You must book in advance through Block Hotels (tel 335807, PO Box 47557), Central Reservation Office, Rehema House, Standard Street, Nairobi. Having booked, you must turn up at the Outspan Hotel in Nyeri not later than 12.30 pm. Here you'll be served with lunch and then driven to the lodge. It isn't necessary to stay at the Outspan the previous night unless you particularly want to.

The Ark is somewhat better appointed than Treetops and is further into the park but it costs much more, too. Full board here including transfer from Mweiga but excluding park entry fees costs KSh 2605 a single and KSh 4585 a double, plus there are 'staterooms' for KSh 4540 a single and KSh 5430 a double. These prices apply year-round. As at Treetops, children under seven years old are not admitted.

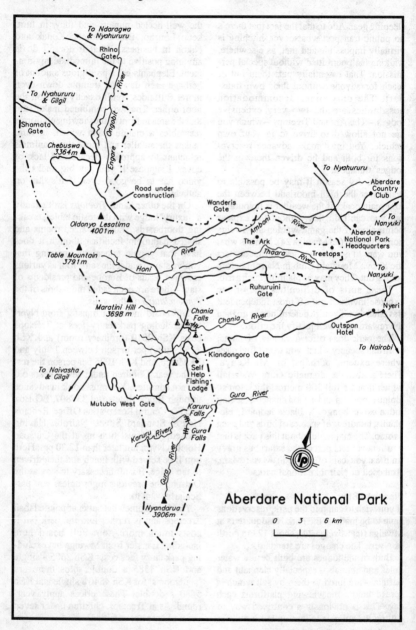

Aberdare National Park

0   3   6 km

You must book in advance through Lonrho Hotels Kenya (tel 723776, PO Box 58581), 5th floor, Bruce House, Standard St, Nairobi. Having booked you must turn up at the Aberdare Country Club at Mweiga, north of Nyeri, on the appointed day and you'll be driven to the lodge.

You can also arrange game drives in the park from The Ark at KSh 1980 (half day) and KSh 3960 (full day) per vehicle.

Other Options If you can't afford the above overnight charges at the lodges there is a somewhat cheaper option and that is to go on a game drive organised by the Outspan Hotel in Nyeri. You can do this into the eastern salient for KSh 350 per person (minimum three people) or anywhere in the park for KSh 515 per person, all excluding park entry fees. You can also rent self-drive vehicles from here for KSh 1200 (salient only) and KSh 1620 (whole park).

NYERI

Nyeri is one of the largest towns in the central highlands, the administrative head-quarters of Central Province, and the usual gateway to Aberdare National Park. It's a lively place with an extensive market, several banks, hardware stores, vehicle repair shops, bookshops and a plethora of other stores selling everything under the sun. It also has a good choice of hotels and restaurants.

It started out life as a garrison town back in the early days of colonialism but quickly became transformed into a trading and social centre for White settlers ranching cattle or growing coffee and wheat. Their watering holes, in the form of the White Rhino Hotel in town and the Aberdare Country Club out at Mweiga are nostalgic reminders of their proclivities though the White Rhino appears to have accepted inevitable decline.

It's a very green area and intensively cultivated for all manner of vegetables, sugar cane, citrus fruits, bananas, tea, coffee and even that Australian import – macadamia nuts! On a clear day, too (usually early morn-

ings), you can see Mt Kenya in all its snow-capped glory over in the distance. Apart from these virtues, however, it's hardly the most magnetic town in Kenya and few travellers stay more than a couple of nights.

Places to Stay – bottom end

If you're down and out, there are some real dives to stay at here such as the *New Alaska Hotel* and the *South Tetu Hotel* but they can't be recommended. One of the best in this range and one which travellers have recommended in the past is the *Bahati Boarding & Lodging* at the front of the upper bus and matatu stand. It's simple and clean and offers rooms for KSh 92 a double without bathroom and KSh 145 a double with bathroom. There's hot water in the mornings. The hotel has its own bar and restaurant. It's a convenient place to stay if you're taking an early bus. If it's full (unlikely), then try the *New 7 Star Boarding & Lodging* across the other side of the road. You can also check out the *Ibis Hotel* or the slightly better *Cedar Tree Boarding & Lodging*.

Places to Stay – middle

The best and most economical place to stay in this range is the *New Thingira Guest House* (tel 4769, PO Box 221, Nyeri) which you get to by turning left and going downhill just after the mosque coming in on the Nairobi-Karatina road. It's a new place and, though it has pretensions of becoming a 'conference centre', the staff are friendly (in fact, almost obsequious) and it's very clean but the architect ought to be shot (or the institute where they trained closed down abruptly)! Badly designed it may be but it's good value at KSh 215 a single and KSh 325 a double with bathroom and hot water. Breakfast costs KSh 35 and lunch or dinner KSh 60. It's wise to order dinner in advance if you intend to eat here. An askari is employed to guard the car park overnight.

Slightly more expensive is the equally modern *Central Hotel* at the top end of town which is less pretentious in its aspirations. Singles/doubles here with bathroom and hot

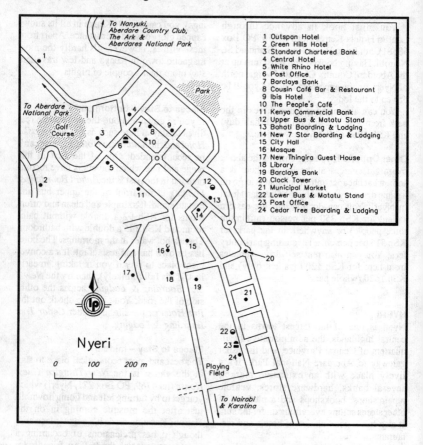

To Nanyuki,
Aberdare Country Club,
The Ark &
Aberdares National Park

Park

To Aberdare
National Park

Golf
Course

1 Outspan Hotel
2 Green Hills Hotel
3 Standard Chartered Bank
4 Central Hotel
5 White Rhino Hotel
6 Post Office
7 Barclays Bank
8 Cousin Café Bar & Restaurant
9 Ibis Hotel
10 The People's Café
11 Kenya Commercial Bank
12 Upper Bus & Matatu Stand
13 Bahati Boarding & Lodging
14 New 7 Star Boarding & Lodging
15 City Hall
16 Mosque
17 New Thingira Guest House
18 Library
19 Barclays Bank
20 Clock Tower
21 Municipal Market
22 Lower Bus & Matatu Stand
23 Post Office
24 Cedar Tree Boarding & Lodging

Nyeri

0   100   200 m

Playing
Field

To Nairobi
& Karatina

water cost KSh 300/420. The hotel has its own bar and restaurant and there's a disco on Friday and Saturday nights.

For a touch of olde-worlde charm at about the same price, though you pay more for nostalgia than the facilities which it offers, there's the old White settlers' watering hole, the *White Rhino Hotel*. It's a popular place to stay, has a terrace bar, lounge, garden and quite a cheap restaurant and offers rooms for KSh 300 a single and KSh 480 a double.

Top of the range is the *Green Hills Hotel* (tel 2017, PO Box 313, Nyeri) which sits on the crest of the hill across the narrow valley

opposite the White Rhino. It's a large place set amongst rolling lawns and has 124 double rooms (though it's not high-rise). It costs KSh 382.50 a single and KSh 589 a double including taxes. Children up to 12 years old occupying the same room are free. There are two restaurants, a bar, sauna, massage facilities, children's playground, swimming pool and guarded parking facilities. Average meal prices are KSh 60 for breakfast, KSh 90 for lunch and KSh 100 for dinner. Checkout time is 10 am. The staff are friendly and the rooms very pleasantly decorated and furnished.

Places to Stay – top end

There's only one top-range hotel in Nyeri itself and that is the *Outspan Hotel*, one of the Block Hotels chain (tel 335807, PO Box 47557, Nairobi). This is the place you have to check in at before being driven to Treetops lodge in the Aberdare National Park. It's sited in beautifully landscaped gardens opposite the golf course and has all the facilities you would expect from a top-range country hotel except that the Mt Kenya Bar has, in fact, no view of Mt Kenya at all – surely a major planning balls-up. Prices depend on the season and the type of accommodation which you take. In the high season (16 December to 31 March and 1 July to 31 August) B&B costs KSh 1870/2100 for singles/doubles and KSh 3070 for a twin cottage. In the low season (1 September to 15 December) the same costs KSh 1680/1860 for singles/doubles and KSh 2770 for a twin cottage. For the rest of the year the prices are KSh 960 for a single room and KSh 1410 for a double. Children under 12 years old are free if sharing the same room with adults.

Self-drive cars can be hired from the hotel to visit Aberdare National Park (see Other Options earlier).

The only other place in this price range is the *Aberdare Country Club* (tel Mweiga 17, PO Box 449, Nyeri), about 12 km north of Nyeri, which is now part of the Lonrho Hotels Kenya group (tel 723776, PO Box 58581), 5th floor, Bruce House, Standard St, Nairobi. Like the Kentmere Club at Limuru and the Norfolk Hotel in Nairobi (also owned by Lonrho), this was once one of the quintessential White planters' watering holes and social foci except that these days it caters for the international leisure set and those with the money to burn on a night or two at The Ark. Full board inclusive of temporary membership costs KSh 2080 a single and KSh 2700 a double.

Self-drive vehicles can be rented from the club for touring Aberdare National Park.

Places to Eat

The most reliable places for a meal are the *White Rhino Hotel* and the *Central Hotel* where you can eat well and relatively cheaply. Forget the *New Thingira Guest House* for a while until they get their cooking act together – there's a menu but rarely is anything available.

The *Cousin Café Bar & Restaurant* is worth a visit if you want cheap, tasty, no-frills food. They have a good range of European and African food here such as ugali with stew for KSh 24, chicken and chips for KSh 40, meat and potatoes for KSh 43, sandwiches for KSh 12 and breakfasts for KSh 35.

Another cheap place for snacks and coffee is the *People's Café* near the post office.

NYAHURURU (THOMSON'S FALLS)

Nyahururu, or 'T Falls' as virtually everyone calls it, was one of the last White settler towns to be established in the colonial era and didn't really take off until the arrival of the railway spur from Gilgil (on the main Nairobi-Malaba-Kisumu line) in 1929. The railway still operates but these days carries only freight. It's one of the highest towns in Kenya (2360 metres) and the climate is cool and invigorating. The surrounding undulating plateau is intensively cultivated for maize, beans and sweet potatoes and well forested, mainly with conifers. The most interesting approach to the town is probably along the newly surfaced road from Nakuru which snakes up hill and down dale through farmlands and forests and offers some spectacular views over the Aberdares.

The falls, on the outskirts of town, are named after Joseph Thomson who was the first European to walk from Mombasa to Lake Victoria in the early 1880s. They're a popular stopover for safari companies en route to Maralal and points further north and well worth a visit. Formed by the waters of the Ewaso Narok River, the falls plummet over 72 metres into a ravine and the resulting spray bathes the dense forest below in a perpetual mist. A series of stone steps leads down to the bottom of the ravine and is the only safe access. Don't attempt to go down

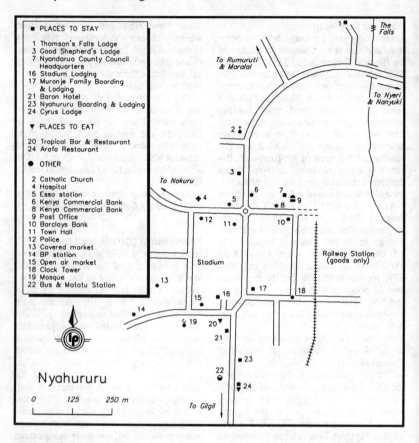

■ PLACES TO STAY

1 Thomson's Falls Lodge
3 Good Shepherd's Lodge
7 Nyandarua County Council
  Headquarters
16 Stadium Lodging
17 Muronje Family Boarding
   & Lodging
21 Baron Hotel
23 Nyahururu Boarding & Lodging
24 Cyrus Lodge

▼ PLACES TO EAT

20 Tropical Bar & Restaurant
24 Arafa Restaurant

● OTHER

2 Catholic Church
4 Hospital
5 Esso station
6 Kenya Commercial Bank
8 Kenya Commercial Bank
9 Post Office
10 Barclays Bank
11 Town Hall
12 Police
13 Covered market
14 BP station
15 Open air market
18 Clock Tower
19 Mosque
22 Bus & Matatu Station

Nyahururu

0   125   250 m

To Rumuruti & Maralal

To Nyeri & Nanyuki

The Falls

To Nakuru

Railway Station (goods only)

Stadium

To Gilgil

any other way as the rocks on the side of the ravine are often very loose. Up above the falls and partially overlooking them (though the view is obscured by a row of ugly souvenir shacks) is the old colonial watering hole, Thomson's Falls Lodge, which has retained much of its quaint atmosphere and is still the most interesting place to stay.

Places to Stay – bottom end

The best place to stay if you have camping equipment is the camp site at *Thomson's Falls Lodge* which is very pleasant and costs

KSh 50 per person per night with as much firewood as you need. Campers are entitled to use all the facilities at the Lodge including hot showers and toilets with toilet paper.

For those without camping equipment there are several budget hotels available in town. Cheapest are the *Muronje Family Boarding & Lodging* and the *Nyahururu Boarding & Lodging* where you can get a room with shared bathroom facilities (cold water only) for KSh 55, but they're both very basic and you shouldn't expect too much. Far better value is the *Good Shepherd's Lodge* which offers self-contained rooms with towel and soap provided for just KSh 60 (one or two people).

It's also sometimes possible to get a room at the *Nyandarua County Council Head-quarters*, next to the post office, which has self-contained rooms with soap, towel and toilet paper provided. They're supposedly single rooms but have double beds and will allow two people to share.

Going up in price, the *Stadium Lodging* is excellent value at KSh 95/165 for singles/doubles with bathroom and hot water. There's a large grille across the entrance so you need have no worries about theft. Similar is the *Cyrus Lodge/Arafa Restaurant* (tel 22190) opposite the bus station.

Places to Stay – middle

The place to stay in this category if you have the money is *Thomson's Falls Lodge* (tel 22006) overlooking the falls. Though it's no longer frequented by White planters, it exudes nostalgia and olde-worlde charm with its polished wooden floorboards and log fires. Accommodation is available either in the main building with its bar, lounge and dining room or in separate cottages scattered over the well-maintained lawns. Rooms here are self-contained with hot water and your own log fire and cost KSh 300/420 for singles/doubles though there is scope for negotiation.

If you prefer modernity and a place in the centre then *Baron Hotel* is the choice. It's clean, well organised and self-contained rooms with hot water go for KSh 180/300 a single/double. The hotel has its own restaurant and the food is good with a choice of three dishes each day – fish, meat or chicken. Prices are very reasonable.

Places to Eat

Most of the budget hotels and many of the bars have a restaurant where you can get standard African food for between KSh 24 and KSh 50, depending on what you order. Meals at the *Baron Hotel* are also excellent value.

For local colour and a barbecued meal, try the *Tropical Bar & Restaurant* round the corner from the Baron Hotel.

For a minor splurge – or if you're staying there – eat at *Thomsons' Falls Lodge*. They do breakfast, lunch and dinner but you need to let them know you intend to eat there if you're taking your meal in the main dining room. A full English-style breakfast will cost you about KSh 65. Three-course lunches or dinners with dessert and tea or coffee cost KSh 120. There's also an open-air grill which operates at lunch time and offers a variety of dishes including soups and various types of nyama choma (barbecued meat). A meat dish will cost you about KSh 50. The Lodge also has the most interesting and one of the liveliest bars in town with deep comfortable armchairs and blazing log fires. All the facilities are open to nonresidents including campers.

For those who want to put their own food together, there's an excellent choice of fruit, vegetables and meat in the covered market.

Entertainment

The *Baron Hotel* has a discotheque every Friday and Saturday night.

Getting There & Away

There are plenty of buses and matatus throughout the day until late afternoon in either direction between Nakuru and Nyeri and Nyahururu. The best bus to take is the once daily OTC bus which runs between Nairobi and Nakuru via Nyeri and Nyahururu. Both roads are in excellent shape and surfaced.

There's also one minibus per day in either direction between Maralal and Nyahururu which leaves early in the morning and costs KSh 85. Get there early if you want a seat. For the rest of the day, hitching is feasible but not easy. The road is surfaced as far as Rumuruti after which it's gravel or *murram* (dirt). Parts of this gravel road are in bad shape but it improves considerably the nearer you get to Maralal.

Mt Kenya & Around

Although a distinctly separate massif from the Aberdares, Mt Kenya also forms part of the central highlands. Africa's second highest mountain at 5199 metres, its gleaming and eroded snow-covered peaks can be seen for miles until the late morning clouds obscure the view. Its lower slopes, like those of the Aberdares, are intensively cultivated by the Kikuyu and the closely related Embu and Meru peoples, along with the descen-

dants of the White settlers who grow mainly wheat on the grassy and largely treeless plains on the northern side. So vast is this mountain that it's not hard to understand why the Kikuyu deified it, why their houses are built with the doors facing the peak and why it was probably never scaled until the arrival of European explorers.

These days it's every traveller's dream to get to the top and take home with them a memory which money cannot buy.

The mountain is circled by an excellent tarmac road along which are the area's main

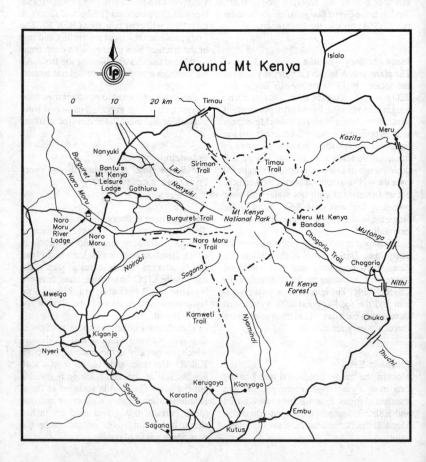

towns – Naro Moru, Nanyuki, Meru and Embu, along with Isiolo at the extreme north-eastern end. We deal first with the towns along this road and then with Mt Kenya itself since the towns are the jumping off points for climbing the mountain.

NARO MORU

The village of Naro Moru on the western side of the mountain consists of little more than a string of small shops and houses, a couple of very basic hotels, agricultural warehouses and the famous Naro Moru River Lodge but it's the most popular starting point for climbing Mt Kenya. There's a post office here but no banks (the nearest are at Nanyuki and Nyeri). The other important thing to bear in mind is that the River Lodge has acquired an exclusive franchise on the mountain huts along the Naro Moru Trail including those at the Meteorological Station so you have to go to this lodge to make bookings. It's all been carefully calculated to sew up the market on this trail but that doesn't prevent you from climbing independently so long as you're prepared to camp and have the appropriate equipment.

Places to Stay

There is just one very basic lodge in the village, the *Naro Moru 82 Bar & Restaurant*, but hardly anyone stays there because it really is the pits and the mattresses stink of urine. Most people head off to the *Naro Moru River Lodge* (tel (0176) 22018, PO Box 18, Naro Moru) which is about 1½ km off to the left down a gravel track from the main Nairobi-Nanyuki road. It's essentially a top-range hotel set in landscaped gardens alongside the Naro Moru River but it does have a well-equipped camp site with hot showers and toilets for KSh 50 per person per night. Campers are entitled to use all the hotel facilities.

Those seeking a degree of luxury either before or after climbing the mountain have the option of self-contained cottages for KSh 1225 a single and KSh 1895 a double including breakfast. The hotel has a swimming pool, restaurant and a cosy bar complete with

log-burning fireplace and decked out with autographed T-shirts of various groups from all over the world who have climbed the mountain at one time or another. Lunch in the restaurant costs KSh 270 and dinner KSh 240 but if you want dinner and are not staying in a cottage then book in advance or you may go hungry. American Express and Visa cards are accepted.

The main reason for coming to this lodge if you're an independent traveller is that it's here you must book and pay for any of the mountain huts which you want to stay at along the Naro Moru Trail. Those at the Meteorological Station cost KSh 165 per person (Kenyan residents KSh 110) and the ones at Mackinder's Camp KSh 275 per person (Kenyan residents KSh 200). You can also pay for the camp sites here which cost KSh 18 per person (no charge for guides or porters). Members of the Mountain Club of Kenya are entitled to a 25% discount on these prices and the accommodation charges at the lodge.

The other reason for coming to this lodge if you don't have a tent, cooking equipment or appropriate clothing is that it runs a comprehensive hire service which is open daily from 7 am to 1 pm and 2 to 8 pm. The charges are similar to those at Atul's in Nairobi and are detailed under the description of climbing the mountain.

There's also an excess baggage store which costs KSh 20 per piece. You can use this service whether you're a guest or not.

The only other place to stay in the vicinity is the *Mt Kenya Hostel*, about 12 km up the road towards the mountain, off the main road to the right. This is a very popular place with budget travellers and campers and it's run by a very friendly and helpful man named Joseph. At one time, there used to be a substantial brick hostel here which was affiliated to the IYHF but it burnt down in 1988. Rebuilding is scheduled to start in early 1990 but meanwhile there are a number of rustic huts to stay in and facilities include hot water showers and cooking facilities. The huts cost KSh 50 per bed and you can camp for KSh 30 (own tent) or KSh 35 (rented tent). The hostel is signposted on the main road up to the mountain. The advantage of staying here is that it's only some four km to the park entrance gate.

Places to Eat

There are no restaurants at Naro Moru so you'll either have to cook your own food or eat at the *Naro Moru River Lodge*. There's very little choice of food available at the shops in Naro Moru so bring your own or, if you have transport, go to Nanyuki to buy it.

Getting There & Away

There are plenty of buses and matatus from Nairobi and Nyeri to Nanyuki and Isiolo which will drop you off in Naro Moru.

The Naro Moru River Lodge also operates a shuttle bus between the lodge and Nairobi on a daily basis. It departs from the lodge at 9 am and from Nairobi at 2.30 pm and costs KSh 600 one way and KSh 1080 return (not cheap!). In Nairobi you have to book the bus on the 1st floor of College House, University Way – ask for Stanley Matiba or ring 337501/8. In Naro Moru, book at the lodge.

NANYUKI

Nanyuki is a typical small country town about halfway along the northern section of the Mt Kenya ring road and a popular base from which to climb the mountain via either the Burguret or Sirimon trails. It was founded by White settlers in 1907 in the days when game roamed freely and in large numbers over the surrounding grassy plains. The game has almost disappeared – shot by the settlers for meat and to protect their crops from damage by foragers – but the descendants of the settlers remain and the town has also become a Kenyan Air Force base as well as a British Army base for the joint manoeuvres conducted by the two armies each year. It's a fairly pleasant town and still has a faint ring of the colonial era to it. There's all the usual facilities here including banks, a post office and a good range of well-stocked stores.

Places to Stay – bottom end

The cheapest place to stay is the *Youth Hostel* (tel 2112) at the Emmanuel Parish Centre, Market Rd, which is pretty basic but has beds for KSh 40 per night. The showers have only cold water. Only slightly more expensive are a number of simple lodges which include the *Silent Guest House* and the *Juba Boarding & Lodging*.

More expensive but a popular place to stay is the *Josaki Hotel* (tel 2181) which has singles/doubles with bathroom for KSh 70/145. There's a bar and restaurant on the ground floor. Equally popular is the *Sirimon Guest House* (tel 22243) fronting the park which offers self-contained rooms with hot water for KSh 100/130 a single/double. Parking is available here. Similar is the *Nyakio Boarding & Lodging* across the other side of the park and the nearby *Landview Boarding & Lodging*.

Further afield up the Nyahururu road is the *Nanyuki Guest House* which is basic but clean and offers self-contained singles (there are no double rooms) for KSh 72. Vehicles can be parked in the hotel compound. Another place which has cheap singles – but only two of them – is the *Simba Lodge* not far from the Catholic church off the road heading to Isiolo at the top end of town. A single here costs KSh 50 or KSh 120 with breakfast. All the other rooms are doubles which go for KSh 300 including breakfast. Vehicles can be parked in the hotel compound and are guarded by an askari.

Places to Stay – middle

One of the nicest places to stay in this range is the *Sportsman's Arms Hotel* (tel 22598), across the other side of the river from the main road. Run by an Asian lady, Mrs Dia, this was once the White settlers' watering hole as the style of the building and the extensive surrounding lawns indicate. It offers self-contained rooms with hot water and breakfast for KSh 310 a single and KSh 540 a double. It used to be possible to camp on the lawns but this is no longer allowed.

At the opposite end of town on the right-hand side just before you enter Nanyuki is

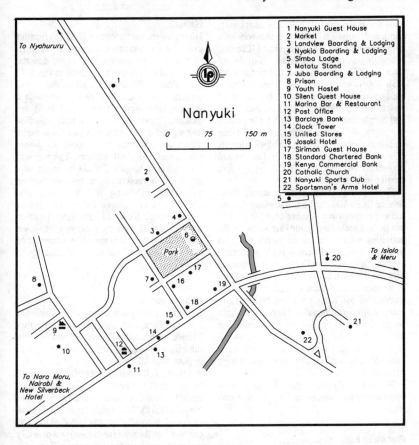

Nanyuki

1 Nanyuki Guest House
2 Market
3 Landview Boarding & Lodging
4 Nyakio Boarding & Lodging
5 Simba Lodge
6 Matatu Stand
7 Juba Boarding & Lodging
8 Prison
9 Youth Hostel
10 Silent Guest House
11 Marina Bar & Restaurant
12 Post Office
13 Barclays Bank
14 Clock Tower
15 United Stores
16 Josaki Hotel
17 Sirimon Guest House
18 Standard Chartered Bank
19 Kenya Commercial Bank
20 Catholic Church
21 Nanyuki Sports Club
22 Sportsman's Arms Hotel

To Nyahururu

0   75   150 m

Park

To Isiolo
& Meru

To Naro Moru,
Nairobi &
New Silverbeck
Hotel

the *New Silverbeck Hotel* (tel 2740). It consists of a main block with bar and restaurant and a collection of wooden cottages which were obviously once very pleasant but are now quite decrepit and in need of major renovation. Part of the reason is that the shower water falls directly onto the wooden floors with just a hole in the boards as a waste outlet (surely the plumbing must have been better than this in the past!?). There are also four new rooms available in a modern concrete block though they're devoid of character. Bucket hot water showers are available ('problems with the water tank' I

was told) and you can have a wood fire in the cottages in the evening. All in all, it's not exceptional value at KSh 505 a single and KSh 790 a double. The Sportsman's Arms is much better value. Also in the hotel compound is a row of souvenir shops and a third (!) Equator sign – the other two are on the main road. Package tourists are traipsed through here by the bus load.

Outside of Nanyuki itself, about two-thirds of the way to Naro Moru, is *Bantu's Mt Kenya Leisure Lodge* (tel (0176) 22787, PO Box 333, Nanyuki) which is tucked away in wooded surroundings just less than a km from the main road. It offers pleasant self-contained cottages with hot showers and fireplaces for KSh 390 a single and KSh 660 a double including breakfast. Half board rates are KSh 535/950 and full board rates KSh 700/1285 respectively. There's also a well-equipped camp site with hot and cold water, toilets, cooking facilities, electricity and ample firewood for KSh 95 per person per night. All prices are inclusive of taxes and service charges. The main block consists of a spacious dining room, bar, lounge and makuti-roofed terrace. The hotel accepts credit cards.

Horse-riding (KSh 150 per hour), trout fishing (KSh 100 per hour including fishing rod and licence) and bird-watching (KSh 100 per person including guide) are some of the activities which the lodge caters for plus there are traditional dances performed each evening from 8.30 pm (KSh 100 per person). The main reason for coming here, however, is to take one of their guided treks to the summit of Mt Kenya via the Naro Moru, Burguret or Sirimon trails. There are a whole range of these to choose from depending on where you want to go and how long you wish to take. The full range of possibilities are outlined in the section dealing with climbing Mt Kenya.

Bantu's Mt Kenya Leisure Lodge is easy to locate on the main Naro Moru to Nanyuki road.

Places to Eat

There are very few restaurants in Nanyuki which are not attached to hotels so take your pick. The *Marina Bar & Restaurant* is a reasonable place to eat in the centre of town and an expats' watering hole. For a splurge, have lunch or dinner at either the *Sportsman's Arms* or the *New Silverbeck Hotel*.

Getting There & Away

There are daily buses from Nairobi and Isiolo to Nanyuki as well as minibuses and matatus from Nyeri and Nyahururu which run throughout the day.

ISIOLO

Isiolo, where the tarmac ends, is the frontier town for north-eastern Kenya – a vast area of forested and barren mountains, deserts, scrub, Lake Turkana and home to the wild and colourful Samburu, Rendille, Boran and Turkana peoples. It's a lively town with a good market and all the usual facilities including petrol stations, a bank, a post office and a good choice of hotels and restaurants. There are also bus connections to places north, east and south of here. The resident population is largely Somali in origin as a result of the resettlement here of Somali ex-soldiers following WW I. It ought, in addition, to be famous for the number of 'rumble strips' (or speed bumps) which force traffic to a snail's pace on the way into town from the south. There are no less than 21 of these and more still at the northern edge of town!

Information

Isiolo is the last place going north which has a bank (Barclays) until you get to either Maralal or Marsabit. There are no banks on the way to or at Lake Turkana (assuming you bypass Maralal).

Likewise, there are no petrol stations north of here until you reach Maralal or Marsabit except at the Samburu Lodge (in Samburu National Park). This doesn't mean that petrol or diesel is totally unobtainable since you can buy it in Baragoi (with ease) and possibly at Christian mission stations elsewhere (with difficulty or not at all if they're low on stock) but you will pay well over the odds for it due to transport costs and irregularity of supply. Stock up in Isiolo!

Travellers about to go to the national parks north of here or to Lake Turkana and who intend to do their own cooking should stock up on food and drink in Isiolo as there's very little available beyond here except at Maralal, Marsabit and (less so) Wamba. There's a very good market in Isiolo adjacent to the mosque for fresh fruit, vegetables and meat. The general stores, too, have a good range of canned food and other items.

Places to Stay – bottom end

There are a number of fairly primitive lodging houses available for those tight on funds which include the *Maendeleo Hotel, Farmers Boarding & Lodging, Savannah Inn, Tawakal Boarding & Lodging, Frontier Lodge, Coffee Tree Hotel* and the *National Hotel*, all offering rooms with shared bathroom facilities (cold water only) starting from KSh 55 a single and KSh 70 a double. The downstairs area of the Frontier Lodge is taken up by a lively bar which sometimes puts on live bands. The Tawakal Boarding & Lodging also has a bar which is open 24 hours a day.

The best place to stay, however, is the *Jamhuri Guest House* which is excellent value and has been popular with travellers for a number of years. It's run by Ibrahim and Arden who are both very friendly and will go out of their way to be helpful. The rooms are very clean and pleasant, mosquito nets are provided and the communal showers have hot water in the mornings. It costs KSh 60 a single and KSh 85 a double. Belongings left in the rooms are quite safe.

Next door to it and similar in price and quality is the *Silent Inn*.

Also good is the *Talent Lodge* on the way to the post office which offers rooms with shared bathroom facilities for KSh 40 a single and KSh 90 a double. There is supposedly hot water all day in the showers (or so the management will assure you). The centre of the hotel and the terrace overlooking the street are taken up by a bar so it's not as quiet as the Jamhuri Guest House.

Going up in the price, there is the *Pasoda Lodge* which is clean and quiet and offers doubles with bathrooms for KSh 130. There are no singles. The hotel has its own restaurant.

Places to Stay – middle

There's only one mid-range hotel in Isiolo and that is the newly constructed *Bomen Hotel* (tel (0165) 2225, PO Box 67, Isiolo). This three storey hotel has a total of 40 spacious rooms, tastefully decorated and furnished and complete with bathrooms and hot

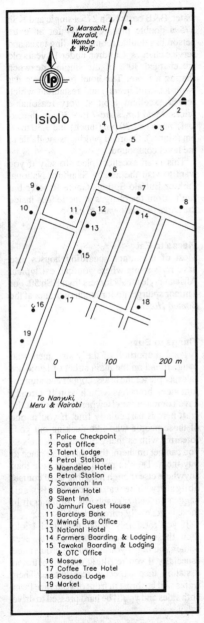

Isiolo

To Marsabit,
Maralal,
Wamba
& Wajir

To Nanyuki,
Meru & Nairobi

0   100   200 m

1 Police Checkpoint
2 Post Office
3 Talent Lodge
4 Petrol Station
5 Maendeleo Hotel
6 Petrol Station
7 Savannah Inn
8 Bomen Hotel
9 Silent Inn
10 Jamhuri Guest House
11 Barclays Bank
12 Mwingi Bus Office
13 National Hotel
14 Farmers Boarding & Lodging
15 Tawakal Boarding & Lodging
    & OTC Office
16 Mosque
17 Coffee Tree Hotel
18 Pasoda Lodge
19 Market

water. B&B costs KSh 275 a single and KSh 375 a double plus KSh 104 for an extra person in a double room including taxes and service charges. Children under 12 years old are charged 30% of the single rate when sharing a room. The hotel has its own bar (with ice-cold beers!) and restaurant which serves excellent food at very reasonable prices. Meal times are 7 to 9.30 am (breakfast), noon to 2.30 pm (lunch) and 7.30 to 10 pm (dinner). Guarded parking is available in the hotel compound.

This is an excellent place to stay if you want to visit the nearby Samburu National Park or Buffalo Springs Game Reserve but can't afford the charges at the lodges inside the parks or don't want to camp.

Places to Eat

Most of the simple boarding houses also have restaurants where you can eat typical African-style meals for less than KSh 50. For a minor splurge, go for lunch or dinner at the *Bomen Hotel.*

Things to Buy

A good proportion of the young men who hang around on the main street of Isiolo are salespeople for the brass, copper and aluminium/steel bracelets which you'll already have come across elsewhere except that the craft here is particularly fine. If you're one of those people who like decking out your forearms with as many of these bracelets as you can get on then, this is the place to buy them. They're much cheaper here than anywhere else though haggling is, of course, obligatory. The same people also sell daggers in leather scabbards but the craft in these is generally unremarkable.

If you're simply *walking* around Isiolo then these salespeople will hardly ever bother you but if you're *driving* around and especially if you're filling up with petrol at a station then expect a real hassle. Their wares will be thrust in front of your face from both sides and you'll be hard pressed to drive away.

Getting There & Away

Both OTC and Mwingi operate buses to Nairobi which take about seven hours. OTC has daily buses at 7 and 7.30 am and 7 pm which cost KSh 115. The Mwingi buses leave daily at 7 am and 7.30 pm. Mwingi has its own little office on the top side of the main street. The OTC booking office is part of the Tawakal Boarding & Lodging on the same side of the main street.

Mwingi also runs buses to Marsabit and Moyale on Tuesday, Thursday and Saturday, which take about six hours to Marsabit and the same, on the following day, to Moyale. The fare for each stage of the journey is KSh 180. These buses only go when full and, consequently, departures are frequently delayed by up to a day. There's no alternative except to simply hang around and wait, or either negotiate a ride on a truck (relatively easy and usually somewhat less than the bus fare) or walk out to the police checkpoint north of town where the tarmac ends and hitch a ride with tourists (not so easy).

To Wajir and Mandera, north-east of Isiolo, Mwingi operate buses three times a week usually on Wednesday, Friday and Sunday. Each stage of the journey takes about nine hours (considerably longer if there are punctures or mechanical problems) and costs KSh 180. Hitching a ride along this route is considerably more difficult than to Marsabit.

Mwingi also operate buses to Maralal every second day (depending on demand) which cost KSh 180.

MERU

Up at the north-eastern end of the ring road around the southern side of Mt Kenya, Meru is an important town which services the intensively cultivated and forested highlands in this part of Central Province. It's quite a climb up to Meru from either Isiolo or Embu and, in the rainy season, you'll find yourself in the clouds up here along with dense forest which frequently reaches right down to the roadside. When the weather is clear there are superb views for miles over the surrounding lowlands. Views of the peaks of Mt Kenya, on the other hand, are hard to come by due mostly to the forest cover.

Although there's a small centre of sorts, Meru is essentially just a built-up area along the main road and, as far as travellers' interests go, there's precious little reason to stay for the night here. It's certainly much too far away from any of the trail heads leading to the peaks of Mt Kenya to be a suitable base to take off from. The nearest of these begins at Chogoria, about halfway between Meru and Embu.

The main thing that Meru is famous for is the quality of its miraa – those bundles of leafy twigs and shoots which you'll see people all over Kenya (and particularly Somalia and Ethiopia) chewing for its stimulant and appetite suppression properties. While it still grows wild here, much of it is now cultivated and it's become a major source of (legal) income for the cultivators and harvesters who supply both the internal market and also export it to neighbouring countries. No doubt the marijuana growers are livid with envy!

Meru National Museum

This small museum just off the main road is worth calling at if you're staying here or passing through. It has the usual display of exhibits detailing the progress of evolution along with stuffed birds, animals and mounted insects, but also a small and informative section concerning the agricultural and initiation practices of the Meru people and their clothing and weapons. Out at the back of the building are a number of appallingly small and sordid cages containing obviously neurotic and pathetically bored specimens of baboon, vervet monkeys and a caracal cat which someone ought to liberate immediately as an act of sheer pity if not humaneness. There's also a reptile pit with a

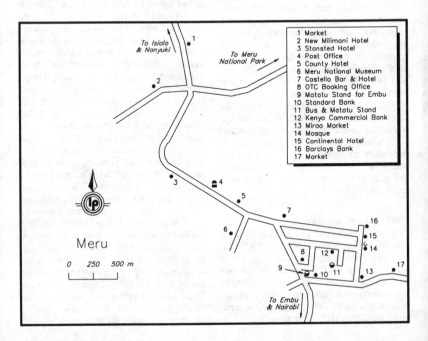

To Isiolo & Nanyuki

To Meru National Park

1 Market
2 New Milimani Hotel
3 Stansted Hotel
4 Post Office
5 County Hotel
6 Meru National Museum
7 Castello Bar & Hotel
8 OTC Booking Office
9 Matatu Stand for Embu
10 Standard Bank
11 Bus & Matatu Stand
12 Kenya Commercial Bank
13 Miraa Market
14 Mosque
15 Continental Hotel
16 Barclays Bank
17 Market

Meru

0   250   500 m

To Embu & Nairobi

notice advising visitors that 'Trespassers will be bitten'.

The museum is open daily from 9.30 am to 6 pm except on Sundays and holidays when it's open from 11 am to 6 pm and 1 to 6 pm respectively. Entrance costs KSh 10 (KSh 5 for children) and KSh 5 for Kenyan residents (KSh 2 for children).

Places to Stay

Two of the cheapest places to stay here are the *Castella Bar & Hotel* and the *Continental Hotel* in the town 'centre'. They're basic and neither is particularly special. Much better value is the *Stansted Hotel* (tel 20360) on the main road past the post office which is clean, quiet and offers self-contained rooms at KSh 75 a single and KSh 100 a double. The hotel has its own bar and restaurant.

Also good value is the *New Milimani Hotel* further up the hill from the Stansted which offers good self-contained rooms with bath and hot water for KSh 100 a double. Vehicles can be parked safely in the hotel compound and, at weekends, there's a disco.

The best mid-range hotel here is probably the *County Hotel*, again on the main road and close to the turn-off for the museum. It's clean, comfortable, has its own restaurant and lively bar and secure parking. Rooms here cost KSh 320 a double with breakfast.

Those with their own transport might like to check out the *Rocky Hill Inn*, about eight km out of town to the north, which is essentially a barbecue and bar but has basic chalets for rent, or the *Forest Lodge* even further out which has a swimming pool, pretensions to being a sort of country club along with expensive chalets.

Getting There & Away

The best way of getting to Meru is by OTC bus from either Isiolo or Nairobi. There is a booking office on the main road at the top of the town 'centre'. Other buses also service this town and have their booking offices in the same central area. The matatu park for transport to Embu can be found on the main road next to the OTC booking office.

EMBU

On the south-eastern slopes of Mt Kenya, Embu is an important provincial centre but spread out over many km along the main road. It has a famous school and hotel and is set in a very hilly area which is intensively cultivated. It's also the provincial headquarters of the Eastern Province though it's on the extreme eastern edge of this and can only have been chosen because of its agreeable climate. Not many travellers stay here overnight and with good reason since there's nothing much to see or do and it's a long way from the only feasible eastern route up Mt Kenya (the Chogoria Trail).

Places to Stay & Eat

There are quite a few cheap hotels spread out along the main road but most of them are very basic and can't be recommended. Right opposite the bus and matatu park is the *New White Rembo Hotel* which offers self-contained rooms for KSh 80 a single, KSh 100 a double and KSh 145 a triple. There's a good restaurant here which serves tasty, reasonably priced food. Similar is the *Al-Aswad Hotel* just a little further up the road which also has a good restaurant where you can eat for just KSh 30. The *Kubukubu Lodge*, further down the hill from the New White Rembo Hotel, is another reasonable choice.

At the top end of this range is the *Valley View Hotel* (tel 20147) where self-contained rooms with hot water cost KSh 165 a single and KSh 300 a double. It's clean and tidy and soap and towel are provided, plus the staff are friendly and helpful. The hotel has its own bar and restaurant. It's also much quieter than the hotels around the bus stand.

If you'd like to splurge then consider a night at the *Izaak Walton Inn* (tel 20128/9) about two km up the main road towards Meru from the town centre. It's right out of the colonial era and set in extensive lawns and gardens with a good restaurant and cosy bar – both with log-burning fireplaces. There's even a yellowing notice in the bar detailing appropriate 'rules' of conduct by inebriated and amorous 'gentlemen' towards

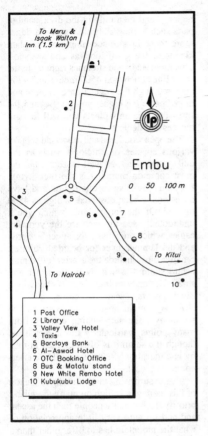

To Meru &
Isaak Walton
Inn (1.5 km)

Embu

0   50   100 m

To Kitui

To Nairobi

1 Post Office
2 Library
3 Valley View Hotel
4 Taxis
5 Barclays Bank
6 Al–Aswad Hotel
7 OTC Booking Office
8 Bus & Matatu stand
9 New White Rembo Hotel
10 Kubukubu Lodge

Getting There & Away

There are daily OTC buses between Nairobi and Embu and this is the safest way to travel between the two places. The booking office is on the top side of the bus and matatu stand. Matatus also offer the same service but they are invariably overcrowded – often dangerously so – and the drivers are like maniacs. 'Accidents' are frequent and often result in everyone on board being killed. This happens on average about once a fortnight so, if you value your life, *don't do this trip by matatu*. It's not that the road is in bad shape – it's an excellent road – but its sweeping curves, high bridges and constant up-hill-down-dale progression seems to encourage total recklessness among drivers. The fare to Nairobi on the matatus is KSh 60 and they terminate on Accra Rd (if you're fortunate to get that far).

The alternative to the buses and matatus is a shared Peugeot taxi. You can find these on the main road at the turn-off for the Valley View Hotel.

The matatus to Meru are not quite the same hair-raising and dangerous prospect since there's not the same pressure on drivers but they're no joy ride either. Take the OTC bus or a Peugeot taxi in preference.

MT KENYA

Africa's second highest mountain at 5199 metres, Mt Kenya was formed between 2½ and three million years ago as a result of successive eruptions of the volcano. It has a diameter at its base of about 120 km. It's probable that when first formed it was over 6000 metres in height and had a summit crater much like that on Kilimanjaro. Intensive erosion, however, principally by glacial ice, has worn away the cone and left a series of jagged peaks, U-shaped valleys and depressions containing glacial lakes or tarns.

In many of these valleys you will come across terminal moraines (curved ridges of boulders and stones carried down by the glaciers) whose position – some as low as 3000 metres – indicates that during the Ice Ages the glaciers must have been far more

'ladies' though it's couched in bar humour and obviously not meant to be taken seriously. Originally a farmhouse and set in 3.4 hectares, it has 42 double rooms (described as 'specious' in the promotional leaflet though they no doubt meant 'spacious'!) each with bathroom and hot water plus a balcony which cost KSh 448 a single, KSh 560 a double and KSh 700 a triple including breakfast. The staff are friendly and helpful and it's definitely *the* place to stay if you have the money.

Even if you don't stay here it's definitely worth turning up for a beer or meal.

extensive than they are today. They began retreating rapidly about 150,000 years ago as the climate changed and the process is still going on today. Since records first began to be kept back in 1893, already seven of the glaciers have disappeared leaving only the current 11 remaining and even these are getting quite thin. It's estimated that if the present trend continues there could be no permanent ice left on the mountain in 25 years.

The volcanic soil and the many rivers which radiate out from the central cone have created a very fertile environment and especially so on the southern and eastern sides which receive the most rain. Human agricultural activity currently extends up to around 1900 metres in what used to be rainforest but which is still well wooded even today in many parts. Above this zone, except where logging takes place, stretches the untouched rainforest characterised by an abundance of different species, particularly the giant camphors, along with vines, ferns, orchids and other epiphytes. This forest zone is not quite so dense on the northern and eastern sides since the climate here is drier and the predominant tree species are conifers. Vines, likewise, are absent.

The forest supports a rich variety of wildlife and it's quite common to come across elephant, buffalo and various species of monkey on the forest tracks. Rhino, numerous varieties of antelope, the giant forest hog and lion also live here but are usually only seen in the clearings around lodges.

On the southern and western slopes the forest gradually merges into a belt of dense bamboo which often grows to 12 metres or more. This eventually gives way to more open woodland consisting of hagena and hypericum trees along with an undergrowth of flowering shrubs and herbs.

Further up still is a belt of giant heather which forms dense clumps up to four metres high interspersed with tall grasses. Open moorland forms the next zone and can often be very colourful because of the profusion of small flowering plants which thrive here. The only large plants to be found in this region – and then only in the drier, sandier parts such as the valley sides and the ridges – are those bizarre specimens of the plant kingdom, the giant lobelias and senecios. This moorland zone stretches right up to the snow line at between 4500 metres and 4700 metres though the vegetation gets more and more sparse the higher you go. Beyond the snow line, the only plants you will find are mosses and lichens.

The open woodland and moorland support various species of antelope, such as the duiker and eland, as well as zebra, but the most common mammal is the rock hyrax. Leopards also live in this region and have occasionally been observed as high as 4500 metres! Of the larger birds which you'll undoubtedly see up here are the verreaux eagles, which prey on hyrax, auger buzzards and the lammergeyer (or bearded vulture). Smaller birds include the scarlet-tufted malachite sunbird which feeds on nectar and small flies and the friendly cliff chat which often appears in search of scraps.

As you might imagine, there are superb views over the surrounding country from many points, particularly the higher ones, though the summit is often clothed in mist by late morning which lasts until late afternoon.

It's not surprising that climbing to the top of this mountain is high on many travellers' priority list but many people rush the ascent and end up with very little appreciation of what the mountain has to offer other than a thumping headache and the thrill of having done it. I've even met people who have been up to the top and back again in just two days! If you take your time, on the other hand, you'll find that the mountain has a great deal more to offer than just an exhilarating climb.

The best times to go, as far as fair weather is concerned, is from mid-January to late February or from late August through September.

Books & Maps

Before you leave Nairobi we strongly recommend that you buy a copy of *Mt Kenya 1:50,000 Map & Guide* by Mark Savage &

Andrew Wielochowski. It has a detailed topographical map on one side and full description of the various trails, mountain medicine, fauna and flora, accommodation, etc on the reverse. This is money well spent and contains everything which most trekkers will need to know. It's stocked by all the main bookshops.

Those who intend to do some climbing (as opposed to walking) should think seriously about getting hold of a copy of the Mountain Club of Kenya's *Guide to Mt Kenya & Kilimanjaro*, edited by Iain Allan. The last edition was published in 1981 but not too much has changed since then especially regarding the main trekking routes and climbing possibilities. This is a much more substantial guide but apparently out of print at the moment. If you want one then try the bookshops in Nairobi or the Mountain Club of Kenya, PO Box 45741, Nairobi. It may also be available from West Col Productions, Goring-on-Thames, Reading, Berks RG8 9AA, UK, and from Stanford's Map Centre, 12/14 Long Acre, Covent Garden, London WC2E 9LP, UK.

The Survey of Kenya also print the map, *Mount Kenya* (1:125,000), which is sufficient for an overall view. It's available from the Public Map Office in Nairobi or from bookshops.

Preparations for Climbing Mt Kenya

Clothing & Equipment The summits of Mt Kenya are covered in glaciers and snow and the temperature at night often drops to below -10°C so you are going to need a good sleeping bag. An air mattress is also advisable if you are going to sleep on the ground as it provides the necessary insulation under your body and is far more comfortable than sleeping without one. A good set of warm clothes is equally important and that should include some sort of headgear and gloves. As it can rain at any time of year – and heavily – you will also need waterproof clothing. A decent pair of boots is an advantage but not strictly necessary. A pair of joggers is quite adequate most of the time though it's a good idea to have a pair of thongs or canvas tennis shoes

available for evening wear if your main shoes get wet.

Remember that it's a good idea to sleep in clothes which you haven't worn during the day because the salt which your day clothes absorb from your skin keeps them moist at night and so reduces their heat retention capabilities.

Those who don't intend to stay in the huts along the way will need a tent and associated equipment.

Unless you intend to eat solely canned and dried food along the way (not recommended) then you'll also need a tent, a stove (kerosene or gas stoves are to be preferred), basic cooking equipment and a water container with a capacity of at least one litre per person as well as water purifying tablets for use on the lower levels of the mountain. Except in an emergency, using wood gathered from the vicinity of camp sites to light open fires is prohibited within the confines of the national park and for good reasons. If you intend to engage porters then you'll also have to supply each of them with a rucksack to carry your gear and theirs.

Hiring Equipment All the sort of gear you need for the climb can be hired in Nairobi at Atul's (tel 25935, PO Box 43202), Biashara St, Nairobi or at the Naro Moru River Lodge (tel (0176) 22018, PO Box 18), Naro Moru. The gear at both places is good and well maintained. Advance booking of gear (from Atul's) is a good idea if you want to be absolutely sure but not normally necessary. Gear cannot be booked in advance at the Naro Moru River Lodge. Here it's first come, first served. Both places carry plenty of stock.

Examples of the sort of daily hire charges and deposits (in KSh) which you'll have to pay at Atul's are:

Item	Hire Cost	Deposit
sleeping bag	30-50	500-800
air mattress	18	800
air mattress pump	10	200
tent	60-180	1000-2000
gas stove	20	400
water containers	5	50
cooking pots	4-6	40-60
woollen socks	15	150
woollen gloves	15	150
climbing boots	40	400
raincoats	40	400

The hire charges at the Naro Moru River Lodge are consistently higher than those at Atul's.

Cooking In an attempt to cut down on baggage, quite a few people forgo taking a stove and cooking equipment and exist entirely on canned and dried foods. You can certainly do it so long as you keep up your fluid intake but it's not the best way to go about it. That cup of hot soup in the evening and pot of tea or coffee in the morning can make all the difference between enjoying the climb and hating it or, at least, feeling irritable.

There are, however, a few things to bear in mind about cooking at high altitudes. The major consideration is that the boiling point of water is considerably reduced. At 4500 metres, for example, it boils at 85°C and at 5500 metres at 82°C. The latter is too low to sufficiently cook rice or spaghetti and you won't be able to brew a good cup of tea from it either (instant coffee is the answer). Cooking times are also considerably

increased as a result (with consequent increased use of fuel).

The best range of suitable foods for the mountain is, of course, to be found in the supermarkets of Nairobi though it's quite a long way to cart food from there to the trail heads. On the western and northern sides of the mountain there's a good range of food at the stores in Nyeri and Nanyuki but precious little at Naro Moru. On the southern and eastern sides the best places to shop are Embu and Meru. Dehydrated foods are not all that easy to find and given the low boiling point of water at high altitudes you really need the precooked variety. Fresh fruit and vegetables are available in all reasonably sized towns and villages.

Take plenty of citrus fruits with you and/or citrus drinks as well as chocolate, sweets or dried fruit to keep your blood sugar levels high on the climb.

One last thing – and this is important to avoid altitude sickness as far as possible: drink at least three litres of fluid per day.

Getting to the Trail Heads
There are seven different routes to the summit but only the three main routes are covered here – Naro Moru, Sirimon and Chogoria. The other trails are much harder to follow and there's a real chance you can get lost without decent maps and the ability to read them, and if you have no experience with a compass.

If you intend to do the climb independently then public transport (buses or matatus) along the Mt Kenya ring road is the first step towards getting to the trail heads. For the Naro Moru Trail it's Naro Moru village where there's a prominent signpost on the right-hand side just outside the village on the way to Nanyuki. For the Sirimon Trail, first go to Nanyuki and then take another matatu about 13 km up the main road to Isiolo where the trail is signposted off to the right. For Chogoria you have the choice of getting off the bus or matatu about three km before Chogoria village on the Embu-Meru road where there's a signpost for Meru Mt Kenya Bandas, or going into Chogoria

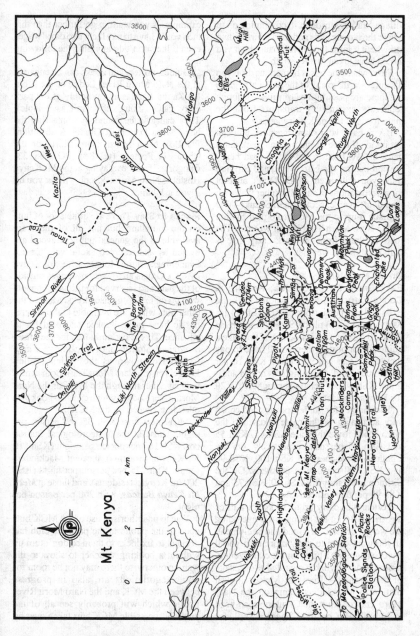

Mt Kenya

village, walking through it, continuing on to where the tarmac ends and then a further two km where it joins the gravel road which you would have taken further south.

From where the buses or matatus drop you it's quite a walk to any of the park entry gates but there are possibilities of private (though relatively expensive) transport from the main roads to the park entry gates.

If you have your own transport, you can get up to all three of the national park entry gates in 2WD but to get to the road heads beyond that on the Naro Moru and Sirimon trails you will need 4WD. Don't attempt these last sections in anything other than that. And don't even expect a small Suzuki 4WD to make it up to the Meteorological Station on the Naro Moru Trail in wet weather. The road up there from the park entry gate is diabolical in wet weather.

On the Mountain
Park Entry Fees, Guides, Porters & Cooks
Entry fees to the national park are KSh 220 per person per night (KSh 50 for Kenyan residents) plus KSh 50 for a vehicle (KSh 20 for Kenyan residents). If you take a guide and/or porters then you'll have to pay their entry fees too which are KSh 10 per person per night. Camping fees are an additional KSh 60 per person per night (KSh 20 for Kenyan residents).

The charges for guides, porters and cooks vary according to the route taken. On the Naro Moru route they are KSh 65, KSh 55 and KSh 65 per day respectively. On the Chogoria route they are KSh 100, KSh 90 and KSh 100 per day respectively. On the Sirimon route they are KSh 90, KSh 75 and KSh 90 per day respectively.

Porters will carry up to 18 kg for a three day trip or 16 kg for a longer trip excluding the weight of their own food and equipment. If you want them to carry more then you'll have to negotiate a price for the extra weight. A normal day's work is regarded as one stage of the journey – from the Meteorological Station to Mackinders Camp on the Naro Moru Trail or from the Chogoria road head to Minto's Hut on the Chogoria Trail, for

example. If you want to go further than this then you'll have to pay them two days' wages even if they don't do anything the following day.

Guides, porters and cooks can be engaged at the Naro Moru River Lodge or the Meru Mt Kenya Bandas and possibly at the park entry gates (though this isn't as reliable). They can also be found by contacting the Naro Moru Porters & Guides Association, PO Box Naro Moru, Naro Moru, or the Chogoria Porters (tel 88), PO Box 33, Chogoria. If you're staying at the Mt Kenya Hostel in Naro Moru, Joseph will fix you up if you ask him.

Places to Stay There are quite a lot of huts on the mountain but not all of them are available to the general public. Several are owned by and reserved exclusively for use by members of the Mountain Club of Kenya (MCK). Others are owned by lodges outside of the park and reserved for the use of people who go on their organised treks. Most of the other huts which are available to the general public have to be booked and paid for in advance. This is certainly true for the *Meteorological Station* and *Mackinders Camp* (otherwise known as the 'Teleki Valley Lodge') on the Naro Moru Trail. Both can be booked either through the MCK or the Naro Moru River Lodge (which can also book you other huts owned by the MCK).

MCK huts cost KSh 35 per person per night. Those at the Meteorological Station cost KSh 165 per person per night (KSh 110 for Kenyan residents), those at Mackinders Camp, KSh 275 per person per night (KSh 200 for Kenyan residents), and those at *Meru Mt Kenya Bandas*, KSh 200 per person per night.

Due to unauthorised use of the MCK huts open to the public in the past, the club has decided to fix locks to them so don't turn up without a booking voucher to show to the warden otherwise there may not be room for you. Negotiations are also in progress between the MCK and the Naro Moru River Lodge which will probably see all of the publicly accessible MCK huts taken over by the lodge. If that happens, *all* the huts will be staffed and there'll be a considerable price hike so don't turn up without booking vouchers.

Shipton's Camp (on the Sirimon trail) is owned by Bantu's Mt Kenya Leisure Lodge and the Meru Mt Kenya Bandas (on the Chogoria Trail) by the local county council. Bookings for Shipton's should be made through the Bantu Lodge in Nanyuki but it's not usually necessary to prebook Meru Mt Kenya Bandas.

The Trails
The normal weather pattern is for clear mornings with the mist closing in from 10 am though this sometimes clears again in the early evening. This means that if you want to make the most of the trek you should set off early every morning and, for the final assault on Point Lenana (the highest point for walkers), you need to make a 5 am start if you want to see the sunrise from the top.

Naro Moru Trail This is the most popular of the trails and the quickest but it's the least scenic. You should allow a minimum of four days for the climb or three if you have transport to and from Naro Moru and the Meteorological Station.

Your starting point here is the village of Naro Moru on the Nairobi-Nanyuki road where the turn-off for the mountain is well signposted just beyond the village. To get there, take one of the daily OTC buses from Nairobi to Naro Moru. The depot is at the junction of Cross Rd and Racecourse Rd. You can also get to Naro Moru from Nyeri by matatu though these are usually very crowded.

The first part of the trail takes you along a relatively good gravel road through farmlands for some 12 km (all the junctions are signposted) to the start of the forest where there's a wooden bridge across a small river. A further five km brings you to the park entry gate at 2400 metres. Having paid your fees, you continue on another eight km to the *Meteorological Station* at 3000 metres where you stay for the night.

If your time is limited you can cut out this part of the trek by taking the Naro Moru River Lodge's Land Rover all the way to the Meteorological Station. This costs KSh 960 plus KSh 15 for the driver's park entry fee and KSh 50 for the vehicle shared by up to eight people. You don't have to be on one of the lodge's organised treks to use this vehicle. Hitching is also possible but the chances of a lift *up* the mountain are limited – it's easier to get a ride on the way down.

On the second day you set out up the Teleki Valley along a well-marked path past the radio relay station and up to the edge of the forest at around 3200 metres. From here you scale the so-called 'Vertical Bog' and up onto a ridge from where you can see Mackinders Camp. The trail divides into two here and you have the choice of taking the higher path which gives the best views but is often wet or the lower path which crosses the Naro Moru stream and continues gently up to Mackinder's Camp (4160 metres). This part of the trek should take you around 4½ hours. Here you can stay the night (bunk houses or camping) or continue on to the *Austrian Hut* (4790 metres). The Austrian Hut is a better choice if you want to be on Point Lenana at dawn the next day since it's only a one hour trek from there. On the third day you continue on up the valley past the rangers' station to where the track divides into two. The main track to the right takes you to the Austrian Hut and Point Lenana (4985 metres and the main summit for walkers) via a swampy area followed by a moraine and a long scree. The final part of the trek up to Point Lenana takes you across a snow-covered glacier though the going is fairly easy. Mackinders Camp to Point Lenana should take about four hours.

Those who are camping and not staying in the bunk houses at either Mackinders Camp or the Austrian Hut have a third choice of where to spend the second night. This is the so-called *American Camp* which you get to by branching off left along a minor track just before the swampy area and above the rangers' station. It's an excellent camp site on a grassy meadow.

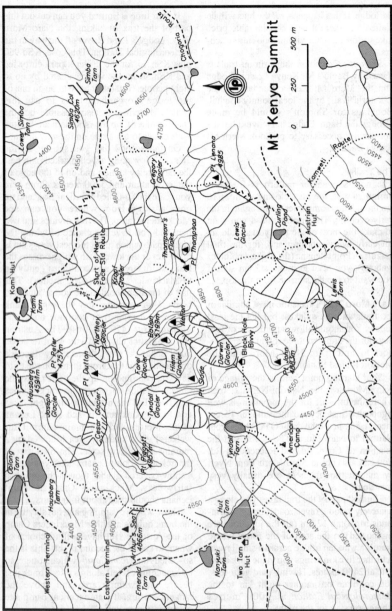

Mt Kenya Summit

From Point Lenana you have the choice of returning to the Meteorological Station back down the same route or continuing round the summit and down either the Chogoria Trail or the Sirimon Trail. Assuming you get to Point Lenana early in the day, you can reach the Meteorological Station the same day.

Sirimon Trail This is the least used of the three main trails but the driest. You should allow a minimum of five days to undertake this trek.

Take the same OTC bus as to Naro Moru but continue on to Nanyuki. If you want to start out up the mountain the same day as you leave Nairobi on this route, you need to take the earliest possible bus leaving Nairobi, otherwise you'll probably have to stay in Nanyuki for the night and leave the following day.

To get from Nanyuki to the start of the Sirimon track take one of the frequent matatus going to Timau on the main Nairobi-Nanyuki road and tell the driver you want to be dropped off at the start of the track (signposted). If you go over a fairly large river (the Sirimon River) then you've gone too far. The start of the trail is about 13 km out of Nanyuki.

On the first day you walk from the main road to the park entrance gate (about 10 km) and on from there to the road head at 3150 metres (a further nine km). It's a fairly easy stroll and you don't gain much in altitude. At the road head there's a good camp site as well as a bunk house. There are no Land Rovers for hire along this part of the route as there are on the Naro Moru Trail. If you have your own vehicle then you'll need 4WD for the last five km as the road is in bad shape.

On the second day you walk from the road head to Liki North Hut (3993 metres). It's an easy morning's walk along a gradually deteriorating trail. If it's still early in the day and you prefer to continue then don't take the trail off to the left at the Liki North stream (which takes you to Liki North Hut) but cross the stream and the ridge beyond and descend into Mackinder Valley. There is a clearly

defined track from here which follows the eastern side of the valley, eventually crosses the main Liki stream and leads you to Shipton's Caves – a formation of obvious rock overhangs where you can camp for the night though it's a poor site. From the road head to Shipton's Caves takes about seven hours.

On the third day (assuming you start from Liki North Hut) take the same route as outlined above to Shipton's Caves and on to Kami Hut (4433 metres). Not far from Shipton's Caves the trail divides into two and you have a choice of routes. The right-hand fork takes you steeply up to Kami Hut and is the best place to head for if you intend to walk around the peaks. Taking this route you can stay in *Kami Hut* for the night or pitch a tent at any of the good camp sites on the ridge just above the hut.

If you take the left-hand fork it leads you further up the Mackinder Valley, past the Shipton's Camp and bunk house, and then up a long hard scree slope to Simba Col. From here you can reach Square Tarn and the junction of the Chogoria Trail and, after that, Point Lenana. The walk from Shipton's Camp to Square Tarn takes about two hours. If you take this route then you'll need a tent unless you intend to carry on to the Austrian Hut for the night – not recommended as this would be a very long day and you'd be exhausted by the end of it.

Assuming you stayed the night at Kami Hut, on the fourth day you go from there to the Austrian Hut via Two Tarn Hut. The first section takes you steeply up a scree slope to Hausberg Col and then down another to Hausberg and Oblong tarns. From here there's a choice of bearing to the right across screes to the Western Terminal or more steeply to the left up to Arthur's Seat from which Two Tarn Hut can be seen. From the col along the Western Terminal route, head down and left towards the lower of the two tarns and then up a little further to Two Tarn Hut. Kami to Two Tarn Hut should take about two hours. There are superb views along this leg of the trail.

From Two Tarn Hut, descend to American

Camp and then on down to the Naro Moru Trail leading to the Austrian Hut.

On the fifth day your options are the same as on the Naro Moru route.

Chogoria Trail This trail, from the eastern side of the mountain, is undoubtedly the most beautiful of the access routes to the summit and certainly the easiest as far as gradients go. From Minto's Hut there are breathtaking views of the head of the Gorges Valley and the glaciers beyond.

To get started on this trail, take an OTC bus from Nairobi direct to Chogoria village or one first to Embu and then a matatu to Chogoria. Unless you get to Chogoria village early on in the day you will probably have to spend the night in Chogoria before setting off up the mountain, as the first day's hike is a long slog (about 24 km) up the forest track with nowhere to stay en route.

The first day is spent walking up to the park entry gate at 2990 metres through superb rainforest and on into the bamboo zone. You have the choice here of staying at the *Meru Mt Kenya Bandas*, about ½ km from the park entry gate, or continuing on a further three km to the *Urumandi Hut* where you can stay free of charge (at present). At the road head itself (3200 metres), six km from the park entry gate, there's also an excellent camp site.

There are possibilities of hitching all the way to the park entry gate from Chogoria as there's at least one official vehicle which does the run daily between the village and the Meru Mt Kenya Bandas, leaving the Bandas between 6.30 and 7 am and returning between 9 and 10 am. There may also be people staying at the Bandas who can help out with lifts.

Alternatively, if you want guaranteed transport, stay at the *Chogoria Cool Inn* (tel 35, PO Box 461, Chogoria) and speak to the proprietor, Francis Njoroge. He has a Peugeot and will take you up to the trail head for KSh 960 shared by up to four people.

The second day is spent walking from either the Meru Mt Kenya Bandas, the Urumandi Hut or the road head camp site to

Minto's Hut with spectacular views all the way. The trail is well defined all along and first crosses the stream up to the ridge which it then follows all the way to Minto's Hut. You need to bring water with you as there are no sources en route. The road head to Minto's Hut should take you about 4½ to five hours. Stay at *Minto's Hut* for the night (recently rehabilitated by a team from Operation Raleigh – a British volunteer organisation) or head further up the valley where there are a number of sheltered camp sites.

On the third day you continue up to the head of the valley, across scree slopes to the right and then left up to Square Tarn. The last section of this leg of the trail is very steep. From the tarn the trail continues straight on to a col below Point Lenana after which it descends briefly and then goes up across a scree slope to the right and onto the Austrian Hut. The trail is well marked with cairns and should take you about 3½ hours. From the Austrian Hut you can scale Point Lenana the same day or stay there for the night and make the ascent the following morning. Point Lenana is about 1½ hours from the Austrian Hut.

The descent from Point Lenana to Minto's Hut should take about two hours after which it's a further three to five hours back down to the Meru Mt Kenya Bandas.

Organised Treks
If your time is limited or you'd prefer someone else to make all the arrangements for climbing the mountain, there are several possibilities.

The Naro Moru River Lodge (tel (0176) 22018, PO Box 18, Naro Moru) can do this for you at a cost of KSh 4200 per person which includes a guide/cook, porters, all meals, park entry fees, camping fees, and transport to and from the trail heads. You spend four nights on the mountain (one of them in a hut and the other three camping) and you go up the Sirimon Trail and come back down along the Naro Moru Trail. These treks take a minimum of seven people.

The Bantu's Mt Kenya Leisure Lodge (tel

Burguret 1 or Nanyuki (0176) 22787, PO Box 333, Nanyuki), between Naro Moru and Nanyuki, also offer a range of organised treks, usually up the Sirimon Trail and down the Naro Moru Trail, taking from three to six days and they have their own huts on the Sirimon Trail where you stay for the night. Costs vary according to the number of days you wish to spend on the mountain and the number of people in the party, though it's cheapest if you can get eight or more people to go on the trek. A three day direct trip to Point Lenana via the Sirimon Trail costs KSh 4560 to KSh 2640 per person (one to eight people respectively), a four day trip along the same route KSh 5640 to KSh 32400 per person (one to eight people respectively) and a six day trip KSh 7200 to KSh 4380 per person (one to eight people respectively). All prices include park entry fees, guide and porters fees, food, transport to and from the trail heads, accommodation, and a special half board deal at the Lodge itself.

Other outfits which can organise walking safaris on Mt Kenya are Tropical Ice Ltd (tel 23649, PO Box 57341, Nairobi), which offer group and individual treks mainly on the Sirimon Trail, and East African Mountain Guides (tel 60728, PO Box 44827, Nairobi), which offers luxury safaris along the Chogoria Trail.

You need to be well prepared when climbing Mt Kenya. We received the following letter from a traveller who had a less than ideal trip:

I'm sure thousands of people agree that your books are extremely useful but the travel survival kit is very aptly named.

I went missing for five days on my own on the descent from Point Lenana. I lost my rucksack, sleeping bag and food. I managed to keep an army surplus bag with my camera, purse belt, hypothermia foil and guide book.

By the end of the fourth day the foil was ripped to shreds and gaining inspiration from the street dwellers in London I ripped out pages from the travel survival kit to cover myself with. I also ate some of the pages on Uganda!

Thanks for helping me survive!

Gillian Tree, UK

Western Kenya

Western Kenya is an area with many attractions, but is often overlooked by travellers, and you won't find a single safari minibus out this way either. For this reason alone it's worth spending a bit of time exploring out here, just to get the feel of Kenya without the tourists.

The countryside is, for the most part, beautiful rolling hills, often covered with the pale green bushes of the rambling tea plantations. Further west you have Lake Victoria and the regional capital of Kisumu on its shore. From here there are plenty of possibilities – just a short distance to the north lies the Kakamega Forest with its lush vegetation and abundant wildlife. Further north still, close to the sleepy regional town of Kitale, are the national parks of Mt Elgon (well worth climbing) and Saiwa Swamp, where the only way of getting around is on foot and the attraction is the rare sitatunga deer.

If you have your sights set on more distant horizons, head west for Busia and Uganda, or south to Isebania and across the border into Tanzania.

This area is the home of Kenya's Luo people. Numbering around two million they make up the third largest ethnic group in the country.

Getting Around

This is the most densely populated part of the country so the road system is good and there are hundreds of matatus of varying shapes and sizes plying the routes. Accidents are unnervingly common, but these seem to happen more amongst the very small matatus which are usually dangerously overloaded. The small-truck size matatus are a lot safer as they generally travel slower and can carry loads with greater ease.

One annoying factor of matatu travel in this region is the way the destination changes suddenly depending on how many passengers there are. So if your matatu is supposedly going from, say, Kakamega to Kitale and it gets to Webuye and everyone gets out, it's a fairly safe bet that you will have to as well. When this happens, and you have paid to the final destination, the driver will find you a seat in another vehicle and fix things with the driver. You will get there in the end, but it may take longer than you think. It took me three matatus to get from Kisumu to Kisii, despite being told when I boarded the first two that they were going all the way.

Lake Victoria

With an area approaching 70,000 sq km, Lake Victoria is obviously the major geographical feature in this part of the continent. Unlike the lakes further west, Victoria is not part of the rift valley system, and so is wide and shallow (only 100 metres deep) compared with, say, Lake Tanganyika which is nearly 1½ km deep.

Lake Victoria touches on three countries – Uganda, Tanzania and Kenya – and it's just a pity that it's not possible to travel between any of the countries via the lake. The only possibilities for excursions are the ferries operating out of Kisumu.

Bilharzia is prevalent in Lake Victoria so don't swim in the water or walk in the grass along its shores – this is the hideout of the snails which are the host for the parasitic flukes which invade your body. Admittedly you face only a very small risk of contracting bilharzia if you spend only a short time here.

KISUMU

Although it hardly feels like it, Kisumu is Kenya's third largest town. It has a very easy-going, almost decaying, atmosphere, possibly partly due to the fact that with the cessation of international ferry services on

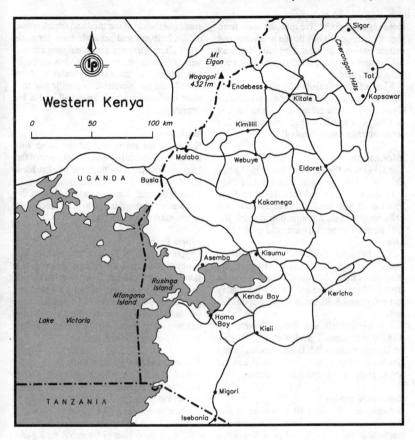

Western Kenya

0   50   100 km

UGANDA

Mt Elgon

Wagagai
4321m

Endebess

Kitale

Sigor

Cherangani Hills

Tot

Kapsawar

Kimilili

Malaba

Webuye

Eldoret

Busla

Kakamega

Kisumu

Asembo

Rusinga Island

Mfangano Island

Kendu Bay

Kericho

Lake Victoria

Homa Bay

Kisii

TANZANIA

Migori

Isebania

the lake, and the decline in through traffic to Uganda, it's a bit of a dead end these days. It was also a busy port from early this century right up until the East African Community split up in 1977, and it seems that from this point on the town has just been marking time.

Don't be put off by that though, as it's the ideal place to head for from the east of the country as the travel connections are excellent. There's also enough to do in the town itself to make it an interesting place to stop for a day or two.

If you've arrived from the higher country further east the first thing that you will notice is the heat and humidity. Kisumu is always a good few degrees hotter than, say, Nairobi and the steamy conditions only add to the general torporific air.

Orientation

Kisumu is sited on the gently sloping shore of Lake Victoria. Although it's a fairly sprawling town, everything you are likely to need is within walking distance. The main drag is Oginga Odinga Rd and along it are virtually all the shops, the banks and the post office.

The railway station and ferry jetty are

close together about five minutes walk from Oginga Odinga Rd, while the noisy bus and matatu station is on Jomo Kenyatta Highway behind the market, about 10 minutes walk from the centre.

Most of the cheap hotels are in the area between Oginga Odinga Rd and Otiena Oyoo St. The best access to the lake itself is at Dunga, a small village about three km south of town along Nzola Rd.

Information

The GPO is in the centre of town on Oginga Odinga Rd and is open Monday to Friday from 8 am to 5 pm and Saturday from 9 am to noon. If you need to make international calls there is a card phone outside and you dial direct. Phonecards are sold at the post office.

The British Council Library is also on Oginga Odinga Rd. It has newspapers and magazines and quite a good library. It is open from 9.30 am to 1 pm and 2 to 5 pm Monday to Friday, and 8.30 am to 12.45 pm on Saturday.

For car rentals see Shiva Travels (tel 43420) or Kisumu Travels (tel 44122), both on Oginga Odinga Rd. Both agencies have a limited number of cars available. Prices are not as good as you can get in Nairobi.

Kisumu Museum

It comes as something of a surprise to find this excellent museum here – it's probably the best in the country and is well worth a visit. It's on Nairobi Rd within easy walking distance of the centre and is open daily from 9.30 am to 6 pm; entry is KSh 20.

The displays are well presented and wide ranging in their variety. There's a very good collection of everyday items from the various different peoples of the area, including agricultural implements, bird and insect traps (including a white-ant trap!), food utensils, clothes, furniture, weapons, musical instruments, a fairly motley collection of stuffed birds and animals and an amazing centrepiece of a lion riding on a wildebeest – both stuffed also.

Outside there is a traditional Luo homestead consisting of the mud and thatch house of the husband and separate ones for each wife. There's usually a man hanging around who will show you around for a few shillings and point out the salient features. Also outside are the inevitable crocodile and tortoise enclosures which are small and a bit depressing.

Market

Kisumu's market is one of the more animated in the country, and certainly one of the largest. Whether you're in the market for a kg of potatoes or are just curious, it's worth a stroll around. You can cut through to the bus station through the hole in the back wall of the market compound.

Hippo Point

Hippo Point is at Dunga, about three km south of town, and the café on the point is a good place to head for. There were no hippos in evidence when I visited but it's a pleasant spot all the same. Known as Dunga Refreshments, it is well signposted once you get out of town along Nzola Rd. This place also has the only camp site in Kisumu.

Places to Stay – bottom end

Accommodation in Kisumu generally seems to be more expensive than similar places elsewhere in Kenya though there's no apparent reason for this. The cheapest option if you don't mind dorm accommodation is the *YWCA* on the corner of Omolo Agar Rd and Nairobi Rd. Beds cost KSh 40, or there are just a few rooms at KSh 120 per person.

As usual, the real budget hotels are brothels and are shabby and extremely basic. Typical of these places is the *PVU Lodge* on Accra St, which charges KSh 60/85/100 for a single/double/triple room with common facilities. A step up the scale is the *New Rozy Lodge* on Ogada St. Rooms here go for KSh 90/165 with common bath; the doubles are definitely overpriced.

On Apindi St there's a couple of places worth a try. *Mirukas Lodge* has small singles but reasonable doubles for KSh 80/110 – not bad value for Kisumu. Right next door is

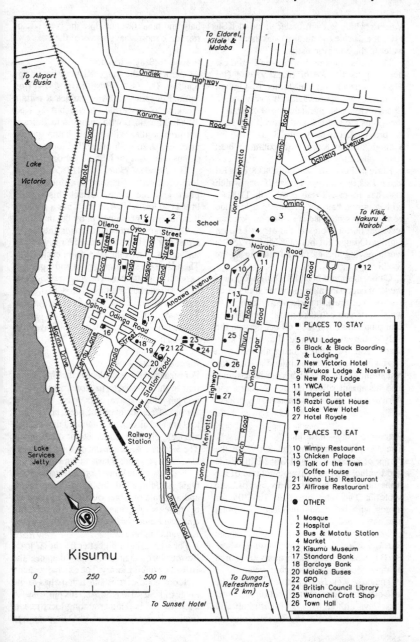

Kisumu

0   250   500 m

To Eldoret,
Kitale &
Malaba

To Airport
& Busia

Lake
Victoria

Ondiek   Highway

Karume   Road

School

Otieno   Oyoo   Street
Street

To Kisii,
Nakuru &
Nairobi

Omino

Nairobi   Road

Anaowa Avenue

Railway
Station

Lake
Services
Jetty

To Dunga
Refreshments
(2 km)

To Sunset Hotel

■ PLACES TO STAY

5 PVU Lodge
6 Black & Black Boarding
   & Lodging
7 New Victoria Hotel
8 Mirukas Lodge & Nasim's
9 New Rozy Lodge
11 YWCA
14 Imperial Hotel
15 Razbi Guest House
16 Lake View Hotel
27 Hotel Royale

▼ PLACES TO EAT

10 Wimpy Restaurant
13 Chicken Palace
19 Talk of the Town
   Coffee House
21 Mona Lisa Restaurant
23 Alfirose Restaurant

● OTHER

1 Mosque
2 Hospital
3 Bus & Matatu Station
4 Market
12 Kisumu Museum
17 Standard Bank
18 Barclays Bank
20 Maloika Buses
22 GPO
24 British Council Library
25 Wananchi Craft Shop
26 Town Hall

Nasim's which is even better value at KSh 110 for a double (no singles) and there's hot water in the common baths.

The pick of the bottom-end places, however, is the *Razbi Guest House* (tel 41312), upstairs on the corner of Oginga Odinga Rd and Kendu Lane. It's very secure (there's a locked grille at the top of the stairs), the rooms are spotless and a towel and soap are provided. The rates are KSh 100/155 for a single/double room with common bath (cold water only).

Right in the centre near Oginga Odinga Rd is the *Talk of the Town Coffee House* which also has rooms. These cost KSh 110/145 with common bath and are not terrific value considering what else is available. Another restaurant with rooms is the *Mona Lisa* on Oginga Odinga Rd but at KSh 90/125 it's worth paying the extra and staying at the Razbi.

Campers should head for *Dunga Refreshments* at Hippo Point, right on the water three km south of town. It takes nearly an hour to walk it, or you can take a taxi for KSh 70. Camping here costs KSh 60 per person, the only disadvantage being that there's no shade. You also need to bring all your own food with you unless you intend to eat in the restaurant as the only shops are in Kisumu. The restaurant offers Indian, Western and African food and is quite reasonably priced.

Places to Stay – middle

The *New Victoria Hotel* (tel 2909) on the corner of Kendu Lane and Gor Mahia Rd is good value, especially if you get one of the front rooms with balcony and views of Lake Victoria. The rates are KSh 165/305 for rooms with bath and breakfast. The hotel also has a good restaurant.

On the next corner down the hill is the *Black & Black Boarding & Lodging* where B&B is KSh 185/275. Bathrooms are shared by three rooms and there is hot water.

The *Lake View Hotel* is much closer to the lake but it barely seems to function as a hotel these days, although the bar is definitely still a bar. The rooms cost KSh 175/350 including bath and breakfast and, like the New Victoria, some rooms have views of the lake.

Places to Stay – top end

At the top of the range Kisumu has a few options. The *Hotel Royale* (tel 44240) on Jomo Kenyatta Highway exudes a certain creaking olde-worlde charm, but at KSh 300/480 for B&B with common facilities is not great value. With private bathroom the price jumps to KSh 505/720. Nonresidents can use the pool for KSh 20 per day.

The *Imperial Hotel* (tel 41485), also on Jomo Kenyatta Highway, is a much newer place and the prices reflect this – KSh 900/1140 for B&B. The hotel has a pool but it is tiny and is hemmed in by the building.

On the southern edge of town, the *Sunset Hotel* (tel 41100) does indeed have views of the sunset, and of the lake, from each room. There's also a swimming pool and a good, if expensive, restaurant. The room rates reflect the position and facilities; KSh 840/1020 for rooms with breakfast. It's part of the African Tours & Hotels Ltd chain and so can be booked in Nairobi in the City Hall Way office by the Hilton.

Places to Eat

For breakfast the best place is the airy restaurant in the *New Victoria Hotel*. For KSh 35 you get juice, papaya, eggs, toast, butter and tea or coffee. It's open for breakfast from 7 to 9 am and also serves standard dishes such as steak, chicken, chips, etc at other times. The *Mona Lisa Restaurant* on the main street also does good breakfasts and meals.

The *Talk of the Town Coffee House* just off Oginga Odinga Rd has good cheap meals and a couple of tables outside. For stand-up or takeaway greasy spoon there's the *Chicken Palace* or the *Wimpy*, both on Jomo Kenyatta Highway.

For something a bit better try the *Alfirose Restaurant* on Oginga Odinga Rd up near the British Council Library. The extensive menu includes good curries and fish dishes in the range of KSh 40 to KSh 90. This place is also licensed and is popular among local expats (mainly Peace Corps and VSO volunteers).

Bodega's is recommended for a cheap fish meal – huge portions of whole fresh fish for KSh 60 to KSh 85.

On Thursday evenings the *Hotel Royale* has a barbecue buffet for KSh 120 which is well worth the money.

If you take a walk out to Hippo Point, the *Dunga Refreshments* café has quite good Indian, Western and African meals and snacks and you can sit outside right on the water's edge.

Things to Buy

Kisumu is about the best place to buy Kisii soapstone carvings and there are pavement stalls set up on the northern side of Oginga Odinga Rd near the British Council Library.

The Wananchi Craft Shop near the town hall is a cooperative selling crafts made by the local women, and they have some interesting items.

Getting There & Away

Air Kenya Airways have 11 flights weekly to Nairobi. The trip takes one hour and costs KSh 650 one way.

Road There are plenty of buses and matatus to all over the place from the large bus station just north of the market. Destinations frequently served include Busia (KSh 50), Kakamega, Homa Bay, Kitale, Nakuru, Kericho and Nairobi. It's possible to book Nairobi buses in advance with Coast Bus at the bus station or Malaika buses in the town centre. Malaika have twice daily buses to Nairobi and Mombasa, and the charge is Kericho KSh 35, Nakuru KSh 60, Naivasha KSh 95, Nairobi KSh 110 and Mombasa KSh 240.

The quickest way to get to Kakamega and Kitale is in one of the fairly new minibuses which leave from right by Jomo Kenyatta Highway and not in the main part of the bus station. Peugeots to Nakuru and Nairobi also leave from here.

Train There are trains to Nairobi daily at 6.30 pm, arriving at 7.35 am the next day. Depending on demand there is often a second daily train. Fares to Nairobi are KSh 380 in 1st class, KSh 179 in 2nd class and KSh 90 in 3rd class. It's advisable to book in advance. The booking office at the station is open daily from 8 am to noon and 2 to 4 pm.

Lake Ferry With the demise of the international services, the Lake Victoria ferries now only go to places close to Kisumu such as Kendu Bay, Homa Bay, Asembo Bay and Mfangano Island. There are three classes on the ferries, none of them ever very crowded, so 2nd or 3rd class is quite OK.

The MV *Alestes* and MV *Reli* have the following services from Kisumu every day except Thursday:

	Arrival	Departure
Kisumu	–	9 am
Kendu Bay	11 am	11.10 am
Homa Bay	2 pm	2.30 pm
Asembo Bay	5 pm	8 am (next day)
Homa Bay	10.40 am	11 am
Kendu Bay	2 pm	2.45 pm
Kisumu	4 pm	–

The fares from Kisumu to Kendu Bay are KSh 50/40/25 in 1st/2nd/3rd class, to Homa Bay KSh 82/65/36, and to Asembo Bay KSh 133/108/52.

The MV *Kamondo* operates between Homa Bay and Mfangano and Rusinga islands twice a week, and between Homa Bay and Kisumu once a week.

AROUND THE LAKE
Kendu Bay

This small lakeside village has little to offer apart from a somewhat strange volcanic lake a couple of km from town. There's basic accommodation in the town, and the ferry jetty is about one km away.

Homa Bay

This is a very nondescript town on a small bay in Lake Victoria. If you've just got off the ferry from Kisumu you'll have to spend the night here, which is no great pleasure. For accommodation there's the *Asego Stores Guest House* which costs KSh 190 for a double with breakfast, or the expensive

Homa Bay Hotel (KSh 390/575). There's transport from here on to Kisii, Migori and Isebania (Tanzanian border) and back to Kisumu.

Rusinga Island

Mbita is the town on Rusinga Island and it is connected by a causeway to the mainland. The only remarkable thing about the island is the mausoleum of Tom Mboya on the northern side of the island – he was born here in 1930 and was shot dead by police in 1969 during political unrest.

There are matatus to Homa Bay, as well as the twice weekly ferry services to Mfangano and Homa Bay.

Mfangano Island

There's little to see here and very little in the way of facilities. The small fishing community is about as far off the beaten track as you can get in Kenya.

There is one cheap hotel and the island is connected to the mainland by twice-weekly ferries to Homa Bay.

Western Highlands

The Western Highlands are the agricultural heartland of Kenya and they separate Kisumu and Lake Victoria from the rest of the country. In the south around Kisii and Kericho lie the vast tea plantations, while further north around Kitale and Eldoret it's all fertile farming land.

The towns of the highlands are really just small agricultural service towns, much the same as you'd find in similar areas in Australia or the USA – and they're about as interesting. For visitors the attractions of the area lie outside these towns – the tea plantations around Kericho, Kakamega Forest near Kakamega, Mt Elgon and Saiwa Swamp national parks both near Kitale, and the Cherangani Hills which lie east of Kitale and Eldoret. They are dealt with in that order in this section.

KISII

As you might expect this is where Kisii soapstone comes from but it's not on sale here at all, the simple reason being that Kisii sees very few tourists and those that do come this way tend to just keep moving. You can, however, visit the quarries if you like. When you get there, ask for Abyce and he'll show you around. Not much happens in Kisii, and even the locals will tell you that it's 'a remote place'. On the other hand, people are friendly and interesting and as so few tourists come here you'll be regarded with curiosity.

Kisii is the main centre of the region

Gusii in traditional dress

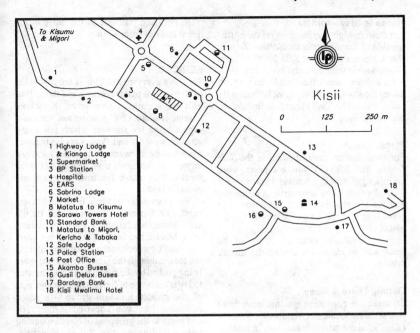

known as the Gusii Highlands, home of the Gusii people. The Gusii, numbering around one million, are a Bantu speaking people in the middle of a non-Bantu area – the Maasai to the south, Luo to the west and north and Kipsigis to the east all speak unrelated languages.

The town centre is compact and, as usual, the market is the liveliest place in the town during the day.

Whilst you're here, it's worth making the four hour round trip to the top of nearby Manga Ridge from which the views – especially over Lake Victoria – are magnificent. You can also see Kisumu in the distance and the coffee plantations of Kericho behind you.

Places to Stay – bottom end

There are two excellent places to stay at in Kisii. The cheaper one is the new *Sabrina Lodge*, just around the corner from the matatu park. It's a very friendly place and has rooms with common facilities for KSh 90/145. The hotel also has a bar and restaurant. Somewhat more expensive is the *Safe Lodge* (tel 202950), opposite the BATA shop, which has friendly staff and costs KSh 130/180 for single/double self-contained rooms. There's hot water, soap and towel are provided and breakfast is included in the price. The single rooms have double beds so a couple could get away with this. It also has an excellent restaurant (dinner KSh 62) which is reminiscent of the sort of place you might find in a small French village. The hotel is also the main social focus of the town – well, the video machine in the restaurant is, anyway.

There's also the *Highway Lodge*, one of the cheapest in town, which has clean, basic rooms for KSh 70/86 with common BATH. The only problem here is that it's right on the main road, so the front rooms cop the noise. Right next door is the *Kiango Lodge* which is clean and costs KSh 95/145 for rooms with bath.

Places to Stay – middle

The modern high-rise building on the northern side of the market is the *Sarawa Towers Hotel*. Rooms here cost KSh 210/330 for a single/double with bath and breakfast.

Otherwise, there's the *Kisii Hotel* for KSh 240 or the *Kisii Mwalimu Hotel*, both slightly out of town. The Kisii Hotel is definitely the best of the two.

Places to Eat

For breakfast try the restaurant in the *Safe Lodge*. For KSh 33 you get juice, fruit, cereals, eggs, sausage, toast and tea or coffee – good value. They also serve good meals, and the fact that there is a video and they serve beer make this a gregarious and lively place, especially in the evenings.

For local tucker there are plenty of the usual sort of restaurant around the matatu station.

Getting There & Away

To make life confusing matatus leave from two separate locations. Matatus for Kisumu (KSh 50, three hours) leave from in front of the market, while those for everywhere else (Migori, Kericho, Tabaka) leave from the station up past the Standard Bank.

For direct buses to Nairobi Akamba has a night bus for KSh 150, and a day bus which also stops at Kericho (KSh 40), Nakuru (KSh 90) and Naivasha (KSh 120) en route. Tickets should be booked one day in advance. Gusii Deluxe Buses across the road has four nightly buses to Nairobi. The trip takes around 8½ hours. EARS also has a night bus to Nairobi at 9 pm for KSh 150.

TABAKA

This is the village where the soapstone is quarried and carved, and on arrival in the village it's easy enough to locate someone who can show you one of the workshops. It's almost just a cottage industry and there are few people who actually work the stone for a living – to most people it's just a handy way to supplement a meagre living made from agriculture.

To get there take one of the fairly infrequent matatus from Kisii.

KERICHO

Tea – it's everywhere! This is the real heart of Kenya's tea plantation area and the rolling hills are a uniform pale green. Kericho's climate is perfect for growing tea, the main aspect being the showers which fall every afternoon year-round. Yes, Kericho is a wet place but the showers are only brief and not unpleasant, and apart from benefiting the tea bushes, they make the town a green and pleasant land.

The town takes its name from the Maasai chief, Ole Kericho, who was killed by the Gusii in the 18th century in a battle over land – the Maasai had been in the area for years and didn't appreciate the Gusii moving into the area, although the Gusii themselves were being pushed by the advancing Luo. The area today is the home of the Kipsigis people, part of the greater Kalenjin group – a name (meaning 'I tell you') devised in the 1950s and given to the grouping of Nandi speaking tribes, including the Pokot, Kipsigis, Marakwet and Nandi.

The town itself has nothing to recommend it but it's not a bad place to stop for the night.

Information

The post office and the two main banks are all on Moi Highway. The banks are open Monday to Friday from 8 am to 1 pm and on Saturday from 8.30 to 11 am.

Tea Plantations

Kenya is the world's third largest producer of tea and typically it accounts for 20% to 30% of the country's export income. Tea picking is obviously one of the main jobs in the area. A top tea picker can pick up to 100 kg per day, and they are paid at the rate of KSh 0.80 per kg. The bushes are picked every 17 days, and the same picker picks the same patches of the plantation each time. If you look closely at one of the fields of bushes you can see how one stalk of a bush is left to grow here and there; these are the markers by which workers identify their patch. The bushes are cut right back to about 50 cm high in January-March every four years, and after 90 days are ready for picking again.

The closest plantation to town is behind the Tea Hotel, itself once owned by the Brooke Bond company. Walk through the hotel grounds behind what was the service station and out through the back gate. This path leads through the tea bushes to the hotel workers' huts. If you're lucky there may be picking in progress.

For a tour of a plantation and processing plant it may be possible to organise one through the Tea Hotel.

Places to Stay – bottom end

Kericho has the usual assortment of scruffy budget hotels at the bottom end of the market. The *Sugutek Hotel* on Tengecha Rd is about as basic as you can get but is cheap enough at KSh 60/95 for a single/double room with common bath. The hotel also has a restaurant.

The *Tas Lodge* is basically a mid-range place but it does have a few good single

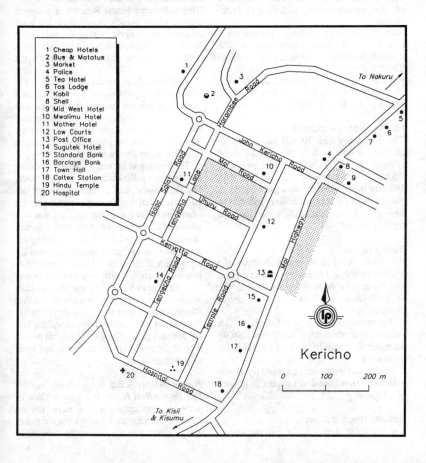

1 Cheap Hotels
2 Bus & Matatus
3 Market
4 Police
5 Tea Hotel
6 Tas Lodge
7 Kobil
8 Shell
9 Mid West Hotel
10 Mwalimu Hotel
11 Mother Hotel
12 Low Courts
13 Post Office
14 Sugutek Hotel
15 Standard Bank
16 Barclays Bank
17 Town Hall
18 Caltex Station
19 Hindu Temple
20 Hospital

To Nakuru

Harambee Road

John Kericho Road

Isaac Sala Lane

Moi Road

Tengecha Lane

Uhuru Road

Kenyatta Road

Moi Highway

Lengecha Road

Temple Road

Kericho

0   100   200 m

Hospital Road

To Kisii
& Kisumu

rooms for KSh 110 with common bath and hot water (in the morning only). Breakfast is also included. It's also possible to camp in the green gardens of this place for KSh 50 per person.

There are a few more basic boarding & lodging places on the road below the matatu station. None of them are up to much.

Places to Stay – middle

The *Tas Lodge* (tel 21112) on the Nakuru road is about the best. KSh 180/275 gets you a big bright room with bath and hot water, and breakfast is included. This hotel has a pleasant garden setting, including an open-air bar.

In the centre of town there's the characterless *Mwalimu Hotel* which charges KSh 215/300 for rooms with bath and breakfast. There's a restaurant and noisy bar in this place. Even more anonymous is the *Mid West Hotel* (tel 20611) on John Kericho Rd, where rooms go for KSh 450/580 with breakfast.

Places to Stay – top end

The *Tea Hotel* (tel 20280) has plenty of charm – it was built by the Brooke Bond company in the 1950s but is now owned by African Tours & Hotels chain. At KSh 840/1020 for B&B, it doesn't do a lot of business, but it's worth a wander around and maybe have a drink (tea, perhaps?) in the lounge or on the terrace.

Places to Eat

For basic African stodge and stews the *Mother Hotel* on Uhuru Rd does as good a job as any, as does the restaurant in the *Sugutek Hotel* on Tengecha Rd – chips, chicken, ugali, etc.

The restaurant in the *Mwalimu Hotel* is a little more sophisticated, while the KSh 95 set lunch or dinner in the *Mid West Hotel* is good value.

For the full treatment you could try a meal at the *Tea Hotel* but don't expect to get out of it lightly.

Getting There & Away

The matatu station is fairly well organised, with matatus on the upper level and minibuses and buses on the lower level.

As is the case throughout the west, there is plenty of transport in any direction. To the town of Kisumu there are occasional Nissan minibuses as well as regular matatus. The companies running buses to Nairobi have small offices at the matatu station.

If you are hitching, the turn-off to Kisumu is about two km south of town along the Kisii road, so you need to get there first, either on foot or by matatu.

KAKAMEGA FOREST RESERVE

The Kakamega Forest Reserve is a superb slab of virgin tropical rainforest in the heart of an intensive agricultural area. It is home to a huge variety of birds and animals and is well worth the minimal effort required to get to it.

The Forest Department maintains a beautiful four room rest house here, as well as a large nursery for propagating trees and shrubs for planting both in this district and for ceremonial occasions around the country. The workers are very amenable and it's no problem to get shown around.

The forest near the rest house is very dense and there are paths leading all over the place. For that reason, and certainly for a greater appreciation of the forest flora and fauna, it's worth engaging one of the staff to guide you around. The most well-known man, Leonard (known to some as Light-Fingered Lenny for reasons I won't go into), is amenable and his knowledge of the trees and birds is extensive. Binoculars are virtually essential, as is wet weather gear as it usually pisses down every afternoon for a couple of hours or so. For that reason also it's best to try and arrive in the morning as you usually have to walk a few km to reach the rest house. The driest period here is from December to April, but even then it rains daily.

Places to Stay & Eat

The *Forest Rest House* is a superb place to put your feet up for a few days. It's an elevated wooden building with a verandah which looks directly on to the seemingly impenetrable forest. There are only four double rooms, and surprisingly they all have a bathroom and toilet. Blankets are supplied but you need to have your own sleeping bag or sheet. It costs KSh 6 to camp here, or KSh 35 per person in the rooms. If the rest house is full when you arrive it is usually possible to sleep on the verandah for KSh 18. If you want to be sure of a room, book in advance through the Forest Officer, PO Box 88, Kakamega.

The only problem here is food. Basically you need to bring your own and preferably something to cook it on, although it is possible to cook on a fire. There is a small kiosk which sells beer, tea and sodas and also cooks basic meals at lunch time, and on request in the evenings – beans or corn and rice is about the limit, but you won't starve. The kiosk closes at 6.30 pm so you need to make sure they know you are coming. There is a small group of dukas about two km back towards Shinyalu, and you can get basic meals and supplies here.

Getting There & Away

The Forest Rest House lies about 12 km east of the A1 Kisumu-Kitale road, about 30 km north of Kisumu. Access is possible either from Kakamega village on the main road when coming from the north, or from Khayaga also on the main road when coming from the south. From both places dirt roads lead east to the small market village of Shinyalu, from where it's a further five km to the rest house, signposted to the left. There are matatus from Kakamega to Shinyalu (KSh 12), and even the occasional one from Khayaga to Shinyalu.

If you want to walk – and it is beautiful walking country – it's about seven km from Khayaga to Shinyalu, about 10 km from Kakamega to Shinyalu. These roads become extremely treacherous after rain and you may prefer to walk when you see how the vehicles slip all over the road. There's very little traffic along either of the roads but you may get a lift with the occasional tractor or Forest Department vehicle. Whatever means you employ to get there, allow half a day

from Kitale or Kisumu. From the turn-off to the rest house the dirt road continues on to Kapsabet so you could also come from that direction but it is a long walk if you can't get a lift.

KAKAMEGA

The town of Kakamega is on the A1 route, 50 km north of Kisumu and 115 km south of Kitale. About the only reason to stay here is if you are heading for the Kakamega Forest and arrive too late in the day to walk or get a vehicle in. It's also the last place to stock up with supplies if heading for a forest sojourn.

The town has the usual facilities – a couple of banks, post office, market and the ubiquitous boardings & lodgings.

Places to Stay

The *New Garden View Lodge* is conveniently close to the matatu station. It is a typical basic Kenyan hotel, and therefore serves as a brothel as well, but is not too bad at KSh 60/85 for a single/double. There is a couple of other places if this one doesn't appeal.

At the absolute other end of the scale is the *Golf Hotel* where rooms go for KSh 660/935 for B&B. The draw card of this place is the attached golf course, and your room rate includes temporary membership.

Getting There & Away

The matatu station is at the northern edge of town. There are buses, matatus or Peugeots to Kisumu, Webuye, Kitale, Nairobi and Busia. Hitching is not too difficult.

ELDORET

There is little to see or do in Eldoret but it may make a convenient stop for the night in your peregrinations around the western highlands, particularly if you are heading to or from the Cherangani Hills which lie to the north of Eldoret.

The town has benefited hugely from the new university here and so it seems likely that it will become one of the few expanding towns in the west.

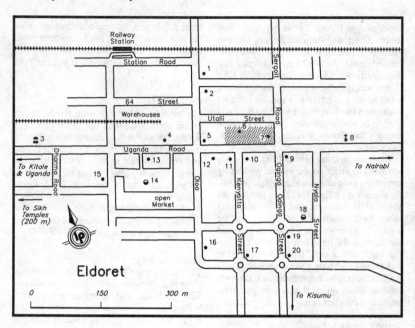

Eldoret

0   150   300 m

To Kitale & Uganda
To Sikh Temples (200 m)
To Nairobi
To Kisumu

1	Eldoret Wagon Hotel
2	Sirikwa Hotel
3	Post Office
4	Police
5	National Bank of Kenya
6	Town Hall
7	Library
8	New Church
9	New Paradise Bar & Lodging
10	Standard Chartered Bank
11	Barclays
12	Otto Cafe
13	Mahindi Hotel
14	Bus & Matatu Park
15	New Miyako Hotel
16	New Lincoln Hotel
17	Eldoret Travel Agency & Sizzlers Cafe
18	Akamba Bus
19	Spark Milk Bar
20	Top Lodge

Information

The post office is on the main street, Uganda Rd, and is open Monday to Friday from 8 am to 5 pm and Saturday from 9 am to noon. There are branches of both Barclays and the Standard Chartered banks, also both on the main street.

For car rental, check out the Eldoret Travel Agency (tel 33351) on Kenyatta St.

Places to Stay – bottom end

Right at the bottom of the range are the two *Sikh Temples* west of the town centre, where I was assured travellers could stay. If you do make use of this hospitality be sure to leave a donation.

For a regular hotel, try the *New Paradise Bar & Lodging* on the corner of Uganda Rd and Oginga Odinga St, or the *Top Lodge*, also on Oginga Odinga St. As usual, the prime function of these cheap places is as brothels but they are quite happy for you to stay a whole night.

Places to Stay – middle

The *Mahindi Hotel* is conveniently close to

the bus and matatu station and is good value at KSh 155/215 for rooms with bath and hot water. They also have cheaper rooms at KSh 120 for singles with common bath. The hotel has a restaurant, and the noise from the Silent Night Bar (!) downstairs can sometimes be distracting. A similar place and also close to the bus station is the *New Miyako Hotel* (tel 22594) which charges KSh 120 for a single with common bath, and KSh 145/215 for singles/doubles with bath.

The *New Lincoln Hotel* (tel 22093) is much quieter and has parking spaces if you're driving. Self-contained rooms with breakfast included are a good bargain at KSh 205/310. The hotel also has its own restaurant and bar.

Places to Stay – top end

Eldoret's top-end offerings are the *Eldoret Wagon Hotel*, which charges KSh 360/540 for rooms with bath and breakfast, and the more modern *Sirikwa Hotel* (tel 31655) which has rooms for KSh 720/900 including breakfast. This place has the only swimming pool in Eldoret.

Places to Eat

A popular lunch time spot is *Otto Cafe* on Uganda Rd. It offers good cheap Western-style meals such as steak, chicken, sausages, eggs, chips and other snacks. Another good place for snacks is the *Spark Milk Bar* on Oginga Odinga St.

For a slightly more upmarket meal or snack try the flash new *Sizzlers Cafe* on Kenyatta St, near the Eldoret Travel Agency. Here they have a whole range of burgers, curries, steak and sandwiches. It's popular but certainly not the cheapest in town.

For over the top meals both the *Sirikwa* and *Eldoret Wagon* hotels have fancy restaurants.

Getting There & Away

Air Air Kenya Aviation have four weekly flights between Nairobi's Wilson Airport and Eldoret. They depart from Nairobi on Tuesday and Thursday at 7 am and 3.45 pm, and from Eldoret at 8.15 am and 5 pm; the trip takes around one hour and costs KSh 1500 one way.

Road The bus and matatu station is right in the centre of town, just off Uganda Rd. There are bus, minibus, Peugeot and matatu departures throughout the day for Kisumu, Nakuru, Naivasha, Nairobi, Kericho and Kitale. Peugeots to Nairobi cost KSh 180 and take just 3½ hours.

Train There are services three times a week for Nairobi on Wednesday, Saturday and Sunday at 9 pm, arriving the next day at 9.30 am. To the Ugandan border at Malaba they depart on Wednesday, Saturday and Sunday at around 4 am.

CHERANGANI HILLS

The beautiful Cherangani Hills are part of the Rift Valley system and extend for about 60 km from the north-east of Eldoret. They form the western wall of the spectacular Elgeyo Escarpment. You could easily spend weeks exploring here, and never come across another mzungu.

The area is best explored on foot as the roads are rough and some of those which scale the Elgeyo Escarpment are incredibly steep. In wet conditions the roads in this area become treacherous. For serious exploration you would need to get copies of the relevant Survey of Kenya maps to the area. Otherwise just follow the dirt roads.

The hills are dotted with small towns and although none of them have any recognised accommodation, it should be possible to arrange something with the local people. If you have a tent it's just a matter of finding a good spot and asking permission.

From Eldoret it should be possible to hitch, or even find a matatu, as far as Kapsowar, 70 km to the north-east in the Kerio Valley and right in the heart of the hills. Coming from the north there is a road which starts from Sigor at the Marich Pass and finds its way to Kapsowar via Tot and the impossibly steep escarpment road, but don't expect much in the way of transport along it.

The hills are the home of the Marakwet (or

Markweta) people, part of the greater Kalenjin grouping. They migrated here from the north and found the area provided good safety and the streams were ideal for agriculture, as the rainfall was low. To this end they have made good use of, and extended, the water distribution channels which were already in existence when the Marakwet first migrated to the area. The channels distribute the water to all the small shambas in the hills.

KITALE

Kitale is another in the string of agricultural service towns which dot the western highlands. It does have a vaguely interesting museum but its main function for travellers is as a base for explorations further afield – Mt Elgon, Saiwa Swamp National Park – and a take-off point for the trip up to Lake Turkana. As such it's a pleasant enough town and can make an enjoyable stopover for a couple of days.

Information

The post office is on Post Office Rd (surprise, surprise) and is open the usual hours. It's possible to make international calls but they have to go through the operator in Nairobi, and this takes time.

Kitale has the usual banks and a busy market.

Kitale Museum

The museum has a variety of indoor exhibits, including good ethnographic displays of the Turkana people. The outdoor exhibits include traditional homesteads of a number of different tribal groups, the inevitable tortoise enclosure and an interesting biogas display. Probably most interesting is the small nature trail which leads through some virgin forest at the back of the museum. There are numbered points along the way and a small guidebook available from the craft shop (KSh 5) explains the points of interest.

The museum is open Monday to Friday from 7.30 am to 6 pm, Saturday from 8 am to 6 pm and Sunday from 9 am to 6 pm; entry is KSh 20.

Places to Stay – bottom end

Best of the usual bunch of cheapies/brothels is the *Star Lodge*. Good sized rooms upstairs are KSh 60/85 with common bath, although they are a bit noisy from the road below.

The *Kahuroko Boarding & Lodging* has double rooms for KSh 120 with common bath. These are in the back yard of the hotel (which has excellent mid-range single rooms upstairs) and are a bit gloomy and also noisy.

There's a stack of other cheap places, and a couple of the better ones are the *New Mombasa Hotel* and the *Hotel Mamboleo*, both on Moi Ave. The Mamboleo's rooms are also on the gloomy side but are not bad value at KSh 85/130 with bath. Up beyond the covered market there is a number of very basic places which charge around KSh 60/85 for basic rooms.

If you want to camp the only place in the area is the *Sirikwa Safaris,* about 20 km north of Kitale on the Kapenguria road. It's run by Mrs Barnley and her daughter and in fact is just their house – they have a couple of rooms (expensive) or you can camp in the garden. It's a very pleasant setting and is a good place to relax for a day or two. Camping costs KSh 60 per person and you need to bring your own supplies, although gargantuan meals are available for KSh 145 for dinner or KSh 110 for breakfast. There's no sign for this place but the matatu drivers usually know where to drop you – ask for Safari Lodge; the driveway is at the top of a rise on the eastern side of the road, and is flanked by three yellow concrete posts.

Places to Stay – middle

For singles, or couples who don't mind sharing a bed, the *Kahuroko Boarding & Lodging* is a good place. Modern rooms with a double bed, bath and hot water cost KSh 145. The *Executive Lodge* on Kenyatta St is similar – large singles with a big bed and bathroom for KSh 180; there are also cheaper rooms with common bath for KSh 95/180.

The *New Kitale Hotel* is the town's old colonial place but these days it's poor value – the whole place has an air of neglect and it

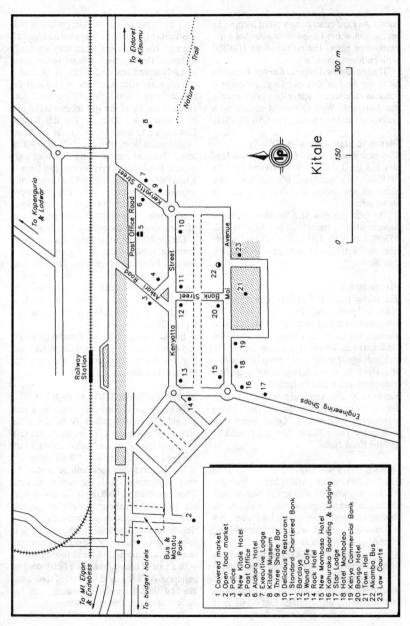

Kitale

To Eldoret & Kisumu

Nature Trail

To Kapenguria & Lodwar

Railway Station

To Mt Elgon & Endebess

To budget hotels

Bus & Matatu Park

Engineering Shops

Kenyatta Street

Post Office Road

Kenyatta Street

Askari Road

Bank Street

Moi Avenue

300 m
150
0

1 Covered market
2 Open food market
3 Police
4 New Kitale Hotel
5 Post Office
6 Alakara Hotel
7 Executive Lodge
8 Kitale Museum
9 Three Shade Bar
10 Delicious Restaurant
11 Standard Chartered Bank
12 Barclays
13 Wandi Cafe
14 Rock Hotel
15 New Mombasa Hotel
16 Kahuroko Boarding & Lodging
17 Star Lodge
18 Hotel Mambeleo
19 Kenyo Commercial Bank
20 Bongo Hotel
21 Town Hall
22 Akombo Bus
23 Low Courts

seems they are generating a bit of income by letting out some rooms to businesses on a permanent basis. The tariff is KSh 180/300 with bath and breakfast.

The brand new *Alakara Hotel* on Kenyatta St is the best in this category, although it remains to be seen whether they can maintain the standard. Well-appointed rooms with bathrooms and hot water cost KSh 215/300.

Places to Stay – top end

The new *Bongo Hotel* (tel 20593) on Moi Ave has good self-contained rooms for KSh 300/360 with breakfast. It's not bad value although the rooms are definitely on the small side.

The best place is Mrs Barnley's *Sirikwa Safaris* where a room with breakfast is KSh 575/865, or KSh 720/1150 with half board. See the bottom-end section for location details.

Places to Eat

The *Wandi Cafe* on Kenyatta St is a popular place at lunch time. They serve basic but tasty meals such as beef stew with rice, and chicken and chips. Another good place is the *Delicious Restaurant* on the same street.

The *Bongo Hotel* on the corner of Moi Ave and Bank St is a slightly more upmarket restaurant and a good place for an evening meal. They also serve alcohol. Right next door is the lively Bongo Bar and there's also a takeaway food section. Other lively bars include the *Three Shade Bar* on Kenyatta St and the *Rock Hotel*.

Getting There & Away

The bus and matatu park is fairly chaotic – it's just a matter of wandering around and finding a vehicle going your way. As is usually the case, competition for passengers is keen and you'll soon be spotted and pointed in the right direction.

For Lodwar and Kalekol in the Turkana district there is a daily JM bus at around 9 am, although it cruises up and down at lunatic speeds for at least two hours prior to that drumming up business. Get on early if you want a choice of seats, otherwise wait near the mosque near the budget hotels past the market (just ask) as they stop and load all the roof baggage there when they are ready to leave. The trip takes around seven hours to Lodwar and costs KSh 125. At around 3 pm (or soon after it arrives in Lodwar) the bus continues on to Kalekol close to the lake shore. This leg of the trip takes around one hour and costs KSh 25. On the Kitale-Lodwar route there is usually at least one large matatu doing the trip daily. They also leave Kitale at around 9 am, but take only around five hours. Every second day there is a minibus doing the trip and this takes only four hours. Although the JM bus is slowest, it is also the most interesting as local Turkana tribespeople in traditional gear get on and off, seemingly in the middle of nowhere.

On the Nairobi route there is a variety of transport – bus, matatu, Peugeot – so it's a matter of finding which suits you. The bus companies have their offices mainly around the bus station area. The exception is Akamba which has its office on Moi Ave. They have daily buses to Nairobi at 9 am and 9 pm; the fare is KSh 155.

For Kakamega there are matatus (KSh 55) and minibuses, the latter en route to Kisumu. For Mt Elgon take one of the frequent matatus to Endebess.

SAIWA SWAMP NATIONAL PARK

This small park north of Kitale is a real delight. The swamp area is the habitat of the sitatunga antelope (*Tragelaphus spekii*), known in Swahili as the Nzohe, and this park has been set aside to protect this habitat.

What makes this park unique is that the only way around inside the park is on foot. There are marked walking trails which skirt the swamp, duckboards right across the swamp in places, and some extremely rickety observation towers. The sitatunga is fairly elusive and really the only way to spot one is to sit atop one of these towers armed with a pair of binoculars and a hefty dose of patience. As is the case in most of the parks, the best time for animal spotting is in the early morning or late afternoon.

This shy antelope is not unlike a bushbuck

in appearance, although larger, and has elongated hooves which are supposed to make it easier for it to get around in swampy conditions – it's hard to see how, but no doubt nature has it all worked out. The colouring is basically grey-brown, with more red noticeable in the females, and both sexes have white spots or stripes on the upper body. The males have long twisted horns which grow up to a metre in length.

The park is also home to the impressive black-and-white colobus monkey (*Colobus polykomos*). It inhabits the higher levels of the trees and, not having the gregarious nature of many primates, is easy to miss as it sits quietly in the heights. When they do move, however, the flowing 'cape' of white hair is very distinctive. Birdlife within the park is also prolific.

With all this on offer it's surprising how few people visit Saiwa Swamp.

Places to Stay

It is possible to camp at the ranger's station inside the park but there is nothing in the way of facilities, otherwise the nearest accommodation is at Kitale or the *Sirikwa Safaris* house of the Barnley family, some few km along the main road to the north (see the Kitale section).

Getting There & Away

Saiwa Swamp National Park lies five km east of the main A1 road, 18 km north of Kitale. Any of the matatus running between Kitale and Kapenguria will let you off at the signposted turn-off, from where you'll probably have to walk to the park as there is little traffic along the dirt road.

MT ELGON NATIONAL PARK

Mt Elgon sits astride the Kenya-Uganda border and, while it offers similar trekking possibilities to Mt Kenya, its location makes it a far less popular goal. The lower altitude also means that the weather on the upper slopes is not quite as severe.

The mountain is an extinct volcano and the national park extends from the lower slopes right up to the border. The highest peak of Elgon, Wagagai (at 4321 metres the 4th highest in Africa) is actually on the far side of the crater in Uganda; the highest peak on the Kenyan side is Koitoboss. There are warm springs in the crater itself, the floor of which is around 3500 metres above sea level.

As access to the national park, which covers 170 sq km, is only officially allowed with a vehicle, those of independent means can take advantage of two other trekking routes to the north and south of the national park.

The mountain's biggest attraction is the elephants, renowned the world over for their predilection for salt, the major source of which is in the caves on the mountain slopes. The elephants are such keen excavators that one school of thought has it that it is the elephants that are totally responsible for the caves. Sadly the numbers of these saline-loving creatures has declined over the years, mainly due to incursions by poachers from the Ugandan side. There are three caves which are open to visitors – Kitum, Chepnyali and Mackingeny. Kitum is the one which you are most likely to see elephants in, Mackingeny the most spectacular. Obviously a good torch (flashlight) is essential.

Less obvious attractions are the ranges of vegetation found on the mountain, starting with forest at the base, then as you ascend it changes to bamboo jungle and finally alpine moorland with the bizarre giant groundsel and giant lobelia plants. The lower forests are the habitat of the impressive black and white colobus monkey along with many other species of birds and animals. Those most commonly sighted include buffalo, bushbuck, giant forest hog and Sykes monkey.

Access to the park is from Endebess, west of Kitale. This is as far as matatu transport goes and is where the bitumen stops. In the dry season it is possible to hire a matatu to take you to the park entrance at Chorlim Gate, but from there you'll have to wait for a lift – and you could be waiting a long time as this is not a popular park. In the wet season the only way in is to have your own 4WD.

Elgon can be a wet place at any time of the year, but the driest months seem to be December, January and February. As well as waterproof gear you are going to need warm clothes as it gets bloody cold up here at night.

If you want to walk in the park, the most popular route is from Kimilili, a small village 36 km south of Kitale on the main A1 road to Webuye and Kisumu. There's basic accommodation here, and matatus going on the seven km to Kapsakwany, from where you start walking. The Kimilili Forest Station is about five km past Kapsakwany and from there it's a further 20 km to the Chepkitale Forest Station, and another seven km past this station to the mountain hut. Obviously it's a long day's walk from Kapsakwany to the hut (32 km for those of you who can't add up) but the rangers at either of the forest stations shouldn't mind if you camp there.

From the hut it takes around four hours to reach the lake known as Lower Elgon Tarn, and from here it's a further one hour walk along a marked trail (cairns and white blazes) to Lower Elgon peak. The pass at the foot of Koitoboss peak and the Suam hot springs are around the crater rim to the right (north-east) and once here you are in the national park. If you reach this point and descend via the park entrance (Chorlim Gate), which is in fact illegal as you're not supposed to walk in the park, expect some difficult questions and be prepared to pay the KSh 220 park entry fee. The options are to return the same way, or via the third route, known as the Masara route, which goes to the small village of Masara on the northern slopes of the mountain, a trek of about 25 km.

Places to Stay

Apart from a very on again/off again lodge, there's no accommodation on the mountain so you need to be fully self- contained. The *Mt Elgon Lodge* officially charges KSh 540/980 for full board – if it's open (don't count on it).

Getting There & Away

As described above, access to the national park is by vehicle only and there's very little traffic so hitching is not an option.

Northern Kenya

This vast area, covering thousands of sq km to the borders with Sudan, Ethiopia and Somalia, is an explorer's paradise hardly touched by the 20th century. The tribes which live here – the Samburu, Turkana, Rendille, Boran, Gabra, Merille and El-Molo – are some of the most fascinating people in the world. The whole area is a living ethnology museum. Like the Maasai, most of them have little contact with the modern world, preferring their own centuries-old traditional lifestyles and customs which bind members of a tribe together and ensure that each individual has a part to play. Many have strong warrior traditions and, in the past, it was the balance of power between the tribes which defined their respective areas.

As late as 1980 there was a clash between the Samburu and the Turkana over grazing land near South Horr which required army intervention. Since most of the tribes are nomadic pastoralists these sort of conflicts have a long history. Nevertheless, settlement of disputes between the tribes is based on compensation rather than retribution so wholesale violence is a rare occurrence.

Change is slowly coming to these people as a result of missionary activity (there are an incredible number of different Christian missions, schools and aid agencies, many of them in very remote areas), employment as rangers and antipoaching patrols in national parks and game reserves, the construction of dams and roads, and the tourist trade. You may well be surprised, for example, to see a young man dressed smartly in Western-style clothes doing some business in a small town and then later on the same day meet him again out in the bush dressed in traditional regalia. It might even turn out that he's a college student in Nairobi for much of the year. Pride in their heritage is one thing these people are very unlikely to lose.

Yet, such examples of sophistication apart, not only are the people another world away from Nairobi and the more developed areas of the country but the landscapes are tremendous. Perhaps no other country in Africa offers such diversity. Much of it is scrub desert dissected by *luggas* (dry river beds which burst into brief but violent life whenever there is a cloud burst) and peppered with acacia thorn trees which are often festooned with weaver bird nests. But there are also extinct and dormant volcanos, barren, shattered lava beds, canyons through which cool, clear streams flow, oases of lush vegetation hemmed in by craggy mountains and huge islands of forested mountains surrounded by sand deserts. And, of course, the legendary 'Jade Sea' (Lake Turkana) – Kenya's largest lake and, as a result of the Leakeys' archaeological digs, regarded by many as the birthplace of mankind.

A long narrow body of water, Lake Turkana stretches south from the Ethiopian border for some 250 km, yet is never more than 50 km wide. While it looks fairly placid most of the time, it is notorious for its vicious squalls which whip up seemingly out of nowhere, and these are largely responsible for the fatalities among the local Turkana and El-Molo people who live along the lake shores.

It was first reached by Europeans in the late 19th century in the form of two Austrian explorers, von Hehnel and Teleki, who named it Lake Rudolf and it wasn't until the early 1970s that the name was changed to Turkana. The Leakeys' fossil discoveries of hominid skulls here are thought to be around 2½ million years old. At that time it is believed that the lake was far more extensive than it is today and supported a richer plant and animal life. Around 10,000 years ago the water level was high enough for the lake to be one of the sources of the Nile, which accounts for the presence of the huge Nile perch still found in the lake.

The contrasts are incredible in this part of

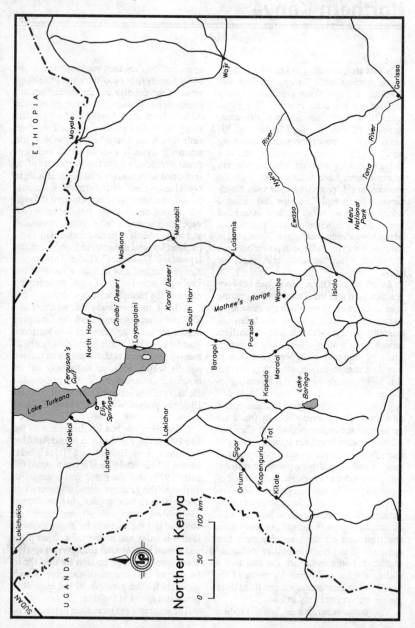

Northern Kenya

0   50   100 km

Kenya and the climate mirrors this. By midday on the plains the temperature can reach 50°C without a breath of wind to relieve the sweat pouring from your brow. Mirages shimmer in the distance on all sides. Nothing moves. Yet in the evening, the calm can suddenly be shattered as the most violent thunderstorm you have ever experienced tears through the place taking all before it. And, just as suddenly, it can all be over leaving you with the clearest, star studded skies you have ever seen. It's adventure country *par excellence*.

A remote region like this with such diverse geographical and climatic features naturally supports a varied fauna. Two species you will see a lot of here (but not elsewhere) are Grevy's zebra, with their much denser pattern of stripes and saucerlike ears, and the reticulated giraffe. Herds of domestic camel are commonplace in the area and often miraculously emerge from a mirage along with their owner when you are bogged down to the axles in soft sand or mud in the middle of the desert. A rope is all you need, although it's a seller's market of course. Lake Turkana also supports the largest population of Nile crocodile in Kenya which feed mainly on the fish living in the lake but which will quite happily dine on incautious humans swimming there. The giant eland finds a sanctuary in the forested hills around Marsabit.

There are several national parks and game sanctuaries in the area, three of them along the Ewaso Nyiro River just north of Isiolo. Further north are the national reserves of Maralal, Losai and Marsabit and right up near the Ethiopian border on the eastern shores of Lake Turkana is the Sibiloi National Park. Others are in the planning stages particularly one in the Mathew's Range north of Wamba which is currently a rhino and elephant sanctuary.

The national parks and game reserves of Marsabit, Maralal, Samburu, Buffalo Springs, Shaba and Meru, on the eastern side, and Saiwa Swamp, on the western side, are all accessible by a combination of public transport and hitching.

Getting There & Around

Hitching Apart from three routes, Kitale-Lodwar, Nyahururu-Maralal-Baragoi and Isiolo-Marsabit-Moyale, there is no public transport in this area of Kenya. You can certainly hitch as far as Maralal or Marsabit (from Nyahururu or Isiolo) on the eastern side and Lodwar (from Kitale) on the western side but that's about the limit of reliable hitching possibilities. There is *very* little traffic on any other routes though I have seen obvious hitchhikers atop trucks heading south out of Loyangalani and met others attempting to hitch north from there to North Horr and Marsabit.

The mission stations/schools invariably have their own Land Rovers (and some have their own light aircraft) but they usually only go in to regional centres of population once a week or once a fortnight. Even so, although most will try to help out if you're stuck, you cannot be guaranteed a lift. The vehicle might be full of people who need urgent medical assistance or (on the return journey) full of supplies. It can be done, of course, but

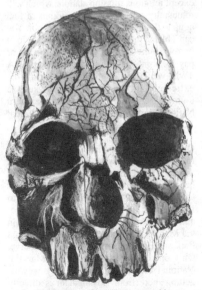

Skull 1470 - 2½ million years old

you must have no deadlines to meet and you must be the sort of person who is quite happy to wait around for days for a ride. In some ways, this could be a very interesting way of getting around and you'd certainly meet a lot of local people but if it is lifts you want you can only do this along the main routes.

You could, of course, buy a camel and do a John Hillaby but this isn't something to approach lightly. It is, however, a distinct possibility especially if you are part of a small group. You'd have the adventure of your life!

Driving For most travellers who want freedom of movement and to see a lot of places it comes down to hiring a vehicle or going on an organised safari. Remember if you are taking your own vehicle to bring a high-rise jack, sand ladders, a shovel, a long, strong rope or chain (that you can hitch up to camels or other vehicles) plus enough fuel and water. The only regular petrol pumps you will find are at Isiolo, Maralal and Marsabit. Elsewhere there's usually nothing except religious mission stations which will reluctantly sell you limited amounts of fuel at up to three times the price in Nairobi. You can't blame them – they have to truck it in in barrels in the back of their Land Rovers or pay for someone else to do it in a truck. A 4WD vehicle is obligatory and you'd be extremely foolhardy to attempt such a journey in anything else except for Samburu National Park and Buffalo Springs National Reserve.

Organised Safaris Most of these last eight to nine days and they all seem to follow much the same route. Starting from Nairobi, they head up the Rift Valley to Lake Baringo, over to Maralal and then up the main route to Loyangalani on Lake Turkana via Baragoi and South Horr. On the return journey, again via Maralal, they take in Samburu National Park and Buffalo Springs National Reserve. Only one or two of them take in Marsabit National Reserve since the only way of getting there from Loyangalani is directly across the Koroli Desert (hazardous after

rain) or via the long loop north through North Horr and Maikona. Even this involves crossing the Chalbi Desert which, like the Koroli, is hazardous after rain. There are also the restrictions on the Marsabit-Isiolo road to contend with – all transport must go in convoy at a certain time of day, usually 10 to 11 am.

The cost of the safaris varies between KSh 3300 and KSh 3960 and includes transport, all meals, park fees and necessary camping equipment. There are all-camping safaris which use open-sided 4WD trucks and are not, therefore, for those in search of luxury. Everyone has their favourite company but a lot depends on the people you find yourself with, what you see en route and the drivers and guides. The following companies all offer Turkana tours, usually once a week but sometimes once a fortnight:

Best Camping
    PO Box 40223, Nanak House, 2nd floor, corner Kimathi and Banda streets, Nairobi (tel 28091, 27203)
Birds Paradise Tours & Travel Ltd
    PO Box 22121, Nairobi (tel 25898)
Safari Camp Services
    PO Box 44801, corner Koinange and Moktar Daddah streets, Nairobi (tel 28936, 330130)
Special Camping Safaris
    PO Box 51512, Gilfillan House, 3rd floor, Kenyatta Ave, Nairobi (tel 338325)
Zirkuli Expeditions
    PO Box 34548, Banda St, Nairobi (tel 23949, 20848)

Some companies also offer flying safaris to Lake Turkana using twin-engined aircraft but they cost more than the truck tours. Two companies which offer this are Birds Paradise Tours & Travel Ltd (address above) and Turkana Air Safaris (tel 26623, 26808), PO Box 41078, Nairobi. These usually go to the western side of the lake and use Lake Turkana Lodge on Ferguson's Gulf as a base. A five day tour costs KSh 6960. You can also combine the Turkana safari with one to Masai Mara but the five day safari then goes up to KSh 9240.

West of Turkana

From Kitale the road north winds through the fertile highlands, passing the turn-off for the tiny Saiwa Swamp National Park (well worth a visit) before reaching Kapenguria, the town most famous for being the place where Jomo Kenyatta and five associates were held and tried in 1953 for their part in the Mau Mau uprising.

The road then snakes its way through the narrow northern gorges of the Cherangani Hills, emerging on to the desert plains through the Marich Pass. The change in scenery is dramatic and there are some fantastic views of the plains. The only town in this part of the hills is Ortum, just off the road. There is basic accommodation in the town if you want to stop and explore the area but the best place to stay in this area is the Marich Pass Field Studies Centre (see below).

Shortly after leaving the Marich Pass is a turn-off to the left to the Turkwel Gorge. There is a huge hydroelectric project nearing completion here and when finished it should supply electricity to a large area of the densely populated highlands – the northern areas will still have to rely on generators.

After km of endless plains and dry creek beds Lokichar is little more than a collection of dismal dukas by the side of the road. The heat here is oppressive and the settlement seems to be gripped by a permanent torpor. The one redeeming feature of the place is that it is possible to buy the basketware and other Turkana trinkets cheaper than you'll find them further north.

MARICH PASS

The best place to stay in this area is the *Marich Pass Field Studies Centre* (tel (0321) 31541), PO Box 2454, Eldoret. This is essentially a residential facility for groups pursuing field courses in geography, botany, zoology, ecology, conservation, geology and rural development, but it's also open to independent travellers who want to spend a day,

a week or a month in a little-known corner of Kenya.

The Centre covers an area of 12 hectares and is surrounded by dense bush and woodland. Birdlife is prolific, monkeys and baboons are 'in residence', while wart hog, buffalo, antelope and elephants are regular visitors. Facilities include a secure camp site (KSh 50 per person per night) with drinking water, toilets, showers and firewood, and several bandas with beds, mattresses and blankets provided (KSh 85 per person per night). English speaking Pokot and Turkana guides are available on request. A dormitory block and basic restaurant are due to be completed shortly.

Most necessities and fresh food are available in local shops and markets but you need to bring with you canned and packet foods if required. Those with their own vehicles should bring sufficient supplies of petrol as there are no service stations between Kapenguria and Lodwar. If you intend walking in the vicinity then you need to be adequately prepared for a variety of weather conditions.

Excursions from the Marich Pass

A few km to the north-west, Mt Sekerr (3326 metres) can be climbed comfortably in a three day round trip via the agricultural plots of the Pokot tribe, forest and open moors. The views from the top are magnificent when the weather is clear.

To the south are the Cherangani Hills, which offer some of the best hill walking possibilities anywhere in Kenya ranging from half-day excursions to week-long safaris by vehicle and on foot. Possibilities include a half-day walk along the old road perched high on the eastern side of the Marich Pass to a local Pokot trading centre; a hard day's slog up the dome of Koh which soars some 1524 metres above the adjacent plains; a safari of several days' duration along the verdant Weiwei Valley to Tamkal and then up to Lelan Forest and the main peaks of the Cherangani.

The Elgeyo Escarpment, which rises in places to more than 1830 metres above the

Kerio Valley and offers spectacular views and waterfalls, is only 1½ hours away from the Centre along a road that passes through several local market centres and intensively farmed garden plots.

The South Turkana National Reserve in dry and rugged hills north-east of the Centre is the domain of Turkana herdsmen and rarely visited by outsiders. The 50 km drive there traverses grazing lands of the pastoral Pokot.

Lastly, the Turkwel Gorge hydroelectric project is only 30 km away along a fine tarmac road. Much of the gorge with its towering rock walls has not been affected by the construction while the dam (the highest of its type in Africa) and connecting road up a sheer mountain face is itself spectacular. The 35 km long lake will eventually be available for fishing, sailing and other water sports.

Getting There & Away
To reach the Field Studies Centre, leave the main Kitale-Lodwar road at the Centre's signpost two km north of the Sigor-Tot junction at Marich Pass and continue south for one km down a clearly marked track. There are three approaches to Marich Pass:

1. The easiest is through Kitale and Kapenguria and then a further 67 km down a tarmac road (described as 'possibly Kenya's most spectacular tarmac road'). There are daily bus services from Nairobi to Kapenguria and matatus (KSh 35) from there to Marich Pass.
2. Through Iten either from Eldoret or via Kabarnet using the new and very scenic road across the upper Kerio Valley from Kabarnet. The all-weather Cherangani Highway can be picked up from Iten to cross the main pass of the Cherangani Hills and join up with the Kitale-Lodwar road near Kapenguria.
3. The roughest of the three approaches is the road from Lake Baringo through the Kito Pass and across the Kerio Valley to Tot but it gives you the chance of a diversion to the hot waterfalls at Kapedo. From Tot, the track

skirts the northern face of the Cherangani Hills and involves fording numerous streams which may be impassable after heavy rain.

LODWAR
The hot and dusty administrative town of Lodwar is the only town of any significance in the north-west. With a bitumen road connecting it with the highlands, and air connections with Nairobi, it is no longer the isolated outpost of the Northern Frontier District that it was during colonial days but is certainly lagging a few steps behind the rest of the country.

Lodwar is also the base for any excursions to the lake from the western side and you will probably find it convenient to stay here for a night at least. There's little to do in the town itself but it has an outback atmosphere which is not altogether unpleasant and just watching the garrulous locals is entertainment in itself. The Turkana have suddenly found that tourists are a good touch when it comes to selling trinkets and they approach with alarming audacity and don't conceal their disgust when you don't want to buy. They are also remarkably persistent. The small market is a good place to watch women weaving the baskets.

Information
The town has a post office and a branch of the Kenya Commercial Bank.

Places to Stay – bottom end
Lodwar is one place where it's worth spending a bit more on accommodation – mainly to get a room with a fan. The rooms in the cheaper places are all hellishly hot and as the mosquitoes are fierce you need to cover up or burn coils if you don't have a net. It seems the recently surfaced road from the south has put Lodwar on the map, and there are new hotels springing up all the time.

Best of the cheapies is the *Mombasa Hotel*, almost next door to the JM Bus office which is where you'll be dropped if arriving that way from Kitale. The friendly Muslim owners charge KSh 60 for single rooms and KSh 95 for doubles. The singles are cooler (it's all relative though) as they have high ceilings. If you have a mosquito net you can sleep in the courtyard.

The *Marira Boarding & Lodging* is a new place and could be worth a try. Another bottom-end cheapie is the *Ngonda Hotel*. Both charge around KSh 60/95 for singles/doubles without fan.

Places to Stay – middle

The *Turkwel Hotel* (tel 21201) is the town's social focus and also has the best accommodation. Single rooms with fan and common bath go for KSh 100, while singles/doubles with fan and bath cost KSh 180/240. There are also a few spacious cottages which are very pleasant and cost KSh 360 for two including breakfast.

Directly opposite the Turkwel is the *New Lodwar Lodge* which has concrete and bamboo cottages situated where they catch the breeze, although they are somewhat overpriced at KSh 180/360.

It is rumoured that a luxury hotel of the African Tours & Hotels chain is to be built on the southern side of the Turkwel River on the approach into town.

Places to Eat

The restaurant at the *Mombasa Hotel* does reasonable local food and has excellent fresh mandazis early in the morning. The *Marira Boarding & Lodging* has little variety but their chips are excellent and freshly cooked to order. For something a bit more sophisticated the *Turkwel Hotel* restaurant does standard Western fare such as steak, chips, etc. Breakfast here consists of a couple of eggs and a sausage and nonresidents are not served until all the hotel guests have finished. The bar here is also a popular place.

Getting There & Away

There are daily JM buses to Kitale at 7 am. The trip takes around seven hours and costs KSh 125. There are also matatus covering this route but they tend to operate on a supply and demand basis. If you can find one they are much quicker than the bus.

The JM bus arriving from Kitale daily at around 3 pm continues on to Kalekol near the lake at around 4 pm. The fare is KSh 20 and the trip takes one hour. If you want to hitch to Kalekol the place where the locals wait is under the tree about 200 metres north of the Kobil station. To give an indication of how long you can expect to wait, there is a chai stall here which also sells mandazis.

KALEKOL

Most travellers head on from Lodwar to Kalekol, a fairly dismal little town a few km from the lake shore. The main building in the one street town is the fish processing factory built with Scandinavian money and expertise and, although fairly new is currently not operating. There is also an Italian sponsored plant closer to the lake shore.

Places to Stay & Eat

A good place to stay is the rudimentary but friendly *George Oyavi's Hotel*. It is right next to the bus office and George meets all incoming buses. The rooms are only rough grass constructions and so thankfully get some breeze. There's a rough and ready shower rigged up and George and his staff somehow muddle through and cook meals although you need to order in advance. Warm beer and sodas are also available. If you want anything more sophisticated to eat than rice, chapatis or fish you'll need to bring it from Lodwar.

There's a second hotel called *Skyway Bar & Lodge* on the right-hand side as you enter Kalekol from the south. Rooms here cost KSh 35/120 a single/double with shared bathroom facilities. Next door is the *Safari Hotel* which has a reasonable restaurant.

Getting There & Away

There is a daily JM Bus to Lodwar and Kitale at 5 am. There is no danger of missing it as the driver revs the engine and honks the horn in plenty of time. The fare to Lodwar is KSh 24, and to Kitale KSh 145.

To get out to the lake it's a hot 1½ hour walk. Someone at George's will guide you, or just walk to the Italian fishing project and cut across the lake bed from there to the lodge.

FERGUSON'S GULF

This is the most accessible part of the lake shore but really it's not particularly attractive, although the sense of achievement in just getting there usually compensates. The water has receded greatly, mainly due to drought in Ethiopia, so you have to walk a long way over the lake bed to actually get to the water. The birdlife along the shore is prolific with flamingos and wild birds. There are also hippos and crocodiles so seek local advice before having a refreshing dip.

There is a small fishing village of grass huts on the far side of the Turkana Lodge and that's about the limit of things.

To get out on the lake you can hire the launches from the lodge to take you to Central Island National Park. By all accounts the trip is worthwhile but it's not cheap. A covered cruiser which takes eight people costs KSh 2340, while the open four-seater long boat costs KSh 1740. Talk to the fishers and they might take you out for a good deal less but make sure their craft is sound – the danger posed by the lake's squalls is not to be taken lightly.

Places to Stay

If you don't mind really roughing it the local villagers will put you up for a few bob, otherwise you'll have to come here just for a day trip from Kalekol or stay at the lodge.

The *Lake Turkana Lodge* is supposedly on an island but the level of the lake has fallen so far in recent years that it's now possible to drive to the lodge, in the dry season at least. It takes around 1½ very hot hours to walk out there from Kalekol – follow the track to the Italian fishing project then head across the lake bed from there. There are children with canoes who will paddle you across the 20 metres or so of channel. By car you just follow the main road through Kalekol and it takes a circuitous route to the far side of the lodge.

Although reportedly busy on weekends, the lodge was deserted when I visited on a weekday and the underworked staff were happy to pass the time playing darts in the bar. The cottages are all self-contained and cost KSh 1020/1585 for full board. If you're just out at the lodge for the day a somewhat meagre plate of fish and chips will set you back KSh 70. Although the water once used to lap at the edge of the bar terrace, it is now more than 100 metres away across a blinding expanse of sand.

ELIYE SPRINGS

This is a far more attractive place than Ferguson's Gulf but, unless you have a 4WD, is inaccessible. The small village here has an army post, a couple of dozen grass huts and a lodge which is of marginal status to say the least. The springs however do provide moisture enough for a curious variety of palm tree to grow here which gives the place a very misplaced tropical island feel. This particular palm tree has an unusually shaped fruit which the locals eat.

If you do make it here you will be greeted by a number of Turkana girls and young women selling trinkets at absurdly cheap prices. With an average of one vehicle a week, it's a real buyer's market. Items for sale include fossilised hippo teeth and fish backbones threaded into necklaces!

Places to Stay & Eat

The *lodge* here is in a state of semidisrepair and, although closed, it still had a full complement of workers milling about. They assured me that the lodge would be reopening but check this in Nairobi in advance before relying on being able to stay. It is possible to camp here at any time. Meals are sporadically available although baked beans from a tin and chapatis was the limit of it and while I sat there and ate, part of the thatch roof gave way and fell to the ground at my feet – which certainly didn't do anything for my confidence about the place ever reopening.

Getting There & Away

The turn-off for Eliye Springs is signposted about halfway along the road from Lodwar to Kalekol. There are a few patches of heavy sand so a 4WD is advisable although you'd probably get through in a conventional vehicle. As there are so few vehicles, hitching is not an option and it's 35 long hot km if you plan to walk it.

LOKICHOKIO

This frontier town is the last on the Pan African Highway before the Sudan border. The road has been sealed all the way here and is in excellent condition but you can't get beyond Lokichokio without a police permit. Even if this was forthcoming the area is not safe as long as the civil war in southern Sudan continues.

Places to Stay

There's a *hotel* of sorts here with a couple of mud huts out the back, and there's a bar in town.

East of Turkana

There are two main routes here. The first is the A2 highway from Nairobi to Marsabit, via Isiolo and Laisamis, and north from there to Moyale on the Ethiopian border. The other is from Nakuru to Maralal, via Nyahururu and north from there to Loyangalani on Lake Turkana, via Baragoi and South Horr. From Loyangalani you can make a loop all the way round the top of the Chalbi Desert to Marsabit via North Horr and Maikona.

Getting There & Away

Bus & Matatu Mwingi runs buses to Marsabit and Moyale from Isiolo on Tuesday, Thursday and Saturday which take about six hours to Marsabit and the same, on the following day, to Moyale. The fare for each stage of the journey is KSh 180. These buses only go when full and, consequently, departures are frequently delayed by up to a day. There's no alternative except to simply hang around and wait or either negotiate a ride on a truck (relatively easy and usually somewhat less than the bus fare) or walk out

to the police checkpoint north of town where the tarmac ends and hitch a ride with tourists (not so easy). A convoy system is in operation in order to deter shiftas from stopping and robbing trucks, buses and cars.

Mwingi also operate buses to Maralal every second day (depending on demand) which cost KSh 180.

North of Maralal, the only public transport is a matatu which plies between Maralal and Baragoi once daily if demand warrants it.

Driving None of the roads in this region are surfaced and the main A2 route is corrugated piste which will shake the guts out of both you and your vehicle depending on what speed you go at. The road connecting Isiolo with Maralal (which branches off the A2 north of Archer's Post) is similarly corrugated but otherwise in good shape. The road from Maralal to Loyangalani, however, is surprisingly smooth though there are bad patches here and there including a diabolical several km section down to Lake Turkana from the plateau.

The main cross route between the two is via Wamba and Parsaloi (though you don't actually go through Wamba itself). This road leaves the main A2 about 20 km north of Archer's Post and joins the Maralal-Loyangalani road about 15 km south of Baragoi. Though a very minor route, this road is very smooth most of the way though there are occasional rough patches. Its main drawback is the steep-sided luggas, none of which are bridged. In the dry season you won't have any problems with a 4WD (impossible with a 2WD) but you can forget about it in the wet season. The worst of these luggas is just outside of Wamba and there's a way around it by taking the Maralal road from Wamba and turning first right along a dirt road once you've crossed an obvious bridge. You'll probably only use it if you want to visit the Mathew's Range.

Forget about the Maralal-Parsaloi road marked on the Survey of Kenya's maps. It's all washed out and you won't even make it in 4WD.

NATIONAL PARKS & GAME RESERVES

Just north of Isiolo are three national reserves, Samburu, Buffalo Springs and Shaba, all of them along the banks of the Ewaso Nyiro River and covering an area of some 300 sq km. They are mainly scrub desert and open savannah plain, broken here and there by small rugged hills. The river, however, which is permanent, supports a wide variety of game and you can see elephant, buffalo, cheetah, leopard and lion as well as dik-dik, wart hog, Grevy's zebra and the reticulated giraffe. Crocodiles can also be seen on certain sandy stretches of the river bank. You are guaranteed close-up sightings of elephant, reticulated giraffe and various species of smaller gazelle in both Samburu and Buffalo Springs but other game is remarkably thin on the ground and particularly on the route into Samburu from Archer's Post. The rhino were wiped out years ago by poachers.

If you are driving round these parks in your own vehicle it's useful to have a copy of the Survey of Kenya map, *Samburu & Buffalo Springs Game Reserves* (SK 85) which costs KSh 80.

The roads inside Buffalo Springs and Samburu are well maintained and it's easy to get around even in 2WD though you might need a 4WD on some of the minor tracks.

Entry to all three parks or game reserves costs KSh 220 per person plus KSh 50 for a vehicle per day. Even though they're contiguous, if you drive from Buffalo Springs to Samburu (or vice versa) in one day then you'll have to pay two lots of park entry fees though, if it's very late in the afternoon when you cross the boundary, the guards will generally postdate your ticket for the following day.

These parks are much less touristed than Amboseli or Masai Mara so, once you're out of the immediate vicinity of the lodges and camp sites, you'll frequently have the place to yourself.

Places to Stay

In Buffalo Springs National Reserve there are four *public camp sites* close to the Gare Mara entrance gate (the nearest to Isiolo and accessible from the main Isiolo-Marsabit road) but none of them are particularly safe as far as robberies go so stick with a group and make sure your tent is guarded when you're out on game drives or pack it up and take it with you. There's also a *special camp site* further west. Camping costs KSh 35 per person per night.

For those with adequate finances, there's the *Buffalo Springs Tented Lodge* (tel 2234, PO Box 71, Isiolo) up at the north-eastern end of the reserve just south of the Ewaso Nyiro River. The lodge consists of 30 tents shielded from the sun by makuti roofs and each with its own bathroom facilities. There are also eight cottages which sleep two to four people. The lodge has a swimming pool and a bar and restaurant overlooking a natural spring where you can sit and observe the wildlife. In the high season, tents or cottages cost KSh 1800/2280 for singles/doubles with full board. In the low season, the costs are KSh 840/1680 with full board. Advance bookings can be made through African Tours & Hotels Ltd (tel 336858, PO Box 30471, Nairobi). The best access to the lodge is either from the Gare Mara Gate or the Buffalo Springs Gate just south of Archer's Post.

In Samburu National Reserve, the most convenient places to stay are the *public camp sites* close to the Samburu Game Lodge and close to the wooden bridge which connects the western extremity of Buffalo Springs to Samburu across the Ewaso Nyiro River. The sites themselves are fairly pleasant and adjacent to the river but the facilities are minimal and the 'toilets' are nothing short of pigsties. The only advantage to staying at them if you don't want to cook for yourself is that they're very close to the lodge with its restaurant and bar. There are also two *special camp sites* further west. Camping costs KSh 35 per person per night.

For those with money, there's a choice of three top-range lodges/tented camps. The most popular is perhaps the *Samburu Game Lodge* which is part of the Block Hotels chain (tel 335807, PO Box 47557, Nairobi).

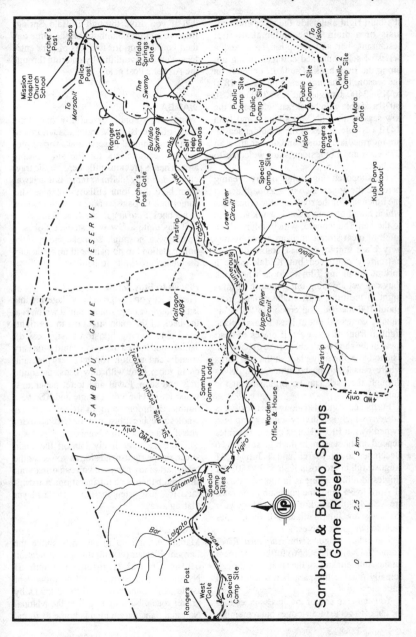

Samburu & Buffalo Springs
Game Reserve

It's built right alongside the river and consists of a main stone and makuti roof restaurant, bar and reception area, and a series of self-contained cottages strung out along the river bank. The tariff depends on the season. In the high season it's KSh 1870 to KSh 2400 a single and KSh 2100 to KSh 3070 a double with breakfast, whereas in the low season it's KSh 960 a single and KSh 1410 a double. Rates in the shoulder season are intermediate. Lunch and dinner are KSh 275 each and nonresidents are welcome to eat here.

The supposed 'highlights' of any evening here are the appearance of a leopard across the other side of the river and the crocodiles which crawl up onto a sandy bank adjacent to the bar. The leopard, which is lured by a hunk of meat strung up from a tree by two very blasé employees just before dusk, is extremely contrived but Kodak make a fortune supplying film to fools who think they can get anything but a picture of midnight in the bush with an Instamatic from about 100 metres. The crocodile 'show' is equally contrived but at least it takes place right in front of you even if pieces of dead meat in the sand don't encourage dynamism. The lodge is the only place in the two parks where petrol can be bought. Game drives through the park can be organised at the lodge.

Further east and also alongside the river is *Larsens* which is a luxury tented camp also owned by the Block Hotels chain. The rates depend on the season. In the high season (16 December to 31 March and 1 July to 31 August) full board costs KSh 5590/7505 for singles/ doubles whereas in the low season (1 April to 30 June) the corresponding rates are KSh 4090/5360. For the rest of the year the costs are intermediate. All these rates include two game drives.

The other lodge is the *Samburu River Lodge* (tel Nairobi 338656) further upstream on the southern side of the river and, though actually outside the park boundary, is still quite close to it.

You can take any of the access gates into the parks to get to these lodges but remember that if you drive through Buffalo Springs Reserve and into Samburu on the same day then you'll be up for two lots of park entry fees. You can avoid this by entering through the Archer's Post gate.

WAMBA

Wamba is a small, essentially one-street town off the Isiolo-Maralal road north of Samburu National Reserve and a sort of provincial headquarters for the surrounding area. There's precious little here for the traveller and its only 'claim to fame' is that it was from here that John Hillaby organised his camel trek to Lake Turkana which resulted in his book, *Journey to the Jade Sea*.

It has quite a few well-stocked dukas, a butchery, a hospital, schools and a large police station but no bank and no electricity despite its proximity to Isiolo.

Places to Stay & Eat

There's only one lodge in the village and that is the *Saudia Lodge* run by Jamal which is at the back of the main street off to the right-hand side coming into town (signposted). Jamal – and indeed his whole family – is very friendly and helpful. You get a very pleasant, clean room here with new beds, mosquito nets and soap, towel and toilet paper provided for just KSh 60 a single and KSh 95 a double. Bathroom facilities are communal. A wholesome breakfast can be provided for you if you order it in advance.

There's a very lively bar on the main street, on the right-hand side as you enter the main part of town, where you can drink your fill though there's no refrigeration. You can't miss it – just listen for the cassette player blaring away!

MARALAL

Maralal is high up in the hills above the Lerochi Plateau (essentially a continuation of the Central Highlands), north of Nyahururu and Nanyuki and north-west of Isiolo, and connected to all these towns by gravel roads. Surrounding it is the Maralal National Sanctuary which is home to zebra,

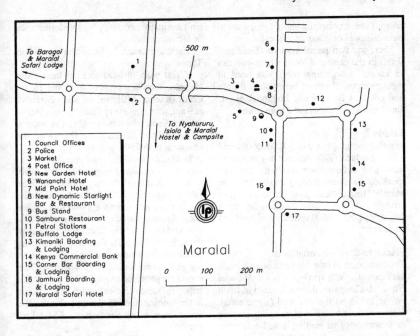

Maralal

1 Council Offices
2 Police
3 Market
4 Post Office
5 New Garden Hotel
6 Wananchi Hotel
7 Mid Point Hotel
8 New Dynamic Starlight
   Bar & Restaurant
9 Bus Stand
10 Samburu Restaurant
11 Petrol Stations
12 Buffalo Lodge
13 Kimoniki Boarding
   & Lodging
14 Kenya Commercial Bank
15 Corner Bar Boarding
   & Lodging
16 Jamhuri Boarding
   & Lodging
17 Maralal Safari Hotel

impala, eland, buffalo, hyaena and wart hog, all of which you can see from the road leading into Maralal from the south or at the Maralal Safari Lodge which has the only permanent water hole in the area.

It's an attractive area of grassy undulating plains and coniferous forests which was once coveted by White settlers in the colonial era. However, their designs for taking it over were scotched by the colonial authorities due to anticipated violent opposition from the Samburu for whom it holds a special significance.

The town itself, while a regional headquarters, retains a decidedly frontier atmosphere with a sense of excitement blowing in the wind which frequently sweeps the plains and whips up the dust in the somewhat ramshackle, but very lively, township with its wide streets and Wild West-type verandahs. It's also the preferred route and overnight centre for the safari companies which take people up to Lake Turkana. People here are very friendly and it's a great place to buy Samburu handicrafts.

There's a post office (with telephone), petrol stations, mechanics, the only bank north of Isiolo other than in Marsabit, shops with a good range of stock, hotels, bars, one of the best camp sites in Kenya, a surprising number of butchers' shops and regular bus transport to Isiolo. There are also matatus to Baragoi which leave from the Shell station. If you're not travelling with a safari company you may well consider spending a few days here. It's a bizarre but captivating place.

Information

The Kenya Commercial Bank is open Monday to Friday from 8.30 am to 1 pm and on Saturday from 8.30 to 11 am. This is the last bank going north apart from those in Marsabit so stock up on cash.

The post office is open normal hours and

the staff are very helpful should you want to make national or international calls.

There are two petrol stations (Shell and Total) in the centre of town where you can be assured of getting what you need at regular prices. North of here you will only find petrol at Baragoi and Loyangalani – if they have it and always at a high price.

Safaris

Regular camel (five days, KSh 6600) and walking safaris (KSh 720 per day including food and accommodation with English speaking Samburu guides) depart from the Maralal Hostel & Campsite and they can also arrange safaris to Lake Turkana by truck (eight days, KSh 6600 including all food and equipment).

Places to Stay – bottom end

The best place to stay here and one which is very popular with travellers is the *Maralal Hostel & Campsite*, three km south of town on the Isiolo-Nyahururu road (signposted). Here you have a choice of camping, staying in a dormitory or renting a self-contained banda. It's been thoughtfully constructed with local materials and is set amongst Samburu manyattas. Facilities include a lounge/library, reference room, self-service restaurant serving local dishes, a shop selling vegetables and canned goods, etc and a bar with cold beers.

The camp site has its own showers and toilets plus there's a manyatta where you can stay the night if you wish. Camping costs KSh 70 per person per night. The dormitories, of which there are two with a total capacity of 30 beds, cost KSh 85 per person. You don't have to be a Youth Hostel member to stay here even though it's affiliated to the IYHF, but if you are there's an 8% discount on the price of a bed. The self-contained bandas cost KSh 360 a single and KSh 565 a double which includes breakfast.

The hostel and camp site are owned and run by Yare Safaris (tel 559313, PO Box 63006, Nairobi) and it's probably a good idea to make advance bookings for the bandas whilst you're in Nairobi though this isn't normally necessary for the dormitories or the camp site.

There are dances by local tribespeople on Thursdays.

If you wish to head straight there from Nairobi, there's transport from the Heron Court Hotel on Milimani Rd every Saturday at 9 am, returning every Friday from Maralal around 8 am, which is free if you're booked on one of Yare Safaris tours. Otherwise, the charge is KSh 190 one way.

In Maralal itself the most popular place to stay is the *Buffalo Lodge* which is a fairly modern structure offering rooms for KSh 145 a single and KSh 290 a double. It's a lively place and there's a video room at the back. Sammy, the barman here, is a real live wire and very friendly. Cheaper but excellent value is the *Kimaniki Boarding & Lodging* which is a two storey wooden building offering good rooms for KSh 60 per person. Clean sheets are provided as well as hot showers (if requested) and vehicles can be parked safely in the hotel compound. There's also the *Mid Point Hotel* which has beds for KSh 60 per person.

Other possibilities include the *Corner Bar Boarding & Lodging, Jamhuri Boarding & Lodging, Maralal Safari Hotel, New Garden Hotel* and *Wananchi Hotel* – all rather basic.

Places to Stay – top end

The only top-range hotel in Maralal is the *Maralal Safari Lodge* (tel 25641, 25941; PO Box 42475, Nairobi) which consists of a main building housing a restaurant, bar and souvenir shop and a series of cottages. It costs KSh 1680 a single, KSh 2630 a double and KSh 3700 a triple for full board. The watering hole, which attracts a varied selection of game, is right in front of the bar's verandah so you can watch the animals whilst sipping a cold beer. You don't have to be a resident to drink or eat here but you will need transport to get there as it's quite a way from the centre of Maralal (about three km), off the road to Baragoi (signposted).

Places to Eat

The liveliest bar in town – and one where you

can get good, tasty, cheap food – is the improbably named *New Dynamic Starlight Bar & Restaurant* which, nevertheless, lives up to its name. The inside rooms are painted with the most bizarre and florid representations of African bush life and there's even a traditionally dressed Samburu hooker here most evenings who does a roaring trade. Unfortunately, there's no refrigeration so the beers are warm but the company makes up for it and some of the characters who come in here have walked straight out of a Breugel canvas. It's a great spot to meet local live wires, get completely out of it and have numerous animated conversations.

An alternative place to eat is the *Samburu Restaurant* near the petrol stations.

There's also the occasional disco in town – ask around when you get there.

Getting There & Away
If you're not coming in on Yare Safaris' transfer bus, Mwingi operate buses every second day to Isiolo which cost KSh 180. They leave from the dirt patch in front of the New Garden Hotel.

There are also matatus to Nyahururu daily which leave early in the morning, and usually one to Baragoi, though this only runs when there's sufficient demand. Matatus leave from in front of the Shell station.

MATHEW'S RANGE
North of Wamba, off the link road between the Isiolo- Marsabit road and the Maralal-Loyangalani road via Parsaloi, is the Mathew's Range. Much of this area is thickly forested and supports rhino, elephant, lion, buffalo and many other species. The highest peak here rises to 2285 metres. The whole area is very undeveloped and populated by Samburu tribespeople but the government is in the process of making it into a game sanctuary especially for the rhino. Some of the tribespeople are already employed to protect the rhino from poachers and there's a game warden's centre.

A few km from this centre (which you have to report to on the way in though there are no charges as yet) is a *camp site* with no facilities other than river water and firewood. At one time it was a well set-up research centre, as the derelict huts indicate. It's a superb site and a genuine African bush experience. You are miles from the nearest village and elephants are quite likely to trundle through your camp in the middle of the night – lions too. During the day, traditionally dressed Samburu warriors will probably visit you to see if you need a guide (which you will if you want to see game or climb to the top of the range as we did). Agree on a reasonable price beforehand (about KSh 60 per person per day) plus a similar amount for the one who stays behind to guard your vehicle. Don't forget that the rules of hospitality will oblige you to provide them with a beer, soft drink or cup of tea, a few cigarettes and perhaps a snack when you get back to camp. They're extremely friendly people. One or two will be able to speak English (the nearest school is in Wamba) but most can converse in Swahili as well as Samburu.

Getting There & Away
Getting to this camp site is not at all easy even with 4WD. There are many different tracks going all over the place and you are going to have to stop many times to ask the way. Perhaps the best approach is from the Wamba-Parsaloi road. Just before Wamba you will get to a T-junction. Instead of going into Wamba, continue north and take the first obvious main track off to the right, several km after the junction. If there are tyre tracks in the sand – follow them. There are two religious mission stations down this track and both have vehicles. You will be able to ask the way at either. One of them is right next to a large river course which generally has some water flowing through it and which you have to ford. If you get lost, ask a local tribesman to come along and guide you but remember that you will have to drive him back to his manyatta after you have found the place. No-one in their right mind walks around in the bush after dark except in large groups – it's too dangerous. It might sound like a *tour de force* getting to this place but it's well worth it!

PARSALOI

Further north, Parsaloi (sometimes spelt Barsaloi) is a small scattered settlement with a few very basic shops but no petrol station. It has a large Catholic Mission which may or may not offer to accommodate you or allow you to camp. There are no lodges. The EEC is funding the building here of quite a large school which was scheduled to finish in 1990.

There are two very rugged and steep-sided luggas at this point on the road, one on either side of the village, and you'll definitely need 4WD to negotiate them.

BARAGOI

Next on is Baragoi, a more substantial settlement full of tribespeople, a couple of very basic lodges, and a few shops. There's also a derelict petrol station but petrol can usually be bought here from a barrel – the local people will show you where to go for it. If you're White, you'll probably be the only one in town and therefore an object of considerable curiosity. Quite a few people speak English around here. The town seems to get rain when everywhere else is dry so the surroundings are quite green.

Be careful not to take photographs in the town as it's supposedly forbidden and the local police are keen to enforce the rule and are not at all pleasant about it.

Places to Stay & Eat

If you ask at any of the restaurants in town they'll usually come up with accommodation but it will be very basic – just a bed in a bare room with no toilet facilities. Some will also allow you to camp in their back yards.

For those with camping equipment, the best place to stay is the *camp site* at the water pumping station about four km to the north of town. To get there, take the road north towards South Horr. After a while you'll go through a small gully and then, a little further on, across a usually dry river bed. Take the next track on the right-hand side and follow this for about one km. It will bring you to a concrete house and a fairly open patch of ground. This is the camp site and there's always someone around. Facilities include toilets and showers and your tent will be guarded by Samburu warriors. It costs KSh 35 per person per night. Trips can be arranged to nearby manyattas for a small fee and you'll be allowed to take photographs.

For food in the town itself, the best is the *Wid-Wid Inn* run by Mrs Fatuma. It's on the top side of the main street and you'll know you've got the right place because all the staff wear garishly pink pinafores! She'll cook you up an absolutely delicious meat stew and chapatis for dinner as well as pancakes, omelettes and tea for breakfast. Either meal costs just KSh 30 per person.

There are also two bars in the town but only one of them – the *Sam Celia Joy Bar*, at the end of the main street going north – usually has beers. The other, on the back street, usually only has conyagi (local firewater) and other spirits.

SOUTH HORR

The next village is South Horr which is set in a beautiful lush canyon between the craggy peaks of Mt Nyiro (2752 metres) and Mt Porale (1990 metres) and Mt Supuko (2066 metres). It's a lively little place with a huge Catholic Mission but there's no petrol available.

Places to Stay & Eat

There are two small and very basic hotels on the main street – the *Mt Nyiro Hotel* and the *Good Tourist Hotel* – where you can find accommodation of sorts as well as a reasonably tasty meal of meat stew, mandazi and tea for around KSh 30 per person. The hotels will generally need up to two hours notice if you want to eat but tea is generally immediately available.

For those with camping equipment, there's a really pleasant *camp site* at the top end of town next to a mountain stream and above the Catholic Mission. The access road for this is on the outskirts of town coming in from the south. Look for signs on the left-hand side before you get to the concrete ford across the stream which read, 'South Horr

Forest Station' and 'Veterinery Office South Horr' and turn off there. The site is used by safari companies going to Loyangalani and there doesn't appear to be any fee at present though this could soon change.

There's another *camp site* (signposted 'Camping' but easy to miss) about 12 km out of town going north on the right-hand side. It's a pleasant site (though the discarded beer bottles and tyres aren't too pretty) and facilities include showers and toilets. There's also plenty of firewood. The charge is KSh 35 per person per night. This site used to be called Kurungu Camp Site and was where most of the safari companies used to put their people up for the night. They no longer stop here and the bandas which used to offer fairly good accommodation have been demolished. Guards can be arranged to watch your tent if you're not cooking your own food and want to eat in town.

South Horr also sports a very lively bar – the *Serima Bar* – on the main road heading north out of town. It's only open in the evenings and seems to have a plentiful supply of beer though there's no refrigeration.

LAKE TURKANA (THE JADE SEA)

Going further north, the lushness of the Horr Valley gradually peters out until, finally, you reach the totally barren, shattered lava beds at the southern end of Lake Turkana. Top the ridge here and there it is in front of you – the Jade Sea. It's a breathtaking sight – vast and yet apparently totally barren. You'll see nothing living here except a few brave, stunted thorn trees. When you reach the lake shore, you'll know why – it's a soda lake and, at this end, highly saline. The northern end of the lake isn't anywhere near as saline because it's fed by the Omo River from Ethiopia (is that where the name of the washing powder came from!?). At this point, most people abandon whatever vehicle they're in and plunge into the lake. If you do this watch out for crocodiles. They're quite partial to a meal of red meat as a change from Nile perch.

LOYANGALANI

A little further up the lake shore and you are in Loyangalani – Turkana 'city'. There is an airstrip, post office, fishing station, luxury lodge, two camp sites, a Catholic Mission (which may reluctantly sell petrol at up to three times the price in Nairobi) and all of it surrounded by the yurtlike, stick and doum-palm dwellings of the Turkana tribespeople. Taking photographs of people or their houses here will attract 'fees'.

If you're an independent traveller, the Oasis Lodge can organise trips to the village where the El-Molo live. Otherwise, ask the drivers of safari trucks at the camp sites if they have room for you – organised safaris to this part of Kenya usually include a trip to the El-Molo village. They're one of the smallest tribes in Africa and quite different from the Turkana though it seems their days are numbered as a distinct tribe. Tourism has also wrought inevitable changes in their lifestyle and you may feel that the whole thing has been thoroughly commercialised. You'll also pay handsomely for taking photographs. As one traveller who felt the tribe had totally prostituted their traditional way of life to make money from tourists put it, 'If they live on fish it must be smoked salmon and caviar'.

Trips to Mt Kulal and Mt Porr can also be arranged at the Oasis Club but they're expensive. The Mt Kulal trip is a part drive, part walking trip up to the forest there and Mt Porr is a well-known fossicking spot. A better thing to do would be to get in touch with Francis Langachar who is a very friendly young Turkana man and ask him to organise something similar for you. He speaks fluent English and his father went on John Hillaby's 'Journey to the Jade Sea' saga.

Places to Stay & Eat

Of the two camp sites, it's hard to favour one over the other though only one has a restaurant and bar. Both are staffed by very friendly people and theft doesn't appear to be a problem at either of them. The first you come to is *El-Molo Camp* (tel 724384, PO Box 34710, Nairobi) which has excellent facilities including good showers and toilets, a swimming pool (KSh 50 fee for use), a large dining hall and bar (with cold beers!) and electricity up to 9.30 pm at night (kerosene lanterns after that). Camping costs KSh 60 per person per night. They also have 20 self-contained bandas for rent which cost KSh 2370 a double with full board.

Meals can be ordered at short notice in the dining room here whether you are staying on the site or not but they take a long time to arrive: 1½ hours is normal. The food, on the other hand, is very good. A dinner of mushroom omelette, boiled potatoes and dressed salad, for instance, cost KSh 95 whereas a breakfast of two fruit salads and a pot of tea or coffee cost KSh 60. Cold beers naturally cost more than in Nairobi but are still very reasonably priced.

The other camp site adjacent to El-Molo is *Sunset Strip Camp,* which also costs KSh 60 per person per night. Facilities include showers and toilets and covered dining areas but you cannot buy food and drink here and there's no electricity.

Neither camp site has firewood so you'll have to bring your own from further south.

Whichever place you camp at, beware of sudden storms which can descend from Mt Kulal. If there is a storm, stay with your tent otherwise it may not be there when you get back and neither will anything else.

Other than the camp sites there is the luxury *Oasis Lodge* (tel 339025, 750034/6, PO Box 14829, Nairobi) which has 25 self-contained double bungalows with electricity (own generator) at KSh 1860 a single and KSh 2640 a double with full board. It's a beautiful place with two spring-fed swimming pools, ice-cold beers and meals available. The only trouble is, if you are not staying there but want to use the facilities, it's going to cost you KSh 200 entrance fee which gives you the use of the bar and swimming pools. It's a lot of money to pay for a brush with luxury but you won't wring any concessions out of the owner (Wolfgang) who can be quite belligerent about this. Basically, he doesn't want what he considers to be 'riffraff' marring the tone of the place and

mingling their sweaty bodies with his otherwise very chic guests.

Other than the El-Molo Camp, there are a couple of basic *tea houses* on the main street of Loyangalani and, if you ask around, you'll meet villagers who will cook up a meal of Nile perch for you in their houses.

Getting There & Away

It's unlikely you'd use the service but Air Kenya (not to be confused with Kenya Airways) operates flights to Loyangalani from Nairobi's Wilson airport three times a week in either direction on Wednesday, Friday and Sunday. The fare is KSh 3600 one way and KSh 6600 return. If there are more than five of you, it's cheaper to charter your own 'plane'.

NORTH HORR

North of Loyangalani the road loops over the lava beds to North Horr. There is a short cut across the desert through the village of Gus.

There are no lodges here and no petrol available but the Catholic Mission is very friendly and will probably offer you somewhere to stay for the night if you are stuck. It's staffed by German and Dutch people.

MAIKONA

Next down the line is Maikona where there is a large village with basic shops (but no lodges) and a very friendly Catholic Mission and school, staffed by Italian people, where you will undoubtedly be offered a place to stay for the night. Please leave a donation before you go if you stay here. The mission usually has electricity and the Father goes into Marsabit once a fortnight in his Land Rover.

MARSABIT

South of Maikona is Marsabit and you are back in relative civilisation. Here there are three petrol stations, a bank, post office, dry cleaners, shops, bars and lodges, buses and an airport. The main attraction here though is the Marsabit National Park & Reserve centred around Mt Marsabit (1702 metres).

The hills here are thickly forested and in

stark contrast to the desert on all sides. Mist often envelopes them in the early morning and mosses hang from tree branches. The views from the communications tower on the summit above town are magnificent in all directions. In fact, they're probably as spectacular as any of the views from Mt Kenya or Kilimanjaro. The whole area is peppered with extinct volcanoes and volcanic craters (called *gofs*), some of which have a lake on the crater floor.

One of the most memorable sights in Marsabit is the colourful mix of tribespeople who you'll see thronging the streets and roads into town. Most noticeable are the Rendille, with their elaborate braided hairstyles and dressed in skins, fantastic multicoloured beaded necklaces and bracelets. These people graze camels and, like the Samburu and Maasai, show little interest in adopting a more sedentary lifestyle, preferring to roam the deserts and only visiting the towns when necessary for trade. They are the major non-Muslim people in what is otherwise a largely Muslim area.

The other major tribes are the Boran and the Gabbra, both of them pastoralists, though with these people it's cattle which they graze

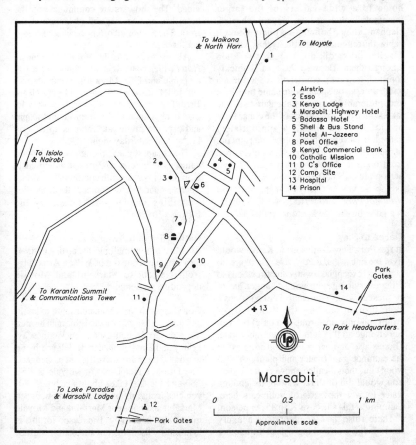

To Maikona
& North Horr

To Moyale

To Isiolo
& Nairobi

1 Airstrip
2 Esso
3 Kenya Lodge
4 Marsabit Highway Hotel
5 Badassa Hotel
6 Shell & Bus Stand
7 Hotel Al-Jazeera
8 Post Office
9 Kenya Commercial Bank
10 Catholic Mission
11 D C's Office
12 Camp Site
13 Hospital
14 Prison

Park
Gates

To Karantin Summit
& Communications Tower

To Park Headquarters

To Lake Paradise
& Marsabit Lodge

Marsabit

Park Gates

0   0.5   1 km

Approximate scale

rather than camels. They're allied to the Galla peoples of Ethiopia from which areas they originated several hundred years ago. Many have abandoned their former transient customs and settled down to more sedentary activities. In the process, many have adopted Islam and the modes of dress of the Somalis with whom they trade and who have also migrated into the area. There are also quite a few Ethiopians in town as a result of that country's tragic and turbulent recent past.

Marsabit National Park & Reserve

The Marsabit National Park & Reserve is home to a wide variety of the larger mammals including lion, leopard, cheetah, elephant, rhino, buffalo, wart hog, Grevy's zebra, the reticulated giraffe, hyaena, Grant's gazelle, oryx, dik-dik and greater kudu among others. Because the area is thickly forested, however, you won't see too much game unless you spend quite some time here and, preferably, camp at Lake Paradise. The lake, which occupies much of the crater floor of Gof Sokorte Guda, is appropriately named. It's an enchanting place and right out in the bush. Entry to the park, which is open from 6 am to 7.15 pm, costs KSh 220 per person plus KSh 50 for a vehicle.

The Survey of Kenya's map, *Marsabit National Park & Reserve* (SK 84), KSh 35, is a good buy if you are touring this park.

Places to Stay

In the Park Few camp sites in Kenya would rival the one at *Lake Paradise*. There are no facilities (except lake water and firewood) so bring everything with you. A ranger has to be present when you camp here so it costs more than an ordinary site (KSh 360 per group and only one group at a time) but you can arrange all this at the park entrance gate. There's also another good *camp site* next to the entrance gate (water and plenty of firewood) but the so-called showers are a joke. You would die of thirst waiting for enough water to wet the back of your ears here. Camping at this site costs KSh 35 per person.

There's also the *Marsabit Lodge*, a luxury safari lodge overlooking a lake in another gof, Sokorte Dika. This costs KSh 980 a single, KSh 1625 a double and KSh 2135 a triple with full board except from 1 April to 15 July when there's a considerable discount. Bookings can be made at Msafiri Inns (tel 29751, 330820; PO Box 42013), 11th floor, Utalii House, Uhuru Highway, Nairobi.

In the Town If you have no camping equipment there's a good choice of lodges available in the town of Marsabit. One of the best is the *Kenya Lodge*. It's very clean and pleasant and costs KSh 60 a single and KSh 85 a double with soap and toilet roll provided. The showers are communal and the hotel has its own bar and restaurant at the front. The restaurant offers excellent Ethiopian food.

Almost as good is the *Marsabit Highway Hotel* which costs KSh 60 a single, KSh 100 a double and KSh 145 a triple with shower and toilet. It's a large place and very clean. Breakfast costs KSh 30. The hotel has its own bar/restaurant open from 11 am to 2 pm and 5 pm to midnight. There is a disco on Friday and Saturday nights.

The cheapest place, though not such good value, is the *Hotel Al-Jazeera* which costs KSh 35 per person with communal showers. There's a bar and restaurant at the front. For something vaguely mid-range, try the *Badassa Hotel*.

Getting There & Away

Air Most of the small private airline companies which operate out of Wilson Airport fly from Nairobi to Marsabit and Moyale depending on demand.

Bus Buses run from Marsabit south to Isiolo and north to Moyale on the Ethiopian border. They depart around 10 am on Wednesday, Friday and Sunday but can be delayed by up to a day if there are not sufficient passengers. The fare to either Isiolo or Moyale is KSh 180 and the trip takes about six hours. All vehicles including buses travelling between Marsabit and Isiolo or Marsabit and Moyale must travel in convoy. The reason for this is to minimise the danger of attack from shiftas.

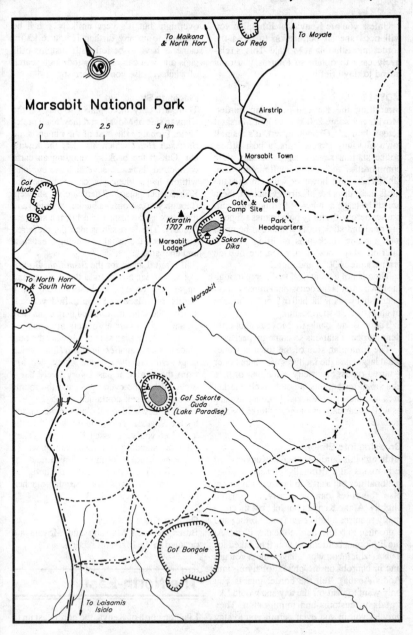

Marsabit National Park

0   2.5   5 km

To Maikona
& North Horr

Gof Redo

To Moyale

Airstrip

Marsabit Town

Gof
Mude

Karatin
1707 m

Gate &
Camp Site

Gate

Park
Headquarters

Marsabit
Lodge

Sokorte
Dika

To North Horr
& South Horr

Mt Marsabit

Gof Sokorte
Guda
(Lake Paradise)

Gof Bongole

To Laisamis
Isiolo

Unless you are Kenyan or Ethiopian you will need special permission to cross the border into Ethiopia at Moyale. This is relatively easy to obtain so long as you only intend to stay briefly.

MOYALE

Straddling the Kenyan-Ethiopian border, Moyale lies some 250 km north of Marsabit across the Dida Galgalu desert. It's a small town of sandy streets, bars, a post office, police station, several shops selling basic commodities and with a small market area. Unlike Marsabit, however, where most of the roofs these days are of corrugated iron, there are still a large number of traditionally built houses here with sturdy pole frames supporting mud and stick roofs which can be up to half a metre thick thus ensuring that the interiors stay cool even when the outside temperature is 30°C and more.

There's not a great deal to do here though the town attracts the occasional intrepid traveller either just for the hell of it or for the sake of an exotic passport stamp.

There is no bank in Moyale and only derelict petrol stations so come prepared.

The Ethiopian side of the town is somewhat larger and the facilities are much better – tarred roads, electricity, a number of bars and small restaurants, a hotel, lively market area and plenty of Marxist-Leninist slogans as well as caricatures of the big three theoreticians.

Crossing into Ethiopia

Although this border is open to Kenyans and Ethiopians, it's officially closed to other nationalities but as it's so far from anywhere else the rules can generally be twisted slightly. At the Kenyan border post this normally requires a little *chai* (small bribe) and a promise to return before the day is out. At the Ethiopian border post you'll be asked for a visa (which you won't have unless you got one in Nairobi on the pretext of flying into Addis Ababa). Tell the border guards you only want to visit for the day and would like to talk to customs and immigration. They *may* let you in and even permit you to stay

overnight but it's very unlikely you'll be allowed to go any further. If you're let in, cameras have to be left with customs officials and you can expect a thorough search of whatever else you are carrying.

Places to Stay & Eat

There are only three places to stay on the Kenyan side of Moyale and they're all pretty basic. Probably the best of the bunch is the *Barissah Hotel* which also has the town's bar. Out at the back surrounding an earth compound there are several basic cubicles without locks where you can rent a bed for KSh 35 per person. There are no showers (though you can order a bucket of water) and the place is far from clean but the staff are friendly. The Barissah is also the preferred place to eat, the usual fare being meat stew and chapatis.

If it's full, head for the *Bismillahi Boarding & Lodging* across from the Barissah and up behind the derelict Esso station. It's a family run place and you'll find yourself sharing the same roof. A bed here costs KSh 30 and facilities are absolutely minimal.

On the Ethiopian side of Moyale, the best place to stay is the *Bekele Molla Hotel* which is government owned and about two km from the border. It has a very lively bar – especially in the evenings – and the rooms are clean and self-contained.

For somewhere to eat closer to the border, try the *Negussie Hotel*, up on the hill to the left after you've crossed the border. They offer the standard Ethiopian fare of wat (a fierce hot sauce) and injera (bread made of millet flour), and there's also a bar here.

Kenyan shillings are acceptable when paying for meals and drinks.

Getting There & Away

Buses between Marsabit and Moyale are detailed in the Marsabit section.

The North-East

Like the north of Kenya, the north-east up to

the border with Somalia covers a vast area of desert and semidesert with very few centres of population and limited public transport possibilities. The main towns are Garissa and Wajir. Most of the area is relatively flat yet it's through here that one of Kenya's major rivers flows – the Tana. The river enters the ocean about halfway between Malindi and Lamu and is the territory of the Orma, Pokomo and Bajun tribes. Straddling this river just north of Garsen is the Tana River Primate Reserve which is included on a few safari companies' itineraries but otherwise difficult to get to. The reserve was set up to protect the red colobus and crested mangabey monkeys both of which are endangered species. The other main river, the Ewaso Nyiro which flows through Samburu and Buffalo Springs national reserves, eventually peters out into the Lorian Swamp, never reaching the ocean.

Few travellers come this way except those taking the back route to Lamu via Garissa and Garsen and those going overland to Somalia via Liboi. It's still possible to enter Somalia via Liboi en route to Kismayu but hardly recommended at present because of internal tensions within Somalia which have led to a lot of fighting and dislocation of the population. There's also been quite an increase in the activities of shiftas as a result both of the fighting and the efforts of the Kenyan government to rid the eastern national parks of poachers who have decimated the elephant and rhino populations. The Somalis have been blamed for much of this and justifiably but the poachers and shiftas have proved hard to control.

There's big money in the sordid ivory and rhino horn business which is fuelled by the refusal of several Arab nations – notably the two Yemens, the United Arab Emirates, Oman and Kuwait – to ban imports and the insatiable appetite of the Chinese market for these animal products. As a result, those who procure the ivory and rhino horn are well armed with automatic weapons and, often, high speed vehicles. They're people to be dealt with very seriously and cautiously and are not averse to taking on units of the Kenyan army or police let alone game wardens and trackers. And, when denied ivory, tourists are an acceptable substitute.

You should think twice before driving a vehicle around Meru National Park (or even taking an organised safari) until the situation is resolved because tourists have been robbed at gunpoint and some of them actually shot dead. If you do go there and you're held up, don't mess about! Get your money and cameras out and hand them over. Any prevarication will invite a bullet in the head. The same possibly applies on the overland route to Somalia through Liboi though we've had no reports of this – maybe because very few people are currently doing this trip. It's unlikely much will change until Siad Barre (the Somali president) is replaced and there's some sort of resolution of the Ethiopian conflicts.

Other than a visit to Meru National Park, which is worth it if security can be guaranteed, and the Tana River area, the north-east isn't a particularly interesting area even for desert fans though Wajir, with its predominantly Somali population, 'Beau Geste' fort and market, would definitely have the edge over Garissa, itself quite a nondescript town hardly worth stopping over in.

MERU NATIONAL PARK
On the lowland plains east of the town of Meru, the Meru National Park is a complete contrast to its more northerly sisters – Samburu, Buffalo Springs and Shaba – where open bush is the norm. Here, abundant rainfall and numerous permanent streams flowing down from the Mt Kenya massif support a luxuriant jungle of forest, swamp and tall grasses which, in turn, provide fodder and shelter to a wide variety of herbivores and their predators. As in other parks, such as Marsabit, where the vegetation is dense, the wildlife is not so easily sighted so you need to spend a few days here if you're to fully appreciate what the park has to offer. If you do that then you are virtually guaranteed sightings of large herds of elephant,

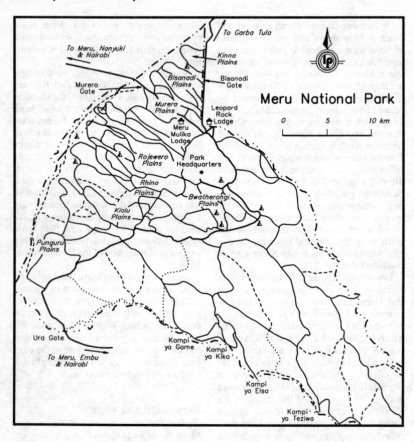

Meru National Park

To Garba Tula

To Meru, Nanyuki & Nairobi

Kinna Plains

Bisanadi Plains

Bisanadi Gate

Murera Gate

Murera Plains

Leopard Rock Lodge

Meru Mulika Lodge

0   5   10 km

Rojewero Plains

Park Headquarters

Rhino Plains

Bwatherongi Plains

Kiolu Plains

Punguru Plains

Ura Gate

To Meru, Embu & Nairobi

Kampi ya Game

Kampi ya Kiko

Kampi ya Elsa

Kampi ya Teziwa

buffalo and reticulated giraffe and, in the more open bush, Grevy's zebra, ostrich and gerenuk. The large predators – leopard and lion, in particular – are only rarely sighted even though there are considerable numbers of them, though lions occasionally visit the Leopard Rock Lodge area. Monkeys, crocodiles and a plethora of bird species are common in the dense vegetation alongside the watercourses.

Meru National Park was also the home of Kenya's only herd of white rhinos which were imported from the Umfolozi game park in South Africa. Jealously guarded 24 hours

a day by rangers to protect them from poachers, these huge animals were quite unlike their more cantankerous cousins, the black rhino, in being remarkably docile and willing to allow their keepers to herd them around the camp sites and park headquarters area during the day and pen them up at night. Sadly, that's all gone now. Heavily armed poachers shot the lot of them and, for good measure, killed their keepers too.

The park is also famous for being Joy and George Adamson's former base where they raised orphaned lion and leopard cubs until they were old enough to be returned to the wild. Both paid for their efforts with their lives – Joy several years ago when she was murdered in Meru park by poachers and George in 1989 when he too met the same fate along with two of his assistants in the nearby Kora National Reserve.

Security in the park has been beefed up since George Adamson was murdered but there is still a real risk of encountering poachers and bandits here so you need to bear this in mind especially if you're driving your own vehicle. It's true to say, however, that the chances of running into bandits is just as great in Masai Mara or Tsavo as it is in Meru. The one major plus about Meru National Park is that you're unlikely to come across another safari vehicle anywhere in the park except outside the lodges.

The tracks through the park are well maintained and signposted though it's a good idea to have with you a copy of Survey of Kenya's map, *Meru National Park*.

Places to Stay

There are several *public camp sites* close to the park headquarters and airstrip where there's plenty of firewood as well as shower and toilet blocks. If you don't have a tent then there are also several simple *bandas* for rent in the same area.

More expensive are the self-contained bandas at *Leopard Rock Lodge* which have electricity, hot water, mosquito nets and fully equipped kitchens. There's a shop at the site which sells basic commodities including canned goods and beer.

At the top of the range is the *Meru Mulika Lodge* (tel 29751, PO Box 42013, Nairobi) which has all the usual facilities of a luxury lodge including a swimming pool (KSh 30 for nonresidents) and where full board costs KSh 1285 a single, KSh 1780 a double and KSh 2300 a triple.

Getting There & Away

Getting to Meru National Park by public transport is a problem. There are no buses or matatus which will take you either to the lodges or the camp sites and park headquarters. Likewise, attempting to hitchhike is basically a waste of time since so few vehicles come into the park and those that do are mainly tour groups so they won't pick you up. It's almost essential to have your own vehicle or be part of a tour group. Quite a few safari companies include Meru National Park on their itineraries but they are all liable to cancel visits at short notice if there has been any trouble with shiftas in the park. Dead or robbed tourists are no good for business.

TANA RIVER PRIMATE SANCTUARY

Well south of Garissa and not too far north of Garsen is the Tana River Primate Sanctuary which, as its name suggests, is a reserve for a number of endangered species of monkey. It's possible to get close to the sanctuary by public transport but there's still a lot of walking involved and the facilities have long fallen into disrepair so you need to take everything with you. Very few safari companies include the reserve on their itineraries. The only one which presently does is Bushbuck Adventures (tel 728737, PO Box 67449, Nairobi) which operates a once-a-year, 12 day Tana River safari taking in the Kora National Reserve, the Primate Reserve, the Tana River delta and Lamu by foot, vehicle, boat and air. Accommodation is in lodges and special camp sites and costs US$2640.

GARISSA

The only reason you would come to Garissa is if you were going overland to Somalia or taking the back route to Lamu direct from Nairobi via Garsen. There's nothing much to see or do here and the heat and humidity are unrelenting but there's a bank (normal hours), petrol stations, bars and a fair choice of places to stay plus the streets are tarmacked.

Places to Stay & Eat

Perhaps the best place to stay for the night is the *Safari Hotel* which offers clean rooms with running water for KSh 60 a single and KSh 95 a double. It has reasonable food in the attached restaurant. The *Garissa Guest House* is somewhat more expensive at KSh 120 per person for B&B with bathroom but the rooms are nothing special and it's quite a walk from the centre of town. If both are full then there's the more basic *Nile Lodging* or the *Kenya Hotel & Lodging*.

Getting There & Away

Air It's possible to fly direct to Garissa from Nairobi's Wilson Airport with one of the small private airlines if there's sufficient demand.

Bus Garissa Express operates a bus from the Kenya Bus Depot in Eastleigh, Nairobi, to Garissa on Monday, Wednesday, Friday and Sunday at 8 am. The depot is a 10 minute matatu ride from Ronald Ngala St (Route No 9). The fare is KSh 95 and the journey takes about eight hours.

There's also a daily Garissa Express bus from the Lamu mainland (Mokowe) to Garissa which leaves at 7 am, costs KSh 180 and takes eight to 10 hours when the weather is dry.

Going further afield, Garissa Express

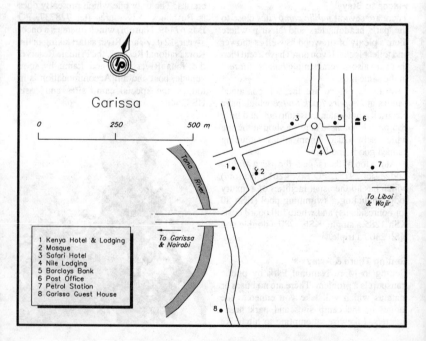

Garissa

0 — 250 — 500 m

To Liboi & Wajir

To Garissa & Nairobi

1 Kenya Hotel & Lodging
2 Mosque
3 Safari Hotel
4 Nile Lodging
5 Barclays Bank
6 Post Office
7 Petrol Station
8 Garissa Guest House

operate buses to Wajir on Tuesday, Thursday and Saturday which arrive the same day and cost KSh 145. These buses continue on the next day to Mandera at the junction of the Kenyan, Ethiopian and Somalian borders. The fare from Garissa to Mandera is KSh 290.

LIBOI
Liboi, right on the Kenya-Somalia border, is a staging post in the *qat* (drug) trade to Somalia. It has only one place to stay, the *Cairo Hotel*.

GARSEN
If you're heading towards Lamu from Garissa then you may have to stay here overnight as it's necessary to change buses – there are none direct from Garissa to Mokowe on the mainland opposite Lamu. There's nothing at all special about Garsen but there are several basic hotels to choose from. The best is the *3-in-1 Lodging & Restaurant* which is fairly clean and has its own restaurant.

For details of buses passing through Garsen, see either the Malindi or Lamu sections.

Amboseli, Masai Mara & Tsavo

AMBOSELI NATIONAL PARK

Amboseli is the next most popular park after Masai Mara, mainly because of the spectacular backdrop of Africa's highest peak, Mt Kilimanjaro, which broods on the southern boundary of the park.

At 392 sq km Amboseli is not a large park, and it certainly doesn't have the profusion of game which you find in Masai Mara. The western section of the park is the dry bed of Lake Amboseli, and although it is occasionally flooded in the wet season, for the majority of the time it is a dry, dusty, shimmering expanse.

Probably the best reason for visiting Amboseli is that it is here that you stand the best chance of spotting a black rhino. Amboseli also has huge herds of elephant, and to see a herd of them making their way sedately across the grassy plains, with Kilimanjaro in the background, is a real African cliché but one which leaves a lasting impression.

Other animals which you are likely to see here include buffalo, lion, gazelle, cheetah, wildebeest, hyaena, jackal, wart hog, Masai giraffe, zebra and baboon.

Amboseli more than any other park has suffered hugely from the number of minibuses which drive through each day. It has a much drier climate than Masai Mara and so for much of the year is a real dust bowl. If you are driving through the park, stick to the defined tracks, and hopefully others will follow suit.

Places to Stay – bottom end

Once again the only budget option is a *camp site*. This one is right on the southern boundary of the park. The only facilities are a couple of long-drop toilets and a kiosk which sells warm beer and sodas, and where you pay the camping fees. The water supply here is extremely unreliable so bring some with you. Elephants are a real problem in this camp site at night and practically everyone

who has stayed here has an elephant story to relate – there are some hilarious (and not so hilarious) ones doing the rounds. At night make sure all food is locked away inside your vehicle. *Don't* keep food in your tent as elephants have a habit of investigating.

Places to Stay – top end

The group of lodges in the centre of the park are strategically situated for views of Kilimanjaro; they (the lodges) couldn't be called pretty. The *Kilimanjaro Safari Lodge* and the *Amboseli Lodge* are both run by the Kilimanjaro Safari Club in Nairobi (tel Nairobi 337510). Prices are around KSh 2640/3600 for a single/double with full board. Also in this group are the *Ol Tukai Lodge* (tel Nairobi 334863) self-catering cottages, but even these aren't cheap.

The *Amboseli Serena Lodge* (tel Nairobi 339800) is of a much more sensitive design and construction; it blends in well with the landscape and the nearby Enkongo Narok Swamp ensures constant bird and animal activity. Room charges are KSh 2880/3480 for a single/double with full board.

Getting There & Away

Air Air Kenya Aviation have daily flights between Wilson Airport and Amboseli. These depart Nairobi at 7.30 am and Amboseli at 8.30 am; the trip takes about 45 minutes and costs KSh 1250 one way.

Road The usual approach to Amboseli is through Namanga, 165 km south of Nairobi on the A104 and the main border post between Kenya and Tanzania. The road is in excellent condition from Nairobi to here. This is the last fuel stop before the park and outside the town's petrol station is a couple of shops selling Maasai crafts. First prices asked are totally ridiculous so bargain fiercely. There's accommodation in Namanga (at the *Namanga Hotel* and others)

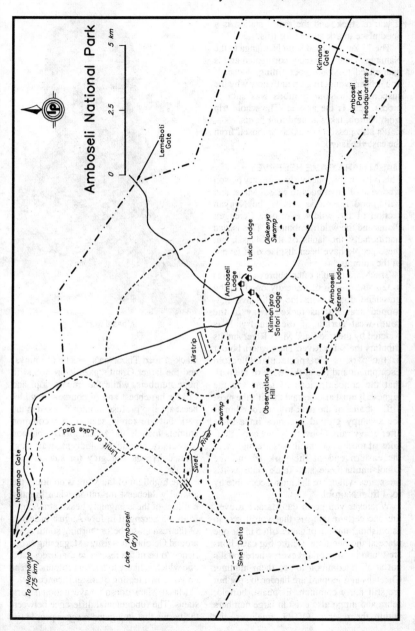

Amboseli National Park

if you're stuck, and the petrol station is a good place to ask around for lifts.

The 75 km dirt road from Namanga to the Namanga Gate is fiercely corrugated and is guaranteed to shake your fillings loose. If you'd been wondering up until now why the suspension in your minibus was shot to pieces, here is the answer. The whole trip from Nairobi takes around four hours.

It's also possible to enter Amboseli from the east via Tsavo.

MASAI MARA GAME RESERVE

This is it – the big one. Virtually every person who visits Kenya goes to Masai Mara, and with good reason as this is the Kenyan section of the wildly evocative Serengeti Plains and the wildlife abounds. This is also traditionally the lands of the Maasai, but these people have been displaced in favour of the animals.

The Mara (as it's often abbreviated to) is a 320 sq km slab of basically open rolling grassland dotted with the distinctive flat-topped acacia trees tucked away in the south-west corner of the country. It is watered by the tree-lined Mara River and its tributary the Talek River. The western border of the park is the spectacular Oloololo Escarpment and it's at this edge of the park that the concentrations of game are the highest. It must also be said that it's the most difficult area of the park to get around in as the swampy ground becomes impassable after heavy rain. Conversely, the concentrations of tourist and minibuses are highest at the eastern end of the park around the Oloolaimutia Gate and Talek Gate as it's these area which are the most accessible by road from Nairobi.

Wherever you go in the Mara, however, the one certain thing is that you'll see an astonishing amount of game, often in the one place at the one time. Of the big cats, lions are found in large prides everywhere and it's not at all uncommon to see them hunting. Cheetahs and leopard are harder to spot but are still fairly common. Elephant, buffalo, zebra and hippo also exist in large numbers within the reserve. Of the antelopes, the

Maasai woman

black-striped Thomson's gazelle (Tommys) and the larger Grant's gazelle are found in huge numbers, while the impala, topi and Coke's hartebeest and of course the wildebeest are also profuse. Rhinos do exist in the park but are rarely seen. Other common animals include the Masai giraffe, baboon (especially around the lodges), wart hog, spotted hyaena and grey (or side-striped) jackals.

The highlight of the Mara is no doubt the annual wildebeest migration when literally millions of these ungainly beasts stray north from the Serengeti in July-August in search of the lush grass, before turning south again around October. It is truly a staggering experience to be in the reserve at that time – and one which is likely to have a profound effect on your own feeling of insignificance.

Masai Mara doesn't have national park status. The fundamental difference between the two is that in a game reserve people (in this case the Maasai) can graze their animals and can also shoot animals if they are attacked. In a national park however, the entire area is set aside exclusively for the wildlife and the natural environment.

Just outside the Oloolaimutia Gate there's a Maasai village which has opened itself up as a tourist attraction. For KSh 120 per person you can walk around and take as many pictures as you like. As you might imagine, it's a real zoo when you have a couple of dozen tourists poking their video cameras and long lenses intrusively everywhere. *If* you can manage to visit when there are no other tourists it's not too bad and you can at least talk to the villagers.

Ballooning
If you can afford the KSh 4000 price tag, balloon safaris are definitely the way to go. For more details see the section on Ballooning under Activities in the Facts for the Visitor chapter.

Places to Stay – bottom end
There is no budget accommodation within the reserve so it's camp or pay high prices at the lodges and tented camps. It's possible to camp just outside the park at any of the gates for a small fee. There are no facilities but you can usually get water from the rangers. The Maasai run the *Oloolaimutia Campsite* between the gate of the same name and the Mara Sopa Lodge at the western extreme of the park. This place is very popular with the budget safari outfits and is usually pretty lively. For KSh 95 per person the Maasai provide firewood and an askari at night. The water supply here is very limited and if you need any you'll have to buy it from the Maasai. The staff canteen of the nearby Mara Sopa Lodge is usually a lively place and you can get meals and warm beer.

There are *official camp sites* along the Talek River by the Talek Gate on the northern border of the park, and just outside the reserve on the banks of the Mara River near the Oloololo Gate. If you want to use any of these sites it's advisable to book them in advance in Nairobi (at Nairobi National Park

main gate) but people who roll up unannounced generally seem to have no problems. The only problem with using these sites is that they are none too secure – baboons and thieves can both take their toll on your gear.

What isn't widely known is that it's possible to camp at *Cottar's Mara Camp* (see below) for KSh 120 per person. They certainly don't encourage it but can't turn you away.

Places to Stay – top end
The lodges and tented camps are all pitched at the top end of the market and should all be booked in advance. For a night's accommodation you are looking at around KSh 2400/3600 for a single/double with full board. The lodges are separate bandas, while the tented camps are often almost identical, the difference being that the rooms have canvas walls – it's certainly stretching things to call them tents.

The *Mara Sopa Lodge* (tel Nairobi 336088) by Oloolaimutia Gate is one of the newer ones and has a commanding view. *Keekorok Lodge* (tel Nairobi 335807) is an older lodge on a grassy plain. The *Mara Sarova Camp* (tel Nairobi 333233) is not far from the Sekenani Gate and has the works, including a swimming pool. The charge here is KSh 2580/3120 for full board. In the centre of the reserve is the *Mara Serena Lodge* (tel Nairobi 339800) with a superb outlook over the Mara River. *Governor's Camp* (tel Nairobi 331871) is the focus of activity in the western part of the reserve. The *Fig Tree Camp* (tel Nairobi 20592) is on the northern boundary of the reserve by Talek Gate.

Other accommodation outside the park north of Oloololo Gate includes the *Kichwa Tembo Camp* (tel Nairobi 335887), the *Mara River Camp* (tel Nairobi 331191) and the *Mara Buffalo Camp*. *Cottar's Mara Camp* (tel Nairobi 882408) is another tented lodge about 15 km from Sekenani Gate. The 'cottages' are dotted around a beautiful green clearing with shady trees, sweeping lawns and flowers. There's an open bar and dining room and a roaring log fire at night. Although

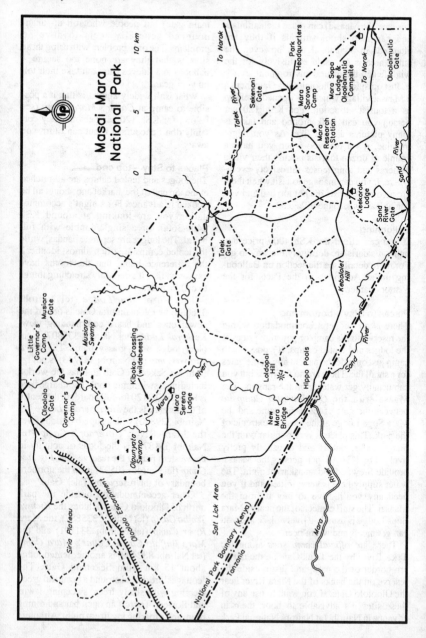

Masai Mara
National Park

it's not actually in the reserve there is a lot of game around the camp itself. They have a baited hide nearby and there's a good chance of seeing leopards. Dawn walks (KSh 140) and night time spotlight game drives (KSh 420) are also organised from the camp.

Even if you can't afford to stay in one of these places, they are usually great places to drop in for a cleansing ale and perhaps a snack although, not surprisingly, prices are high. On a more practical level, the Mara Sarova Camp, Keekorok Lodge and Mara Serena Lodge all sell petrol (KSh 10 per litre) and will usually part with it to nonguests.

Getting There & Away

Air Air Kenya Aviation Ltd has twice daily flights between Nairobi's Wilson Airport and Masai Mara, departing Nairobi at 10 am and 3 pm, and from the Mara at 11 am and 4 pm. The one-way fare is KSh 1585, but to these you have to add the cost of chartering a vehicle in the park.

Road The Mara is not a place you come to without transport. There is no public transport to or within the park, and even if there was there's certainly no way you could do a game drive on a matatu! If you are patient and persistent you should be able to hitch a ride with other tourists, but get yourself to Narok first.This is the main access point to the reserve and is a small provincial town a few hours drive west of Nairobi. As most vehicles stop to refuel here (it's the last place to do so before the park itself) the town is chocker with souvenir shops and hawkers. There are a couple of banks and a few basic budget hotels if you get stuck for the night. There are frequent buses and matatus buzzing between Nairobi and Narok.

From Narok onwards the bitumen runs out and public transport dries up. It's almost 100 km from here to any of the park gates.

It's also possible to approach the reserve from Kisii and the west along reasonably well-maintained dirt roads. You can get closer to the park by public transport but there are far fewer tourist vehicles to hitch with. Matatus run as far as Kilkoris directly

south of Kisii, or Suna on the main A1 route close to the Tanzanian border.

TSAVO NATIONAL PARK

At just over 20,000 sq km Tsavo is the largest national park in Kenya, and for administrative purposes it has been split into Tsavo West National Park, with an area of 8500 sq km, and Tsavo East National Park, which covers 11,000 sq km.

The northern area of Tsavo West, west of the Nairobi-Mombasa A109 road, is the most developed and has some excellent scenery. Tsavo East is much less visited and consists of vast rolling plains with scrubby vegetation. The entire area north of the Galana River, and this constitutes the bulk of the park, is off limits to the general public. This is due to the ongoing campaign against poachers, who still find the relative remoteness of Tsavo a good prospect. Happily it seems the authorities are winning the battle, but in the meantime the rhino population has been absolutely decimated – from around 8000 in 1970 to less than 100 today.

When driving around the park, all track junctions have a numbered cairn which makes navigation fairly simple.

Tsavo West National Park

The focus here is the watering holes by the Kilaguni and Ngulia Lodges. Both attract huge varieties of animals and birds, particularly during the dry season when water may be scarce elsewhere.

The Mzima Springs are not far from Kilaguni Lodge and the pools here are favourite haunts of both hippo and crocodile. The much vaunted underwater viewing chamber was designed to give you a view of the hippos' submarine activities but they have retreated to the far end of the pool. The springs are the source of the bulk of Mombasa's fresh water and there is a direct pipeline from here to the coast.

Also in the area of the lodges is the spectacular Shaitani lava flow and caves. Both are worth investigating although for the caves you need to exercise caution and carry a torch (flashlight). The Chaimu Crater just

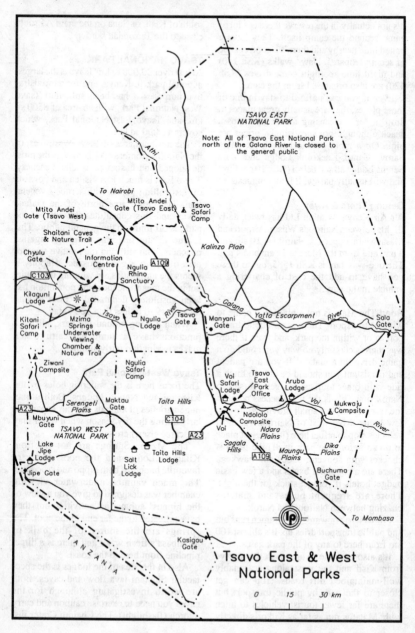

TSAVO EAST
NATIONAL PARK

Note: All of Tsavo East National Park
north of the Galana River is closed to
the general public

Tsavo East & West
National Parks

0   15   30 km

south of Kilaguni Lodge can also be climbed. It's worth remembering while walking on any of these nature trails that the park animals are far from tame, and while there's little danger, you do need to keep your eyes on what's happening around you. These nature trails are also the only places where you are permitted to get out of the vehicle.

There is an information centre at the Kilaguni Lodge and if it's open it may be worth checking to see where the most recent animal sightings have been.

Places to Stay – bottom end Tsavo West has a number of *camp sites*, namely at each of the three gates (Tsavo, Mtito Andei and Chyulu) and the *Ziwani Campsite* on the western boundary of the park.

The self-service accommodation at the *Ngulia Safari Camp* and the *Kitani Safari Camp* (tel Nairobi 340331 for both) is, by park standards, quite cheap at KSh 120 per person in the fully equipped bandas.

Places to Stay – top end The *Ngulia Lodge* (tel Nairobi 336858) charges KSh 2400/3000 for singles/doubles for full board. The water hole here is a constant attraction, both for the animals and therefore the visitors.

The *Kilaguni Lodge* (tel Nairobi 336858) is slightly more expensive at KSh 2520/3240, also for full board. Here is a recent visitor's account of a day spent at Kilaguni Lodge:

The lodge is beautifully situated looking out over the rolling hills. The large water hole, floodlit at night, is right in front of the lodge and you can sit in the bar or restaurant, or on the verandah in front of your room, and watch the wildlife. You can even lie in bed with your binoculars to hand – every room faces a water hole. All this luxury, including a swimming pool and lush garden, doesn't come cheap, but where else do you need a pair of binoculars and a field guide at hand while you eat?

We arrive in time for lunch and watch the comings and goings at the water hole. To the left there are impala and a couple of waterbuck; back from the water there's a small group of ostrich, and off to the right there's a herd of oryx. Marabou storks lounge around in the foreground while right in front of the restaurant are groups of smaller birds and mongoose.

There's so much activity it's hard to concentrate on lunch – and this is just after the wet season when the game are less concentrated at the water holes!

The scene is only spoilt by the idiots who persist, in spite of numerous posted warnings, in throwing bread out to the animals. This has already taught some of the storks (notoriously efficient scavengers) to line up in front of the restaurant wall. It would be all too easy to turn this wonderful scene into a cheap zoo with animals begging for handouts. This is the same Africa of Ethiopia and Mozambique and there's something obscene about dumb tourists hurling whole bread rolls just for amusement and a better shot with the Instamatic.

After lunch we watch from the verandah of our room – some zebra and two more ostrich appear but all the storks have left and gradually the animals wander off as the afternoon wears on. By 4.30 pm there's only the solitary waterbuck left; even the ostrich finally troop off in a stately line.

Down at the north end of the lodge grounds there's a tree full of weaver bird nests with twittering hordes of the bright yellow birds furiously at work. Some of their nests, mainly older ones, have fallen out of the tree, and on close examination they are amazingly intricate and neatly woven; coconut-size with a funnel-like entrance underneath. Right in front of our room a small squad of mongooses appear, cavort around for a few minutes, then wander away. By 5 pm it's baboon time again and the tribe wanders down to the water hole again for their evening visit. A few of them come up to our room to hassle us but soon give it away. Rock hyrax scamper around, one even coming right into our room, and the mongooses come and go. Gradually the impala reappear.

Dinner time, unhappily, is the one blot on the perfect experience. Once again there are the idiotic food hurlers at work and a hyaena trots up and waits expectantly for handouts, joined by a slender mongoose-like genet. With much shouting, loud conversation and cameras flashing madly there's a distinct theatre-restaurant feel to the whole meal and we're glad to get back to the quiet of our rooms.

The baboons leave soon after dark and by bedtime it's basically the impalas and zebras. I get up several times in the night to check what's up but, apart from bats swooping around, the scene seems static until dawn. The impala keep watch all night long.

At dawn the zebra wander off, the oryx reappear, the whole baboon tribe wanders back and immediately start carousing merrily. A couple of pairs of impala bucks square off for a morning duel and the whole cycle starts again.

Although we didn't see elephants or lions we still enjoyed every minute of it. Now if only they could put those 'don't feed the animals signs' on every table…

Tony Wheeler

In a fairly isolated spot on the western boundary of the park and almost on the Tanzanian border, the *Lake Jipe Lodge* (tel Nairobi 27623) is one of the cheaper places, with a tariff of KSh 1920/3000 for a single/double with full board.

Getting There & Away The main access is through the Mtito Andei Gate on the Mombasa-Nairobi road at the northern end of the park. The park HQ is here and there's a camp site. From the gate it's 31 km to the Kilaguni Lodge. A further 48 km along the main road away from Nairobi is the Tsavo Gate, where there's another camp site. This gate is 75 km from the Kilaguni area, so if you're hitching the Mtito Andei Gate is much closer and far busier.

From Voi there is access past the Hilton-owned Taita Hills and Salt Lick lodges (tel Nairobi 334000 for both) via the Maktau Gate. This road cuts clear across the park, exiting at the Mbuyuni Gate, to Taveta from where it's possible to cross into Tanzania and the town of Moshi at the foot of Kilimanjaro.

Tsavo East National Park

The southern third of this park is open to the public and the rolling scrub-covered hills are home to huge herds of elephants, usually covered in red dust.

The Kanderi Swamp, not far into the park from the main Voi Gate and park HQ, is home to a profusion of wildlife and there's a camp site here. Further into the park, 30 km from the gate, is the main attraction in this part of the park, the Aruba Dam built across the Voi River. Here too you'll encounter a wide variety of game – without the usual hordes of tourists; very few people visit Tsavo East.

Places to Stay – bottom end There are *camp sites* at the Voi Gate, Kanderi Swamp (Ndololo Campsite), Aruba Lodge and the *Makwaju Campsite* on the Voi River 50 km in from the main gate.

Places to Stay – top end The *Voi Safari Lodge* (tel Nairobi 336858) is five km inside the park from the Voi Gate. As you might imagine, things are a good deal more peaceful here than at the lodges in Tsavo West. Charges for a rooms are KSh 1980/2640 in the high season for full board.

The *Aruba Lodge* (tel Nairobi 340331) is in a good shady location by the dam. The small shop here sells basic provisions.

Getting There & Away The main access point and the park HQ is Voi Gate on the Nairobi-Mombasa road. Further north near the Tsavo Gate entrance of Tsavo West is the Manyani Gate. The murram road from here cuts straight across to the Galana River and follows the river clear across the park, exiting at Sala Gate on the eastern side, a distance of 100 km. From Sala Gate it's a further 110 to Malindi.

Uganda

Introduction

Uganda's long string of tragedies since independence in 1962 have featured in the Western media to such an extent that most people probably regard the country as dangerously unstable and to be avoided.

Yoweri Museveni's National Resistance Army has ruled effectively since coming to power in 1986. In the past, predictions of the stability of a regime have been premature. However, Museveni is taking Uganda into the 1990s with brighter prospects than it has had for many years. Stability has returned to most parts of the country, Kampala has virtually returned to normal and the process of getting the country back on a firm footing is well under way.

Before independence Uganda was a prosperous and cohesive country. Its great beauty led Winston Churchill to refer to the country as the 'Pearl of Africa', but by early 1986 Uganda lay shattered and bankrupt, broken by tribal animosity, nepotism, politicians who had gone mad on power and military tyranny. While a lot of the blame can be laid squarely at the feet of the sordid and brutal military dictatorship of Idi Amin, who was overthrown in 1979, others have a great deal to answer for. Indeed, there was really little difference between any of Uganda's pre-1986 rulers. All appear to have been spawned from the same degenerative mould.

Yet despite the killings and disappearances, the brutality and the fear and destruction of the past, Ugandans appear to have weathered the storm remarkably well. You will not meet a sullen, bitter or cowed people. Rather, though hard to believe, they still smile and find the enthusiasm to carry on and rebuild after the nightmare years. In fact these days there's an air of optimism as people realise that the years of terror and bloodshed are finally over.

Undoubtedly, the main reason is the regime headed by Museveni which has made a clean sweep of the government, the civil service and the army. Despite the huge odds against him and an empty treasury, during his early years in power Museveni made a lot of effort to get the country back on its feet. There was a clampdown on corruption, political meetings were banned to prevent a resurgence of intertribal rivalry and squabbling among power brokers, and a real effort was made to reassure tribal elders that Museveni's administration was balanced. Perhaps of chief importance, Museveni's army is the most disciplined that Uganda has ever seen, despite the astonishing (to Westerners) sight of fatigued teenagers among its ranks – some as young as 14. Gone are the days when every road was littered with checkpoints staffed by drunken, surly soldiers intent on squeezing every last penny from civilians, or when soldiers took anything they wanted from stores at gunpoint. There are still roadblocks, but politeness and courtesy are what you're most likely to encounter now.

For the traveller, all this means that Uganda is once again a safe and friendly country to visit. Certainly the level of comfort is not what you might be used to in Kenya, but the Ugandan people are among the friendliest on the continent and there are some unforgettable sights. Don't be afraid to go there. It's a beautiful country and it has a great deal to offer.

Facts about the Country

HISTORY

Early Settlers

Until the 19th century there was very little penetration of Uganda from outside. Despite the fertility of the land and its capacity to grow surplus crops, there were virtually no trading links with the East African coast. Some indigenous kingdoms came into being from the 14th century onwards, among them Buganda, Bunyoro, Toro, Ankole and Busoga, with Bunyoro initially being the most powerful.

Over the following centuries, the Baganda (the people of the Buganda tribe) eventually created the dominant kingdom. They make up about 20% of Uganda's population and were once ruled by a *kabaka* (king).

During the reign of Kabaka Mwanga in the mid-19th century, contacts were finally made with Arab traders from the coast and European explorers. The Christian missionaries who followed the explorers made themselves very unpopular with the rulers of Buganda and Toro, and there were massacres of both Christians and Muslims.

The Colonial Era

After the Treaty of Berlin in 1890, which defined the various European countries' spheres of influence in Africa, Uganda, Kenya and the islands of Zanzibar and Pemba were declared British Protectorates in 1894. The colonial administrators adopted a policy of indirect rule giving the traditional kingdoms a considerable degree of autonomy but, at the same time, they also favoured the recruitment of Baganda for the civil service.

Other tribespeople, unable to acquire responsible jobs in the colonial administration or to make inroads on the Baganda-dominated commercial sector, were forced to seek other ways of joining the mainstream. The Acholi and Lango, for example, chose the army and became the tribal majority in

the military. Thus were planted the seeds for the intertribal conflicts which were to tear Uganda apart following independence.

Independence

Unlike Kenya and, to a lesser extent, Tanzania, Uganda never experienced a large influx of European settlers and the expropriation of land which occurred with it. Instead, tribespeople were encouraged to grow cash crops for export through their own cooperative organisations. As a result, nationalist organisations sprouted much later than those in neighbouring countries and when they did it was on a tribal basis. So exclusive were some of these that when independence began to be discussed the Baganda even considered secession. By the mid-1950s, however, a Lango schoolteacher, Dr Milton Obote, managed to put together a loose coalition which led Uganda to independence in 1962 on the promise that the Baganda would have autonomy. The kabaka was the new nation's president and Milton Obote was its prime minister.

It wasn't a particularly propitious time for Uganda to come to grips with independence. Civil wars were raging in neighbouring southern Sudan, Zaïre and Rwanda and refugees streamed into the country adding to its problems. Also, it soon became obvious that Obote had no intention of sharing power with the kabaka. A confrontation was inevitable.

Obote moved fast, arresting several cabinet ministers and ordering his army chief of staff, Idi Amin, to storm the kabaka's palace. The raid resulted in the flight of the kabaka and his exile in London, where he died five years later. Obote had himself made president, the Bagandan monarchy was abolished and Idi Amin's star was on the rise.

The Amin Years

Events started to go seriously wrong after

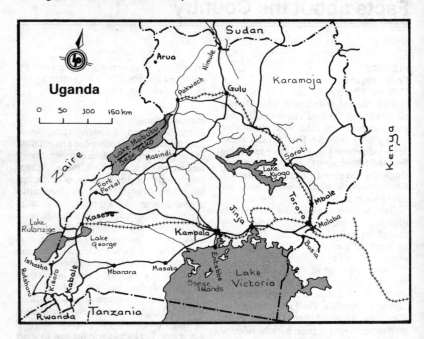

that. Obote had his attorney general, Godfrey Binaisa (a Bagandan), rewrite the constitution to consolidate virtually all powers in the presidency. He then began to nationalise foreign assets.

Then, in 1969, a scandal surfaced with the revelation that US$5 million in funds and weapons allocated to the Ministry of Defence could not be accounted for. An explanation was demanded from Amin. When it wasn't forthcoming, his deputy, Colonel Okoya, and some junior officers demanded his resignation. Shortly afterwards Okoya and his wife were shot dead in their Gulu home and rumours began to circulate about Amin's imminent arrest. It never came. Instead, when Obote left for Singapore in January 1971 to attend the Commonwealth Heads of Government conference, Amin staged a coup. The British, who had probably suffered most from Obote's nationalisation programme, were one of the first countries to recognise the new

regime. Obote left Singapore and went into exile in Tanzania.

So began Uganda's first reign of terror. All political activities were quickly suspended and the army was empowered to shoot on sight anyone suspected of opposition to the regime. Over the next eight years an estimated 300,000 Ugandans lost their lives, often in horrifying ways: bludgeoned to death with sledgehammers and iron bars or tortured to death in prisons and police stations all over the country. Nile Mansions, next to the Conference Centre in Kampala, became particularly notorious. The screams of those who were being tortured or beaten to death there could often be heard around the clock for days on end. Prime targets of Amin's death squads were the Acholi and Lango who were decimated in waves of massacres. Whole villages were wiped out. Next he turned on the professional classes. University professors and lecturers, doctors, cabinet ministers, lawyers, businesspeople and even military officers who might have posed a threat to Amin were dragged from their offices and shot or simply never seen again.

Next in line was the 70,000-strong Asian community. In 1972 they were given 90 days to leave the country with virtually nothing more than the clothes they wore. Amin and his cronies grabbed the US$1000 million booty they were forced to leave behind and quickly squandered it on new toys for the army and frivolous luxury items. Amin then turned on the British and nationalised, without compensation, US$500 million worth of investments in tea plantations and other industries. Again the booty was squandered.

Meanwhile, the economy collapsed, industrial activity ground to a halt, hospitals and rural health clinics closed, roads cracked and filled with potholes, cities became garbage dumps and their utilities fell apart. The prolific wildlife was machine-gunned down by soldiers for meat, ivory and skins and the tourist industry evaporated. The stream of refugees across the border became a flood.

Faced with chaos and an inflation rate which hit 1000%, Amin was forced to delegate more and more powers to the provincial governors who became virtual warlords in their areas. Towards the end, the treasury was so bereft of funds that it was unable to pay the soldiers. At the same time, international condemnation of the sordid regime was strengthening daily as more and more news of massacres, torture and summary executions leaked out of the country.

About the only source of support for Amin at this time was from Libya under the increasingly idiosyncratic leadership of Gaddafi. Libya bailed out the Ugandan economy, supposedly in the name of Islamic brotherhood (Amin had conveniently become a Muslim by this stage), and began an intensive drive to equip the Ugandan forces with sophisticated weapons.

The rot had spread too far, however, and was way past the point where it could be arrested by a few million dollars worth of Libyan largesse. Faced with a restless army in which intertribal fighting had broken out, Amin was forced to seek a diversion. He chose a war with Tanzania, ostensibly to teach that country a lesson for supporting anti-Amin dissidents. It was his last major act of insanity and in it began his downfall.

Post-Amin Chaos

On 30 October 1978 the Ugandan army rolled across north-western Tanzania virtually unopposed and annexed more than 1200 sq km of territory. Meanwhile, the airforce bombed the Lake Victoria ports of Bukoba and Musoma. President Julius Nyerere ordered a full-scale counterattack but it took months to mobilise his ill-equipped and poorly trained forces. By the following spring, however, he had managed to scrape together a 50,000-strong people's militia composed mainly of illiterate youngsters from the bush. This militia joined with the many exiled Ugandan liberation groups (united only in their determination to rid Uganda of Amin). The two armies met. East Africa's supposedly best equipped and best trained army threw down its weapons and fled and the Tanzanians pushed on into the heart of Uganda. Kampala fell without a fight and by the end of April organised resistance had effectively ceased. Amin fled to Libya where he remained until Gaddafi threw him out following a shoot-out with Libyan soldiers. He now lives in Jeddah on a Saudi Arabian pension.

The Tanzanian action was criticised, somewhat half-heartedly, by the Organisation for African Unity (OAU), but it's probably true to say that most African countries breathed a sigh of relief to see the madman finally thrown out. All the same, Tanzania was forced to foot the entire war bill, estimated at US$500 million. This was a crushing blow for an already desperately poor country. No other country has ever made a contribution.

The rejoicing in Uganda was short-lived. The 12,000 or so Tanzanian soldiers who remained in the country, supposedly to assist with reconstruction and to maintain law and order, turned on the Ugandans as soon as their pay wasn't forthcoming. They took what they wanted from shops at gunpoint, hijacked trucks arriving from Kenya with international relief aid and slaughtered more wildlife.

Once again the country slid into chaos and gangs of armed bandits began to roam the cities, killing and looting. Food supplies ran out and hospitals could no longer function. Nevertheless, thousands of exiled Ugandans began to answer the new president's call to return home and help with reconstruction.

Usefu Lule, a modest and unambitious man, was installed as president with Nyerere's blessing, but when he began speaking out against Nyerere he was replaced by Godfrey Binaisa, sparking riots supporting Lule in Kampala. Meanwhile, Obote bided his time in Dar es Salaam.

Binaisa quickly came under pressure to set a date for a general election and a return to civilian rule. Although this was done, he found himself at odds with other powerful members of the provisional government on ideological, constitutional and personal grounds – particularly over his insistence that the pre-Amin political parties not be allowed to contest the election.

The strongest criticism came from two senior members of the army, Tito Okello and David Ojok, both Obote supporters. Fearing a coup, Binaisa attempted to dismiss Ojok, who refused to step down, and instead placed Binaisa under house arrest. The government was taken over by a military commission which set the election for later that year. Obote returned from exile to an enthusiastic welcome in many parts of the country and swept to victory in an election which was blatantly rigged. Binaisa returned to exile in the USA.

The honeymoon with Obote proved to be relatively short. Like Amin, Obote favoured certain tribes. Large numbers of civil servants and army and police commanders belonging to the tribes of the south were replaced with Obote supporters belonging to the tribes of the north. The State Research Bureau, a euphemism for the secret police,

was re-established and the prisons began to fill once more. Obote was about to complete the destruction that Amin initiated. More and more reports of atrocities and killings leaked out of the country. Mass graves were unearthed that were unrelated to the Amin era. The press was muzzled and Western journalists were expelled. It was obvious that Obote was once again attempting to achieve absolute power. Intertribal tension was again on the rise and in mid-1985 Obote was overthrown in a coup staged by the army under the leadership of Tito Okello.

The NRA Takeover

Okello was not the only opponent of Obote. Shortly after Obote became president for the second time, a guerrilla army opposed to his tribally biased government was formed in western Uganda. It was led by Yoweri Museveni, who had lived in exile in Tanzania during Amin's reign and who had served as defence minister during the chaotic administrations of 1979-80.

From a group of 27 men grew a guerrilla force of about 20,000, many of them orphaned teenagers. In the early days, few gave the guerrillas, known as the National Resistance Army, much of a chance. Government troops frequently made murderous sweeps across the notorious Luwero Triangle and artillery supplied by North Korea pounded areas where the guerrillas were thought to be hiding. Few people outside Uganda even knew of the existence of the NRA due to Obote's success in muzzling the press and expelling journalists. At times it seemed that Museveni might give up the battle – he spent several months in London at one point – but his dedicated young lieutenants kept fighting.

The NRA was not a bunch of drunken thugs like Amin's and Obote's armies. New recruits were indoctrinated in the bush by political commissars and taught that they had to be the servants of the people, not their oppressors. Discipline was tough. Anyone who got badly out of line was executed. Museveni was determined that the army would never again disgrace Uganda. Also, a

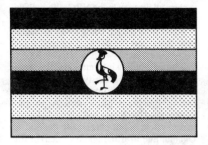

central thrust of the NRA was to win the hearts and minds of the people, who learnt to identify totally with the persecuted Bagandans in the infamous Triangle.

By the time Obote was ousted and Okello had taken over, the NRA controlled a large slice of western Uganda and was a power to be reckoned with. Recognising this, Okello attempted to arrange a truce so that the leaders from both sides could negotiate on sharing power. However, peace talks in Nairobi failed. Wisely, Museveni didn't trust a man who had been one of Obote's closest military aides for more than 15 years. Neither did he trust Okello's prime minister, Paulo Mwanga, who was formerly Obote's vice president and minister of defence. Also, Okello's army was notorious for its lack of discipline and brutality. Units of Amin's former army had even returned from exile in Zaïre and Sudan and joined with Okello.

What Museveni wanted was a clean sweep of the administration, the army and the police. He wanted corruption stamped out and those who had been involved in atrocities during the Amin and Obote regimes brought to trial. These demands were, of course, anathema to Okello who was up to his neck in corruption and responsible for many atrocities.

The fighting continued in earnest and by late January 1986 it was obvious that Okello's days were numbered. The surrender of 1600 government soldiers holed up in their barracks in the southern town of Mbarara, which was controlled by the NRA,

brought the NRA to the outskirts of Kampala itself. With the morale of the government troops at a low ebb, in February the NRA launched an all-out offensive to take the capital. Okello's troops fled, almost without a fight, although not before looting whatever remained and carting it away in commandeered buses. It was a typical parting gesture, as was the gratuitous shooting-up of many Kampala high-rise offices.

During the following weeks Okello's rabble were pursued and finally pushed north over the border into Sudan. The civil war was over apart from a few mopping up operations in the extreme north-west and Karamoja Province. The long nightmare was finally over. Although there are occasional reports of units of Okello's army raiding frontier areas, it's a spent force. There is no mistaking which of the two armies Ugandan civilians prefer.

Despite Museveni's Marxist leanings (he studied political science at Dar es Salaam University in the early 1970s and trained with the anti-Portuguese guerrillas in Mozambique), he has proved to be pragmatic since taking control. Despite many of his officers' radical stands on certain issues, he appointed several arch-conservatives to his cabinet and made an effort to reassure the country's influential Catholic community.

In the late 1980s peace agreements were negotiated with most of the guerrilla factions who had fought for Okello or Obote and were still active in the north and north-east. Under an amnesty offered to the rebels, by 1988 as many as 40,000 had surrendered and many were given jobs in the NRA. In the north-west of the country, almost 300,000 Ugandans have returned home from across the Sudanese border.

The economy is now the country's main problem, but if peace can be maintained Ugandans can look forward with optimism. Factories which have lain idle for years are finally getting back into production.

Museveni is likely to face political pressure, for as peace spreads, so too will demands to relax the ban on political parties and move towards a multiparty democracy.

GEOGRAPHY

Uganda has an area of 236,580 sq km, of which about 25% is fertile arable land capable of providing a surplus of food. Lake Victoria and the Victoria Nile, which flows through much of the country, together create one of the best watered areas of Africa.

The land varies from semidesert in the north-east to the lush and fertile shores of the lake, the Ruwenzori Mountains in the west and the beautiful, mountainous south-west.

The tropical heat is tempered by the altitude, which averages over 1000 metres.

CLIMATE

As most of Uganda is fairly flat with mountains only in the extreme east (Mt Elgon), extreme west (Ruwenzori) and close to the Rwanda border, the bulk of the country enjoys the same tropical climate with temperatures averaging about 26°C during the day and 16°C at night. The hottest months are from December to February when the daytime range is 27°C to 29°C. The rainy seasons in the south are from April to May and October to November, the wettest month being April. In the north the wet season is from April to October and the dry season is from November to March. During the wet seasons the average rainfall is 175 mm per month. Humidity is generally low outside the wet seasons.

GOVERNMENT

Uganda is a republic and a member of the British Commonwealth. The president is head of state, government and the armed forces. The governing 80-member National Resistance Council (NRC) is made up of members of various political organisations including the National Resistance Movement (the political wing of the NRA), the UPM, Democratic Party, Uganda People's Congress, the Conservative Party and two guerrilla organisations.

At the base of the NRM political policy is the Resistance Committee (RC) – a village-based administration tool which is responsible for village matters – members of which can in theory be elected and pass through the system all the way to the NRC, although this has not yet happened.

Apart from the RC being a way to channel new faces into the political system, it provides the NRM with a direct line to disseminate policy information to the people and has improved security at a local level.

Constitutional reform is another big task facing President Museveni. A political system must be chosen and adopted. A multi-party system is not necessarily the best for Uganda due to tribal and/or sectarian frictions. Hopefully a lot of the debate over reform will take place as planned at the village level through the RCs.

Despite the other reforms which have taken place, change is slow and corruption among officials at all levels is still a large problem.

ECONOMY

Before Amin's coup, Uganda was approaching self-sufficiency in food, had a small but vital industrial sector and profitable copper mines. Boosting export income were the thriving coffee, sugar and tourist industries. Under Amin the country reverted almost completely to a subsistence economy. The managerial and technical elite was either expelled, killed or exiled and the country's infrastructure was virtually destroyed. Some cash crops made a tentative recovery under Obote, but Museveni's government inherited massive problems.

In 1987 there was a massive devaluation, a new currency was issued, an International Monetary Fund (IMF) restructuring deal was accepted and the government made a real attempt to tackle its economic problems. Despite this, inflation was running at more than 100% within a year and another massive devaluation followed.

Uganda's problems stem from its almost total reliance on coffee, which accounts for 98% of exports, plus the fact that 60% of foreign earnings is used to pay off its large foreign debt.

The remainder of the exchange reserves are spent on items aimed at bringing about improvements in the long term. Short-term benefits are few and poverty is widespread.

One of the more interesting aspects of the Ugandan economy is the barter system, whereby the country makes deals with foreign trading partners, exchanging goods (usually coffee) for much needed imports. So far it has struck deals with Algeria, Cuba, Czechoslovakia, Germany, Italy, Libya, North Korea, Rwanda, Somalia, Sudan and Yugoslavia.

Inflation remains a critical problem and it seems the government has lost control of the currency – inflation is running at more than 200% and the black market is flourishing (the value of the shilling is three times the official rate).

Despite the obvious problems, the Ugandan economy appears set for large improvements, as agricultural and manufacturing output and construction have all increased in the past few years.

Agriculture is the single most important component of the Ugandan economy. It accounts for 70% of gross domestic product (GDP) and employs 90% of the workforce. Coffee, sugar, cotton and tea are the main export crops. Crops grown for local consumption include maize, millet, cassava, sweet potato, beans and cereals.

The manufacturing sector's share of GDP has shrunk from 12% in 1970 to less than 4% now. Manufactured goods include textiles, soap, cement and steel products. Foreign aid is mostly used to supply vital imported fuel and purchase spare parts to get factories back to full production.

POPULATION

Uganda's population of 16 million is increasing at the alarming rate of 2.8%. It is made up of a complex and diverse range of tribes. Lake Kyoga forms the northern boundary for the Bantu speaking peoples who dominate much of east, central and southern Africa and, in Uganda, include the Bagandans and several other tribes. In the north live the Lango (near Lake Kyoga) and the Acholi (towards the Sudan border) who speak Nilotic languages. To the east are the Teso and Karamojong who are related to the Maasai and who also speak Nilotic languages. Pygmies live in the forests of the west.

RELIGION

While about two-thirds of the population is Christian, the remaining one-third still practices animism while a small percentage is Muslim. There were sizeable numbers of Sikhs and Hindus in the country until Asians were expelled in 1972.

HOLIDAYS & FESTIVALS

January
    New Year's Day (1st)
    Start of NRM Government (26th)
April
    Good Friday
    Easter Monday
May
    Labour Day (1st)
October
    Independence Day (9th)
December
    Christmas Day (25th)
    Boxing Day (26th)

LANGUAGE

The official language is English, which most people can speak. The other major languages are Luganda and Swahili, although the latter isn't spoken much in Kampala.

Facts for the Visitor

VISAS

Visas are required by all, except nationals of Commonwealth countries, Denmark, Finland, Iceland, Ireland, Italy, Norway, Spain, Sweden or Turkey. Visas cost about US$20 and generally allow an initial stay of up to two weeks, but can be extended. Travellers who don't require visas are also permitted a two week initial stay. This can be extended to two months maximum at any district commissioner's office, at no cost.

Embassies

There are Ugandan embassies in Addis Ababa (Ethiopia), Beijing (China), Bonn (Germany), Brussels (Belgium), Cairo (Egypt), Canberra (Australia), Copenhagen (Denmark), Khartoum (Sudan), Kigali (Rwanda), Kinshasa (Zaïre), London (UK), Nairobi (Kenya), New Delhi (India), Ottawa (Canada), Paris (France), Tokyo (Japan) and Washington DC (USA).

In Nairobi, the visa section of the high commission is on the 4th floor, Baring Arcade, Phoenix House, Kenyatta Ave. It's not a good place to get a visa as it costs US$20 which must be paid in cash dollars or by travellers' cheque! The office is open from 9.30 am to 12.30 pm and 2.30 to 4 pm. The two week visa takes 24 hours to issue and requires one photo.

In Kigali, the embassy (tel 76495) is on the 3rd floor of the building on Ave de la Paix near the corner of Ave des Collines. It's open Monday to Friday from 8 am to 3.30 pm. Visas take 48 hours to issue, require two photos and cost RFr 2000.

If you haven't got a visa, it's still worth turning up at the border. You may well be allowed in on payment of the usual visa fee, but don't blame us if you're not!

Other African Visas

Burundi Don't plan on getting a visa for Burundi in Uganda as these are only issued to Ugandans and Ugandan residents. If you

want to try, the embassy (tel 545840) is at 2 Katego Rd, near the Uganda Museum. It's open Monday to Friday from 8.30 am to 12.30 pm and 2.30 to 5 pm.

Kenya The high commission (tel 231861) is at Plot No 60, Kira Rd, near the Uganda Museum. It's open Monday to Friday from 8.30 am to 12.30 pm and 2 to 4.30 pm. Visas cost US$2.70, are issued in 24 hours and two photos are required. Apply before noon and the visa can usually be issued the same day.

Rwanda The embassy (tel 241105) is on the 2nd floor, Baumann House, Obote Ave (Parliament Ave). It's open from 8.30 am to 12.30 pm and 2.30 to 5 pm, but visa applications are accepted in the morning only. Think carefully when stating which date you will be entering Rwanda as the visa is only valid from that date. Visas are sometimes issued the same day, otherwise it takes 24 hours. The cost is US$2.20 for a one week visa, US$4.30 for one month and US$8.60 for two to six months. There is no extra charge for multiple entries, so it's worth asking for this, especially if you've planned to go from Bukavu (Zaïre) to Bujumbura (Burundi) by road.

Sudan The embassy (tel 243518) is on the 4th floor, Embassy House, King George VI Way, on the corner of Obote Ave (Parliament Ave). It's open Monday to Friday from 9 am to 3 pm and on Saturday from 10 am till noon. Visa applications are only accepted on Monday and Thursday. A one month tourist visa costs US$10 (shillings are not accepted), requires two photos, a letter of introduction from your embassy and an onward ticket. It can take anything up to a month to issue as all applications have to be referred to Khartoum.

Tanzania The high commission (tel 56755) is at 6 Kagera Rd and is open Monday to

Top: Matatu station, Kampala, Uganda (GE)
Bottom: School children, Kampala, Uganda (GE)

Friday from 9 am to 3 pm. Visa costs vary according to your nationality, but range from US$2.20 to US$9.30. Visas are valid for three months, take two days to issue and require two photos.

Zaïre Don't come to Kampala with the idea of picking up a Zaïre visa. The fee, at US$70 for a one month single entry visa and US$100 for multiple entry, is nothing short of extortion. It must be paid in hard currency too! It's scandalous, especially as the same visa in Nairobi costs the equivalent of about US$7.50. If you still want to apply, the embassy (tel 23377) is at 20 Philip Rd, Kololo District. While it's open Monday to Friday from 8 am to 3 pm, visa applications are only accepted before noon. A letter of introduction from your embassy and two photos are required, and the visa is issued in 24 hours.

MONEY

US$1 = USh 340 (official)
US$1 = USh 750 (black market)

The Ugandan shilling (USh) is a highly volatile currency and is constantly losing value. The rate given here was applicable in 1990, but will probably look laughable now. The big difficulty is that prices quoted in Ugandan shillings here will be way off the mark in a very short time, which is why prices are quoted in US dollars, using the exchange rate in this book. This way you should still get a fairly good idea of current prices. Items quoted are payable in Ugandan shillings unless stated otherwise.

The other trouble with the continuing devaluation of the Ugandan shilling is the sheer volume of banknotes it's necessary to carry. The largest denomination (at the time of writing) was USh 100! Change US$100 (on the black market) and you have at least 750 banknotes to cart around – conceal them in case you are checked, although this is extremely unlikely. Carting these notes around and counting them is the economy's only major growth sector. The other notes in circulation are USh 50, USh 20 and USh 10 (no coins).

Black Market

You'll have no trouble finding someone to change your money. Cash and travellers' cheques can be changed on the street market, though expect quite a bit less for cheques per US dollar than cash. Shop around for the best rates. These are usually found in clothing stores, automobile parts shops, photographic shops and any store which sells imported goods, especially electronic appliances. Simply go in and ask.

Kampala is the best place to change money, although rates at places like Kasese and Kabale are only marginally less. At Malaba on the Uganda-Kenya border the exchange rates are generally poor because

moneychangers assume that tourists don't know the current maximum rates (often true). You'll be lucky to get more than about USh 600 to the dollar. Change only enough to get to your next destination and make a point of asking other travellers who have recently been to Uganda what the rates are.

If you're going to use the black market (and unfortunately for Uganda, there are very few travellers who can afford not to) use US dollars and to a lesser extent pounds sterling. Anything else is virtually useless.

Currency Declaration Forms

These forms are usually issued at the border on entry, but whether or not you'll have to show the money you declare varies from day to day and from border to border. Officials at the Malaba crossing with Kenya are now keen to search bags and money belts for undeclared cash, so hide it well.

It's a good idea to officially change a minimal amount of money and get a bank stamp on your form. For a start, you won't get into any national park unless you have proof that you've changed money officially. Also, it's likely that you'll be asked for the form when leaving the country. As long as it has a stamp it's unlikely to raise questions. If your form is blank you may have to resort to bribery. Your chances of getting through without parting with some money are slim. Some travellers report having their form checked at roadblocks within Uganda.

A far more altruistic reason for changing money officially is so that, hopefully, it will help buy medicines, fuel and other essential imports. Consider it a donation towards helping a destitute country get back on its feet and try not to think that your money could go towards guns for the army or limousines for government bigwigs.

It occasionally happens that some Ugandan borders run out of forms, which makes a total nonsense of the whole operation. Another piece of absurdity regarding currency forms is that the Ugandan Hotels Corporation, which runs a chain of top hotels throughout the country, demands payment in hard currency. They won't accept shillings,

even when there are sufficient bank stamps on your currency form to prove that you've changed money in a bank at the official rate. Naturally, if you don't have the exact amount in hard currency to pay your hotel bill they'll give you the change in shillings (not hard currency) at the official rate of exchange.

The same is true when buying airline tickets in Uganda. You must pay for these in hard currency – Uganda Airlines internal flights too. There are no cheap deals. This makes flying out of Uganda expensive. Similarly, some embassies will no longer accept shillings for visa fees. However, you can still pay for postage and telephone calls in shillings, which makes it cheap by East African standards, especially when compared with places like Rwanda and Burundi.

COSTS

Uganda is not the travel bargain it was a few years ago. At black market rates, goods and services are affordable (on a par with Kenya) but there are no real bargains. Using the official rate you'll find that your money disappears at an incredible pace.

You can pay for all the necessities of life with shillings – accommodation, food, drink, transport, post and telecommunications. The exceptions are hotels belonging to the Ugandan Hotels Corporation, air fares and national park fees.

Transport and food are especially cheap since the prices must, to some extent, reflect the capacity of the average Ugandan to pay. Hotel prices are proportionally higher, in line with catering for a more affluent clientele.

TOURIST INFORMATION

There is a tourist office in Kampala but it has very little printed information.

GENERAL INFORMATION
Post & Telephone

Despite the ravages of the civil wars, international postal and telephone services are excellent, at least from Kampala. I sent several letters and parcels to Australia from Kampala and all of them arrived. Poste restante also functions efficiently.

AIDS continues to be a huge problem in Uganda with the number of cases running at about 20,000 – a figure that will double every year. The epidemic is worst in the south-west of the country where it is estimated that 20% of the population are AIDS carriers. A government campaign focuses on preventing infection through fidelity and abstinence rather than by encouraging the use of condoms. Blood is screened in main medical centres and the incidence of cases arising from contaminated blood is on the decrease. (For more information see the Health section in the introductory Facts for the Visitor chapter.)

Internal telephone connections have improved greatly in the past few years and are generally not a problem.

Time
The time is GMT plus three hours.

Banking Hours
Banking hours are Monday to Friday from 8.30 am to 12.30 pm.

MEDIA
Newspapers
Quite a few English-language newspapers have reappeared on the streets since order has been re-established. These include the government-owned *New Vision*, the *Star* and the *Independent Observer*. They offer very little in the way of international news but give an interesting insight into how the country is gradually pulling itself out of the mire. Newspapers published in Luganda include *Munno, Ngabo* and *Taifa*.

HEALTH
You must take precautions against malaria. Also, bilharzia is a serious risk in any of Uganda's lakes (Victoria, Kyoga, etc) and rivers. Avoid swimming and walking around barefoot, especially where there are lots of reeds (the snails which are the intermediate host for the bilharzia parasite live in areas such as these).

DANGERS & ANNOYANCES
More than any other East African country, Uganda has suffered incredibly from misgovernment, corruption, civil war, coups and badly disciplined armies. As a result, it has an image as a dangerous and unstable country to visit. Only in the past few years have tourists started to visit Uganda once more. With the stability that has been established with the Museveni government, travellers have found that Uganda is once again a safe, friendly and interesting country.

There is no need to have any fears about travelling in Uganda. Yet staff at some embassies are still warning travellers about dangers. If you are concerned, check with other travellers as they are generally a far more reliable source of information than a government official behind a desk in another country. It's true that there are still areas where your safety cannot be guaranteed, but this is limited to the extreme north along the border with Sudan and the north-east of the country along the border with Kenya. If you want to visit these areas, make enquiries before setting off. As for the rest of the country, it's safe to travel. Ugandans are generally very friendly people.

FILM & PHOTOGRAPHY
Bring all your own equipment and film. In Kampala there are limited quantities of Konica print film, but it's not cheap. In other

parts of the country don't count on being able to get anything. Slide film is unobtainable anywhere.

Although there are no official restrictions on photography, there is a certain amount of paranoia about photos being taken of anything which could be interpreted as poverty or deprivation. This is only a recent phenomenon and the situation varies from place to place. Always ask permission before taking photos of people. Usually they will be more than happy to be photographed, but respect their feelings if they aren't. Quite a few Ugandan homes are proudly displaying family portraits which I took and, having received the photos, they always write to wish you every happiness in the world. So if you promise a copy, please send it.

Getting There

Possible access routes into Uganda are by air and road. There are railways but no international trains, even though the line is continuous with the Kenyan system. One day it may be restored, making it again possible to travel all the way from Kasese to Mombasa by train.

AIR

International airlines serving Uganda include Aeroflot, Air Tanzania, Ethiopian Airlines, Kenya Airways, Sabena and Uganda Airlines.

Few travellers enter Uganda by air because most of the discounted air fares available in Europe and North America use Nairobi as the gateway to East Africa. International airline tickets bought in Uganda have to be paid for in hard currency (Ugandan shillings are not acceptable). This, coupled with the fact that there are no discounted fares available in Kampala, makes flying out of Uganda expensive. It's possible, however, that you might find a cheap Aeroflot ticket to a European city via Moscow, but it doesn't fly often. Flights to Kenya can be booked out for a week or two in advance because these flights are used a lot by international aid workers, banking officials and government delegations.

OVERLAND
To/From Kenya

The two main border posts which most overland travellers use are Malaba and Busia, with Malaba being by far the more commonly used. You would probably use Busia only if you were coming directly from Kisumu and wishing to go directly to Jinja or Kampala, bypassing Tororo.

Nairobi to Kampala via Malaba There are trains from Nairobi to Malaba via Nakuru and Eldoret on Tuesday, Friday and Saturday, leaving at 3 pm and arriving at 8.30 am the next day. In the opposite direction they depart Malaba on Wednesday, Saturday and Sunday at 4 pm and arrive at 9.30 am the next day. The fares are KSh 440 in 1st class, KSh 207 in 2nd class and KSh 107 in 3rd class. The trains don't connect with the Ugandan system, so you must go by road between Malaba and Tororo (and beyond, unless you want to take the extremely slow train from Tororo to Jinja or Kampala).

Buses with different companies travel daily between Nairobi and Malaba, departing both places at about 7.30 pm and arriving at about 5.30 am the next day. The fare is KSh 160. If you prefer to travel by day there are several daily buses between Nairobi and Bungoma, in each direction, which depart both places at about 8 am and arrive at about 5 pm the same day.

There are plenty of matatus between Bungoma and Malaba which cost KSh 20 and take about 45 minutes. If you stay in Bungoma overnight there are plenty of cheap hotels to choose from.

The Kenyan and Ugandan border posts are about one km from each other at Malaba. You will have to walk. When leaving Kenya you will be asked for your currency declaration form, which isn't checked, and whether you have any Kenyan shillings (it's illegal to export them), but otherwise there's no fuss or baggage searches.

When entering Uganda, firstly you'll be issued with a currency declaration form. Upon its completion, go through the gate to the stinking hot tin hut on the right for a baggage search and money check, then it's just a matter of queuing to go through immigration, then customs (over the road). The whole process takes anything up to 1½ hours, but usually less. Ugandan customs and immigration are usually closed for an hour at lunch.

On the Kenyan side there are hordes of moneychangers who will greet you, both before you clear Kenyan immigration and while you're on your way to the Ugandan post. It's safe enough to change with them although their rates are poor (about US$1 = USh 500; they also change Kenyan shillings). They'll also tell you there's no bank on the Ugandan side, which is a lie. The bank at Malaba is open seven days a week, although on Sundays entry is through the back door. It's probably a good idea to change a small amount at the border post officially, otherwise how will you pay for the onward matatu? Plenty of people are willing to change money for you in Malaba; expect about USh 600 for US$1. There's also a couple of basic lodges at Malaba if you need to stay overnight. The Paradise Inn has basic singles/doubles for US$2/3.40 and a good restaurant and bar.

There are frequent matatus in either direction between Malaba (in Uganda) and Tororo which cost US$0.30 and take less than one hour. Between Malaba and Jinja (US$2, two hours) or Kampala (US$3, three hours) matatus are frequent until the late afternoon. The road has been resurfaced and is excellent, although it does mean that drivers can reach terrifying speeds, especially between Jinja and Kampala. There's also a train from Tororo to Kampala but it only runs three times a week and is diabolically slow.

Taking a vehicle through this border crossing is fairly straightforward and doesn't take more than a couple of hours.

To/From Rwanda

The two crossing points between Uganda and Rwanda are at Gatuna/Katuna on the Kigali-Kabale road and at Cyanika on the Ruhengeri-Kisoro road. Both border posts are very easy-going.

Kigali to Kabale There are frequent minibuses from Kigali to Katuna which cost RFr 250 and take about two hours. The border is very easy-going and it's only 100 metres to the Ugandan post. There are moneychangers on the Rwandan side and you can buy Ugandan shillings (with either Rwandan francs or dollars), although you do need to know the current rate or you're a sitting duck to be ripped off. From the border, minibuses which go frequently to Kabale cost about US$0.40 and take about 30 minutes.

Ruhengeri to Kisoro From Ruhengeri to Cyanika there are regular minibuses which take about an hour and cost RFr 70. You may have trouble finding anyone who sells Ugandan shillings at this border, but the customs officials have been known to oblige! The road on the Ugandan side is little more than a dirt track which sees hardly any traffic. You may have to walk the 12 km to Kisoro, although hitching is possible – it just takes time.

To/From Sudan

The only point of entry from Sudan is via Nimule north of Gulu, but this is the area into which the retreating troops of Amin and Okello were pushed by the NRA in early 1986 so it may still not be safe. Make enquiries before setting off.

There's also a civil war going on in southern Sudan between the Muslim north and the Christian/animist south, so it is almost certainly impossible to get from Juba to Nimule. At present it's certainly impossible to go overland from Khartoum to Juba without risking your life, so if you're heading north from Uganda you need to think seriously and ask around before setting off. There are a few intrepid travellers who make it through between Nimule and Juba when hostilities are on the back burner, but don't undertake it lightly. Getting a visa for Sudan is the first of many problems you'll encounter.

To/From Tanzania

Trying to go overland across the Kagera salient from Bukoba to Masaka via Kyaka will prove extremely frustrating. The road has been in very bad condition ever since Tanzanian troops repelled Idi Amin's forces in 1979 and went on to take Kampala. The road and border is open but we haven't heard from (or of) anyone who's done this route for years.

To/From Zaïre

The two main crossing points are south from Rutshuru to Kisoro, and north-west from Beni to Kasese via Katwe and Kasindi. The Ishasha crossing between Kasese and Rutshuru is also open. There are less used border posts further north between Mahagi and Pakwach and between Aru and Arua. If you're thinking of crossing between Aru and Arua, you'd be wise to make enquiries about security before setting off. Ratbag remnants of Amin's, Obote's and Okello's troops may still be a nuisance in this area.

Rutshuru to Kisoro The most reliable crossing is that between Rutshuru and Kisoro, a distance of about 30 km. You'll probably have to hitch and the road is very rough. The actual crossing is very straightforward. A basic hotel on the Zaïre side of the border charges Z600 for a single room.

Rutshuru to Kasese The Ishasha border is another possibility. As there's a Friday market at Ishasha, this is probably the best day to go because trucks from Rutshuru to Ishasha leave early in the morning (about 5.30 am) and return in the evening. There's also a Saturday market at Isharo (about halfway between Rutshuru and Ishasha), so there are trucks from Rutshuru early on Saturday mornings.

On the Ugandan side, the Ishasha River Camp is 17 km from Ishasha, inside the Ruwenzori (Queen Elizabeth II) National Park. You'll have to wait for a lift as walking in this part of the park is prohibited due to the lions. There are no supplies of any sort (apart from Primus beer from Zaïre), although the rangers will cook something up if you're desperate. Camping costs US$2 and *bandas* (circular, grass-thatched traditional-style houses) are US$4.

From Ishasha, the road to Katunguru (marked on most maps as a 2nd class road) is impassable at present, so don't try it! The alternative route is the road through Kihihi and Rukungiri to Ishaka on the Kasese-Mbarara road. There is a steady trickle of traffic along this route so hitching from Ishaka shouldn't be too much of a problem and there's even the occasional matatu. The Ugandan customs official at the Ishasha border lives at Kihihi so it may be possible to hitch with him.

Beni to Kasese The route from Beni to Kasese via Kasindi, Mpondwe and Katwe involves hitching unless you can find a matatu. Depending on the day you go, this could involve a considerable wait (hours rather than days), whichever of the two routes you use from the Ugandan border to Kasese.

Kasindi has a couple of hotels, a bar and a restaurant of sorts. A hotel room costs Z700. It's three km from Kasindi to the border post at Bwero. You'll probably have to walk. When crossing the border hide any excess zaïres well, as everyone wants them – from customs officials to drivers and waitresses.

In Bwero, the Modern Lodge Hotel is a clean and very friendly concrete place. Rooms cost US$1 per night, and coffee and omelettes are available across the road. Pickups leave at about 7 am for the trip to Kasese (US$0.70).

LAKE

To/From Tanzania

The ferry service between Jinja and Mwanza (in Tanzania) across Lake Victoria is primarily for freight. While there's room for passengers, getting permission to travel on the ferries is virtually impossible. If you want to try, see the chief traffic manager of the Uganda Railways. You can find him lurking in an office on the 1st floor of the Kampala Railway Station.

There is talk of a service connecting Mwanza and Bukoba with Entebbe, but at this stage it's just that – talk.

Getting Around

AIR

Uganda Airlines services all internal routes. Tickets must be paid for in hard currency. Ugandan shillings are not acceptable even with a currency form and bank stamps to prove that you have changed money officially. There are usually several flights per week between Entebbe and most major centres of population but they're often cancelled at short notice.

BUS

Uganda is the land of minibuses (matatus) and shared taxis and there's never any shortage of them. Fares are fixed and they leave when full. The only trouble is that 'full' is usually the equivalent of 'way beyond capacity'. Most matatus are like sardine cans, but this isn't always the case. Many drivers are speed maniacs who go much too fast to leave any leeway for emergencies. So-called accidents are frequent.

Normal buses also connect the major towns. They're cheaper than matatus and much slower because they stop a great deal to pick up and set down passengers. They're also a lot safer.

Most towns and cities have a bus station/matatu park, so simply turn up and tell people where you want to go. On the open road, just put out your hand.

TRAIN

There are two main lines in Uganda. The first starts at Tororo and runs west all the way to Kasese via Jinja and Kampala. The other line runs from Tororo north-west to Pakwach via Mbale, Soroti, Lira and Gulu.

Travelling by train is a good way of getting from Kampala to Kasese, but elsewhere services are either suspended or terribly slow. There are three classes on Ugandan trains: 1st class, which consists of tiny two-berth compartments; 2nd class, the same as 1st class but with six berths; and economy class, which has seats and is

usually very crowded. All the carriages have seen better days. It would be unusual to find one where the lights or flush toilets work. Second class is adequate, especially if you're part of a group. Economy class is bearable, although you need to keep a close watch on your gear at night. Sexes are separated in 1st and 2nd class unless your group fills a compartment.

It's advisable to book in advance if you want a ticket in one of the bunk classes, though you can only do this the day before the scheduled departure. When buying a ticket, first get a reservation (not necessary in economy) then join the queue to pay.

Most trains have dining cars, which are actually far more pleasant places to ride in than the claustrophobic compartments. The lights and fans work too! Meals, beer and soft drinks are available at reasonable prices. There are often no connecting doors between

the carriages so you may be stuck in the dining car for some time, although it's usually less than an hour between stops. There's also food at stalls at most stations. These stalls are usually very cheap and offer items like barbecued meat, roast maize, ugali (maize meal), stewed meat dishes, fruit, tea and coffee.

The train schedules are largely wishful thinking, as delays, derailments and cancellations are all common. The train I caught from Kampala departed 10 hours late and was even further behind time when it finally arrived in Kasese.

DRIVING

There's a system of sealed roads between most major centres of population, though the conditions vary from unbelievably good (Kampala-Jinja, Kabale-Kisoro) to diabolically bad (Mbarara-Kabale). Minor roads are usually badly potholed and become impassable after heavy rain.

HITCHING

Hitching is virtually obligatory in some situations, such as getting into national parks to which there's no public transport. Most of the lifts you will get will be on trucks, usually on top of the load at the back, which can be a very pleasant way to travel, although sun protection is a must. Free lifts on trucks are the exception rather than the rule, so ask before you get on.

Other sources for lifts are international aid workers, missionaries, businesspeople and the occasional diplomat, but you may have to wait a long time in some places before anyone comes along. There were not many privately owned vehicles that were not 'requisitioned' by Okello's retreating troops. There must be a lot of rotting vehicles lying by the side of the road in northern Uganda.

Kampala

The capital, Kampala, suffered a great deal during the years of civil strife that began with Idi Amin's defeat in 1979 at the hands of the Tanzanian army and ended with the victory of Yoweri Museveni's NRA in early 1986. The city is still getting back on its feet and services continue to be gradually restored. Kampala still carries the scars of street fighting and looting, the enforced departure of its Asian population and years of corruption.

Unless you've had previous experience of upheavals like these, it's hard to believe the amount of gratuitous destruction and looting that went on: office blocks and government offices had the bulk of their windows shattered; the buildings were riddled with rifle fire; plumbing and electrical fittings and telephone receivers were ripped from walls; buses were shot up and abandoned; and stores were looted of everything down to the last bottle of aspirin or the last odd shoes.

Now Kampala is much more like a normal city – the electricity works, water comes out of the taps, buildings are being rehabilitated (notably the old Apollo Hotel which is now a spanking new Kampala Sheraton) and the shops and markets are once again well stocked. The major roads are in fairly good condition and matatus and taxis ply the streets regularly. Perhaps Uganda is also the flavour of the '90s with international aid agencies, as it seems every second vehicle in Kampala belongs to one of them.

It's quite safe to walk around Kampala at any time of the day or night. The people are friendly and there's quite a bit to see.

Orientation

The city is said to be built on seven hills, though it's more than likely you will spend most of your time on just one of them, Nakasero Hill, in the city centre. The top half of this hill is a type of garden city with wide, quiet avenues lined with flowering trees and large, detached houses behind imposing fences and hedges. Here you'll find many of the embassies, international aid organisations, top class hotels, rich people's houses, the High Court and government buildings. Between here and the lower part of the city is Kampala's main thoroughfare – Kampala Rd (which turns into Jinja Rd at one end and Bombo Rd at the other). On this road are the main banks, the post and telecommunications office, the railway station, the immigration office and a few hotels and restaurants.

Below Kampala Rd, towards the bottom of the valley, are heaps of different shops and small businesses, budget hotels and restaurants, the market, the immense *gurdwaras* (temples) of the very much depleted Sikh community (one has been converted into a school) and the bus and matatu stations. It's a completely different world to that on the top side of Kampala Rd. There are potholed, congested streets thronged with people, battered old cars and minibuses, overflowing garbage skips, impromptu street markets and pavement stalls offering everything from rubber stamps to radio repairs. There are hawkers, hustlers, newspaper sellers and one of the most mind-boggling and chaotic matatu stands you're ever likely to see. This is Nairobi's River Rd all over again.

Apart from Kololo which is a fairly exclusive residential area, the other hills of Kampala tend to be a mixture of the two extremes.

Information

Tourist Office The Ministry of Tourism & Wildlife (tel 32971) acts as a tourist office. It's on Obote Ave (Parliament Ave), PO Box 4241, opposite the British High Commission and the American Embassy. The staff are very friendly and helpful and do their best under trying circumstances. They usually sell an excellent large-scale street map of Kampala for US$0.25, but very little else. They may also have a free leaflet detailing the prices and current state of repair of national park lodges and hotels belonging to the Ugandan Hotels Corporation.

Post The GPO is on the corner of Kampala Rd and Speke Rd. It's open on weekdays and Saturday from 8 am to 5 pm, and on Sunday from 9 to 11 am.

The poste restante service is well organised and there's no charge for collecting letters. There's even a reasonable philatelic department.

It's also economical to post parcels from here. For example, a seven kg parcel sent airmail to Australia costs US$10.

Telephone The post office also houses the international telephone department and, because it's quite cheap to make an international call, you'll often see travellers here. The service is usually very efficient – expect five to 10 minutes wait for a call to the USA or Australia. Calls to Australia, the USA or UK cost US$5.10 for three minutes.

Money The Uganda Commercial Bank office on Kampala Rd next to the Nile Grill is open Monday to Friday from 8.30 am to 12.30 pm and 2 to 4 pm, and on Saturday and Sunday from 9 am till noon.

Foreign Embassies There are embassies or high commissions for Algeria, Burundi, France (Embassy House, King George VI Way – issues visas for Central African Republic, Chad, etc), Germany, India, Italy, Kenya, Nigeria, Rwanda, Somalia, Sudan, Tanzania, UK, USA and Zaïre.

Bookstores Excellent large-scale maps of Uganda (Series 1301, Sheet NA-36) with a lot more detail than any of the usual maps of East Africa (Michelin, Bartholomew's, etc) can sometimes be bought from the Uganda Bookshop on Colville St. If it has no stock the only other place to try is the Department of Lands & Surveys office in Entebbe.

For English-language publications the best place to try is the Uganda Bookshop.

Uganda Museum
The Uganda Museum on Kira Rd has been closed for renovations since 1985 but should be open now, although I wouldn't guarantee it. Before it closed the museum had good ethnological exhibits covering hunting, agriculture, war, religion and witchcraft, as well as archaeological and natural history displays. Perhaps its most interesting feature, however, is a collection of traditional musical instruments.

Kasubi Tombs
Another 'must see' are the Kasubi Tombs (also known as the Ssekabaka's Tombs) on Kasubi Hill just off Masiro Rd. Here you will find the huge traditional reed and bark cloth buildings of the kabakas (kings) of the Baganda people. The group of buildings contains the tombs of Muteesa I, his son Mwanga, Sir Daudi Chwa and his son Edward Muteesa II, the last of the kabakas. He died in London in 1969, three years after being deposed by Obote.

The kabaka's palace is also here, but is closed to the public.

The entry fee to the tombs is US$0.40 which includes a guide, although a tip is half expected. Remove your shoes before entering the main building. You can get to the tombs by minibus, either from the matatu park in the city centre (ask for Hoima Rd), or from the junction of Bombo and Makerere Hill roads. The minibuses you want are the ones which terminate at the market at the junction of Hoima and Masiro roads. The tombs are a few hundred metres walk up the hill from here (signposted).

Religious Buildings
Also worth a visit are the four main religious buildings in Kampala – the gleaming white Kibuli Mosque dominating Kibuli Hill on the other side of the railway station from Nakasero Hill; the huge Roman Catholic Rubaga Cathedral on Rubaga Hill; the Anglican Namirembe Cathedral where the congregation is called to worship by the beating of drums; and the enormous Sikh Temple in the city centre.

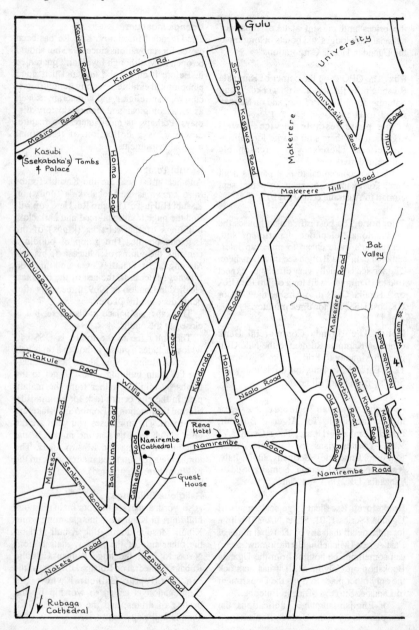

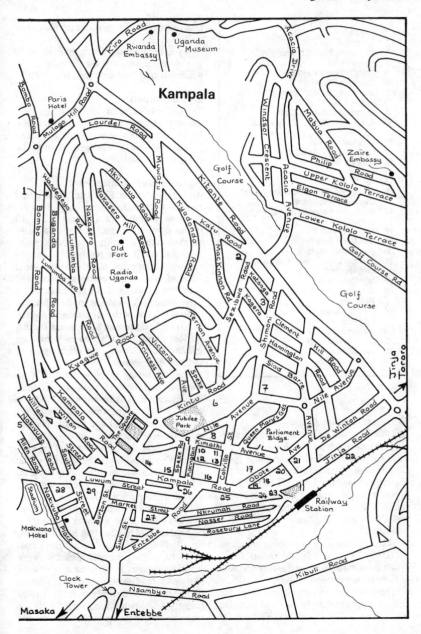

1	YMCA
2	Fairway Hotel
3	Tanzanian High Commission
4	Gloria Hotel
5	Splendid House Hotel
6	Kampala Sheraton
7	International Conference Centre
8	Speke Hotel
9	Standard Chartered Bank
10	Ethiopian Airlines, Air Tanzania, Aeroflot
11	Uganda Airlines
12	China Palace Restaurant
13	Uganda Bookshop
14	Grindlays Bank
15	GPO
16	Air France, British Airways, Kibimba Chinese Restaurant
17	American Embassy, British High Commission
18	Tourist Office
19	City Bar & Sports Club
20	Rwandan Embassy
21	French, Libyan, Sudanese and German Embassies
22	Immigration
23	City Springs Hotel, Iceland Restaurant
24	Tourist Hotel
25	Nile Grill
26	Barclays Bank
27	Nakasero Market
28	Bus Station
29	Matatu Station

Botanical Gardens & Zoo

Outside Kampala at Entebbe are the Botanical Gardens which are worth visiting if you have half a day available. Laid out in 1901, they're along the lake side between the Sailing Club and the centre of Entebbe. Even if you're not particularly interested in botany there are some interesting and unusual trees and shrubs and the grounds are fairly well maintained.

There's also a very depressing zoo close by (US$0.20 entry, US$0.40 camera fee) – worth avoiding in the hope that it might close if there are not enough visitors.

There are frequent minibuses from the central matatu park in Kampala to Entebbe. They cost US$0.40 and take about 25 minutes. Get off before you reach the end of the line.

If you need a meal, snack or drink while you're in the area try the Entebbe Club, which has cold beer and meals for US$1.

Entebbe Airport

There's little of great interest in Entebbe unless you have a yen to see the airport where Israeli commandos once stormed a hijacked jet and liberated the hostages, much to the chagrin of Idi Amin.

Places to Stay – bottom end

Accommodation in Kampala is not cheap and you get little for your money. Even the cheapest dumps/brothels cost US$3.40 (street rates) for a double that's basically uninhabitable. In other words, it's much more than you'd pay in Nairobi for a comparable place. It's not until you pay about US$5.40 that you get something decent, and even then it's nothing flash. Single rooms are very rare. Thank goodness for the YMCA.

So at this end of the price range the situation is fairly desperate. Most hotels are in a terrible state and it's obvious that the minimum time, money and effort has been spent on maintenance.

The one saving grace is the *YMCA* on Buganda Rd, about 15 minutes walk from the city centre. A floor mat costs US$0.70 and US$1.20 gets you a mattress, if there are any left. It's a popular and friendly place to stay, although somewhat inconvenient as you must pack up and be out by 8 am each day as it's used as a school on weekdays. The showers are erratic and the toilets could do with a good scrub, but it's really the only habitable cheap place in Kampala.

If you really want a hotel room, the best of a bad bunch is the *Splendid House Hotel* on Nakivubo Rd in a bustling part of the city. Small double rooms (no singles) cost US$3.40 and there are only bucket showers. It's just habitable. In the same league is the *Makwano Hotel* on Nakivubo Place near the bus station. Extremely scruffy rooms (mostly windowless) cost US$2.40/3 a single/double, there are bucket showers and the toilets are full of shit – only for the desperate.

Places to Stay – middle

Things improve rapidly if you are prepared to pay a bit more. The *Nakasero Hotel* opposite the Nakasero Market is convenient and the rooms are fairly clean and not too small. At US$3.20/4.70 a single/double with a common bath it's about the best value in this price range.

The *City Springs Hotel* next to the railway station is in an incredible state of disrepair, but still charges US$4.20 for double rooms. The bathrooms are filthy, with plumbing hanging out of the walls and blocked drains. The place is slowly being renovated so there may be some decent rooms by the time you get there. There is also a noisy disco on Saturday nights in the bar below the rooms.

Just a few minutes walk from the centre, the *Gloria Hotel* on William St is not bad value at US$5.40 for large clean doubles. It's on a quiet street and has its own bar and restaurant. Close by is the *Equatoria Hotel* which has certainly seen better days and looks closed most of the time. Shabby double rooms (no singles) with a balcony cost US$5.60 and the hotel has a bar.

The new *Rena Hotel* is on Namirembe Rd, a matatu ride from the centre, but is good value at US$4.80 for clean doubles with a common bath and US$6.40 with a private bath. Take a Namirembe matatu from the matatu park. Further out along the same street is the *Namirembe Guest House* opposite the Mengo Hospital. It's set in spacious grounds in a quiet suburb, and is good value at US$4 for a double, US$3.20 for a bed in a double and US$2.90 for a bed in a triple. Breakfast costs US$1 and dinner costs US$2.20. Take a Namirembe matatu and ask for Mengo Hospital.

Up the price scale a bit (and a quantum leap as far as quality goes) is the renovated *Tourist Hotel*, next to the City Springs Hotel on Kampala Rd. Large, clean rooms with a bath and hot water cost US$6.40/8 a single/double. A good breakfast of omelette, toast and tea costs US$0.70.

The *College Inn* on Bombo Rd past the YMCA has good clean rooms with a bath, toilet and hot water for US$6.70. It has a good restaurant.

Places to Stay – top end

All accommodation in this price bracket has to be paid for in hard currency, so forget it unless you're spending someone else's money. The *Speke Hotel*, one block up the hill from Kampala Rd, still bears the scars of the past and is fire damaged in one wing. It's not good value by any stretch of the imagination at US$54/66 a single/double. The *Fairway Hotel* on Kafu Rd near the golf course is owned by the Ugandan Hotels Corporation, costs much the same as the Speke and is much better value.

The old Apollo Hotel which dominated the city skyline has been completely renovated and is now the *Kampala Sheraton* (tel 244590), the city's only true five-star hotel. Rooms cost US$115/125 plus tax.

Places to Eat – cheap

If you're staying at the YMCA (as most travellers do) there are a couple of cheap local restaurants by the roundabout. There's also the *College Inn 2000* which has good meals of roast chicken or steak and chips for US$1.60. For really cheap local food, try the shed in the car park on De Winton Rd, on the right side going down. It's run by Disgoro, a disabled persons' enterprise. A meal will cost you less than a beer does in most places.

Below the City Springs Hotel on the railway station side is the small and very mellow *Iceland Restaurant*. It not only serves excellent huge meals at very reasonable prices, but has a good music selection and cold beers – recommended.

Places to Eat – more expensive

A popular meeting place in the city centre on Kampala Rd is the *Nile Grill*. It's not the cheapest place to go, but it is popular with expatriate aid workers and well-to-do locals. Outside there are tables with umbrellas. The food is expensive and not that great (chips for US$1.40) but if you're hanging out for a steak or roast chicken it's the place to head for. Many people come here for a coffee or a beer. It's open from 9 am to 9 pm daily, except Sunday when it closes at 4 pm. Between noon and 3 pm there's a minimum charge of US$1.40.

If you feel like lashing out, there are a few places worth trying. For Chinese food you can't beat the new *China Palace Restaurant*, poorly signposted on the 1st floor of the building on Pilkington St; you'll probably have to ask directions. Main dishes cost from US$1.60 to US$2.70, so expect to pay from US$3.40 to US$4 per person, plus drinks. It's open Tuesday to Sunday for lunch and dinner. Also highly rated by many people is the *Kibimba Chinese Restaurant* on Kampala Rd, up from and opposite the Nile Grill.

Another good splurge is the buffet breakfast at the *Kampala Sheraton*. It costs US$3.70 (payable in shillings) and is open from 7.30 to 10.30 am. There's a mind boggling array of food which you can dig into as often as you like, and the views of Kampala are excellent – not to be missed. For just a beer and a snack the *Lion Bar* in the grounds of the Sheraton is a good spot. There are tables inside and out and the prices are a lot more reasonable than you might expect.

The *Fairway Hotel* does an 'Afro' buffet for lunch on Sundays in its very pleasant dining room. There's a good spread of food and it's yours for US$4.70.

Entertainment

Nightlife in Kampala is much improved on what it was a few years ago. The *California Bar* puts on bands most evenings at 6 pm. The *Bat Valley Club* on Bombo Rd next to UNICEF and near the YMCA has live music on weekends. All-night dance clubs include *Club Clouds* on Nkrumah Rd, *Club Tropicana One-Ten* on Jinja Rd and *Ange Noire*, also on Jinja Rd. Entry to these places is about US$2 on weekends.

There are a few disco and 'day and night clubs' down in the area of the Nakasero Market, but they're basically pick-up joints. The *City Bar & Sports Club* on Kampala Rd opposite the Tourist Hotel has music some evenings and there are tables outside.

Getting There & Away

Bus Buses leave for Kasese daily at 7 am and go via Fort Portal. There is no advance booking, so be there an hour before and fight your way on, otherwise you could be standing the entire way. The trip takes eight hours to Kasese and costs US$4.30; to Fort Portal it's one hour less and costs US$3.50.

There are buses every morning to Kabale via Masaka and Mbarara. The entire trip takes 10 hours and costs US$4.70. Be there early to get your bum on a seat.

Matatu Tororo-Kampala by matatu costs US$2.70 and takes about 3½ hours. Jinja-Kampala costs US$1.10 and takes about one hour. By ordinary bus the fare is less but the journey takes over two hours.

To Busia by matatu takes about four hours and costs US$2. Entebbe-Kampala by matatu costs US$0.40 and takes 25 to 30 minutes. An ordinary taxi (which private cars suddenly turn into as soon as their drivers clap eyes on White people) costs US$1.40. Mbarara-Kampala by matatu costs US$6.70 and takes 4½ to five hours.

Train The train schedules from Kampala should be taken with a large pinch of salt. Delays and cancellations are the order of the day.

Trains to Tororo depart on Sundays, Tuesdays and Thursdays at 9 am, arriving at about 4 pm. The trains are economy class only. The fare is US$1 to Tororo and US$0.60 to Jinja. Few travellers take this train as the matatus are a lot quicker and more convenient.

To Kasese, the 1st and 2nd class service leaves Kampala on Mondays, Wednesdays and Fridays at 3 pm, arriving at 6 am (if you're lucky). An economy class service runs on Tuesdays and Thursdays, leaving Kampala at 7 pm. The fare is US$3.10 in 1st class, US$2.30 in 2nd class and US$1.60 in economy class. Sleeping berths should be booked at 8 am on the day before departure.

Ferry From Kampala's Port Bell there are ferries two or three times a week to the Sese Islands.

Getting Around
The international airport is at Entebbe, 35 km from Kampala. It has a duty-free shop, restaurant, bank, post office and a hotel/car hire reservations office. There are public matatus between Kampala and Entebbe but only a taxi service for the last three km between the airport and Entebbe centre.

Around the Country

South-Eastern Uganda

TORORO

At the eastern railhead of Uganda, just over the border from Kenya, is Tororo. It must have looked particularly beautiful once, with its flowering trees. It also must have had a substantial Asian community, as the two large Hindu temples suggest. One has been taken over by the Muslim community for use as an educational centre!

Now there is little of interest in this somewhat derelict town. Its only redeeming feature is the intriguing, forest-covered volcanic plug that rises up abruptly from an otherwise flat plain at the back of the town.

The views from the top are well worth the climb.

Information

It's difficult to change money in Tororo after banking hours, even if you have cash. This is one place where you will have to look for moneychangers rather than the other way around.

Places to Stay & Eat

The only cheap place worth considering is the *Tororo Christian Guest House*, diagonally opposite the Total petrol station on Mbale Rd. It's clean enough and the people who run it are very friendly. It costs US$4 for a single room which will sleep three

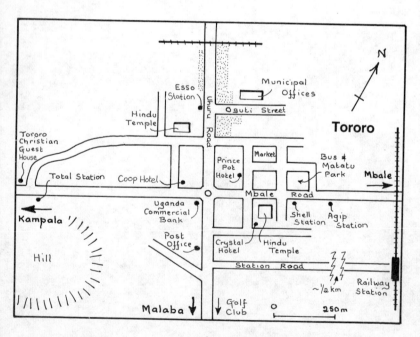

people at a push. There are no showers, the toilets are filthy and you'll have to get your meals in town.

The next best place is the *Crystal Hotel* which has clean rooms with a bath for US$6. It also has a restaurant. The clean and friendly *Coop Hotel* charges US$2.40 a double and has bucket showers. The *Prince Pot Hotel* is just one of a few grubby hotels and costs US$2.40 a double.

For somewhere to eat try the *New Safari Hotel* on the corner of Mbale and Uhuru roads.

Getting There & Away
Matatu A matatu to Kampala costs US$2.70 and takes about 3½ hours. To Malaba on the Kenyan border, it's a short ride costing US$0.30.

Train Tororo is a train junction for trains north and west, although with the northern service still suspended and the service west to Kampala being slow and infrequent, most travellers in this area use matatus.

Trains depart from Tororo to Kampala on Mondays, Wednesdays and Fridays. The fare is US$1 to Kampala, US$0.60 to Jinja and the complete journey takes about 9½ hours.

Another line runs north-west to Pakwach via Mbale and Gulu. If the service is ever restored there should be a daily train in either direction.

JINJA
Jinja lies on the shores of Lake Victoria and is a major marketing centre for southern Uganda. It's an interesting little place with almost a ghost town feel to it even now, years after the sizeable Asian community was forced to leave. The town didn't suffer as badly as many others during the last civil war so it doesn't wear the same air of dereliction. According to local residents, Okello's retreating troops were told in no uncertain terms that they wouldn't be welcome.

Jinja is close to what used to be the Owen Falls, where the Victoria Nile leaves the lake. Now there is a hydroelectric station which supplies Uganda with the bulk of its electric-

ity. There are good views over Lake Victoria and the Saturday market is extremely lively.

Owen Falls Dam
At the source of the Victoria Nile, this dam is worth visiting. The actual falls have disappeared under the lake which has been created. Photography is prohibited. It's several km west of the town towards Kampala on a main road which crosses the top of the dam. The best way to get there is to catch one of the bicycle taxis which hang around outside the market.

Jinja Sailing Club
Although it seems that many years have gone by since any sailing took place, the Sailing Club is well maintained and has green lawns which run to the edge of the lake. The shade bandas give welcome relief from the sun, and cold beer and soft drinks are sold, as are basic meals. On Friday and Saturday nights it's the town's focal point when the disco starts up.

The club is 200 metres past the port. Walk (about 20 minutes) or take a bicycle taxi (US$0.20).

Places to Stay
The *Victoria View Hotel* has a name which might be wishful thinking, but it is clean and very pleasant and costs US$3.40 a double with a bathroom (there are no singles). Clean sheets, a towel and table are provided. The door locks are purely cosmetic but the place seems safe enough. The hotel is on Kutch Rd and it has a restaurant.

A few doors along is the *Fairway Guest House* which is cheaper at US$2/2.70 a single/double in rooms with a common bath. It's perfectly adequate although a bit noisy during the day.

More expensive, but reasonable value, is the *Belle View Hotel* on Kutch Rd. It's nothing special but is comfortable and charges US$4.70/6 a single/double with a bath and breakfast. The hotel also has a good restaurant, bar and TV lounge.

At the top end is the *Sunset Hotel* which overlooks the river, the railway bridge and the Owen Falls Barrage. Self-contained

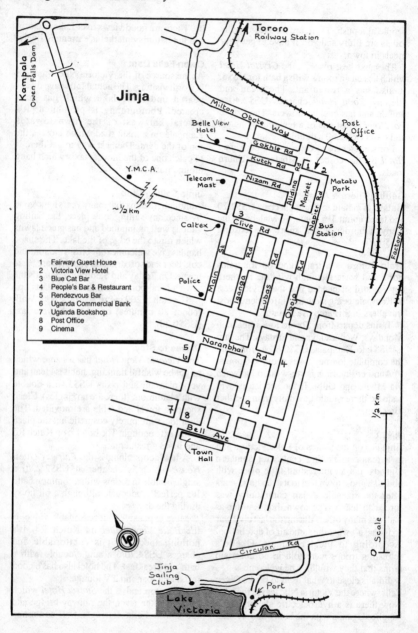

Jinja

Kampala
Owen Falls Dam

Tororo
Railway Station

Milton Obote Way

Belle View
Hotel

Gokhle Rd

Kutch Rd

Post
Office

Y.M.C.A.

Telecom
Mast

Nizam Rd

Aldina Rd

Market

Napier Rd

Matatu
Park

~½ km

Caltex

Clive Rd

Bus
Station

Factory St

Police

Main St

Ganga Rd

Lubas Rd

Obote Rd

1 Fairway Guest House
2 Victoria View Hotel
3 Blue Cat Bar
4 People's Bar & Restaurant
5 Rendezvous Bar
6 Uganda Commercial Bank
7 Uganda Bookshop
8 Post Office
9 Cinema

Naranbhai Rd

Bell Ave

Town
Hall

½ km

Scale

0

Circular Rd

Jinja Sailing
Club

Port

Lake
Victoria

rooms with breakfast cost US$12. Even if you can't afford to stay it's worth having a drink in the gardens.

The *Ripon Falls Hotel*, overlooking the harbour, is a splendid colonial relic which is in an advanced state of decay.

Places to Eat

For a cheap local meal of beans, rice and vegetables (US$0.20) go to the market opposite the Victoria View Hotel. It closes at 9.30 pm.

The best eatery in town is the restaurant in the *Belle View Hotel*. A Spanish omelette with chips and salad costs US$1.20, while goat, chips and salad costs US$1.80. The beers are cold too. The *Victoria View Hotel* serves basic meals for lunch and omelettes and bread for breakfast.

Getting There & Away

Bus & Matatu From Kampala to Jinja by matatu costs US$1.10 and takes about one hour on a very good road. By ordinary bus the fare is marginally less but the journey takes more than two hours.

There is supposedly a direct bus (Peoples Bus Company) daily to Busia, departing at 8 am, but it's unreliable. A better bet is a matatu to Busia (US$2) or a bus from Jinja to Iganga (US$0.60, two hours) and then a taxi to Busia (US$1.10, two hours).

Train Jinja is on the Tororo-Kampala main railway line. A train runs in each direction three times a week. (See the Tororo or Kampala Getting There & Away sections.) The railway station is about one km out of town on the Tororo road; US$0.15 by bicycle taxi.

Ferry Ugandan Railways ferries operate to Mwanza in Tanzania but unfortunately don't take passengers. To get a ride you need clearance from the chief traffic manager at Kampala Railway Station. Permission is not generally granted to travellers. You may want to try your luck with staff at the dock in Jinja. If you get on, you'll have to clear

immigration at the district administration office in the town hall.

Western Uganda

FORT PORTAL

Fort Portal is a small, pleasant and quiet town at the northern end of the Ruwenzori Mountains. Some travellers choose it as a base from which to organise a trek in the mountains, but it's not as convenient as Kasese as it's much further from the starting point at Ibanda. Most people come through here either because they're en route to Gulu and the Kabalega National Park or because they want to visit the hot springs and pygmy tribes on the way to Bundibugyo on the other side of the Ruwenzori.

Places to Stay

The best of the budget hotels and a popular spot with travellers is the *Wooden Horse Hotel* in Lugard Rd. It has single rooms for US$3.20 and a double with a bath for US$4. There's a bar and a reasonable restaurant.

A good, popular second choice is the *Hot Spring Lodge* above a hair salon on Ruwdi Rd. It charges US$1.15/1.80 a single/double. If this is full and you want another cheap place to stay, try the *Kyaka Lodge* on quiet Kuhadika Rd. It's scruffy but costs only US$1.10/2 a single/double.

Lastly, for budget travellers, there is the *Mwenge Lodge* between Babitha and Kahinju roads where the matatus arrive and depart. It has tiny singles for US$1.60 and better value doubles for US$2. It's poor value considering what you can get for your money in this part of Uganda and that the hotel is pretty scruffy.

If you have in mind more commodious accommodation and services, go to the *Mountains of the Moon Hotel*, part of the Ugandan Hotels Corporation chain. You must pay in hard currency so it works out to be very expensive at US$60 for a double.

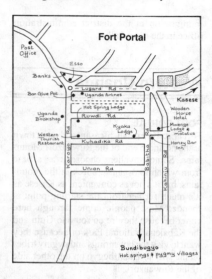

Fort Portal

Places to Eat
There's good, cheap food at the *Wooden Horse Hotel*. For a change, try the *Western Tourist Restaurant* on Kuhadika Rd.

Two good bars are the *Bar Glue Pot* on Karoye Rd and the *Honey Bar Inn* on Babitha Rd.

Getting There & Away
A matatu from Kasese costs US$0.80 and takes about an hour. Going south, there is a daily morning bus (except Sunday) to Kabale, via Kasese and Mbarara. You can also do this journey by matatu, but there isn't a lot of room for backpacks. Each morning there is the bus from Kasese on its way to Kampala. The bus from Kampala to Kasese passes through Fort Portal in mid-afternoon.

AROUND FORT PORTAL
Semliki Valley
While there's little to see in Fort Portal, it's definitely worth organising a day trip (at least) to Bundibugyo in the Semliki Valley on the other side of the Ruwenzori. Get a small group together and hire a matatu, because the ordinary matatus which simply transport passengers between the two towns often won't stop along the way to allow time to explore. Agree on what the driver is going to do and where he will take you before setting off.

The two main attractions are the hot springs near Sempaya and the pygmy tribes near the village of Ntandi in the forest of the Semliki Valley, a few km before Bundibugyo. In any case, the drive there is worthwhile, just for the magnificent views over the rainforest and savannah and into Zaïre. Unfortunately these pygmy tribes have gone the way of those in eastern Zaïre and are now horribly commercialised. They have become something of a sideshow, standing by the side of the road calling for you to stop and visit their village (for a price), while the younger ones ask for pens, etc. Opium smoking has become a real problem among men.

Places to Stay
A Ugandan called Morence offers accommodation to travellers to help raise money for the orphans he looks after. Accommodation space is strictly limited so it's best to write or phone in advance. The place is also difficult to find – it's about 15 km past Fort Portal on the road to Bundibugyo, just past Kihondo village. Matatus are few and far between, as is other traffic for hitching. The address is Kichwamba (tel 2245), Nyaukuku Resting Place, PO Box 317, Fort Portal.

In Ntandi village there's a man called John at the trading centre (ask in town) who will let you sleep on his floor, or you can pitch a tent in front of his hut.

North-Western Uganda

GULU
Gulu is the largest Ugandan town in the north of the country and is on the railway line between Tororo and Pakwach. It's a starting point for a visit to Paraa on the Victoria Nile, which runs through the spectacular Kabalega National Park. Thirty km north of Gulu at Patiko is Baker's Fort which was built by the

British in the 1870s as a base from which to suppress the slave trade.

This area hasn't seen tourists for years because of the threat of rebel activity, but is now reportedly safe for travelling. To be extra safe, check with an embassy in Kampala before setting off.

Places to Stay & Eat

A good, cheap place and also excellent value is the *Church of Uganda Guest House*. Other places recommended are the *New Gulu Restaurant* in Pakwach Rd and the *Luxxor Lodge* opposite the truck park.

The top hotel is the *Acholi Inn*, part of the Ugandan Hotels Corporation, so you must pay in hard currency.

Getting There & Away

Buses and trucks go between Kampala and Gulu. Gulu is on the railway line between Tororo and Pakwach. Other main towns on the route include Mbale, Soroti and Lira, but there are no passenger trains along the route.

South-Western Uganda

KASESE

Kasese is at the western railhead of Uganda and is the base from which to organise a trip up the Ruwenzori Mountains or to the Ruwenzori National Park (Queen Elizabeth II National Park). It's a small, quiet town but was once important to the economy because of the nearby copper mines at Kilembe (copper was Uganda's third most important export during the 1970s), although these are now closed.

Like Kabale, Kasese has been controlled by the NRA for several years and was spared the looting and destruction which befell other Ugandan towns further east.

At the time of writing, all foreigners arriving in Kasese had to check in with the local police. The police, however, are friendly and the procedure is simple and straightforward. Currency declaration forms are checked but there's no hassle as long as you have changed

some money officially. Some of the cheaper hotels will not allow you to stay unless you have a letter of clearance from the police.

The town is infested with mosquitoes so make sure you have some coils or a net at night.

Things to See

Kasese has no attractions, but if you have half a day to kill, hire a bicycle and cycle the 13 km up to Kilembe for an interesting diversion. It is a long gradual uphill climb, which makes for hard work on the way there but is great fun on the way back! The manager of the Saad Hotel can arrange bicycle hire at the rate of US$0.30 per hour.

If you're organising a trek to the Ruwenzori, enquire at the Saad Hotel as there are a couple of guys who can help with guides, porters, etc.

Places to Stay

By far the best place to stay is the *Saad Hotel* (tel 157/9) on Ruwenzori Rd. The staff are very friendly and the rooms are pleasant and spotlessly clean. It only has double rooms (with two single beds) which have a shower and toilet and cost US$4. Three people can share a room. It's very popular with travellers. The manager is very friendly and can help with bicycle hire and other information.

The *Ataco Holiday Inn* on Stanley St provides basic but adequate lodgings. The rooms are set around a yard and there are communal showers. The charge is US$1.60/2 a single/double, and it's acceptable to have three in a room. There's a bar which is not a bad place for a (warm) beer.

The *Highway Bar & Lodge* is 100 metres along the same street and is similar, although it won't allow foreigners to stay unless you have written proof that you've registered with the police, which is a nuisance.

Slightly cheaper, but not as good, are the *Paradise Bar & Lodging* and the *Ruwenzori Guest House* on Speke St near the market. Both are pretty basic and charge about US$2.40 a double with common facilities. On the same street is the *Kaghasera Hotel*

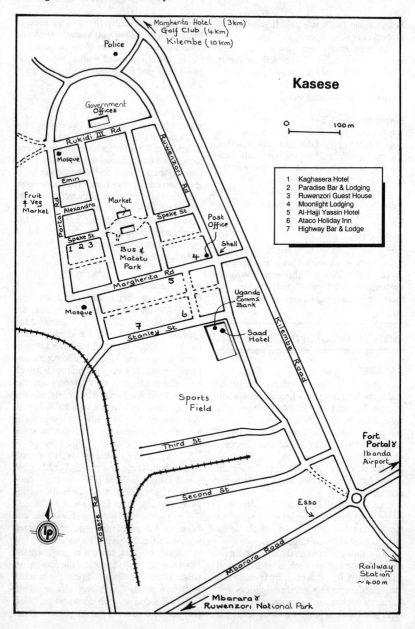

Kasese

0   100m

1 Kaghasera Hotel
2 Paradise Bar & Lodging
3 Ruwenzori Guest House
4 Moonlight Lodging
5 Al-Hajji Yassin Hotel
6 Ataco Holiday Inn
7 Highway Bar & Lodge

Margherita Hotel (3km)
Golf Club (4km)
Kilembe (10km)

Police

Government Offices

Rukidi III Rd

Mosque

Emin

Portal Rd

Alexandra

Fruit & Veg Market

Market

Speke St

Speke St

Ruwenzori Rd

Post Office

Shell

1 2 3

Bus & Matatu Park

Margherita Rd

5

Mosque

6

Uganda Comms Bank

7   Stanley St

Saad Hotel

Kilembe Road

Sports Field

Third St

Kogete Rd

Second St

Esso

Fort Portal & Ibanda Airport

Railway Station ~400m

Mbarara Road

Mbarara & Ruwenzori National Park

which has big double rooms with a bath for US$2.40.

At the top end is the *Margherita Hotel*, three km out of town on the road up to Kilembe. It's part of the Ugandan Hotels Corporation and payment (US$40 a double) is expected in hard currency. The setting is certainly beautiful – looking out towards the Ruwenzori on one side and the golf course on the other and surrounded by flowering trees – but it's hardly value for money. It's also a long way to walk with a backpack.

Places to Eat

There are several inexpensive restaurants around the matatu park and market where you can get traditional staples like meat stews, matoke, beans and rice. On Margherita Rd the *Al-Hajji Yassin Hotel* is a shop and restaurant run by a friendly Yemeni family, offering good meals and friendly service. It's open late at night.

Otherwise the meals at the *Saad Hotel* are hard to beat – tilapia (fish) with chips and salad for US$0.70 and dishes in the US$0.40 to US$0.70 range. Breakfast is equally good value.

Getting There & Away

Bus Daily buses between Kampala and Kasese in either direction cost US$4.30 and take about eight hours. From Kasese the bus leaves at 6 am, so be there early to ensure that you get a seat.

From Monday to Saturday there is a bus in either direction between Fort Portal and Kabale via Kasese and Mbarara. Going south it leaves Kasese at about 9 am, takes about 9½ hours and costs US$3.80 (US$2.40 to Mbarara, US$2.70 Mbarara to Kabale). The last part of the journey south crosses a mountain pass from which, weather permitting, you'll be rewarded with spectacular views to the west of the volcanoes along the Uganda-Rwanda border.

Matatu Matatus between Kasese and Fort Portal cost US$0.80 and take about one hour. There's one matatu daily to the Ruwenzori National Park. It leaves at about 10 am and

goes to Katwe, but will drop you at the park gate (US$0.80), from where it's an eight km walk or an easy hitch. To hire a matatu to the gate costs US$9.40. To do a day trip to the park from Kasese, hire a matatu for a 'special ride' which costs US$16 return. In a group, it's a good way to see the park.

Train There are economy class trains to Kampala on Wednesdays and Fridays for US$1.60, although these are very crowded and you need to watch over your gear at night. There is a 1st and 2nd class train to Kampala on Tuesdays, Thursdays and Saturdays at 4 pm, provided of course that it arrives on time on the outward journey from Kampala on the morning of that day. The fare is US$3.10 in 1st class and US$2.30 in 2nd class. Tickets should be booked the day before departure.

MASAKA

In 1979 Masaka was virtually destroyed by the Tanzanian army in the closing stages of the war which ousted Idi Amin. A lot of rebuilding has taken place, but a lot more is required. There's very little to do in Masaka and for most travellers it's just a way station, but it's from here that you can visit the Ssese Islands in Lake Victoria.

Places to Stay & Eat

Most lodges are on the main street. A good place to stay is the *Masaka Safari Lodge* about three minutes walk from the bus station. It's very clean and cheap.

About 20 km east of Masaka is Lake Nabugabo where you can stay at the *Church of Uganda Holiday & Conference Centre* which has bandas for hire. The proprietors are very pleasant and there's also a beautiful camp site.

THE SSESE ISLANDS

This group of 84 islands lies off the north-western shores of Lake Victoria, east of Masaka and south of Entebbe. Masaka is the departure point to visit them.

Although rarely visited by travellers, the islands offer an interesting and refreshingly

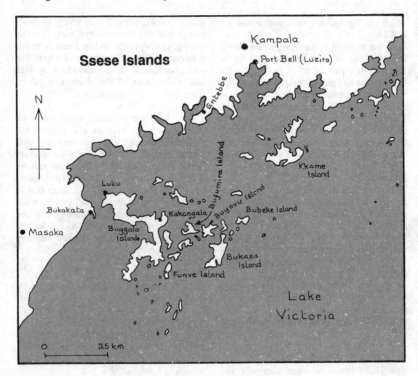

different facet of Uganda which is worth exploring. Unlike the mainland, these islands escaped the ravages of the civil wars and so remain largely unspoiled. The people, known as the Basese, form a distinct tribal group with their own language, culture and folklore. As so few foreigners visit the islands, you're assured of a warm welcome.

Most islanders are members of one or other of the various Christian sects. A minority are Muslims. Communities are tightly knit and there are no dangers associated with wandering around the islands on foot. In fact, this is the best way to see them.

Most Basese are fishers and farmers of coffee, sweet potato, cassava, yams and bananas. As you might expect, fish forms a major part of their diet.

The main islands of Buggala, Bufumira, Bukasa, Bubeke and Kkome are hilly and, where not cultivated, are forested with a wide variety of trees. Animals you're likely to come across include various species of monkey, hippos, crocodiles and many different types of bird but there are no large predators (other than crocodiles).

Many spots afford beautiful views over the lake and across to the other islands. You'll have no problems persuading the fishers to take you out on their boats. Swimming is also possible off most of the islands as long as you observe the usual precaution about avoiding reedy areas (where the snails which carry the bilharzia parasite live).

All up, you're looking at a very mellow and peaceful time on these islands. There is a plentiful variety of food and most of the time there is not another tourist in sight. Spend sufficient time here and you'll end up with many good friends.

Places to Stay & Eat

Most of the accommodation on the islands will be in private houses and this is also where you'll eat. Simply ask around in any town or village and you'll quickly find somewhere to stay. There are no standard charges. Indeed most people will probably offer you free accommodation and meals. If that's the case, remember the rules of hospitality and be generous in what you give.

Other than accommodation in private houses, there are several lodges and guest houses in the main towns. There's a guest house on Bukasa Island established by a former elder, J Lutaya Kaganda. On Buggala Island is the *Malaanga Ssese Safari Lodge* (tel Kalangala 26), PO Box 1165, in Kalangala town. It's owned by Mr P T Andronico Ssemakula, a school teacher who speaks fluent English. His lodge is approved by the Ministry of Tourism & Wildlife. It supplies bedding, all meals and drinks. There's a TV, a library and bicycles for hire.

There's another small lodge at Luku on Buggala Island owned by Mr Kalwangi. Also enquire at the missions in Kalangula.

Getting There & Away

Two ferries go to the islands from the mainland departure points of Bukakata (east of Masaka) and Port Bell (in the Luzira area of Kampala).

From the mainland, the ferry from Bukakata goes to Luku on Buggala Island daily at 5 pm and in the opposite direction at 8.30 am. There are also smaller taxi-boats every hour or so between the two ports.

From Port Bell there's a steamer to Kkome, Bubeke, Bukasa, Bufumira and Buggala islands on Tuesdays, Thursdays and Saturdays at 8.30 am.

A third way of getting to the islands is by motorised native boats from Kasenyi, a fishing village on the Entebbe Peninsula. These go every day to the main islands, though there's no regular schedule – they leave when there are sufficient passengers or cargo.

Getting Around

It's fairly easy to find local paddle or motorised boats between the islands. Simply ask around in the fishing villages or towns. Rates are negotiable. Otherwise, use the Port Bell steamer connections.

A UTC bus and matatus connect the main towns on Buggala Island, the largest of the group.

MBARARA

There's little of interest in Mbarara and there was a lot of destruction during the war, but you may find yourself staying there overnight if you're coming from or going to Kampala.

Places to Stay

Perhaps the best place to stay, and certainly one of the cheapest, is the *Church of Uganda Hostel*, which many travellers have recommended. Next to the bus station and near the market, it has dormitory beds for US$1.

If you're after more comfort, try the *New Ankole Hotel* on the main road past the police station. It has doubles with a bathroom and hot water (usually) but is not all that cheap. The hotel is set in beautiful grounds and has a good restaurant.

Getting There & Away

There are frequent matatus to and from Kampala and the journey takes 4½ to five hours. Mbarara is also on the routes from Kampala to Kabale and from Kasese to Kabale, so see the respective Getting There & Away sections.

There are matatus to Kabale and it's a fairly easy road to hitch along.

KABALE

Kabale is in the Kigeza area, which tourist brochures often and inappropriately refer to as the 'Little Switzerland of Africa'.

This south-western corner of Uganda is certainly very beautiful with its intensively cultivated and terraced hills, forests and lakes, but it reminded me much more of the hill stations of West Bengal in India. It doesn't offer breathtaking views of an endless range of massive, snow capped mountains like in Darjeeling, but there are equally impressive views of the Virunga chain of volcanoes from the summits of various passes (such as the one just before you drop down into Kabale on the road from Mbarara, and from the Kanaba Gap, 60 km from Kabale on the road to Kisoro). There are also tea-growing estates all the way from Kabale to the Rwandan border at Gatuna.

Kigeza is superb hiking country and the area is honeycombed with tracks and paths, hamlets and farms. A visit to Lake Bunyonyi is particularly recommended.

Kabale is Uganda's highest town (about 2000 metres) and it turns cool at night, so have warm clothes handy. Unlike many Ugandan towns further east, Kabale has been controlled by the NRA for a long time so it's in better shape than towns which were controlled by Obote's or Okello's troops.

Information

For information on visiting the gorillas in the Impenetrable Forest near Kisoro, head up the hill to the wildlife office opposite the White Horse Inn. As of mid-1990 the area was closed to tourists, but this may have changed.

Things to See

Go walking down any of the tracks in this area and let them take you where they will. There are always good views over the surrounding countryside and local people are very friendly and keen to talk with you.

Perhaps the best trip is to Lake Bunyonyi, a famous beauty spot over the ridge to the west of Kabale. It's a large and irregularly shaped lake with many islands, and the surrounding hillsides, as elsewhere in this region, are intensively cultivated. Many of the villagers have boats and you shouldn't have any difficulty arranging a trip onto the lake.

There are two ways of getting to the lake. Either walk all the way up and over the ridge from Kabale by picking your way through the tracks on the hillside (about three hours if you pick the right tracks) or hitch a ride on the road to Kisoro and get off where the road touches the lake (about halfway). It isn't always easy to hitch to Kisoro but there are reasonably frequent matatus going there as well as a daily UTC bus at 8 am.

Places to Stay – bottom end

If you are camping there is a free site close to the White Horse Inn but there are no facilities. In fact it's just a field of long grass and, as there's no fence, security may be suspect.

The cheapest place to stay is *St Paul's Training Centre & Hostel* where single/double rooms cost US$0.70/1.40. Basic meals of matoke and beans are available for US$0.40.

Of the hotels, the cheapest is the *Paradise Hotel* but it's pretty basic. For US$1.10 you get a single cell with common facilities.

A much better bet is the *Capital Motel* which charges US$1.40/2 a single/double for large rooms. Facilities are shared and hot water is available by the bucket for US$0.15. The entrance is around the back through the car park.

Better still is the *Victoria Inn* which is one of the best value-for-money places in the country. Immaculate rooms with a bath and toilet cost US$2.70/3.40 a single/double. A towel and soap are provided and hot water is available on request. The hotel also has a very pleasant bar and lounge.

Places to Stay – middle

The only mid-range place is the *Highlands Hotel* where single rooms cost US$2.70, or US$4 with a bath and toilet. Hot water is provided by the bucket. It's not a bad place and you can make international phone calls if necessary.

Places to Stay – top end

Kabale's best hotel is the *White Horse Inn* up on the hill overlooking the town. It's part of the Ugandan Hotels Corporation chain so you have to pay in hard currency (US$30 for a double, no singles). It's perhaps one of the most attractive of the hotels belonging to this chain but it's obviously not for the impecunious. The hotel has a bar and restaurant.

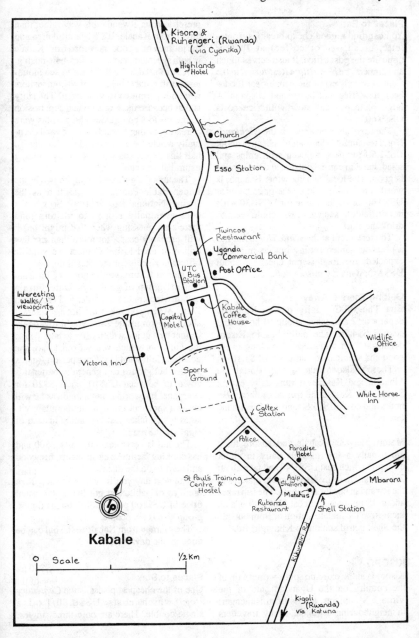

Kisoro &
Ruhengeri (Rwanda)
(via Cyanika)

Highlands
Hotel

Church

Esso Station

Twincos
Restaurant

Uganda
Commercial Bank

UTC
Bus
Station

Post Office

Kabale
Coffee
House

Interesting
Walks/
viewpoints

Capital
Motel

Victoria Inn

Sports
Ground

Wildlife
Office

White Horse
Inn

Caltex
Station

Police

Paradise
Hotel

Mbarara

St Paul's Training
Centre &
Hostel

Agip
Station

Matatus

Rubanza
Restaurant

Shell Station

Kikungiri Rd

Kabale

0   Scale   1/2 Km

Kigali
(Rwanda)
via Katuna

Places to Eat

You can find a good cheap breakfast (omelette, bread, tea or coffee) at *Twincos* opposite the post office. It also serves lunch and dinner. The *New Hilton Restaurant* in the Capital Motel serves the usual local food – beef stew, rice and beans and chapatis. A large plate of beef stew with rice costs US$0.60.

The best value, however, is the *Highlands Hotel* restaurant. Meals aren't cheap at about US$1.50 for roast chicken with chips and salad, but you can eat outside and the service is good. The local banana wine, Banapo, is worth a try and is sold by the glass here for US$0.40, or by the bottle for US$1.30 – it's not difficult to see why few people seem to drink the stuff.

The restaurant at the *White Horse Inn* has a pleasant garden setting but, as might be expected, the food is not cheap at about US$2 for a main course.

Getting There & Away

Bus The UTC's daily bus to Kampala departs at 7 am, takes about 10 hours and costs US$4.70. The daily bus to Kisoro departs at 8 am, takes 2½ hours along a very good and scenic road and costs US$1.10.

There's also a bus to Fort Portal via Mbarara and Kasese. It runs daily except Sunday. To Kasese the trip takes about 9½ hours and costs US$3.80 and to Mbarara the fare is US$2.70.

Matatu Between Kabale and Kisoro there are usually a few matatus daily in either direction which cost US$1.40 and take about 2½ hours. There are also frequent matatus to the Rwandan border at Gatuna. The trip takes about 45 minutes and cost US$0.40. Catch them from the matatu station or from outside the Shell petrol station on Kikungiri Rd.

KISORO

Kisoro is at the extreme south-western tip of the country on the Ugandan side of the Virunga Mountains, across from Ruhengeri in neighbouring Rwanda. Many travellers prefer to enter Rwanda this way rather than direct from Kabale. It's a beautiful area and the journey on a good, new road from Kabale is both spectacular and, at times, hair-raising.

Kisoro used to be the place to see mountain gorillas but at the time of writing visitors were not permitted to visit them. The story is that because there was no real supervision of the visitors and guides, the gorillas were retreating further towards Rwanda and eventually would have left Uganda altogether. To halt this retreat and to survey the gorillas, a naturalist was called in.

The area the gorillas live in, known as the Impenetrable Forest, was gazetted as the Bwindi National Park in 1989. So when it does eventually reopen to visitors (and there's no guessing when that might be) it will probably cost a lot more than the few dollars it used to be. Contact the wildlife officer in Kabale for the latest info.

Once in Kisoro, you're not very far from the first group of gorillas in Zaïre. Take a matatu nine km to the border and cross into Zaïre. When you reach the hotel/restaurant about one km inside Zaïre you'll invariably be met by a guide who'll offer to take you to the hut from which you set out to see the gorillas. He'll want US$5 per person for this service but groups can generally barter this down to between US$10 and US$20 for everyone. It's worth using a guide as he will know a short cut through the mountain villages which takes just two hours instead of eight via the road.

The hut is very pleasant, costs Z500 and has cooking facilities, clean sheets, firewood and staff to do the dishes.

The next day you'll be taken to see three families of habituated gorillas at the usual price of US$100 per person. The maximum group size is six people.

The journey from Kabale to the hut can be done in one day.

Places to Stay

One of the cheapest places is the *Centenary Hotel* which costs US$0.80/1.60 a single/double. There are only three singles.

It's popular with budget travellers although the toilets and showers are a bit on the nose.

The *Mubano Hotel* is much better value. A double room with an immaculately clean bathroom costs US$2 (no singles). There are even VIP rooms for US$3.40.

Top of the range in Kisoro is the *Travellers' Rest*. Although part of the Ugandan Hotels Corporation, payment in local currency is permitted, so it's not bad value at US$2.20/2.90 a single/double.

Places to Eat

The *Mubano Hotel* has a restaurant and serves excellent food – about US$0.70 for lunch or dinner. Breakfast is also good.

The *Happy Cafe* by the bus stop does good potatoes, cabbage and beans for US$0.35.

Getting There & Away

Between Kabale and Kisoro there are usually a few matatus (US$1.40) and at least one bus daily in either direction. See the Kabale Getting There & Away section.

To reach the Zaïre and Rwanda borders, the best days for finding a lift are Monday and Thursday as these are market days in Kisoro. Lifts to the Zaïre border are easy to find and cost about US$0.60. Less traffic uses the road to Cyanika (Rwanda border). You may have to wait a while or hire a taxi for US$4.

National Parks & Ruwenzori Mountains

KABALEGA NATIONAL PARK

This park covers 3900 sq km, through which the Victoria Nile flows on its way to Lake Mobutu Sese Seko (formerly Lake Albert).

Kabalega National Park used to contain some of the largest concentrations of game in Uganda. Unfortunately, poachers and the retreating troops of Idi Amin and then of Okello, both armed with automatic weapons, wiped out practically all game except the more numerous (or less sought after) herd species. There are now no lions, only a few rhinos and a 20-head herd of elephants. There are still plenty of Ugandan kobs, buffaloes, hippos and crocodiles. The game is recovering slowly from the onslaught but it will be a long time before it returns to its former numbers – if ever.

Despite this it's still worth visiting Kabalega if only for the animals which are left and for the Murchison and Karuma falls on the Victoria Nile within the park boundaries. The falls were once described as the most spectacular thing to happen to the Nile along its 6700 km length.

The Nile bisects the park and is safe for travel south of the river. Also safe is the three hour launch trip upriver to a point where you can opt to walk for a couple of hours to the falls. En route you see crocodiles and hippos, thousands of birds and usually elephants. The only drawback is the price (US$19, payable in shillings), but this is a popular place among aid workers and diplomatic staff so it shouldn't be too difficult to hitch a ride, especially on weekends. Try asking in Paraa, where there is a radio and it is generally know, in advance if someone is coming.

Game drives north of the Nile are more problematic. There is a real (although slight) risk of ambush. However, the road through the park is an important supply route to southern Sudan, so if conflict continues so do the daily convoys with military escort. A lift on one of these through the park is your best bet. There's not much game left after the

years of slaughter but you should see giraffe, oribi, kob and kongoni.

Packwach is the town at the northern end of the park. Either lodge there or return to Paraa – there is plenty of traffic in either direction.

This area of the country gets quite hot. The best remedy is a dip in the Nile at Paraa. Bilharzia is a possibility but the fast-flowing river and the absence of settlements upstream reduce the likelihood considerably. You're far more likely to get chewed up by a hippo, so inspect the bathing site carefully before plunging in. You will inevitably attract a huge crowd of curious locals who will probably laugh at you. If you're at all shy or self-conscious this may be more of a deterrent than the bilharzia. They will also warn of people-eating crocodiles, but the last incident occurred more than 20 years ago and the poor creatures have been so heavily poached that they steer clear of human habitation.

Places to Stay

Paraa has a very primitive *camp site* with earth toilets and very little else – you'll need a tent and there's plenty of water in the Nile. The Paraa Lodge across the river has been bombed, burnt and looted. While you can't stay there, it's worth taking the ferry across the river to wander around the ruins.

Food supplies (and beer) are available in Paraa but it's cheaper to bring them from Masindi.

Getting There & Away

Getting to the park is fairly easy. From Kampala, a bitumen road carries plenty of buses all the way to Masindi, where there are lodges. From Masindi, it's not difficult to get a lift along the very scenic (but tsetse fly infested) road to Paraa.

Top: Cattle on the Masaka-Mbarara road, Uganda (PP)
Bottom: Fort Portal, Uganda (GE)

Top: Volcanoes, Zaïre-Rwanda border (GC)
Bottom: Gorillas, Ruhengeri National Park, Rwanda (GE)

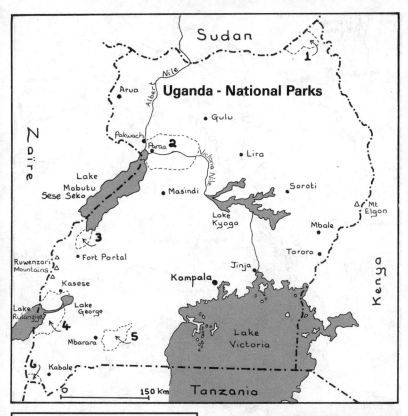

Uganda - National Parks

1. Kidepo Valley National Park
2. Kabalega National Park / Murchison Falls
3. Toro Game Reserve
4. Ruwenzori National Park
5. Lake Mburo National Park
6. Bwindi National Park (Gorilla Sanctuary)

RUWENZORI NATIONAL PARK

Formerly the Queen Elizabeth II National Park, this reserve covers 2000 sq km and is bordered to the north by the Ruwenzori Mountains and to the west by Lake Rutanzige (Lake Edward).

The Ruwenzori National Park was once a magnificent place to visit with its great herds of elephants, buffaloes, kobs, waterbucks, hippos and topis. But like Kabalega, most of the game was wiped out by the retreating troops of Amin and Okello and the Tanzanian army which occupied the country after Amin's demise. They all did their ivory and trophy-hunting best. There's now very little game in the park apart from gazelles, buffaloes, hippos and a couple of small herds of elephants. But it's worth a visit just to see the hippos and the birds. There are few places in Africa where you will be able to see so many hippos.

Every visitor takes a launch trip up the Kazinga Channel to see the thousands of

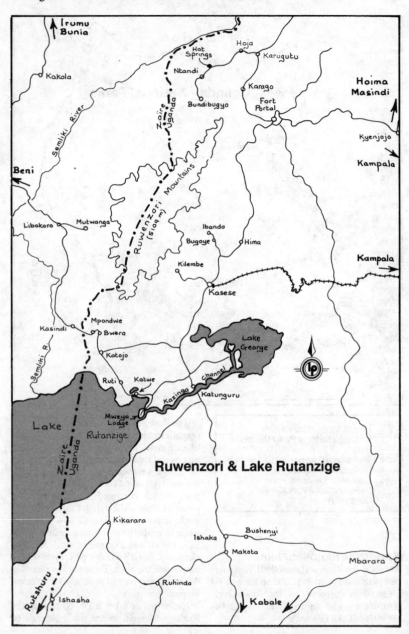

Ruwenzori & Lake Rutanzige

hippos and the pelicans. If you're lucky you will also catch sight of one of the elephant herds and very occasionally see a lion or leopard. The two hour trip costs foreigners a prohibitive US$50 (launch hire) but Ugandan residents pay only US$8 (payable in shillings), so try to hitch a lift or share the cost with visitors at the lodge. As the boat holds about 50 people and there's rarely more than 10 in one group, it's not too difficult to hitch a ride, especially at weekends. The lifts are usually with foreign aid workers and diplomatic staff. The best time to go is from dawn till 9 am and after 4 pm if you want to see anything other than hippos, pelicans and buffaloes.

A much less visited area of the park is that around Ishasha on the border with Zaïre. Once you get to Ishasha (see the Getting There chapter) the only problem is getting a lift for the 17 km from the gate to the camp. Rangers usually visit the gate once a day and provide lifts. Hitching is prohibited because of the lions.

The lions in this area were once famous for their habit of climbing trees, but it seems they've given it up. The attraction now is the beautiful setting. You can bathe in the river (watch out for hippos) and walk in the forest, the only danger there being the buffaloes – make lots of noise as you walk.

Entry to the park costs US$2.70 per day, payable in shillings if you have changed something officially on your currency form, otherwise it's US$10 per day, payable in hard currency. If you leave by the Katunguru Gate there's a good chance they won't check how many days you've stayed.

There's a small museum next to the Mweya Lodge which contains skulls and a few other things. It's open weekdays from 3 to 6 pm and at weekends from 10 am till noon.

Places to Stay

The best place is the *Institute of Ecology Hostel* next to the expensive Mweya Lodge. Large basic singles/doubles cost US$2.70/4 (payable in shillings) and have common facilities. Bed linen and pillows are not pro-

vided. The only other cheap option is the *Student Hostel*, a km or so further along the small peninsula. If you have a tent this is the place to stay (US$1.40 per person), as the eight-bed dorms are poor value at US$2.70 per person.

The *Mweya Safari Lodge* has a stunning position on the raised peninsula, with excellent views over Lake Rutanzige (Lake Edward) to Katwe and Zaïre, and in the other direction along the Kazinga Channel. Sitting on the terrace with a cold drink at sunset is perfect.

As the lodge is part of the UHC chain, payment for accommodation must be in foreign currency at the rate of US$40/60 a single/double. During the week the place is almost deserted but it gets busy on weekends. You can change money (at bank rates) here and print film is available in the small gift shop.

The *camp sites* near Ishasha are very basic – toilets are all that's provided. The only supplies available are beer (Primus from Zaïre), so come prepared. If you're desperate the rangers will cook some local stodge for you. If you don't have a tent there are several bandas, including one lovely old thatched colonial building which is falling down but is still infinitely more agreeable than the recently erected brick monstrosities. Camping costs US$2 per person; the bandas US$4.

Places to Eat

The *Ecology Hostel* provides basic meals, otherwise the *Mweya Lodge* offers excellent dishes for US$2.30, but you must order in advance if you're not staying there. Snacks are available for about US$0.80.

Getting There & Away

The main gate is on the Kasese-Katwe road and there's usually one matatu from Kasese daily at about 10 am. The fare to the gate is US$0.70 and the trip takes about one hour. A taxi from Kasese to the gate costs US$10 one way or US$16 return, including a drive in the park.

From the gate it's seven km to the lodge

and although the rangers don't seem too keen they do actually let you walk this stretch. Vehicles are reasonably frequent so you shouldn't have to wait too long if you decide not to walk.

There's another gate near the village of Katunguru where the Kasese-Mbarara road crosses the Kazinga Channel. There is much less traffic from this gate to the lodge, but you'd get there eventually. If you do get stuck there is a basic lodge in Katunguru.

Hitching out of the park is easy – just stand by the barrier at the Mweya Lodge and flag down any vehicle that passes. A couple of hours is all you should have to wait. Even if there's no tourist traffic there's at least one vehicle each morning taking the fish, caught by the local villagers, to Katunguru.

LAKE MBURO NATIONAL PARK

Between Mbarara and Masaka and covering an area of 290 sq km, this national park is mainly savannah with scattered acacia trees. There are 14 lakes, the largest of which is Lake Mburo. Gazetted in 1983, this park features some of the rarer animals such as impalas, elands, roan antelopes, reedbucks, klipspringers and topis, as well as zebras, buffaloes and hippos.

TORO GAME RESERVE

This is a small game reserve to the north of Fort Portal. It stretches as far as Ntoroko on the shores of Lake Mobutu Sese Seko. You really need your own transport to see this reserve as there has been nowhere to stay since the Semliki Safari Lodge burnt down quite a few years ago.

KIDEPO VALLEY NATIONAL PARK

Surrounded by mountains and notable for its ostriches, cheetahs and giraffes, this park is in the extreme north-east of Uganda along the border with Sudan. It covers an area of 1450 sq km and may still be a dangerous area to visit because of scattered bands of Okello supporters and so-called Karamoja cattle duffers (rustlers), as yet uncontrolled by the NRA. Make enquiries in Kampala about safety before heading off in this direction.

RUWENZORI MOUNTAINS

These fabled, mist-covered mountains on Uganda's western border with Zaïre are almost as popular with travellers as Kilimanjaro and Mt Kenya, but they are definitely harder to climb. They have a well-deserved reputation for being very wet at times. This was best summed up by a comment on the wall of Bujuku hut: 'Jesus came here to learn how to walk on water. After five days, anyone could do it.' Be prepared and take warm, waterproof clothing.

The mountain range, which is not volcanic, stretches for about 100 km. At its centre are several peaks which are permanently snow and glacier-covered: Mt Stanley (5590 metres); Mt Speke (5340 metres); Mt Baker (5290 metres); Mt Gessi (5156 metres); Mt Emui (5240 metres) and Mt Luigi di Savoia (5028 metres). The two highest peaks are Margherita (5590 metres) and Alexandra (5570 metres) on Mt Stanley.

The climbing varies from the easy ascent of Mt Speke, which requires only limited mountain experience, to the harder routes on Stanley and Baker which should not be attempted unless you are of alpine standard. Climb to the top only if you want to, otherwise the guides will be happy to take you around the lower reaches.

Five days is the absolute minimum for a visit to the range, but seven or eight days is better, with one or two days at the top huts. The best times to climb are from late December to the end of February and mid-June to mid-August when there's little rain. But even at these times the higher reaches are often enveloped in mist, though this generally clears for a short time each day.

Books & Maps

Before attempting a trek up the Ruwenzori Mountains it's strongly recommended that you obtain a copy of *Ruwenzori – Map & Guide* by Andrew Wielochowski (1989). This is an excellent large-scale contoured map of the mountains complete with all the main trails, huts and camping sites marked as well as other features.

On the reverse side are detailed descriptions of the various possible treks as well as sections on history, fauna and flora, weather and climate, necessary equipment, useful contacts, costs and advice in the event of an accident. It's for sale in most Nairobi bookshops (KSh 100) or you can get it from Ian Munro/Mark Savage, PO Box 44827, Nairobi, Kenya, or Andrew Wielochowski, 32 Seamill Park Crescent, Worthing BN11 2PN, UK.

It may also still be possible to get hold of a copy of *Guide to the Ruwenzori* by Osmaston & Pasteur (Mountain Club of Uganda, 1972). This was the first comprehensive account of the mountains to be published and, although somewhat out of date, it's still very useful for serious climbers (those wanting to scale the peaks). It can only be bought from the publishers, West Col Productions, 1 Meadow Close, Goring-on-Thames, Reading, Berks, UK, and at Stanfords Map Centre, Long Acre, Covent Garden, London WC2, UK. It costs UK£8.95 plus postage.

Organisation
Preparations for a climb are best made from Kasese since there's a good selection of foodstuffs and equipment there. First contact a member of the Ruwenzori Mountaineering Services (PO Box 33, Kasese, Uganda).

They can usually be found at the Saad Hotel in Kasese. If not, ask the manager of the hotel to put you in touch with them. The organisation is run by John Matte (formerly of the Mountain Club of Uganda) who lives at Ibanda (the trail starting point).

The RMS will organise a guide and porters. The guide will make all the necessary food and clothing purchases for the porters, get permission from the District Commissioner for your climb and arrange transport to Ibanda. The guide will also take responsability for the management of the porters and the safety of the baggage carried by them. You will be responsible for the purchase of your own food and the provision of cooking pots and *pangas* (machetes) as well as camping equipment (if you don't intend to use the mountain huts). There's nowhere in Kasese to hire equipment, so you'll have to bring it with you.

There are agreed types and amounts of food which you are required to provide for the guide and porters along with cigarettes, a blanket and a sweater.

Porters are compulsory and, on the usual six to seven day trip, once loaded with their own requirements they can only carry a few kg of your gear, so you almost need two porters per person. No footwear is necessary for guides/porters as far as Bujuku Hut (4400 metres). Any who wear their own boots above this level are entitled to an additional daily allowance.

Equipment
Since night temperatures often drop below zero, you'll need a good sleeping bag, an insulating pad/air bed and suitable warm clothing. This should include a woollen hat (up to 30% of body heat is lost through your head). Boots aren't absolutely necessary; joggers will do but they will get very wet so you'll need another pair to change into at the hut or camp.

Another essential item is a waterproof jacket as it's almost impossible to stay dry in these mountains. Waterproof trousers (or at least a waterproof covering) are advisable. All your extra clothing, sleeping bag and perishable food should be protected from water by wrapping them in strong plastic bags. The best way to carry them is inside a frameless rucksack (or one with an internal frame). A small day pack is useful if porters are going to be carrying the bulk of your equipment.

Don't forget insect repellent, factor 15-plus sun cream, sunglasses, a torch (flashlight), water bottle, first-aid kit, cutlery and a cup.

Cooking pots are expensive in Kasese so, if possible, bring them from Kenya and remember that one pot needs to be large.

Guides and porters will not go onto snow or ice unless provided with proper clothing and footwear. So if you plan to do this you'll also have to provide ice axes, ropes and crampons.

Costs

For a seven day trek you're looking at US$30 per porter for food and equipment plus about US$1 per day for his salary (double rates for rainy days or walking on snow or to the higher altitude huts) and the guide's salary. There's also an entry fee of US$14 per person (which includes use of the huts) and US$5 for transport to Ibanda, the starting point. Add to this the cost of your own food and a tip for the guide and porters at the end and it works out at about US$85 to US$90 per person, assuming there is a minimum of five. If there are only a couple of people the cost will escalate to about US$120 each.

The cost of going onto ice or snow are proportionally higher as you'll have to provide the guide and porters with appropriate equipment.

By going to Ibanda yourself, organising porters and arranging their supplies, it's possible to save a small amount but it involves a lot of messing about and simply isn't worth it. In any case, you will still have to hire a guide.

Accommodation

With heavy American investment, many improvements are being made to the tracks. There are new bridges over the larger rivers.

the huts now have essentials such as walls and roofs (which they lacked not long ago) and there's a wooden pathway over the bog. All this is being done to lessen the impact of walkers on the fragile environment. But because of the increasing numbers of walkers, it's a good idea to bring a tent as there's a good chance the huts will be full.

Altitude Sickness

Be aware of the dangers of high altitude sickness. In extreme cases it can be fatal. High altitude sickness usually becomes noticeable above 3000 metres and is a sign of your body adjusting to lower oxygen levels. Mild symptoms include headaches, mild nausea and a slight loss of coordination. Symptoms of severe altitude sickness include marked loss of coordination, severe nausea, severe headaches, abnormal speech and behaviour and persistent coughing spasms. When any combination of these severe symptoms occurs, the afflicted person should immediately descend 300 to 1000 metres. When trekking, such a descent may even have to take place at night. There are no known indicators as to who might suffer from altitude sickness (fitness, age and previous high altitude experience all seem to be irrelevant), and the only cure is immediate descent to lower altitudes.

The Trails

Ibanda is the starting point for a climb in the Ruwenzori. If you haven't arranged transport in Kasese, head down the road to Fort Portal for about 10 km and turn left where you see the sign 'Ruwenzori High School' and 'Bugoye Sub-Dispensary'. There's an electrical substation by the turn-off. There's plenty of transport as far as the turn-off but the remaining 12 km along a gravel road to Ibanda are very difficult to hitch. You may have to walk. People along this road are very friendly and there is warm beer (but no soft drinks) available at the tailor's shop in Bugoye.

You can camp at Ibanda free of charge or rent a bunkhouse for a small fee at the RMS headquarters. This may soon change as

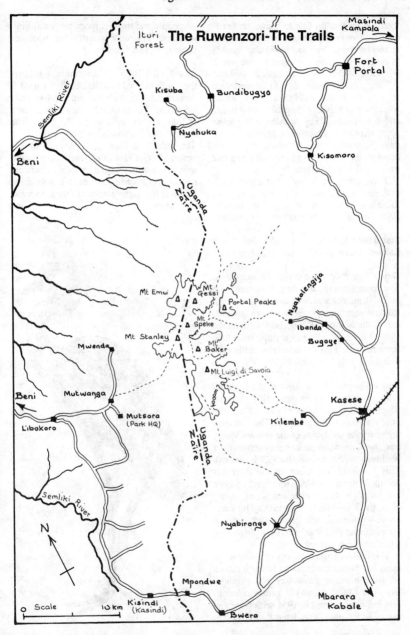

The Ruwenzori-The Trails

there's a project on line to move the head-quarters five km up the trail to Nyakalengija at 1600 metres. The Saad Hotel also intends to construct a cheap bunkhouse there which will include showers and a basic restaurant.

There are two basic trails up the mountain starting from Ibanda/Nyakalengija which will take you between the peaks of Mt Baker and Mt Stanley. They both have the same approach as far as Nyabitaba Hut on the first day. After that they form a sort of loop between the two peaks so you can go up one trail and down the other.

There are quite a few other minor trails both up the mountain and across the top into Zaïre and down to Mutwanga (the Uganda-Zaïre border essentially crosses the peaks).

Ibanda/Nyakalengija to Lake Bujuku & Lake Kitandara
This route takes four days:

Day 1 This involves a walk of about 4½ to five hours from the Ibanda to Nyabitaba Hut at 2620 metres and will take you through tropical vegetation, over two minor streams, across the Mahoma River and finally up the side of a steep valley to a ridge on which there is a *hut*. This hut is in reasonable condition but only has rainwater.

Day 2 The trail drops down to the Mubuku River close to its confluence with the Bujuku River. Both rivers must be crossed and the only way is over the boulders. The trail continues up the north side of the Bujuku Valley past the Kanyasabu rock shelter and on over boulders to *Nyamuleju Hut* (3300 metres). This hut is in bad shape as the floor has collapsed but it will sleep up to eight people and there's a rock shelter and water supply close by. The walk to Nyamuleju Hut takes about 4½ hours. Few groups stay here for the night and prefer to press on to *Bigo Hut*, a further 2½ hours away.

The trail to Bigo involves crossing more open but boggy countryside through stands of giant heather, groundsel and bamboo. Bigo Hut (3400 metres) is a round aluminium building erected in 1951 with floor and bunks added nine years later. It sleeps up to

12 people and there is room for tents. Firewood is available nearby for open-air cooking in fine weather.

Day 3 After Bigo, the trail initially follows the south side of the Bujuku River until it crosses over to the north side and ascends steeply to skirt the north-east shore of Lake Bujuku and on to Cooking Pot Cave. The *Bujuku Hut* is about 15 minutes further on. The trek from Bigo Hut takes about 2½ hours. Bujuku Hut (3993 metres) is an old iron shack with its door missing. There are good *camp sites* in the area. It's possible to return to the starting point at Ibanda in about nine hours.

Day 4 To get on the trail which leads between the peaks and on to Lake Kitandara it's necessary to backtrack from Bujuku Hut to Cooking Pot Cave and then take the trail which heads south over swampy ground and streams and through stands of giant groundsel. You'll reach a narrow gully at the top of which are good viewing points.

After this the trail divides, the right-hand fork leading to the Elena Hut on one of Mt Stanley's glaciers and the other going down through a groundsel forest, over boulders and a scree up to Scott-Elliot Pass at 4372 metres. From the pass the trail heads down into the Kitandara Valley, passing the steep walls of the west face of Mt Baker, and ends up at the higher of the two lakes. *Kitandara Hut* (4000 metres) is at the north-eastern end of the lower lake. It's a beautifully positioned wooden hut which is in good shape and can sleep up to 16 people. Walking time from Bujuku Hut is about three hours. From the hut you can either return to Ibanda the way you came or descend via the Mubuku Valley.

Ibanda/Nyakalengija to Lake Kitandara

Day 1 On the first day you take the same walk as the previous route.

Day 2 Instead of taking the left-hand fork past the Nyabitaba Hut, continue along the ridge for about one km and then bear right to drop gently into the valley of the Mubuku River. Having reached the river, wade across it and follow the gently rising trail – often very boggy – to Kichuchu (2987 metres) where there's an overhanging cliff which affords limited shelter. The walk from Nyabitaba to here takes about 2½ hours. From here the trail rises steeply along the cliff line and you need to exercise caution climbing it as it's exposed and slippery (porters don't like climbing it fully loaded but don't mind descending it when their loads are lighter). From here the valley widens and eventually leads to a dry rock shelter, known as *Kabamba* (3600 metres), beside a waterfall. Walking time to here from Nyabitaba is about six hours. You'll need to

camp here overnight as the next stage to Kitandara Hut takes five hours.

Day 3 From Kabamba, continue on to Bujongolo at 3780 metres where there's an extensive sheltered area, and then along a muddy path through tussock grasses to Freshfield Pass (4360 metres). The trail gradually dries out as it approaches the pass. It next descends steeply to Lake Kitandara and a hut at the northern end of the lake. The entire journey takes about five hours including one hour from the pass to the hut. If you're going in the reverse direction, allow four hours from the hut to the top of the pass. From the Kitandara Hut you can either return to Ibanda the way you came or return via the Bukuku Valley.

Other Routes There are several detours off the two main routes detailed. If you follow them, ensure you have made adequate preparations and are aware of the huts and camp sites where you can stay for the night. They're described in detail in *Ruwenzori – Map & Guide*. There are several new huts which have been constructed along the main trails, including the John Matte Hut (3400 metres) which is a large wooden hut with eight bunks and more due to be added, and the Guy Yeoman Hut, between Kitandara and Nyabitaba huts.

Pre-Arranged Climbs It is possible to have a climb fully organised before you arrive. The main company which does this is Executive Wilderness Programmes Ltd (tel (0903) 37565), 32 Seamill Park Crescent, Worthing BN11 2PN, UK, or you can contact them in the Nairobi office (tel 60728) at PO Box 44827. It naturally costs more this way but it does relieve you of all the organisational hassles and the need to cart camping equipment all the way from Kenya.

BWINDI NATIONAL PARK
This is Uganda's newest national park, gazetted in September 1989. It's in the southwestern corner of the country and encompasses the mountain gorilla habitat in

what was formerly known as the Impenetrable Forest.

When writing this the park was not open to visitors as the gorillas were being habituated by a naturalist, so seeing the gorillas cheaply in Uganda is no longer an option. However, the park may be open now, so check at the wildlife office in Kabale.

Rwanda, Burundi & Eastern Zaïre

Rwanda

Many travellers come to Rwanda mainly to visit the Parc National des Volcans in the north where the borders of Rwanda, Uganda and Zaïre meet. The thickly forested slopes are one of the last remaining sanctuaries of the mountain gorilla.

Like Burundi, Rwanda is one of the world's most densely populated countries. To feed the people, almost every available piece of land is under cultivation (except for the Akagera along the border with Tanzania and the higher slopes of the volcanoes). Since most of the country is mountainous, this involves a good deal of terracing. The banded hillsides are similar to those in Nepal or the Philippines. Tea plantations take up considerable areas of land.

Facts about the Country

HISTORY
Early Settlement
As in neighbouring Burundi, the original inhabitants of Rwanda, the Twa pygmies, were gradually displaced from 1000 AD onwards by migrating Hutu tribespeople who, in turn, came to be dominated by the Watutsi from the 15th century onwards. The Watutsi used the same methods for securing domination over the Hutu as in Burundi. Namely, this was the introduction of a feudal land system and a lord-peasant relationship with regard to services and the ownership of cattle, which represented wealth. There the similarities with Burundi end. The Rwandan *mwami's* (king's) authority was far greater than that of his opposite number in Burundi, and the system of feudal overlordship which developed in Rwanda was unsurpassed outside Ethiopia.

Not only was the Rwandan mwami an absolute ruler in every sense of the word, with the power to exact forced Hutu labour and to allocate land to peasants or evict them,

but the Watutsi overlordship was reinforced by ceremonial and religious observances. Military organisation, likewise, was the sole preserve of the Watutsi. Rwanda, however, was more intensively farmed than Burundi and, in the process of growing food on all available land, the Hutu eventually denuded the hills of trees. The consequent erosion, lack of fuel and competition for land with the Watutsi pastoralists frequently threatened the Hutu with famine. Indeed, in the 20th century alone there have been no less than six famines.

Faced with such a narrow margin of security, something was bound to give sooner or later among the Hutu who, in this country, account for 89% of the population. However, the process was interrupted by the colonial period.

The Colonial Era
In 1890 the Germans took the country and held it until 1916 when their garrisons surrendered to the Belgian forces during WW I. At the end of the war, Rwanda and Burundi were mandated to the Belgians by the League of Nations. From then until independence, the power and privileges of the Watutsi were increased as the Belgians found it convenient to rule indirectly through the mwami and his princes. They were not only trained to run the bureaucracy but had a monopoly on the educational system operated by the Catholic missionaries.

The condition of the Hutu peasantry deteriorated and led in 1957 to a series of urgent demands for radical reform. Power and its props are rarely given up voluntarily in Africa, however; in 1959, following the death of Mwami Matara III, a ruthless Watutsi clan seized power and murdered Hutu leaders.

Independence
The Watutsi power grab was a serious miscalculation and fired a massive Hutu

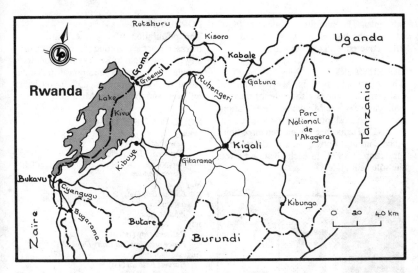

uprising. About 100,000 Watutsi were butchered in the bloodletting which followed and many thousands fled into neighbouring countries. The new mwami fled into exile. Faced with carnage on this scale, the Belgian colonial authorities were forced to introduce political reforms. When independence was granted in 1962 it brought the Hutu majority to power under Prime Minister Gregoire Kayibanda.

Certain sections of the Watutsi were unwilling to accept the loss of their privileged position. They formed guerrilla groups which mounted raids on Hutu communities, thus provoking further Hutu reprisals. In the bloodshed which followed, thousands more Watutsi were killed and tens of thousands of their fellow tribespeople fled to Uganda and Burundi.

Since those dark days, tribal relations have cooled, though there was a resurgence of anti-Watutsi feeling in 1972 when Hutu tribespeople were being massacred in neighbouring Burundi.

Disturbances in Rwanda during this time prompted the army commander, Major General Juvenal Habyarimana, to oust Kayibanda. He has ruled the country ever since and has managed to keep it on an even keel. This is despite depressed prices for tea and coffee (the country's major exports) and an influx in 1988 of 50,000 refugees from the ethnic conflict in neighbouring Burundi. He has also managed to stay clear of needing to apply for IMF loans which have certain strictures. How long Habyarimana can continue to do this, given the population pressures, remains to be seen.

GEOGRAPHY
Rwanda's mountainous terrain occupies 26,338 sq km. Land use is about 35% arable, 20% pasture and 11% forest.

CLIMATE
The average day temperature is 30°C with a possible maximum of 34°C, except in the highlands where the day range is between 12°C and 15°C. There are four discernible seasons: the long rains from mid-March to mid-May, the long dry from mid-May to mid-October, the short rains from mid-October to mid-December and the short dry from mid-December to mid-March.

It rains more frequently and heavily in the north-east where volcanoes are covered by rainforest. The summit of Kalisimbi (4507 metres), the highest of these volcanoes, is often covered with sleet or snow.

GOVERNMENT

The head of state is Major General Habyarimana who is also leader of the only political party, the Mouvement Révolutionnaire National pour le Développement (MRND). He has been re-elected three times since coming to power in a bloodless military coup in 1973. In each election he was the sole candidate.

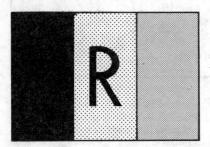

ECONOMY

The economy is agriculturally based with coffee by far the largest export, accounting for about 75% of export income. Tungsten, tin, pyrethrum and tea are also important, but the tin industry is presently in limbo following the forced liquidation of the state mining company after the collapse of the International Tin Agreement in 1985.

The country is a major recipient of international aid, particularly from the People's Republic of China, Belgium and Germany.

Agriculture is the main employer and export earner and contributes about 40% of GDP. The principal food crops include plantain, sweet potato, beans, cassava, sorghum and maize.

The manufacturing sector contributes nearly 20% to GDP. Local produce includes cigarettes, soap, plastics and textiles.

Inflation is running at a very respectable 4% per annum.

POPULATION

The population of about 6.7 million is increasing at the alarming rate of 3.7% annually (almost equal to Kenya). The country's population density is the highest in Africa. About 65% are Christians, 25% follow tribal religions and the rest are Muslims.

HOLIDAYS & FESTIVALS

January
  New Year's Day (1st)
  Democracy Day (28th)
March-April
  Easter Monday
May
  Labour Day (1st)
  Ascension
  Whit Monday
July
  National Day (1st)
  Peace and National Unity Day (5th)
August
  Harvest Festival (1st)
  Assumption (15th)
September
  Culture Day (8th)
  Kamarampaka Day (25th)
October
  Armed Forces Day (26th)
November
  All Saints' Day (1st)
December
  Christmas Day (25th)

Many shops and offices tend to be closed between 1 July and 5 July.

LANGUAGE

The national language is Kinyarwanda. The official languages are Kinyarwanda and French, which enables you to get by in most areas. Kinyarwanda is the medium of school instruction at primary level; French at secondary level (only 8% of the population reach secondary level). Little English is spoken but KiSwahili is useful in some areas.

Facts for the Visitor

VISAS

Visas are required by everyone except

nationals of Germany. Avoid applying for your visa outside East Africa as this often involves a lot of red tape. They cost about US$10 in most countries, require two photos, permit a one month stay and generally take 24 hours to issue.

There are a couple of points to consider when applying for a Rwandan visa. The first is that you have to give the exact date you intend to enter the country as the visa becomes valid from that date and lasts only for the period you have specified. You cannot legally enter the country before the specified date, although some people have done so without any problems. As a one month visa is not expensive, it's best to get this as it gives you some flexibility as to the date you turn up at the border.

The second consideration is whether to request a multiple-entry visa, especially if you intend to re-enter Rwanda from Zaïre. There's no extra cost and it again gives you flexibility. The main reason for this is that one of the routes between Bukavu (Zaïre) and Bujumbura (Burundi) is via Rwanda and for this you may need a Rwandan visa, even though only one-third of the road is through Rwanda and you have no intention of getting off the bus, truck or car. Rwandan transit visas (valid for 12 hours) cost about US$10 so you might as well apply for a tourist visa initially. There are alternatives to this route so a Rwandan visa is not absolutely essential.

Letters of introduction from your own embassy and onward tickets are no longer required. No-one will ask to see (or count) how much money you are carrying.

Embassies

There are Rwandan embassies in Brussels (Belgium), Ottawa (Canada), Cairo (Egypt), Addis Ababa (Ethiopia), Paris (France), Bonn (Germany), Abidjan (Ivory Coast), Tokyo (Japan) and Washington DC (USA).

In East Africa, visas can be obtained from Rwandan embassies in Bujumbura (Burundi), Nairobi (Kenya), Dar es Salaam (Tanzania), Kampala (Uganda) and Kinshasa (Zaïre). There is a consulate in Mombasa (Kenya).

Burundi The embassy (tel 26865) is at 24 Ave Zaïre, Bujumbura, next to the Zaïre Embassy. One month multiple-entry visas cost BFr 2500, require two photos and are issued in 24 hours. Office hours are Monday to Friday from 8 am to 4 pm and Saturday from 8 to 11.30 am.

Kenya The embassy (tel 334341) is on the 12th floor, International House, Mama Ngina St, Nairobi. It's open Monday to Friday from 8.30 am to 12.30 pm and from 2 to 5 pm. One month visas cost KSh 200, require two photos and take 24 hours to issue.

Tanzania The embassy (tel 20115) is at 32 Upanga Rd. Visas cost TSh 2500 or US$20, require two photos and are issued in 24 hours. Office hours are Monday to Friday from 8 am to 2.30 pm and Saturday from 8 am till noon.

Uganda The embassy (tel 241105) is on the 2nd floor, Baumann House, Obote Ave (Parliament Ave), Kampala. It's open Monday to Friday from 8.30 am to 12.30 pm and from 2.30 to 5 pm, but visa applications are accepted in the morning only. Visas are issued the same day if things are not busy, otherwise it takes 24 hours. The cost is US$2.20 for a one week visa, US$4.30 for one month and US$8.60 for two to six months (all payable in local currency). There is no extra charge for multiple entries, so it's worth requesting this.

Zaïre There are no Rwandan consulates at either Bukavu or Goma in eastern Zaïre so it's advisable to get your visa in Kinshasa (or elsewhere) if you're coming from the west. On the other hand, it appears from letters that Rwandan transit visas are available at the border for RFr 1600. We've also had reports that it's possible to get a *permis provisoire* (a type of transit visa) which is valid for one week for about US$46 on demand at the Goma-Gisenyi border. If you have the time, a tourist visa also seems available from the Belgian Consulate in Goma for about

US$17. The latter takes two weeks to issue and you have to leave your passport with them. The same may be true for the Belgian Consulate in Bukavu. Regulations change constantly so don't rely on this possibility.

Visa Extension

Tourist visas can be extended in the capital, Kigali, at the immigration office, Rue du Commerce, next to the Air France office. The cost is about US$17. Transit visas obtained at a border can also be extended (for seven days) in Kigali, but at a cost of US$40.

Other African Visas

Kigali, the capital of Rwanda, is a small city and most foreign embassies are within easy walking distance of the centre.

Burundi The embassy (tel 73465) is on Rue de Ntaruka off Ave de Rusumo. Visas are issued only to Rwandan residents so don't waste your time. Burundi transit visas are available at the border.

Kenya The embassy (tel 74771) is on the Blvd de Nyabugogo just off the Place de l'Unité Nationale next to the Panafrique Hotel. It's open Monday to Friday from 8.30 am till noon and from 2 to 4.30 pm. Visas cost RFr 700, require two photographs and are issued the same day if you apply before 11.30 am. No onward tickets or minimum funds are asked for.

Tanzania The embassy (tel 76074) is on Ave Paul VI close to the junction of Ave de Rusumo. Visas generally take 48 hours to issue, cost from RFr 1000 to RFr 2700 (depending on your nationality) and require two photos. The embassy is open Monday to Friday from 9 am to 2 pm.

Uganda The embassy (tel 76495) is on the 3rd floor of the building on Ave de la Paix near the corner of Ave des Collines. It's open Monday to Friday from 8 am to 3 pm. Visas take 48 hours to issue, require two photos and cost RFr 2000.

Zaïre The embassy (tel 75327) is on Rue Député Kamuzinzi off Ave de Rusumo. Don't plan to get a visa here unless you have about US$70 to spare – outright banditry. One month single-entry visas cost RFr 6500; two month multiple-entry visas cost RFr 9500. Three photographs are required for any visa and these are generally issued in 24 hours. A letter of recommendation from your own embassy is generally not needed nor is an onward ticket, but these regulations change from time to time.

MONEY

US$1 = RFr 80	official	
US$1 = RFr 115	black market (cash)	
US$1 = RFr 95	black market (TCs)	

The unit of currency is the Rwandan franc (RFr). It's divided into 100 centimes but it's unlikely you'll come across these.

Travellers with only travellers' cheques (TCs) are at a considerable disadvantage in Rwanda since the bank commission rates are little short of banditry. Even at the Banque Commerciale de Rwanda in Kigali it costs RFr 250 per transaction. In other banks you can expect RFr 370 per transaction. On one occasion my travelling companion was charged RFr 440 for changing a US$20 travellers' cheque at the Banque Commerciale de Rwanda in Gisenyi. The moral of the story is to bring cash to Rwanda and change it on the street market or in shops. The best rates are to be found in Kigali, Cyangugu and Gisenyi (US$1 = RFr 110 to RFr 115). The rates in Gatuna are relatively poor (US$1 = RFr 100).

The Kigali street market is more or less controlled by a few individuals and, if you find it, you'll get about 10% above the rates quoted, though we obviously can't identify exactly where you will find those people. Try walking around the Rue de Travail or the Blvd de la Révolution. You can often change money in minibuses on the way to Kigali. You'll find quite a few people around the petrol station on the main street in Gisenyi. They'll offer to change US dollars, Rwandan francs, zaïres, etc and their rates aren't too bad if you know what the current rate is. In Kigali the moneychangers hang around the main post office.

The Banque Nationale de Kigali will change US dollar bank cheques into Bank America US dollar travellers' cheques for a 1% commission.

Rwandan banking hours are Monday to Friday from 8 to 11 am. Outside of these hours, armed only with travellers' cheques, you are in dire straits. You can change travellers' cheque on the black market, but only in Kigali and only at a slight premium over the bank rate. Basically only the banks want them. Don't come to Rwanda without at least some cash.

Credit cards are generally accepted only in relatively expensive hotels and restaurants in places such as Kigali and Gisenyi. The most useful cards are American Express, Diners Club and Visa.

Currency declaration forms are not issued at the border.

COSTS

Rwanda is expensive, possibly because of the dense population and the many expatriates. In this landlocked country a lot of export earnings are spent importing food, drink and transport requirements for the expatriates. As a budget traveller you will be hard pressed even if you stay in mission hostels. There is no way you can exist here on a Kenyan, Tanzanian or Ugandan budget and student cards are only useful to get into the national parks at a discount.

A trip to the gorillas in the Parc National des Volcans will cost you an arm and a leg. You're looking at US$18 park entry fee plus US$100 to see the gorillas, including a guide, plus about US$5 per person to camp (your tent – none for hire) or US$9 per person to rent a bed in one of the cottages at the park headquarters. Firewood is extra. Also add on food (no local restaurants) and transport (no buses – hitch and pay) and it becomes a very expensive, though memorable, three to four hours tête-à-tête with a family of mountain gorillas.

Transport (by minibus) and food in a roadside restaurant is much the same price as in the rest of East Africa so long as you don't

want meat with your meal. Meat will just about double the price. Anything on which culinary expertise has been lavished will cost you a week's budget. If you have a yen for French cuisine, however, there are some excellent restaurants in the capital, or so I'm told.

Super petrol costs RFr 66 per litre.

TOURIST INFORMATION

The tourist office (tel 76514) in Kigali is open long hours (7 am to 9 pm) but its main function is to take bookings to see the gorillas. There is very little printed information or maps, although it does have a list of the current prices for the middle and top-end hotels around the country.

GENERAL INFORMATION
Post

Overseas postal rates are relatively high. A postcard, for example, costs RFr 60 (well over US$0.50 at the official exchange rate).

Telephone

International calls are similarly expensive. In Kigali you can dial your own calls at the main post office, so connection is immediate. Charges are RFr 800 per minute to Australia, RFr 480 to the USA and RFr 400 to the UK and Europe.

Time

Rwanda time is GMT plus two hours.

MEDIA
Newspapers & Magazines

Newspapers and periodicals are published mainly in Kinyarwanda and French.

Radio

There are two AM and five FM radio stations which generally broadcast in either Kinyarwanda or French. There are also programmes in KiSwahili and English.

HEALTH

As with most African countries you should take precautions against malaria whilst in Rwanda, but mosquitoes generally are not a problem.

Expatriate residents suggest that you should take special care in Rwanda to avoid illness and/or treatment which could require a blood transfusion. A recent study of prostitutes in this country indicated that about 80% carry the AIDS antibody. If you think you'll need any injections whilst you're there buy your own disposable syringe.

There are certain parts of Lake Kivu where it is very dangerous to swim as volcanic gases are released continuously from the bottom and, in the absence of wind, tend to collect on the surface of the lake. Quite a few people have been asphyxiated as a result. Make enquiries or watch where the local people swim and you'll probably be safe. Bilharzia is also a risk in Lake Kivu. Stay away from shore areas where there is a lot of reedy vegetation. Also keep away from slow moving rivers.

It's advisable not to drink tap water. Purify all water used for drinking except that obtained from mountain streams and springs above any human habitation. Soft drinks, fruit and beer are available even in the smallest places.

Other than the necessary precautions mentioned here, you'll find Rwanda a fairly healthy place to live, especially as much of the country is considerably higher than neighbouring Tanzania, Uganda and Zaïre. Cholera vaccination certificates are compulsory for entry or exit by air. If entering overland, the check is cursory but officials sometimes ask about it.

FILM & PHOTOGRAPHY

Bring plenty of film with you as it is very expensive and the choice is extremely limited – usually only 64 ASA and 100 ASA colour negative film and then only in places like Kigali and Gisenyi. Slide film is almost impossible to obtain. If you buy film, check the expiry dates carefully.

To take photos of the gorillas in the Parc National des Volcans you will need high speed film. It's often very dark in the jungle where they live, so normal film will produce very disappointing results when developed. Use 800 ASA or 1600 ASA fast film, which in East Africa can only be found in Kenya.

Warning

Don't take photographs of anything connected with the government or the military (post offices, banks, bridges, border posts, barracks, prisons, dams, etc). Your film and maybe your equipment will be confiscated. I walked up the hill at the back of the prison in Ruhengeri to take shots of the volcanoes late one afternoon (not knowing the prison was at the base of the hill) and before I knew it I was escorted at gunpoint by three soldiers down to the prison to see the commandant. What did I think I was doing? Didn't I know it was strictly forbidden to take photographs of the prison? Was I a spy? Luckily I speak reasonable French (necessity was the mother of invention where my memory failed) and was able to convince the commandant that there was no subversive intent in my activities. Nevertheless, he wanted to see all my documents, retained my camera and film and

told me to come back the next morning to see his superior.

I ended up talking to the lower echelons of the general staff the next day and they were as helpful as could be given the constraints of their position. In the end, not only were they happy with just the film from the camera but they promised to return any frames which didn't include the prison. Unfortunately, I couldn't wait that long (the film had to be sent to Kigali for processing), so I asked the person dealing with this if he would forward them to me in Australia if I paid his expenses. I never expected to see them again but there they were when I returned home! That's quite something in Africa. I've heard stories of travellers who were not so fortunate. Be careful!

ACCOMMODATION
Hostels

If you don't mind dormitory accommodation at the mission hostels you're looking at between US$2.50 and US$3.50 per night without food. A private double room at the hostels will cost from US$7 to US$12.50 per night.

Mission hostels seem to attract an exceptionally conscientious type of people who take the old adage that 'Cleanliness is next to godliness' fairly seriously. You might not get hot water but your bed and room will be spotless. The one catch with mission hostels is that they're often full, particularly on weekends or in places where there is only one mission hostel in town. Also, the door is usually closed at 10 pm (or earlier).

Hotels

Hotels, as opposed to mission hostels, are considerably more expensive and rarely worth the extra amount, especially at the bottom end where hotels are little better than squalid flea pits. You're also likely to be woken up at dawn by the sound of chickens being strangled in preparation for lunch. There are exceptions, but not many.

Camping

The national parks will burn a hole in your

pocket unless you have your own tent and, unlike Kenya or Tanzania, organised safaris don't cater for budget travellers. They cater for intrepid megadollar travellers with two or three weeks to spare and to whom expense is no object.

Getting There

You can enter Rwanda by air or road. There are no railways in Rwanda. There are lake ferries on both the Rwandan and Zaïrois sides of Lake Kivu but they connect towns only on their respective sides of the lake.

AIR

International airlines flying into Rwanda are Aeroflot, Air Burundi, Air France, Air Tanzania, Air Zaïre, Ethiopian Airlines, Kenya Airways and Sabena.

Air Rwanda flies internationally from Kigali to Brussels (Belgium) and Goma (Zaïre) once a week, Bujumbura (Burundi) twice a week, Entebbe (Uganda) twice a week and Nairobi (Kenya) once a week.

Its main office (tel 73793) is on Blvd de la Révolution, BP 808, Kigali, opposite the US Embassy. There are offices at Kigali Airport (tel 85472), Butare (c/o SORIMEX), Gisenyi (tel 40282, c/o Hôtel Edelweiss) and Kamembe (tel 407, c/o Garage Ruzimeca). Air tickets bought in Rwanda for international flights are very expensive and compare poorly with what is on offer in Nairobi.

OVERLAND
To/From Burundi
Bujumbura to Butare The main crossing point between Rwanda and Burundi is via Kayanza on the Bujumbura-Butare road. The road is sealed all the way. There are daily minibuses which charge BFr 300 for the trip from Bujumbura to Kayanza, from where there are minibuses to the border on Tuesdays, Fridays and Sundays for BFr 150. Otherwise hire a taxi or hitch.

The border crossing is easy, although there is usually a cursory baggage search on both sides. The two posts are only about 200 metres apart. There are infrequent minibuses between the border and Butare for RFr 200. The trip takes an hour or so.

Bujumbura to Cyangugu It's also possible to go from Bujumbura to Cyangugu via the border at Bugarama in the far south-western corner of Rwanda. This is another possibility for the Bujumbura to Bukavu (Zaïre) route. If that's where you're headed it is the way to go if you don't have a visa to re-enter Zaïre (and you have a Rwanda visa) as the road is in much better condition than the Uvira-Bukavu road.

There's no shortage of traffic along this route. Minibuses from Bujumbura to Rugombo cost BFr 200 and take about 2½ hours. From Rugombo to the border village of Luhwa is 12 km and to the Rwandan border post of Bugarama it's eight km. You'll probably have to hitch the entire 20 km. From Bugarama there are minibuses to Cyangugu. Using this route it's easy enough to get from Bukavu to Bujumbura in one day. (See the Eastern Zaïre Getting There section.)

To/From Tanzania
Getting into Rwanda from Tanzania is much easier than it used to be. First take a bus from Mwanza to Ngara (though you have to get off at Lusahanga). The buses leave Mwanza (usually daily) at 4 am and arrive after dark. They're operated by the New El-Jabry Bus Co in Mwanza. To make sure you catch the bus, stay at the Penda Guest House next to the bus terminal. It's a dump but it's convenient.

Lusahanga is an overnight truck stop for petrol trucks supplying Kigali and Bujumbura from the Tanzanian coast. It's easy to get a lift to Rusumo (the first Rwandan town) or even to Kigali. If you only get as far as Rusumo, there's a daily bus from there to Kigali which costs RFr 450. Alternatively, you can take a shared taxi from Rusumo to Kibungo for RFr 200 and a minibus from there to Kigali for RFr 350.

To/From Uganda

Between Rwanda and Uganda there are two main crossing points: Kabale to Kigali via Gatuna/Katuna; and Kisoro to Ruhengeri via Cyanika. Both border posts are very easygoing.

Make sure you get to the border before 11 am as there is a one hour time difference between Rwanda and Uganda (so 11 am in Rwanda is noon in Uganda) and the Ugandans take a long lunch break.

Kabale to Kigali There are frequent daily matatus between Kabale and the Katuna border post. The trip costs US$0.40 and takes about 45 minutes. They leave Kabale from the matatu park by the market or you can pick them up outside the Shell station on Kigungiri Rd. The two border posts are about 100 metres apart.

On the Rwandan side at Gatuna you'll be besieged by moneychangers. It's all very open and appears to be quite safe. As usual, you need to know the current rate or you'll get a lousy deal. When the black market rate was US$1 = RFr 115 in Kigali, you could get RFr 100 at this border. For Ugandan shillings you get RFr 180 for USh 1000.

From the Rwandan side of the border there are frequent minibuses to Kigali until mid-afternoon. They cost RFr 250 and take about two hours.

Kisoro to Ruhengeri Kisoro is about 12 km from the Uganda-Rwanda border at Cyanika. Not a lot of traffic uses this route so you may have to walk unless you can find a matatu or a lift. To hire a taxi costs US$4. The road is little more than a dirt track. From the border there are several minibuses daily along a good road to Ruhengeri. They cost RFr 70 and take about an hour. It can be difficult to get Rwandan francs at Cyanika as very little traffic comes this way.

To/From Zaïre

The two main crossing points from Rwanda to Zaïre are between Goma and Gisenyi (at the northern end of Lake Kivu) and Bukavu and Cyangugu (at the southern end of Lake Kivu). These borders are open between 6 am and 6 pm (for non-Africans). For Africans they are open from 6 am until midnight.

Goma to Gisenyi The two crossing points are the Poids Lourds crossing (a rough road) along the main road north of the ritzy part of Gisenyi, and a sealed road along the lake shore. It's only two to three km either way. From Goma it's a km or two to either post; a motorcycle will cost Z250.

The easier of the two routes is along the lake shore, but from the border you'll have to take a taxi (RFr 350) or a taxi-motor (RFr 50) into Gisenyi. I arrived at this border at 7.30 am one morning and was through within five minutes! The officials at the Poids Lourds post are apparently not quite as amenable. There are minibuses into Gisenyi from this post.

Bukavu to Cyangugu From Bukavu it's a three km walk or Z500 taxi ride to the Ruzizi border post. It's an easy border crossing and you can walk between the two posts.

On the Rwandan side, Cyangugu is the actual border post but Kamembe is the town and transport centre. From the border, minibuses make the half-hour ride to Kamembe for RFr 30. You'll be able to catch one to Bugarama if you're heading straight to Bujumbura.

Getting Around

AIR

Internally, Air Rwanda flies from Kigali to Gisenyi and Kamembe (close to Cyangugu). There are six flights a week to Kamembe and twice weekly flights to Gisenyi. There are also connecting flights between Gisenyi and Kamembe.

BUS

Rwanda has an excellent road system, mainly due to massive injections of foreign aid. The only unsealed roads now are those to Kibuye on the shore of Lake Kivu.

There are plenty of modern, well-maintained minibuses serving all the main routes. Between dawn and about 3 pm at the bus station in any town you can almost always find one going your way. Destinations are displayed in the front window and the fares are fixed (ask other passengers if you're not sure).

Minibuses leave when full and this means when all the seats are occupied, unlike in Kenya, Uganda and Tanzania where most of the time they won't leave until you can't breathe for the people sitting on your lap and jamming the aisle. You should not be charged for baggage. Many minibuses have decent sound systems so you might hear some good African music which isn't ear-splitting.

There are also modern government buses (many of them bearing the Japan-Rwanda assistance programme logo) on quite a few routes. These are cheaper than minibuses but take longer and are far less frequent.

FERRY

The ferries on Lake Kivu used to connect Rwandan ports with Zaïrois ports but these days Rwandan ferries only call at Rwandan ports and Zaïrois ferries only at Zaïrois ports. The small modern motor ferry *Nyungwe* covers the route from Cyangugu to Kirambo, Kibuye and Gisenyi. It leaves Cyangugu on Mondays and Thursdays and Gisenyi on Wednesdays and Saturdays, all at 6 am. The full trip takes about six hours and costs RFr 765. This is just a tiny boat but it rarely gets crowded. In Gisenyi, make enquiries at the boat or, if it's not there, at the bus depot next to the post office.

HITCHING

If you are hitching in Rwanda you may find a list of vehicle licence plates useful as they indicate the province of origin of the vehicle (though that doesn't mean they are going there!). They are:

AB	Kigali
BB	Gitarama
CB	Butare
DB	Gikongoro
EB	Cyangugu
FB	Kibuye
GB	Gisenyi
HB	Ruhengeri
IB	Byumba
JB	Kibungo

If you're looking for lifts on trucks from Kigali to Uganda, Kenya, Burundi or Zaïre, go to MAGERWA (short for Magasins Généraux de Rwanda) in the Gikondo suburb about three km from the centre. Have your pick from the scores of trucks at the customs clearance depot. To get there, head down the Blvd de l'OUA and turn right when you see the sign. It's sometimes possible to find a free lift all the way to Mombasa, but usually it's a matter of negotiating a fare with the driver.

LOCAL TRANSPORT
Taxi-Motor
Most towns are compact enough to get around on foot, but where you need transport the taxi-motor is a good bet. It's just a motorcycle and you ride on the back. The driver can usually sling your pack across the petrol tank and they generally drive pretty safely, though of course there's no helmet for the passenger.

Around the Country

KIGALI
The tourist organisation describes Rwanda as the 'Land of Eternal Spring'. It's an appropriate motto which Kigali, the capital, displays to the full. Built on a ridge and extending down into the valley floors on either side, it's a small but beautiful city with an incredible variety of flowering trees and shrubs. From various points on the ridge there are superb views over the surrounding intensively cultivated and terraced countryside. The mountains and hills seem to stretch forever and the abundant rainfall keeps them a lush green.

Many international organisations have bases here – the United Nations (UN), Food & Agriculture Organisation (FAO) and the European Economic Community (EEC) for instance – and there is a large number of resident expatriates, mainly from Europe and the Far East. So it's a fairly cosmopolitan city. Don't miss the Chinese Embassy as it must be one of the largest and most impressive buildings in the country. It puts both the American and Soviet embassies to shame. China funds many aid projects in Rwanda.

The only trouble with Kigali is that, unless you have friends or contacts who will introduce you to the social life of the city, there isn't much to do (apart from enjoying the tremendous views and pleasant walks). Restaurants, bars and cafés are few and far between. European-style restaurants, in particular, tend to be well outside most travellers' budgets.

Information

Tourist Office The national tourist office, Office Rwandais du Tourisme et des Parcs Nationaux (tel 76514), BP 905, is on the Place de l'Indépendance, opposite the post office (PTT). It's open daily, including Sundays and public holidays, from 7 am to 9 pm. It has a few leaflets (in French) about the mountain gorillas, but little else. Reservations must be made here to see the mountain gorillas in the Parc National des Volcans.

Post & Telephone The poste restante is quite well organised. Staff will let you look through the log book of letters. It's unlikely that you'll miss anything which was sent to you for collection, including parcels. Each letter collected will cost RFr 20. The post office is open Monday to Friday from 7.30 am to 6 pm, and on Saturday from 8.30 am to 1 pm. The telephone office is also here and is open the same hours.

Foreign Embassies Neighbouring countries with diplomatic offices in Kigali include Burundi, Kenya, Tanzania, Uganda and Zaïre – see the Visas entry in the Facts

for the Visitor section earlier in this chapter. There are also embassies for Belgium (tel 75551), the People's Republic of China, Egypt (tel 75755), France (tel 75225), Germany and the USA (tel 75327). A British Consulate (tel 75905) is at 55 Ave Paul VI.

Airline Offices These include Air Rwanda (tel 73793), Air France (tel 75566), Ethiopian Airlines (tel 75045), Kenya Airways (tel 73999), Sabena (tel 75290) and Aeroflot (tel 73646).

Immigration The immigration office is on Ave du Commerce next to the Air France office in a building set back from the road.

Bookstores There are a few bookstores in Kigali, selling mainly French-language publications. The best is probably Librairie Caritas, next to the immigration office on Ave du Commerce.

Camping Goods The so-called disposable Campingaz cartridges can be bought at the Rwanda Petrolgaz shop below the market or at the Janmohammed's shop on Rue du Travail. As with most things in Rwanda, they're not cheap.

Emergency In the case of a medical emergency, call 76466.

Places to Stay – bottom end

Mission Hostels Most travellers stay at the *Auberge d'Accueil* (tel 73640) at the Église Presbytérienne au Rwanda, 2 Rue Député Kayuku. Staff are friendly and the accommodation is excellent, but there are only cold water showers. It costs RFr 650/1100 a single/double and RFr 350 for a dormitory bed. Private rooms have a washbasin and clean sheets are provided. There are no objections to you doing your own laundry. Breakfast costs RFr 150 (good value). Soft drinks and beer are available from the canteen which is usually open in the early evening. The auberge closes at 10 pm, except by prior arrangement, and is a 15 minute downhill walk from the bus station.

Kigali

Kabale (Uganda) via Gatuna

Ruhengeri, Gisenyi, Butare

Riviere Mpazi

1 Logement Bon Accueil
2 Restaurant Métropole & Belle View
3 Restaurant Novotel
4 Unity Restaurant
5 Restaurant Bar aux Heures Douces
6 Motel Le Calme
7 Market
8 Gloria Hôtel
9 Janmohammed's
10 Air Rwanda
11 Town Hôtel Restaurant
12 Eden Garden Restaurant
13 Post Office
14 Place de l'Indépendance
15 Immigration, Air France, Librairie Caritas
16 Ugandan Embassy, La Cave Restaurant
17 Snack Tam-Tam
18 Restaurant La Sierra
19 Tourist Office
20 Hôtel des Milles Collines
21 Burundi Embassy
22 Banque Commerciale du Rwanda
23 American Embassy, USIS
24 Ethiopian Airlines
25 Tanzanian Embassy
26 Auberge d'Accueil
27 Zaire Embassy
28 Belgian Embassy
29 Chinese Embassy
30 Hôtel des Diplomates
31 Restaurant Impala

Kenyan Embassy
Hôtel Bienvenue
Place de l'Unité Nationale
Restaurant Umagnanura
Restaurant Café Flora
Gare Routière (Bus Station)
Rwanda Petrolgaz

Rue de l'Akagera
Rue des Parcs
Rue de la Députée Kamuzinzi
Rue du Mont Juru
Rue de Kigoma
Rue de Kiyouki
Rue Kajangwe
Rue de Rusumo
Rue des Grands Lacs
Ave des Députés
Ave Paul VI
Boulevard de l'OUA
Rue de la Concorde
Rue de Ntaruka
Blvd de la Révolution
Ave de la République
Ave de l'Armée
Ave des Milles Collines
Ave de la Paix
Ave de la Jeunesse
Ave du Commerce
Rue Karisimbi
Rue du Travail
Rue du Commerce
Rue du Lac Ihema
Rue de la Justice
Ave de la Justice
Blvd de Nyabugogo
Ave de la Démocratie
Ave de la Gendarmerie
Rue du Lac Nasho
Ave de Nyokobanda

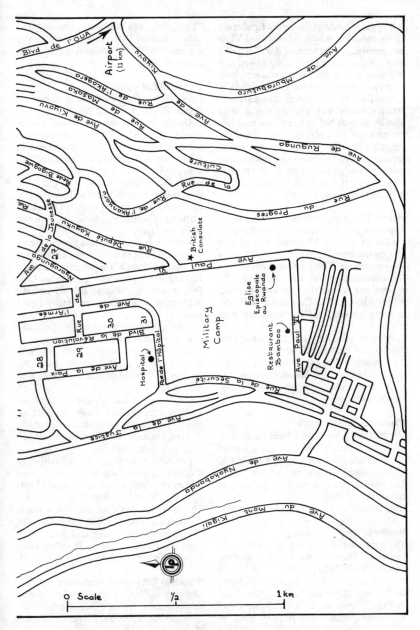

The *guest house* at the Église Épiscopale au Rwanda (tel 76340), 32 Ave Paul VI, is less popular, mainly because it is a long way from the city centre (really only an option if you have transport). The rooms are clean, bright and plentiful, so you should always be able to find accommodation. There are cold water showers only and there is a large laundry area. A bed in one of the six triple rooms costs RFr 600 including breakfast (eggs, bread, coffee or tea). The three double rooms cost RFr 1100 without breakfast. The gate closes at 10 pm and there's no check-in after 9 pm. If you want to walk, it's 30 minutes from the city centre.

Hotels The cheapest habitable hotel is the *Logement Bon Accueil* on Rue du Travail in the bus station area. It's basic but clean, with singles/doubles for RFr 600/900 with a shower cubicle. There are other cheapies in this area, such as the *Motel Le Calme*, but the rooms are generally claustrophobic, windowless cells. Compared with the mission hostels they're extremely poor value.

Another possibility are the rooms at the *Town Hôtel Restaurant* (tel 76690) on Ave du Commerce. The only redeeming features of this place are the hot showers and the excellent restaurant. Singles/doubles cost RFr 750/1000.

Places to Stay – middle

Up the scale a bit is the *Gloria Hôtel*. This place has definitely seen better days but that is not reflected in the prices – RFr 1200/1600 a single/double with a bath and hot water. The hotel has no sign but is the building on the corner of Rue du Travail and Ave du Commerce.

Places to Stay – top end

The remainder of the hotels in Kigali are all top range. These include the *Hôtel des Diplomates* (tel 75111), 43 Blvd de la Révolution; *Hôtel Kiyovu* (tel 75106), 6 Ave de Kiyovu; *Hôtel des Milles Collines* (tel 76530), 1 Ave de la République; *Hôtel Umubano-Méridien* (tel 82177), Blvd de l'Umuganda; and the *Village Urugwiro* (tel 6656), Blvd de l'Umuganda. It will cost a minimum of RFr 3500/4500 a single/double at any of these.

Places to Eat – cheap

Good breakfasts are available at the mission hostels (if you're staying there).

Despite the poor value of its hotel accommodation, the *Town Hôtel Restaurant* offers some of the cheapest and best meals in Kigali, especially for lunch. The tilapia (fish) with chips and salad for RFr 150 is excellent value. Other dishes include chicken, beef, goat, beans, potatoes and rice. If you've just come from Uganda you may find the salads particularly welcome. Many travellers rate this place highly.

Another excellent place is the *Restaurant Bar aux Heures Douces*, down a small lane off Rue du Travail. The set menus for RFr 250 and RFr 300 are very good value. Cold Primus beer is cheap at RFr 85 and the outdoor bar is lively in the evenings – a good place.

Although the rooms at the *Motel Le Calme* near the market can't seriously be recommended, the restaurant is quite good, with nothing over RFr 150. A similar place is the *Restaurant Novotel* on Rue Préfecture near the bus station.

On Ave de la Justice, about 15 minutes walk from the centre, is the *Restaurant Café Flora*. The set menu is not bad value at RFr 450 and à la carte fish dishes cost about RFr 300; meat dishes RFr 500.

For those staying at the Auberge d'Accueil, a good place to eat at night is the *Restaurant Umaganura* on Blvd de l'OAU opposite the end of Rue Député Kayuku. This is a very basic African eatery but is cheap, friendly and the food is quite OK. The closest restaurant to the Église Épiscopale au Rwanda guest house is the *Restaurant Bambou*, around the corner on Ave Paul VI.

Places to Eat – more expensive

Going up-market, try the *Eden Garden*, Rue de Karisimbi, which offers Western-style food and bamboo decor. Tilapia with French fries and salad costs RFr 600. Beef or chicken with French fries and salad costs RFr 700.

On Ave de la Paix close to the Ugandan Embassy is *La Cave*. Pizza, spaghetti or steak costs between RFr 400 and RFr 600 and breakfast is available for RFr 300. The entrance is down the steps under the photo developing shop.

For just a snack, try sitting outside at the *Snack Tam-Tam* on Blvd de la Révolution. The service can be incredibly slow and the food is not that cheap with sandwiches at RFr 300, salads for RFr 350 and pizza for RFr 600. It is, however, a good place for a beer or a coffee. Just a few doors along is the *Restaurant La Sierra*. This is an expensive place with full waiter service.

The *Restaurant Impala*, Blvd de la Révolution next to the Hôtel des Diplomates, is worth a visit if you have the money. Brochettes (kebabs) are a lunch time speciality and there's a good bar. If you are really stuck for ways to toss your money away you could try one of the restaurants at any of the top-class hotels.

Entertainment

Apart from bars, there is not much cheap entertainment available. There are *nightclubs* in the big hotels, but apart from being expensive you need to be well dressed to get in. Jeans and T-shirts don't make it. It's worth enquiring at both the *US Information Service* (USIS), next door to the US Embassy, and at the *Centre Culturel Français*, Ave de la République close to the Place de l'Unité Nationale, to see if they have anything happening. The latter often puts on concerts and films in the afternoons and evenings. Local events are also advertised at the tourist office. There's also a *cinema* on the Blvd de la Révolution opposite the Banque Commerciale du Rwanda.

Getting There & Away

Matatus run from the main bus station to towns all over Rwanda, including Butare (RFr 400, about three hours), Gitarama (RFr 200), Katuna (RFr 250), Kibuye (RFr 400),

Ruhengeri (RFr 300, about two hours), Rusumu (RFr 450), Cyangugu (RFr 800) and Gisenyi (RFr 450). See the respective towns.

Getting Around

The international airport is at Kanombe, 12 km from the city centre. A taxi costs RFr 1000 but you can get there cheaper by taking a minibus to Kabuga (RFr 30) and getting off at the airport turn-off, from where it's a 500 metre walk.

GISENYI

Gisenyi is a resort town for rich Rwandans and expatriate workers and residents. Their beautifully landscaped villas, plush hotels and clubs take up virtually the whole of the Lake Kivu frontage and are quite a contrast to the African township on the hillside above.

For those with the money there's a wide variety of water sports available plus night-clubs and restaurants. For those without, there are magnificent views over Lake Kivu and, looking north-west, the 3470 metre high volcano of Nyiragongo. Swimming and sun-bathing on the sandy beach are also free. It's a pleasant town to stay in but, as you might expect, expensive, especially if you want some action.

Information

Money If you are carrying only travellers' cheques, try to avoid having to change money at the banks as commission rates are outrageous (up to US$5 per transaction). Moneychangers (cash transactions only) hang out around the market and the ERP petrol station outside. There are others at the craft stalls on Ave de l'Indépendance at the back of the Hôtel Palm Beach. Their rates are as good as you'll get in Kigali – about RFr 115 to the US dollar, or zaïres at the rate of about Z400 for RFr 100.

Visas There is no Zaïre Consulate here so you must obtain your visa elsewhere if you intend going to Zaïre. The nearest embassy is in Kigali.

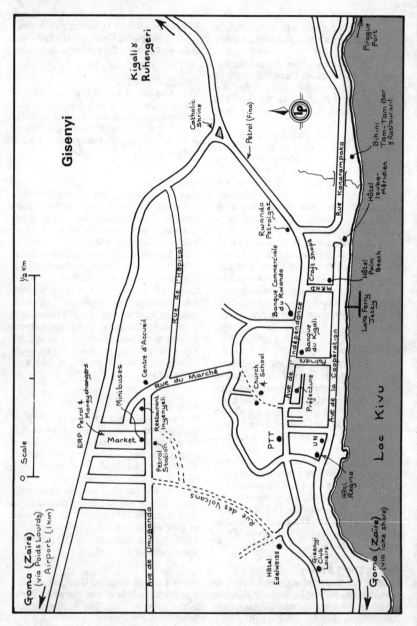

Gisenyi

Places to Stay – bottom end

There are a few small hotels up in the African part of town but they're hard to find (no signs) and the standard of accommodation is low. Most travellers stay at the Mission Presbytérienne's *Centre d'Accueil* (tel 40522) about 100 metres from the market and bus station. It costs RFr 300 per person in a dorm or RFr 500/900 a single/double with common facilities. There's mosquito netting on the windows, which is an important consideration when choosing somewhere to stay here. It's good value for money and rarely has more than a couple of guests. The views over the lake from the front lawn are excellent. This is better value than anything across the border in Goma.

Places to Stay – middle

Apart from the hostel there is no decent cheap place to stay in Gisenyi. All the acceptable hotels are near the lake front. The most reasonably priced of these is the *Hôtel Edelweiss* (tel 40282) run by a Belgian and his Zaïrois wife. As the name suggests, it's built in the style of an alpine cottage. Although a fairly old building, it's homely and clean and the verandah is a delightful place to sit and have a beer and watch the lake. It costs RFr 1700 for a double room with a private toilet and hot shower. There are no singles.

Next up in price are the *Hôtel Palm Beach* (tel 40304) and the *Hôtel Regina* (tel 40263), both on Ave de la Coopération – the palm-shaded lakeshore drive. Hôtel Palm Beach costs RFr 2600 a double with a private toilet and hot shower, while the Regina is cheaper at RFr 1500/2000 a single/double. The Palm Beach doesn't have single rooms and the staff are likely to treat backpackers with a considerable degree of disdain (as are the clientele).

Places to Stay – top end

The *Hôtel Izuba-Méridien* (tel 40381) is the equivalent of the Hôtel des Diplomates in Kigali and costs RFr 5800/6800 a single/double.

Places to Eat

Several simple restaurants on the main road in the African part of town serve cheap meals (usually matoke, rice, beans and a little meat), but the standard isn't up to much. Much better is the *Restaurant Inyenyeli* opposite the Centre d'Accueil. It has a reasonably priced and varied menu with dishes for about RFr 150.

The restaurant at the *Hôtel Edelwiess* looks good but unfortunately the food is grossly overpriced and you can grow old waiting for your meal to arrive, so avoid eating here.

More reasonable is the curiously named *Bikini Tam-Tam Bar & Restaurant* on the beach on Rue Kanarampaka. A main course costs about RFr 600. Alternatively, put your own meals together from the wide variety of fruit and vegetables available at the main market.

Entertainment

If you're looking for action at night, the *Gisenyi Club Loisirs*, close to the Hôtel Edelweiss, is open to nonmembers and puts on rock bands on Saturday nights. Entry to the hall where the band plays costs RFr 400 but you can go into the bar free of charge if you want to check the music out before paying.

If it's just a quiet drink you're after, the balcony of the *Hôtel Edelweiss* is hard to beat, or for something with a bit more local colour, try the *bar* next to the Restaurant Inyenyeli.

Getting There & Away

Air The Hôtel Edelweiss is the agency for Air Rwanda. There are twice weekly flights to Kigali and one flight a week to Kamembe.

Matatu A matatu from Ruhengeri to Gisenyi takes about 1½ hours and costs RFr 150. It's a beautiful journey through upland forest and villages and finally there are panoramic views of Lake Kivu as you descend into Gisenyi. There are two border posts into Zaïre (see the Zaïre Getting There section).

Ferry The ferry across Lake Kivu operates

twice a week to Kibuye and Cyangugu. See the main Getting Around section at the beginning of this chapter.

KIBUYE

A small town about halfway along Lake Kivu, Kibuye has an excellent beach and water sports facilities. It's a pleasant place to relax for a few days. If coming here by road from Gisenyi try not to miss the waterfall at Ndaba (Les Chutes de Ndaba). It's more than 100 metres high.

Places to Stay

A very popular place among travellers is the *Hôme St Jean* about two km from town up the Kigali road. If you're not sure of the way, ask at the Catholic church in town. The Hôme St Jean is on a superb site overlooking the lake and is excellent value at RFr 100 for one night in a dorm bed (RFr 50 for subsequent nights). Singles/doubles cost RFr 500/900.

The only other place to stay is the *Guest House Kibuye* on the lake side. It's expensive at RFr 2400/3200 a single/double, but it does have a good outdoor bar with cold beers for RFr 115 and a diving board which anyone can use.

Places to Eat

Excellent meals are available at the *Hôme St Jean* for RFr 440 (fish, potatoes and vegetables) and RFr 340 (meat, potatoes and vegetables). Vegetables alone cost RFr 120.

Two cheap places, the *Restaurant Nouveauté* and *Restaurant Moderne*, are at the eastern end of town. They have the same menu (goat stew, beans, rice, potatoes, omelettes) and you can eat well for about RFr 30. Cold beers are RFr 100 and soft drinks cost RFr 25.

Getting There & Away

From Kigali the road is partly sealed and minibuses cost RFr 400. The fare from Gitarama is RFr 250.

CYANGUGU

At the southern end of Lake Kivu and close to Bukavu (Zaïre), Cyangugu is an attractively positioned town on the lake shore and the Zaïre border. Kamembe, a few km from the border, is the main town and an important centre for the processing of tea and cotton. Nearby is the Rugege Forest, home for elephant, buffalo, leopard, chimpanzee and many other mammals and birds.

The waterfalls of the Rusizi River and the hot springs of Nyakabuye are here and it's also the ferry departure point for the other Rwandan towns on Lake Kivu, Kibuye and Gisenyi.

Places to Stay

A convenient place to stay if you're heading for Zaïre (or coming from there) is the *Mission St François* at the border. It's spotlessly clean, friendly and charges RFr 400/700/1050 a single/double/triple. The only problem is that couples may be separated. The only other option is the expensive *Hôtel du Lac* opposite.

Places to Eat

The meals at the *Mission St François* are excellent. Breakfast costs RFr 150, a three course lunch or dinner costs RFr 250 and there's unlimited tea and coffee.

Getting There & Away

Matatu Matatus between Cyangugu and Kamembe cost RFr 30 and from Kamembe to Butare cost RFr 450 (four hours both legs). This is an incredibly spectacular road in parts and it passes through the superb Nyungwe rainforest.

From Kamembe, matatus to Kigali (via Butare) cost RFr 800. If you're heading straight for Bujumbura, minibuses go from Cyangugu to the Burundi border at Bugarama.

Ferry The small ferry *Nyungwe* connects Cyangugu with Kibuye and Gisenyi twice a week. See the main Getting Around section at the beginning of this chapter.

RUHENGERI

Most travellers come to Ruhengeri on their

way to or from the Parc National des Volcans. It's a small town with two army barracks, a very busy hospital and magnificent views of the volcanoes to the north and west – Karisimbi, Visoke, Mikeno, Muside, Sabinyo, Gahinga and Muhabura.

Forget any ideas you may have about climbing the hill near the post office as it's a military area and access is prohibited.

Information

Post The post office (PTT) is open Monday to Friday from 8 am till noon. It's also open Monday to Thursday from 2 to 6 pm and on Saturday from 8 am to 1 pm. Service can be slow.

Money Banks are open Monday to Friday from 7.45 to 11 am and 2 to 3 pm. Commission rates for travellers' cheques are about the same as in Kigali.

Places to Stay – bottom end

The only place to consider seriously is the *Centre d'Accueil* on Ave de la Nutrition close to the grass airstrip. It's clean and has dorm beds for RFr 250; singles/doubles for RFr 450/650. The only problem is that the beds are very old and saggy. The communal showers (cold water only) and toilets are clean. A motorcycle from the bus drop is RFr 50, otherwise it's a 10 minute walk.

In contrast, the *Hôme d'Accueil* on Ave du 5 Juillet in the town centre has eight small rooms and charges an outrageous RFr 1000 a double for what is basically a dump.

Places to Stay – top end

At the top end of the market is the *Hôtel Muhabura* (tel 46296), Ave du 5 Juillet, which even local people rate as very overpriced at RFr 2500/3000/3500 a single/double/triple, all with private bathrooms (hot water) and toilet. Breakfast costs from RFr 250 to RFr 400 and lunch or dinner costs RFr 1000.

Places to Eat

The *Centre d'Accueil* offers excellent dinners (stewed meat, beans, cabbage, sautéed potatoes) for RFr 250, but the breakfasts aren't such good value at RFr 100 (tea, bread, margarine, jam). Cold beers cost RFr 80 and there's a common room for residents.

There are a couple of simple restaurants in the town centre which offer standard African food. One such place is the *Restaurant Amahoro* on the main street where meals cost about RFr 200. The *Hôtel Urumuli*, down a small side street off Rue du Marché, has an outdoor area where you can get good meals in the evening (excellent brochettes for RFr 40) and very cold beers.

For a splurge, it's well worth going to the *Restaurant Touristique*, Rue du Commerce, where the food is excellent. The set menu of four courses is RFr 850, or you can order à la carte (about RFr 400 for a main course).

If you are putting your own meal together there's a good variety of meat, fish, fruit and vegetables at the market in the town centre.

Getting There & Away

Matatu From Kigali, matatus take about two hours and cost RFr 300. The road ascends and descends magnificently over the intensively cultivated mountains. From Cyanika on the Rwanda-Uganda border, matatus cost RFr 100 to Ruhengeri. From Gisenyi on the Rwanda-Zaïre border, they cost RFr 150 for the 1½ hour trip.

Taxi-Motor If you're heading for the Parc National des Volcans, the best way to get up to the entrance on the morning of the day of your visit is to get a ride on a taxi-motor. It costs RFr 500 and it means that you don't have to stay overnight at the cottages if you don't have a tent. A safer way of getting there, perhaps, is to hitch, but you would need to do this the day before your gorilla visit as there's no guarantee that you'd get there in time.

Getting Around

Bicycles are for hire near the market, but they're not that cheap at RFr 500 per day.

BUTARE

Butare is the intellectual centre of Rwanda

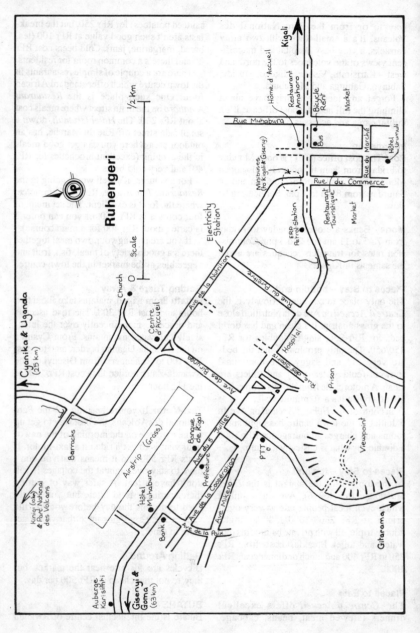

Ruhengeri

Kigali

Home d'Accueil
Restaurant Amahoro
Bicycle Rent
Market
Rue Muhabura
Bus
Hôtel Urumuli
Minibuses (to Kigali /Gisenyi)
Rue du Marché
Rue du Commerce
Restaurant Touristique
Market
ERP Station
Petrol Station

Scale
0   ½ km

Cyanika & Uganda (25 km)

Church
Centre d'Accueil

Ave de la Nutrition
Rue du Préfecture

Electricity Station

Hospital

Rue des Sports

Ave des Bigogo

Prison

Viewpoint

Barracks

Airstrip (Grass)

Hôtel Muhabura

Bank

Bank de Kigali
Ave du 5 Juillet
Préfecture
Ave de la Coopération
Ave Mikeno
Ave de la Paix

PTT

Kinigi (6 km) & Parc National des Volcans

Gitarama

Auberge Karisimbi
Gisenyi & Goma (63 km)

and it's here that you'll find the National University, the National Institute of Scientific Research (folklore dance displays) and the excellent National Museum.

In the surrounding area are several craft centres such as Gihindamuyaga (10 km) and Gishamvu (12 km). If you're thinking of buying anything at these places first look at the quality and prices of what's for sale at the two top-range hotels in town, the Hôtel Ibis and Hôtel Faucon.

Those interested in trees should visit the Arboretum de Ruhande.

National Museum

This huge museum was opened in 1989 and is probably the best museum in East Africa. It's certainly the most amazing building in the country. A gift from Belgium to commemorate 25 years of independence, it's well worth a visit for its ethnological and archaeological displays. The museum is open on Monday from 2.30 to 4.30 pm, Tuesday to Friday from 9 to 11.30 am and 2.30 to 4.30 pm, Saturday from 2 to 5 pm and Sunday from 9 am till noon and 2 to 5 pm. Entry is RFr 100, or RFr 50 if you have a student card. It's about 15 minutes walk north of the centre, past the minibus station.

Places to Stay – bottom end

The best place to stay is undoubtedly the Procure de Butare, which is a very attractive building surrounded by flower gardens. It costs RFr 400 per person and, although they do have double and triple rooms, usually only singles are available. These are large, well-furnished rooms and the sheets are crisp! There are no signs for this place so you must ask directions, but it's at the opposite end of town to the minibus station (about a 20 minute walk), so take a taxi-motor. The door closes at 9 pm sharp.

If you want a hotel, there are a few along the street near the market. The clean and friendly Weekend Hôtel has singles/doubles for RFr 600/1000. Better value is the International Hôtel across the road. It has double rooms with good beds, a bath and hot water for RFr 1000.

Places to Stay – top end

There are two top hotels here, the Hôtel Faucon (tel 30391) and the Hôtel Ibis (tel 30335). The Ibis charges RFr 3000/3600 a single/double with all facilities. It also has a good terrace bar which serves drinks and snacks. The Faucon is more expensive.

Places to Eat

The Procure du Butare has good, cheap meals, with breakfast available for RFr 150 and excellent dinners for RFr 250 (three courses; all you can eat). Otherwise, the Restaurant Chez Nous near the market has good local food. Also, next door to the International Hôtel in a pleasant setting, the Jacaranda Restaurant has a very good three course set menu for RFr 400.

Getting There & Away

The matatu station is just a patch of dirt about one km north of the town centre by the stadium. Arriving matatus often drop you in the centre of town, but when leaving you have to get yourself to the station. Taxi-motors abound, so it's not a problem.

To Kigali, matatus cost RFr 400 and take about three hours. To Gitarama it's about RFr 200 and to Kamembe (Cyangugu) it's RFr 450 along a road which is spectacular in parts. It passes through the Nyungwe Forest which contains some amazing virgin rainforest between Uwinka and Kiutabe.

To the Burundi border there are infrequent matatus which cost RFr 200 and take about an hour once they set off. The one I travelled on waited for 1½ hours before it finally filled up and left.

The National Parks

PARC NATIONAL DES VOLCANS

This area along the border with Zaïre and Uganda has to be one of the most beautiful sights in Africa. There is a chain of no less than seven volcanoes, one of them more than 4500 metres high.

But it's not just the mountains which

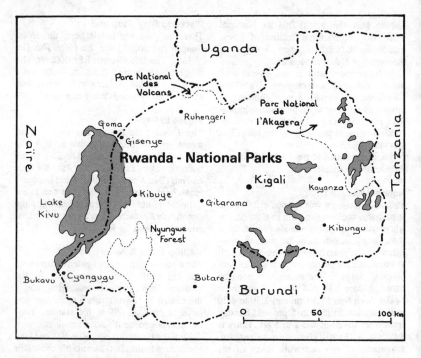

attract travellers. On the bamboo and rainforest covered slopes is one of the last remaining sanctuaries of the mountain gorillas (*gorilla beringei*). These animals were studied in depth first by George Schaller and, more recently, by Dian Fossey. Fossey spent the best part of 13 years living at a remote camp high up on the slopes of Visoke in order to study the gorillas and to habituate them to human contact.

She'd probably still be there now had she not been murdered in December 1985, most likely by poachers with whom she made herself very unpopular. Without her tenacious efforts to have poaching stamped out, however, there possibly wouldn't be any gorillas left in Rwanda by now. It remains to be seen what will happen to the four known groups which survive.

It isn't just poaching which threatens them. Another major factor which is clawing away at their existence is local pressure for grazing and agricultural land and the European Common Market's pyrethrum project – daisylike flowers processed into a natural insecticide. This project was responsible for the removal in 1969 of more than 8900 hectares from the park – almost half its area! The park now covers only 0.5% of the total land area of Rwanda.

Fossey's account of her years with the gorillas and her battle with the poachers and government officials, *Gorillas in the Mist* (Penguin Books, 1985), makes fascinating reading. Pick up a copy before coming here. Her story has also been made into a film of the same name and following its success the tourism industry in the country has boomed, making it even more difficult to make a visit to the mountain gorillas because not only do you have to pay a large amount of money, the park is often booked out weeks ahead.

Visiting the Gorillas

Many travellers rate this visit as one of the highlights of their trip to Africa. It isn't, however, a joy ride. The guides can generally find them within one to four hours of starting out but it often involves a lot of strenuous effort scrambling through dense vegetation up steep, muddy hillsides sometimes to more than 3000 metres. It also rains a lot in this area. If you don't have the right footwear and clothing you're in for a hard time.

An encounter with a silverback male gorilla at close quarters can also be a hair-raising experience if you've only ever seen large wild animals in the safety of a zoo. Some people return with soiled underwear (gorillas actually do much the same thing when fleeing from danger!). Despite their size, however, they're remarkably non-aggressive animals and it's usually quite safe to be close to them. For most people it's a magical encounter, but Tarzan myths die hard.

The only drawback to seeing the gorillas in Rwanda is the cost (about US$120 plus accommodation and food) and the fact that there's no transport between Ruhengeri and the park headquarters at Kinigi (hitch, walk or hire a taxi-motor). If you can't afford this sort of money for what amounts to a day trip, go to Zaïre where it costs US$100 to see gorillas (see the Eastern Zaïre chapter).

In the Parc National des Volcans, the four gorilla groups you can visit are known as Groups 9 (six gorillas), 11 (12 gorillas), 13 (10 gorillas) and SUSA (29 including two silverbacks). Any of the groups can be seen in one day, though a visit to the SUSA group involves a more rugged trip starting at 5.30 am rather than 8 am.

Reservations To see any group you must make advance reservations at the tourist office in Kigali, Office Rwandais du Tourisme et des Parcs Nationaux (tel 76514), BP 905. Otherwise you can not be guaranteed a place on the day you want to go. Groups 11 and 13 are often booked up weeks ahead especially during the European summer holiday season, but there are lots of cancellations so it's often possible to join a group if you are at the park headquarters before 8 am. Also, a single person can often get a place in a group just two or three days in advance.

The maximum group size is eight people, but unfortunately (for the gorillas) the pressure of numbers means this limit is often exceeded. Children under 15 years of age cannot visit the gorillas.

Having made a booking, present yourself at the park headquarters between 7 and 8 am on the day of the visit to pay fees or have your permit checked. Be at the various departure points by 9.15 am. This can be problematical without your own transport. The park doesn't lay on any and tourists with cars are often reluctant to take you. Also, there's very little local transport so it may not be possible to hitch. A possible solution is to take a taxi-motor from Ruhengeri in the morning (RFr 500) or stay at the park gate the night before.

To see the SUSA gorillas, you must pay your fees at the park headquarters by 5 pm on the day before your visit. You then have to turn up at 5.30 am the next day at the park entry point at Gashinya. To get there catch a Gisenyi minibus from Ruhengeri and get off at Busoyo, then walk the seven km to Gashinya. This entails an overnight stay at the park gate unless you have transport.

Kinigi village is about 18 km from Ruhengeri and the park headquarters is another two km from there (signposted 'Bureau du PNV'). It's not too difficult to

Gorilla Gorilla Beringei

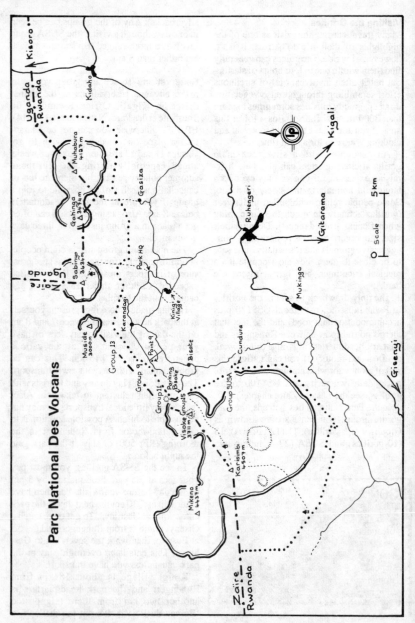

hitch from Ruhengeri to the turn-off for the park headquarters (expect to pay about RFr 50 for a lift).

Park Fees These are RFr 11,000 per person for a gorilla visit (including compulsory guide) plus RFr 2000 per person for park entry. Porters (optional) are available (20 kg maximum) at RFr 300 per day plus RFr 500 per night. If you have an international student card the fee is RFr 8000 plus RFr 1000 park entry, which still isn't cheap.

Places to Stay & Eat If you have a tent (none for hire) you can camp at the partially covered *site* 100 metres from the park headquarters for RFr 500 per person per night and use the same facilities as the chalets across the road. Be very careful about thieves at the camp site. Don't leave anything of value in an unguarded tent. Thieves even steal from tents in which the occupants are sleeping.

Without a tent you'll have to stay in one of the *chalets* opposite the camp site. There are four of these, each with five beds and a fireplace (a couple often get a whole chalet to themselves). They cost RFr 850 per person. Clean sheets are provided but firewood costs RFr 200 per bundle. Toilets and showers are communal and not very clean. Valuables left in the chalets appear to be safe.

A common room/bar which is open all day until late at night serves soft drink, beer (RFr 120), wine and spirits. There's also a barbecue in another building in the same compound which offers brochettes (RFr 50 each), chicken (RFr 400 for a whole chicken) and French fries (RFr 100).

Climbing the Volcanoes
There are several possibilities for trekking up to the summits of one or more of the volcanoes in the park. These range from several hours to two days or more. For all these a guide is compulsory (at the usual fee) but porters are optional. The ascents take you through some remarkable changes of vegetation ranging from thick forests of bamboo, giant lobelia or hagenia on to alpine meadows. If the weather is favourable you'll

be rewarded with some spectacular views over the mountain chain. It is forbidden to cut down trees or otherwise damage vegetation in the park and you can only make fires in the designated camping areas. Among the more popular treks are:

Visoke (3711 metres) Return trip takes six to seven hours from Parking Bisoke. The ascent takes you up the very steep southwestern flanks of the volcano to the summit where you can see the crater lake. The descent follows a rough track on the northwestern side from which there are magnificent views over the Parc National des Virungas (Zaïre) and Lake Ngezi.

Lake Ngezi (About 3000 metres) Return trip takes three to four hours from Parking Bisoke. This is one of the easiest of the treks and, if you get there at the right time of the day, you may see a variety of animals coming to drink.

Karisimbi (4507 metres) Return trip takes two days. The track follows the saddle between Visoke and Karisimbi and then ascends the north-western flank of the latter. Some five hours after beginning the trek you arrive at a metal *hut* which is where you stay for the night (the hut keys are available at Parking Bisoke). The rocky and sometimes snow-covered summit is a further two to four hours walk through alpine vegetation. You descend the mountain the following day. To do this trek you need plenty of warm clothing and a very good sleeping bag. It gets very cold, especially at the metal hut which is on a bleak shoulder of the mountain at about 3660 metres. The wind whips through, frequently with fog, so you don't get much warmth from the sun.

Sabinyo (3634 metres) Return trip takes five to six hours from the park headquarters at Kinigi. The track ascends the south-eastern face of the volcano, ending up with a rough scramble over steep lava beds along a very narrow path. There's a metal *hut* just before the start of the lava beds.

Gahinga & Muhabura (3474 metres & 4127 metres) Return trip takes two days from Gasiza. The summit of the first volcano is reached after a climb of about four hours along a track which passes through a swampy saddle between the two mountains. There is a metal *hut* here which offers a modicum of shelter but it's in a bad state of repair. The trip to the summit of Muhabura takes about four hours from the saddle.

PARC NATIONAL DE L'AKAGERA

Created in 1934 and covering an area of 2500 sq km, Akagera is one of the least visited but most interesting wildlife parks in Africa. One reason for this is its three distinct environments. Large areas of the park are covered with treeless savannah but there is an immense swampy area about 95 km long and between two and 20 km wide along the border with Tanzania. This contains six lakes and numerous islands, some of which are covered with savannah, others with forest. Thirdly, there is a chain of low mountains (ranging from 1618 to 1825 metres high) which stretches through much of the length of the park. The vegetation here is variable, ranging from short grasses on the summits to wooded savannah and dense thickets of xerophilious (adapted to a dry habitat) forest on the flanks.

There's an extraordinary variety of animals to be seen here and they're often much easier to find than in other wildlife parks. In just a two to three day trip you can usually come across topi, impala, roan antelope, giant eland, bushbuck, oribi, various types of duiker, buffalo, wart hog, red river hog, baboon, vervet monkeys, lion, leopard, hyaena, zebra, hippo, crocodile and, at night, hare, palm civet, genet, galago (bushbaby) and giant crested porcupine. There are also herds of elephant.

The best time to visit the park, in terms of access, is during the dry season from mid-May to mid-September. November and April are the wettest months.

Tsetse flies can be troublesome in the north and east but you could be bothered by the odd one anywhere in the park, so bring a fly swat and/or insect repellent.

Hiring a guide is a waste of money. You won't find any more animals with a guide than you will without. All you need is a map of the park, your eyes and a pair of binoculars. Park maps, for sale at the tourist office in Kigali, are remarkably accurate despite the way they appear – you can't buy these at the park. A wildlife handbook is also useful. Take all your own food, drinking and washing water and fuel. It's best to assume you won't be able to get these in the park. Sometimes fuel is available at the hotels but they're very reluctant to sell it.

Places to Stay

The *hotels* in the park are very expensive (RFr 3700/5050 a single/double) so to keep costs down you'll have to camp. You can do this on good sites at both of the hotels. There are also designated *camp sites* at various other points inside the park but that's all they are – 'designated'. There are no facilities and no protection. Some people do camp out but it's not recommended and can be dangerous (sleep in the car instead).

One exception to this is at *Plage Hippos*, halfway up the park and close to the Tanzanian border. Here there are covered picnic tables, good waste bins and toilets but the site is no more protected than anywhere else. It's a beautiful place and there are plenty of hippos and crocodiles, monkeys and birdlife. Don't swim here, not only because of the hippos and crocodiles but also because there's a fair chance of catching bilharzia.

Getting There & Away

The only problem with getting to Akagera is that you need your own transport or to join an organised safari. Safaris do not, as in Kenya and Tanzania, cater to budget travellers. Check out car hire and safari prices in Kigali at: Rwanda Travel Service (tel 2210), Hôtel des Diplomates, 45 Blvd de la Révolution; Umubano Tours Agency (tel 2176), BP 1160; and Agence Solliard (tel 5660), 2 Ave de la République.

Park entry fees are RFr 1500 per person

plus RFr 800 for a car or RFr 1000 for a jeep. Camping costs RFr 1000 per person. A guide costs RFr 500 per day and a fishing licence costs RFr 1500 per day.

The best entry into the park is either at the Gabiro Hôtel in the mid-north or the Akagera Hôtel in the south, but the quickest is the Nyamiyaga entrance about 16 km from the sealed road going through Kayonza.

NYUNGWE FOREST CONSERVATION PROJECT

Despite not being a national park, the Nyungwe Forest ranks among Rwanda's foremost attractions. One of the largest protected montane rainforests in Africa, it covers 970 sq km and offers superb scenery overlooking the forest and Lake Kivu as well as views to the north of the distant volcanoes of the Virunga.

The conservation project began in 1988 and is sponsored by the American Peace Corps, the New York Zoological Society and the Rwandan Government. It aims to promote tourism in an ecologically sound way while studying the ecology of the forest and educating local people about its value.

The main attraction is the guided tours to view large groups of black-and-white colobus monkeys (up to 300 per group). The lush, green valleys also offer outstanding hiking across 20 km of well-maintained trails passing through enormous stands of hardwoods, under waterfalls and through a large marsh. There are about 270 species of trees, 50 species of mammal, 275 species of bird as well as an astonishing variety of orchids and butterflies.

The guided tours depart the project headquarters at Uwinka three times daily at 8 and 11 am and 2 pm. An information centre is also at the headquarters. The tours cost RFr 500 per person and you should expect to walk for about an hour. Sturdy shoes, binoculars and rain gear are advisable.

Another guided tour (RFr 500 per person) goes to the Kamiranzovu March where the area's six remaining elephants reside in the forest.

In addition to the tours there are six other trails, ranging from one km to nine km in length, along which you're free to hike without a guide.

Places to Stay

There are *camp sites* at the Uwinka HQ but you must bring everything you need – tent, sleeping bag, cooking equipment, water, food and warm clothes (the nights are cool at 2400 metres). There is nothing here other than toilets, charcoal and wood. Camping fees are RFr 200 per person per night. The nearest towns for provisions are Cyangugu and Butare. Plans are being made to connect the existing trails with other camp sites to enable those who prefer backpacking to take two to three-day treks in the forest.

Uwinka sits on a ridge overlooking the forest and offers impressive views in all directions.

There's also a *camp site* at Karamba about 14 km towards Cyangugu from Uwinka.

Getting There & Away

The Nyungwe Forest lies between Butare and Cyangugu. From Kigali, head south to Butare and then west towards Cyangugu. Minibuses leave from Kigali (RFr 800) and Butare throughout the day. Another option is to take the large, crowded green bus which leaves Kigali daily at 7 am and costs only RFr 600. The Uwinka headquarters is just past the 90 km post and is marked by a board on which a black-and-white colobus monkey is painted. The trip from Kigali takes between four and six hours.

From Cyangugu, take a minibus towards Butare and get off at Uwinka which is just past the 54 km post. The journey takes about one hour and costs RFr 300.

Burundi

Burundi is a small and beautiful mountainous country. Sandwiched between Tanzania, Rwanda and Zaïre, it has magnificent views over Lake Tanganyika. Burundi has had a stormy history full of tribal wars and factional struggles between the ruling families. This has been further complicated in recent times by colonisation, first by the Germans and later by the Belgians. It is one of the most densely populated countries in the world with 145 people per sq km. Despite this, there are few urban centres. The only towns of any size are the capital, Bujumbura, and Gitega. Most people live in family compounds known as *rugos*.

Facts about the Country

HISTORY
Early Settlement
The original inhabitants of the area were the Twa pygmies who now comprise only 1% of the population. They were gradually displaced from about 1000 AD onwards by migrating Hutu, mostly farmers of Bantu stock, who now make up 85% of the population.

In the 16th and 17th centuries the country experienced another wave of migration. This time it was the tall, pastoralist Watutsi from Ethiopia and Uganda who now make up 14% of the population. The Watutsi gradually subjugated the Hutu into a type of feudal system, similar to that which operated in mediaeval Europe. The Watutsi became a loosely organised aristocracy with a *mwami*, or king, at the top of each social pyramid. Under this system the Hutu relinquished their land and mortgaged their services to the nobility in return for cattle – the symbol of wealth and status in Burundi.

The Colonial Era
At the end of the 19th century, Burundi and Rwanda were colonised by Germany. However, they were so thinly garrisoned that the Belgians were easily able to oust the German forces during WW I. After the war, the League of Nations mandated Burundi (then known as Urundi) and Rwanda to Belgium.

Taking advantage of the feudal structure, the Belgians ruled indirectly through the Watutsi chiefs and princes, granting them wide-ranging powers to recruit labour and raise taxes. The Watutsi were not averse to abusing these powers whenever it suited them. After all, they considered themselves to be a superior, intelligent people, born to rule, while the Hutu were merely hardworking but dumb peasants. The Christian missions encouraged this view by concentrating on educating the Watutsi and virtually ignoring the Hutu. As the missions had been granted a monopoly on education, this policy remained unchallenged.

The establishment of coffee plantations and the resulting concentration of wealth in the hands of the Watutsi urban elite further exacerbated tensions between the two tribal groups.

Independence
In the 1950s a nationalist organisation based on unity between the tribes was founded under the leadership of the mwami's eldest

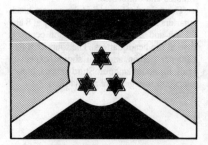

son, Prince Rwagasore. However, in the run-up to independence the prince was assassinated with the connivance of the colonial authorities who feared their commercial interests would be threatened if he came to power.

Despite this setback, when independence was granted in 1962, challenges were raised about the concentration of power in Watutsi hands. It appeared that the country was headed for a majority government. This had already happened in neighbouring Rwanda where a similar tribal imbalance existed.

Yet in the 1964 elections, even though Hutu candidates collected the majority of votes, the mwami refused to appoint a Hutu prime minister. Hutu frustration boiled over a year later in an attempted coup staged by Hutu military officers and political figures. Though the attempt failed, it led to the flight of the mwami into exile in Switzerland. He was replaced by a Watutsi military junta. A

wholesale purge of Hutu from the army and the bureaucracy followed, but in 1972 another large-scale revolt saw more than 1000 Watutsi killed.

The military junta responded to this challenge with what was nothing less than selective genocide. Any Hutu who had received a formal education, had a government job or had wealth was rooted out and murdered, often in the most horrifying way. Certainly few bullets were used and convoys of army trucks full of the mutilated bodies of Hutu rumbled through the streets of Bujumbura for days on end, initially even in broad daylight. Many Hutu were taken from their homes at night while others received summonses to police stations.

It is hard to believe how subservient the Hutu had become to their Watutsi overlords. Even the most uninformed peasant was aware of what was occurring. After three months, 200,000 Hutu had been killed and

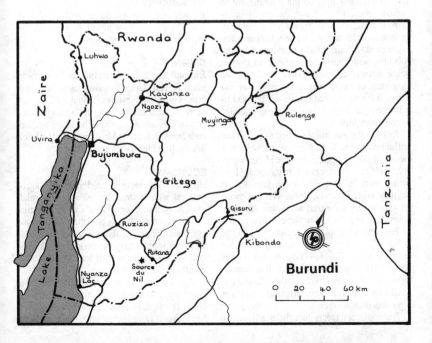

100,000 had fled to Tanzania, Rwanda and Zaïre. More refugees have poured into Tanzania since.

Neither the Christian missions inside the country nor the international community outside raised any protest against this carnage. Indeed, whilst it was in full swing, an official of the Organization of African Unity (OAU) visited Bujumbura to congratulate President Michel Micombero on the orderly way the country was being run!

In 1976 Jean-Baptiste Bagaza came to power in a bloodless coup and in 1979 formed the Union pour le Progrès National (UPRONA), ruling with a central committee and small politburo. As part of a so-called democratisation programme, elections in 1982 saw candidates (mostly Watutsi and all approved by UPRONA) voted into the National Assembly. Hutu people have only ever held about 25% of government ministries.

During the Bagaza years there were some half-hearted attempts by the government to remove some of the main causes of intertribal conflict, but these were mostly cosmetic. The army and the bureaucracy were (and still are) totally dominated by the Watutsi, with the Hutu confined to menial jobs, agriculture and cattle raising. The government even vetoed international aid when it suspected that this might be used to educate or enrich the Hutu, and so eventually breed opposition.

In 1985 the government tried to lessen the influence of the Catholic Church, which it believed was sympathetic to the Hutu majority. Its fears of a church-organised Hutu revolt were heightened by the fact that in neighbouring Rwanda, Hutus were in power. Priests were put on trial and some missionaries were expelled from the country.

Bagaza was toppled in September 1987 in a bloodless coup led by his cousin Major Pierre Buyoya. This latest regime has gone a long way towards mending the fences between the government on one side and the Catholic Church and international aid agencies on the other.

Burundi very rarely hits the headlines of the world's press, but an outbreak of intertribal violence in the north of the country in August 1988 was big news. However, the event was given only minor coverage, especially when one considers that, depending on whose figures you believe, somewhere between 4000 and 24,000 people were massacred while thousands more fled into neighbouring Rwanda. The blood bath was a major setback for Buyoya who had been trying to play down the ethnic divisions within the country, even to the point of refusing to state how many of his ministers were Watutsi and how many were Hutu (the numbers are 16 and four respectively).

It's unlikely, as a visitor, that you will become aware of all the internal tensions. Outwardly the country appears calm and seems destined to stay that way for the foreseeable future. Few travellers stay long in Burundi in any case. Most are en route to or from Tanzania or Rwanda.

GEOGRAPHY

Burundi occupies a mountainous 27,834 sq km. The capital, Bujumbura, is on the northern tip of Lake Tanganyika.

CLIMATE

Burundi has a variable climate. The lower land around Lake Tanganyika is hot and humid with temperatures around 30°C. In the more mountainous north, the average temperature is around 20°C. The rainy season lasts from October to May and there is a brief dry spell in December and January.

ECONOMY

Burundi's economy is predominantly agricultural with coffee, the main commercial crop, accounting for 65% of export income. The government has been trying to encourage development of the noncoffee sector in an effort to diversify the economy. Consequently, the production of tea has increased greatly in the past few years.

Agriculture is the mainstay of the economy and accounts for more than 50% of GDP. It employs about 85% of the workforce. Apart from coffee, cash crops include tea, cotton, palm oil and tobacco. Subsistence crops (which occupy most of the cultivated land) include cassava, bananas, sweet potatoes, maize and sorghum.

The manufacturing sector, based in Bujumbura, accounts for 15% of GDP and output includes cigarettes, glass, textiles, cement, oxygen and coffee processing.

Unfortunately, wood is used to meet most of the energy requirements at the village level. Major energy needs are met through oil imports from the Persian Gulf and electricity from Zaïre.

Inflation is running at about 7.5%.

POPULATION
The population of five million is about 14% Watutsi and 85% Hutu.

HOLIDAYS & FESTIVALS
Public holidays are 1 January, 1 May, Good Friday, Easter Sunday, Ascension Day, 1 July, 15 August, 18 September, 13 October, 1 November and 25 December (Christmas).

LANGUAGE
The official languages are Kirundi and French. KiSwahili is also useful. Hardly anyone speaks English.

Facts for the Visitor

VISAS
Visas are required by all. Citizens of South Africa are not admitted.

Visas cost about US$10 and allow for a stay of up to 60 days. When applying for a tourist visa you must nominate the date you will be entering the country and how long you will be staying. Don't get too concerned about this as the visa can be valid for up to three months from the date of issue and, as there's no price difference between a one day or a two month visa, it's worth asking for more time rather than less. There's also no extra charge for requesting multiple-entry. If there's any chance you could use this facility, get it now rather than later.

It's also possible to get a three day transit visa at the border.

Embassies
Visas can be obtained from Burundi embassies in Addis Ababa (Ethiopia), Algiers (Algeria), Cairo (Egypt), Dar es Salaam (Tanzania), Kinshasa (Zaïre), Nairobi (Kenya) and Tripoli (Libya). There are embassies in Kampala (Uganda) and Kigali (Rwanda) but at present they only issue visas to nationals and residents of those countries.

Outside Africa there are embassies in Beijing (People's Republic of China), Bonn (Germany), Brussels (Belgium), Bucharest (Romania), Geneva (Switzerland), Moscow (USSR), Washington DC (USA), Ottawa (Canada) and Paris (France). There are Burundi consulates in Bukavu (Zaïre) and Kigoma (Tanzania).

The visa application story in East Africa is as follows:

Kenya At the embassy in Nairobi (tel 728340), 14th floor, Development House, Moi Ave, visas cost KSh 200, require two photographs and take 24 hours. Apply only on Monday and Wednesday and collect it on Tuesday and Thursday at 4 pm. The embassy is open Monday to Thursday from 8.30 am to 12.30 pm and 2 to 5 pm.

Rwanda At the embassy in Kigali (Rue de Ntaruka) visas are only issued to Rwandan nationals and foreigners resident in Rwanda.

Tanzania At the consulate in Kigoma visas cost TSh 3000, require two photographs and are issued the same day. The consulate is open Monday to Friday from 8 am to 3 pm.

In Dar es Salaam the same visa costs TSh 4000 (or US$20), requires two pictures and takes 24 hours to issue. The embassy is on Lugala Rd next to the Italian Embassy and is open Monday to Friday from 8 am to 2 pm.

Uganda Don't plan on getting a visa for Burundi in Kampala as they are only issued to Ugandans and Ugandan residents. If you still want to try, the embassy (tel 545840) is at 2 Katego Rd near the Uganda Museum. It's open Monday to Friday from 8.30 am to 12.30 pm and 2.30 to 5 pm.

Zaïre At the consulate in Bukavu (SINELAC Building, 184 Ave du Président Mobutu) Burundi visas cost Z4600, require two photographs and take 24 hours to be issued. The consulate is open Monday to Friday from 7.30 am till noon and 2.30 to 5 pm.

Visa Extensions
Visa extensions can be obtained from the immigration office in Bujumbura. These cost BFr 1000 per month and take 24 hours to be issued.

Other African Visas
Visas available in Bujumbura for neighbouring African countries include:

Rwanda The embassy (tel 26865) is at 24 Ave du Zaïre, Bujumbura, next to the Zaïre Embassy. A one month multiple-entry visa costs BFr 2500, requires two photos and are

issued in 24 hours. Office hours are Monday to Friday from 8 am to 4 pm and Saturday from 8 to 11.30 am.

Tanzania The embassy is on Ave de l'ONU, around the corner from the Rwandan and Zaïre embassies on Ave du Zaïre. Visa costs vary according to your nationality (BFr 1250 to BFr 1750). They require two photographs and are issued in 24 hours. The embassy is open Monday to Friday from 8 am till noon and 2 to 5 pm.

Zaïre The embassy is on Ave Zaïre next to the Rwandan Embassy. A one month single-entry visa costs BFr 2000, two months is BFr 3000 and three months is BFr 4000. It costs an extra BFr 500 to have multiple entry on any of these visas. One photo is required and a visa is issued in 24 hours. The embassy is open only in the morning from 8.30 am till noon.

MONEY
US$1 = BFr 177   official
US$1 = BFr 200   black market

The unit of currency, the Burundi franc (BFr), is divided into 100 centimes, which you're highly unlikely to come across. Notes in circulation are BFr 5000, BFr 1000, BFr 500, BFr 100, BFr 50 and BFr 10. The only coins are BFr 5 and BFr 1.

The exchange value of the Burundi franc fluctuates according to the international currency market, particularly the value of the US dollar and the French franc, and devaluations are not uncommon. Currency declaration forms are not issued on arrival.

Commission rates for changing travellers' cheques amount to outright banditry at most banks – some charge up to 7%! The Banque de la République du Burundi charges only BFr 3 commission per transaction and, surprisingly, will change small amounts of dollar travellers' cheques to dollars cash. Banking hours are Monday to Friday from 8 to 11.30 am. Outside of these hours you can change travellers' cheques at one of the large hotels in Bujumbura (eg Novotel, Chaussée du Peuple Burundi). Their rates are fractionally below those offered by the banks, though they charge no commission.

There's a relatively open street market in Bujumbura, but beware of moneychangers as now the bank rates are nearly fair in Burundi and the only way for them to make some money is by ripping you off. Dealers generally hang around the front of the main post office. Rates obviously vary according to the official exchange rate and the amount you want to change (large bills are preferred). For currencies other than the US dollar, you're better off at the bank.

Tanzanian shillings can also be bought here, which is handy if you're heading for Kigoma or Nyanza Lac, but the rate is not that good: for BFr 110 you get TSh 100 and for US$1 you get TSh 200.

If you take your own food on the Lake Tanganyika steamer, MV *Liemba* (and don't want to buy drinks), there's no need for shillings, but for the Nyanza Lac and Gombe Stream route you'll need some. If you're taking the *Liemba* all the way to Mpulungu you'll need shillings, if only to stock up with goods in Kigoma.

At the border post between Uvira (Zaïre) and Bujumbura you'll run into a lot of moneychangers. Their rates (zaïres to Burundi francs but not hard currency to Burundi francs) are quite reasonable so long as you know the current street rates for the Burundi franc.

COSTS

Burundi can be an expensive place to stay if you want to be near the town centre in Bujumbura, but there are reasonably cheap places in the suburbs. Elsewhere, meals can usually be found at a reasonable price and transport costs are about the same as in Rwanda.

GENERAL INFORMATION
Post

The postal service is reasonably efficient, but the poste restante service at the main post office (PTT) in Bujumbura is poorly organised. Make sure you check not only the pile for your surname but any other possible ones as well. It's open Monday to Friday

from 8 am till noon and 2 to 4 pm, and on Saturday from 8 to 11 am.

Telephone
Rates for international calls are extremely high at BFr 3200 for three minutes to Australia, Europe or the USA. Connections from the main post office take no more than a few minutes.

Time
The time in Burundi is GMT plus two hours.

Business Hours
Official business hours (other than banks) are Monday to Saturday from 8 am till noon and 2 to 5 pm.

MEDIA
Newspapers
The main newspaper is the French-language daily, *Le Renouveau du Burundi*.

Radio
Local radio stations broadcast in Kirundi, French and KiSwahili. There are occasional broadcasts in English on the local FM station (98.10 MHz). This station also plays some pretty decent African music.

HEALTH
As with most African countries you should take precautions against malaria in Burundi. There is a good beach (with expensive hotels and restaurants) at the northern end of Lake Tanganyika between Bujumbura and the Burundi-Zaïre border. It's probably safe to swim there but you should avoid bathing in this lake wherever there is reedy vegetation, due to the risk of contracting bilharzia.

Getting There

You can enter Burundi by air, road or lake ferry. There are no railways.

AIR
International airlines servicing Burundi are Aeroflot, Air Burundi, Air France, Air Tanzania, Air Zaïre, Cameroon Airlines, Ethiopian Airlines, Kenya Airways and Sabena.

If you're heading for Tanzania and thinking of flying internally from Kigoma to Dar es Salaam, it's worth making a reservation at the Air Tanzania office in Bujumbura. You don't have to pay for the ticket until you get to Kigoma but Air Tanzania staff will give you written confirmation of the reservation. No matter where you make the reservation you'll still have to pay the full whack (US$235). It's actually far cheaper to fly to Dar es Salaam from Bujumbura (US$166)!

The Air Tanzania flight to Dar es Salaam departs every Sunday and flies via Mwanza. Air France flies to other cities in the region on its twice weekly run from Paris to Bujumbura via Nairobi and Kigali.

OVERLAND
To/From Rwanda
There is a choice of two routes. Which one you take will depend on whether you want to go from Kigali direct to Butare and on to Bujumbura, or via Cyangugu (Lake Kivu).

Butare to Bujumbura From Butare, take a minibus (infrequent) to the border for RFr 200. You'll be met by a gaggle of moneychangers who'll change dollars or Rwandan francs into Burundi francs.

The border is easy-going although you should expect cursory baggage searches on both sides. From the Burundi border village it's possible to catch a minibus to Kayanza (BFr 150) on Tuesdays, Fridays and Sundays (market days in Kayanza); at other times you'll have to hitch or hire a taxi. There are frequent minibuses to Bujumbura (BFr 300, two hours) from Kayanza.

Cyangugu to Bujumbura From Cyangugu take a minibus to the border village of Bugarama. You'll probably have to hitch the next eight km to the Burundi border post at Luhwa and the following 12 km to the village of Rugombo. From Rugombo there are minibuses to Bujumbura for BFr 200 (1½ hours).

There's quite a lot of traffic along this route, so it's easy enough to travel between Cyangugu (or Bukavu in Zaïre) and Bujumbura in a day.

To/From Zaïre

There are two possible routes:

Bukavu to Bujumbura via Cyangugu (Rwanda) Having crossed from Bukavu to Cyangugu this route is identical to the route described above.

Bukavu to Bujumbura via Uvira This is the longer and less comfortable route. First read about travel between Bukavu and Uvira in the Eastern Zaïre chapter, as this route has two options, one through Rwanda and the other direct to Uvira.

Once in Uvira the route into Burundi is across the top of Lake Tanganyika. From Uvira, shared taxis leave until late in the afternoon and take about 15 minutes. From the Zaïre border post to the Burundi border post it's about one km which you'll probably have to walk. You may be able to find a minibus going from the Burundi border post to Bujumbura, but usually you will have to get a shared taxi (BFr 50, about 15 minutes).

LAKE

To/From Tanzania

The two routes available both use Lake Tanganyika at different points. A direct route is from Kigoma on the venerable MV *Liemba*. However, a more interesting route is via Nyanza Lac and Gombe Stream National Park, the chimpanzee sanctuary across the border in Tanzania.

Ferry The MV *Liemba* connects Tanzania with Burundi (and Zambia). It used to operate in conjunction with a sister ship, the MV *Mwongozo*, but this boat now only services ports on the Tanzanian part of the lake (see the Tanzania Getting Around chapter).

The schedule for the MV *Liemba* is more or less regular but it can be delayed for up to

24 hours at either end depending on how much cargo there is to load or unload. Engine trouble can also delay it at any point, though not usually for more than a few hours.

It departs Mpulungu (Zambia) on Friday at about 5 pm, arrives at Kigoma (Tanzania) on Sunday at 10 am, leaves Kigoma at 4 pm the same day and arrives in Bujumbura (Burundi) on Monday at 7.30 am. From Kigoma the fares are:

Destination	1st class	2nd class	3rd class
Bujumbura	128	920	420
Mpulungu	3050	2330	1040

Tickets can be bought from the railway station in Kigoma. For full details of classes and conditions on board and a rundown of the *Liemba's* chequered history, see the Tanzania Getting There chapter.

Lake Taxi The alternative route is to travel by lake taxi between Kigoma and the Tanzanian border village of Kagunga (there is no road) via the Gombe Stream National Park. However, before taking this route into Burundi it's worth noting that the entrance fee for Gombe Stream is now a ludicrous US$50, so a visit to see the chimps is going to cost you at least US$70 just in park fees and accommodation! Unless the authorities were under pressure by the researchers to reduce the number of visitors to Gombe Stream it's hard to understand why the fees have skyrocketed. Maybe it's sheer greed. On the other hand, both Zaïre and Rwanda charge US$100 to see the gorillas.

From Kigoma the lake taxis leave from the small village of Kalalangabo, about three km north of town. The trips to Gombe Stream and on to Kagunga take about half a day each and the fare is TSh 250 per person. These boats are not totally reliable and do not operate on Sundays. When catching a lake taxi, try to get one with a cover as it becomes stinking hot on the lake in the middle of the day. These boats are small, wooden affairs, often overcrowded not only with people but also produce. They offer no creature comforts. They're good fun when the weather is fine, but if there's a squall on the lake you may be in for a rough time.

The border crossing is very straightforward. Tanzanian formalities are taken care of at Kagunga. From there to the Burundi post it's a two km walk along a narrow track. Once into Burundi take a minibus (BFr 100) to Nyanza Lac and check in with Burundi immigration. The office is about one km from the centre of town towards the lake. From Nyanza Lac there are minibuses to Bujumbura (BFr 400). If you get stuck at the border for the night there are a couple of restaurants where you can bed down.

If you intend leaving Tanzania by this route, check with immigration officials in Kigoma as to whether you need to be stamped out in Kigoma or in Kagunga. In the past there has been confusion about this.

Getting Around

AIR
Air Burundi, the national airline, does not have regular internal flights.

BUS
Like Rwanda, Burundi used to be difficult to travel in, especially during the rainy season, because of the lack of decent roads and public transport. Now most of the major routes are sealed.

There are plenty of modern, Japanese minibuses which are fairly frequent, not overcrowded and cheaper than shared taxis. Destinations are displayed in the front window and they depart when full. You can usually find one heading in your direction any day between early morning and early afternoon at the *gare routière* (bus station) in any town or city.

Government OTRACO buses serve the area around Bujumbura.

Around the Country

BUJUMBURA
Sprawling up the mountainside on the northeastern tip of Lake Tanganyika, Bujumbura overlooks the vast wall of mountains in Zaïre on the other side of the lake. The Burundi capital is a mixture of grandiose colonial town planning (wide boulevards and imposing public buildings) and dusty crowded suburbs like those which surround many African cities. It's also one of the most important ports on Lake Tanganyika.

Like Kigali in neighbouring Rwanda, Bujumbura has a sizeable expatriate population of international aid organisation workers, medicos, missionaries and businesspeople. Even Colonel Gaddafi has made his mark here in the form of a large and beautifully conceived Islamic Cultural Centre and mosque which must have cost a

1	BP & FINA Stations
2	Hôtel Au Bon Accueil
3	Hôtel Panama
4	Au Château Fort Hôtel
5	Sonaco (MV *Liemba* tickets)
6	Novotel
7	Tourist Office
8	Restaurant Pizza Oasis
9	Ethiopian Airlines
10	Alliance Française, Boulangerie-Pâtisserie Trianon
11	Aux Délices Restaurant
12	Hôtel Burundi Palace
13	Air Tanzania
14	American Cultural Centre
15	Restaurant Aux Beaux Lilas, Airlines' Agent
16	Aeroflot
17	New Tourist Hôtel
18	Banque de la République du Burundi
19	Banque du Crédit de Bujumbura, Sabena
20	Post Office
21	Market, Minibuses
22	Banque Commerciale du Burundi, American Embassy
23	Zaïre & Rwandan Embassies
24	Hôtel Résidence
25	Tanzanian Embassy

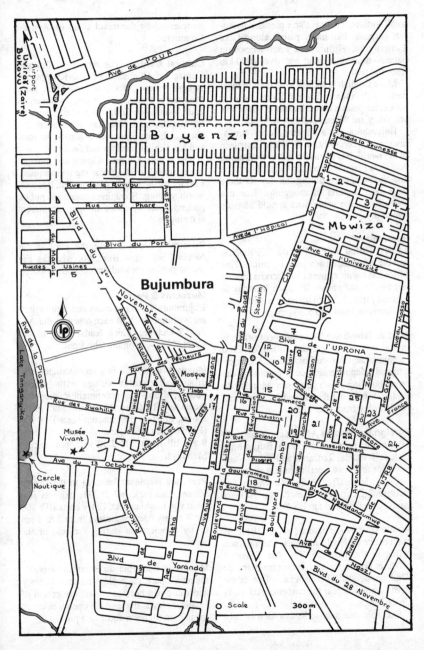

small fortune. There is also a pleasant botanical surprise: like many places along Lake Tanganyika, Bujumbura sports coconut palms – most unusual at well over 1000 km from the sea!

More English is spoken here than in most parts of Rwanda or Eastern Zaïre. Another noticeable point is how tall many of the people are – they are Watutsi and they're huge!

Bujumbura has a slightly sleazy atmosphere and is certainly not the friendliest place in the world. It is advisable not to walk along Ave de la Plage between the Cercle Nautique and the port, even during the day, as there have been reports of muggings. Rue des Swahilis in the same area should also be avoided.

Information

Tourist Office It's on Blvd de l'UPRONA, and the information available is limited. This office has a wide range of handicrafts for sale but they're not cheap. It's open Monday to Saturday from 7.30 am till noon and Monday to Thursday from 2 to 5.30 pm.

Post & Telephone The main post office is in the city centre on the corner of Blvd Lumumba and Ave du Commerce. The international telephone service is housed in the same building. Both are open Monday to Friday from 8 am till noon and 2 to 4 pm, and on Saturday from 8 to 11 am.

Foreign Embassies African countries with diplomatic representation in Bujumbura include Rwanda, Tanzania and Zaïre – see Facts for the Visitor earlier in this chapter.

Consular offices include those for Belgium, Denmark, France, the Netherlands, Germany and the USA.

Airline Offices Air France (tel 26310) has its main office on Blvd Lumumba and a branch office in the Novotel. The Air Tanzania office is also in the city centre on Place de l'Indépendence. The Sabena office is on Blvd Lumumba near the corner of Ave de la Croix Rouge.

Other airlines, such as Kenya Airways, are represented by the travel agent on Ave du Commerce.

Cultural Centres The American Cultural Centre on Chaussée Prince Rwagasore screens video news from the USA from Monday to Friday at 5.15 pm. Its library is open Monday to Friday from 2 to 8 pm and on Tuesday and Thursday from 9 am till noon. Alliance Française is across the road and has similar services and facilities.

The Islamic Cultural Centre and mosque is a beautiful building near the main square. Paid for by the Libyan government, it is well worth visiting. Sometimes there are public performances by dance troupes, drummers and singers.

Swimming Pool To use the pool at the Novotel will cost BFr 500, whereas the public pool at the stadium costs BFr 300.

Museums & Park

Bujumbura's two museums and reptile park are within a block of each other on the Ave du 13 Octobre which leads down to the Cercle Nautique on the lake front.

Musée Vivant This is a reconstructed traditional Burundian village with basket, pottery, drum and photographic displays. Occasionally there are traditional drum shows. Entry to the museum costs BFr 100 (BFr 50 for students) and it's open daily from 9 am till noon and 2.30 to 5 pm, except Mondays.

Parc des Reptiles Adjacent to the Musée Vivant, this park (tel 25374) exhibits just what you might expect. Entry costs BFr 200 but it's only open Saturdays from 2 to 4 pm or by appointment during the rest of the week.

Musée de Géologie du Burundi Opposite the reptile park, the geology museum is dusty and run-down but has a good collection of fossils. Entry is free and it's open weekdays from 7 am till noon and 2 to 5 pm.

Places to Stay – bottom end

It can be difficult to find a reasonably priced place to stay in Bujumbura, especially at weekends or if you arrive late in the day. Also, many of the cheaper places are more or less permanently filled with expatriate aid workers. You may have to do some leg work!

For years now budget travellers have found a warm welcome at the *Vugizu Mission* (tel 32059) run by the Johnson family. There's a two-bed caravan and a tent (which sleeps two) in the garden of the mission for travellers' use. These facilities plus an excellent breakfast are free and there are no chores to do. The mission is on a beautiful site overlooking the lake near the University Hospital in Kamenge.

The mission is a considerable distance from the centre so catch a bus or taxi. A taxi from the city centre to the mission costs about BFr 400. The best bus is the OTRACO bus to Gisenyi which takes you almost to the mission, but there are only three buses each morning and afternoon. It's easier to get a minibus (from the main bus stand) to Kamenge. These leave frequently. Get off at the large road junction where there are the petrol stations and ask for directions to Johnson's – about a 500 metre walk.

If you're coming into Bujumbura on a bus from Kayanza or Bugarama, ask to be let off at the large road junction at Kamenge.

Another place to pitch a tent is at the *Cercle Nautique* (yacht club) on the lake shore, a 15 minute walk from the city centre.

For regular hotels, the cheapest are in the suburb of Mbwiza, about 10 minutes walk north-west of the city centre and 15 minutes east of the port. It's a fairly depressed district with car bodies rusting in the dirt streets, inadequate drainage and an air of neglect. None of the streets are signposted, but 6th Ave is the one which runs alongside the BP station, almost opposite the small post office on Chaussée du Peuple Burundi. Fifth Ave is the next one back towards the city centre, alongside the FINA station.

The cheapest of the habitable places is the *Hôtel Panama* on 5th Ave. Singles/doubles cost BFr 850/1250 and are basic but OK.

The *Au Château Fort Hôtel* is also on 5th Ave, a couple of blocks further from Chaussée du Peuple Burundi. It has a variety of rooms ranging from BFr 630 for a cupboard to BFr 1250 for a double. There are so many security grilles and gates that the place seems like a prison. It also makes you wonder about the likelihood of getting out in a hurry if there was a fire.

A better place on the same street is the *New Bwiza Hôtel* which charges BFr 800 for a single or BFr 1200 for a couple in the same room; no doubles. It's a friendly place and there's mosquito netting on the windows.

If you can afford the extra, the friendly *Hôtel Au Bon Accueil* on 6th Ave in Mbwiza is well worth it. The rooms are all upstairs and have outward facing windows which catch any breeze that's going. The common facilities are kept reasonably clean and there's a good bar and restaurant downstairs. Singles/doubles cost BFr 1500/3000. If it's not busy and you are catching the MV *Liemba* at 4 pm, staff will often let you keep the room until 3 pm.

The *Hôtel Résidence* (tel 23886) is close to the city centre and has a variety of rooms ranging from BFr 1500 to BFr 2800 for singles or couples. It charges half as much again for two people of the same sex (a common practice here and in Eastern Zaïre).

Places to Stay – middle

To stay in the city centre the cheapest place is the *Hôtel Burundi Palace* which has singles/doubles for BFr 2450/3150 and BFr 1200 for an extra bed.

The *New Tourist Hôtel* on Place de l'Indépendance has been renovated and charges BFr 3000 for a single or a double.

Places to Stay – top end

The *Novotel*, Chaussée du Peuple Burundi, is everything you would expect a hotel of this type to be. Rooms are from BFr 11,500.

The *Hôtel Club des Vacances* on the lake shore is popular with the local expatriate population at weekends. Entry to the beach costs BFr 500 and there's a nightclub as well.

A taxi from the city centre costs about BFr 500.

Places to Eat – cheap

If you're staying in Mbwiza and want to eat basic African street food, try the *Restaurant des Jeunes* behind the FINA petrol station on Chaussée du Peuple Burundi. It's as basic as you can get, but the food is fine and very cheap – rice and beans cost BFr 90, or try potato, plantains and spinach. No English is spoken so you need to know the food names in KiSwahili.

On almost every corner in Mbwiza there seems to be a makeshift stall selling brochettes, although the hygiene at some places leaves a lot to be desired. Another place in Mbwiza is the *New Nusura Restaurant* on 7th Ave.

We heard bad reports about the *Restaurant Aux Beaux Lilas*, Ave du Commerce, in the city centre. It has apparently become expensive and many items on the menu are missing.

A good place for excellent coffee and home-made ice cream is the *Café Polar* on Chaussée Prince Rwagasore, one block back from the Ave du Zaïre. Coffee costs BFr 50, ice cream BFr 100 and a tortilla BFr 250 (very filling).

The *Cotton Club* in the Asian part of town has cheap food and good rock or folk music all the time. Don't be late as food runs out early.

Super-Snack-Sympa behind the market has good pizzas, lasagna and a special 'hamburger', all with vegetables, cream and tortilla bread for US$1.50.

Other places to try include the *Polar,* up on Rwagasore, which has good coffee, marakuja juice, hamburgers and ice cream, and the *Caf'Snack 2000*.

For travellers staying at the Vugizu Mission in Kamenge, there's a place selling kebabs on the main road where you catch the buses to Bujumbura. The kebabs sell for US$0.50

On the same road, but further along (about one km), are several nice and cheap bars.

There's also the *Mukate Papa* restaurant which is good value.

Places to Eat – more expensive

The *Boulangerie-Pâtisserie Trianon* on Chaussée Prince Rwagasore is a popular place for breakfast. For good snacks and main meals, the nearby *Aux Délices* is also popular, although the main attraction seems to be the video rather than the food. Meals are from BFr 1000 to BFr 1500 and snacks range from BFr 500 to BFr 1000. The service is not exactly fast as the waiters also find the video interesting.

Back in Mbwiza, the *Hôtel Au Bon Accueil* has a good restaurant and bar. The back lawn becomes a very pleasant beer garden and al fresco restaurant in the evening. Cold Primus beer costs BFr 140.

For a splurge you could do worse than try the *Restaurant Pizza Oasis* on the corner of Ave Victoire and Blvd de l'UPRONA. It's open Monday to Saturday from noon till 2 pm and from 7 to 10 pm, and is expensive. Another more expensive place is the *Cercle Nautique* (tel 2559) on the lake front at the end of Ave du 13 Octobre. You can eat very well here for between BFr 800 and BFr 1000 whilst enjoying the views which include the occasional hippo. It's a great place to sip a cold beer even if you don't want to eat. The Cercle is open daily, except Tuesday, from 5 pm and on Sunday from 11 am.

Entertainment

Most nightclubs are by the lake shore in the vicinity of the Hôtel Club des Vacances. The best ones are the *Black & White* and the *Bamboo*. A taxi from the centre costs about BFr 500; it's not safe to walk.

Getting Around

The international airport is 11 km from the city.

GITEGA

Gitega is the second largest town in Burundi and is home to the National Museum. Although small, the museum is well worth a visit and is very educational. Entry is free.

There might be a folklore performance – ask if the *tambourinaires* are playing. They usually play at Gishola, about 10 km away, on the last Sunday of every month.

Places to Stay
The *Mission Catholique* is probably the best place to enquire for budget accommodation. It has a huge guest house.

KAYANZA
Kayanza is on the road north to Kigali, not far from the Rwandan border. It has a good market on Mondays, Wednesdays and Saturdays.

Places to Stay
The missions won't take guests so stay at the *Auberge de Kayanza* which costs BFr 960 a double.

Getting There & Away
Matatus from Bujumbura cost BFr 300 and take about two hours. See the Getting There chapter for details on getting from Kayanza to the Rwandan border.

KILEMBA
The principal attraction are the Kibabi Hot Springs, 16 km from town. There are several pools of differing temperature, the main one hovering around 100°C. A little further uphill is a waterfall and another deep pool where it's safe to swim.

Places to Stay
Most people stay at the *Swedish Pentecostal Mission* which has a very good guest house. A bed in the dormitory costs BFr 150. Private rooms with a shower and toilet and the use of a fully equipped kitchen cost BFr 600 per person.

SOURCE DU NIL
This is the southernmost source of the Nile. It's possible to stay at the *Mission Catholique* in Rutana seven km away.

Eastern Zaïre

This section covers a narrow strip of eastern Zaïre from the northern tip of Lake Tanganyika to Lake Mobutu Sese Seko, along the borders with Burundi, Rwanda and Uganda. It is included because it is an integral part of the mountainous area that forms the western wall of the Rift Valley. It is also considerably easier to get to from East Africa than it is from the west coast, which entails a journey through the jungles of the Congo Basin.

A full history of Zaïre would not be appropriate since only a small part of Kivu Province is covered and many of the historical events which have taken place in the western parts of Zaïre have no connection with events on the eastern borders.

There's some magnificent countryside and a lot of things to see and do in eastern Zaïre, such as mountain climbing and visiting gorilla sanctuaries and pygmy settlements.

Facts about the Country

HISTORY

Because of the altitude and the fertile soil in eastern Zaïre, the Belgian colonialists developed many coffee plantations early in the 20th century. They also built up the lake resort towns of Bukavu and Goma and several mountain retreats further north. These days it is Mobutu, president of Zaïre since 1965, and his cronies who maintain summer palaces here, partly to ensure that their presence is felt in this far flung corner.

It isn't only Mobutu, however, who is keen to maintain a presence here. In few other areas of East Africa will you encounter so much Christian missionary activity. The number of different sects hard at work saving souls is little short of amazing. The whole range of Catholic and Protestant sects are involved, as are the ubiquitous Seventh Day Adventists, Mormons and Jehovah's Witnesses. It's probably a good idea that they have chosen to work this area so intensively, as their schools and hospitals provide many people with their only educational and medical facilities. Few funds are available for these sorts of facilities from the central government and, because Mobuto's regime is so corrupt and only interested in hanging onto power, the funds shrink every year.

In the early years following independence in 1960, there was very little direct control of Kivu Province by the central government in Kinshasa and, consequently, local governors enjoyed virtual autonomy. The attempted secession by the southern province of Shaba (formerly Katanga) under Moise Tshombe, and the subsequent intervention by the United Nations is well known. These events prompted the overthrow and murder of Zaïre's first prime minister, Patrice Lumumba, and his replacement by Joseph Kasavubu with assistance from Mobutu, the army commander at the time. What is less well known is that after the Katangan secession had been crushed, Kasavubu was faced with armed revolt by the governors of the eastern provinces, including Kivu Province. His failure to crush the rebellion and bring the governors to book led to his overthrow by Mobutu in 1965.

Mobutu has certainly restored a high level of centralised control to Zaïre since he came to power, but the costs in terms of wasted resources, repression, jailings, executions, corruption and a decaying infrastructure have been enormous.

It is unlikely that Mobutu will be replaced until he dies. He is a cunning and ruthless politician who has perfected a personality cult in a way few other African presidents have been able to match. These days he rules as a half-god, half-chieftain, combining the sophisticated techniques of 20th century communication with traditional tribal symbolism. His photograph is to be seen everywhere, often accompanied by one of

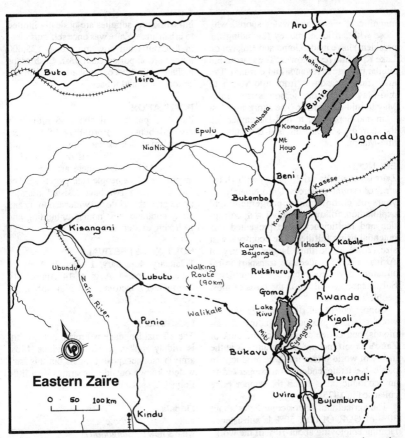

Eastern Zaïre

0   50   100 km

the many slogans underlining his indispens-ability and benevolence, such as 'Mobutu: The Unifier'; 'Mobutu: The Pacifier'; 'Mobutu: The Guide'. It would almost be a comic opera if it wasn't so serious, as one day the people of Zaïre will have to pay for the extravagance and neglect.

GEOGRAPHY

Geographically this area is quite different from the rest of Zaïre. It is a land of huge volcanoes and vast, deep lakes. Some of the volcanoes, such as those at the northern end of Lake Kivu, have erupted in the last decade and Nyiragongo is still smoking but the rest

are currently dormant. Others, where the borders of Zaïre, Rwanda and Uganda meet, haven't erupted in living memory and their upper slopes are among the last remaining sanctuaries for the rare mountain gorillas.

The Ruwenzori Mountains along the border with Uganda are the highest in the region and the only ones with permanent snow cover on the peaks. These are not typical as they are not volcanic. It's a wild and beautiful area of Africa.

CLIMATE

Eastern Zaïre enjoys a Mediterranean climate. This is one reason, apart from the magnificent views and water sports, why those with sufficient money (including the president) have made Goma and Bukavu on Lake Kivu into resort towns. The seasons are similar to those in Rwanda and Burundi. The main rainy season is from mid-March to mid-May and the dry season is from mid-May to mid-September. The short rains last from mid-September to mid-December and the short dry season from mid-December to mid-March.

ECONOMY

Zaïre is potentially a rich country with a huge array of natural resources. Unfortunately the years of colonial mismanagement and exploitation, followed by civil war, corruption and inefficiency have prevented this potential being fulfilled. The country's vast size (Zaïre is the third largest country in Africa) and its inadequate transport infrastructure have exacerbated the problems. Subsistence agriculture is the basis of most people's existence.

Copper, cobalt, oil, diamonds (Zaïre is the world's largest producer of industrial diamonds) and coffee account for the bulk of Zaïre's export income. The country is at the mercy of world prices for these products. In particular, its dependency on copper led to an economic crisis when the copper price collapsed in 1975.

The agricultural sector contributes about 30% of GDP. Of that, 50% is subsistence farming employing about 70% of the workforce. The main subsistence crops include cassava, maize and rice. With the terrible

infrastructure, supplies are basically limited to urban areas. Zaïre was once self-sufficient in foodstuffs but now more than 125,000 tonnes are imported each year. Cash crops include coffee, cocoa, rubber, tea, palm oil, cotton, sugar and tobacco.

POPULATION

Zaïre's population of about 35 million is divided between more than 200 tribes, several of which extend into neighbouring countries. Eastern Zaïre is one of the few areas in Africa where there are significant numbers of Twa people (the pygmies). The forest-dwelling Twa have resisted attempts to integrate them into the wider economy and many continue their nomadic, hunting and gathering existence.

HOLIDAYS & FESTIVALS

1 January, 4 January, 1 May, 20 May, 24 June, 30 June, 1 August, 14 August, 14 October, 27 October, 17 November, 24 November, 25 December.

LANGUAGE

The official language is French but Swahili is widely spoken in Kivu Province. Most army personnel speak Lingala but this isn't widely known outside the army. Very little English is spoken.

Lingala

hello	*mbote*
what's new?	*sangonini?*
nothing new	*sangote*
go	*nake*
depart	*kokende*
where?	*wapi?*
where are?	*okeyi wapi?*
why?	*ponanini?*
OK/thanks	*malam*
very far	*musika*
tomorrow	*lobi*
house	*ndako*
home	*mboka*
to eat	*kolia*
to drink	*komela*
things to eat	*biloko yakolia*
water	*mai*

manioc	*songo*
bananas	*makemba*
rice	*loso*
beans	*madeso*
salted fish	*makaibo*
fresh fish	*mbisi*
meat	*nyama*
peanuts	*injunga karanga*
market	*nazondo*
strong	*makasi*
a lot	*mingi*
new	*sango*
dog	*mbwa*

Facts for the Visitor

VISAS

Visas are required by everyone. The cost of a visa depends on whether you want a one month, two month or three month visa and whether you want single or multiple entries. If there's any chance that you'll need a multiple-entry visa get it at the start and save a lot of hassle.

All visa applications must be accompanied by a letter of introduction from your own embassy (except in Bangui and Harare). Some embassies issue these free while others charge for them. British embassies charge about US$7.50! You may also be asked for an onward ticket and vaccination certificates (cholera and yellow fever). On the visa application form it may say, 'Entry through Kinshasa only', but this isn't stamped in your passport so it doesn't matter.

Embassies

In Africa visas can be obtained from Zaïrois embassies in Abidjan (Ivory Coast), Accra (Ghana), Addis Ababa (Ethiopia), Algiers (Algeria), Bangui (Central African Republic), Brazzaville (Congo), Bujumbura (Burundi), Cairo (Egypt), Conakry (Guinea), Cotonou (Benin), Dakar (Senegal), Dar es Salaam (Tanzania), Harare (Zimbabwe), Kampala (Uganda), Khartoum (Sudan), Kigali (Rwanda), Lagos (Nigeria), Libreville (Gabon), Lomé (Togo), Luanda (Angola), Lusaka (Zambia), Maputo (Mozambique), Monrovia (Liberia), Nairobi (Kenya), Nouakchott (Mauritania), N'Djamena (Chad), Rabat (Morocco), Tripoli (Libya), Tunis (Tunisia) and Yaoundé (Cameroon), and from the Zaïre Consulate in Kigoma (Tanzania).

Outside Africa there are embassies in Berlin and Bonn (Germany), London (UK), Madrid (Spain), Paris (France), Rome (Italy) and Washington DC (USA).

Although the cost of a visa is quite reasonable in Nairobi (US$7.50), Bujumbura (US$10) and Kigoma (US$8), in Kampala, Kigali and Dar es Salaam they cost an outrageous US$70 minimum, so avoid applying in those places.

Kenya The embassy (tel 29771) is at Electricity House, Harambee Ave, Nairobi. A one month visa costs KSh 160, a two month visa is KSh 280 and a three month visa is KSh 350. There is no extra charge for multiple entry; just request it on your application form. Four photographs and a letter of introduction from your own embassy are required and the visa is issued in 24 hours. Staff are pleasant and the embassy is open Monday to Friday from 9 am till noon.

Rwanda In Kigali the embassy (tel 75327) is on Rue Député Kamuzinzi off Ave de Rusumo. Don't get a visa here unless you have about US$70 to spare – banditry again! One month single-entry visas cost RFr 6500; two month multiple-entry visas cost RFr 9500. Three photographs are required for any visa and they are generally issued in 24 hours. A letter of recommendation from your own embassy is generally not needed nor is an onward ticket, but regulations change from time to time.

There are no Zaïrois consulates in either Gisenyi or Cyangugu.

Tanzania In Dar es Salaam the Zaïre Embassy is on Malik Rd near the junction with United Nations Rd. Visas cost US$80, require three photographs and a letter of introduction from your own embassy. It's difficult to get anything other than a one month, single-entry visa. Visas take 48 hours to be issued. The embassy is open on Monday, Wednesday and Friday from 11 am to 2 pm.

At the Zaïre Consulate in Kigoma on Lake Tanganyika, a one month single-entry visa costs TSh 2000, requires four photos and is issued in 24 hours. Office hours are Monday to Friday from 9 am till noon.

Uganda Don't come to Kampala with the idea of picking up a Zaïre visa. It is nothing short of extortion at US$70 for a one month single-entry visa and US$100 if you want multiple entry – paid for in hard currency! It's scandalous, especially as the same visa in Nairobi costs the equivalent of about US$7.50! If you still want to apply, the embassy (tel 23377) is at 20 Philip Rd, Kololo District. It's open Monday to Friday from 8 am to 3 pm, although visa applications are only accepted before noon. A letter of introduction from your own embassy and two photos are required and the visa is issued in 24 hours.

Visa Extension
Visa extensions can be obtained in Bukavu. Travellers report that extensions for up to three months are easy to get here.

Other African Visas
Burundi At the consulate in Bukavu (SINELAC Building, top floor, 184 Ave du Président Mobutu) visas cost Z4600, require two photographs and are issued in 24 hours. The consulate is open Monday to Friday from 7.30 am till noon and 2.30 to 5 pm.

Rwanda There are no Rwandan consulates at either Bukavu or Goma in eastern Zaïre, so it's advisable to get your visa in Kinshasa (or elsewhere) if you're coming from the west. Several travellers have reported that it's possible to get a *permis provisoire* (a type of transit visa), valid for one week, for about US$46 on demand at the Goma-Gisenyi border or, assuming you have the time, a tourist visa from the Belgian Consulate in

Goma for about US$17. The latter takes two weeks to be issued and you have to leave your passport with them. The same may be true for the Belgian Consulate in Bukavu. The regulations change constantly so don't rely on this possibility.

It's probably wise to have both Rwandan and Zaïrois multiple-entry visas if you intend to go by road between Bukavu and Bujumbura as there are a couple of alternatives and a multiple-entry visa gives you flexibility. On the other hand, the latest reports indicate that Rwandan transit visas are available at the border for RFr 1600.

Kenya, Tanzania & Uganda There are no consulates for these countries in eastern Zaïre. The nearest embassies are in Kigali (Rwanda) and Bujumbura (Burundi).

MONEY
US$1 = Z400

The unit of currency is the zaïre, which is equivalent to 100 makutas, although you're not likely to see anything smaller than Z1 now, and even then only when you change money in a bank. At current rates the Z1 note is worth approximately US$0.0025! Notes in circulation are Z5000, Z1000, Z500, Z100, Z50, Z20, Z10, Z5 and Z1.

There are old and new banknotes in circulation. They're all legal tender but the designs differ and the old notes are huge and usually in an advanced state of decrepitude. Most notes carry a government health warning. Banks love giving them to you, perhaps as a joke, but more probably because they're usually low denominations so it's easy for them to miss a few out without you noticing.

There is very little difference between the bank exchange rate and the street rate. Changing cash on the street does, however, save you a lot of time and you don't pay commission. You can expect up to Z450 for the US dollar. It's not always easy to find someone who wants to change money (Asian and European shopkeepers are your best bet) but most people can be persuaded if you accept something near the bank rate.

If you have travellers' cheques, shop around before changing them as commissions can vary from 1% to 20%! Some banks won't even change travellers' cheques (the Banque de Kinshasa in Goma and the Banque de Zaïre in Bukavu, for example). The Banque Commerciale Zaïroise is probably the best bet as their commission is negligible and you can usually have your cheque cashed in half an hour. At the Union des Banques Zaïroises, some travellers have been charged 20% commission.

Banking hours are Monday to Friday from 8 to 11.30 am, but if you're changing travellers' cheques, you must arrive before 11 am as they won't entertain you after that.

There are lots of hilarious stories circulating about banks and travellers' cheques in eastern Zaïre. One traveller spent all day at a bank in Bukavu (he didn't say which one) trying to change a travellers' cheque. They wouldn't change it because it didn't have 'Specimen' printed across it like the bank's sample! We heard another story about a manager who wouldn't change a US$100 cheque because his sample was a US$50 cheque. Others may refuse if your cheque is issued by a company which has a different

name to the manager's sample. You should not run into anything as silly as this at the Banque Commerciale Zaïroise in either Goma or Bukavu, but you cannot change travellers' cheques at the bank in Uvira.

Currency declaration forms were abolished in May 1986 but that doesn't mean that this information has percolated down to every customs and immigration officer at every border post. In early 1990 the border between Kisoro (Uganda) and Rutshuru was still issuing them. If you're issued with one you can safely ignore it.

The import or export of local currency is officially prohibited and you may well be asked if you have any when leaving Zaïre. It's very unlikely that you will be searched. Moreover, there will be some occasions when you simply have to take zaïres into Zaïre (at weekends, for instance, if you only have travellers' cheques, or any day of the week if you're crossing to Uvira from Bujumbura where banks won't change cheques). You must hide them though.

COSTS

Like Uganda, eastern Zaïre is not the travel bargain it used to be. You'll be spending much the same as you spend in Rwanda or Burundi. A basic single room in a hotel costs

about Z1500. Once again the mission hostels are good value for money, if a little austere.

It's usually fairly cheap to travel in Zaïre and there's a much better selection of hotels and restaurants in most towns than you would find in neighbouring Burundi or Rwanda. Where there are no public buses (and there are not many) you will be reliant on overcrowded pick-ups or hitching rides on trucks. The fares are negotiable but you shouldn't have to pay more than the local people.

A visit to the mountain or plains gorillas will set you back US$100, payable in hard currency (cash or travellers' cheques) at the entrance to the Parc National de Kahuzi-Biega or at the tourist office in Goma for the Parc National des Virunga. Other national park entry fees are US$50 regardless of how long you stay. Climbing Nyiragongo Volcano attracts a US$30 fee.

GENERAL INFORMATION

Post

There's a small charge for each letter collected from poste restante.

Time

Eastern Zaïre is GMT plus two hours.

HEALTH

Take precautions against malaria. If you stay in Zaïre a long time you could pick it up. I've met very few American Peace Corps volunteers in Zaïre who haven't had at least one bout of malaria, despite the fact they were taking prophylactics.

Tap water is not safe to drink, so purify it first.

Another condition you might pick up, especially if you only wear thongs, is jiggers (tropical fleas which burrow under your skin). Get them pulled out at a clinic. They're easy to remove if you know what you're doing.

FILM & PHOTOGRAPHY

Bring all your film requirements to Zaïre. About the only places where you can buy film are Bukavu and Goma, and it's expensive. Check the expiry date carefully.

When entering Zaïre, customs officers may demand that you buy a photography permit for each camera that you have. The usual charge is about US$3. It's my firm belief that these 'permits' are an unbridled act of creativity on the part of the customs officers and that the money they fleece from travellers merely supplements their pay. I've seen receipts issued on Republic of the Congo note paper (Zaïre hasn't been called the Congo since 1971). I'm not sure what the answer to this is. After all, who do you complain to? Crossing from Gisenyi to Goma, this is only sprung on you at the Poids Lourds post, not at the lakeshore post.

Don't take photographs of anything vaguely connected with the military or of government buildings, banks, bridges, border posts, post offices or ports. If anyone sees you the chances are you'll lose your film. There is intense paranoia about spies in some places (Uvira is one of them) because Zaïre doesn't get on well with Burundi, Rwanda or Tanzania. On a visit to Burundi and Rwanda in 1985, Colonel Gaddafi stated that Mobutu's assassin would be guaranteed a place in paradise! They also haven't forgotten the Katanga secession in the 1960s, the invasions from Angola in the 1970s and the more recent raids from Tanzania. If you don't want to run into problems while snapping pics, get a written OK from the Sous-Régional Commissioner. You may have to cross his palm to get it but don't offer unless it's strongly indicated. Travellers have been arrested for taking pictures of such innocent scenes as markets.

Getting There

AIR
The national airline, Air Zaïre, flies into Goma from Kinshasa and Kisangani on a fairly regular basis but occasionally it can be diverted, depending on cargo requirements. The jet is sometimes commandeered by the president on his visits to Goma and Bukavu. You may be able to get student discounts if you're under 26 years of age, but it usually involves a lot of talking!

OVERLAND
To/From Burundi
There are two routes to Zaïre from Burundi.

Bujumbura to Bukavu via Cyangugu (Rwanda) This route goes from Bujumbura via the Burundi-Rwanda border at Bugarama to Cyangugu in Rwanda, from where it's just a short hop across the Zaïre border into Bukavu. See the Rwanda Getting There section for details on the Bujumbura to Cyangugu leg. For details of the Cyangugu-Bukavu border crossing see To/From Rwanda in this section.

Bujumbura to Bukavu via Uvira (Zaïre) The second route goes from Bujumbura to Bukavu via Uvira (in Zaïre, just across the border from Bujumbura). This route has two variations: the first (and less comfortable) is the direct road between Uvira and Bukavu (see the Bukavu section); the second also goes from Uvira to Bukavu but mostly through Rwanda to make use of the far superior Rwandan roads. To take this route you'll need a Rwandan visa and a multiple-entry

Zaïre visa to re-enter Zaïre. In the past, border formalities have sometimes been dispensed with so that officially you never left Zaïre. This was because the amount of time you spent in Rwanda was minimal and you had no intention of staying in that country. This doesn't seem to happen any more, so check that you have the necessary visa stamps. If you do have a Rwandan visa the best bet is to use the route direct from Bujumbura to Bukavu via Bugarama and Cyangugu anyway. You certainly don't miss anything by bypassing Uvira.

To/From Rwanda
The two main crossing points between Rwanda and Zaïre are between Gisenyi and Goma and between Cyangugu and Bukavu. These borders are open for non-Africans from 6 am to 6 pm.

Gisenyi to Goma There are two border crossing points between Gisenyi and Goma – the Poids Lourds crossing (a rough road) along the main road north of the ritzy part of Gisenyi, and a sealed road along the lake shore. It's between two and three km either way. Minibuses run to the border along the Poids Lourds route but not along the lake shore.

The easier of the two routes is along the lake shore, but you'll have to take a taxi (RFr 350) or a taxi-motor (RFr 50) or walk to it. I strolled through this border at 7.30 am one morning and was in Goma within five minutes! The officials at the Poids Lourds post are apparently not quite as amenable.

From either post, once on the Zaïre side it's a couple of km into Goma. You can get a motorcycle for Z250.

Cyangugu to Bukavu Cyangugu is the actual border post here, but Kamembe is the town and transport centre and is where you'll be let down if arriving from elsewhere in Rwanda. From here there are minibuses (RFr 30) for the 15 minute ride to the border at Cyangugu. It's an easy border crossing and you can walk between the two posts. From the Zaïre side it's a Z500 taxi ride or a three km walk into Bukavu.

To/From Uganda

The two main crossing points are south from Kisoro to Rutshuru and west from Kasese to Beni via Katwe and Kasindi. The Ishasha crossing between Kasese and Rutshuru is also open. There are less used border posts further north between Mahagi and Pakwach and between Aru and Arua. If you're thinking of crossing between Aru and Arua you'd be wise to make enquiries about security before leaving. Ratbag remnants of Amin's, Obote's and Okello's troops may still be making a nuisance of themselves in this area.

Kisoro to Rutshuru The most reliable crossing is between Kisoro and Rutshuru, a distance of about 30 km. There are matatus from Kisoro to the border (nine km) for USh 250. Ugandan officials at the border will demand to see your currency declaration form and bank receipts but are usually amenable if you don't have the receipts. On the Zaïre side, your bags will be searched and vaccination certificates checked but otherwise there are no problems. From here you'll have to hitch and the road is very rough. There's a basic hotel on the Zaïre side of the border which charges Z600 a single.

It's possible to visit the gorillas before going on to Rutshuru. A guide will meet you at the restaurant about one km from the border post. He will offer to take you to the hut in the Parc National des Virunga. The guide knows a short cut which takes two hours instead of eight via the road. The walk is through mountain villages and is very interesting. He'll expect US$5 per person for this, but large groups can barter (US$10 to US$20 for everyone).

Kasese to Rutshuru The Ishasha border is another possibility, although the road between Katunguru and Ishasha (marked on most maps as a second class road) is impassable – don't try it! The alternative route is the road from Ishaka (on the Kasese-Mbarara road) through Rukungiri and Kihihi. There

is a steady trickle of traffic along this route so hitching from Ishaka shouldn't be too much of a problem; there's even the occasional matatu. There's a market on Fridays at Ishasha, so this is probably the best day to go. The Ugandan customs official stationed at this border post actually lives in Kihihi, so it may be possible to hitch to the border with him. For a place to stay in Kihihi, check out the Hilltop Lodge.

For an interesting diversion from Ishasha, the Ishasha River Camp is 17 km inside the Ruwenzori National Park from Ishasha on the Ugandan side. You'll have to wait for a lift as walking in this part of the park is prohibited because of lions. There are no supplies of any sort (apart from Primus beer from Zaïre), though the rangers will cook something up for you if you're desperate. Camping costs US$2 and bandas are US$4 (payable in Ugandan shillings).

Kasese to Beni The route from Kasese to Beni via Katwe, Mpondwe and Kasindi involves hitching unless you can find a matatu. Again, depending on the day you go, this could involve a considerable wait (hours rather than days), whichever of the two turn-offs you take going west. If you want to take this route it would be a good idea to make enquiries in Kasese before you set off.

From Kasese there are occasional matatus to the border post at Bwero (US$0.70) where accommodation is available on the Ugandan side for US$1 at the Modern Lodge Hotel. Once across the border there is accommodation in a basic hotel (Z700) in Kasindi and from here there are connections to Beni.

To/From Central Zaïre

Kisangani to Goma The main route at present between eastern Zaïre and Kisangani on the Zaïre River is from Komanda on the Beni to Bunia road via Mambasa, Epulu, Nia Nia and Bafwasende. There are some diabolical stretches of road en route but it's generally passable even in the wet season. Trucks cover the route regularly. The journey can take as little as 2½ days but three would be usual at the best of times. In the wet season you should count on six days or even more (without breakdowns).

There's also the occasional possibility of negotiating a lift with one of those overland trucks which cart pseudo-adventurers from one end of the continent to the other at vast expense. If you're an independent traveller it might be barely tolerable for a few days. For further details of this route you'll need a copy of Lonely Planet's *Africa on a shoestring*.

Kisangani to Bukavu This is perhaps the easiest route between Kisangani and the Lake Kivu region but it does involve a trek of about three days through the jungle – interesting and not at all dangerous. Travellers are increasingly using this route and they

Mask from Zaïre

rave about it as one of the best thing they did in Zaïre – second only to the river trip from western Zaïre to Kisangani.

The walk is along the route of the new road being constructed between Kisangani and Bukavu, so how far you have to walk depends on the speed of the road crews. Early in 1990 there was still a distance of about 60 km uncompleted but this is gradually being reduced. The western section of the road is being constructed by Germans and the eastern section by Chinese. It's an impressive road.

From Kisangani, hitch to Lobutu (Z1000) and from there to the German depot at Amisi. The total distance of about 400 km can be done in just four to five hours along an excellent road – amazing for Zaïre! Many travellers have reported excellent hospitality at this depot but it's usually extended only to those who have walked from the east rather than those arriving from the west. Either way, don't take it for granted. The depot is on a hill from which there are views of jungle on all sides. From the depot you may be offered a lift to a truck depot at Osso village and from there to where the bulldozers are pushing the jungle aside. From here you start the walk proper.

The route is an easy to follow path which connects many of the villages and is well used by the locals. In sequence, the villages you pass through from Mondindi are Maula, Andre, Kibati, Ondofea, Mabek, Kuba, Biruwe, Obianda, Mafombi, Loyo, Kanyama, Chingala and Ossukari. The hospitality you encounter can be disarming, although this will undoubtedly change as the route is used by more foreigners. Remember to give a gift that covers costs to anyone who offers you somewhere to stay for the night. There are also three mission stations en route – at Ossukari (Catholic), Biruwe (Catholic) and Ondofea (Protestant) – where you may be able to find accommodation. It's probably a good idea to carry some food with you but it's usually available from the *mamas* in the larger villages – normally rice and beans or cassava leaves cooked in palm oil (Z100 to Z200 for a large plate). Other food is scarce, though bananas are usually available. Some tinned food (sardines) is also sold but expect to pay at least four times the normal price.

Along this trail you'll pass many gold mines where gold can be bought (unofficially) for about US$8 to US$10 a gram.

At the end of the trail (Mondindi) you will meet the Chinese road crews who may give you a lift to Walikale (their base) where there's a small hotel and a few shops. From Walikale there is regular truck and minibus transport to Bukavu. The trucks are preferable. They take nine hours and charge Z4000. The minibuses take far longer.

If you are coming in the opposite direction (from Bukavu), you may be able to find a lift with the Chinese to Walikale – try the Club Sportif.

It is hoped that the road will be completed by 1992, but anything is possible and most things are impossible in this part of the world, so don't hold your breath!

LAKE
To/From Tanzania
It is no longer possible to cross Lake Tanganyika from Kigoma in Tanzania to Kalemie in Zaïre unless you can find a friendly skipper who's prepared to take you on a cargo boat – it's a long shot.

Getting Around

AIR
Quite a few private airline companies operate small planes between various places in eastern Zaïre. If you're in a desperate hurry, these might be of interest. VAC flies the half-hour between Goma and Bukavu twice daily for Z19,000. Scibe-Airlift operates a similar service. VAC also flies between Bukavu and Kisangani for Z32,000.

ROAD
With a few exceptions, getting around Zaïre is an exercise in initiative, imagination, patience, persistence and endurance. It's archetypal Africa and it promises some of the most memorable adventures you're ever likely to experience. To enjoy it and not end up with a frazzled brain, forget your fetish for getting from A to B in a certain time or eating food and staying in accommodation of a particular standard. Few things can be guaranteed, nothing runs on time and, in the wet season, you could be stranded for days or even weeks waiting for a lift or for the road to dry out sufficiently to give you a fighting chance of getting through. On the other hand, the beer rarely runs out. Aside from Australia and Germany, there are few other countries which place such a high priority on their beer supplies.

Roads are often in a diabolical state of repair, with potholes large enough to swallow a truck, but they do tend to get smoothed out as the dry season progresses.

BOAT
There are three boats which ply between Goma and Bukavu on Lake Kivu. It's a pleasant trip with incomparable views of the Virunga volcanoes across the lake. None of the boats call at Rwandan ports nor do the Rwandan ferries call at Zaïrois ports.

The boats are the *Karisimbi*, the *Vedette* and the *Mulamba*. The first two are government owned and operated. The *Vedette* is purely a passenger boat while the *Karisimbi* takes freight (including motorcycles) too. Both are crowded and not particularly comfortable.

The *Mulamba* is a privately owned vessel which carries beer from the Primus factory in Bukavu to Goma once a week. It is a far more comfortable boat to travel on (if you go 1st class) and is only Z50 more than the *Vedette*. The 1st class area is not crowded and there's a small lounge where reasonable meals are served. As you might expect, there's plenty of warm Primus beer for sale! Second class on the *Mulamba* is the cheapest way to cross the lake but it is crowded and you're exposed to the elements – it's hot and often wet as well.

All three boats take from seven to eight hours to make the crossing. Tickets should be bought a day in advance – see the Goma and Bukavu sections. The schedule for the *Mulamba* varies; the other two are fixed. The schedules and fares are:

vessel	ex Goma	ex Bukavu	fare
Karisimbi	Sun 11 am	Fri 10 am	Z3030
Vedette	Sat 10 am	Fri 10 am	Z4550
	Wed 10 am	Tue 10 am	Z4550
Mulamba	Sun 10 am	Thu 10 am	Z5000/2500

HITCHING

There are very few regular buses of any description and most of the time you will have to hitch lifts on trucks. Free lifts are the exception unless you meet the occasional Somali or Kenyan driver. Usually you will have to pay for lifts and the price often reflects the difficulty of the journey rather than the distance, but it's more or less 'fixed'. This doesn't mean you'll be quoted the price local people pay straight away. Negotiation is the name of the game. There's generally a truck park in every town where drivers congregate and it's here that you'll find a lift. In small places it's usually around the petrol station.

Transport on the main route (between Bunia on Lake Mobutu Sese Seko and Uvira on Lake Tanganyika) is more or less guaranteed, but once you leave the main route you may well have to do a lot of walking. You must be in the right frame of mind to do this and it helps if you have a light pack. It's quite safe to walk around in this area (no one has ever been mugged, maimed or murdered that we've heard about). Hospitality is usually excellent so long as you observe village protocol. The rewards are well worth the discomfort. Many places haven't seen a tourist for years, if ever.

Although it's safe to travel in the north, don't attempt to go by road south from Uvira to Kalemie. The road over the mountains via Fizi and Baraka is reportedly the hideout of the remnants of the Simbas from the 1965-67 insurgency.

There's little point in quoting hitching costs on trucks since these will change and, to some extent, they'll depend on your bargaining ability. To get the best price, don't be in a hurry and ask around before you have to leave. Free lifts are available in some places if you can make the contacts.

Eastern Zaïre from North to South

BUNIA

This is a large town in the hills above Lake Mobutu Sese Seko and is one of the starting points for the trip west to Kisangani via Komanda, Mambasa and Nia Nia.

Places to Stay & Eat

Most hotels are on the main street. One of the most popular places is the *Hôtel Palace* which has double rooms for Z2500. Two places in the town centre are the *Hôtel Semliki* and the *Hôtel Ituri*. Both charge about Z3500 a double.

The *Hôtel Semliki* has a good restaurant where you can eat well for Z2000.

Getting There & Away

There are a few buses each week between Goma and Bunia but, as with all transport in this region, it's extremely variable.

KOMANDA

Komanda has a small market and a bakery. The *Hôtel LL* is about 50 metres from the monument on the Bunia road. Spacious single rooms cost Z700 and the hotel is very clean. Nearby, several small restaurants serve meat and rice for Z500.

Getting There & Away

Trucks between Epulu and Komanda take eight hours along a very good road. The trip costs about Z3000, though many drivers are reluctant to take foreigners.

BENI

Beni is the starting point for climbing the Ruwenzori Mountains from the Zaïre side (also possible from the Ugandan side – see the Ugandan national parks chapter). Several of the hotels offer excess baggage storage facilities, though you can also leave gear at the park warden's office in Mutsora.

Places to Stay

One of the cheapest places is the *Hôtel Jumbo* which offers doubles for Z1500. The hotel has bucket showers but no electricity. A similar place which is also good to meet travellers at is the *Hôtel Lualaba*, about 100 metres down the Kasindi road from the roundabout. Like the Jumbo, it has bucket showers. Staff don't mind if you cook your own food but the hotel also has a good, cheap restaurant. You can leave excess baggage safely at either hotel while you climb the Ruwenzoris.

Other hotels recommended include the *Hôtel Virunga*, the *Hôtel Busa Beni*, the *Hôtel Isale* (very clean and friendly; Z2400 a double) and the *Hôtel Bashu*. The *Hôtel Sina Makosa* opposite the Hôtel Lualaba has rooms for Z1500.

Places to Eat

The restaurant at the *Hôtel Lualaba* offers rice and beans, meat and rice and omelettes. Their bread is baked on the premises.

Good breakfasts are available from the *Restaurant du Rond Point* on the roundabout. The snacks outside the *Paradisio Club* (a disco) are also recommended.

For a splurge, try the plat du jour (Z5000) at the *Hôtel Busa Beni*.

Next to the Hôtel Lualaba is a small well-stocked market. The Semliki Grocery Store has a good range of provisions. This is useful if you're organising a trek up the Ruwenzoris as there's only a very limited range of food-stuffs at the market in Mutsora.

Getting There & Away

There are frequent pick-ups and minibuses available between Beni and Butembo. In Beni, both the minibuses and trucks leave from the petrol station which is down the Komanda road from the roundabout. Pick-ups to Komanda cost Z300 and take about six hours. Trucks to Mutwanga cost Z1000.

For lifts out of Beni ask at the CAPACO

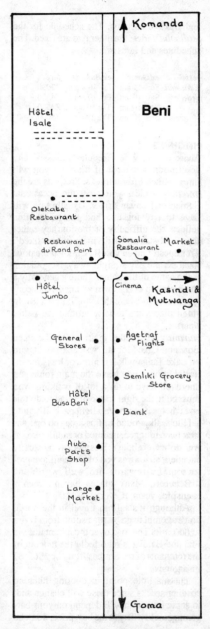

depot about trucks to Goma. The manager is very friendly and may organise a free lift. The journey often takes about 24 hours.

BUTEMBO

With a population of 100,000, Butembo is a large town about halfway between Goma and Bunia. It has a good market and excellent views of the surrounding countryside.

Places to Stay

Two good cheap places are the *Logement Apollo II*, which has electricity in the evenings and bucket showers, and the *Semuliki Hôtel*, which has a good restaurant.

Somewhat more expensive is the *Hôtel Ambiance*. It's very pleasant, has electricity, running water, showers and washing facilities.

The *Oasis Hôtel*, a deteriorating colonial place displaying a delightful air of elegance, used to be popular but, sadly, it has closed. Maybe someone will resurrect it.

Places to Eat

Apart from the *Semuliki Hôtel*, the *Restaurant Cafétéria* near the market is recommended.

Getting There & Away

There are four buses a week to Goma, depending on breakdowns. The journey takes at least 10 hours.

Hitching a truck along this stretch could take two days because of stops en route. If you do decide to hitch, trucks leave from outside a group of shops on the left towards the southern end of the main street.

Between Butembo and Beni there are frequent pick-ups and minibuses available. The trip takes about five hours and costs Z1000. To get to Komanda takes 14 hours and costs Z2000.

KAYNA-BAYONGA

This town is a truck stop on the road between Goma and Butembo, particularly if you're heading south since drivers are not allowed to travel through the Parc National des Virunga at night. As far as views are concerned, this is to your advantage, as otherwise you would miss the Kabasha escarpment.

Places to Stay

Although there are a few small places in the town centre, most truck drivers (and thus travellers looking for a lift) stay at the *Hôtel Italie* about three km north of the town. It has clean, concrete toilets and bucket showers (cold water). There's no electricity so kerosene lamps are provided.

Places to Eat

If you stay at the *Hôtel Italie* you'll probably have to eat there too, although the food is relatively expensive. On the other hand, they don't mind cooking for those who arrive late (say, up to 10 pm).

If you stay in the town centre there are three places where you can pick up food. Two are on the main street but one is really only a bar which has bread. The *restaurant* on the main street offers the best value with meat, rice and tea, though the proprietor may try to charge you a tourist price. The other *restaurant* is down an alley off the main street and has similar food and prices. There's a good daily market if you want to put your own meal together.

Getting There & Away

The bus from Butembo to Goma is supposed to pass through here four times a week, but this depends on breakdowns.

Trucks leave for Goma early in the morning between 5.30 and 6 am, either from the Hôtel Italie or from the market. Otherwise you'll have to rely on transport passing through from elsewhere.

RUTSHURU

Rutshuru is perhaps the most convenient departure point for a visit to the mountain gorillas in the Parc National des Virunga, where they are found on the slopes of Muside and Sabinyo volcanoes (which Zaïre shares with Rwanda and Uganda). First make your way to Djomba (sometimes spelt Jomba).

The turn-off for this place is about two km south of Rutshuru and is clearly signposted.

If you're coming from or going to Uganda you will probably also come through Rutshuru unless you are going to cross the border further north between Beni and Kasese via Kasindi.

Places to Stay & Eat

Probably the best place to stay in Rutshuru is the *Catholic Mission Guest House*. Showers and meals are available and they may let you camp in the mission grounds without charge.

A cheaper option is the unnamed *lodging house* about 50 metres north of the police station on the opposite side of the road. It has basic rooms, bucket showers and an earth toilet. The owner is very friendly and may help you find transport.

The *Hôtel Gremafu* is very clean and has singles/doubles for Z1300/1600. It also has a bar and restaurant where meals cost about Z800 (meat, chips and salad) but must be ordered an hour in advance. It's just beyond the truck park (on the main street) at the northern end of town and off to the right. It's possible to leave excess baggage here if you want to see the gorillas or Rwindi National Park.

Getting There & Away

There is a daily bus to and from Goma which takes about two hours and costs Z1500. You can hitch with a truck for about the same price, though, in this case, it's advisable to make an early start (say 5 am) as breakdowns and/or punctures often prolong the journey. To get to Butembo in a pick-up takes about 11 hours and costs Z4000.

It's also possible to hitch to the Ugandan border and head for Kisoro. There's a basic hotel at the border. (See the Uganda Getting There chapter.)

GOMA

Goma sits at the foot of the brooding Nyiragongo Volcano at the northern end of Lake Kivu. This is not far from the chain of volcanoes which make up the Parc National des Virunga on the border between Zaïre and Rwanda. Like Bukavu, it's an important business, government and resort town and has a fairly cosmopolitan population. There's quite a contrast between the ritzy landscaped villas down by the lake shore and the *cité* behind it. President Mobutu maintains a palatial villa, but keep away from it.

Goma is a dusty, somewhat run-down town with many unsealed roads. Nevertheless, it has the only international airport in this part of Zaïre.

Information

Tourist Office The small tourist office one block north of Ave Mobutu and not far from the post office is the place to book a visit to the gorillas in the Parc National des Virunga. It's also possible to book at Rwindi at the radio shack, but you may have to wait a week for confirmation.

Bank If you're changing travellers' cheques, the best bank is the Banque Commerciale Zaïroise. It shouldn't take longer than half an hour and its commission charge is minimal. If you need to change cash or travellers' cheques outside banking hours, ask at the Hôtel des Grands Lacs; if they can't help they'll put you on to someone who can.

Places to Stay – bottom end

The best value for money in this category is the mission hostels. The *Mission Catholique* is an anonymous yellow building about 300 metres from the post office along Ave du Rond Point. Although not the friendliest place in the world, it's exceptionally clean, quiet and is totally secure. The rooms are very small, cost Z2000/3000 a single/double and have a washbasin. Breakfast at Z500 is definitely not for big eaters (coffee/tea, bread, sausage). The hostel is usually full on Sundays and there's a 10 pm curfew.

Next door is the *Centre d'Accueil Protestant* which is a good deal less austere than its Catholic neighbour. Accommodation prices are the same but the rooms are much larger and the price includes breakfast and hot

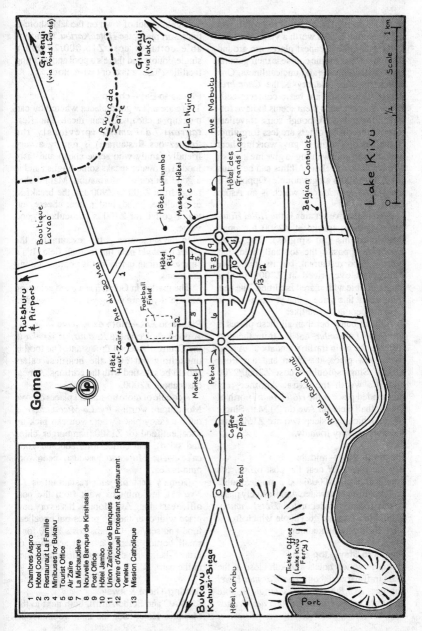

Goma

Scale
0   ½   1 km

Lake Kivu

Rutshuru & Airport

Gisenyi (via Poids Lourds)

Gisenyi (via lake)

Rwanda
Zaïre

Boutique Lavao

Hôtel Lumumba

Masques Hôtel

VAC

La Nyira

Ave Mobutu

Hôtel des Grands Lacs

Belgian Consulate

Hôtel Rif

Football Field

Hôtel Haut-Zaïre

Ave du 20 Mai

Market

Petrol

Coffee Depot

Petrol

Ave du Rond Point

Bukavu
Kahuzi-Biega

Hôtel Karibu

Ticket Office
(Lake Kivu Ferry)

Port

1   Chambres Aspro
2   Hôtel Cooboki
3   Restaurant La Famille
4   Minibuses for Bukavu
5   Tourist Office
6   Air Zaïre
7   La Michaudière
8   Nouvelle Banque de Kinshasa
9   Post Office
10 Hôtel Jambo
11 Union Zaïroise de Banques
12 Centre d'Accueil Protestant & Restaurant
     Yeneka
13 Mission Catholique

water showers. The hostel is often full and the restaurant is also worth a visit.

As usual, the cheapest places are around the market. Par for the course is their general state of decrepitude and uncleanliness. One which fits this category is the *Chambres Aspro*. The rooms are basic concrete cells and whoever cleans them seems to have forgotten the toilets. Although some travellers tolerate this place, others are less forgiving: 'I had hassles from a guy working here knocking at night wanting to give me kisses', wrote a male traveller! All this can be yours for Z700/1500 a single/double. Opposite is the *Macho kwa Macho* which is an Aspro clone.

Also in the market area is the *Hôtel Haut-Zaïre*, nothing special at Z2500 for small double rooms (no singles). The *Hôtel Cooboki*, opposite the football field, has quite a good restaurant, but its rooms are dingy and overpriced at Z2000/3000 a single/double with shared facilities. The best thing about this place is that you can cram in as many people as you like.

A much better bet than all these places is the *Hôtel Lumumba*, not far from the post office at the main traffic roundabout. A relatively new place, it's clean and has flush toilets. Singles/doubles cost Z2000/2700 and it's worth the extra. Another recommended place is the *Hôtel Amari* north of the football field on Ave du 20 Mai. Single rooms which can sleep two are Z1500 and the staff are very friendly.

Places to Stay – middle

Try the *Hôtel Rif* near the post office. It's good value at Z4000/6400 a single/double with a bath and hot water. A more lively place is the recently redecorated *Hôtel Jambo*, behind the Banque du Peuple which fronts on to the main roundabout.

Places to Stay – top end

Goma's two top hotels are both close to the main traffic roundabout. The *Masques Hôtel* charges Z13,800/17,250 a single/double with cold water, while the *Hôtel des Grands Lacs* is more expensive.

Eight km out of town on the lake shore is the resort place, the *Hôtel Karibu*. Comfortable cottages cost Z15,000/20,000 a single/double and there's a pool and sporting facilities. Take a taxi or taxi-motor.

Places to Eat – cheap

There are a few good places where you can pick up a cheap African meal. The *Restaurant La Famille* (previously the Rendezvous Restaurant) is run by a very friendly family who serve cheap and tasty food. The owner speaks some English and is a good source of information. Main dishes range from Z400 to Z900 and the breakfast of omelette, bread, butter, jam, cheese and tea or coffee for Z700 is particularly good value.

In the same area is the restaurant in the *Hôtel Cooboki* near the football field. It's a simple African eatery but is popular among the locals.

The market in Goma has a good selection of food if you are doing your own cooking.

Places to Eat – more expensive

A good choice is the *Restaurant Yeneka* at the Centre d'Accueil Protestant. The food is unexciting but even the heartiest eaters should be satisfied with the portions. A meal costs about Z2000.

A couple of more up-market places on Ave Mobutu are worth a try. *La Michaudière* is quite a fancy place where you can pick up excellent food for Z1500 (hamburger, chips and salad), real coffee for Z200 and good cakes. The *Mupendo* has also been recommended.

Goma's best bar and restaurant is *La Nyira*, a few minutes walk from the post office east along Ave Mobutu. It's a very new place with over the top prices but excellent food and service. Guiness costs Z750 for a small bottle. There's a good selection of French-language current affairs magazines in the bar.

Getting There & Away

Air VAC and Scibe-Airlift, both next to the Masques Hôtel near the main roundabout, have flights from Goma to Bukavu. See the Getting Around section at the beginning of this chapter. The Air Zaïre office on Ave Mobutu has regular flights to Kinshasa.

Bus There is a daily bus in both directions between Goma and Rutshuru. It's a bit hard to pin down, but it leaves in the early afternoon and takes a couple of hours. The customary place to wait for it is outside the Boutique Lavao, a small shop on the Rutshuru road, 500 metres north of Ave du 20 Mai. Sometimes there's a bus in the morning too. The fare is Z1500 and the journey takes from two to 2½ hours. You can also hitch this section on a truck for the same price, though it generally takes longer.

To get to Butembo the connections are even more tenuous. The road is in a bad way and the bus is in equally poor shape. It's supposed to leave four times a week from outside the Centre d'Accueil Protestant. Buy tickets and make enquiries there as to where the bus is and its current state of disassembly – running repairs are carried out all the time. The trip costs Z6000 and takes at least 10 hours.

Minibus If you don't want to take a lake ferry, there are daily minibuses to Bukavu from near the Hôtel Rif. Buy your ticket the day before from the office with the corrugated iron front in the first building back from the main road which skirts the back of the post office.

Minibuses leave daily at about 7 am and the trip costs Z4000. However, think seriously about doing this journey by road. The so-called road is diabolical – a single-lane dirt track full of large potholes – and the trip is exhausting. The minibuses are thoroughly overcrowded (up to 33 people plus produce) and, although you may be told that the journey takes only 10 hours, it can take up to 24 hours. There are also articulated trucks to contend with which, if they break down, can block the road for days. Bring sufficient food and drink with you in case of difficulty.

Ferry The three ferries between Goma and

Bukavu are the *Vedette*, the *Karisimbi* and the *Mulamba* – see the Zaïre Getting Around section. The port is about a 20 minute walk from the market area and slightly less from the mission hostels.

Hitching Often there are Kenyan trucks outside the coffee depot on Ave Mobutu, waiting to load coffee to haul to Mombasa. The drivers are mostly Somalis and are a friendly bunch. It shouldn't be too difficult to arrange a ride, although you won't be breaking any speed records if you go this way – they take about 10 days to get to Mombasa via Kigali and Kampala.

BUKAVU

Built over several lush tongues of land which jut out into Lake Kivu, and sprawling back up the steep mountainside behind, Bukavu is a large and very attractive city with a fairly cosmopolitan population.

It's effectively divided into two parts following the lines of Ave des Martyrs de la Révolution, which heads south straight up a valley from the lake shore, and Ave du Président Mobutu, which winds its way east above the lake shore. The two parts are separated by the grassy saddle of a hill. Most of the budget hotels and restaurants, the main market (Marché Maman Mobutu) and truck parks are in the south of the city. The business centre, government offices, consulates, the huge cathedral and the ritzier parts of the city are along Ave du Président Mobutu.

More English is spoken here than in the other francophone cities of the region, mainly because of the large American Peace Corps Training Centre. The city also has a more than adequate number of mosquitoes, so have a net or coils on hand.

Information

National Parks Office This office (Institut Zaïrois pour la Conservation de la Nature) is at 185 Ave du Président Mobutu and is open Monday to Friday from 8.30 am to 3 pm and on Saturday from 8.30 am till noon. The staff are friendly and helpful.

If you want to visit the plains gorillas in

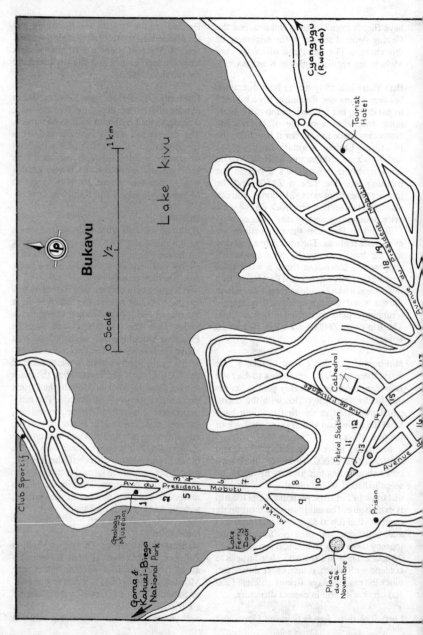

Bukavu

Lake Kivu

Cyangugu (Rwanda)

Tourist Hotel

Goma & Kahuzi-Biega National Park

Club Sportif

Geology Museum

Av. du President Mobutu

Market

Lake Ferry Dock

Place du 24 Novembre

Prison

Patrol Station

Cathedral

Avenue de l'Afrique

Avenue du President

Avenue du

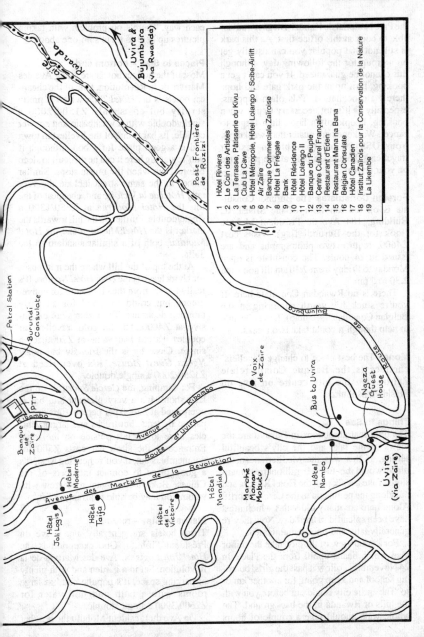

1 Hôtel Riviera
2 Le Coin des Artistes
3 La Terrasse, Pâtisserie du Kivu
4 Club La Cave
5 Hôtel Métropole, Hôtel Lolango I, Scibe-Airlift
6 Air Zaïre
7 Banque Commerciale Zaïroise
8 Hôtel La Frégate
9 Bank
10 Hôtel Résidence
11 Hôtel Lolango II
12 Banque du Peuple
13 Centre Culturel Français
14 Restaurant d'Eden
15 Restaurant Mana na Bana
16 Belgian Consulate
17 Hôtel Canadien
18 Institut Zaïrois pour la Conservation de la Nature
19 La Likembe

the Parc National de Kahuzi-Biega it's advisable to book at this office first. As this park is still not that popular you can usually get on a group for the following day, although this cannot be guaranteed. If you can't get a booking, turn up at the park gate and hope there's a cancellation. This often happens, especially as it's not necessary to pay when booking. People often book then forget to cancel. Weekends are busier than weekdays. Your US$100 fee (payable in cash or travellers' cheques) is paid at the park gate on your arrival.

Foreign Consulates The Burundi Consulate is on the top floor of the SINELAC Building, 184 Ave du Président Mobutu (look for the Burundi flag). Visas cost Z4600, require two photographs and are issued in 24 hours. The consulate is open Monday to Friday from 7.30 am till noon and 2.30 to 5 pm.

There is no Rwandan Consulate here. If you're stuck it's worth enquiring at the Belgian Consulate (see map). It may be able to help though it could take two weeks.

Money The best place to change travellers' cheques is the Banque Commerciale Zaïroise in the city centre on Ave du Président Mobutu.

Things to See

The only real attractions in Bukavu are the views of the lake and the city's beautiful setting. If this was the Mediterranean the place would be full of millionaires' mansions. Take a walk past the Hôtel Riviera and out along the peninsula to the Cercle Sportif. Along here are many old villas which must have been splendid in their day. Now they're generally tatty and poorly maintained.

For a good view of the city, take the minor road which heads uphill from the Place du 24 Novembre. Follow it past the girls' boarding school and keep going for another km or so. The entire city is laid out before you with the hills of Rwanda in the background. The whole walk should take a couple of hours

each way. There's no problem with taking pictures up here as there's no-one about.

Places to Stay – bottom end

Most of the budget hotels are along Ave des Martyrs de la Révolution. One of the cheapest hotels is the *Hôtel Taifa* which is pretty scruffy but costs only Z1500/2000 a single/double with a washbasin and shower cubicle. Its bar is one of the liveliest in town and is a good place for a bop, although if you're staying here it can be difficult to sleep before 1 am when the music stops. Similar places in the same street include the very tatty *Hôtel de la Victoire* and, cheapest of the lot, the *Hôtel Moderne* at Z850/1300 a single/double. Further up the hill towards the market is the *Hôtel Mu-ungu* and the *Hôtel Mundial*, both of a similar standard to the Taifa.

At the top of the hill where the minibuses for Uvira leave is the cosy *Hôtel Nambo*. It's really too far from the city centre for convenience but could be good for an early morning departure. Twin rooms are expensive at Z4000, but for solo travellers or couples it's not bad value at Z2000 for a single. Close by is the friendly but noisy *Ngeza Guest House*. It's overpriced at Z1250/2000 a single/double.

For camping, the *Cercle Sportif* is on the lake shore. It's a very pleasant site but is overpriced at Z2000 per person. Cars can be parked by tents, but trucks and larger vehicles have to be left outside on the road. Entrance to the site's bar costs Z500 for nonmembers but, if you're heading west, it's a good place to contact members of the Chinese Bukavu-Kisangani road crew with whom you may be able to arrange a lift.

Places to Stay – middle

These hotels are generally along Ave du Président Mobutu. One exception is the *Hôtel Joli Logis* on Ave des Martyrs de la Révolution. Set in a garden and with plenty of parking space, it's popular and has large rooms with a bath and hot water for Z2600/3900 a single/double.

On Ave du Président Mobutu the best bet

is the *Hôtel Canadien*. About one km north of the city centre, almost opposite the Burundi Consulate, it's a friendly place and some English is spoken. Huge singles/doubles with a bath cost Z2400/2800, although the plumbing needs attention. Still, it's about the best value in this range.

Up the scale a bit is the *Hôtel Métropole*, very conveniently situated in the city centre. It's seen better days but is still not bad value with singles/doubles from Z3000/4500 up to Z5000/7000 for deluxe. Almost next door is the *Hôtel Lolango I* which has large singles/doubles for Z3300/4900 without a bath and up to Z8000 for a double with a bath and hot water. The common bathrooms also have hot water. The *Hôtel Lolango II* further up Ave du Président Mobutu is owned by the same people and has similar prices.

Close to the Hôtel Résidence is the *Hôtel La Frégate*, an older style place with good-sized doubles from Z3000 to Z6000. It's not a bad place.

Places to Stay – top end

The *Hôtel Résidence* is in the city centre on Ave du Président Mobutu. Rooms start at Z12,000 and have all the facilities you'd expect for that price. Have a look at the downstairs bar if you want to see how the other half lives.

The *Hôtel Riviera* has a cramped location on the edge of the lake at the bottom end of town. It's a comfortable hotel and the service is good.

Places to Eat – cheap

There's a good choice of cheap, African eateries in Bukavu. One of the simplest, and perhaps the most atmospheric in the entire region, is the colourfully named *Restaurant Docteur Wa Tumbo*, near the Place du 24 Novembre. It's practically a hole in the wall, there's no electricity and only bench seating for 10 people at a squeeze. The owner is very amenable and the food, although extremely basic, is filling and cheap. The view out the back door isn't bad either! An omelette with tomato and onion, plus bread, butter and coffee costs just Z350; beans or meat and rice is also Z350.

The *Café du Peuple* next door is similar but only open for breakfast and lunch. The entrance is well hidden – it's between the two goat meat stalls down from the fruit and vegetable market.

Just up from the market, on the corner of Ave du Président Mobutu, brochette stalls set up in the evening, and a couple of brochettes with bread are a cheap filler. Similar African fare is also available from any of the many local restaurants by the main market on Ave des Martyrs de la Révolution. For something a little better try the *ABC Restaurant*, on the same street, next door to the Hôtel Joli Logis, It has good cheap local food and is open daily from 8 am to 4 pm. Breakfast costs Z500, rice and beans are Z300 and meat and chips are Z750.

Places to Eat – more expensive

For a full breakfast of eggs, bread and coffee, the somewhat dreary *Pâtisserie du Kivu* on Ave du Président Mobutu does a reasonable job for Z850. The restaurant in the *Hôtel Lolango I* is popular, although the service is haphazard. Expect to pay from Z1200 to Z1500 for a main course; soup is free. On the same street, opposite the Union des Banques Zaïroises, the *Café Negrita* is not that cheap, but the set menu is good (soup, steak, chips and salad for Z1800) and the beer is cold (Z400). This is a popular place with the many peace corps volunteers in Bukavu.

Entertainment

There are dozens of small bars along Ave des Martyrs de la Révolution. Although they're mostly just beer-swilling places or brothels, they can be great fun if you're in the mood. Some of them get pretty wild as the night wears on. African music is usually playing, as it is in most bars in Zaïre. The bar at the *Hôtel Taifa* is popular and the music goes until 1 am.

If it's just a cooling ale or a soft drink you're after, the outdoor area at the *Hôtel*

Métropole is not a bad spot – Bukavu's equivalent of the Thorn Tree Café in Nairobi, although a good deal less pretentious.

Things to Buy

Bukavu has a couple of good craft shops and there are street hawkers outside the Hôtel Résidence, although the latter's prices need deflating. Le Coin des Artistes on Ave du

Nail fetish figure

Président Mobutu and La Likembe on the same street both have a good selection of local masks, drums and other wooden artefacts.

Getting There & Away

Air There are quite a number of private airline companies operating small planes between various places in eastern Zaïre and there are several flights a day between Goma and Bukavu, amongst others (see the Goma section). Two such companies are Scibe-Airlift which has an office next to the Hôtel Lolango I and VAC which has an office in the Hôtel Residence.

Minibus Minibuses going north usually start from the Place du 24 Novembre but they often do at least one run up the Ave des Martyrs de la Révolution to collect passengers. If you're heading for the Parc National de Kahuzi-Biega, hitch or catch a minibus heading for Miti.

Minibuses to Uvira (via Rwanda) leave when full from the Place Major Vangu (at the very top of the Ave des Martyrs de la Révolution opposite the Hôtel Nambo). The trip takes about four hours and costs Z2000. It is possible to go from Bukavu to Cyangugu (Rwanda), then south to the Rwanda-Burundi border at Bugarama and then on to Bujumbura (the Burundi capital). There are minibuses and taxis all the way. See the Burundi Getting There section.

Most travellers who simply want to get from Bukavu to Goma take the Lake Kivu ferry since it's quicker, cheaper and smoother than going by road. However, there is one minibus daily between the two towns. The trip takes about eight hours and costs Z4000.

Ferry Three ferries ply between Bukavu and Goma on Lake Kivu: the *Vedette*, the *Karisimbi* and the *Mulamba* (see the Getting Around section at the beginning of this chapter).

The *Vedette* and *Karisimbi* dock at the port, just off Place du 24 November. The *Mulamba* does the beer run so it docks at the

BRALIMA brewery, two km along the Goma road, although when arriving from Goma it often stops at a small jetty about halfway between the brewery and the port to let passengers disembark.

All ferries should be booked one day in advance. Tickets for the *Vedette* and *Karisimbi* can be bought at the port while tickets for the *Mulamba* are sold on board. You'll have to show your passport to buy a ticket, so if you're buying tickets for other people make sure you have their passports as well.

Hitching The main truck parks are around the Marché Maman Mobutu and around the Place Major Vangu.

The Place du 24 Novembre is from where you can hitch a ride to Walikale if you plan to do the 90 km walk to Lubutu. You can also pick up trucks going north from the BRALIMA brewery about two km from the Place du 24 Novembre along the Goma road.

Getting Around
There are plenty of dilapidated yellow taxis. Drivers generally hike the prices when they see a foreigner, so bargain hard.

UVIRA
Uvira is on the north-western tip of Lake Tanganyika facing Bujumbura across the lake. It's not a particularly attractive or interesting place. Avoid army personnel and keep that camera out of sight – there's a lot of mercenary paranoia in the area.

The actual port area, Kalundu, is four km south of Uvira. You'll be very lucky to find a boat going south – most travellers have drawn a blank – and the road south is not safe.

Places to Stay
One of the cheapest places is the *Hôtel Babyo 'La Patience'*, Ave Bas-Zaïre near the mosque. If it's full, try the *Pole Pole*. There's no running water but it has a bar and good brochettes for sale. Another good place which is clean and quiet is the *Hôtel Rafiki*.

Places to Eat
A good place to eat is the *Tanganyika Restaurant*, down the road from La Patience hotel. Run by Ugandan refugees, the food is good, the staff are pleasant and English is spoken. For a splurge, try the *Hôtel La Côte* which offers very good three-course meals.

For nightlife, try the *Lobe Disco* which becomes very crowded after 9.30 pm. The *Nyanda au Grand Lac* sometimes has music.

Getting There & Away
There are two possible routes between Uvira and Bukavu. The first goes entirely through Zaïrois territory and involves finding a lift on a truck (there are usually several daily). The route takes a mountain road on the western side of the Rusizi River via Kamanyola and Nya-Ngezi through stunning countryside. Minibuses are available between Uvira and Kamanyola if you can't find a truck.

The second route goes some of the way through Rwanda to take advantage of the excellent Rwandan road system. There are plenty of minibuses, the trip takes three to four hours and costs Z2000. If you use this route, you'll need a Rwandan transit or tourist visa and a multiple-entry visa to get back into Zaïre, although in the past this rule has not always been enforced; officially you never left Zaïre. Rwandan transit visas are available at the border for RFr 1600.

Taxi Taxis to the Zaïre-Burundi border post run all day until late afternoon, take 10 minutes and cost Z100. It's a very easy-going border (see the Zaïre or Burundi Getting There section).

National Parks

PARC NATIONAL DE KAHUZI-BIEGA
Lying between Bukavu and Goma, this park was created in 1970 with an initial area of 600 sq km but was expanded to 6000 sq km in 1975. It was primarily created to preserve the habitat of the eastern lowland (plains)

gorilla (*Gorilla gorilla graueri*) which was once found all the way from the right bank of the Zaïre River to the mountains on the borders with Uganda and Rwanda. Now this gorilla is an endangered species, as is the mountain gorilla which lives on the slopes of the volcanoes on the borders between Zaïre, Rwanda and Uganda.

Many other animals also live in this park. These include chimpanzee, many other species of monkey, elephant, buffalo, many species of antelope, leopard, genet, serval and mongoose. The bird life is prolific.

The altitude varies between 900 metres and 3308 metres (Mt Kahuzi) and the average annual rainfall is fairly heavy at 1900 mm, with the largest falls in April and November. The dry season runs through the months of June, July and August. Most areas of the park have a temperate climate with a fairly constant average temperature of 15°C.

Because of the heavy rainfall and the varying altitude there's a wide variety of vegetation, ranging from dense rainforests at the lower levels, through bamboo forests between 2400 metres and 2600 metres and finally heath and alpine meadows on the summits of the highest mountains. Many animals tend to live in the denser parts of the forest and so are often difficult to see.

Visiting the Gorillas

There are several groups of gorillas, although you will usually only see one of the groups which has become accustomed to humans. In 1990 there were 27 gorillas in the family group. Each year they become more and more accustomed to seeing humans. It's usually possible to get within a metre or two of the silverbacks and large females.

The gorillas can be visited any day of the year, including public holidays. Children under 15 years of age are not allowed. Ideally you should make a reservation with the national park office in Bukavu (Institut Zaïrois pour la Conservation de la Nature, 185 Ave du Président Mobutu), but often if you just turn up at Station Tshivanga (the park entrance and departure point) by 8 am there's no problem. As most people use

Bukavu as a base it's easy to make a booking, in which case there is no need to be at the gate until 9 am. The visit ends back at the gate at about 1 pm.

The cost is US$100, payable in hard currency (cash or travellers' cheques) at the park entrance on the day of your visit. Payment in zaïres is not accepted. The ticket you get is valid for seven days, but although you could stay in the park for seven days, it is only good for one trip to the gorillas.

The fee includes a guide, trackers (who chop the vegetation to make a track) and a gun-toting guard (who scares off elephants). They all expect a tip at the end – so would I if I had to chop my way through thick jungle with a bunch of tourists every day! The average tip is a bottle of beer, given to each of them back at the gate.

You must have appropriate footwear and clothing, preferably a pair of stout boots and waterproof clothes – this is not a picnic. It's often very muddy and hard going up steep slopes. You need to be careful about what you grab hold of to pull yourself up as many vines and other plants carry thorns or will sting. A pair of gloves is a good idea. It can rain even in the dry season.

The guides can generally locate a group of gorillas within two hours although it can be up to five hours or as little as five minutes (unusual). If you don't see any the first day your fee covers you for another attempt the next. No refunds are possible if you can't return the next day.

To photograph the gorillas you need the fastest film you can get – ASA 1600 is the best or ASA 800 at the very least. Anything less and you'll be very disappointed when you get home. When you finally find a group of gorillas, the trackers start hacking away at the bush to give you a better view. Depending on how much time it's taken to locate the gorillas, you spend about an hour with them. Don't let the guide rush you into heading back to the gate too soon. After all, he sees the gorillas every day and doesn't pay US$100 for the privilege.

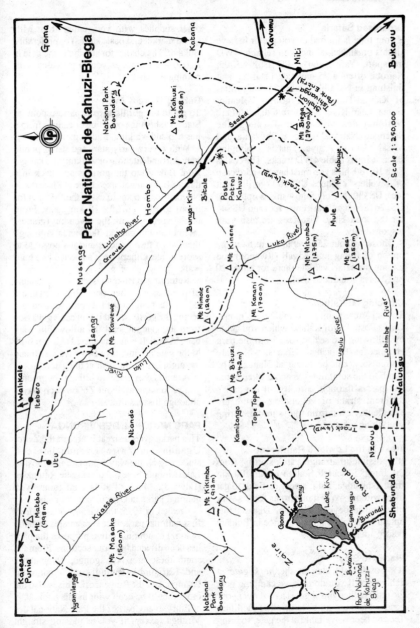

Parc National de Kahuzi-Biega

Scale 1 : 250,000

Organised Safaris

If your time is limited or you prefer to have all this organised, along with reliable 4WD transport, Yare Safaris, PO Box 63006, Nairobi, offers a 25 day safari starting and finishing in Nairobi. It takes in the gorillas of Kahuzi-Biega, Nyiragongo Volcano, Goma, Lake Kivu, Rutshuru Falls, the Parc National des Volcans in Rwanda, the Serengeti National Park in Tanzania and Masai Mara in Kenya. This is a camping safari using reliable 4WD trucks. The cost is KSh 10,780, plus you must have in hard cash or travellers' cheques US$100 (gorilla visit fee), US$30 (Nyiragongo – this is optional), US$26 (Serengeti park entry fee) and US$44 for the food kitty. Visa fees are also your responsibility.

Those without 25 days to spare have the option of flying into Kigali (Rwanda) and joining the safari vehicle there for either 20 or 12 days at reduced cost.

Climbing Mt Kahuzi

The departure point for climbing this mountain is Poste Patrol Kahuzi which you get to by following the sealed road from the park entrance at Tshivanga. Guides, which are compulsory, can be found at Kahuzi. The climb to the summit takes about three hours and passes through virtually all the park's different strata of vegetation. There are excellent views from the summit. Bring everything you need.

Treks in the Lowland Rainforest

It's possible to arrange a trek starting from the Irangi Research Station about 100 km from Tshivanga, but it's very difficult to get there without 4WD transport as there's very little traffic beyond Hombo. Discuss this option at the national park office in Bukavu before attempting it.

Places to Stay

It's possible to stay at the *park gate* at Tshivanga. If you don't have camping gear the only shelter you'll get is a roof over your head – there are no beds or other facilities. Tea and beer is available at the gate, so bring

other supplies with you, either from Miti (good market and basic stores) or preferably Bukavu. The charge for staying at the gate is Z1000 – a rip-off as you're provided with nothing but shelter.

Getting There & Away

To get to the gorilla trips departure point at Station Tshivanga combine or choose from a bus trip and walking, hitching or a taxi.

With a very early start and using public transport and hitching or walking you can get from Bukavu to the gorillas and back in a day. In Bukavu you need to be at Place du 24 Novembre by 6 am to catch the first bus (or hitch) to Miti (Z700), 18 km away. From there expect to walk the seven km (gradual incline) to the gate at Tshivanga, although there are a few vehicles and it's possible to score a ride. Otherwise it's about a two hour walk.

Returning to Bukavu is easier for a couple of reasons: it's often possible to arrange a ride with people with a vehicle who are seeing the gorillas; and if you can't get a ride from the gate, at least it's a downhill walk back to Miti. If you are worried about getting to the gate in time, take two days and spend the night before the visit at the gate.

A taxi is only feasible if there's a group – you're looking at about Z6000 each way – although it saves time.

PARC NATIONAL DES VIRUNGA

This park covers a sizeable area of the Zaïre-Uganda and Zaïre-Rwanda borders, stretching all the way from Goma almost to Lake Mobutu Sese Seko via Lake Rutanzige (Edward). Much of it is contiguous with national parks in Uganda and Rwanda.

Created in 1925, the Virunga was Zaïre's first national park. It covers an area of 8000 sq km. For administrative purposes the park has been divided into four sections. From the south these are: Nyiragongo, Nyamulgira and Karisimbi; Rwindi and Vitshumbi; Ishango; and the Ruwenzori. This is also the order they'll be dealt with in this book.

Entry to any part of the Parc National des Virunga (except if you're passing straight

Top: Bujumbura, Burundi (GC)
Bottom: Boyoma Falls, Kisangani, Eastern Zaïre (EE)

Top: Children at Catholic Mission, near Goma, Eastern Zaïre (PP)
Left: Mt Ruwenzori, Eastern Zaïre (EE)
Right: Karasimbi Volcano, near Nyiragongo, Eastern Zaïre (EE)

through on transport between Rutshuru and Kayna-Bayonga) costs US$50 for a seven day permit plus Z50 for a camera permit. You can go from one part of the park to another without paying twice, just as long as your permit is still valid.

Nyiragongo, Nyamulgira & Karisimbi

This section includes the three volcanoes which give it its name, and also the sanctuaries of the mountain gorilla (*Gorilla gorilla beringei*) at Djomba, on the slopes of Muside and Sabinyo volcanoes along the border with Rwanda, and at Bukima.

The Gorilla Sanctuaries The sanctuaries are managed by the Institut Zaïrois pour la Conservation de la Nature. If you want to be absolutely sure of getting on a gorilla viewing group, book at the tourist office in Goma. The office is open daily between 9 and 11 am and sometimes later, but it's not easy to find so see the Goma section for details. If you don't book you can still see the gorillas if there is room on the one group per day which visits them. Usually there is, but if an overland truck arrives you might have to wait several days before they fit you in. The fee is US$100 per person, payable in cash or travellers' cheques.

Djomba To see the gorillas, you must be at the departure point by 8 am. The fee includes a compulsory guide who will expect a tip at the end. They can usually find a group of gorillas within an hour or two. There are two groups, one known as Oscar and the other known as Marcel. Only two people may visit the Oscar group at any one time but up to six may visit the Marcel group.

To get to Djomba, first go to Rutshuru (see the Rutshuru section). The turn-off for Djomba is about two km before Rutshuru and is clearly signposted. The Michelin map of this area is not very precise as on the map it appears that the road goes off from the town centre. This isn't the case. The turn-off you want branches from a roundabout with a petrol station about four km from the actual centre of Rutshuru. The signposts saying you

are in Rutshuru are misleading as the city's boundaries start about two km from the roundabout and six km from the town centre.

There's another right fork in the town centre which leads to Uganda via Ishasha. The bus from Goma goes into the centre unless you request to be let off elsewhere. From the turn-off on the Goma-Rutshuru road it's about 26 km to Djomba over a very rough road (4WD). Transport is sporadic.

From Djomba it's a seven km, gradual uphill walk to the starting point and a *hut* where you can stay for Z1000 per person per night. It has a stove but you must take all your own food or have the villagers cook for you. They have a limited range of food which they'll sell if you want to do your own cooking but the nearest stores are in Djomba. Camping costs Z500.

If you don't want to stay in the hut there's a *Catholic Mission* in Djomba and also an *American Baptist Mission* at Rwanguba, five km uphill from Djomba, but neither is very welcoming towards travellers. Djomba is about seven km from the Ugandan border.

Bukima After booking in Goma, get to the Station de Rumangabo on the Rutshuru road, 45 km from Goma (about a two hour drive). A guide will take you up the mountain (about a four hour walk) where you stay overnight in a *hut*. The next morning there's a two hour walk to find the gorillas after which you return the same day to Rumangabo – a long day. There's a cleared *camp site* with no facilities here, otherwise get a *room* with one of the locals. They're open to negotiation. There's also a *gîte* which you can use for Z500 but it has no beds, curtains or water. The guides are heavily into *cadeaux* (gifts) and will advise you to take food and drink which they will expect you to share with them.

If you're coming from Kisoro in Uganda, a guide may meet you about one km past the border post at the restaurant and offer to take you to a hut in the national park. He knows a short cut which will get you to the hut in two hours as opposed to eight hours via the road. The walk is through mountain villages

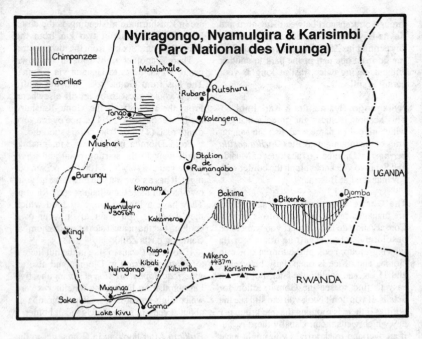

Nyiragongo, Nyamulgira & Karisimbi (Parc National des Virunga)

and is very interesting. He expects US$5 per person for this but large groups can barter him down to US$10 to US$20 for everyone. The *hut* costs Z500, is very pleasant and has cooking facilities, firewood, clean sheets and staff to do the dishes.

The next morning you visit three habituated families of gorillas for the usual fee of US$100. Six people is the maximum per group. Coming this way, you completely bypass Djomba and can arrive at the hut in one day from Kabale (Uganda).

Nyiragongo This volcano (3470 metres), which broods over Goma, used to be a spectacular sight when it was erupting, but now it's merely smoking. It's still worth climbing to the top for the views. Since it only takes five hours up and three hours down it can be done in one day if you set off very early. However, a one day trip isn't recommended because the summit is only clear of mist or

cloud in the early morning and again, briefly, in the late afternoon. So it's better to make it a two day event.

The starting point is at Kibati about 15 km north of Goma on the Rutshuru road. Here you find the Camp des Guides which is a long, white, unmarked building set back above the road at the foot of the volcano. Either hitch or walk to this place.

The US$30 entry fee is paid at the camp and includes the services of a guide (who will expect a tip at the end – Z1000 seems to be the going rate). Porters can also be hired at Kibati. The trouble with porters and guides is that they'll set off with neither food nor bedding so you'll have to provide this if you want to make the climb a two day event. Bring all your food and drink from Goma as there's nothing for sale at Kibati. Firewood is also in short supply.

It's possible to stay at the *Camp des Guides* the day before you go up the mountain but there's no regular accommodation.

Many travellers buy the head guide a bottle of beer and end up sleeping on his floor – he's friendly and interesting. Otherwise you can camp at the free *camp site* about two km south of the Camp des Guides.

On the first day you need to start out before 1 pm as it's a three hour walk to the base of the crater cone proper and then another hour to the huts (which are in bad shape). On the way up you pass some interesting geological formations and vegetation – tropical forest, hardened lava flows (recent, old and ancient) and giant lobelia.

On the second day you need to get up early and put on some warm clothes so you can set off by 6.30 am. It's a half-hour walk to the crater rim and the weather should be clear. Looking down into the base of the crater you'll probably still see wisps of steam and vapour coming from the walls while the base itself is an uneven cooled mass of lava. Sulphur fumes hang in the air. The views of Goma, Lake Kivu and over into Rwanda are terrific. By about 9.30 am the mist will start closing in for the day and you lose the views. The descent takes about three hours.

Nyamulgira You'll need at least three days to climb Nyamulgira (3056 metres), but you shouldn't have to pay the park entry fee again if you haven't used all your original seven days. As for Nyiragongo, you'll have to tip the guides extra. Bring all your food requirements and, as there's nowhere to stay at the Nyamulgira base camp, you'll need a tent.

The trip starts at Kibati (as for Nyiragongo) and the first part involves a 45 km walk (two days) to the base camp through beautiful countryside. The next stage involves a six hour climb through an incredibly varied landscape ranging from old and recent lava flows (some of them pocked with lava pools) to dense upland jungles. You may be lucky to catch sight of elephants, chimpanzees, buffaloes and antelopes but you'll definitely see and hear hundreds of different birds.

The first night on the mountain is spent at a decaying but rambling *hut* (for which you pay extra) though it is possible to return to

the base camp the same day if you set off early enough. Camping is an alternative. The guides generally cook their own food.

The next day you set off for the crater rim. It takes about one hour to reach the tree line and then another hour to get to the crater rim across recent lava flows (slippery when wet). As from Nyiragongo, the views from the summit are magnificent. You descend the mountain the same day.

Rwindi & Vitshumbi

The main attraction in this part of the park is the game – lions, elephants, hippos, giraffes, antelopes, hyaenas, buffaloes and many others. The Ruwenzori National Park in neighbouring Uganda (which is contiguous with the Parc National des Virunga) used to be much the same but it was sadly depleted of wildlife during that country's civil wars. You cannot hire vehicles to tour this part of the Virunga so you'll be reliant on tourists and they're not always keen to pick up strangers.

The *lodge* at Rwindi is somewhat expensive although if you wait until the bar closes it may be possible to bed down by the swimming pool. The more people do this the sooner there will be a clampdown, as camping is officially forbidden in or around the lodge. If you can't afford to stay at the lodge enquire about *rooms* in the drivers' quarters; you may be lucky and get a cheap room. There's also a small *guest house* in the nearby village but they're not keen on taking tourists.

While you're in this area you should pay a visit to the fishing village of Vitshumbi at the southern end of Lake Rutanzige (Edward). A visit to the fishing village of Kiavinyonge at the northern end of the lake near Kasindi is also interesting.

Ishango

This is similar to the Rwindi/Vitshumbi part of the park except that there are no elephants. Ishango is just a park camping area with a small airstrip and a derelict lodge which you can use free of charge – it's usually filthy with bat droppings. Camping is preferable but you'll be charged for this. There are no fences so it's advisable to be careful at night. Campers have encountered hyaenas and leopards that have come too close for comfort.

Those who know the area well say that it's possible to swim in either Lake Rutanzige (Edward) or in the Semliki River which flows into it. While there's apparently no danger of bilharzia, they do give a strong warning about hippos. If you decide to swim, watch closely for 10 to 15 minutes to make sure there are no hippos anywhere near you. One traveller who ignored the warnings had a buttock bitten. There are no hospitals close by in Zaïre, but he was lucky because the Ugandans allowed him through to their nearest hospital (after a long hassle). The wildlife and particularly the bird life is prolific where the Semliki flows into the lake.

To get to Ishango, first get to Kasindi either from Beni (Zaïre) or Kasese (Uganda). It's possible to hitch as there are usually a fair number of trucks on the road between the two places. Wait at the turn-off in Kasindi for a lift into the park. If you get stuck at the turn-off, it's three km to the park entrance. You can generally rent a bedroom in one of the park buildings, but you will have to pay the park entrance fee again if your seven day permit expires. There is a way around this if you don't want to go to Ishango. If that's the case, tell them you are going to Kiavinyonge which is 10 km beyond Ishango and is not strictly in the national park. No one else pays to get there as the only road in is through Kasindi and Ishango. The trip involves a ferry crossing over a river literally swarming with hippos.

Kiavinyonge

This large fishing village has a spectacular setting at the foot of a mountain range leading down to the northern end of Lake Rutanzige (Edward). Herds of hippo wallow close to the beach and large marabou birds are everywhere. At about 6 am the village becomes a hive of activity as fishing boats land their catches on the sandy beach in front of the restaurant and houses. The men look after the nets and the women sort the fish which are then smoked during the day. Few tourists visit so you're in for a treat.

The *Logement Spécial* at the west end of the village has cheap rooms. Don't be put off if they're not sure what to do with you when you turn up! There's a *restaurant* on the lake shore which sells coffee, tea, bread and hot corned beef (of all things!) but the best thing to buy is fish and rice – it won't be found fresher anywhere else! The restaurant is open from 6 am to 8 pm.

To leave Kiavinyonge, enquire about trucks taking fish to Butembo. These leave at about 8 am and take about four hours. It's an incredible journey up over the mountains on a dirt road with many hairpin bends. This is not the normal Kasindi-Butembo road.

Ruwenzori

This is the most northerly part of the Parc National des Virunga and its major appeal for travellers is the climb up the Ruwenzori Mountains. It is also possible to climb from the Ugandan side since the border between the two countries passes along the summits. Don't underestimate the difficulties of this trek from either side. It's much tougher than climbing up Kilimanjaro. True, some people do make it in joggers and normal clothes but they suffer for it. Anywhere above Hut Three (about 4200 metres) you can almost freeze to death without adequate clothing and a warm sleeping bag. Snow is not unusual either at or above this point. Prepare for it properly and it will be one of the most memorable trips in your life.

Before even considering doing this trek, obtain the appropriate footwear, clothing and a good sleeping bag. Don't forget a woollen hat and gloves. Pots and pans are very useful and will repay their cost several times over, especially if you're trying to economise on weight by taking dried soups. You need to take all your own food including enough to feed the guide and any porters hired. A stove is also very useful but not absolutely essential.

Many of the huts where you will stay overnight are in poor shape. There is no glass in the windows, so sheets of plastic pinned across the holes can work wonders for your wellbeing. Hopefully this state will improve as an ex-Peace Corps volunteer by the name of Leo is rebuilding some of the huts.

The guide and porters are very partial to cigarettes at the end of a day. If you run out, they can become unpleasant. Leave your 'clean and healthy living' fetishes at home; these people are not trekking for fun. Sure, they're being paid but it's not a king's ransom. Before setting off make sure that all parties agree on what are your and their responsibilities, who pays for what, where exactly you are going and how many days the trip will take. Be firm, but remember that other trekkers will follow, so try to keep them happy. If they end up wanting to string you up from the nearest tree, I don't want to be on the trek which follows yours. Five days or more is a long time to be with people who want to battle with you at every turn.

The best selection of food is at Beni but there are also some fairly well-stocked shops and a reasonable market (meat, fruit, vegetables, beer, sodas, etc) in Mutwanga. This is where the guides and porters get their supplies.

The actual trek starts when you get to the park headquarters in Mutsora, about four km from Mutwanga. Both of these places are about halfway between Beni and Kasindi on the road to Uganda. There are trucks from close to the Hôtel Lualaba in Beni to the turn-off to Mutsora and Mutwanga. From there you walk, although it is possible to get a lift all the way to Mutwanga. It's about 13 km from the turn-off on the Beni-Kasindi road to either Mutsora or Mutwanga.

At the park headquarters in Mutsora you pay the necessary fees (US$50 for a seven day permit, payable in cash or travellers' cheques) and arrange for guides and porters. You pay for all food but the guide and porters provide their own equipment. The charge for porters is Z850 per day (Z500 wage plus Z350 for food) plus an extra Z350 per day for the guide's food (his wage is included in the park fee).

If you like you can stay at the *park head-*

quarters. Camping costs Z500 and there's a river nearby for bathing and drawing water. Most budget travellers go to Mutwanga, about four km away, to stay at the *Ruwenzori Hôtel* which was abandoned for years but is now slowly being rebuilt. There's no charge for staying here but you should tip the caretaker. Meals may be available. As for going up the Ruwenzoris, the standard trek takes five to six days.

There are variations on this route and scheduling, but you must arrange these before setting off.

Before attempting to ascend the Ruwenzori it's a very good idea to get hold of a copy of *Ruwenzori – Map & Guide* by Andrew Wielochowski. Published in 1989, it has an excellent large-scale contoured map with the Ruwenzori on one side and information on geology, fauna and flora, walking routes, hire of guides and porters, costs, equipment, useful contacts and weather on the other side. It's available from Nairobi bookshops for KSh 100 or from 32 Seamill Park Crescent, Worthing BN11 2PN, UK (tel (0903) 37565).

It may still be possible to get hold of a copy of Osmaston & Pasteur's *Guide to the Ruwenzori*, last published in 1972. The only places I know of where you can buy this book are West Col Productions, 1 Meadow Close, Goring-on-Thames, Reading, Berks, UK, and Stanfords Map Centre, Long Acre, Covent Garden, London WC2, UK.

Day 1 From Mutwanga/Mutsora (1700 metres) it's a two hour walk along a gently rising path through the cultivated foothills to *Kiandolire Hut* (or Guides' Hut) at 1700 metres. Few trekkers stay here although it will sleep 10 people and water is available. Leaving the hut, the path enters thick forest and fords two major streams. You'll reach *Kalonge Hut* (2138 metres) after a three hour trek; it appears about 10 minutes after fording the second stream. This hut can sleep 16 people and there's space for camping. It's in excellent condition and water and firewood are available.

Day 2 The path from Kalonge Hut veers off east and drops steeply down to another stream. It then climbs very steeply to a ridge at 2440 metres and after that to a knoll at 2910 metres. This section takes about three hours. From the knoll it's two hours to *Mahungu Hut* (3310 metres), made tough by giant heather and deep mosses. This hut sleeps up to 16 people. There is space for tents and water is sometimes available from a small well close to the hut. If the well is dry the porters know another water source a considerable distance from the hut.

This part of the trek and the first part of the following day is the toughest as it's mostly uphill and is very hard going between roots and vines. For much of the way the ground is very wet and rain can fall frequently outside the wet season.

Day 3 The trek continues through giant heather and mosses for about two hours until the heather thins and a small stream is reached. A further hour takes you through more open countryside to Kampi ya Chupa, a ridge at 4030 metres, from which there are beautiful views over the rainforests of Semliki Valley on the one side and down to Lac Noir on the other. On the way up you'll pass some superb stands of giant groundsel, lobelia, senecio and helichrysum. A further hour from Kampi ya Chupa brings you to *Kiondo Hut* (4300 metres) from which there are fine views of the Stanley peaks, weather permitting. The hut can sleep 12 people and there's space for tents. Water is available from a nearby stream.

Day 4 This begins from a col just east of the hut from which the path descends to a rocky step protected by a cable. It continues to descend more steeply, through a muddy gully to Lac Vert at 4160 metres after which it climbs steeply from the northern end to Lac Gris where there is a good *camp site*. This section takes about two hours. About 45 minutes further on you arrive at *Moraine Hut* (or Glacier Hut) at 4495 metres after which the snowfield starts. The hut can sleep four people and there's space for one tent nearby.

The hut is damp and can be extremely cold at night, so be prepared. Going beyond this point demands that you have suitable equipment and preferably experience of climbing on snow and ice. Porters will not go beyond this point.

Days 5 & 6 If you're reasonably fit, you can descend along the same route in two days with an overnight stop at *Mahungu Hut* which is about an eight hour walk from Mutwanga.

Mt Hoyo

Mt Hoyo is about 13 km off the Beni-Bunia road close to Komanda. Its draw cards are the waterfall known as the Chutes de Vénus, the grottoes (small caves) and the pygmy villages nearby. It also used to be possible to climb Mt Hoyo (a two day trek) but the track is now overgrown and there's no longer a hut at the top. This shouldn't deter those who are determined; guides can be found at the hotel.

The waterfall and grottoes are managed as an extension of the Parc National des Virunga so you must pay for a seven day permit, which includes the services of a compulsory guide. The guide may tell you that you have to pay him direct but this isn't true; you must pay at the Auberge. The tour of the waterfall and grottoes lasts about two hours and takes you to three different cavern systems (illuminated with a kerosene lantern) and finally down to the base of the waterfall.

The pygmy villages have seen too many tourists and are very commercialised. Be prepared for being hassled to death and having to pay for every photograph you take. If you have the time, it's better to spend a few days here and gradually build up a relationship with the pygmies by trading with them or buying food from them before visiting their village.

A better place to visit the pygmies is at Loya, at the first bridge over the Loya River south of the Mt Hoyo turn-off. There is a small carpark south of the bridge (with a very small sign on the roadside). Park there and someone will soon appear. A trip to their village by pirogue and back costs about Z500 for two hours. So far these people are far less commercialised and don't give you the hard sell.

If you come here on the Eka Massambe bus from Butembo (Monday and Thursday from Butembo, about seven hours) it will drop you at the Mt Hoyo turn-off at about 5 pm, which means you'll have to make the 13 km walk to the hotel at night. It's possible to hire porters for this three hour walk. Seven km down the road is a fruit plantation which has pineapples, papayas, avocados and bananas for sale. Buy some while you have

the chance because food at the hotel is very expensive.

The hotel, *Auberge de Mont Hoyo*, is not cheap for a room with three beds, and you will literally have to beg for electricity. It's possible to camp cheaply, the cost for which includes use of a toilet and showers. If you have no tent and cannot afford the hotel there's a small room adjoining the toilet and bathroom which you can rent fairly cheaply (it sleeps up to four people on the floor). Meals are very expensive. Some food can be bought from pygmies who come up to the hotel.

Tanzania

Facts about the Country

INTRODUCTION

Tanzania, with its magnificent wildlife reserves, is East Africa at its best. Famous parks such as Serengeti or the wonderful crater of Ngorongoro offer some of the best safari opportunities on the continent. While these two may be the best known of the country's numerous parks and reserves, many others deserve a visit. These range from the tiny Gombe Stream National Park chimpanzee sanctuary near the Burundi border to the huge and virtually untouched Selous Game Reserve in the south-east.

Parks and wildlife are not all Tanzania has to offer. In the north near the Kenyan border is snow-capped Mt Kilimanjaro, the highest mountain in Africa. Scaling this 5895 metre peak is the goal of many visitors. Offshore in the Indian Ocean are several islands including exotic Zanzibar, one of those truly magical travel names like Kathmandu or Timbuktu.

All these sights and attractions are mixed in with Tanzania's single-minded and erratic system of government which, unfortunately, has in the past few years led to continuing major price increases in park entry fees and costs. The huge disparity between the official bank rate of exchange and the widely utilised black market also adds to the confusion. Still, it's a beautiful country and well worth seeing.

HISTORY

No other African country has been moulded so closely in the image of its president. Known as Mwalimu (teacher) in his own country and often referred to as the 'conscience of Black Africa' elsewhere, Tanzania's first president, Julius Nyerere, is one of Africa's elder statespeople.

He ruled his country as president for over 20 years until he stepped down in 1985 to become the chairman of his party, Chama Cha Mapinduzi (CCM – Party of the Revolution).

Like many other first presidents of post-colonial Africa such as Nkrumah (Ghana), Sekou Touré (Guinea) and Kaunda (Zambia), Nyerere was firmly committed to radical socialism and nonalignment. He was always in the forefront of African liberation struggles and Dar es Salaam has been home to many a political exile or guerrilla fighter. Likewise, he has never missed an opportunity to condemn the South African regime.

Certainly his sincerity cannot be faulted, but a more pragmatic attitude to solving his country's problems might well have been more realistic than rigid adherence to ideology. On the other hand, his popularity among the people cannot be doubted. In the 1975 and 1980 elections he picked up more than 90% of the vote. None of his party colleagues have come even close to matching this performance.

Since November 1985 Ali Hassan Mwinyi has been the president though, out of respect to Nyerere, their photographs appear side by side in all offices, hotel foyers, restaurants, etc.

Early History

Not a great deal is known about the early history of the Tanzanian interior except that by 1800 AD the Maasai, who in previous centuries had grazed their cattle in the Lake Turkana region of Kenya, had migrated down the Rift Valley as far as Dodoma. Their advance was only stopped by the Gogo, who occupied an area west of the Rift Valley, and the Hehe to the south of Dodoma. Because of their reputation as a warrior tribe, the Maasai were feared by the neighbouring Bantu tribes and avoided by the Arab traders, so the northern part of Tanzania was almost free from the depredations of the slave trade and the civil wars which destroyed so many villages and settlements in other areas of the country.

Now the Maasai occupy only a fraction of their former grazing grounds and have been

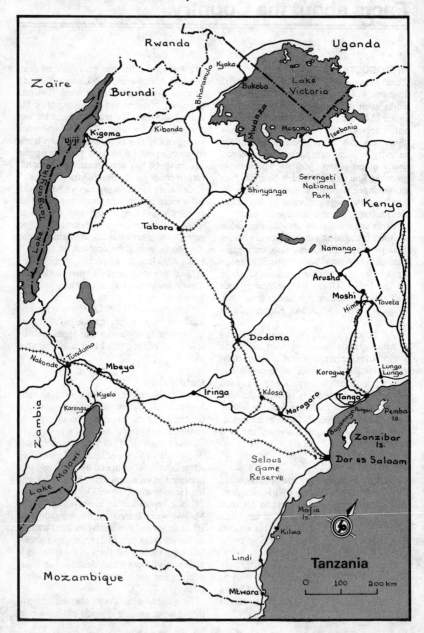

forced to share it with some of Tanzania's most famous national parks and game reserves. Although some of the southern clans have built permanent villages and planted crops, their northern cousins have retained their pastoral habits and are the least affected by, or interested in, the mainstream of modern Tanzania. Most of the other tribes of this country have more or less given up their traditional customs under pressure from Nyerere's drive to create a unified nation which cuts across tribal divisions.

Though the coastal area had long been the scene of maritime rivalry, first between the Portuguese and Arab traders and later between the various European powers, it was Arab traders and slavers who first penetrated the interior as far as Lake Tanganyika in the middle of the 18th century. Their main depots were at Ujiji on the shores of Lake Tanganyika and Tabora in the central plain. Their captives were generally acquired by commerce rather than force and were taken first to Bagamoyo and then to Zanzibar, where they were either put to work on the plantations there or on Pemba, or shipped to the Arabian Peninsula for sale as domestic servants.

Zanzibar, which had been ruled for decades from Oman at the mouth of the Persian Gulf, had, by the first half of the 1800s, become so important as a slaving and spice entrepôt that the Omani Sultan, Seyyid Said, moved his capital there from Muscat in 1832. Though cloves had only been introduced to Zanzibar from the Moluccas in 1818, by the end of Seyyid Said's reign it was producing 75% of the world's supply.

British Influence

Britain's interest in this area stemmed from the beginning of the 19th century when a treaty had been signed with Seyyid Said's predecessor to forestall possible threats from Napoleonic France to British possessions in India. The British were only too pleased that a friendly Oriental power should extend its dominion down the East African coast rather than leave it open to the French. When Seyyid Said moved to Zanzibar the British set up their first consulate there.

At that time Britain was actively trying to suppress the slave trade and various treaties limiting the trade were signed with the Omani sultans. But it wasn't until 1873, under the threat of a naval bombardment, that Sultan Barghash (Seyyid Said's successor) signed a decree outlawing the slave trade. The decree certainly abolished the seaborne trade but the practice still continued on the mainland for many years as it was an integral part of the search for ivory. Indeed, slavery probably intensified the slaughter of elephants since ivory was now one of the few exportable commodities which held its value, despite transport costs to the coast. Slaves were the means of transport.

European explorers began arriving around the middle of the 19th century, the most famous of whom were Stanley and Livingstone. Stanley's famous phrase, 'Dr Livingstone, I presume', stems from their meeting at Ujiji on Lake Tanganyika. Other notable explorers in this region included Burton and Speke who were sent to Lake Tanganyika in 1858 by the Royal Geographical Society.

The German Colonial Era

A little later the German explorer Carl Peters set about persuading unsuspecting and generally illiterate chiefs to sign so-called treaties of friendship. On the strength of these the German East Africa Company was set up to exploit and colonise what was to become Tanganyika. Though much of the coastal area was held by the Sultan of Zanzibar, German gunboats were used to ensure his compliance. The company's sphere of influence was soon declared a protectorate of the German state after an agreement was signed with Britain which gave the Germans Tanganyika while the British took Kenya and Uganda.

Like the British in Kenya, the Germans set about building railways to open their colony to commerce. Unlike Kenya's fertile and climatically pleasant highlands, eminently suitable for European farmers to colonise, much of Tanganyika was unsuitable for agriculture. Also, the tsetse fly made cattle grazing or dairying over large areas of central and southern Tanganyika impossible. Most farming occurred along the coast and around Mt Kilimanjaro and Mt Meru.

The detachment of the sultan's coastal mainland possessions didn't go down too well with his subjects, so Bagamoyo, Pangani and Tanga rose in revolt. These revolts were crushed, as were other anti-German revolts in 1889; the Maji Maji revolt in 1905 was only put down at a cost of some 120,000 African lives.

The British Era & Independence

The German occupation continued until the end of WW I after which the League of Nations mandated the territory to the British. Nationalist organisations came into being after WW II, but it wasn't until Julius Nyerere founded the Tanganyika African National Union (TANU) in 1954 that they became very effective. The British would have preferred to see a 'multiracial' constitution adopted by the nationalists so as to protect the European and Asian minorities, but this was opposed by Nyerere. Sensibly, the last British governor, Sir Richard Turnbull, ditched the idea and Tanganyika attained independence in 1961 with Nyerere as the country's first president.

The island of Zanzibar had been a British Protectorate since 1890, as had a 16 km wide strip of the entire Kenyan coastline which was considered to belong to the sultan. It remained that way until Zanzibar and Kenya attained independence in 1963. The Sultan of Zanzibar was toppled about a year after independence in a communist-inspired revolution in which most of the Arab population of the island was either massacred or expelled. The sultan was replaced by a revolutionary council formed by the Afro-Shirazi Party. A short time later, Zanzibar and the other offshore island of Pemba merged with mainland Tanganyika to form Tanzania.

Socialist Tanzania

Nyerere inherited a country which had been largely ignored by the British colonial authorities since it had few exploitable resources and only one major export crop, sisal. Education had been neglected too, so that at independence there were only 120 university graduates in the whole country.

It was an inauspicious beginning and the problems it created eventually led to the Arusha Declaration of 1967. Based on the Chinese communist model, the cornerstone of this policy was the Ujamaa village – a collective agricultural venture run along traditional African lines. The villages were intended to be socialist organisations created by the people and governed by those who lived and worked in them. Self-reliance was the key word in the hundreds of villages that were set up. Basic goods and tools were to be held in common and shared among members whilst each individual was obligated to work on the land.

Nyerere's proposals for education were seen as an essential part of this scheme and were designed to foster constructive attitudes to cooperative endeavour, stress the concept of social equality and responsibility and counter the tendency towards intellectual arrogance among the educated.

At the same time, the economy was nationalised as was a great deal of rental property. Taxes were increased in an attempt to redistribute individual wealth. Nyerere also sought to ensure that those in political power did not develop into an exploitative class by banning government ministers and party officials from holding shares or directorships in companies or from receiving more than one salary. They were also prohibited from owning rental properties. Nevertheless, corruption remained widespread.

In the early days of the Ujamaa movement progressive farmers were encouraged to expand in the hope that other peasants would follow their example. This resulted in little improvement in rural poverty and the enrichment of those who were the recipients of state funds. Thus this approach was abandoned in favour of direct state control and peasants were resettled into planned villages with the object of modernising and monetising the agricultural sector of the economy. The settlements were to be well provided with potable water, clinics, schools, fertilisers, high-yielding seeds and, where possible, irrigation. Again they failed, since this was well beyond the country's financial resources and there was a lot of hostility and resentment among the peasants towards what they regarded as compulsory resettlement, without any consultation or influence over the decision-making process.

Following the second failure a third scheme was adopted. This was based on persuading the peasants to amalgamate their small holdings into large, communally owned farms, using economic incentives and shifting the emphasis to self-reliance. In this way, the benefits reaped by the members of Ujamaa settlements would be a direct reflection of the dedication of those who lived there. This scheme has had its critics but has been relatively successful and has prompted the government to adopt a policy of compulsory 'villagisation' of the entire rural population.

Despite lip service to his policies there was little development aid from the West so Nyerere turned to the People's Republic of China as a foreign partner. China built Tanzania's brand-new, modern railway from Dar es Salaam to Kapiri Mposhi (the TAZARA railway) in the copper belt of Zambia, at a cost of some US$400 million. For a while it was the showpiece of eastern and southern Africa and considerably reduced Zambia's dependence on the Zimbabwean (at that time Rhodesian) and South African railway systems. OPEC's oil price hike at the beginning of the 1970s, however, led to a financial crisis and Tanzania was no longer able to afford any more than essential maintenance of the railway. There were also serious fuel shortages. As a result, the railway no longer functions anywhere near as well as it did when first built, although recently things have been improving slightly.

Tanzania Today

Tanzania's experiment in radical socialism and self-reliance might have been a courageous path to follow in the heady days following independence, and even during the 1970s when not only Tanzania but many other African countries were feeling the oil price pinch, but only romantics would argue with the assessment that it has failed. The transport system is in tatters, agricultural production is stagnant, the industrial sector limps along at well under 50% capacity, the capital, Dar es Salaam, is dusty and down-at-heel and all economic incentives seem to have been eliminated. Obviously, many factors have contributed to Tanzania's woes and many of them have been beyond its control, not least the fact that it is one of the world's poorest countries. At least that is true of the mainland, for Zanzibar was one of the most prosperous countries in Africa at the time of independence.

The trouble is that Nyerere has no intention of changing and he tolerates no dissent. In 1979 Tanzanian jails held more political prisoners than South Africa, though more than 6000 were freed late that year and a further 4400 the following year. Even though Nyerere is no longer president, it is unlikely there will be any significant changes until after his death.

Tanzania has been one of the most consistently outspoken supporters of African liberation movements, particularly in the south. Nyerere joined with Zambia's Kaunda in supporting the guerrillas fighting for the independence of Angola and Mozambique

against the Portuguese, and also those fighting to overthrow the White minority government of Rhodesia during Ian Smith's regime. This support has continued to cost both countries dearly, though these days the cost is spread between the so-called Front Line States of Angola, Botswana, Mozambique, Tanzania, Zambia and Zimbabwe.

Tanzania also provided asylum to Ugandan exiles during Idi Amin's regime, including Milton Obote and the current president, Yoweri Museveni. This support almost bankrupted Tanzania. In October 1978, Idi Amin sent his army into northern Tanzania and occupied the Kagera salient, and also bombarded the Lake Victoria ports of Bukoba and Musoma. It was done, so he said, to teach Tanzania a lesson for supporting exiled groups hostile to his regime, but it's more likely that it was a diversionary movement to head off a mutiny among his restless troops. As Tanzania had hardly any army worth mentioning it took several months to scrape together a people's militia of 50,000 men and get them to the front. They were ill-equipped and poorly trained but they utterly routed the Ugandans – supposedly Africa's best trained and best equipped army. The Ugandans threw down their weapons and fled and the Tanzanians pushed on into Uganda. A 12,000-strong Tanzanian contingent stayed in the country for some time to maintain law and order and to ensure that Nyerere could exert a significant influence over the choice of Amin's successor. The war cost Tanzania around US$500 million and it received not a single contribution from any source.

Not only that but it was half-heartedly condemned by other African countries within the Organisation of African Unity (OAU). One of the cardinal principles of the OAU is that African borders are inviolable and member states must not interfere in the internal affairs of others. It wasn't the first time that Tanzania had interfered in the affairs of its neighbours. Nyerere had helped to topple two other regimes, once in the Comoros Islands in 1975 and again in the Seychelles in 1977.

Perhaps Tanzania's economy wouldn't have got into such a parlous state if the East African Economic Community had been allowed to work. At the time of independence, Kenya, Tanzania and Uganda were linked in an economic union which shared a common airline, telecommunication and postal facilities, transportation and customs. Their currencies were freely convertible and there was freedom of movement. Any person from one country could work in another. It fell apart in 1977 due to political differences between socialistic Tanzania, capitalistic Kenya and the military chaos that stood for government in Uganda.

As a result of Kenya grabbing the bulk of the economic community's assets, Nyerere closed his country's border with Kenya. Though one idea behind this was to force tourists to fly directly to Tanzania rather than entering via Kenya, all it achieved was an alarming loss of tourism for Tanzania. The border remained closed for years and although it is now open again the government continues to display a propensity for economic suicide.

GEOGRAPHY

A land of plains, lakes and mountains with a narrow coastal belt, Tanzania is East Africa's largest country. The bulk of the 945,087 sq km country is a highland plateau, some of it desert or semidesert and the rest savannah and scattered bush. Much of the plateau is relatively uninhabited because of the tsetse fly which prevents stock raising. The highest mountains – Meru (4556 metres) and Kilimanjaro (Africa's highest at 5895 metres) – are in the north-east along the border with Kenya.

Along the coast is a narrow low-lying coastal strip and offshore are the islands of Pemba, Zanzibar and Mafia. More than 53,000 sq km of the country is covered by inland lakes, most of them in the Rift Valley.

CLIMATE

Tanzania's widely varying geography accounts for its variety of climatic conditions. Much of the country is a high plateau where the altitude considerably tempers what would otherwise be a tropical climate. In many places it can be quite cool at night.

The coastal strip along the Indian Ocean together with the offshore islands of Pemba, Zanzibar and Mafia have a hot, humid, tropical climate, tempered by sea breezes. The high mountains are in the north-east along the Kenyan border and this area enjoys an almost temperate climate for most of the year.

The long rainy season is from April to May when it rains almost every day. The short rains fall during November and December though it frequently rains in January, too.

ECONOMY

Tanzania, or Tanganyika as it once partly was, was always the poor cousin of the British colonial Kenya-Uganda-Tanganyika trio. Although it did not have the problem of a large influx of European settlers, Tanzania was still a seriously underdeveloped country at the time of independence. Things have not improved, the economy is still overwhelmingly agricultural and overall it has been marked mostly by mismanagement and decline.

Sisal, a fibre plant used for cordage, is the leading export. Other products are cloves (80% of world supply), coffee, cotton, coconuts, tea, cashew nuts and timber. Diamond, gold, tin and mica are mined.

POPULATION

The population of Tanzania is about 20 million. There are more than 100 tribal groups, the majority of which are of Bantu origin. The Arab influence on Zanzibar and Pemba islands is evident in the people, who are a mix of Shirazis (from Persia), Arabs and Comorians (from the Comoros Islands).

HOLIDAYS & FESTIVALS

January
  Zanzibar Revolution Day (12th)
February
  CCM Foundation Day (5th)
April
  Union Day (26th)
May
  Workers' Day (1st)
July
  Peasants' Day (7th)
December
  Independence Day (9th)
  Christmas Day (25th)

Variable public holidays are Good Friday, Easter Monday, Id-ul-Fitr (end of Ramadan) and Id-ul-Haji.

LANGUAGE

KiSwahili and English are the official languages but there are also many local African languages. Outside of the cities and towns far fewer local people speak English than you would find in comparable areas in Kenya. It's said that the KiSwahili spoken in Zanzibar is of a much purer form than that which you find in Kenya (at least, that's their story) and quite a few travellers come here to learn it since the Institute of KiSwahili & Foreign Languages is on the island.

Facts for the Visitor

VISAS

Visas are required by all except nationals of Commonwealth countries, Scandinavian countries, the Republic of Ireland, Rwanda, Romania and Sudan. For these people a free visitor's pass, valid for one to three months, is obtainable at the border (you'll be asked how long you want to stay). Nationals of South Africa are not admitted.

Visa costs vary depending on your nationality; two photographs are required and they're generally issued in 24 hours.

Some Tanzanian borders have acquired bad reputations for hassling travellers. At the Tunduma-Nakonde (Tanzania-Zambia) border you can expect hassles whether you cross by road or on the TAZARA railway. Make sure your papers are in order and everything else is satisfactory. The Kyela-Karonga (Tanzania-Malawi) border is probably the worst. Your bag will be minutely searched and all your travellers' cheques and cash counted. The border crossing points into Kenya are generally a breeze (Namanga and Lunga Lunga) and take just a few minutes. They don't even collect currency forms at Namanga.

If you take a car across the border into Tanzania you will have to buy a 90 day road permit for TSh 1000.

Warning

You will probably be refused a visa or visitor's pass if you have South African stamps in your passport or the stamps of border posts to South Africa. This is especially true at the Malawi-Tanzania border and the Zambia-Tanzania border. If you think you are going to have problems you can hedge your bets by getting a visitor's pass at the Tanzanian High Commission in Harare, Zimbabwe. It's free, there's no fuss and it takes 48 hours to be issued. Don't bother applying in Lusaka, Zambia, as it takes three weeks to come through!

Even with this pass you cannot be guaran-

teed entry. We have heard of people being refused after doing all the right things. New passports also evoke suspicion, especially if issued in Botswana, Zambia or Zimbabwe. Even stamps showing that you entered and left Lesotho or Swaziland by air may evoke suspicion. If they're sure you've been to South Africa your passport may well be endorsed 'undesirable alien' or 'illegal immigrant'. Some travellers have had this stamped in their passports just for arguing too forcefully with immigration officials. If you have to convince them that you haven't been to South Africa then do it politely and don't get agitated.

Embassies

You can obtain visas for Tanzania from the following neighbouring countries:

Burundi The Tanzanian Embassy in Bujumbura is on Ave de l'ONU, around the corner from the Rwandan and Zaïre embassies on Ave du Zaïre. Visa costs vary according to your nationality (BFr 1250 to BFr 1750). Two photographs are required and visas are issued in 24 hours. Opening hours are Monday to Friday from 8 am till noon and from 2 to 5 pm.

Rwanda The embassy (tel 76074) is on Ave Paul VI close to the junction with Ave de Rusumo. Visas generally take 48 hours to be issued, cost from RFr 1000 to RFr 2700 (depending on your nationality) and require two photos. The embassy is open Monday to Friday from 9 am to 2 pm.

Kenya In Nairobi the embassy (tel 331056/7) is on the 4th floor, Continental House, on the corner of Harambee Ave and Uhuru Highway. It's open Monday to Friday from 9 am to 5 pm. Visas cost from KSh 100 to KSh 600 (depending on your nationality), require two photographs and take 48 hours to be issued.

Uganda The Tanzanian High Commission (tel 56755) is at 6 Kagera Rd. It's open Monday to Friday from 9 am to 3 pm. The cost of a visa varies according to your nationality but ranges from USh 1600 to USh 7000. The visas are valid for three months, take two days to be issued and two photos are required.

Other Countries There are Tanzanian embassies also in Addis Ababa (Ethiopia), Bonn (Germany), Brussels (Belgium), Cairo (Egypt), Conakry (Guinea), Geneva (Switzerland), The Hague (Netherlands), Harare (Zimbabwe), Khartoum (Sudan), Kinshasa (Zaïre), Lagos (Nigeria), London (UK), Lusaka (Zambia), New Delhi (India), New York (USA), Ottawa (Canada), Paris (France), Rome (Italy), Stockholm (Sweden), Tokyo (Japan) and Washington DC (USA). Avoid getting your visa in Zambia as they take three weeks to come through.

Other African Visas
Burundi The embassy (tel 38608) is at Plot 1007, Lugalo Rd, Dar es Salaam, next door to the Italian Embassy and at the back of the Palm Beach Hotel. Office hours are Monday to Friday from 8 am to 2.30 pm and on Saturday from 8 am to 12.30 pm. Visas cost TSh 4000 or US$20, require two photos and are issued in 24 hours. There's also a Burundi Consulate in Kigoma on Lake Tanganyika.

Kenya The high commission (tel 31526, 37337) is on the 14th floor, NIC Investment House, Samora Ave, at the junction with Mirambo St, Dar es Salaam. Visas cost TSh 1000, require two photographs and take 24 hours to be issued. It is open Monday to Friday from 9 am to 3 pm but visa applications are only dealt with between 9 am and noon.

Rwanda The embassy (tel 30119/20) is at 32 Upanga Rd, Dar es Salaam. Visas cost TSh 2500 or US$20, require two photographs and take 24 hours to be issued. They're valid for a stay of one month. Office hours for visa

applications are Monday to Friday from 8 am to 2.30 pm and Saturday from 8 am to 12.30 pm.

Uganda The high commission (tel 31004/5) is on the 10th floor, IPS Building, Maktaba St, Dar es Salaam. Office hours are Monday to Friday from 8 am to 12.30 pm and 2 to 4 pm.

Zaïre The embassy (tel 24181/2) is at 438 Malik Rd, Dar es Salaam. Visas cost a ridiculous US$80, require three photographs, a letter of recommendation from your own embassy and are issued in 48 hours. They will only issue one month, single-entry visas. Office hours are Monday to Friday from 8.30 am to 3 pm.

If you're heading for Kigoma, get the visa there as you can pay in local currency and, apart from Nairobi, it's the only place in the region where you can get a Zaïre visa at a remotely sensible price. At the consulate in Kigoma on Lake Tanganyika, a one month single-entry visa costs TSh 2000, requires four photos and is issued in 24 hours. Office hours are Monday to Friday from 9 am till noon.

Zambia The high commission (tel 27261/3) is at 5/9 Sokoine Drive, Dar es Salaam. Office hours are Monday to Friday from 8 am till noon and 2 to 4.30 pm.

Zambian visas also appear to be available at the Tunduma-Nakonde border if you're travelling on the TAZARA train from Dar es Salaam to Kapiri Mposhi. At the border they cost US$10 or Kw 100, but don't take this for granted.

Francophone Countries Dar es Salaam is a good place to stock up on francophone country visas (Central African Republic, Chad, etc). As there are very few of these embassies in the capital you must get them all from the French Embassy (tel 34961/3) which is at the corner of Bagamoyo and Kulimani roads. It's open Monday to Friday from 8.30 am to 2 pm.

CUSTOMS

Before clearing Tanzanian customs and immigration you have to change US$50 (or the equivalent) into Tanzanian shillings at the bank. Likewise, and despite the fact that this is supposed to be a united republic, you have to change US$40 (or the equivalent) into Tanzanian shillings on entry into Zanzibar – see the Zanzibar chapter.

MONEY

US$1 = TSh 191

The unit of currency is the Tanzanian shilling, which is equivalent to 100 senti. There are bills of TSh 500, TSh 200, TSh 100, TSh 50 and TSh 20 and coins of TSh 10, TSh 5 and TSh 1.

The export of Tanzanian shillings is officially limited to TSh 200. Import is prohibited.

Banking hours are Monday to Friday from 8.30 am to 12.30 pm and on Saturday from 8.30 to 11.30 am.

Black Market

The December 1989 devaluation of the shilling (following IMF pressure) has brought it much closer to a realistic exchange rate with the US dollar, but there is still quite a gap between the official and black market rates. The unofficial rate varies between TSh 280 and TSh 310, depending on where you change and whether you change small or large denomination US dollar bills. Zanzibar, Dar es Salaam and Arusha are the best places to change (in that order) and the best rates are for US$50 and US$100 bills.

Be very cautious when using the black market as police are well aware of what is going on. Never, under any circumstances, change money on the street or with a taxi driver. If you do, the chances are that you'll be dealing with an undercover agent or a police informer. This will cost you not only the money you wanted changed but a hefty bribe also – US$100 to US$200 is not unusual.

Many travellers have been caught out this way. Some would say it serves them right for being greedy but that doesn't take into account police corruption. We've never heard of any traveller being taken to court for breach of currency regulations. Avoid anyone who offers to change money on Maktaba St or Sokoine Drive, Dar es

Salaam, or outside the post office in Arusha. You're being set up.

Forget about buying Tanzanian shillings in Nairobi unless you know the rate. There are lots of sharp operators here who dupe travellers into accepting half the normal rate (which is less than the bank rate!).

Hard Currency

These days shillings bought on the black market are only of limited use. All national park camping and entry fees, airline tickets and virtually all hotel accommodation costing more than US$10 have to be paid in hard currency (shillings are not acceptable even with bank receipts). Not only that, if you don't have the exact amount in hard currency the change will be given in local currency at the official rate. Even if you hand over a US$100 bill or travellers' cheques for something which costs US$10, the change will be in Tanzanian shillings. There's no way you'll be given hard currency in return.

With this in mind, *it's essential that you arrive in Tanzania with plenty of small denomination hard currency bills or travellers' cheques* – US dollars preferably since that is what everything is priced in. If you don't, you'll end up with a mountain of local currency which you can only use for buying meals, land transport and souvenirs and which cannot be exported or reconverted, even if you're flying out.

In theory, it is possible to change hard currency travellers' cheques into US dollar bills at certain banks on both the mainland and in Zanzibar but, as many travellers have found to their cost, this can take a lot of time and involve an inordinate amount of frustration. Some have done it in Dar es Salaam by saying they're going to the national parks and need their US$100 travellers' cheques broken into smaller denominations in order to pay for park entry and camping fees. On Zanzibar, everyone will tell you that the People's Bank of Zanzibar at the back of the fort will do the same thing since *all* hotel accommodation has to be paid for in US dollars. Go and try it! Admittedly, others have been luckier, but it took one friend three

days of begging, scraping and pleading to get them to do it. It's even worse on Pemba Island where they'll say they simply don't have the hard cash – understandable since there are very few tourists, though they did eventually find US$20 for me.

As in Uganda, Kenyan shillings are almost as good as hard currency when you want to change money, although it's officially illegal to take them out of the country. Expect KSh 1 to fetch you you TSh 10.

Diners Club, American Express and, to a lesser extent, Visa credit cards are generally only acceptable at major hotels and the like.

Currency Declaration Forms

These are issued on arrival, except at the Rusumo (Tanzania-Rwanda) border where they're handwritten. It's rare that officials will ask you to verify what you write on the form on arrival. It's far more likely that officials will demand you do this when you leave. This is especially true at the Tanzania-Malawi border between Kyela and Karonga. This border has acquired the reputation for being one of the heaviest in Africa. Here they'll tear your baggage apart and maybe even strip search you. If you've got something to hide, they'll find it.

The Nakonde-Tunduma (Tanzania-Zambia) border on the TAZARA railway, on the other hand, is relatively easy-going, though as soon as the authorities read this you can expect the heat to be turned up. Another border to watch out for is that at Borogonja, between Serengeti and Masai Mara national parks. This is a little used crossing between Tanzania and Kenya and the officials don't have much else to do except check that the cash you have on you matches what you declared on your currency form.

As usual, exit via the Namanga border (Tanzania-Kenya) involves little drama since so many people use it every day.

Make sure that all payments you make in foreign currency or travellers' cheques are recorded on your currency form.

In the past there used to be a lively trade on the black market in forged bank stamps and bank receipts which you paid for by a lower exchange rate. It's a complete waste of time these days, so forget it. If you use the black market, make sure that you never have more shillings on you than you're supposed to have according to your currency form. In the event of being stopped and your wallet or money belt being checked, any excess will be confiscated and you may be hassled for a bribe.

TOURIST INFORMATION
Local Tourist Offices
The Tanzania Tourist Corporation (TTC) has offices in Dar es Salaam (tel 2761/4, PO Box 2485), Zanzibar (tel 32344, PO Box 216) and Arusha (tel 3842) on Boma Rd.

The TTC can make bookings for you at any of the large hotels in Tanzania and at most of the national park lodges.

Overseas Reps
The TTC also has offices in the following countries:

Germany
    Kaiserstrasse 13, 6000 Frankfurt Main 1 (tel (0611) 280154)
Italy
    Palazzo Africa, Largo Africa 1, Milano (tel 432870, 464421)
Sweden
    Oxtorgsgatan 2-4, PO Box 7627, 102 94 Stockholm (tel (08) 21 6700)
UK
    43 Hertford St, London W1
USA
    201 East 42nd St, New York, NY 10017 (tel (212) 986 7124)

National Parks
The national parks are managed by the Tanzania National Parks Authority (tel 3471), PO Box 3134, Arusha. Their main administrative office is on the 6th floor, Kilimanjaro Wing, Arusha International Conference Centre. If you call in they may well have a range of descriptive leaflets about the national parks and a reasonably good road map of the Serengeti National Park (there's a nominal charge).

Better still is the recently published series of well-produced and illustrated booklets which cover most of Tanzania's principal national parks. Published by the Tanzania National Parks Authority in cooperation with the African Wildlife Foundation, they cost about US$5 each and are excellent safari companions. The series includes *Arusha National Park, Kilimanjaro National Park, Tarangire National Park* and *Ngorongoro Conservation Area*, among others. They're available from bookshops and hotel stores.

Another good source of information about the parks is the booklet, *A Guide to Tanzania National Parks* by Lilla N Lyogello, which is superb value at less than US$0.50.

GENERAL INFORMATION
Post
The poste restante is well organised and you should have no problems with expected letters not turning up. The same is true for telegrams. There's no charge for collecting letters. Because of the favourable street exchange rate for hard currency, posting parcels from Tanzania is cheaper than it is from Kenya.

Telephone

Extelcoms House on Samora Ave in Dar es Salaam has an efficient international exchange. You can usually get a connection in just a couple of minutes, but they're expensive! Expect to pay US$8.30 *per minute* at the official rate of exchange. A deposit is payable before they will connect you. Reverse charge (collect) calls cannot be made from here.

You can also make overseas calls through a hotel switchboard, but they'll add on a commission of about 25%.

Time

The time in Tanzania is GMT plus three hours.

MEDIA

Newspapers & Magazines

The only English-language newspaper is the *Daily News* which you can get in Dar es Salaam, Arusha, Zanzibar and one or two other places. It's essentially a 'what the president did today' type of publication. Foreign news coverage is minimal. International magazines and periodicals can be found at stalls along Samora Ave and Maktaba St in Dar es Salaam and around the post office in Arusha. Kenyan daily newspapers are usually at the same places.

HEALTH

As in most African countries you must take precautions against malaria. Most of the lakes and rivers of Tanzania carry a risk of bilharzia if you bathe in them or walk along the shores without footwear, especially where the vegetation is very reedy. Tsetse flies are distributed over large areas of the central plateau, though they're only a real nuisance in a few places. Insect repellent and a fly whisk are useful in such places.

FILM & PHOTOGRAPHY

Bring all your photographic requirements with you as very little is available outside of Dar es Salaam, Arusha and Zanzibar. Even at these places the choice is very limited and prices are high. Slide film is a rarity – colour negative and B&W film are what's mostly available. If you're desperate for film, the large hotels are probably your best bet. You'll be extremely lucky to find film at any of the national park lodges.

Don't take photographs of anything connected with the government or the military (government offices, post offices, banks, railway stations, bridges, airports, barracks, etc). You may well be arrested and your film confiscated if you do. If you're on the TAZARA train from Dar es Salaam to Kapiri Mposhi (Zambia) and want to take photographs of game as you go through the Selous Game Reserve, get permission first from military personnel if possible or, failing that, from railway officials. You might think that what you are doing is completely innocuous, but they may well think otherwise.

Getting There

It's possible to enter Tanzania by air, road, rail or boat. Rail access is only from Zambia. Even though the Tanzanian railway system is continuous with the Kenyan system there are no through services. Likewise, although there are steamers on the various parts of Lake Victoria belonging to Kenya, Tanzania and Uganda, none sail from one country to the next. The exception is an occasional cargo ship between Jinja (Uganda) and Mwanza (Tanzania) which may have room for a few passengers. What is certain is that there are dhows which ply between Mombasa (Kenya) and Zanzibar via Pemba, and there's also the Lake Tanganyika steamer which connects Burundi with Tanzania and Zambia.

AIR

International airlines serving Tanzania either through Kilimanjaro or Dar es Salaam international airports include Aeroflot, Air France, Air India, Alitalia, British Airways, EgyptAir, Ethiopian Airlines, Kenya Airways, KLM, Linhas Aereas Mocambique, Lufthansa, PIA, Sabena, SAS, Somali Airlines, Swissair and Uganda Airlines.

Quite a few travellers use Tanzania as a gateway to Africa although it is not as popular as Nairobi. There's not a lot of difference between the fares to Nairobi and those to Dar es Salaam or Kilimanjaro. International flight tickets bought in Tanzania have to be paid for in hard currency. You cannot buy them in shillings, even with bank receipts.

From Kenya

The cheapest options to fly between Tanzania and Kenya are the flights between Dar es Salaam and Nairobi (about US$50) and Zanzibar and Mombasa (about US$28), though you must add the US$20 departure tax to these prices. The Zanzibar-Mombasa flight with Kenyan Airways is very popular, so ticket demand is heavy. Book at least two weeks ahead to be sure of securing a seat.

OVERLAND
To/From Kenya

Bus Several bus companies run from Mombasa to Dar es Salaam via Tanga and vice versa, though usually only once a week in either direction. The companies include Coast, Cat and Tawfiq. The trip takes anything from 16 to 24 hours to Dar es Salaam and eight hours to Tanga. The border at Lunga Lunga-Horohoro is quite straightforward but it takes as much as four hours to clear all 50 or so people through both posts. The fare from Dar es Salaam to Mombasa is TSh 2500. The Cat office in Dar es Salaam is on Msimbazi St close to the Kariakoo Market and the Caltex station.

You can also do the journey in stages. From Mombasa to Lunga Lunga there are frequent matatus for the one hour trip. Once you're through the Kenyan border post there is a six km walk to the Tanzanian post at Horohoro. There's very little traffic along here so hitching is difficult. From Horohoro there are a couple of buses a day along the rough single-lane dirt road to Tanga (TSh 300). If you walk the few km from Horohoro to the first Tanzanian village you'll have a better chance of getting a ride to Tanga.

If you're going in the other direction, from Dar es Salaam to Tanga, a much more comfortable alternative (only about TSh 300 more expensive) is to take the overnight train 1st class to Tanga where you can pick up one of the Dar es Salaam to Mombasa buses (TSh 700) at about 8 am.

Going from Nairobi to Arusha and Moshi, the Kilimanjaro Bus Service operates a regular luxury bus along this route. The bus departs Nairobi at 9 am on Tuesday, Friday and Sunday, arriving in Arusha at 3.30 pm. In the opposite direction, the bus departs Arusha at 9 am on Monday, Thursday and Saturday and arrives in Nairobi at 3.30 pm.

Another service departs Moshi at 7 am on Monday, Thursday and Saturday and arrives in Arusha at 9 am and Nairobi at 2.30 pm. The fares are KSh 150/TSh 1250 from Nairobi to Moshi and KSh 140/TSh 1150 from Nairobi to Arusha. Book in advance. The booking office in Nairobi is at Goldline (tel 25279), Cross Rd. In Arusha and Moshi the bus office is at the bus station.

Matatu & Shared Taxi It's just as easy to do this journey in stages. As the Kenyan and Tanzanian border posts are next to each other at Namanga, there's no long walk involved. There are frequent matatus and shared taxis from Nairobi to Namanga every day which go when full and cost KSh 80 and KSh 120 respectively. The journey by taxi takes about two hours and by matatu about three hours. Both leave from outside the petrol station on Ronald Ngala St close to the junction with River Rd. From the Tanzanian side of the border there are frequent matatus and shared taxis to Arusha which cost TSh 500 and from TSh 1000 to TSh 1300 (negotiable) respectively. The taxis normally take about 1½ hours though there are some kamikaze drivers who are totally crazy and will get you there in just one hour.

The crossing between Moshi and Voi via Taveta is also reliable as far as transport goes – buses, matatus and shared taxis – but between Kisii and Musoma in the north there's very little traffic and you'll have to rely on hitching a ride or doing a lot of walking, especially in the border area.

To/From Malawi
The one crossing point here is between Karonga and Mbeya at the top of Lake Malawi, via Tukuyu and Kyela. The Tanzanian side of this border is notorious for officialdom, especially if you're leaving the country. Expect a full baggage search and possibly a body search. Make absolutely sure that the money you have matches what you declared on your currency form. If it doesn't, you're in for a major hassle. If you're entering Tanzania, officials will be on the lookout

for any indication that you have visited South Africa. This includes overland entry stamps into Zimbabwe, Botswana, Lesotho and Swaziland. Many travellers have been refused entry on such 'evidence' and those that have argued about it have had 'prohibited immigrant' stamped in their passports. If it appears that you're heading in that direction, get your passport back and try a different border crossing (Nakonde-Tunduma or Kigoma via the Lake Tanganyika ferry from Mpulungu in Zambia).

On the other hand, this is the border crossing which most people now use between the two countries rather than the ones via Nakonde (Zambia) and Chitipa (Malawi), along which transport can be problematical.

Bus A daily bus from Karonga to the border at Iponga on the Songwe River departs between 2.30 and 3 pm and takes about four hours. The bus goes via Kaporo where you get your Malawi exit stamp. The border closes at 6 pm which means you'll get there too late to cross and will have to stay the night. You'll find this most inconvenient as there are no facilities whatsoever – no food, accommodation or running water. Nor will you be allowed to sleep on the bus, so bring what you need to make an uncomfortable night tolerable. The bus returns to Karonga at 6 am the next morning.

In the morning you cross over to the Tanzanian side after which it's about seven km to the main Kyela-Mbeya road. You'll have to hitch a ride or walk this stretch. Once on the main road, buses to Mbeya (about a five hour trip) pass two or three times a day, but it's often more convenient to hitch a ride. There's no need to go into Kyela along this route as the town is five km south-east of the junction, and so in the wrong direction for Mbeya.

Going in the opposite direction from Tanzania, if you can't find a bus from Mbeya to Kyela, take another to Tukuyu which is on the same road (TSh 200, about three hours) and then another to Kyela (TSh 100, 1½ hours). If it's very early in the day make sure that you're dropped at the border road turn-off which is five km from Kyela, then hitch or walk the seven km to the border. Doing it this way you might make the 6 am bus from the Malawian border to Karonga. If it's getting late, stay at a hotel in Kyela otherwise you're up for a night on the Malawian border. Don't attempt to cross this border on a Sunday as there's hardly any traffic and you'll have to do a lot of walking.

A fortnightly bus in either direction between Mzuzu and Dar es Salaam is operated by Momaga Motor Ltd. It leaves Mzuzu at 6 am on Wednesday and arrives at Karonga at noon, after which it continues on to Kyela where you stay the night. The next day it arrives at Mbeya at noon and at Dar es Salaam at about 1 pm on Friday. The fare from Mzuzu to Dar es Salaam is Kw 60. In the opposite direction, the bus departs Dar es Salaam on Sunday morning and arrives in Mbeya at 7 pm on Monday. It continues on to Kyela where you stay the night and the next day continues on to Karonga, arriving at 9 am. Mzuzu is reached at 3 pm the same day. This bus can be picked up in Mbeya if there are spare seats.

To/From Rwanda

Entering Tanzania from Rwanda is much easier than it used to be. First take a matatu to Kibungo (RFr 350) from where you get a shared taxi (RFr 200) to the border at Rusumo (Chutes de Rusumo). Otherwise take the 7 am direct bus from Kigali to Rusumo.

From Rusumo you will have to hitch to Ngara or Lusahanga. The Lusahanga-Rusumo-Kigali road is the main route used by petrol trucks supplying Kigali and Bujumbura, so there's plenty of traffic.

From Ngara, a bus (usually daily) goes to Mwanza via Lusahanga, setting off very early at about 4 am and arriving after dark. The buses are operated by the New El-Jabry Bus Co in Mwanza. Lusahanga is an overnight truck stop for petrol tanker drivers and it's where the tarmac road starts.

Alternatively, organise a lift all the way from Kigali. Take a Gikondo matatu from the

Place de l'Unité Nationale in Kigali and go about three km down the Blvd de l'OUA to the STIR truck park and ask around there. Many trucks leave daily from here at about 9 am, heading for Tanzania. Most of the drivers are Somalis and, if you strike up a rapport with them, you may well get a free lift all the way to a major city in Tanzania. If not, you're looking at about US$20 from Kigali to Mwanza.

If you're entering Rwanda from Tanzania, get the bus from Mwanza to Ngara but make sure you get off at Lusahanga. Buses leave Mwanza (usually daily) at 4 am and arrive after dark. To make sure you catch the bus, stay in Mwanza at the Penda Guest House next to the bus terminal. It's a dump but it's convenient.

To/From Uganda

Road transport between Masaka or Kampala and Bukoba is almost impossible to find. There are no buses and trucks are like hens' teeth. Ever since the Tanzanians invaded Uganda to push out Idi Amin the roads have been atrocious, although there are plans to upgrade them. We haven't heard of anyone going this way for years.

To/From Zambia

The usual route is on the TAZARA railway but there's also road transport from Mbeya to Tunduma on the Tanzania-Zambia border. From the border you walk to Nakonde on the Zambian side and take a bus from there to Kasama and Lusaka. Not many people use the road route. This border used to be notorious for officialdom but has cooled off a lot in recent years, though it's wise to be on your guard.

Train The TAZARA railway runs between Dar es Salaam and Kapiri Mposhi in the heartland of the Zambian copper belt, via Morogoro, Mbeya and Tunduma/Nakonde. The line was built by the Chinese in the 1960s and passes through some of the most remote countryside in Africa, including part of the Selous Game Reserve. It is Zambia's most important link with the sea but, unfortunately, maintenance hasn't matched the energy with which the Chinese first constructed the railway. As a result, schedules can be erratic. There are usually three trains per week in either direction.

The express train usually departs Kapiri Mposhi at about 8.45 pm on Tuesdays and at about 4.45 pm from Dar es Salaam on the same day. The journey takes between 42 and 48 hours and the fares are or TSh 4310 (1st class), TSh 2970 (2nd class) and TSh 1360 (3rd class).

The ordinary train departs Kapiri Mposhi at 9.45 am on Monday and Friday and at 12.30 pm from Dar es Salaam on the same days. The journey takes about 52 hours and the fares are TSh 4080 (1st class), TSh 2740 (2nd class) and TSh 1130 (3rd class). Tickets can be bought at the booking office (tel 213232) in Lusaka. In Dar es Salaam, buy tickets at the TAZARA Railway Station on Pugu Rd. This is not the same station as the one in central Dar es Salaam where Central Line trains arrive and depart. The TAZARA station is about halfway to the airport. Get there on an airport bus from the junction of Sokoine Drive and Kivukoni Front, opposite the Cenotaph and Lutheran Church. A taxi will cost TSh 500.

Book tickets at least five days ahead. Don't expect any 1st or 2nd class tickets to be available beyond this point, unless you have 'contacts' such as government officials and diplomats. It's remarkable how easy it is to get a 1st class ticket the day before departure if you know someone like this! Third class tickets are sold only on the day of departure.

Student discounts of 50% are available for International Student Card holders but getting authorisation for this can be time consuming. The normal procedure is to pick up a form from the TAZARA station and take it to the Ministry of Education beside State House where you fill in more forms and get the appropriate rubber stamp. Then you take the form back to the TAZARA station and buy your ticket. It's a lot of fuss for a few dollars!

As on Kenyan trains, men and women can only travel together in 1st and 2nd class if they occupy an entire compartment.

Meals are usually available on the train and can be served in your compartment, though food supplies generally run out towards the end of a journey. If this happens, there are always plenty of food and drink vendors at the stations en route. Don't take photographs on this train unless you have discussed the matter beforehand with the police.

LAKE
To/From Burundi
Ferry The main ferry on Lake Tanganyika is the historic MV *Liemba* which connects Tanzania with Burundi and Zambia. It operates a weekly service connecting Bujumbura (Burundi), Kigoma (Tanzania) and Mpulungu (Zambia). It's a great way to travel.

The MV *Liemba* is a legend among travellers and must be one of the oldest steamers in the world still operating on a regular basis. Built by the Germans in 1914 and assembled on the lake shore after being transported in pieces on the railway from Dar es Salaam, it first saw service as the *Graf von Goetzn*. Not long afterwards, following Germany's defeat in WW I, it was greased and scuttled to prevent the British getting their hands on it. In 1922 the British colonial authorities paid the princely sum of UK£4000 for it. Two years later they raised it from the bottom of the lake, had it reconditioned and put back into service as the MV *Liemba*. The fact that it's still going after all these years is a credit to its maintenance engineers.

The schedule for the MV *Liemba* is more or less regular but it can be delayed for up to 24 hours at either end, depending on how much cargo there is to load or unload. Engine trouble can also delay it at any point, though not usually for more than a few hours.

Officially it departs once a week from Bujumbura on Monday at about 4 pm and arrives in Kigoma (Tanzania) on Tuesday at 8 am. It leaves Kigoma at about 4 pm on Wednesday and arrives in Mpulungu (Zambia) on Friday at 8 am. It calls at many small Tanzanian ports en route between Kigoma and Mpulungu, but rarely for more than half an hour.

The fares from Bujumbura in BFr are:

	1st class	2nd class	3rd class
Kigoma	254	1820	810
Mpulungu	7150	5590	2335

The fares from Kigoma in TSh are:

	1st class	2nd class	3rd class
Bujumbura	1285	920	420
Mpulungu	3050	2330	1040

In addition, port fees of BFr 200 are payable upon boarding in Bujumbura. Tickets for the ferry can be bought from SONACO, Rue des Usines off Ave du Port, Bujumbura, on Monday morning from 8 am.

Tickets bought in Mpulungu for the trip north to Kigoma or Bujumbura must be paid for in US dollars. Kwacha and shillings are not acceptable. The fares from Mpulungu to Kigoma are US$60 (1st class), US$42 (2nd class) and US$20 (3rd class).

To save money when going all the way from Bujumbura to Mpulungu, first buy a ticket to Kigoma and once the boat sails buy a ticket for the rest of the journey to Mpulungu from the purser using Tanzanian shillings bought on the street market in Bujumbura. Do this as soon as possible after departing Bujumbura if you want a cabin between Kigoma and Mpulungu.

When travelling from Bujumbura direct to Mpulungu you have to stay on the boat for the 36 hours or so that it docks in Kigoma, although you are allowed into town during the day.

Third class consists of bench seats either in a covered area towards the back of the boat or in another very poorly ventilated area with bench seats in the bowels of the vessel. The best plan is to grab some deck space. The 2nd class cabins are incredibly hot, stuffy and claustrophobic. They have four bunks and are also very poorly ventilated. If you want a cabin go the whole hog and take a 1st class one. These have two bunks, are on a higher deck, have a window and fan and are clean

and reasonably cool. Bedding is available for TSh 70.

Third class is not usually crowded between Bujumbura and Kigoma, so to save money this is a reasonable possibility, especially as it's only overnight. It's no problem to sleep out on the deck – the best spot is above the 1st class deck, although you need to be discreet as it's supposedly off limits to passengers. On the lower decks you need to keep your gear safe as some petty pilfering does sometimes occur. If you're travelling 3rd class between Bujumbura and Kigoma, and want to upgrade to a cabin for the Kigoma-Mpulungu leg, make sure you see the purser soon after leaving Bujumbura. At the start of this leg 3rd class is very crowded with people hanging off everywhere, although it rapidly thins out as the boat stops at Tanzanian ports along the way.

Meals and drinks are available on board and must be paid for in Tanzanian shillings. Bring enough shillings to cover this – exchange rates on board are naturally poor. Three course meals of soup, chicken and rice followed by dessert are not bad value at TSh 400. Warm Primus beer is available for TSh 250 or Tanzanian Safari for TSh 210. Breakfasts are also very good value at TSh 200.

Coming from Bujumbura, the MV *Liemba* arrives at Kigoma at about 5 am but you can't get off until 8 am when customs and immigration officials arrive. So, instead of packing your bags and hanging around it's a good idea to have breakfast.

Lake Taxi & Matatu The alternative to the MV *Liemba* is to travel partly by matatu and partly by lake taxi between Bujumbura and Kigoma via the Tanzanian border village of Kagunga and the Gombe Stream National Park. The national park is primarily a chimpanzee sanctuary and well worth a visit, but it does cost US$50 entry fee plus US$20 for accommodation. If you can't afford this then simply stay on the lake taxi which will take you all the way to Kigoma.

From Bujumbura, matatus go daily to Nyanza Lac for BFr 400. You must go through immigration here and the office is about one km from the town centre towards the lake. After that you take a matatu (BFr 100) to the Burundi border post. From this post to the Tanzanian border post at Kagunga it's a two km walk along a narrow track. The Kagunga border post often runs out of currency declaration forms and this may create problems if you intend to visit Gombe Stream National Park. If that's the case, try to get *something* on paper with an official stamp. From Kagunga, there are lake taxis to Kigoma (actually to Kalalangabo, about three km north of Kigoma) which cost TSh 500 and take most of the day. The taxis call at Gombe Stream (about halfway) where you can get off if you like. The fare to Gombe Stream is TSh 250, as is the fare from there to Kigoma.

The lake taxis are small, wooden boats, often overcrowded not only with people but with their produce, and they offer no creature comforts whatsoever. They're good fun when the weather is fine though if there's a squall on the lake you may be in for a rough time. If you have a choice, try to get a boat with a cover as it gets stinking hot out on the lake in the middle of the day. These boats do not operate on Sundays.

To/From Kenya
Dhow It used to be possible to get from Mombasa to Pemba, Zanzibar and Dar es Salaam by the *Virgin Butterfly* hydrofoil but the service has been suspended (see the Dar es Salaam chapter). There are now only occasional dhows between these places. To find one, you'll have to hang around the dhow dock in Mombasa and be persistent. It could take you several days to find one. The trip to Dar es Salaam takes anything from 24 to 36 hours and costs KSh 200 for which you get zilch in the way of facilities or comfort. Bring everything with you. There are similar dhows between Mombasa and Zanzibar.

There are no steamers on Lake Victoria which connect Kenya with Tanzania.

To/From Uganda
Boat In the early stages of researching this book we were told that cargo boats between Jinja and Mwanza no longer took passengers. Later on, I met a German expatriate working in Tanzania who was involved in exporting cotton from East Africa. He knew the ferry situation on Lake Victoria very well and assured me there were cargo boats between Uganda and Tanzania which took passengers but that there was no regular schedule. So it seems there are still possibilities. Make enquiries if you are interested.

To/From Zaïre
There is no land border between Tanzania and Zaïre (separated by Lake Tanganyika) and there are no passenger ferries between the two countries either. However, there are cargo ships and some of the captains will take passengers. Enquire at the dock in Kalemie (or at Kigoma if you are going in the opposite direction).

To/From Zambia
See the To/From Burundi entry for details about MV *Liemba's* services on Lake Tanganyika.

LEAVING TANZANIA
Departure Tax
The international airport departure tax for international flights is US$20 or UK£18 payable in hard cash. Travellers' cheques are not acceptable and neither are UK£1 coins so, if you pay in pounds sterling you'll have to give them UK£20 and get change in local currency. Very convenient!

The departure tax for domestic flights is payable in local currency and varies between TSh 300 and TSh 500.

Getting Around

AIR

Air Tanzania, the national carrier, serves all internal routes. Small jets are used between the main airports – Dar es Salaam, Kilimanjaro, Mwanza and Zanzibar. Propeller planes are used on routes which service smaller airports at places such as Bukoba, Dodoma, Iringa, Kigoma, Kilwa, Lindi, Mafia, Mbeya, Musoma, Mtwara, Pemba, Shinyanga, Songea, Tabora and Tanga.

There are supposedly scheduled flights to all these places but *never ever* rely on them. Air Tanzania would be better renamed Air Maybe. Cancellations and long delays are the order of the day, and don't waste time and energy complaining about it because no-one is going to lift a finger to help you. To be fair, there simply are not enough planes to service their routes, but that's only part of the story. Ask for a flight schedule or a list of current fares (even at the head office in Dar es Salaam) and you'll be told 'We don't have them – it's all on computer'. Just the ticket if you want to plan ahead, and guaranteed to increase the queues in front of the computer operators.

Nevertheless, you do need to plan ahead if only because of the backlog of frustrated passengers left stranded because of cancellations and heavy demand for tickets on certain routes. The busiest are Dar es Salaam to Zanzibar and Dar es Salaam to Kilimanjaro for which you must book at least a week in advance. Other routes aren't quite so bad.

All nonresident foreigners must pay for tickets in hard currency (cash or travellers' cheques) or by credit card (American Express, Diners Club and Visa are acceptable). You cannot pay for flights in shillings, even if you have bank receipts. And beware! If you pay for a flight with cash or travellers' cheques and it's cancelled, any refund will be in shillings! There's no way you'll get your hard cash back. Still, flights are relatively cheap. For example, Dar es Salaam to Zanzibar costs US$23 one way.

Domestic airport departure taxes vary. At the large airports it's TSh 500 and at the smaller ones it's TSh 300.

BUS & MATATU

Tanzania's economy is definitely on the mend but there's still very little spare cash for road or rail maintenance. So expect the worst and, when it's better than that, be grateful. Except for certain sections – Namanga, Arusha, Moshi, Himo and Dar es Salaam to Morogoro – the roads are poor. At one time many roads were sealed but the tarmac has since broken up, large potholes have formed and they're now worse than a poorly maintained gravel road. Traffic meanders from one side of the road to the other like a cavalcade of drunken ants in an often vain attempt to avoid the larger holes. It's not particularly dangerous, especially during daylight hours, because no-one can travel at high speed. Comfortable it is not and slow it certainly is.

What has improved recently is the fuel supply in Tanzania. Petrol and diesel are readily available and there's generally no restrictions on the amount you can buy. Pump prices are TSh 93 for regular, TSh 97 for premium and less for diesel.

On the main long-haul routes there's generally a choice between so-called luxury buses and ordinary buses. The distinction in terms of comfort is often academic. The main difference is in the time they take to get to their destination – ordinary buses pick up and put down more frequently, so take longer; they're also marginally cheaper.

On short hauls the choice is between ordinary buses and matatus and, for those who want to get somewhere fast and have the money, shared taxis. Ordinary buses and matatus leave when full and the fare is fixed. Only rarely will the conductor attempt to charge you more than what anyone else is paying. Advance booking on long hauls is definitely advisable. Don't expect to turn up an hour or so before departure and be able to buy tickets.

A few Tanzanian towns have central bus and matatu stations (Moshi and Arusha) so it's easy to find the bus you want. Other places, Dar es Salaam being the prime example, don't have a central bus stand so buses depart from several locations, some of which are not at all obvious. In circumstances like this you will have to ask around before you find the bus you want.

Beware of pickpockets and thieves at bus stations. There are usually scores of them and they're all waiting for you! Don't let your attention wander, even for a moment. Arusha is notorious for them, with Moshi a close second.

If you have the option, it's always better to travel 1st or 2nd class on a train for long hauls rather than go by bus. Take a look at the haggard faces of travellers who stumble off the so-called luxury buses between Dar es Salaam and Moshi and you won't need any further convincing!

Finding a place to put your pack on a bus can sometimes present problems. The racks above the seats are generally too small to accommodate rucksacks but there's usually room up front near the driver. On long hauls, don't allow your bag to be put on the roof if there's any possibility of passengers being up there with it. There won't be much left in it by the time you arrive at your destination. The safest thing to do is to insist that it goes under your seat or in the aisle where you can keep your eye on it. Another option on short hauls is to pay for an extra seat and pile your bags on that.

TRAIN

Apart from Arusha, Tanzania's major population centres are connected by railway. The Central Line linking Dar es Salaam with Kigoma via Morogoro, Kilosa, Dodoma and Tabora was built by the German colonial authorities between 1905 and 1914. Later it was extended from Tabora to Mwanza by the British. The other arm of this line links Dar

es Salaam with Moshi and Tanga via Korogwe.

The other major line is the TAZARA railway linking Dar es Salaam with Kapiri Mposhi in the heartland of the Zambian copper belt via Morogoro, Mbeya and Tunduma/Nakonde. It is Zambia's most important link with the sea. This line was built by the People's Republic of China in the 1960s and passes through some of the most remote country in Africa, including part of the Selous Game Reserve. The line involved the construction of 147 stations, more than 300 bridges and 23 tunnels. It was the most ambitious project ever undertaken by the Chinese outside their own territory. Unfortunately, maintenance hasn't matched the energy with which the Chinese first constructed the railway so schedules are erratic, though there are usually three trains in either direction each week.

As with bus travel, keep an eye on your gear at all times, particularly in 3rd class. Even in 1st and 2nd class make sure that the window is jammed shut at night. There is usually a piece of wood provided for this as the window locks don't work. It's common practice for thieves to jump in from the window at night when the train stops at stations.

Classes

There are three classes on Tanzanian trains: 1st class (two-bunk compartments), 2nd class (usually six-bunk compartments) and 3rd class (wooden benches only). Second class on the Dar es Salaam to Moshi and Dar es Salaam to Tanga trains is seats only. You'd have to be desperate to go any distance in 3rd class – it's very uncomfortable, very crowded and there are thieves to contend with. It's definitely not recommended. Second class is several quantum levels above 3rd class in terms of space and comfort (though the fans may not work) and it's an acceptable way to travel long distances. The difference between 1st and 2nd class is that there are two people to a compartment instead of six. Men and women can only travel together in 1st or 2nd class if they occupy the whole compartment.

Some trains (Dar es Salaam to Kigoma, Mwanza, Moshi and Tanga) have restaurant cars which serve good meals (TSh 400 dinner, TSh 300 breakfast), soft drinks and beer. Bed rolls are available in 1st and 2nd class at a cost of TSh 150, regardless of how long the journey is. These can be a good investment on the long runs from Dar es Salaam to Mwanza or Kigoma.

Reservations

Buying a ticket can be a daylight nightmare, especially in Dar es Salaam and Moshi. It's chaos at the stations and nowhere will you find any schedules. The only information that's usually posted is a list of fares but this is often out of date. Even when you try to book a ticket several days in advance you may well be told that 1st and 2nd class is sold out. The Central Line station in Dar es Salaam is notorious for this. The claim is usually pure, unadulterated rubbish, but it helps to secure 'presents' for ticket clerks. If you are told this, see the station master and beg, scrape and plead for his assistance. It may take some time but you'll get those supposedly 'booked' tickets in the end. The claim is generally true, on the other hand, on the day of departure.

BOAT
Ferry

Lake Tanganyika See the Tanzania Getting There chapter about transport from Tanzania to Burundi aboard the MV *Liemba* on Lake Tanganyika. This connects Tanzania with Burundi and Zambia and also operates between Tanzanian ports on the lake.

The MV *Mwongozo* operates services only in Tanzania, connecting Kigoma with the small Tanzanian ports to the south and north. On Sundays it sails south from Kigoma to Kasanga near the Zambian border. On Thursdays and Saturdays it heads north for Kagunga near the Burundi border.

Lake Victoria Two ferries serve ports on Lake Victoria: the MV *Victoria* connects Bukoba and Mwanza while the MV *Bukoba* serves Bukoba, Mwanza and Musoma. See the Lake Victoria section for schedules and fares.

Offshore Islands & South Coast See the Dar es Salaam and Zanzibar chapters for details on the services to the islands off the Tanzanian coast and to the ports south of Dar es Salaam.

Dhow

Dhows have sailed the coastal waters of East Africa and across to Arabia and India for centuries. Although now greatly reduced in number, they can still be found if you're looking for a slow but romantic way of getting across to the islands or up to Mombasa.

Most of the dhows are motorised but it's still possible to find the smaller ones which rely entirely on their sail. Dependent on the wind and tides, they only sail when these variables are favourable otherwise too much tacking becomes necessary. This may mean that they sail at night which, on a full moon, is pure magic. There's nothing to disturb the silence except for the lapping of the sea against the sides of the boat. Remember that they are open boats without bunks or luxuries. You simply bed down wherever there is space and where you won't get in the way of the crew. Fares are negotiable but are often more than you would pay on a modern vessel for the same journey.

The larger, motorised dhows are a standard form of public transport connecting Dar es Salaam to Zanzibar, Pemba and Tanga. They run on regular schedules and are easily found. Fares are generally fixed. The smaller dhows are a little harder to find. Make enquiries at the dhow docks (usually in a different location from those which service modern shipping).

DRIVING
Car Rental

This is a relatively expensive option for getting around Tanzania and certainly way beyond a budget traveller's means unless shared with several others. Examples of rates are:

	per day	per km
Saloon Cars	TSh 1500	TSh 100
Land Rover	TSh 1500	TSh 120
VW Combi	TSh 1500	TSh 120
Nissan Minibus	TSh 2000	TSh 220

They all have a 100 km per day minimum charge.

Dar es Salaam

Dar es Salaam, the 'Haven of Peace', started out as a humble fishing village in the mid-19th century when the Sultan of Zanzibar decided to turn the inland creek, which is now the harbour, into a safe port and trading centre. It became the capital in 1891, when the German colonial authorities transferred their seat of government from Bagamoyo because the port there was unsuitable for steamships.

Since then it has continued to grow and is now a city of about 1½ million people. Although quite a few high-rise buildings have appeared in the centre and at various places in the suburbs, it remains substantially a low-rise city of red-tiled roofs, with its colonial character substantially intact. The harbour is still fringed with palms and mangroves, and Arab dhows and dugout canoes mingle with huge ocean-going vessels.

Like all large African capital cities, there are substantial contrasts between the various parts of the city. Yet you won't find the same glaring disparity in living standards between the slums and the more salubrious suburbs that you would in Nairobi. The busy, dusty streets and concrete buildings around the Kariakoo market and clock tower are certainly another world away from the wide, tree-lined boulevards of the government and diplomatic quarters, but there's no way you would describe them as slums.

From being a relatively unrewarding place for nightlife in the mid to late 1980s, Dar es Salaam has considerably livened up, particularly if you're willing to head towards Oyster Bay.

Information

Tourist Office The TTC office (tel 2485) is on Maktaba Rd near the junction with Samora Ave and opposite the New Africa Hotel. It's open Monday to Friday from 9 am to 5 pm and Saturday from 9 am till noon. It has a limited range of glossy leaflets about the national parks and other places of interest, a map of the city and a 1:2,000,000 scale map of Tanzania, but they're often out of stock of all of these. If the maps are unavailable it can be difficult to find any street map of Dar es Salaam, but the road map is sometimes available from the Kilimanjaro Hotel shops.

The TTC can also make reservations at any of the larger hotels in Tanzania and at most of the national park lodges (payment in foreign currency only) but they can't help you with budget accommodation. It's better to book national park lodges through a travel agency as they may offer special deals.

Banks Banking hours are Monday to Friday from 8.30 am to 12.30 pm and on Saturdays from 8.30 to 11.30 am. If you need to change money at a bank outside these hours there is a branch of the National Bank of Commerce in the Kilimanjaro Hotel open daily except Sunday from 8 am to 8 pm.

Foreign Embassies Embassies in Dar es Salaam include:

Algeria
    34 Upanga Rd (tel 20846). Open Monday to Friday from 8 am to 2 pm and on Saturday from 8 am to 1 pm.
Angola
    10th floor, IPS Building, Maktaba St (tel 24292). Open Monday to Friday from 8 am to 3 pm and on Saturday from 8 till noon.
Belgium
    7th floor, NIC Investment House, Samora Ave (tel 20244/5). Open Monday to Friday from 8 am to 1 pm.
Burundi
    Plot 1007, Lugalo Rd (tel 38608). Open Monday to Friday from 8 am to 2.30 pm and on Saturday from 8 am to 12.30 pm.
Canada
    Pan African Insurance Co Building, Samora Ave (tel 35752). Open Monday to Friday from 7.30 am to 3 pm.
Denmark
    Ghana Ave (tel 27077/8). Open Monday to Friday from 8 am to 1 pm.

Top: Pride, Ngorogoro Crater, Tanzania (GE)
Bottom: Tusker, Ngorogoro Crater, Tanzania (GE)

Top: Arusha, Tanzania (GE)
Left: Game drive, Ngorogoro Crater, Tanzania (GE)
Right: Ebony carvings, Tanzania (SB)

Finland
9th & 10th floors, NIC Investment House, Samora Ave (tel 30396).
France
Corner Bagomoyo and Kulimani roads (tel 34961/3). Open Monday to Friday from 8.30 am to 2 pm.
Germany
10th floor, NIC Investment House, Samora Ave (tel 23286/8). Open Monday and Thursday from 7 am to 1.15 pm and 2 to 4 pm, and Tuesday, Wednesday and Friday from 7 am to 1.30 pm.
India
11th floor, NIC Investment House, Samora Ave (tel 28197). The consular section is at 28 Samora Ave (tel 20295/6). Open Monday to Thursday from 8 am to 3.30 pm and on Friday from 8 am to 6 pm.
Italy
316 Lugalo Rd (tel 29961). Open Monday and Tuesday from 7.30 am to 1 pm and 3.30 to 6 pm, Wednesday and Friday from 7.30 am to 1 pm, and Thursday from 7.30 am to 1 pm and 3.30 to 7 pm.
Japan
Plot 1018, Upanga Rd (tel 31215/9). Open Monday to Friday from 8.30 am to 3.30 pm.
Kenya
14th floor, NIC Investment House, Samora Ave (tel 31526). Open Monday to Friday from 8 am to 3 pm.
Madagascar
143 Malik Rd (tel 29442). Open Monday to Friday from 8 am to 2 pm and Saturday from 8 am till noon.
Malawi
9th floor, IPS Building, Maktaba St (tel 37260/1). Open Monday to Friday from 8 am till noon and 2 to 5 pm.
Mozambique
25 Garden Ave (tel 33062/5). Open Monday to Friday from 8.30 am to 4 pm.
Netherlands
New ATC Building, corner Garden Ave and Ohio St (tel 26767/9). Open Monday to Friday from 8 am to 3 pm.
Norway
Extelecoms House, Samora Ave (tel 25195/7). Open Monday to Friday from 7.30 am to 2.30 pm.
Rwanda
32 Upanga Rd (tel 30119, 30120). Open Monday to Friday from 8 am to 2.30 pm and Saturday from 8 am to 12.30 pm.
Spain
IPS Building, Samora Ave (tel 23203).
Sudan
64 Upanga Rd (tel 32022). Open Monday to Friday from 8.30 am to 3 pm.
Sweden
Extelecoms House, Samora Ave (tel 23501/6). Open Monday to Friday from 8 am to 3 pm and Saturday from 8 am till noon.
Switzerland
17 Kenyatta Drive, Oyster Bay (tel 34903). Open Monday to Wednesday and Friday from 7.30 am to 2.30 pm and Thursday from 7.30 am to 3 pm.
Uganda
10th floor, IPS Building, Maktaba St (tel 31004/5). Open Monday to Friday from 8 am to 12.30 pm and 2 to 5 pm.
UK
Hifiadhi House, Samora Ave (tel 29601/9).
USA
36 Laibon Rd (tel 37501/4). Open Monday to Friday from 7.30 am to 3.30 pm.
Zaïre
438 Malik Rd (tel 24181/2). Open Monday to Friday from 8.30 am to 3 pm.
Zambia
5/9 Sokoine Drive at Ohio St (tel 27261/3). Open Monday to Friday from 8 am till noon and 2 to 4.30 pm.
Zimbabwe
Plot 439, Malik Rd (tel 30455). Open Monday to Friday from 8 am to 12.30 pm and 2.30 to 4.30 pm.

The nearest Australian High Commission is in Nairobi and the nearest New Zealand High Commission is in Harare.

Airline Offices Airlines with offices in Dar es Salaam are:

Aeroflot
Eminaz Mansion, Samora Ave (23577)
Air France
Peugeot House, corner Upanga Rd and UWT St
Air India
corner Upanga Rd and UWT St (tel 23525)
Air Tanzania
ATC House, Ohio St (tel 38300) and Tancot House, Sokoine Drive
Air Zaïre
IPS Building, Maktaba St (tel 20836)
Alitalia
Peugeot House, Upanga Rd
British Airways
Coronation House, Samora Ave (tel 20322)
EgyptAir
Matasalamat Mansion, Samora Ave (tel 23425)
Ethiopian Airlines
TDFL Building, Samora Ave (tel 24174)
Kenya Airways
Peugeot House, Upanga Rd

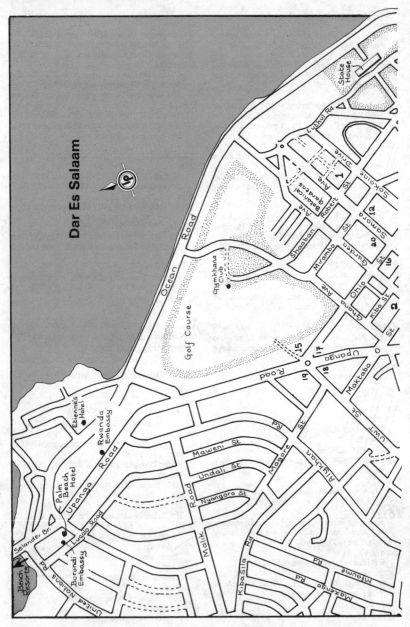

Dar Es Salaam

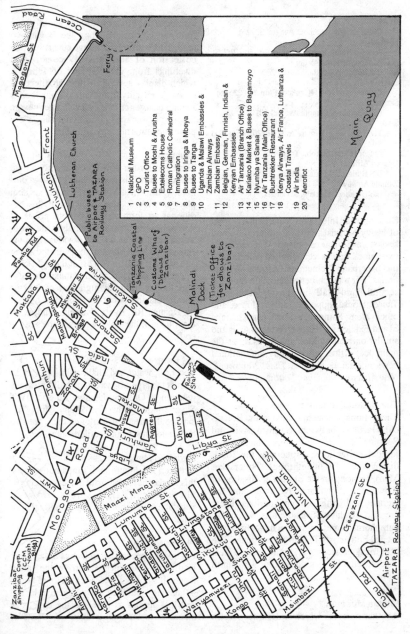

1   National Museum
2   GPO
3   Tourist Office
4   Buses to Moshi & Arusha
5   Extelecoms House
6   Roman Catholic Cathedral
7   Immigration
8   Buses to Iringa & Mbeya
9   Buses to Tanga
10 Uganda & Malawi Embassies &
    Zambian Airways
11 Zambian Embassy
12 Belgian, German, Finnish, Indian &
    Kenyan Embassies
13 Air Tanzania (Branch Office)
14 Kariakoo Market & Buses to Bagamoyo
15 Nyumba ya Sanaa
16 Air Tanzania (Main Office)
17 Bushtrekker Restaurant
18 Kenya Airways, Air France, Lufthanza &
    Coastal Travels
19 Air India
20 Aeroflot

KLM
TDFL Building, Samora Ave (tel 33725)
Lufthansa
Peugeot House, corner Upanga Rd and UWT St
Pakistan International Airlines
IPS Building, Maktaba St (tel 26944)
Pan Am
Kilimanjaro Hotel, Kivukoni Front (tel 23526)
Sabena
AMI Building, Samora Ave (tel 30109)
SAS
TDFL Building, Samora Ave (tel 22015, ext 845)
Swissair
Luther House, Sokoine Drive (tel 22539)
Uganda Airlines
IPS Building, Maktaba St (tel 30359)
Zambia Airways
IPS Building, Maktaba St (tel 29071)

Bookstores Unless you're particularly fond of heavy Marxist tomes, there are no good bookstores in Dar es Salaam. The ones that exist stock only a very limited selection of the paperback Heinemann African Writers Series. For a much better selection there's a second-hand stall on the street outside Tancot House, opposite Luther House, and others along Samora Ave between Maktaba St and Extelecoms House. At these stalls and similar ones along Maktaba St, as far as the main post office, you can buy international news magazines such as *Time*, *Newsweek*, *New African Magazine*, *South*, etc.

The National Museum

The National Museum is next to the Botanical Gardens between Samora Ave and Sokoine Drive. It houses important archaeological collections, especially the fossil discoveries of Zinjanthropus (Nutcracker Man), sections on the Shirazi civilisation of Kilwa, the Zanzibar slave trade and the German and British colonial periods. There are also displays of handicrafts, witchcraft paraphernalia and traditional dancing instruments. Entry costs TSh 50 for residents, TSh 200 for nonresidents and students are free. The museum is open daily from 9.30 am to 6 pm.

Village Museum

Another museum which is definitely worth visiting is the Village Museum, about 10 km from the city centre along the Bagamoyo road. This is an actual village consisting of a collection of authentically constructed dwellings from various parts of Tanzania which display several distinct architectural styles. Open daily from 9 am to 7 pm, there's a small charge for entry plus another charge to take photographs. Traditional dances are performed on Thursday and Sunday.

Mwenge

Three km further down the Bagamoyo road at Mpakani Rd is a *makonde* carving community. Known as Mwenge, it is an excellent place to pick up superb pieces of this traditional art form at rock-bottom prices. If you're heading this way by public transport, watch carefully as it's not obvious from the Bagamoyo road. Stay up front with the driver and ask him to drop you off at the right spot.

Another good place to find makonde carvings, though at slightly higher prices, is at the beer garden in front of the Palm Beach Hotel on Upanga Rd. Every evening vendors do the rounds of the tables with examples of the craft.

Art Centre

Local oil, water and chalk paintings can be seen at the Nyumba ya Sanaa building at the junction of Ohio St, Upanga Rd and UWT St, overlooking the Gymkhana Club. You can see the artists at work and there are also makonde carvers and batik designers.

Kariakoo Market

Between Mkunguni and Tandamuti streets, this market has a colourful and exotic atmosphere – fruit, fish, spices, flowers, vegetables, etc – but very few handicrafts for sale.

Places to Stay

Finding a place to stay in Dar es Salaam can be difficult. The later you arrive, the harder it gets. It's not that there aren't a lot of hotels – there are – but they always seem to be full and this applies as much to the expensive places as to the budget digs. So, whatever else you do on arrival in Dar es Salaam, *don't* pass up a vacant room. Take the room and then look for something else if you're not happy with it. You can always make a booking for the following day if you find something better.

Most of the cheaper hotels are scattered between Maktaba and Lumumba streets with several others in the vicinity of the Kariakoo market. The expensive places are either on Maktaba St or to the north and east of it.

All the Tanzania Tourist Corporation hotels – New Africa Hotel, Kilimanjaro Hotel, Kunduchi Beach Hotel – offer 50% discounts from the Monday following Easter Sunday until 30 June each year.

Dar es Salaam has water and electricity problems. Basically, supply doesn't match demand so certain sections of the city are shut off from time to time. This affects practically all hotels, even the New Africa Hotel, but not the Kilimanjaro which has its own generator.

Places to Stay – bottom end

Don't expect too much for your money – a scruffy room with equally scruffy communal showers and toilets are the rule, but there are one or two exceptions.

Mission Houses & the Ys Two places stand head and shoulders above all the rest as being excellent value for money. The first is *Luther House* (tel 32154, PO Box 389), Sokoine Drive, next to the characteristically German church at the junction of Sokoine Drive and Kivukoni Front. It costs TSh 950/1300 a single/double with a bathroom and including breakfast. It's clean and secure, mosquito nets are provided and there's hot water. As you might expect, it's a very popular place to stay. So popular in fact that it's likely to be booked out at least a week in advance, so to be sure of a room write to them in advance requesting a booking and, preferably, enclosing a deposit.

Equally popular is the *YWCA* on Maktaba St, next to the GPO, which takes couples as well as women. It's very clean and secure and there are a lot of rules which are enforced

but everything works as a result (shorts are not allowed in the canteen, for instance). Mosquito nets and laundry facilities are provided. Doubles cost TSh 900 including a good breakfast. Be polite and look clean and tidy when asking about accommodation here otherwise they'll tell you it's full. Like Luther House it's advisable to book in advance, but there's more chance of getting a room here as you can only stay a maximum of seven nights.

The *YMCA*, Upanga Rd, isn't such good value and has no single rooms. Also, you must watch your belongings as there's the occasional theft from the rooms. Doubles cost TSh 1600 including a fairly poor breakfast.

Another mission guest house, recommended by a traveller, is *Sister Sandra Guest House* (tel 22749), Kibasila Rd, at the back of the National Library which is on UWT St. I've never heard of anyone else staying there but they apparently have double rooms with hot showers for TSh 1200. It's very clean and a large breakfast is included in the price.

Hotels One of the cheapest of the budget hotels is the *City Guest House* (tel 22987, PO Box 1326), Chagga St , which is pretty clean and costs TSh 300/400/500 a single/double/triple with a shared bath. Checkout time is 10 am. This place is hard to see as the sign is broken. Similar to this is the *Holiday Hotel*, Jamhuri St, which has singles/doubles with a shared bath for TSh 500/550 and doubles with a private bath for TSh 650. Likewise, the *Traffic Light Motel* (tel 23438), corner Jamhuri St and Morogoro Rd, offers B&B for TSh 700 a single (shared bath) and TSh 1050 a double with a private bath.

Further afield in the vicinity of the clock tower are several other cheapies. The *Delux Inn* (tel 20873), Uhuru St, is reasonable value at TSh 700/900 a single/double with a shared bath, as is the *Kibodya Hotel* (tel 31312) on Nkrumah St, which has doubles with bathroom for TSh 1200. The Kibodya has no singles and is often booked out three days in advance. Nearby on Lindi St, the

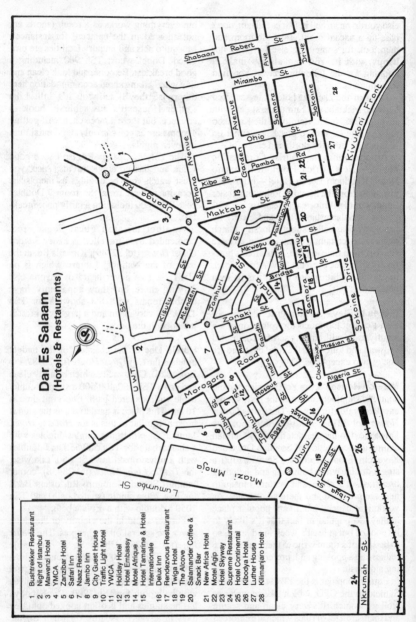

Dar Es Salaam
(Hotels & Restaurants)

1   Bushtrekker Restaurant
3   Night of Istanbul
4   Mawenzi Hotel
5   YMCA
6   Zanzibar Hotel
7   Safari Inn
8   Naaz Restaurant
9   Jambo Inn
10 City Guest House
11 Traffic Light Motel
12 YWCA
13 Holiday Hotel
14 Hotel Embassy
15 Motel Afrique
16 Hotel Tamarine & Hotel
    Internationale
17 Delux Inn
18 Rendezvous Restaurant
19 Twiga Hotel
20 The Alcove
    Salaamander Coffee &
    Snack Bar
21 New Africa Hotel
22 Motel Agip
23 Hotel Skyway
24 Supreme Restaurant
25 Hotel Continental
26 Kibodya Hotel
27 Luther House
28 Kilimanjaro Hotel

Hotel Tamarine (tel 20233, 20573) has doubles with a shared bath for TSh 600 and doubles with a private bath for TSh 750. In theory you can have single occupancy of a double with a shared bath for TSh 400, but that depends on demand. A hotel is being built next door to the Tamarine which, according to the sign, will be called *Fatman's Hotel*! On the opposite side of the road is the *Hotel Internationale* (tel 22785) which has doubles with a shared hot water bath for TSh 800, but the receptionist told me I had to pay in hard currency (US$7)! This is pure nonsense. No-one pays for a hotel under US$10 in hard currency.

Going up in price a little, one of the best places to stay and one which has become very popular with travellers recently is the *Safari Inn* (tel 38101, PO Box 21113), Band St, off Libya St behind the Jambo Inn. It's new, very friendly and has a reasonably useful notice board. It's excellent value at TSh 1500 a single, TSh 1800 a double (double bed) and TSh 2200 a double (twin beds), plus there are several doubles with air-con at TSh 3000. Checkout time is 11 am. There's a sign saying, 'Women of moral terpitude not allowed'!

The *Jambo Inn* (tel 35359, 21552) on Libya St seems reasonable value at TSh 1500/2000 a single/double with a bathroom and TSh 2500/3000 for air-conditioned doubles/suites. Taxes of 17.5% must be added to these prices but room rates include breakfast. However, a few travellers have complained recently that standards of cleanliness leave something to be desired. The Jambo Inn has its own restaurant which is good value. If you stay at this hotel, under no circumstances be tempted to change money with the employee named Abdul. He's believed to be a police informer.

Places to Stay – middle

Worth a try in this category is the *Hotel Continental* (tel 22481), Nkrumah St. It was the only mid-range hotel in Dar es Salaam which I came across that would accept local currency as payment. There are no singles and self-contained doubles cost TSh 4600

including breakfast. Similar in price is the *Motel Afrique* (tel 31034), corner Kaluta and Bridge streets, which has self-contained doubles for US$20 (TSh 3500 for residents). The trouble here is that the staff are somewhat indifferent.

The *Hotel Skyway* (tel 27061), corner Sokoine Drive and Ohio St, is similarly priced at US$22 a single and US$25 a double with bathroom, but I've never heard from anyone who has stayed there.

A little further from the city centre is the *Mawenzi Hotel* (tel 27761), on the corner of Upanga Rd and Maktaba St at the roundabout, opposite the YMCA. This hotel has undergone a major refurbishment and is now very good value and a popular place to stay. Tariffs for nonresidents are US$25/30/35 a single/double/triple or TSh 3500/4200/4600 for residents. All rooms are self-contained and the hotel has a bar and restaurant.

If you're prepared to stay even further out of the centre (a 15 to 20 minute walk – even in the hot sun!), then you can't beat the Greek-owned *Palm Beach Hotel* (tel 28892), Upanga Rd, near the junction with Ocean Rd. This is the Heron Court Hotel of Nairobi in Dar es Salaam. The outdoor beer garden/barbecue area is a favourite watering hole for expatriates from all over the world as well as Tanzanian entrepreneurs and local women looking for a man to take them to the Oyster Bay Hotel disco when the bar closes. It's an excellent place to make useful contacts. The hotel is efficiently run, secure and hassle-free, has friendly staff and is as clean as a whistle. There are a variety of rooms, all with air-con and telephone, at US$21/30 a single/double with a shared bath and US$27/35/39 a single/double/triple with a private bath. Prices for residents are TSh 2835/4050 and TSh 4707/6217 respectively. Prices include breakfast (extra charge for eggs) and the hotel has a laundry service. The restaurant has an indoor area (basically seafood and meats) and a beer garden barbecue area where you can eat alfresco for TSh 400 to TSh 500 (doner kebab, kebab and chicken). It's very lively and is packed out every night.

Not far from the Palm Beach Hotel is *Etienne's Hotel* (tel 20293) on Ocean Rd. This used to be a favourite Peace Corps volunteers hang-out and some of them still stay here when they're in town. It has a kind of engaging leafy degeneracy about it with hints of a down-at-heel obscure rural English pub and comes complete with one of the world's most indolent bartenders. It's tropical languor *par excellence*. Fans groan lazily above your head, the springs on the lounge seats succumbed to posterior pressure long ago, the lights are dim and people talk in conspiratorial tones. There's a beer garden and meals are available but these didn't look particularly great when I was last there. Officially they're only allowed to take Tanzanian residents as guests at TSh 3080 a double as they don't have a licence to take foreign currency, but if you told them you were a resident I doubt they'd ask for proof.

Last in this range is the *Twiga Hotel* (tel 22561), Samora Ave, which doesn't have anywhere near the same atmosphere as the preceding two hotels but is very central and does have a good rooftop restaurant. Singles/doubles cost US$30/32 for nonresidents or TSh 4500/5500 for residents, including breakfast and all taxes. All rooms are self-contained.

Places to Stay – top end

There are only four top-end hotels in the city centre, two of which are privately owned while the others are operated by the Tanzania Tourist Corporation.

Of the privately owned, probably the best is the *Hotel Embassy* (tel 30006, PO Box 3152), 24 Garden Ave , which has 150 rooms – all self-contained with air-con, a telephone and 24-hour room service – at US$70 a double (TSh 13,250 for residents) including breakfast and all taxes. There's a swimming pool, bar, grill, restaurant and all the usual services. American Express cards are accepted. Similarly priced and of much the same standard is the *Motel Agip* (tel 23511), Pamba Rd, at the back of the New Africa Hotel.

The first of the TTC hotels is the *New Africa Hotel* (tel 29611) in Maktaba St. A well-known landmark, it's currently being extended to double its size. The rooms are well appointed and fully air-conditioned and the hotel has all the usual facilities except for a swimming pool. Singles/doubles which include a continental breakfast cost US$68/78 plus 22.5% taxes and service charge. Credit cards are accepted.

Top of the range is the TTC *Kilimanjaro Hotel* (tel 21281), Kivukoni Front, where singles/doubles/triples with a continental breakfast cost US$77/87/92 plus 22.5% taxes and service charge. Like the New Africa Hotel, all the rooms are well appointed and fully air-conditioned and the hotel has all the usual facilities including a swimming pool and a popular rooftop restaurant which overlooks the harbour. Credit cards are accepted.

Places to Eat – cheap

There are many small restaurants in the city centre where you can buy a cheap traditional African meal or Indian food (usually the latter). Some of these places are attached to hotels.

Currently popular with travellers is the *Sheesh Mahal*, India St, which offers good, cheap Indian food. Equally popular is the *Imran Restaurant*, Chagga St, offering Indian curries which are rated by some travellers as the best in town. Also very popular, especially for lunch, is the *Salamander Coffee & Snack Bar*, Samora Ave at Mkwepu St, where you can either eat inside or outside on the verandah. An average lunch costs about TSh 400. Other good cheapies include the *Pop-In*, the *Naaz Restaurant*, Jamhuri St (samosas, fruit salad and ice cream only) and the *Nawaz Restaurant*, Msinhiri St, between Mosque St and Morogoro Rd, which has cheap rice and meat dishes.

Possibly the best vegetarian Indian restaurant in Dar es Salaam is the *Supreme Restaurant*, Nkrumah St. This place has been operating for years and has a well-deserved reputation. The *Royal Restaurant*, Jamhuri St, between Mosque St and Kitumbini St, also does vegetable curries and the like.

Slightly more expensive but very good is the restaurant at the *Jambo Inn*, Libya St. It has soups, chicken curries, various red-meat dishes and fish or chicken with rice or chips.

Ice cream freaks should make at least one visit to the *Sno-Cream Parlour*, Mansfield St, near the junction with Bridge St. Mansfield St runs part of the way between Samora Ave and Sokoine Drive. This place has the best ice cream in Tanzania and is well on the way to becoming a legend among travellers. You should see the number of Indian families who come here on Sundays! Lastly, for fruit juices, peanut brittle and gooey cakes go to *Siefee's Juice Shop*, Samora Ave. It also has good samosas.

Places to Eat – more expensive

For a not too expensive splurge, the *Chinese Restaurant* in the basement of the NIC Building, Samora Ave at Mirambo St, is excellent value and has been a popular place for a small spree for years, especially if you want a break from Indian or African food. Likewise, you'll find a lot of travellers eating lunch at the restaurant on the ground floor of the *New Africa Hotel*, if only to squeeze a cold beer out of them (they're forever pretending to run out of this desirable commodity if you're just drinking and not having a meal). The cuisine varies from average to good and a full meal will cost from TSh 700 to TSh 800 including taxes. The food is basically continental though they also attempt Chinese. Similar to this is the rooftop restaurant at the *Twiga Hotel*, Samora Ave, opposite Extelecoms House. Many travellers recommend this place. Expect to pay about TSh 500 for a main course, although lobster will cost TSh 900.

Meals at the *Motel Agip* have been described by a few Italian travellers as 'as good as a first class restaurant in Rome with better service and at a fraction of the cost'.

For a very refreshing change, treat your taste buds to an evening meal at the *Night of Istanbul*, corner Zanaki St and UWT St. This restaurant is owned and run by a Turk so there's all the usual Turkish dishes such as doner kebab, shish kebab, hummus, etc. It

isn't particularly cheap at TSh 1000 for a meal but it's highly rated by everyone who goes there. Another place of similar standard is *Shari's Dar Bar*, UWT St, which offers huge servings of Tandoori chicken, beef and salad for about TSh 500. It's described by one traveller as 'the best eats in Dar'.

Further out of town it's worth heading for the very popular outdoor barbecue at the *Palm Beach Hotel*, Upanga Rd, especially if you're thinking of doing some serious drinking afterwards (they never run out of beer, even if you're not eating). Barbecued chicken or doner kebab with chips and salad costs TSh 500. An indoor restaurant offers somewhat more expensive standard European dishes but the food is only average. The nearby *Etienne's Hotel*, Ocean Rd, also offers lunch and dinner and is recommended by Peace Corps volunteers, but the meals I saw didn't look very special.

For a real splurge there's a choice of three restaurants. One of the most popular is *The Alcove*, Samora Ave, which offers Indian and Chinese dishes in air-conditioned comfort amid soft lighting. The food would rate a mention in any international restaurant guide. Average prices for a main course are TSh 800. Only imported beers are served and these are quite expensive at between TSh 355 and TSh 400. The Alcove is open for lunch and dinner. Get there early or reserve a table if you don't want to stand around.

More expensive still but a superb place to eat is the *Bushtrekker Restaurant* overlooking the Gymkhana Club on the roundabout where Upanga Rd, Ohio St and UWT St meet. It's very up-market, with starched linen tablecloths and an extensive wine list plus a choice of eating alfresco on the covered balcony or inside with the air-con fully on. Main dishes average from TSh 1300 to TSh 1500 with a few at TSh 3500 (lobster, beef tenderloin, etc); starters are from TSh 500 to TSh 900; soups are about TSh 500 and desserts are from TSh 300 to TSh 600.

Most people have at least one meal at the rooftop restaurant in the *Kilimanjaro Hotel*. The views over the harbour at night are superb and the food is usually good, though the last time I was there I was served a particularly dry and tasteless piece of fish, so perhaps the quality of the food is not consistent. It's popular with businesspeople, local expatriates and well-heeled tourists. Prices are roughly the same as at The Alcove's.

Entertainment

Definitely the most popular place for a cold cleansing ale in the city centre is the street level patio bar of the *New Africa Hotel* on Maktaba St. Most travellers come here at one time or another and you can always get into a lively conversation. It gets very busy between 4.30 and 7 pm. The only trouble here is that they frequently pretend they've run out of beer (except for clients who are eating in the adjacent restaurant). Since no other hotel in Dar es Salaam ever runs out of beer this is clearly nonsense. Others have recommended the bar at the *Motel Agip*.

A much livelier bar than the New Africa is the one at the *Palm Beach Hotel*, Upanga Rd, though it is further out of town so you'll have to take a taxi (TSh 200) at night. In the evenings it's always full of a gregarious mixture of Africans and working expatriates (both male and female) and although the beers get warmer as the night wears on, they never run out. The bar closes at about 11 pm. The nearby *Etienne's Hotel*, Ocean Rd, is also worth a visit though it's much quieter.

Probably the most popular disco in Dar es Salaam is the one at the *Oyster Bay Hotel*, though you'll definitely need a taxi (TSh 400) to there from the centre unless you're offered a lift from the Palm Beach Hotel when its bar closes. This is an open-air disco with a *makuti* (palm leaf) roof (the old roof was blown away by the December 1989 cyclone but will no doubt have been replaced by now). Live bands often play and entry is TSh 1000. There's a disco every night of the week.

There are other discos at the main hotels in the centre of Dar es Salaam and at the beach resort hotels.

The *Yacht Club*, about four km beyond Oyster Bay, is recommended as a good place to meet expatriates. A taxi to the club from central Dar es Salaam costs TSh 600.

The *British Council* (tel 22716), Samora Ave, has free film shows on Wednesday afternoons or evenings and sometimes on Mondays. Similar social evenings are organised by the *Goethe Institute* (tel 22227), IPS Building, Samora Ave, and the *US Information Service* (tel 26611), Samora Ave.

Getting There & Away

Air Dar es Salaam is the major international arrival point for flights from overseas. See the Getting There and Getting Around chapters for details on international and domestic flights.

Bus As there's no central bus station in Dar es Salaam, buses to various parts of the country leave from a variety of places within the city.

Buses for Bagamoyo leave throughout the day until about 3 pm from outside the Kariakoo market on Swahili St. They depart when full, cost TSh 160 one way and take between two and three hours.

Heading for Moshi and Arusha, buses depart from the bus station on the corner of Morogoro Rd and Libya St. Luxury buses cost TSh 3000 and ordinary buses TSh 2300 and the journey takes up to 24 hours. The road is a nightmare as far as Moshi, as anyone who's done it will tell you, so make sure you take a luxury bus at the very least!

Buses to Tanga and Mbeya and other points west and south depart from the so-called Country Bus Station on Libya St on the bottom side of the park between Uhuru and Nkrumah streets. The buses to Tanga take between seven and eight hours and those to Mbeya take about 20 hours. See the individual towns for details on fares and schedules.

Train The Central Line station booking office in Dar es Salaam is an example of near chaos. To make advance bookings you'll simply have to join the rabble and have as much time as it takes to get to the front of the nonexistent queue. It can also be very frustrating unless you book well in advance because of the practice of claiming that 1st and 2nd class tickets are sold out when they're actually not. This enables ticket clerks to extract bribes from those who are willing to pay. Persistence sometimes helps but, if not, an appeal to the station master often turns up the goodies.

Trains depart from Dar es Salaam to Mwanza and Kigoma on Tuesday, Wednesday, Friday and Sunday at 6.10 pm. Heading for Moshi and Tanga, trains depart on Tuesday, Thursday and Saturday at 4 pm. Fares (in TSh) from Dar es Salaam are:

	1st class	2nd class	3rd class
Dodoma	2045	940	320
Kigoma	4790	2145	745
Mbeya	3430	1995	1220
Moshi	2320	1050	370
Mwanza	4720	2115	725
Tabora	3390	1525	530
Tanga	1685	770	270

For information about the TAZARA service between Tanzania and Zambia see the Getting There chapter.

Boat To get to Zanzibar and Pemba, the Zanzibar Shipping Corporation (tel 30749, PO Box 1395), Umoja wa Vijana, Morogoro Rd, operates what amounts to a weekly service between Dar es Salaam, Zanzibar and Pemba. The ship is the MV *Maendeleo*. The fare to Zanzibar is TSh 1048 (2nd class; two cabins available only), TSh 740 (tourist class) and TSh 540 (3rd class) and the trip takes four hours. There is no fixed schedule so make enquiries. The Umoja wa Vijana building is just past the Swami Narayan Hindu temple.

To go south of Dar es Salaam, the Tanzanian Coastal Shipping Line, or Kampuni ya Meli Mwankao Tanzania (tel 26192, PO Box 9461), Sokoine Drive, operates boats which connect Dar es Salaam with Mombasa, Tanga, Mafia Island, Kilwa, Lindi and Mtwara. The schedules vary since their vessels are essentially cargo boats, but they all take passengers. Projected sailings are chalked on a blackboard outside the office and you should book according to what is written there. The company owns several boats, including the MS *Mtwara*, MV *Lindi*, MV *Kilindoni*, BP *Ushirikiano* and MV *Junior 'D'*. The fares in KSh are:

	Mafia	Kilwa	Lindi	Mtwara
Dar es Salaam	350	470	650	680
Mafia	–	170	440	470

The average times of journey are 12 hours to Tanga, eight hours to Mafia and 16 hours to Kilwa.

During late 1988 and part of 1989 a hydrofoil service operated between Dar es Salaam and Zanzibar. The *Virgin Butterfly* service took less than one hour and proved to be very popular, though fares for non-Tanzanian residents had to be paid in hard currency and it cost almost as much as the Air Tanzania flight (without the TSh 500 departure tax).

The service has been suspended indefinitely, though the sign for the *Virgin Butterfly* is still on Sokoine Drive. There are various bizarre stories about the demise of this service but the most reliable one I heard was that the hydrofoil had been taken to Mombasa for repairs, from where it was hijacked and taken to Malta! Apparently there was some financial dispute between the owners and the operators of the hydrofoil. When it will return – if it ever does – is anyone's guess.

Dhows Dhows operate out of the Malindi Dock alongside Sokoine Drive and are the means by which most budget travellers get to Zanzibar from Dar es Salaam. The fare is TSh 500 and the journey takes from six to eight hours. The dhows are large, wooden, motorised vessels which on average can take about 200 passengers – these are not the small dhows with lateen sails that you see around Tanga and Lamu (Kenya).

There's usually one dhow per day in either direction. To book, go down to the Malindi Dock and buy a ticket the morning before the dhow sails. The booking office is on the right-hand side just inside the metal gates at the bottom of the tarmac ramp which goes down from Sokoine Drive. It's labelled 'East & Southern Boat Transporters'. These dhows don't sail on Sundays or public holidays.

Departure times vary (the one I went on left at 6 am the following morning), but you have to check in at the customs shed two hours before departure – you'll be told what time when you buy the ticket. This customs shed is where you see the *Virgin Butterfly* sign – not the place where you bought the ticket. No food or drink is available on the boat so bring your own. There's generally a toilet on board which hangs off the back of the dhow.

Getting off the dhow at Zanzibar is like extricating yourself from a rugby scrum. *Wazungu* are generally the last to leave as it's a major effort to climb over the side of a dhow with a rucksack on your back and into a flimsy bucking aluminium motor launch whilst a hundred Zanzibaris claw and elbow you out of the way. Good luck! It's fun.

Getting Around

Airport Transport Dar es Salaam airport is 13 km from the city centre. Bus No 67 connects the two but, if you get on at the airport, make sure that it is going right into the city centre as some don't.

A shuttle bus between the centre of Dar es Salaam and the airport is operated by Takims Holidays, Tours & Safaris. It departs from the New Africa Hotel, Maktaba St, at 8 and 10 am, noon, 2, 4 and 5 pm, and from the airport at 9 and 11 am, 1, 3, 5 and 6 pm. The fare is TSh 200. A taxi to or from the airport costs from TSh 800 to TSh 1000 for up to four people.

Bus Local buses are operated by both government (UDA buses) and private firms (Dala Dala). Neither type are numbered. Instead they have their first and last stop indicated in the front window. The bus to the TAZARA Railway Station is marked Posta-Vigunguti. Fares are fixed and cost only a few shillings, but all buses are very crowded.

Taxi Taxis are without meters and charge a standard TSh 200 per journey inside the city centre. Slightly outside this area they'll charge TSh 300. To Oyster Bay taxis cost TSh 400 and to the TAZARA Railway Station they cost TSh 500.

Beaches Around Dar es Salaam

Oyster Bay is the nearest beach, six km north of the city centre and on the fringes of where the affluent and the foreign ambassadors have their residences. As you might expect, it's a particularly beautiful stretch of tropical coastline fringed with coconut palms, but keeping it that way has become a bone of contention between local environmental groups and the city council. It seems that various groups of young, well-to-do revheads have been chewing up the foreshore at weekends with their 4WD dune buggies and not giving a damn about the damage they do or the work which local residents have put into conserving the area. Some people have been arrested for attempting to plant coconut palms intended to replace those which will soon die. That's a sad indictment of the city council's policies and very short-sighted. This beach is, after all, a major recreation area for the city.

There are other beaches a little further up the coast from here but the major resort area is 25 km to 27 km north of the city, east of the Bagamoyo road. Strung out along the coast here, from south to north, are the Kunduchi Beach Hotel, Silversands, Rungwe Oceanic Hotel and the Bahari Beach Hotel. This is Dar es Salaam's answer to the Shelly, Tiwi and Diani beaches south of Mombasa. It's an idyllic mixture of sea, sand, sun and landscaped tropical extravagance. The only drawback, as with the Mombasa beaches, is the copious amounts of seaweed which makes swimming at high tide very unpleasant. When the tide goes out, however, the seaweed tends to stay on the beach thus providing clear sea in which to enjoy yourself. There are also several wooded islands with good beaches offshore which the beach hotels run boats to.

If you stay at any of these beach resorts, don't walk from one to the other either along the beach or along the connecting roads unless you're with a large group. Many people have been robbed, some of them with violence. Always take a taxi or get a lift.

Boat trips to offshore islands such as Mbudya, where you can swim, snorkel or sunbathe, are available from the Kunduchi Beach Hotel, the Rungwe Oceanic Hotel and the Bahari Beach Hotel. Charges to Mbudya from the Kunduchi are TSh 800 return and from the Bahari they're TSh 1200 return. There are three trips per day from Monday to Saturday and 12 trips on Sundays and public holidays. You need a minimum of four people unless you're willing to pay a surcharge. You can also go sailing from these places for TSh 700 per person (minimum of eight) and and rent a catamaran (TSh 700 per hour) or a sailboard (TSh 500 per hour). It used to be possible to do day trips to Zanzibar but these appear to have been discontinued.

Places to Stay

The *Oyster Bay Hotel* (tel 68631), Touré Drive, about six km from the city centre, is the first of the beach hotels north of Dar es Salaam. All rooms face the sea and it's definitely top of the range at US$95 a double including breakfast. The management has a very condescending attitude to anyone without a shiny car or who is not just plain rich. Perhaps that's intentional. The disco here, on the other hand, is very popular and you don't need Gucci to get in, just a spare TSh 1000.

Of the other hotels further up the coast, the TTC *Kunduchi Beach Hotel* (tel 47621) is quite pleasant and all rooms face the ocean. Self-contained singles/doubles with continental breakfast cost US$43/53 plus 22.5% taxes and service charge. Temporary daily entry for nonresidents costs TSh 200 plus a further TSh 150 to use the swimming pool, but you don't pay this if you arrive on the State Transport Corporation shuttle bus since they assume you're going to stay there or go further up the coast to one of the other hotels. A barbecue dinner costs TSh 1200.

Next up the coast is the *Rungwe Oceanic Hotel* (tel 47021) which is favoured by overland truck companies since it's the only beach hotel where camping is permitted. Therefore it's the only one within reach of the budget traveller. Camping costs TSh 100 per person per night but the site is somewhat run-down and water is rarely available. It's possible to leave a vehicle here for TSh 100 per night whilst you go to Zanzibar.

Top of the range is the *Bahari Beach Hotel* (tel 47101), a stunningly beautiful construction in coral rag and makuti, and very thoughtfully landscaped with flowering trees and coconut palms. Apart from the reception and dining areas, the Bahari consists of a series of two-storey chalets, each with four bedrooms, private showers, individual balconies and air-con. There's a swimming pool and a very popular weekend disco. Singles/doubles with a continental breakfast cost US$70/90 (TSh 13,090/ 16,830 for Tanzanian residents) including taxes. Temporary daily entry costs TSh 200 on weekdays and Saturdays and TSh 300 on Sundays when there's live music. Bookings should be made through Bushtrekker Safaris, PO Box 5350, Dar es Salaam (telex 41178).

Places to Eat

It's more than likely you'll eat at the hotel you're staying at, but if you're just a day guest you can also eat lunch and dinner at any of the hotels. The cost for either meal is about US$10 to $US12 (payable in shillings). Those relying on the State Transport Corporation shuttle bus from Dar es Salaam to the hotels only have the option of taking lunch since the last bus back to Dar es Salaam leaves at about 6 pm. If you're staying for dinner, you'll need your own transport back.

Getting There & Away

It is possible to get to the Kunduchi beach

resorts using local buses from the centre of Dar es Salaam but these will drop you in the village from where it's quite a walk to the hotels. Also, there's a good chance of being robbed. It's much safer and more convenient to take the State Transport Corporation shuttle bus from the New Africa Hotel in Dar es Salaam. The shuttle bus leaves the New Africa Hotel Monday to Friday at 9 am, noon, 2 and 5 pm and on Saturday and Sunday at 9 and 11 am and 1, 3 and 5 pm. In the opposite direction it returns to Dar es Salaam Monday to Friday at 7.45 and 9.45 am and 1, 3 and 6 pm. On Saturday it returns at 7.45 and 10 am and 2, 4 and 6 pm. On Sunday and public holidays it returns at 8 and 10 am, noon, 4 and 6 pm. The fare is TSh 300.

The Coast

BAGAMOYO

The name of this coastal town, 75 km north of Dar es Salaam, derives from the word 'bwagamoyo' meaning 'lay down your heart'. It's a reminder that it was once the terminus of the slave trade caravan route from Lake Tanganyika. This was the point of no return where the captives were loaded onto dhows and shipped to Zanzibar for sale to Arab buyers.

Bagamoyo later became the headquarters of the German colonial administration and many of the buildings which they constructed still remain. However, its history goes back to the 14th century when the East African coast was being settled by Arabs and Shirazis from the Persian Gulf. The ruins they left at Kaole, just outside Bagamoyo, are similar to those at Gedi and around the Lamu archipelago further north in Kenya.

Bagamoyo hasn't entirely left its infamous history behind as now it's notorious for thieves and muggers. Be careful if you're on your own, although the last time I visited (on my own) in 1990 I didn't feel threatened in any way.

Around Town

The tourist literature would have you believe that Bagamoyo is a miniversion of Zanzibar or Mombasa with an historical centre of narrow, winding alleys, tiny mosques, cafés and whitewashed German colonial buildings. There's certainly a small section of town down by the waterfront which corresponds to such a description but it has all seen better days and the most lasting impression is one of near terminal decay. Restoration is being carried out on the customs house at the beach but the other colonial buildings show only benign and mildewy neglect. All in all, it's debatable whether what remains is worth a four to six hour return bus trip. Personally, I think not, and so do many other travellers.

Out of Town

The Catholic Mission north of town maintains a museum with relics of the slave trade and displays about the early European explorers Burton, Speke and Stanley. The chapel where Livingstone's body was laid before being taken to Zanzibar en route to Westminster Abbey is also here. Don't walk to this museum alone as there's a good chance you'll get mugged. To visit the 14th century ruins at Kaole you'll need to hire a taxi, and they're very hard to find in Bagamoyo.

Places to Stay & Eat

There's only one hotel (well signposted) in Bagamoyo, but it's very basic and essentially used only by prostitutes and their clients. It's better to head out to the *Badeco Beach Hotel*. Even this place is somewhat run-down, the water supply is erratic and there are no mosquito nets. However, the excellent beach compensates for the hardships. The cook at the hotel will prepare food for a small fee but don't expect anything fancy. You can buy lobster and other seafood from the fishers near the old German customs building. They land their catches here in the late morning and late afternoon.

Things are looking up, however, and there will soon be a brand-new beach resort to be known as the *Gogo Beach Resort*. It will offer self-contained doubles, a restaurant, picnic and camping area and a swimming pool. Before heading this way, call 36006 in Dar es Salaam and enquire whether it has opened yet.

Getting There & Away

Buses depart from Dar es Salaam throughout the day until about 3 pm from outside the Kariakoo market. They leave when full, are very crowded, cost TSh 160 one way and take two to three hours, depending on the number of stops en route.

PANGANI

Pangani is a small village north of Bagamoyo and some 50 km south of Tanga. It's on a beautiful stretch of coast with many reefs and islands offshore. From Pangani you can organise fishing trips to the reefs and snorkelling at the two islands of Mawe Mdogo and Mwamba Mawe. There's also a small marine park on the island of Maziwi and boat trips are possible to see the wildlife up the Pangani River.

Places to Stay & Eat

The *YMCA* is more than six km north of Pangani, so it's really only suitable for those with their own transport or a penchant for walking more than 1½ hours to the nearest restaurant. The manager, however, is a live wire and well worth tracking down for an animated conversation.

A more convenient place to stay in Pangani is the *Pangadeco* at the beach end of the main street on the high-water mark, about 50 metres through the coconut palms. The rooms are clean and mosquito nets are provided, though you may not be too impressed with the sky-blue decor. There's no running water so bucket showers are the order of the day. It costs TSh 355 a single and food is available on request.

There are two other guest houses: the *River Inn* is on the road running alongside the river, about halfway from the boat yard to the ferry stage, and the *Udo* is on the same road but nearer the ferry.

Entertainment

Pangani is a Muslim town, and there's only one bar which is noisy despite an average clientele of only six people per night. However, here you can meet the District Commissioner and District Administrator who are both charming when sober and keen to help tourists have a good time.

Getting There & Away

Buses go to and from Tanga three times daily and depart between 8 am and noon. Trips by motor boat (from the frozen-fish factory) are expensive – TSh 2800 for two hours, for example.

TANGA

Strolling around Tanga, amid its sleepy, semicolonial atmosphere, you'd hardly be aware that this is Tanzania's second largest seaport. Seen from the air, however, it's a remarkably large town which sprawls well into the hinterland. It was founded by the Germans in the late 19th century and is a centre for the export of sisal. Not many travellers come here apart from those looking for a dhow to Pemba Island or heading north to Mombasa.

Tanga briefly hit the headlines in early 1990 when, after a tip-off, police uncovered hundreds of elephant tusks buried in the sand in gunny sacks on a tiny offshore island. Those involved were obviously intent on smuggling them out of the country one dark night but there were no reports of subsequent arrests. Sound like a familiar tale?

Amboni Caves

This area is predominantly a limestone district and the Amboni Caves, off the road to Lunga Lunga, are not too far from town.

Tongoni Ruins

The Tongoni Ruins are 20 km south of Tanga on the Pangani road. There's a large ruined mosque and more than 40 tombs, the largest concentration of such tombs on the East African coast.

According to accounts which came into the hands of the Portuguese when they first arrived at Kilwa in 1505, both Kilwa and Tongoni were founded at the end of the 10th century by Ali bin Hasan, the son of Sultan Hasan of Shiraz in Persia. Certainly the method of construction of the mosque is unlike that used by the Arabs who came from the Arabian Peninsula in later centuries. Yet Persian script has only been found once and that is on one of the tombstones at Tongoni, though Persian coins are common at other sites along the coast, such as at Malindi.

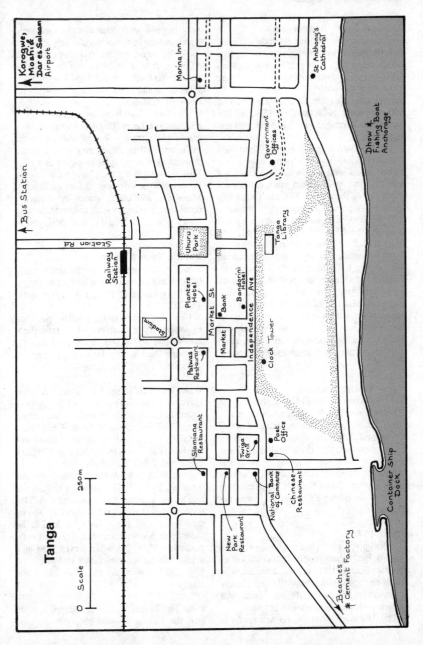

Tanga

Scale

0   250m

Korogwe,
Moshi &
Dar es Salaam
Airport

Bus Station

Station Rd

Railway Station

Stadium

Uhuru Park

Planters Hotel

Market St

Patwas Restaurant

Slamiana Restaurant

New Park Restaurant

Twiga Grill

National Bank of Commerce

Chinese Restaurant

Post Office

Market

Bank

Bandarini Hotel

Independence Ave

Clock Tower

Tanga Library

Government Offices

Marina Inn

St Anthony's Cathedral

Dhow & Fishing Boat Anchorage

Container Ship Dock

Beaches & Cement Factory

Places to Stay – bottom end

Overlooking the harbour on Independence Ave, the *Bandorini Hotel* is a very twee place which many travellers rate highly. It offers matchless English colonial-style living (reflecting the owners' nationality) and its seven rooms are often full. Singles cost TSh 600 and breakfast (optional) is TSh 150. The owners can arrange boat trips to Pangani and elsewhere.

The *Usabara Guest House* on Third St is similarly priced and the rooms have a fan, clean sheets and a towel. The staff are friendly and your belongings are secure when left in the rooms. You can't miss this place as it's painted in large bright stripes.

If the Bandorini and the Usabara are full then try the *Planters Hotel* (tel 2041) on Market St. It's a huge, rambling, old wooden hotel surrounded by an enormous verandah and with a bar and restaurant downstairs. Aussies from Queensland will love this place – it's home away from home. The rooms are clean and have a hand basin but the communal showers have cold water only. If these hotels are too expensive the *Mkwakwani Lodgings*, behind the maternity hospital and dispensary, has clean doubles with fans for TSh 500.

Places to Stay – middle

The most convenient mid-range hotel is the *Marina Inn* which is a modern, well maintained hotel offering air-conditioned doubles for around TSh 1000 including breakfast. There are no singles. The hotel has a bar and restaurant, but if you're going to spend this amount of money it's probably better to stay at the *Baobab Hotel* (tel 40638), about five km from the centre. Prices are similar to the Marina Inn.

Places to Eat

The best place for a cheap, tasty meal is the *Patwas Restaurant*, opposite the market in the town centre. It's a very clean and friendly Asian-run restaurant which offers extremely reasonably priced meals for lunch and dinner, with snacks and tea in between.

The *Marine Restaurant* on Market St is very popular with local people for lunch. Meals are cheap but the food is only average.

For a minor splurge you can eat at the *Planters Hotel*. They're a bit on the slow side getting food together but it's worth the wait. Fish, chips and salad or curried prawns with rice costs TSh 600.

The *Yacht Club* is the focus of the lives of resident foreigners (English, Dutch, Norwegian and German), though alcohol is the main motivation for coming here and the conversation is pretty uninspiring as a rule. Still, the club is a good place to track down people who are driving to Dar es Salaam, Mombasa and other places in relatively comfortable vehicles such as Land Cruisers. So it's worth checking this place out if you're heading in that direction.

Getting There & Away

Bus There are usually one or two buses daily (at night only) from Dar es Salaam to Tanga. The trip takes seven to eight hours and costs TSh 800.

For the Tanzanian border post of Horohoro, try to catch one of the infrequent buses from the bus station. Otherwise hitch, although there's very little traffic. See the Tanzania Getting There chapter.

Train Trains to Tanga from Dar es Salaam leave on Tuesday, Thursday and Saturday at 4 pm. In the opposite direction they depart Tanga at 7.30 pm on Monday, Wednesday and Friday. The trip takes about 13 hours and fares are TSh 1685 (1st class), TSh 770 (2nd class) and TSh 270 (3rd class).

From Tanga to Moshi trains leave on Tuesday, Thursday and Saturday at 7.30 pm and arrive at about 9 am the next day. The train arrives at Korogwe at about 11.30 pm then waits until about 3 am for the Dar es Salaam to Moshi train to arrive. A lively platform café at Korogwe serves food and drink. The fares from Tanga to Moshi are TSh 1615 (1st class) and TSh 755 (2nd class).

Boat The Tanzanian Coastal Shipping Line (see the Dar es Salaam chapter) operates boats to Tanga from Dar es Salaam but there's no regular schedule, so enquire. The boats are essentially freighters but they do take passengers.

It is possible to find dhows operating between Tanga and Pemba Island but they're nowhere near as easy to find as the dhows between Dar es Salaam and Zanzibar.

Zanzibar

History
The annals of Zanzibar read like a chapter from *The Thousand and One Nights* and doubtless evoke many exotic and erotic images in the minds of travellers. Otherwise known as the Spice Island, it has lured travellers to its shores for centuries, some in search of trade, some in search of plunder and still others in search of an idyllic home. The Sumerians, Assyrians, Egyptians, Phoenicians, Indians, Chinese, Persians, Portuguese, Omani Arabs, Dutch and English have all been here at one time or other. Some, notably the Shirazi Persians and the Omani Arabs, stayed to settle and rule.

It was early in the 19th century under the Omani Arabs that the island enjoyed its most recent heyday, following the introduction of the clove tree in 1818. Not long afterwards, the sultan's court was transferred from Muscat, near the entrance to the Persian Gulf, to Zanzibar. By the middle of the century Zanzibar had become the world's largest producer of cloves and the largest slaving entrepôt on the east coast. Nearly 50,000 slaves, drawn from as far away as Lake Tanganyika, passed through its market every year.

As a result, Zanzibar became the most important town on the East African coast. All other centres were subject to it and virtually all trade passed through it. However, this changed with the establishment of the European Protectorates towards the end of the 19th century and the construction of the Mombasa-Kampala railway. The Omani sultans continued to rule under a British Protectorate until 1963, when independence was granted, but were overthrown the following year in a bloody revolution instigated by the Afro-Shirazi Party. This occurred prior to the union with mainland Tanganyika.

The many centuries of occupation and influence by all these various peoples has left its mark and the old Stone Town of Zanzibar is one of the most fascinating places on the east coast. Much larger than Lamu or the old town of Mombasa, it's a fascinating labyrinth of narrow, winding streets lined with whitewashed, coral-rag houses, many with overhanging balconies and magnificently carved brass-studded doors. Regrettably, many of these doors have disappeared in recent years.

There are endless quaint little shops, bazaars, mosques, courtyards and squares, a fortress, two former sultans' palaces, two huge cathedrals, former colonial mansions, a Persian-style public bath house and a bizarre collection of foreign consulates.

Outside of town there are more ruined palaces, other Shirazi remains, the famous Persian baths and that other perennial attraction – magnificent, palm-fringed beaches with warm, clear water ideal for swimming and snorkelling.

Information
Tourist Office The Tanzania Friendship Tourist Bureau (tel 32344, PO Box 216) has an office in Livingstone House. It has an excellent map of Zanzibar town (1:10,000) and one of the island (1:200,000). The town map is worth buying for exploring the alleys of the old town, though you'll probably still get lost from time to time. It costs TSh 200 and is also available at the tourist office in Dar es Salaam.

Bookings for island beach chalets are made at the tourist office.

Money On arrival in Zanzibar by dhow or ship you'll be required to change US$40 (or the equivalent) into shillings at the so-called bank next to the immigration office. The bank is actually an untidy little office staffed by one person, and you have to queue up on the street, rain or shine. Since you'll already have been through immigration and there's usually a gaggle of foreigners outside the bank, it's easy to simply walk away without changing money. No-one is going to ask for your currency form to confirm that you did change the US$40.

In theory, you can change hard currency travellers' cheques into cash dollars at the People's Bank of Zanzibar behind the fort. In practice, this is a lot harder than many people would have you believe. It took a friend three days to finally make it, but you might be luckier. There's a limit of US$50 per day, which is useful to know if you have only large denomination travellers' cheques.

Foreign Consulates The island has consulates for Germany, the Sultanate of Oman, the USSR, Egypt, India, Mozambique and the People's Republic of China. The first three are in the old Stone Town while the others are on the road to the airport.

The Old Stone Town

The old Stone Town of Zanzibar is a fascinating place to wander around and get lost in, though you can't really get lost for too long as, sooner or later, you'll end up either on the seafront or on Creek Rd. Nevertheless, every twist and turn of the narrow alleyways will present you with something of interest – be it a school full of children chanting verses from the Koran, a beautiful old mansion with overhanging verandahs, a shady square studded with huge old trees, a collection of quaint little hole-in-the-wall shops selling everything from Panadol to pawpaws or a gaggle of women in *bui-bui* sharing a joke and some salacious local gossip.

You'll see a lot of crumbled and crumbling buildings as you walk around the Stone Town and it's a great pity that so much of the fabric of this historic place has been allowed to fall into disrepair. A determined effort is now being made to restore a lot of the more important buildings, but it's high time that the entire Stone Town was declared a World Heritage site and appropriate funds were

provided to stop the rot. Tourist receipts have gone a long way to encourage the local authorities to do something about the decay but priorities are elsewhere and money, as usual, is in short supply.

It's not really possible to suggest any sort of 'itinerary' or route since it's impossible for a newcomer to come to grips with the town's layout for at least a week, even with a map (though a map does help!). Still, it's worth putting in the effort to see some of the town's major features.

Beit-el-Ajaib One of the most prominent buildings in the old Stone Town is the Beit-el-Ajaib or House of Wonders, formerly the sultan's palace and one of the largest structures in Zanzibar. Built in 1883 by Sultan Barghash (1870-88), it's an elegant four-storey structure surrounded by wide verandahs. In 1896 it was the target of a British naval bombardment, the object of which was to force Sultan Barghash to abdicate in favour of a British nominee. Now it's the local political headquarters of the CCM (Chama Cha Mapinduzi). Beside it is a more modest palace which Barghash's successor moved to after vacating the Beit-el-Ajaib in 1911.

Fort On the other side of Beit-el-Ajaib is the 'Arab' fort, a typical massive, crenellated and bastioned structure. Originally built by the Portuguese in 1700, there's little inside the fort other than a craft gallery in a poor state of repair, though restoration is soon to begin if the notice outside is to be believed. There might be an entry fee, but the last time I visited the guard was fast asleep on the table.

The craft gallery has an excellent selection of first-rate batiks, worth a look even if you don't like batiks.

Old Slave Market Another prominent landmark is the Old Slave Market alongside Creek Rd, but there's very little to see as the first Anglican cathedral in East Africa, the UMCA Cathedral (United Mission to Central Africa), stands here.

St Joseph's Cathedral The towers of this Roman Catholic cathedral, set back from the fort, are easily spotted on arrival at the island by dhow. Yet it's deceptively hard to find in the narrow confines of the adjacent streets.

Hamamni Persian Baths Perhaps worth a visit are these baths built by Sultan Barghash as public baths. They're a protected monument and are locked, but if you show a passing interest the guardian (who runs a shop a few metres away) will rush up with the key and show you around, then ask you for a 'donation'. There's no water inside anymore so it's not that interesting, especially if you've ever been inside a functional Persian/Turkish bath.

Livingstone House This was the base for the missionary/explorer's last expedition before he died. It's out on Malawi Rd and is now the tourist office.

Mosques As Zanzibar is essentially a Muslim society there are quite a few mosques scattered around the Stone Town, but if you would like to visit any of these talk to local people first. You may be invited in – suitably dressed, etc – but you may not, so play it by ear. None are part museums.

The National Museum The two buildings of the museum present a catalogued history of the island. It's worth visiting, although it's becoming run-down. Entry costs TSh 50.

Festivals

The festival of Id-ul-Fitr (the end of Ramadan) lasts about four days and if you visit the island at this time don't miss the Zanzibarian equivalent of the tug-of-war at Makunduchi in the south of the island. Men from the south challenge those from the north by beating each other silly with banana branches. After that the women of the town launch into a series of traditional folk songs and then the whole town eats and dances the night away.

Places to Stay

All accommodation on the island has to be paid for in foreign currency (preferably US dollars) unless you're a Tanzanian resident. There are no exceptions. Even staying with friends on the island supposedly requires a special permit, though it's easily obtained.

Places to Stay – bottom end

One of the cheapest places to stay is the small *Flamingo Guest House* (tel 32850), Mkunazini Bazaar. It's very friendly but lacks character. Rooms with a fan and mosquito net cost US$5 per person. Just as cheap and very close to the dock is the *Warere Guest House* at the back of the Ciné Afrique. This is very clean, well kept and was freshly repainted in late 1989. A bed costs US$5 as long as you're prepared to share the room if necessary, otherwise doubles cost US$10. All bathrooms are shared.

My nomination for best place to stay (with which many travellers would agree) is the *Malindi Guest House* (tel 30165), Funguni Bazaar, also very close to the dock. This is a beautiful place with bags of atmosphere, superbly maintained and constantly being repainted. The staff are very friendly. B&B costs US$8/12/18 a single/double/triple, plus there's a type of dormitory where you can have a bed for US$5 per head. The rooms are spotless and comfortable and are provided with clean sheets, a fan and mosquito nets. The shared bathrooms are squeaky clean and there's hot water. A laundry service is also available.

Another place which is quite popular is the *Victoria Guest House* (tel 32861) between Vuga and Kaunda roads at the back of the Omani Consulate. It's a modern place, the staff are friendly and B&B costs US$6/12 a single/double with shared bathroom facilities. Self-contained doubles cost US$18. It's a good choice if the Malindi Guest House is full.

Back up the other end of town and close to the main police station and Minara Mosque is the newly opened *El Khattab Guest House* (tel 32054). Although a good place to stay it lacks character. Beds cost

Zanzibar – Old Town

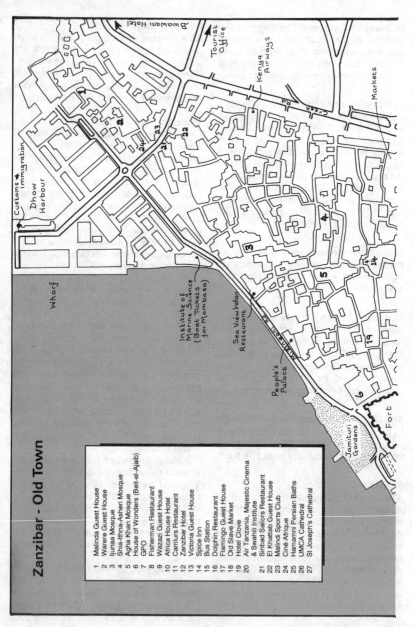

1   Malinda Guest House
2   Warere Guest House
3   Ijunaa Mosque
4   Shia-Ithna-Asheri Mosque
5   Agha Khan Mosque
6   House of Wonders (Beit-el-Ajaib)
7   GPO
8   Fisherman Restaurant
9   Wazazi Guest House
10 Africa House Hotel
11 Camlurs Restaurant
12 Zanzibar Hotel
13 Victoria Guest House
14 Spice Inn
15 Bus Station
16 Dolphin Restaurant
17 Flamingo Guest House
18 Old Slave Market
19 Hotel Clove
20 Air Tanzania, Majestic Cinema
    & Swahili Institute
21 Sinbad Sailors Restaurant
22 El Knattab Guest House
23 Malindi Sports Club
24 Ciné Afrique
25 Hamamni Persian Baths
26 UMCA Cathedral
27 St Joseph's Cathedral

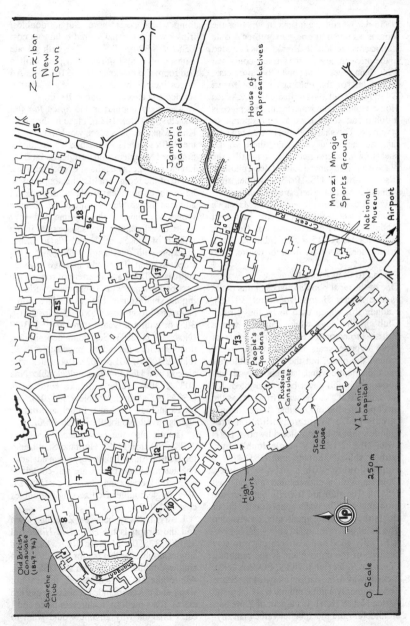

US$6 per person regardless of whether the room is occupied by one, two or three people – all rooms are double. Breakfast is included in the price and the rooms are self-contained with clean sheets, a fan and mosquito nets.

The last of the cheapies is the *Wazazi Guest House* (tel 2961) adjacent to the Africa House Hotel on the waterfront. This place is a dump and you'd have to be desperate to stay here. The shared showers are Dickensian, the fans died years ago, there are no sheets or mosquito nets and, generally, the place is in an advanced state of decrepitation. It's a rip-off at US$10/15 a double/triple without breakfast. There are no singles.

Outside the Stone Town is *Musa Maisara's Guest House* on Nyerere Rd, just past Abdallah Mzee Rd on the seafront. He offers B&B for US$10/15 a single/double. It's a good place but too far from the centre.

Places to Stay – middle
One of the most popular places in this range is the *Africa House Hotel* (tel 30708), Kaunda Rd, which used to be the 'British Club' in the days when Zanzibar was a British Protectorate. Esoteric reminders of those bygone years are still to be found around the place, but the billiard table has been dismantled and, somehow, you just know that it will never be reassembled. All the same, as it's on the waterfront, it has the most popular bar in Zanzibar (there are only three!) and a major rehabilitation programme should be completed by now. B&B costs US$12/18/30 a single/double/triple with a shared shower and US$14/21 a single/double with a private shower. Doubles with a shower and air-con cost US$24. The staff are friendly but there are problems with the water supply on the upper floors though none, apparently, downstairs. The hotel has a restaurant above the bar.

Equally good and a superb place to stay because of the atmosphere is the rambling *Zanzibar Hotel* (tel 30708/9, PO Box 392), tucked away in the narrow alleys of the Stone Town and only a three minute walk from the Africa House Hotel. It's a gem of Zanzibari architecture and much better value than anything which costs more. Singles/doubles/triples with a fan and shared bathroom cost US$12/18/30 or US$14/21/35 with private bathroom. Singles/doubles/triples with a bathroom and air-con cost US$16/24/40. All prices include breakfast. There's a laundry service and checkout time is 10 am.

Also very popular is the *Spice Inn* (tel 30728/9, PO Box 1029), close to the Agha Khan Mosque. This place would have to be the Raffles Hotel of Zanzibar. It's decidedly Somerset Maughan with its timeless 1st floor lounge full of easy chairs and local antiques. Some of the rooms are like this too, but you have to choose carefully and book in advance if possible, as some of the cheaper rooms are plain in the extreme and very basic. Overlooking a tiny square right in the middle of the Stone Town, it's a former mansion with overhanging balconies, polished wooden floors and massive wooden staircases. There are a variety of rooms, the best being those with a verandah overlooking the small square. Singles/doubles with a shared bathroom cost US$19/25 (Nos 206 & 305) or with a private bathroom US$23/28 (Nos 202 & 203). Self-contained singles/doubles with a fan or air-con cost US$28/33 (Nos 201, 204, 301 & 302). Two suites with air-con cost US$35/40 a single/double (Nos 303 & 304) while a deluxe suite costs US$45/50 a single/double (No 205). All prices include breakfast. Lunch and dinner are also available for about TSh 1000.

There's also the new *Hotel Clove* (tel 31785, PO Box 1117), Hurumzi St, close to the Beit-el-Ajaib. This is very clean but lacks character. All the rooms are self-contained with a refrigerator and a fan and cost US$24/30 a single/double. Deluxe singles/doubles cost US$30/35.

Lastly, halfway between Zanzibar town and the airport is the *High Hill Hotel* (tel 30000, 32550), Nyerere Rd, which has singles/doubles with a fan for US$25/32 and singles/doubles with air-con for US$30/38. All rooms are self-contained, there's hot water and prices include breakfast (eggs are extra). It's a modern, featureless place and I can't imagine why anyone would want to stay here. Nor do I know why it was built where it is other than to gain commissions for taxi drivers. They'll tell you there's a free hotel shuttle bus available to take you into town but there isn't. It's a very inconvenient place to stay.

Places to Stay – top end
At the top of the range but totally character-less is the *Bwawani Hotel* (tel 30200, PO Box 670) overlooking Funguni Creek. To think that someone had the opportunity and money to construct a top-range hotel in an historic place like Zanzibar and came up with something so utterly ordinary and boring is beyond belief! Still, for those without a shed of imagination, this is it. There are ordinary self-contained and air-conditioned singles/doubles for US$49/62 and suites ranging from US$97 to US$146. Room rates include a continental breakfast, taxes and a service charge. Checkout time is noon. The hotel has all the usual facilities, including a swimming pool (often empty), tennis and squash courts, restaurant, bar (expensive beers!) and the island's only discotheque (9 pm to 2 am and open to nonresidents). American Express and Diners Club cards are accepted.

Places to Eat – cheap
Undoubtedly the most pleasant and cheapest place to eat in the evening, along with a good slice of the population of Zanzibar, is in the Jamituri Gardens in front of the fort. The townspeople gather here at that time to socialise, talk about what's happened and watch the sun go down. Food stall vendors sell spicy curries, roasted meat and maize, cassava, smoked octopus, sugar cane juice and ice cream – all at extremely reasonable prices.

Just about as cheap and very popular, especially with local people, is the café at the *Ciné Afrique* where basic African dishes are available. Many travellers have also recommended the *Al Jabri Restaurant* close to Kenya Airways on Creek Rd. Here you can get cheap excellent food which is described by some as 'the best on the island'. The ambience is pleasant, too.

Just to the left of the Africa House Hotel as you face the entrance is a recently opened cheap *restaurant* with a blackboard outside the door detailing the day's offerings. It has no name as yet (though this will change if it's successful) but has the words 'Local Food' at the top of the blackboard.

Somewhat more expensive but very popular with travellers is the *Dolphin Restaurant*, close to the GPO on Kenyatta Rd. The Dolphin has been going for years and offers all the usual seafood dishes plus a few other items.

Places to Eat – more expensive
For a not too expensive splurge, there's a choice of three very popular restaurants.

The first is *Sinbad Sailors Restaurant*, diagonally opposite the Ciné Afrique on Malawi Rd. The food is excellent, the staff are friendly and the service is fast. It offers all the usual seafood plus spaghetti and curry dishes. Prices vary from as little as TSh 400 (fish & French fries) to TSh 1500 (lobster). The fish dishes are particularly succulent. It's open from about 11 am to 10 pm.

Second is the *Fisherman Restaurant* on Shangani St near the Starehe Club. Set up in a traditional Zanzibari house which makes for an intimate atmosphere, the restaurant offers a full range of excellent seafood at very competitive prices. Salads and soups average TSh 150, main courses TSh 500 to TSh 2000 (fish, crab, prawns, lobster, etc), and desserts TSh 150. It's open Monday to Saturday from 8 to 10 am (breakfast), 1 to 3 pm (lunch) and 6 to 10 pm (dinner). On Sunday it's open from 7 to 10 pm only. Get there early for dinner if you want the best choice of dishes because they tend to run out of certain items later in the evening.

The third choice is the *Sea View Indian Restaurant* on Mizingani Rd overlooking the harbour on the 1st floor. This restaurant has the best location of any on the island and offers a choice of eating outside on the balcony or inside. It's also the only restaurant in town (other than at the Africa House Hotel) where you can have a cold beer with your meal. They offer a full range of seafood plus, as you might expect, Indian curries. It's a very pleasant place to dine, but the service can be deadly slow – so slow at times that the starters occasionally turn up after you've finished the main course! This is partly because the chefs insist on cooking everything in the traditional manner over charcoal and disdain the use of a gas oven, even though they have one. If you plan to eat here in the evening it's advisable to pop in earlier in the day and choose your menu so that they have time to organise it. Also book a table if you want to eat on the balcony.

The *Africa House Hotel* has a restaurant on the floor above the bar but few people seem to eat here. Perhaps this is because for several years the food wasn't up to much, but recent reports suggest things have improved greatly. Prices are comparable with the three restaurants already mentioned in this section.

The *Zanzibar Hotel* also caters for nonresidents and may well be a good choice for a night out, but you must make advance reservations as you can't just turn up.

More expensive still is lunch or dinner at the *Spice Inn*, also open to nonresidents and with no advance booking necessary. An average meal costs about TSh 1000.

Lastly, there's the *In By The Sea Resort* (tel 31755) next to the Bwani ruins, off the road to the airport and just past the Chinese Consulate. The restaurant is right by the sea and is open for lunch and dinner. It serves chicken and chips for between TSh 300 and TSh 600 and has one of the few bars on the island. It's a long way to go and you'd have to take a taxi, which would make it expensive unless a group of you shares the cost.

Entertainment
Virtually everyone goes for a cold beer in the late afternoon/early evening at the *Africa House Hotel*. The bar is on the 1st floor terrace overlooking the ocean and is a favourite spot to watch the sun go down. The beers are reasonably priced and generally cold though, depending on demand, they get warmer as the evening wears on. The bar is open throughout the day from around 10 am to 11 pm. It's an excellent place to make contacts for visits to Changuu Island and for Spice Tours or to meet people you last saw in Nairobi, Lagos or wherever.

Another bar which surprisingly few people go to is the *Starehe Bar* on Shangani St. It's quite a large place and right next to the beach overlooking the harbour. Since it rarely has too many customers, the beers are always ice cold. It has an occasional disco in the evenings for which there might be a small cover charge.

If you want to party on until 2 am without spending a lot of money, there's good news in the form of the *Wazazi Bar*, next to the Africa House Hotel. It's a makuti-roofed bar at ground level and is very popular with local young people (including prostitutes and gays) and wazungu who are not in a hurry for an early night. There's African taped music and sometimes a live band. It opens late in the afternoon and there are always taxis outside if you don't want to walk home afterwards.

The bar at the *Hotel Bwawani* is deadly boring and the beers are expensive, but the hotel has the island's only regular disco (9 pm to 2 am) which is open to nonresidents. There's a cover charge and the disco generally takes place about three times a week, so enquire before going there.

Getting There & Away
Air Air Tanzania operates two (sometimes three) daily flights in either direction between Zanzibar and Dar es Salaam. These flights are heavily subscribed and cancellations are frequent so be prepared for a lot of messing about. Delays are standard. Advance booking at least a week ahead is essential to be sure of a seat.

The Air Tanzania office is on Vuga Rd and is open Monday to Friday from 8 am to 12.30 pm and from 2 to 4.30 pm. On Saturday it's open from 8 am to 12.30 pm. The airport departure tax is TSh 500.

If the Air Tanzania flights are full there's an outside chance of getting a seat on the 'Daily News' flight which operates once a day in either direction. It's a small chartered plane which basically delivers newspapers to the island but has room for seven passengers at TSh 3000 each. The booking office in Zanzibar is at the bookshop behind the market. Try to book at least five days in advance.

Another very popular flight is the daily Kenya Airways Mombasa-Zanzibar-Mombasa run which costs US$28 one way plus US$20 airport tax. Again, book well in advance to be sure of a seat. The Kenyan Airways office is on Creek Rd.

Boat The majority of budget travellers come to Zanzibar by motorised dhow and return to Dar es Salaam the same way. There's a dhow in either direction daily which leaves early in the morning (about 6 am), costs TSh 500 and takes about eight hours. Bring your own food and drink as none is available on the dhows.

To book in Zanzibar, go to the Malindi Sports Club directly opposite Sinbad Sailors Restaurant on the morning before departure. Tickets are sold here. This is also where you book a passage on a dhow to Pemba Island – the dhows dock at Mkoani in the south of the island.

The Zanzibar Shipping Corporation operates the MV *Maendeleo* between Dar es Salaam, Zanzibar and Pemba on an approximately weekly basis. See the Dar es Salaam chapter. In Zanzibar, the booking office is down by the wharf.

Dhows and other boats also run between Zanzibar and Mombasa usually once or twice a week in either direction. To find out the schedule and to book, go to the Institute of Marine Science workshop on Mizingani Rd – there's a small sign at the gate (which is flanked by the Tanzanian and Zanzibari flags) which says, 'Tickets for Dar, Pemba, Mombasa'. The fare is TSh 2000 or US$11 and the journey takes about 12 hours but can take quite a bit longer depending on the currents.

Getting Around
Airport Transport Municipal buses run between the airport and town for a few shil-

lings. They're marked 'U'. A taxi will cost TSh 600.

Bicycle Rental It's becoming difficult to rent bicycles in Zanzibar because of their theft from the beaches. If you just want to ride around town then you have more chance of getting one. It's probably best to first enquire at your hotel, but there is a shop near the market set back from Creek Rd. Bicycles can be put on the roofs of local buses if you get tired of pedalling.

Those with money to spend might consider renting a motorcycle. These can be hired from a shop in the Old Slave Market area and cost TSh 3500 per day. It's a good way of getting to the east coast.

AROUND ZANZIBAR
Historical sites around the island which are worth visiting include the Maruhubi Palace, built by Sultan Barghash in 1882 to house his harem but unfortunately largely destroyed by fire in 1899; the Persian Baths near Kidichi, built by Sultan Seyyid Said for his Persian wife at the highest point on the island (153 metres); and the Mangapwani Slave Caves (used for illegal slave trading after it was abolished by the British in the late 1800s), about 16 km north of Zanzibar town. To get to the Slave Caves under your own steam, take bus No 2 from the bus station on Creek Rd opposite the market in Zanzibar town.

Spice Tours
To visit all the above sites separately involves a lot of effort and/or money. It's much better to take one of the popular Spice Tours. Perhaps the best person to tour with is an elderly Indian man named Mitu who owns a taxi and has been doing this trip for years. Mitu originally put this trip together and has trained quite a few others who now operate on their own. Another bunch which has been recommended is Triple M. Mitu can be contacted either outside or inside the café adjacent to the Ciné Afrique (opposite Sinbad Sailor's Restaurant) before 9.30 am

or after 6 pm daily. Just ask around – everyone knows him. Triple M usually hang around the bar of the Africa House Hotel early in the evening. It's advisable to arrange a tour one day in advance.

Spice Tours also go to the various spice and fruit plantations around the island. Along the way you'll be invited to taste all the spices, herbs and fruits which the island produces. Lunch is included.

To get a tour going you need four people to share a taxi. A typical tour begins at about 9.30 am and returns by 5 pm and costs TSh 6000 (shared between four), plus the price of the fruit you eat (minimal). These tours are excellent value and are very popular.

Mbeweni Palace Ruins
Just south of Zanzibar town off the airport road are the Mbeweni Palace ruins which might interest you if you have a yen for Arab architecture, but which otherwise are totally neglected and largely overgrown.

Mvuleni Ruins
Close to the top of the island and north of Mkokotoni are the ruins of Mvuleni which date from the Portuguese maritime heyday when they made an abortive attempt to colonise the island.

Shirazi Mosque Ruins
Near Kizimkazi in the south, the ruins of the Shirazi Dimbani Mosque has an inscription around the mihrab dated 1107 – the oldest inscription found in East Africa. Excavations have indicated the existence of an earlier mosque on the same site.

Jozani Forest
South-east of Zanzibar town and close to Pete is the Jozani Forest, now a nature reserve and the last remaining sanctuary in the world of the red colobus monkey, of which only some 500 remain.

THE BEACHES
There are some superb beaches, particularly on the east coast of the island, which so far are totally unspoilt. This is mainly because there's been no development, so the locals are untainted by tourism and life goes on the way it has for centuries. It will probably remain that way for quite some time because the accommodation is not for those who can't do without electricity, hot and cold running water, swimming pools and night entertainment. Paradise here is simple and uncomplicated, involves a little effort but enables you to immerse yourself in the lives of the local people. It's totally relaxing and, unlike many of the beaches on the western side of the island close to Zanzibar town, there are no concerns about being robbed or mugged.

Places to Stay & Eat
Beach Bungalows The tourist office in Zanzibar maintains several bungalows at the best beaches – Bwejuu, Chwaka, Jambiani, Makunduchi and Uroa. Most of these are priced on the basis that they will sleep five people comfortably, but they will take six at a pinch. As with other accommodation on Zanzibar, payment is in foreign currency and the bungalows must be booked and paid for at the tourist office in Zanzibar. However, I have heard of travellers who have simply asked around the villages for accommodation in local houses and paid in shillings. Most people rate Jambiani and Bwejuu as the best beaches. The rates for the various beach bungalows are:

Bwejuu, Chwaka 2, Makunduchi 1 & 2: US$16 for up to five people sharing plus US$2 for each extra person.

Chwaka 1, Jambiani & Uroa: US$20 for up to five people sharing plus US$2 for each extra person.

Kerosene lanterns are provided at all the above bungalows and water is usually drawn from a well. Most people opt to have food prepared for them either by the caretaker or local people but you can, if you prefer, put your own meals together. At Jambiani, for instance, the caretaker Hassan Haji and his English-speaking assistant, Abul, are very

Zanzibar Island

friendly and will provide fresh seafood for TSh 150 (enough for four people) plus TSh 200 to cook it (regardless of how many are eating). They can also provide rice, potatoes, pineapples and other fruits and vegetables at very low cost. Soft drinks are also available. Snorkelling on the offshore coral reef can be done from dugout fishing boats at TSh 250 per person plus TSh 75 for a mask and snorkel. It's a stunningly beautiful area, the food is delicious and the local people are extremely friendly.

Guest Houses There are several private guest houses which are usually cheaper than the bungalows.

At Chwaka, the *Kichipwi Guest House* (tel 32371) costs US$15 for up to four people plus US$2 for each extra person. For bookings, contact Ali Khamis, PO Box 25, Zanzibar.

At Bwejuu, the *Dere Guest House* costs US$10 per room. Rice and fish meals are available for TSh 180 per person or lobster and crab meals for TSh 1550 split three ways – delicious.

At Jambiani, the *Jambiani Guest House* run by Mr Abu Abbi Mussa (ask for Mr Abu) is highly recommended. On the beach, it costs US$15 per day and can easily sleep up to eight people. Mr Abu is a great person, speaks very good English and can arrange anything you want or would like to do – a lobster for dinner, some item from the shops in Zanzibar town, a boat to go out snorkelling – you name it. To book, write to PO Box 229, Zanzibar.

Getting There & Away
To get to the east coast beaches you'll have to take a local bus. The bus station is on Creek Rd opposite the market.

Bus No 9 goes to Jambiani (10 am and 4 pm, three hours, TSh 80) and also to Bwejuu (different from the bus to Jambiani – ask). Otherwise get a group together and rent a minibus (TSh 700 per person among nine). The return bus from Bwejuu to Zanzibar departs the village at about 2 am and reaches the market in Zanzibar by 6.30 am. Bus No 10 goes to Makunduchi, No 6 goes to Chwaka (1½ hours) and the No 6 'Special' goes to Uroa.

OFFSHORE ISLANDS
Just offshore from Zanzibar town are several islands ringed with coral reefs. Three are simply sandbanks which partially disappear at high tide but the other four (including Chumbe Island to the south where there is a lighthouse) are well-forested, idyllic tropical islands with superb beaches.

Changuu Island

Also known as Prison Island, it's the most famous of the offshore islands. In the 19th century this island was owned by an Arab who used it, as the sign says, for housing 'recalcitrant slaves'. It was later bought by a Briton who constructed a prison, yet apparently this was never used although the ruins remain. Now it's used by day trippers from Zanzibar and by yuppies as a kind of low-key retreat from the main island.

The beach is superb, the sea crystal clear and there's a whole family of (frequently copulating) giant land tortoises which roam around the main landing spot. It's thought they were brought to the island from Aldabra in the Seychelles at around the turn of the century.

The island has a double-storey house with a verandah, a bar and a restaurant, adjacent to which there are several basic rooms to rent. Lunch (seafood, chips and salad) costs about the same as on the main island and cold beers are TSh 250 (you can drink without eating).

The island is run by the TTC which charges an entry fee of US$1, UK£1 or DM 2 payable in *cash* – neither shillings nor UK£1 coins are accepted. If you don't have that spare dollar, tough shit – sit on the boat all day!

Activities here include windsurfing (TSh 700 to TSh 1200 per hour depending on board size, plus harnesses at TSh 200 per hour and lessons at TSh 700 per hour), sailing (TSh 1500 per hour), aquacycling (TSh 1000 per hour) and snorkelling (TSh 200 per hour or TSh 500 per day for equipment).

Getting There & Away

It's easy finding transport across from Zanzibar. Simply sit in the bar at the Africa House Hotel any evening and someone will ask if you want to go there the next day. Motorised boats cost TSh 2500 shared by up to 10 people. They generally leave at 9 am and return by 4.30 pm (departure and return times are entirely up to you).

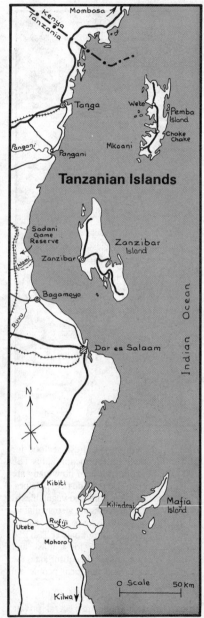

Tanzanian Islands

Other Islands

PEMBA

While most travellers make it to Zanzibar, very few ever make the journey to Pemba Island, north of Zanzibar. It's perhaps not surprising since, in terms of tourism, there's precious little to do or see. Also, the beaches and whatever historical sites there are tend to be difficult to get to because of the lack of public transport off the island's only main road. Nevertheless, it's quite a contrast to Zanzibar.

For a start, the island is much more hilly and far more densely wooded than Zanzibar, due to the higher rainfall and greater fertility of the soil. There are no extensive historic sections in the island's three main towns, though Chake Chake works hard at this.

The island is very laid back and the people are friendly and interested in where you come from and why you're there. It's the sort of place where you make an effort to get to know people and find out what's going on rather than go to see things in the usual tourist mode.

My one enduring impression of the island is the number of schoolchildren who flock onto the roads twice a day on their way home. There are thousands and thousands of them so one must assume that education has a very high priority on this island. It's heartening to see that all these children are taught practical agriculture as part of the curriculum. Indeed, when it's clove harvest time (about once every five months), the schools close and everyone turns out to help.

Cloves are the mainstay of the island's economy and the crop is three times as large as the crop from Zanzibar. There are 3½ million clove trees on Pemba, many of which date from the early 19th century when they were introduced from the Moluccas. Most are owned by small farmers who would typically have between 10 and 50 trees on their plots. There are very few large plantations of the sort you might find on Zanzibar. Everywhere you go on this island you'll see the ripe cloves laid out to dry in the sun and you'll smell their characteristic aroma.

Although Pemba was never as important as Zanzibar or other settlements on the Tanzanian coast, it has had some interesting and remarkable associations during its history. The island's earliest ruins are those of Ras Mkumbu on the peninsula west of Chake Chake where the Shirazis settled about 1200 AD. This site has several houses and pillar tombs and the remains of a large 14th century mosque.

At Pujini on the island's east coast there is a fortified settlement and the remains of a palace destroyed by the Portuguese in 1520. These were apparently built by conquerors from the Maldive Islands! It seems they were not particularly welcome as one of the rulers of this town was known as Mkame Ndume (Milker of Men) because of the amount of work he extracted from his subjects. Later, after the expulsion of the Portuguese from this part of East Africa, Pemba was taken over first by the rulers of Paté in the Lamu archipelago, then by the rulers of Mombasa, and finally by the sultans of Zanzibar.

Come here if you want to see something different but don't expect historical romance or ready-made entertainment.

Wete

This is the most northern of the island's main towns and has the second most important port through which most of the clove crop is exported. It's essentially a one-street town which snakes up the hillside from the docks. A branch of the People's Bank of Zanzibar is on the main road, but it won't change travellers' cheques. You must go to Chake Chake for this.

Places to Stay & Eat The only accommodation is the government-owned *Hoteli ya Wete* (tel 4301) on the main street at the top end of town. Rooms cost US$10 (payable in hard currency) whether you occupy them singly or as a double. Clean sheets, toilet paper, a towel and soap are provided. All rooms are self-contained and have a fan.

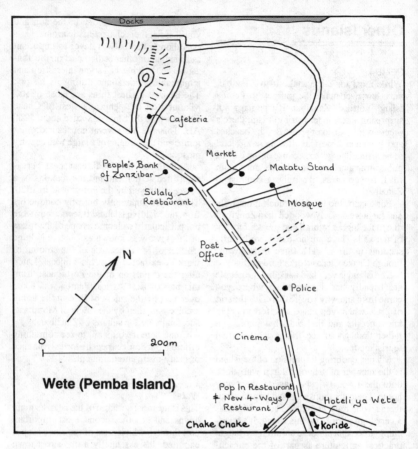

Wete (Pemba Island)

They're clean and well maintained, the staff are very friendly and English is spoken. Checkout time is 10 am.

Breakfast costs TSh 260 (fruit, eggs, bread and coffee) and lunch or dinner costs TSh 650 (usually soup plus a meat and potato stew or Portuguese-style fish with chips). Ice-cold beers are available at normal prices (so long as the nearby police canteen still has a supply of them!).

For a slight change of diet you could try one of the other restaurants in town, though they're all pretty basic. They include the *Sulaly Restaurant, Pop-In Restaurant* and the *New 4-Ways Restaurant*. The latter two are opposite the hotel.

Getting There & Away Dhows from Tanga often dock at Wete, though not always. These dhows are not usually motorised, so sailing times depend on the tides and the winds. Nor are they always easy to find. In addition, you might need permission from the District Commissioner before you can sail.

Getting Around Pick-ups and wooden-sided trucks with bench seats (remarkably similar to the jeepneys of the Philippines!)

connect Wete with Chake Chake (No 6) and Koride further north (No 24) throughout the day. The fare to Chake Chake is TSh 60 and the trip takes about 45 minutes. The people who use them are garrulous and good fun. Inevitably you'll be the only *mzungu* on board. The road is sealed and in excellent condition.

Chake Chake

This is Pemba's principal town and a lively place to wander around in the early mornings and late afternoons. It has a well-defined but small old centre, complete with bazaar, and it sits on top of a ridge overlooking a largely silted-up creek into which dhows occasionally sail when the tides allow. The overall impression of the town from the ridge is one of a mixture of makuti and rusty old tin roofs, but times are changing rapidly here. Nearing completion is a brand-new hospital, funded by the European Economic Community, and a huge sports stadium on the outskirts of town. Chake Chake also has the island's only airport, about seven km from town off the road to Mkoani.

Information The tourist office (tel 2121) is

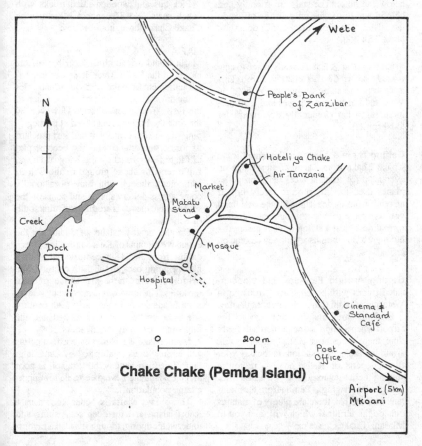

Chake Chake (Pemba Island)

next door to the Hoteli ya Chake and is staffed by a very friendly woman. Unfortunately, they have no literature (only limited information) and can't supply you with a copy of the detailed map of Pemba which is on the office wall.

The People's Bank of Zanzibar changes travellers' cheques and can provide you with cash US dollars to pay your hotel bill against hard currency travellers' cheques (though they don't particularly like doing this). The staff are friendly and efficient.

The Air Tanzania office (tel 2162) is on the main road which goes through town, below the hotel. The staff are friendly and helpful and this is the only airline office on the island. The airport (tel 2357) departure tax is TSh 300.

Places to Stay & Eat The only place to stay is the *Hoteli ya Chake* (tel 2069, 2189). This is exactly the same design as the hotel in Wete and has the same prices and facilities, including a bar (frequently dry except for local spirits).

Getting There & Away Air Tanzania flies to Chake Chake from Zanzibar and Tanga on average three times a week. F27 propeller planes used for this run are rarely full. If arriving from or departing for the mainland you will have to pass through immigration formalities – just a stamp in your passport – but there's no compulsory money change on arrival.

Getting Around Pick-ups and wooden-sided trucks with bench seats (No 6) go to Wete and Mkoani (No 3) throughout the day.

Pick-ups and matatus only go to the airport when a flight is due (as that's the only time there's business at the airport). Ask around at the matatu station on the day your flight departs or at the hotel – if you're staying there they may give you a free lift.

If you're arriving at Pemba from the mainland or Zanzibar, there are plenty of matatus outside the terminal which will take you to Mkoani, Chake Chake or Wete.

Mkoani

This is the last of Pemba's main towns and the most important port. You arrive here if you're coming to Pemba by dhow from Zanzibar. However, if you're coming from Tanga, you may arrive in Wete. The boats from Zanzibar are much more predictable and are easy to get on. Book at the Malindi Sports Club in Zanzibar. Sailing time is about 12 hours.

The only hotel in town is the *Hoteli ya Mkoani*. It's exactly the same design as the hotels in Chake Chake and Wete and both the prices and facilities are the same.

Pick-ups and wooden-sided trucks with bench seats (No 3) connect Mkoani with Chake Chake throughout the day.

MAFIA

Mafia Island lies south of Zanzibar off the mouth of the Rufiji River. It was an important settlement from the 12th to 14th centuries in the days when the Shirazis ruled much of the East African coastal area. However, by the time the Portuguese arrived at the beginning of the 16th century, it had lost much of its former importance and had become part of the territory ruled by the King of Kilwa. Little remains above ground of the Shirazi settlement, though you may occasionally come across pottery shards and coins on the shore where the sea is eroding the ruins south of Kilindoni.

On the nearby island of Juani are the extensive remains of Kua, a much later town dating from the 18th century but with a history going back to the 14th century. The principal ruins here are those of five mosques. The town was destroyed by raiders from Madagascar in the early 19th century when the entire town was sacked and the inhabitants eaten by the invaders!

Mafia Island is covered by coconut palms and cashew trees established by Omanis in their Zanzibari heyday, but the soil is poor and the island has never been able to support a large population.

These days Mafia is better known as a resort island and for deep sea fishing and underwater diving, though it's also a favourite breeding ground for giant turtles which come up onto the white coral sands to lay their eggs.

You're unlikely to meet any traveller who has been to Mafia Island. The reasons are simple – accommodation and transport. The accommodation available is expensive and transport can involve long waits in Dar es Salaam as the boats operated by the Tanzania Coastal Shipping Line are infrequent (see the Dar es Salaam chapter). Air Tanzania usually has a flight to the island at least once a week.

Places to Stay & Eat If you have a tent, you can find a suitable spot to pitch it and buy fruit, vegetables and fish from local people. If not, ask around among the locals for a room.

For those with money, the TTC-owned *Mafia Island Lodge* (tel 23491), Fisherman's Cove, has 30 air-conditioned rooms with private showers, etc, overlooking the sea. Rooms cost US$32/41/92 a single/double/triple including breakfast, plus 22.5% taxes and service charge.

Around the Country

North towards Kenya

MOSHI

Moshi is the gateway to Kilimanjaro and the end of the northern railway line from Dar es Salaam, but otherwise not a very interesting place. Rather than stay here, many travellers head straight out to Marangu and arrange a trek up the mountain from there, but this might not always be the best thing to do. The pros and cons are discussed in the National Parks & Game Reserves chapter.

Information

Telephone International telephone calls can be made from the post office but there's only one booth and a long queue of very bored people.

Immigration Office The Moshi immigration office can renew your visa or stay permit. It's in Kibo House close to the clock tower on the road leading to the YMCA. The office is open Monday to Friday from 7.30 am to 2.30 pm and on Saturday from 7.30 am to 12.30 pm.

Airline Office The Air Tanzania office is next to the Moshi Hotel. It's open Monday to Friday from 8 am to 12.30 pm and from 2 to 4.30 pm and on Saturday from 8 am to 12.30 pm. Airport shuttle buses leave from here about two hours before scheduled flight departures.

Places to Stay – bottom end

It used to be possible to sleep on the floor of the *Sikh Community Centre* and use the showers but we haven't heard of anyone who's stayed there for a long time. If it's still available, to get there you turn left out of the railway station and continue until you see a football pitch on the left-hand side with a sign saying 'Members Only'. That's the

place. If it looks closed, see the caretaker. Leave a donation if you stay.

The vast majority of travellers stay at the *YMCA* on the roundabout about 300 metres from the clock tower. It's a large, modern building with a gymnasium, swimming pool (always empty), dining room and a TV lounge/coffee bar. The rooms are spotlessly clean and well furnished and some face Mt Kilimanjaro. It costs TSh 850/1400 a single/double including breakfast (fruit, eggs, bread and butter and tea/coffee). The showers (cold water only) and toilets are communal. Lunch and dinner cost TSh 600 and are good value. A travel office here can arrange treks up Kilimanjaro and there's a store which sells toiletries and the like. It's a friendly place and there's a guarded car park.

Cheaper but more basic is the *Kilimanjaro Hotel* just down from the clock tower towards the railway station. It offers singles/doubles with communal showers (cold water only) for TSh 300/500. It has a restaurant and bar.

Further away from the centre and up beyond the YMCA is the *Green Cottage Hostel*. It's in a very pleasant area and has safe parking. Singles/doubles with shared bathroom facilities cost TSh 500/800 and doubles with a bathroom are TSh 1000. There are hot water showers. It's a small place and run by friendly people.

If you don't mind a bit of walking on arrival (about one km) there are two other places which are off the road to Marangu. The best is the *Rombo Cottage Hotel* (tel 2112). It's well maintained, has friendly staff and is excellent value at TSh 1200 a double with a bathroom and hot water. There's a bar, a restaurant and safe parking. The other place is the *Sengia Guest House* (tel 4942) which has several simple rooms for rent but often there's no-one around.

Back in the town centre, close to the clock tower, is the *Coffee Tree Hotel* on the 2nd and 3rd floors of the large office block. There's

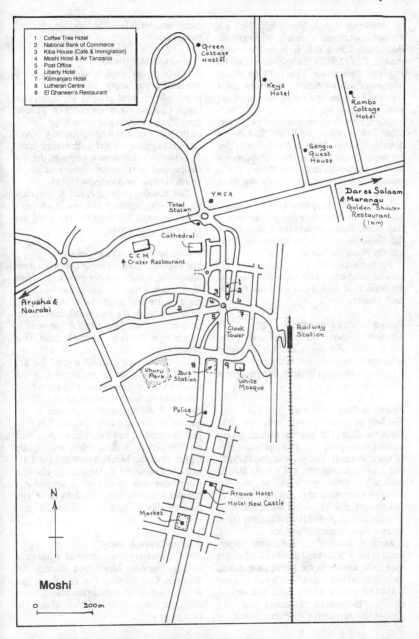

1 Coffee Tree Hotel
2 National Bank of Commerce
3 Kiba House (Café & Immigration)
4 Moshi Hotel & Air Tanzania
5 Post Office
6 Liberty Hotel
7 Kilimanjaro Hotel
8 Lutheran Centre
9 El Ghaneen's Restaurant

Green Cottage Hostel

Keys Hotel

Rombo Cottage Hotel

Sengia Guest House

YMCA

Dar es Salaam & Marangu

Golden Shower Restaurant (1 km)

Total Station

Cathedral

CCM
Crater Restaurant

Arusha & Nairobi

Clock Tower

Railway Station

Uhuru Park
Bus Station

White Mosque

Police

Arawa Hotel
Hotel New Castle

Market

N

Moshi

0   200m

no prominent sign, so you might think it's not there, but the entrance is in the courtyard. B&B costs TSh 630 a single with a shared shower, TSh 1260/2310 a single/double with a private shower (or TSh 1575 for single occupancy of a double). There are great views of Kilimanjaro from the restaurant and some of the rooms.

Other travellers recommend the *Motel Silva* which offers B&B for TSh 800 a double. It's very clean and excellent value but there's no hot water. Many of the rooms have a private balcony and there's a restaurant where good food can be had for about TSh 200.

Several other cheap hotels are at the southern end of town but very few people seem to stay there. These include the *Arawa Hotel*, the *Korini Hotel*, *Mlay's Residential Hotel* and the *Hotel Taj Mahal*.

For campers, there's a site adjacent to the playing field about two km out of town on the main road to Arusha. Facilities include cold showers.

Places to Stay – middle
The hotel of choice is the *Hotel New Castle*. It's a fairly new place and has plenty of self-contained rooms with hot water. Singles/doubles cost US$8/9, also payable in local currency.

Places to Stay – top end
The best value in this range is the new *Keys Hotel* (tel 2250, PO Box 933) which is very tastefully designed and is in a pleasant area of town. A small double room costs US$25 and a large double with a TV costs US$50 (prices for Tanzanian residents are TSh 3000/5000 respectively). All the rooms are self-contained and have hot water. There are no singles. The ground floor is entirely taken up by a large restaurant and bar.

More expensive but somewhat impersonal is the TTC-owned *Moshi Hotel* which used to be known as the Livingstone Hotel. Self-contained doubles/suites cost US$44/66 plus a 22.5% taxes and service charge. Tanzanian residents pay TSh 2300/4320 respectively. Prices include a continental breakfast. The hotel has a bar and restaurant.

Places to Eat – cheap
Apart from the YMCA, cheap meals are available at the *Liberty Hotel* which is very popular with local people, especially for lunch. *Chrisburger*, a few doors up the road from the clock tower and towards the YMCA on the left-hand side is also popular. It serves excellent eggburgers and fresh orange juice. *El Ghaneen's Restaurant*, opposite the bus station and next to the white mosque, is worth visiting for Asian specialities.

The *Rombo Cottage Hotel* is certainly worth visiting for lunch or dinner if you don't mind the walk. The food is very good and prices are competitive.

Places to Eat – more expensive
For a splurge, you can choose between three places. Right in the centre of town, the *Moshi Hotel* offers a lunch or dinner menu of soup, main course and coffee for about TSh 850 including taxes. It's also worth considering an evening at the *Keys Hotel* if you want to dine in style. Prices are similar to those at the Moshi Hotel.

My favourite, though it's a good 1½ km out of town on the Marangu road, is the *Golden Shower Restaurant*. This place has a much more intimate atmosphere and offers a choice of dining inside or outside in the garden. It also has a very cosy bar. The food here is excellent and individually presented and the service is fast. Prices are slightly higher than the Moshi Hotel but the little extra is well worth it. Despite the distance from town this restaurant is surprisingly popular with travellers, especially those who have climbed Kilimanjaro and feel like celebrating.

Getting There & Away
Air Kilimanjaro International Airport is halfway between Moshi and Arusha. Air Tanzania flies between Dar es Salaam and Kilimanjaro in either direction usually twice daily, but you must book well in advance to be sure of a seat.

Bus There are several buses daily in either direction between Dar es Salaam and Moshi. Many of these continue on to Arusha. Departures are at night and it's fair to describe the trip as a nightmare due to the state of the road. The fare is TSh 3000 and the journey should take about 12 hours but can take considerably longer. Don't attempt to save a few shillings by taking an ordinary bus. You'll regret it. Always take one of the so-called luxury buses.

There are frequent daily buses and matatus between Arusha and Moshi which depart when full. The fare is TSh 160 and the trip takes 1½ hours along a good, sealed road. A shared taxi between the two places will cost TSh 7000.

Train Trains depart Dar es Salaam for Moshi on Tuesday, Thursday and Saturday at 4 pm. In the opposite direction, they leave Moshi for Dar es Salaam on Monday, Wednesday and Friday at 4 pm. The journey takes from 15 to 18 hours and the fares are TSh 2320 (1st class), TSh 1050 (2nd class) and TSh 370 (3rd class). Bedding costs TSh 150 and dinner is available in the buffet car. Advance booking is essential for 1st and 2nd class since no-one, out of choice, goes by bus. Buying a ticket at Moshi station is an exercise in tenacity and determination. It's a little short of chaos and you'll just have to join the rabble.

Getting Around

Airport Transport The State Transport Corporation operates shuttle buses to the airport which depart from the Air Tanzania office about two hours before flight departure. The fare is TSh 500. The airport departure tax is TSh 500 for domestic flights.

Matatu & Taxi There are frequent matatus throughout the day between Moshi and Marangu (the village below the Kilimanjaro park entry gate). A taxi will cost TSh 6500 shared between four or possibly five people. Taxis around Moshi cost TSh 300 per journey, though why they cost more than in Arusha is a mystery. They'll baulk if you offer TSh 200.

ARUSHA

Arusha is one of Tanzania's most attractive towns and was the headquarters of the East African Community in the days when Kenya, Tanzania and Uganda were members of an economic, communications and customs union. It sits in lush, green countryside at the foot of Mt Meru (4556 metres) and enjoys a temperate climate throughout the year. Surrounding it are many coffee, wheat and maize estates tended by the Waarusha and Wameru tribespeople whom you may see occasionally in the market area of town. For travellers, Arusha is the gateway to Serengeti, Lake Manyara and Tarangire national parks and the Ngorongoro Conservation Area. It's to Arusha that you come to arrange a safari. Mt Meru can also be climbed from here.

Arusha is a pleasant town to walk around and take in the sights and the market area is particularly lively, but the main concern of most travellers will be arranging a safari and taking off for the national parks.

The town is in two parts, separated by a small valley through which the Naura River runs. The upper part, just off the main Moshi-Namanga road, contains the government buildings, post office, the top class hotels, safari companies, airline offices, curio and craft shops and the huge International Conference Centre. Further down the hill and across the valley is the commercial and industrial area, the market, many small shops, many of the budget hotels and the bus station.

Information

Tourist Office The office (tel 3842) is on Boma Rd just down from the New Safari Hotel. It generally has a few glossy leaflets about the national parks but its main function is to make bookings for TTC-owned hotels, including the national park lodges. Safari companies can also make these bookings if you're going on a trip with them. They may also be able to arrange special deals.

Telephone The exchange is opposite the New Safari Hotel and is the best place from which to make calls, both domestic and international. It's often crowded in the morning but usually deserted in the evening. It's open Monday to Saturday from 8 am to 10 pm and from 9 am to 8 pm on Sunday.

Airline Office The Air Tanzania office is open Monday to Friday from 8 am to 12.30 pm and from 2 to 4.30 pm and on Saturday from 8 am to 12.30 pm. Bookings are computerised and American Express cards are accepted.

Newspapers & Bookstores Local newspapers can be bought on the street opposite the clock tower. International magazines and Kenyan daily newspapers can be bought from the bookstore at the New Arusha Hotel. It also has a reasonable selection of novels and books about the national parks.

National Parks The Tanzania National Parks headquarters (tel 3471, PO Box 3134) is on the 6th floor, Kilimanjaro Wing, International Conference Centre. It usually stocks a few leaflets about the national parks but otherwise you probably won't need to come here unless you're a journalist searching for information. The quarterly reports make interesting but often distressing reading, especially as far as poaching is concerned.

Safari Companies Quite a few safari companies have offices in the International Conference Centre while others are along Boma Rd, Sokoine Rd and India St.

The National Museum

At the top of Boma Rd, this place simply has to be a joke. It consists of one corridor about 20 metres long by five metres wide with facsimiles of the evolutionary progress of Homo sapiens based on the digs at Olduvai Gorge. You've seen it all before. It's open Monday to Friday from 7.30 am to 5 pm and on Saturday from 7.30 am to 4.30 pm. Entry costs TSh 50 (TSh 10 for Tanzanian residents).

Places to Stay – bottom end

The cheapest place to stay is *St Theresa's Catholic Guest House* which has been popular for years, but they sometimes refuse to take foreigners. If you manage to get in, it costs TSh 300 on the floor and TSh 400/600 a single/double. It's just below the Catholic church in the valley between the two parts of town. There's no hot water in the showers (and often no water at all) and nowhere to lock away your gear during the day but it's unlikely anything will be stolen.

Another cheap place and superb value if you can get in is the *Lutheran Centre* on Boma Rd, opposite the New Safari Hotel, but like the Catholic Guest House, they generally won't take foreigners. The story is that it can officially only put up church workers as the centre doesn't have a commercial licence.

Many travellers stay at the *YMCA/Arusha Inn* on India St. It's fairly clean and well furnished but the toilets won't flush and the showers often don't work. Still, it's an excellent place to meet people, especially if you're trying to get a group together to go on safari. B&B costs TSh 800/950 a single/double with shared toilet facilities (cold water only). The breakfast isn't up to much – boiled egg, dry bread and butter plus tea – but the staff are very friendly, your gear is safe and there's a laundry service. Downstairs is the Silver City Bar but it closes early in the evening so there's no problem about noise. Get here early if you want a room.

Also fairly popular is the Indian-run *Greenland Hotel* though, like the YMCA, it's long overdue for major renovations. There are no singles and doubles/triples cost TSh 800/1200 with shared bathroom facilities. Better, perhaps, is the *Continental Hotel*, opposite the Hotel Arusha by Night, which is basic but has clean sheets and shared bathroom facilities at TSh 400 a double. Many Somalis stayed here in early 1990, most of them trying to get out of the way of Siad Barre's purges. They're a friendly bunch of people.

Much better value, but often full, is the new *Amazon Hotel*, Zaramo St, close to the bus station. It's basic but very clean and excellent value at TSh 800 a double. Also excellent value and popular with travellers is the *Miami Beach Guest House* north of the bus station. It's well maintained, the staff are very friendly and there are hot showers. Singles/doubles with shared bathroom facilities cost TSh 500/1600. The hotel has its own restaurant.

Other travellers and local people have recommended the *Meru Guest House* which costs the same as the Miami Beach and has clean sheets, hot water and good security. Yet others have recommended *Nonye's Guest House* up the road past the Golden Rose Hotel. It's very pleasant, spotlessly clean, has hot water and costs TSh 400/500 a single/double. Similar to this is *Amigo's Guest House* at TSh 250/400 a single/double with hot showers. Another good place is the *Mt Kilimanjaro Guest House* in Mosque St, between the market and Sokoine Rd and next to the mosque. It's clean and costs TSh 400 per person. There's no running water but bucket showers are available.

There are many other budget hotels in the market area of town, all more or less of a similar standard and price. They include the *Central Guest House*, *Town Guest House*, *New Central Hotel*, *Silver Guest House*, *Robannyson Hotel*, and the *Twiga Guest House*.

Places to Stay – middle

One of the cheapest of the mid-range hotels is the *Naaz Hotel* on Sokoine Rd. Very clean and pleasant, secure and well maintained, it costs US$10 for a single or a double (shillings not accepted) with shared toilet facilities. This is reasonable value for a double room but poor value for a single.

Next is the very popular *Hotel Arusha by Night* on Swahili St. Depending on the time of day you arrive you may be quoted US$10 or US$15 for a double with a bathroom and hot water. An annexe to the hotel is on the top side of the stadium. This is almost as large as the original hotel and costs the same. If there is a choice, it's probably best to get a room in the annexe because the main hotel

has a disco on the 1st floor which rocks until about 2 am nightly. Both branches have a bar and restaurant.

The *Arusha Resort Centre* is popular with travellers and we've had several recommendations. The staff are friendly and helpful and a double room with a hot shower costs US$20.

More expensive but very good value is the new *Golden Rose Hotel* (tel 7959), Stadium Rd, which has doubles with twin beds, bathroom with hot water, telephone and balcony at US$25 or US$20 for single occupancy, including breakfast (fruit, eggs, bread, butter and jam plus tea/coffee). Towels, soap and toilet paper are provided. There's a bar and the restaurant serves excellent lunches and dinners for about TSh 500.

A new hotel, the *Hotel Pallsons*, Market St, is probably open by now. Tariffs are likely to be in the upper mid-range.

Places to Stay – top end

At the top end are four hotels, three of which are on Boma Rd – the TTC-owned *New Safari Hotel* (tel 2857, PO Box 303), the Bushtrekker Safaris-owned *New Arusha Hotel* (tel 3241/4, PO Box 88) and the *Equator Hotel* (tel 3127/9, PO Box 3002).

The New Safari Hotel has self-contained singles/doubles in the old wing for US$22/ 34 and in the new wing for US$34/40, all plus 22.5% taxes and service charge. All prices include breakfast. The hotel has a restaurant, a beer garden and a weekend disco.

The Equator Hotel, opposite the New Safari, has self-contained rooms at US$65 for singles or doubles, including breakfast. It has a restaurant, a bar and a beer garden and there's often live African music at weekends. Further down the hill at the roundabout and clock tower is the much larger New Arusha Hotel which has self-contained rooms with full English breakfast for US$65/75/83 a single/double/triple. There's a residents' bar, a public bar, a beer garden and a fast food cafeteria as well as craft shops and a newsagent/bookstore.

Top of the range is the *Novotel Mount*

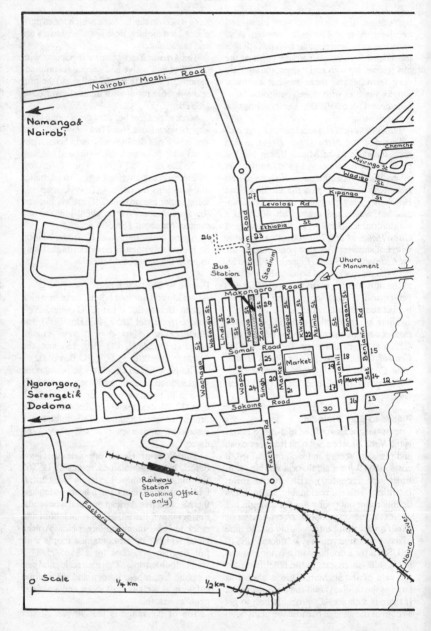

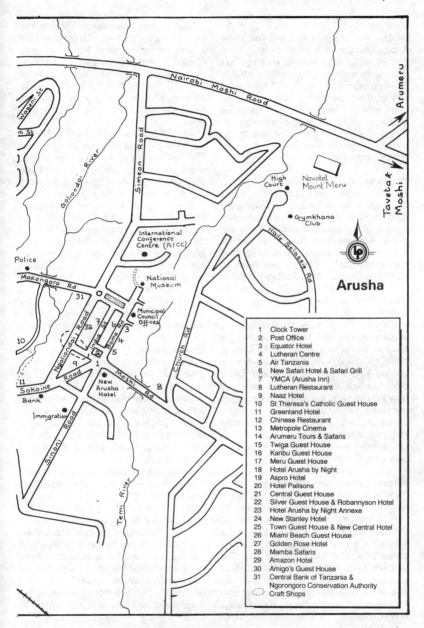

Arusha

1   Clock Tower
2   Post Office
3   Equator Hotel
4   Lutheran Centre
5   Air Tanzania
6   New Safari Hotel & Safari Grill
7   YMCA (Arusha Inn)
8   Lutheran Restaurant
9   Naaz Hotel
10 St Theresa's Catholic Guest House
11 Greenland Hotel
12 Chinese Restaurant
13 Metropole Cinema
14 Arumeru Tours & Safaris
15 Twiga Guest House
16 Karibu Guest House
17 Meru Guest House
18 Hotel Arusha by Night
19 Aspro Hotel
20 Hotel Pallsons
21 Central Guest House
22 Silver Guest House & Robannyson Hotel
23 Hotel Arusha by Night Annexe
24 New Stanley Hotel
25 Town Guest House & New Central Hotel
26 Miami Beach Guest House
27 Golden Rose Hotel
28 Mamba Safaris
29 Amazon Hotel
30 Amigo's Guest House
31 Central Bank of Tanzania &
    Ngorongoro Conservation Authority
    Craft Shops

Meru (tel 2712, 2728; PO Box 877), set in landscaped grounds just off the main Arusha-Moshi road. It has all the usual facilities including a swimming pool and has singles/doubles/triples for US$70/84/102 in the high season (1 January to 16 April and 1 July to 30 November) or US$55/66/84 in the low season (17 April to 30 June). Breakfast is included in the rates as are all taxes and service charges. The swimming pool can be used by nonresidents on payment of a temporary membership fee.

Places to Eat – cheap

Plenty of simple cafés and cheap restaurants in the lower part of town along Sokoine Rd offer standard Afro-Indian fare – curries, ugali or ndizi (plantains) with meat stew and beans, sambusa, biriyani and the like for about TSh 300. Bars and discos usually have barbecued food – kebabs and chips or matoke for about TSh 200. Try the *Silver City Bar*, attached to the YMCA, or the *Naura Yard Bar* next to the Chinese Restaurant.

It's also worth wandering around the streets close to the bus station in the evening and looking out for verandah cafés. They're easily identified – just look for someone grilling kebabs over charcoal and frying chips in a large metal pan. I had some very tasty kebabs, chips and salad at such a place one evening and it cost just TSh 150.

The fast food cafeteria in the *New Arusha Hotel* has MacDonalds-type food as well as samosas, but late in the day they often have only a fraction of what's on the menu.

Places to Eat – more expensive

For a splurge, most travellers go to one of two restaurants – the *Safari Grill* next to the New Safari Hotel or the *Chinese Restaurant*. Probably the most popular is the Safari Grill which has a good range of fish and meat dishes as well as soups and desserts. The food is well cooked and presented and costs an average of TSh 120 for soups and from TSh 400 to TSh 500 for main courses plus 15% taxes and service charge. It also serves very cold beers.

The Chinese Restaurant, Sokoine Rd, close to the bridge, is equally good and has a very extensive menu which includes seafood, though this tends to be expensive. Prices are generally higher than those at the Safari Grill but the food is very good and it's a popular place to eat. It's open for breakfast, lunch and dinner and menu prices include taxes.

The restaurant at the *Golden Rose Hotel* is also very good and the menu changes daily. The chef has obviously trained overseas so watch out for some delicious Eastern European specialities. Average prices for lunch and dinner are TSh 500.

Some travellers recommend the restaurant at the *Ark Grill Hotel*, Swahili St, which offers excellent European-style food and fast, friendly service. Another traveller suggests eating at *La Terrace*, a new restaurant run by a Dutch. The traveller says it's very reasonable but you'll need to get a taxi there as it's near the bottling factory.

For Indian specialities, check out the *Meenar Restaurant* on Ngoliondoi Rd, though it appears to be open for dinner only.

Entertainment

Two of the liveliest and cheapest bars are the *Silver City Bar* next to the YMCA and the *Naura Yard Bar* next to the Chinese Restaurant. It's easy to strike up a conversation with local people or travellers at both these places. Cold beers cost TSh 180, both have barbecue grills and the Naura has a deafeningly loud spit-and-sawdust disco each Sunday which is free.

The indoor bar at the *Hotel Equator* often has live bands at the weekend which rage all day and all night and are very popular. There's usually a cover charge of TSh 200 but if they play during the week it's free.

In the basement of the New Safari Hotel is the *Cave Disco* which is very popular at weekends (nothing during the week) when it rocks all afternoon until very late at night. The tourist literature describes it as 'a sensation'. That's far from accurate, but deafening it certainly is. Entry costs TSh 200.

The only nightly disco is at the *Hotel Arusha by Night*. This goes on until about 2 am and is very popular with local people and wazungu. There are no hassles, drinks are the normal price and the sexes are about equally matched in number. There's plenty of dancing space and the lights are low. Entry costs TSh 200.

Things to Buy

There are several very good craft shops along the short street between the clock tower and Ngoliondoi Rd. They have superb examples of makonde carving at prices lower than in Dar es Salaam. If I wanted to buy an example of this beautiful and traditional art form I would look for it here.

Getting There & Away

Air Kilimanjaro International Airport is halfway between Arusha and Moshi and is serviced by Air Tanzania, Ethiopian Airlines and KLM, all of which have offices on Boma Rd close to the New Safari Hotel. Air Tanzania generally has two flights per day between Dar es Salaam and Kilimanjaro in either direction. Advance booking is essential as the service is heavily subscribed. The fare is US$124 (TSh 9000 for Tanzanian residents).

Road There are several buses daily in either direction between Dar es Salaam and Arusha via Moshi. The fare on the 'luxury' bus is TSh 3000 and on the ordinary bus it's TSh 2300, but no-one in their right mind would take anything other than a 'luxury' bus because the journey is a nightmare due to the atrocious state of the road. The trip is overnight and takes about 12 hours though it can take considerably longer if you have punctures or a breakdown. Bus companies which do this trip include Mrakama Bus Service, Mavanja Bus Service and Tawfiq Luxury Coach. It's a good idea to book in advance at their offices at the bus station.

Tanga African Motor Transport has daily buses between Tanga and Arusha which cost TSh 1200 (luxury) and TSh 878 (ordinary).

Kajoi Bus Service has a bus every second day which does the Moshi-Arusha-Mwanza route and vice versa. The fare is TSh 3000 and the journey takes about 24 hours. Advance booking is essential – there's an office at the bus station. The same company also has buses to Tabora.

There are buses and matatus all day, every day until late between Arusha and Moshi which leave when full. The fare is TSh 160 and the journey takes 1½ hours over a good, sealed road. Shared taxis between the two places cost TSh 7000.

Getting Around

Airport Transport The State Transport Corporation operates shuttle buses to the airport about two hours before flight departures. The fare is TSh 500.

Taxi Arusha is a small place so it's easy to get from one place to another on foot. Taxis charge TSh 200 per journey during the day and TSh 300 at night.

USAMBARA MOUNTAINS

This area between Moshi and Korogwe and the Kenyan border is a spectacularly beautiful area which you shouldn't miss if you have the chance to visit. The Michelin map marks the road up to Soni and Lushoto as 'scenic' which is a major understatement. Getting up there involves negotiating a series of huge hairpin bends with sheer drops on the outer lane virtually the whole way. Yet despite the steepness, the mountains are cultivated from the bottom to the top (with the usual maize, bananas, pineapples, beans and tree plantations), so the landscape looks as if it's had a chequered green tablecloth thrown over it.

This is walking country, especially for those who like to get to the top of mountains without too much effort. There is an endless number of gently graded tracks which zigzag up the mountains with breathtaking views at every turn. It's almost impossible to get lost as long as you stick to the track. One of the most popular tracks takes you to what's known as the Viewpoint – a slab of rock at the top of a cliff face looking out over the Mombo-Tanga road and the Masai Plain. It's about a 45 minute walk from Lushoto. To get there, head towards Irente and ask for the Children's Home (the regional orphanage). When you get there, ask someone to show you the right track. The views from here are simply incredible.

Lushoto

Lushoto, the main centre of population in the Usambara Mountains, sits in a valley, although the town is built on several levels which produce a feeling of space. Most of the houses are built from locally manufactured mud bricks and have pitched roofs. The main government buildings are European in style and indeed Lushoto was once slated to become the capital of German East Africa back in colonial times. These days it's a religious centre of sorts with a bewildering variety of churches and missions as well as mosques. Everyone is hard at it here making converts, and even if you're not hot on religion, it can be fun eavesdropping on religious politics.

Information The immigration officer at the municipal office building will extend visas without the usual queueing or hassle. He's a very pleasant safari-suited Maasai. You may well meet him after hours in the bar of the Kilimani Guest House where he'll ask the usual questions and scrutinise your passport over a cup of tea. Office hours are from 8.30 am to 2.30 pm.

If you stay here for a while you'll run into quite a few helpful people who will direct you to things you might otherwise miss. Two such people are Pious, the deputy manager of the post office, and the manager of the Christian Book Shop. Both men speak English and the bookshop manager's wife, a middle-aged English woman, has a useful ordinance survey map of the area (there are none available locally).

Other interesting characters include Gerard, a Dutch soil scientist and longtime African resident who advises local farmers on irrigation and soil conservation, and Gregory, a German aid worker who is busy reafforesting the area with native and exotic trees. Another interesting pair are Carter, a

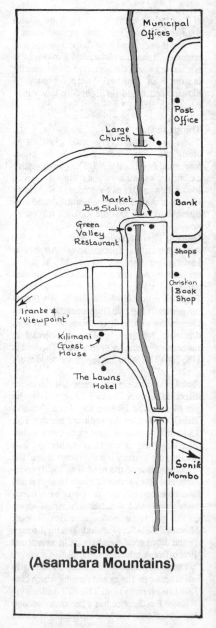

Lushoto
(Asambara Mountains)

young American writer, and George, who live about an hour's walk from Lushoto. Both are keen hang gliders and George is involved in training buzzards and falcons to assist glider pilots in staying airborne indefinitely, the idea being that these birds are far more capable than humans of reading the landscape and finding thermals. Once the pilot has been guided to the thermals, they sit on the steering bar until the glider wishes to land! You can often find these two at The Lawns Hotel or the Kilimani Guest House or at the Green Valley disco on Saturday nights.

Places to Stay The most expensive hotel is *The Lawns Hotel* which is positioned at the highest point with views over the valley. It's a fairly typical colonial-style hotel with a large front lawn mown by two cows and has a verandah with easy chairs and a well-stocked bar. The rooms cost TSh 2300 a double or triple. Owned by a resident expatriate, the service leaves a little to be desired.

The *Kilimani Guest House* has rooms set around a rectangular courtyard at the centre of which is a bar. Singles/doubles cost TSh 200/400. The rooms are given privacy by an inner slatted fence that lines the courtyard. The beds are comfortable and have clean linen and there's a table and chair. The women who run it speak two words of English between the four of them, but they're very friendly and helpful as well as being excellent cooks. There's no running water, but a bucket of hot water and a mug will be provided on request.

To get there, leave the main street in Lushoto at the sign for The Lawns Hotel and continue past it. Up to your left you come to a village green running along the top of the ridge. At The Lawns end is the guest house.

Places to Eat The *Green Valley Restaurant* in the centre of town is the best place to eat if you're not eating where you stay. The staff are pleasant and the food is very good.

Getting There & Away To get to Lushoto, take a bus from Mombo on the main Moshi-Korogwe road. Anyone in Mombo will show

you where the bus departs from. The journey takes about 1½ hours and the fare is TSh 160. Buses are usually crowded but the road is well maintained and sealed all the way.

There are also direct buses between Tanga and Lushoto. If you have to stay in Mombo overnight then try the *Usambara Inn*, next to the petrol station on the corner of the road to Lushoto. It's something of a time warp but has a garden, bar and restaurant. Single rooms have a sink, a towel and a large fan and cost TSh 355.

Lake Victoria

MWANZA

Mwanza is Tanzania's most important port on the shore of Lake Victoria and the terminus of a branch of the central railway line from Dar es Salaam. It's a fairly attractive town flanked by rocky hills and its port handles the cotton, tea and coffee grown in the fertile western part of the country. In the area live the Wasukuma people who make up the largest tribe in the country. Lake ferries go from Mwanza to the Tanzanian ports of Bukoba and Musoma and occasionally ferries go to Jinja (Uganda).

If you'd like to explore the area further north of Mwanza, there are regular ferries from Mwanza to Ukerewe Island.

Sukuma Museum

About 15 km east of Mwanza on the Musoma road, the Sukuma Museum (sometimes called the Bujora Museum) was originally put together by a Quebecois missionary. Its displays are about the culture and traditions of the Wasukuma tribe. There is an excellent drum collection and about once a week the museum puts on traditional tribal dances including the spectacular Bugobogobo, the Sukuma Snake Dance. It's well worth enquiring in town about when the next performance is to be. Entry costs TSh 100 (or TSh 200 if you want to take photographs). To get there, take a local bus from the bus station in Mwanza to Kisessa from where it's about a one km walk. It's also possible to camp at the museum or rent a banda.

Places to Stay

You can generally camp for free at the *Sukuma Museum* but if you have no tent there are two-bed bandas for rent. It's a lovely spot and many travellers stay here.

You can also camp free of charge at the *Saba Saba Showground* near the airport on the outskirts of town, though occasionally someone will masquerade as a guard and attempt to charge you a fee. Facilities consist of a tap and toilet only. There are no showers.

In Mwanza there's quite a choice of reasonably priced hotels. The *Zimbabwe Guest House* near the bus station is adequate

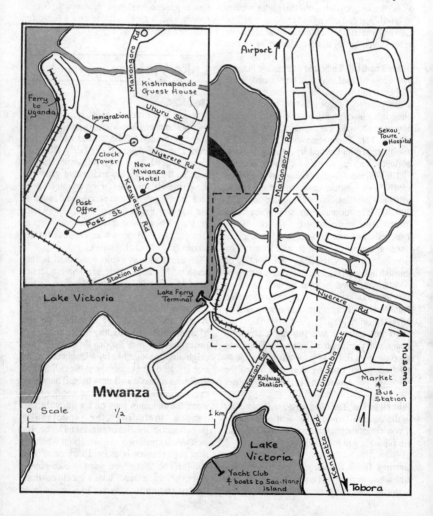

for most budget travellers' needs and the staff are friendly. Mosquito nets and towels are provided.

Similar places include the *Mwanza Guest House*, Uhuru St, which has singles/doubles for TSh 260/320, the *Capitol Guest House* at TSh 450 a double, the *Mutimba Guest House* at TSh 700 a double and the *Hotel Victoria* at TSh 500 a double.

Other cheapies which have been recommended in the past are the *Shinyanga Guest House*, *Furaha Guest House*, *Wageni Salim's Guest House*, *Jafferies Hotel* and the *New Safari Lodge*.

Going up in price, try the *Kishinapanda Guest House*, a new place which is very good but fills up early in the day. The rooms are self-contained and have fans and mosquito nets. To get there from the bus station, take the first street on the right (on Nyerere Rd) after the Mutimba Guest House and then the second on the left. About 50 metres down this road you come to the Delux Hotel and the Kishinapanda is just around the corner from there. If you're coming from the harbour, take the first street on the left before the Mutimba Guest House and then the second street on the left. The *Delux Hotel* is also worth checking out if you want a mid-range hotel. The restaurant here is excellent.

Places to Eat

There are several good cheap local restaurants along Lumumba St. Try the *Cairo* next to the Shinyanga Guest House. In the evenings between 5.30 and 6.30 pm you can eat well for a song at the food stalls opposite the Victoria Hotel.

A favourite with travellers is *Al Shah's African Restaurant* where you can get a very cheap meal of fish or meat with vegetables and potatoes or rice. At the rear of this place a lively disco runs on Saturdays and Sundays (African music) which costs TSh 200 entry (free if you eat there).

The *Delux Hotel* is definitely worth a visit if you like Indian Moghlai food. It's not cheap but the food is very good and the beers are cold.

Other reasonably priced restaurants which

are recommended include the *Kunaris Restaurant*, the *Furaha Restaurant* and the *Rex Hotel*.

If you are preparing your own meals you can buy cheap fish at the market near the ferry terminal.

Getting There & Away

Bus Buses run every second day between Mwanza and Arusha. The trip takes 24 hours, costs TSh 3000 and the service is operated by the Kajoi Bus Service. Advance booking is advised.

Train The railway line from Dar es Salaam runs due west as far as Tabora where it splits, one line continuing west to Kigoma while the other runs north to Mwanza. Trains depart Dar es Salaam for Mwanza on Tuesday, Wednesday, Friday and Sunday at 6.10 pm. In the opposite direction, they depart Mwanza for Dar es Salaam on the same days at 7 pm. Fares are TSh 4720 (1st class), TSh 2115 (2nd class) and TSh 725 (3rd class). The journey takes about 36 hours but can take 40 hours.

Travelling from Mwanza to Kigoma there are only 1st and 2nd class reservations available as far as Tabora. Beyond that point you cannot be guaranteed a reservation in the same class on the connecting train. The station manager at Tabora used to be very helpful about arranging onward reservations but he's apparently been replaced so you'll have to take pot luck.

MUSOMA

Musoma is a small port on the eastern shore of Lake Victoria close to the Kenyan border. It's connected to Bukoba and Mwanza by lake ferry.

Places to Stay & Eat

Most travellers stay at the very clean, cheap and friendly *Mennonite Centre*. The only drawback is that it's a long way from the ferry terminal. If it's too far then try the reasonably priced *Embassy Lodge* in the town centre or the slightly more expensive *Musambura Guest House* around the corner.

The *Sengerema Guest House* close to the market and bus station has also been recommended by travellers in the past.

One of the best mid-range hotels is the *Railway Hotel*, about half an hour's walk from the town centre. It's worth coming here for a meal whilst you're in town, even if you don't stay.

BUKOBA

Bukoba is Tanzania's second largest port on Lake Victoria but few travellers come here now because it's something of a dead end – there's hardly any transport north to Uganda and getting to Rwanda involves backtracking to Biharamulo.

Places to Stay

One of the cheapest places to stay is the *Nyumba wa Vijana* (Youth Centre) at the Evangelical Lutheran Church on the road to the hospital. The dormitory beds are very cheap and you can leave your gear here safely. The *Catholic Mission* has similar facilities.

For a cheap private room there are many budget hotels around the bus station. If you'd prefer a mid-range hotel then try the *Lake Hotel* (tel 237), a beautiful old colonial building with a verandah overlooking the lake. It's about two km from the town centre past the police station and the council offices. The *Coffee Tree Inn* (tel 412) is similar.

Getting Around

The lake ferries jetty is about 2½ km from the town centre.

Western Tanzania

DODOMA

Dodoma is the CCM party political headquarters and is slated to become the capital of Tanzania sometime towards the end of the century, though economic constraints may delay this. In the meantime there's little of interest here for the traveller. It is, however,

the only wine producing area of Africa south of Morocco and north of South Africa. Bacchanalians shouldn't get too excited though as Tanzanian viniculture has a long way to go before it will interest anyone with a taste for anything other than wine vinegar.

Places to Stay & Eat

The *Central Province Hotel* (tel 21177) is a reasonable place to stay. To get there, leave the front entrance of the railway station and turn right along the road running parallel with the tracks. Continue to the first roundabout and turn right. Walk to the next roundabout and turn right again. The hotel is 50 metres down the first street on the left.

Also within walking distance of town is the *Horombo Malazi*, Nyumba wa Wagena, a simple local guest house where you can get a double room for just TSh 150 per person. The owner is friendly and you'll probably be the only wazungu there.

Another place worth trying is the *Ujiji Guest House* near the bus station. It's clean and provides mosquito nets.

The best value, however, is the *Christian Council of Tanzania Guest House* (ask people for the CCT) which has double rooms with a cold shower, towels and mosquito nets for TSh 450. It's exceptional value and the canteen serves reasonable meals for about TSh 220 (omelette and chips).

For those seeking comfort, the *Dodoma Hotel* offers double, self-contained rooms for US$35. Its restaurant offers excellent breakfasts (all you can eat buffets for TSh 250 per person) and dinners (set menu for TSh 650 and à la carte for TSh 410). The bar, a hang-out for local expatriates, has beers at TSh 210.

Getting There & Away

Bus The daily bus to Arusha departs at about 6 am from the Caltex station. While the trip is supposed to take 13 hours, it often takes 21 hours due to the diabolical state of the road and breakdowns. The fare is TSh 1500 and you should book a day in advance to guarantee a seat. Don't be surprised if, at one point on the journey, you have to alight the bus and walk to the top of a hill. The bus can't make it otherwise!

Train The Dar es Salaam to Kigoma or Mwanza railway line runs through Dodoma. Departures are the same as for Mwanza or Kigoma. Fares from Dar es Salaam are TSh 2045 (1st class), TSh 940 (2nd class) and TSh 320 (3rd class).

TABORA
Tabora is a railway junction town where the central railway line branches for Mwanza and Kigoma. You may have to stay the night if you're changing trains and can't get immediate onward reservations.

Places to Stay & Eat
The *Moravian Guest House* is probably the best place to stay and is exceptionally cheap. It's pleasant and the staff are friendly. If you'd like more creature comforts then try the more expensive *Railway Hotel* where meals are reasonably good.

Getting There & Away
Train The railway line north-west of Dar es Salaam splits at Tabora, one line continuing west to Kigoma on Lake Tanganyika, the other heading north to Mwanza on Lake Victoria. Departures from Dar es Salaam are the same as for Kigoma or Mwanza. The fares from Dar es Salaam are TSh 3390 (1st class), TSh 1525 (2nd class) and TSh 530 (3rd class).

KIGOMA
Kigoma is the most important Tanzanian port on Lake Tanganyika and the terminus of the railway from Dar es Salaam. Many travellers come through here en route to or coming from Bujumbura (Burundi) or Mpulungu (Zambia) on the Lake Tanganyika steamer MV *Liemba*. It's a small but pleasant town with one main street which is lined with huge shady mango trees. Life ticks over at a slow pace. If you get stuck waiting for the train (a few days is not uncommon) or the boat (a day or two) you'll have to amuse yourself with

walks around town and visits to Ujiji. There's very little of interest in the Kigoma township, but it's a good base for visits to Gombe Stream National Park (see the National Parks & Game Reserves chapter).

Don't bother trying to climb any of the hills that flank the town in search of a view as these are military zones and are off limits to mere mortals. The best (accessible) view of the town is from outside the new church which is just to the left of the main road as you head up the hill towards Muwanga.

Information
Kigoma has consulates for Burundi and Zaïre (see the Visas entry in the Facts for the Visitor chapter).

It's no longer necessary to visit immigration in Kigoma if you're heading north to Gombe Stream National Park. All exit formalities are now dealt with at Kagunga, the last Tanzanian village before you cross the border into Burundi.

Places to Stay – bottom end
The best value for money is the *Kigoma Hotel* on the main street in the middle of town. Its double rooms are huge and excellent value while the singles are smaller but still good. Singles/doubles with common facilities cost TSh 400/500. The *Lake View Hotel*, a bit further up the hill on the left-hand side, is very similar to the Kigoma, but marginally more expensive.

The *Mapinduzi Hotel* is a basic African hotel which charges TSh 340 for doubles that can accommodate four people without any problem. There are no singles.

All the other hotels are further up the hill and are hardly worth the walk. The *Safari Lodging* is about as far up as you need to go. It charges TSh 320 a double with common facilities, but it is opposite the mosque. Further up the hill still there are at least another dozen budget hotels.

Places to Stay – top end
Kigoma's only up-market place is the *Railway Hotel* overlooking the lake, a few hundred metres south of the centre. The posi-

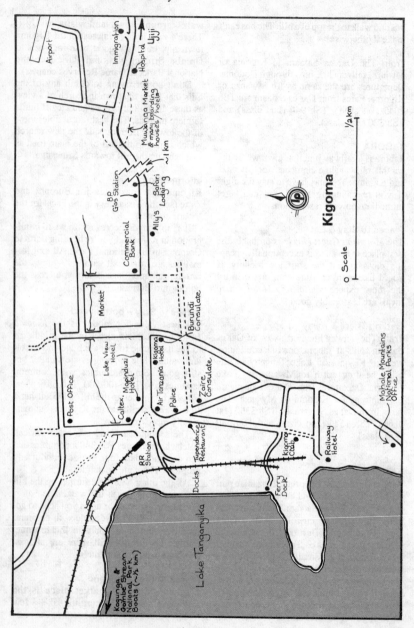

Kigoma

tion is excellent and the views are good, but you have to pay in hard currency. The rates are US$14 a double.

Places to Eat

Lunch is the main meal of the day here and there is far less variety available in the evenings. There are several good places to eat though. One of the cheapest is the *Kigoma Hotel* where you can get a meal of soup, fish, sauce, rice and a piece of fruit for TSh 200. The cardammon chai is also excellent at TSh 20. The *Lake View* has similar meals and prices and is the place to head to for breakfast – papaya, porridge, two eggs, bread and two cups of tea for TSh 150.

A bit further up the hill is the Muslim-owned *Ally's*. Although the service is slow, this place has the best range of food in Kigoma, especially in the evenings when there is little available elsewhere. Chips are cooked on request, although these take half an hour or so.

The *Tupendance Restaurant*, near the police station, has excellent ndizi and chicken for lunch, and also has a fan. These are a necessity in this restaurant at least; when I ate there you had to sit under one so that the flies would be discouraged by the blast of moving air – this place has squillions of them!

For what amounts to a splurge in Kigoma you could try a meal at the *Railway Hotel*. They're not bad but nothing to write home about. Lunch or dinner costs TSh 400.

Entertainment

The *Kigoma Hotel* has a reasonable bar and warm beer. The music system has seen better days so the distortion levels are high. The *Railway Hotel* has a disco on Saturday night for TSh 300 and another one on Sunday afternoon for TSh 100.

Getting There & Away

Air The air fare between Dar es Salaam and Kigoma with Air Tanzania is a ridiculous US$235! If you are a Tanzanian resident the fare is much less as it can be paid in shillings.

The flight leaves Kigoma weekly on Mondays.

If you're coming from Burundi and want to fly to Dar es Salaam it's much cheaper to take the Air Tanzania flight from Bujumbura (US$166).

Train In theory there are four trains a week in each direction between Kigoma and Dar es Salaam. In practice this is usually the case, although derailments and other incidents often result in cancellations.

Trains depart Kigoma on Tuesday, Thursday, Friday and Sunday at about 7 pm. The journey takes about 36 hours, but when heading for Dar es Salaam it's best to get off at Morogoro and catch one of the frequent minibuses (TSh 400), thus knocking around five hours off the trip.

The fares from Dar es Salaam to Kigoma are TSh 4790 (1st class), TSh 2145 (2nd class) and TSh 745 (3rd class). See the Chief Booking Clerk at the station in Kigoma for 1st class bookings. The train is often booked out in 1st and 2nd class but with persistence you can usually get a booking, at least as far as Tabora. From there you're at the mercy of the Travelling Ticket Examiner on the train. He will try to find you a berth on to Dar es Salaam or Dodoma but this is not always possible, in which case you'll end up in 3rd class for the night.

Ferry For details of the MV *Liemba's* services to Mpulungu and Bujumbura, see the Tanzania Getting There chapter. The 'dock' for boats to the Gombe Stream National Park is about an hour's walk up the railway tracks from the station.

Hitching The buses in this area only serve local towns, but it is possible to find trucks to Mwanza if you are prepared to wait a few days. Ask around in the shops on the main street.

Getting Around

Air Tanzania runs a minibus from their office in town to the airport. There's a small charge.

UJIJI

Down the lake shore from Kigoma, Ujiji is one of Africa's oldest market villages and it's a good deal more interesting than Kigoma. This is where the famous words, 'Dr Livingstone, I presume', were spoken by the explorer and journalist Henry Stanley. There's the inevitable plaque at the site where this event is alleged to have occurred; there is a similar plaque in Burundi! The site is to the right of the main road (when coming from Kigoma) down the side street next to the Bin Tunia Restaurant – just ask for Livingstone and the bus driver will make sure you get off at the right place.

The two mango trees growing in the walled compound at the site are said to have been grafted from the original tree growing there when the two men met. A museum is planned, the building for which is already finished. It presently houses a few pictorial representations by local artists of Livingstone's time here. The pictures bear captions such as: 'Dr Livingstone sitting under the mango tree in Ujiji thinking about slavery.' Entry is by voluntary donation, which seems to go straight into the caretaker's pocket.

About 500 metres past the compound along the same street is the beach and the local boat builders. This seems to be a thriving local industry and there may be as many as a dozen boats in various stages of construction. No power tools are used and construction methods have hardly changed in generations.

Places to Stay

The *Matunda Guest House* on the main street is a cosy place to stay and costs TSh 250 a double.

Getting There & Away

There are frequent buses to Ujiji from outside the railway station in Kigoma. The fare is TSh 20.

MBEYA

Until recently, few travellers stayed overnight in Mbeya but this has changed since the opening of the direct route to Karonga in Malawi via Kyela. Now it is a busy overnight stopover town. The surrounding area is very fertile with banana, tea, coffee and cocoa plantations, but there's little of interest for the traveller.

However, if you have a day to spare, it's worth climbing the mountain which overlooks the town to the north. The views from the top are amazing, though it's probably wise to stay away from the radio mast as people might think you're a spy. To get there, head from the roundabout towards the waterworks but turn left before you reach the gates along a gravel track (about 150 metres from the roundabout). You will pass a quarry on the right-hand side after 50 metres or so and then a few houses below a eucalypt forest. The track then goes to the left of a clearing where maize is grown. From there follow one of the paths which go to the mountain top. It will take about two hours to get to the top.

Places to Stay & Eat

If at all possible you should try to arrive early in the day as places fill up rapidly by late afternoon. One of the best places is the very clean and friendly *Moravian Youth Hostel* near the radio tower. It costs TSh 450 a double and breakfast and dinner are excellent value at TSh 60 and TSh 170 respectively. Back in town, the *Karibuni Guest House* (tel 3035) is worth trying and is pleasant and clean. It costs TSh 300 per person.

For a mid-range hotel, the *Mbeya Hotel* opposite the football stadium is recommended. Managed by the Tanzanian Railways Corporation, it's a very pleasant, colonial-style hotel with comfortable rooms, clean sheets, mosquito nets and hot showers. B&B costs TSh 2600/3500 a single/double, though they have cheaper rooms with shared bathroom facilities. Dinner is good value at TSh 450.

The Tanzanian Coffee Board has a *coffee shop* on the corner of the market square where you can get a good cup of coffee for a few shillings.

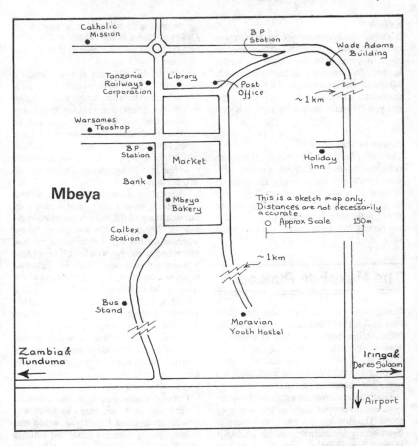

The following labels appear on the map:

Catholic Mission

BP Station

Wade Adams Building

Tanzania Railways Corporation

Library

Post Office

~1 km

Warsames Teashop

BP Station

Market

Holiday Inn

Bank

Mbeya

Mbeya Bakery

This is a sketch map only. Distances are not necessarily accurate.

Approx Scale   150m

Caltex Station

~1 km

Bus Stand

Moravian Youth Hostel

Zambia & Tunduma

Iringa & Dar es Salaam

Airport

Getting There & Away

Bus There are several daily express buses between Dar es Salaam and Mbeya which cost TSh 1300 and take about 18 hours. The last eight hours of the journey are pretty rough as the road is bad. The buses depart from the main bus station which is about 10 minutes walk from the Moravian Youth Hostel. Zainabs bus company has been recommended as being clean, fast and comfortable. Advance booking is essential. The Dar es Salaam to Mbeya road goes through the Mikumi National Park and there's a lot of game visible during the day, including elephant, giraffe, zebra and gazelle. For details on the trip from Mbeya to Karonga in Malawi, see the To/From Malawi section in the Getting There chapter.

Train Trains on the TAZARA railway to Dar es Salaam are heavily booked, so make a reservation well in advance (see the Train section in the Getting Around chapter). Fares between Dar es Salaam and Mbeya are TSh 3430 (1st class), TSh 1995 (2nd class) and TSh 1220 (3rd class).

KYELA

If it's early in the day and you're on your way to the Malawi border, there's no need to come to Kyela as the turn-off to the border is about five km back up the road towards Mbeya. From the turn-off, it's seven km to the border which is open until 6 pm. If it's late you may have to stay the night at Kyela.

Places to Stay

The *Ram Hotel*, not far from the bus stand, is excellent value at TSh 300 a double with clean sheets and mosquito nets. The hotel has its own generator (so there are lights after dark) and good food is available. The *Salaam Hotel* on the main road has beds for TSh 200 per person, but the showers have cold water only.

The Makonde Plateau

Hardly any traveller ever visits the south-eastern part of Tanzania adjacent to the Mozambique border, but this is where the famous makonde carvings originally came from (they've since been copied by artisans all over Tanzania and even in Kenya). It's also a very beautiful part of the country.

Getting there involves a series of bus journeys and overnight stays in the towns en route. The first leg is a bus from Mbeya to Njombe via Makumbako on the TAZARA railway line. Njombe is one of the highest and coldest areas of Tanzania and you'll need plenty of warm clothes. It's a prosperous

agricultural area and you can stay at the *Lutheran Guest House* which will provide breakfast (but no other meals) if booked in advance.

Between Njombe and Songea there's a new British-built road over a stunningly beautiful mountain area where a lot of coffee is grown. There are regular minibuses between the two towns and seats can be booked in advance. There are also regular buses between Songea and Dar es Salaam which take about 24 hours. There are plenty of lodgings in Songea which cost about TSh 250 per person.

The next leg of the journey is from Songea to Tunduru on a terrible road which goes through some of the most deserted country-side in Tanzania. It can sometimes take a week to do the 272 km between the two towns in a truck, but with luck it won't take you more than a day. There are only two buses per week, so the rest of the time you'll have to hire private Land Rovers. These should cost about TSh 1200 and take about 12 hours. Lodgings are available in Tunduru for about TSh 250 per person.

Between Tunduru and Masasi there's an all-weather gravel road but the bus service is erratic and always very crowded. The journey usually takes about three hours but it can occasionally take 10.

Once at Masasi you're on the Makonde Plateau and there are buses to Lindi and Mtwara on the coast. Cargo boats which take passengers ply between Lindi and Mtwara and Dar es Salaam and are operated by the Tanzanian Coastal Shipping Line (see the Dar es Salaam chapter).

National Parks & Game Reserves

Kenya may well have the better stocked game parks and easier access to them but Tanzania has the world famous Serengeti National Park and Ngorongoro Crater with the Olduvai Gorge sandwiched between them plus, of course, Mt Kilimanjaro.

Serengeti has a huge animal population and they're easy to see in the flat grassland of the park. At Ngorongoro the park is in the crater of a huge extinct volcano which is said to be the world's largest caldera.

Tanzania has many other national parks, but getting to the more remote western or southern parts of the country where they are can be either problematical or expensive or both. Accommodation at these more remote parks also tends to be limited if you're not camping. This doesn't mean that they're not worth the effort – they certainly are, especially the Selous Game Reserve which is Tanzania's largest park. The Selous was also the very first game park to be set up in Tanzania, yet it remains a vast wilderness with facilities available only on the north-eastern fringes.

The border closure with Kenya which began in 1977 and lasted for years did a great deal of damage to Tanzania's tourist industry. During that period tourist facilities were nowhere near as numerous or as easily accessible as Kenya's, except in the northern parks and game reserves. This all changed once the border reopened for normal usage. Now there are plenty of safari companies, budget and luxury, which can take you to the more popular parks.

Until 1989 only locally registered safari companies were allowed to operate out of Arusha, Dar es Salaam and elsewhere but, since then, foreign-based companies have been allowed to set up shop. They've taken quite a lot of business from local companies and there's a degree of disquiet about this, but the big companies generally cater for the more affluent. What does seem unfair, to a degree, is that the large companies can afford to throw capital at their operations, something which the smaller ones don't have the resources to do. Instead, they depend on turnover to make a go of it.

The national parks are open from 6 am to 7 pm. You are not permitted to drive in the parks at any other time.

WILDLIFE ORGANISATIONS

If you want to get involved in antipoaching measures and conservation activities in Tanzania (and help is needed in a big way), contact either the Tanzania Wildlife Protection Fund, PO Box 1994, Dar es Salaam, or the African Wildlife Foundation, PO Box 48177, Nairobi, Kenya, or 1717 Massachusetts Ave NW, Washington DC 20036, USA. The Wildlife Conservation Society of Tanzania, PO Box 70919, Dar es Salaam, does similar work.

All these societies do their best to protect wildlife and their habitats, to help the recovery of endangered animal and plant species and fund research into the management of wildlife and the impact of human beings on their habitats. Enquiries are welcome.

PARK ENTRY FEES

All national park fees must be paid in hard currency (cash or travellers' cheques) unless you are a Tanzanian resident in which case you may pay in local currency. The following fees are for each 24 hour period or part thereof:

Fees	Nonresident	Resident
Adult entry	US$ 15	TSh 100
Child entry	US$ 5	TSh 30
Vehicle entry (up to 2000 kg)	US$ 30	TSh 300
Vehicle entry (over 2000 kg)	US$150	TSh 7500
Camping (established sites)	US$ 10	TSh 100
Camping ('special' sites)	US$ 40	TSh 200
Camping (children)	US$ 5	TSh 40
Guide (where appropriate)	US$ 10	TSh 100

A child's rate is applicable for children between the ages of three and 16. Children under three are free.

The only exception to this fee structure is at the Gombe Stream National Park on Lake Tanganyika where the park entry fee is US$50 or TSh 500 for residents.

Charges for vehicle recovery in the event of an accident are TSh 50,000 (up to 2000 kg) and TSh 100,000 (over 2000 kg).

It's important to bear in mind that if you don't have the exact amount in hard currency to pay these fees, the change will be given in local currency. If you're with a group on safari, sort this out between yourselves before you arrive at a park entry gate.

You'll occasionally hear (as we do) of travellers who have managed to negotiate part payment in local currency at some entry gates. You can safely assume that they've been lucky. At most entry gates this would simply be a waste of time.

BOOKS & MAPS

In contrast to the mid-1980s, there's now a considerable amount of literature available on the various national parks. The best is a series of booklets written in association with the Tanzania National Parks, the African Wildlife Foundation or the Wildlife Conservation Society of Tanzania. They are priced between TSh 1000 and TSh 1200. These booklets include detailed descriptions of the national parks, their geography, fauna and flora and tourist facilities, and include sketches and maps. The series includes *Kilimanjaro National Park, Ngorongoro Conservation Area, Serengeti National Park, Tarangire National Park* and *Arusha National Park*. These booklets are available at the bookshops of the large hotels in Arusha and Dar es Salaam and sometimes at park entry gates.

Another excellent booklet which covers all of the national parks and includes maps and sketches is *A Guide to Tanzania National Parks* by Lilla N Lyogello (Travel Promotion Services Ltd, 1988). It costs only TSh 70 which is an absolute bargain.

It may still be possible to buy a very detailed map of the Ngorongoro Conservation Area from Ngorongoro Crater House if they haven't sold out. Crater House is basically a craft shop on Boma Rd in Arusha, close to the New Safari Hotel.

GETTING THERE & AROUND

You can safely assume that attempting to hitch into the national parks is a complete waste of time. You may well be able to get to the entry gates of the most popular parks but it's very unlikely you'll get any further, and the only parks you are allowed to walk in are Selous, Mahale and Gombe Stream. Most people arriving at a park entry gate will either be part of an organised safari group (in which case you've got next to no chance) or in their own vehicle (in which case they probably have lodge bookings and/or are loaded to the roof with supplies and camping equipment, etc so they'll be extremely reluctant to overload the vehicle with you and your gear or get involved in complications about where you're going to stay).

This being so, there are basically only two

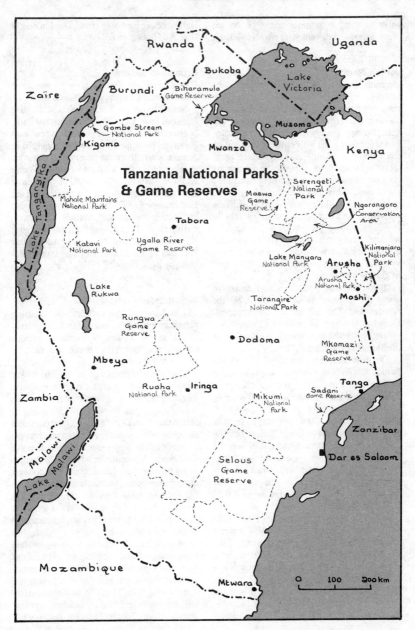

ways to visit a national park: go on an organised safari or rent your own vehicle.

Vehicle Rental

Tanzania is not Kenya when it comes to renting a vehicle. Not only are there very few companies which rent vehicles but those that do charge an arm and a leg and many of the vehicles are poorly maintained. Maintenance (or lack of it) isn't entirely the fault of the companies. Until recently, spare parts were very hard to come by because of government restrictions on foreign currency purchases. This has been relaxed (to a degree) but it will be years before the effects are visible. In other words, renting a vehicle is not a viable proposition for anyone without money to burn – even if you can find a company that will rent you a self-drive vehicle. You will also need a 4WD to be sure of getting anywhere.

If you do rent a vehicle, fuel costs are about the same as in Kenya – TSh 93 for regular and TSh 97 for premium petrol. Diesel is less. These prices will obviously escalate with the continuing devaluation of the Tanzanian shilling.

The next best thing to a self-drive vehicle (which amounts to a quasisafari) is to rent a vehicle plus driver. The average charge in Arusha for a Land Rover is US$40 per day plus US$0.80 per km plus the driver's allowance (about TSh 2000 per day). To this expense you will have to add fuel and all the entrance fees for the vehicle and driver. On the plus side it gives you more flexibility than a standard organised safari. If this interests you, contact Serengeti Select Safaris/Tarangire Safari Lodge in the AICC Building, Arusha.

In Dar es Salaam, the hire rates appear to be cheaper. A Land Rover or VW Kombi costs a US$20 standing charge per day plus US$0.90 per km plus a TSh 2000 driver's allowance. A Nissan minibus goes for a US$25 standing charge plus US$2 per km and the driver's allowance. The minimum km per day for both is 100. Contact Classic Tours (tel 36520, 30006 ext 515), c/o Juma Hamisi & Co, Embassy Hotel, Garden St, PO Box 70250, Dar es Salaam.

Organised Safaris

Going on an organised safari is the way most travellers visit Tanzania's national parks.

Safaris to Arusha National Park, Tarangire National Park, Lake Manyara National Park, Ngorongoro Conservation Area and Serengeti National Park are best arranged in Arusha where there are plenty of companies to choose from. Visits to Sadani Game Reserve, Mikumi National Park, Ruaha National Park and Selous Game Reserve are best arranged in Dar es Salaam while those to Gombe Stream and Mahale Mountains national parks are best arranged from Kigoma. Getting to Rubondo Island National Park (in Lake Victoria) is only feasible by light aircraft.

Which Safari Company?

This is dangerous ground! As far as camping safaris go everyone has a different tale to tell. Before recommending or dismissing various companies, however, there are several factors to consider.

If a bunch of people go on a safari with a certain company, have an excellent time and there are no serious hitches such as vehicle breakdowns, then those people are going to recommend that company to others. If the company also fixes it for them to pay for part of the trip in local currency then that's a double plus. The trouble, however, is that for many travellers all that is required to convert an enthusiastic recommendation into a scathing condemnation is for the vehicle to break down for half a day, especially on a four to five day tour of Lake Manyara, Ngorongoro Crater and Serengeti.

We get letters all the time from travellers expressing contrary points of view about particular companies (as in Kenya). Some of the complaints are justified but others are simply bad luck. There's obviously a lot which companies can do to head off foreseeable problems, in particular by having well-maintained vehicles, reasonable spare tyres and sufficient tools to fix minor problems. In Tanzania, however, this is often easier said than done for reasons already mentioned.

Also, if the company you go through is trying hard to cater for budget travellers and is allowing you to pay partially in local currency, then it's hardly fair to be enthusiastic about this and then totally condemnatory when you lose half a day because of a breakdown. All the same, you'd be surprised how many people want their bread buttered on both sides.

So, if you do have a breakdown, don't whinge, count your blessings, get out and lend a hand, get your hands dirty and get back on the road. This is a safari after all!

Bear all this in mind when choosing which safari company to use and get several quotes first.

From Arusha Arusha is the safari capital of Tanzania and there's a plethora of companies which offer a range of possibilities to suit all tastes and pockets, though cost and reliability vary widely. To a large extent you get what you pay for.

The safaris available vary from just one day to 15 days. A one day safari takes you to Arusha National Park and a two day safari to Tarangire National Park. Most travellers, however, prefer longer safaris – four to six days on average. You need a minimum of three days and two nights to tour Lake Manyara and Ngorongoro Crater, four days and three nights to tour Lake Manyara, Ngorongoro Crater and Serengeti, and six days and five nights to tour Lake Manyara, Ngorongoro Crater, Serengeti and Tarangire. These are absolute minimum tour lengths. If you can afford to stay longer, then do. You'll see a lot more and you won't come back feeling that half the driving time was taken up just getting to and from Arusha. A longer tour will also enable you to make more economical use of park entry fees. If you leave one park within 24 hours and enter another (between Ngorongoro Crater and Serengeti,

for instance) you'll be up for two lots of park entry fees (US$30 per person) instead of one.

If you want to have a good look at Lake Manyara, Ngorongoro Crater and Serengeti then plan on a five to six day safari. On a seven day safari you could see Lake Manyara, Ngorongoro Crater, Serengeti and Tarangire at a relatively leisurely pace. On a 15 day safari you could take in all the places mentioned plus Lake Natron and Arusha National Park.

Most safari companies have offices in the Arusha International Conference Centre (AICC). Others are along India St, Boma Rd, Sokoine Rd and Set Benjamin Rd. We recommend you check out the following companies first before deciding on a particular one. For camping safaris try:

Dice Safaris
> PO Box 284, Sokoine Rd, just below the clock tower, Arusha (tel 3090, 3625). Run by the very able and informative Terry Rice, who must have East Africa tattooed on the palms of her hands by now, this company will organise wherever you want to go at a price you can afford. She doesn't bullshit, there are no hidden extras and the vehicles are well maintained. An excellent first contact.

Sengo Safaris Ltd
> PO Box 207, Room 153-5, Ngorongoro Wing, AICC, Arusha (tel 3181 ext 1518/19/20). Another first port of call and recommended by safari companies in Nairobi (with justification). Again, no bullshit, reliable vehicles and drivers.

Arumeru Tours & Safaris
> PO Box 730, Seth Benjamin Rd, Arusha (tel 2780)

Star Tours
> PO Box 1099, Room 138/140, Ngorongoro Wing, AICC, Arusha (tel 3181 ext 2281/2285 after hours)

This is by no means a comprehensive list of companies which offer camping safaris. There are plenty more on just about every floor of the AICC building. You could easily spend half a day or even a whole day checking out the various offices.

Virtually all the companies which offer camping safaris can also arrange a lodge safari. The following companies can be recommended:

Hoopoe Safaris Ltd
PO Box 2047, India St, Arusha (tel 7541). This is a very reliable company and can be highly recommended. It gets nothing but praise from those who have used it.
Wildersun Safaris & Tours
PO Box 930, Sokoine Rd, Arusha (tel 3880, 6471)
Simba Safaris
PO Box 1207, between India St and Ngoliondoi Rd, Arusha (tel 3509, 3600)
Equatorial Safaris Ltd
PO Box 2156, Arusha (tel 2617)

Takims Holidays, Tours & Safaris Ltd
PO Box 6023, Suite 421, Ngorongoro Wing, AICC, Arusha (tel 3174, 7500)
Bushtrekker Safaris
PO Box 3173, Arusha (tel 3727)
United Touring Company Ltd
PO Box 2211, corner Ngoliondoi Rd and Sokoine Rd, Arusha (tel 7931). This could well be *the* most expensive safari company.

Again, this is by no means a comprehensive list of companies offering lodge safaris. There are many more in the AICC building.

Costs The cost of a safari depends on two main factors: whether you camp for the night or stay in a lodge or luxury tented camp; and how many people are on the safari.

A camping safari is obviously much cheaper than one which uses lodges for overnight accommodation. The exact cost depends partly on how long you want to go for and where you want to go. In general, you're looking at US$150 to US$200 per day shared between up to six people. This includes the vehicle, the driver and the driver's food, accommodation and entry fees. Other companies quote between US$60 and US$85 per person per day. You need to add to this the cost of your own food, park entry fees and camping fees plus the cost of any other accommodation you might need.

Most companies will allow you to pay in local currency (though there's officially nothing they can do about park entry and camping fees which have to be paid in hard currency). Some companies demand payment in hard currency for everything.

So, at official rates of exchange and assuming there are five people sharing the cost of the vehicle and driver plus the driver's expenses, you're looking at a minimum of US$60 to US$70 per person per day including park entry and camping fees and the cost of your food. If there are less than five people, the cost per day will increase sharply. With a lot of running around, it's possible to find a company which will quote you less for their component of the costs, but it's probably true to say that their vehicles won't be particularly well maintained. We do get letters from travellers who have managed to do this. Some have had a relatively trouble-free safari (just lucky?) while for others it's been a disaster with multiple breakdowns and delays. The choice is yours.

On safaris where you stay at lodges or luxury tented camps overnight you're looking at about double the cost, regardless of the length of the safari and assuming that there is *a minimum of six people* on the safari. If this is the case, average costs vary from US$100 to US$145 per person per day. If there are less than six people then the cost per day increases sharply. Taking a typical six day, five night safari to Lake Manyara, Ngorongoro Crater and Serengeti, for instance, the cost per person per day will be US$134 (five people), US$138 (four people), US$168 (three people), US$184 (two people).

All the lodge safaris assume that single travellers are willing to share accommodation. If you want your own room you'll be up for a 'single supplement' which is an extra US$25 per day.

Lodge safaris invariably have to be paid for entirely in hard currency (under government regulations most of what you pay for – lodge accommodation and food, park entry fees, etc – has to be paid in hard currency anyway). Lodge safari costs are generally all-inclusive – transport, accommodation, meals, park entry fees, etc.

From Dar es Salaam There are far fewer safari companies in Dar es Salaam and they are scattered throughout the city centre rather than being concentrated in one building, as in Arusha. They cater mainly for safaris to Mikumi, Ruaha and Selous and there are guaranteed departures, usually once a week, to all these parks. If you have a group together a safari can leave at any time you're ready.

Safaris to Mikumi typically last two to three days, to Mikumi and Ruaha five days, and to Selous five days. Safaris which take in all three parks last for nine days.

The possibilities of camping in these parks

is much more limited than in the northern parks. On most safaris you'll stay in lodges or semiluxury tented camps. Check out the following companies which offer lodge-based safaris:

Takims Holidays, Tours & Safaris
   PO Box 20350, Jamhuri St, Dar es Salaam (tel 25691, 30037)
Bushtrekker Safaris
   PO Box 5350, Dar es Salaam (tel 31957, 32671)
Tanzania Safari Tours Ltd/Rufiji River Camp
   PO Box 20058, Dar es Salaam (tel 64177, 63546). The office is on Pugu Rd, diagonally opposite the TAZARA Railway Station. This company caters only for safaris to Selous and you stay at the company's Rufiji River Camp. Most people make their own arrangements for getting there (either by vehicle or plane) but the company can arrange transfer.

Costs As with safaris from Arusha, costs usually depend largely on where you stay for the night and how many go on any particular safari.

A two day tour of Mikumi National Park costs about US$160 per person and a three day tour is US$250, assuming there are seven people. If there are less than seven on the two/three day tours you should expect to pay, per person, about US$171/264 (six people), US$188/284 (five people), US$214/315 (four people), US$256/366 (three people), US$339/470 (two people) and US$591/778 (one person).

A five day tour of Mikumi and Ruaha national parks costs US$472 per person for seven people and up to US$1451 for one person.

A five day tour of Selous by Land Rover costs US$601 per person for seven people and up to US$1572 for one person, whereas an eight day tour costs US$908 for seven people and up to US$2167 for one person. A nine day tour of all three parks costs from US$1007 (seven people) to US$2967 (one person).

All these safaris assume that if you are a single traveller you will be willing to share a room or tent at night with someone else. If you're not willing to share, there will be an additional 'single supplement' charge of about US$25 to US$30 per night.

Costs quoted here are all-inclusive and include transport, accommodation, all meals, park entry fees, etc. There is far less scope in Dar es Salaam for paying partly in local currency, so it's best to assume you will have to pay entirely in hard currency.

Tipping Regardless of whether you go on a camping safari or a lodge safari, the driver/guide and the cook(s) (where provided) will expect a reasonable tip at the end of the journey. Be generous. You may think you've paid a lot of money for your safari but most of it will have gone to the national parks, the lodges and the safari company. The wages of the driver and cooks will have been minimal. Remember that others will come after you and there's nothing worse than a driver/guide and/or cooks who couldn't care less and who feel exploited.

Organising your own Safari

Tanzania is not Kenya as far as this goes because of the difficulties of hiring self-drive vehicles. Essentially it's not worth it without your own vehicle and if you bring a foreign registered vehicle into Tanzania then the park entry fees for the vehicle alone will be US$30 per 24 hours as opposed to just TSh 300 for a locally registered vehicle. Also, if you intend to stay at lodges you won't be entitled to the discounts which agents can get for group bookings so you'll be up for the full cost (the agents' commission for booking lodges is usually 10%).

KILIMANJARO NATIONAL PARK

An almost perfectly shaped volcano which rises sheer from the plains, Mt Kilimanjaro is one of the African continent's most magnificent sights. Snow-capped and not yet extinct, at 5895 metres it is the highest peak in Africa.

From cultivated farmlands on the lower levels, it rises through lush rainforest onto alpine meadow and finally across a barren lunar landscape to the snow and ice-capped summit. The rainforest is home to many animals including elephant, buffalo, rhino, leopard and monkey. You may encounter herds of eland on the saddle between the summits of Mawenzi and Kibo.

History

Geologically, Kilimanjaro is only a relative newcomer to the Rift Valley and didn't even exist between one and two million years ago. At that time, where Kilimanjaro now stands, there was just an undulating plain with a few old eroded mountains. But that all changed with movements of the earth's crust associated with the rift. Lava poured out from the fractures that were created and eventually gave rise to an enormous ridge which is now represented by the nearby peaks of Ol Molog, Kibongoto and Kilema.

Kilimanjaro began to grow about 750,000 years ago as a result of lava spewing out of three main centres – Shira, Kibo and Mawenzi. It kept growing until their cones reached a height of about 5000 metres about half a million years ago. About this time, Shira collapsed into a caldera and became inactive but Kibo and Mawenzi continued to erupt until their peaks reached about 5500 metres. Mawenzi was the next to die but Kibo continued to be active until about 360,000 years ago during which time there were some particularly violent eruptions, including one which filled the old eroded caldera of Shira with black lava.

From an estimated final height of 5900 metres, Kibo then gradually fell silent and, although intermittent eruptions continued for thousands of years, the whole mountain began to shrink and Kibo's cone collapsed into a series of concentric terraces. Erosion, in the form of glaciers which came and went, wore the peaks down even more as did a huge landslide about 100,000 years ago which created the Kibo Barranco.

Kibo finally died after a last fling of violent activity which created the present caldera and the lava flows known as the Inner Crater and Ash Pit. Then the glaciers returned to continue their work. Meanwhile, the forests and alpine vegetation claimed what they could of the mountain, and streams sculpted the sides of the massif into the shape it is now. Interestingly, it appears that Kilimanjaro, like Mt Kenya, is gradually losing its glaciers.

Books & Maps

Before climbing Kilimanjaro I recommend that you buy a copy of *Kilimanjaro – Map & Guide* by Mark Savage. It has an excellent large-scale topographical map of Kilimanjaro on one side and details of the geology, fauna and flora, weather and climate, history, costs, walking and climbing route on the other side. It's available from most bookshops in Nairobi for KSh 100, or you can get it from 32 Seamill Park Crescent, Worthing BN11 2PN, UK.

An excellent booklet to take on your trek is *Kilimanjaro National Park* written by Jeanette Hanby in association with the Tanzania National Parks and the African Wildlife Foundation (1987). It contains descriptions of all the possible routes up Kilimanjaro, the climate, fauna and flora, mountain medicine and tourist facilities, complete with maps and illustrations. It's for sale in Arusha (at bookshops in the large hotels) and in Dar es Salaam.

For those intending to rock climb, as opposed to walk, the *Guide to Mt Kenya & Kilimanjaro* edited by Iain Allan (Mountain Club of Kenya, 1981) is also worth chasing up, although it's presently out of print. You may be able to get a copy from the Mountain Club of Kenya (PO Box 45741, Nairobi) or from bookshops in Nairobi. You will not be able to buy it in Tanzania.

For any other information, get in touch with the Kilimanjaro Mountain Club, PO Box 66, Moshi, Tanzania.

Preparation

Too many people try to scale Mt Kilimanjaro without sufficient acclimatisation and end up with altitude sickness or, at the very least, nausea and headaches. This is obviously going to detract from your enjoyment of going up there and prevents quite a few people from reaching the summit. Scaling a 5895 metre high mountain is no joy ride!

To give yourself the best chance of reaching the top it's a very good idea to stay at the Horombo Hut for two nights instead of one, though this will not guarantee you plain sailing. You won't get the same benefits from staying two nights at the Kibo Hut as it's too high and you won't be able sleep very much. Remember the old mountaineering adage: 'Go high, sleep low'. Also, whatever else you do, walk *pole pole*, drink a lot of liquid, suck glucose tablets and don't eat too much (you won't feel like eating too much anyway!). Staying two nights at the Horombo Hut is going to make the trek into a six day affair and increase your costs, so bear this in mind and make sure that the guides and porters understand what you have in mind before setting off.

There's a very funny but beautifully accurate description of what it's like climbing Kilimanjaro in Mark Savage's *Kilimanjaro – Map & Guide*. Make sure you read it!

No specialist equipment is required to climb Kilimanjaro but you do need a strong pair of good boots, plenty of warm clothing including gloves, a woollen hat and waterproof overclothes. If you lack any of these they can be hired from the two hotels in Marangu village or at the park entrance.

Kilimanjaro can be climbed at any time of year but there's usually a lot of rain during April, May and November.

Organised Climbs

It is a traveller's dream to scale the summit, watch the dawn break and gaze out over vast expanses of East African bushland. Who would come to East Africa and not climb Kilimanjaro? Certainly not many, but you should know that it's going to cost you between US$350 and US$380 for a standard five day climb, excluding the hire of camping gear and transport to Marangu (the starting point for the climb). The bulk of this is payable in hard currency – cash or travellers' cheques.

Most people who climb Kilimanjaro, unlike Mt Kenya, opt to go on an organised tour. There are good reasons for this. Most of the charges are standard and a guide is compulsory in any case. Also, as the climb takes a minimum of five days, organising your own climb involves a lot of running around and this is difficult without your own transport – food supplies are very limited at Marangu so you'll have to do most of your shopping in Moshi. By the time you have the whole thing together you will have saved very little. Not only that, but most people find that they have very little energy left for cooking at the end of a day's climb. Having someone to do it for you can very well make the difference between loving and hating the trek. Likewise, hiring porters to carry the bulk of your gear is going to add considerably to your enjoyment of the mountain.

There are three places which offer reliable organised climbs – one in Moshi and the other two in Marangu.

In Moshi, Trans-Kibo Travels Ltd (tel 4734, 2923), PO Box 558, Moshi, inside the YMCA, offers the cheapest deal. For a five day trek it charges US$380 (one climber), US$360 per person (two climbers) and US$350 per person (three or more climbers). To stay longer it costs US$80 per person for each extra day. This price includes park entry fees, hut fees, rescue fees, guide and porters (two porters per climber) and food, but it excludes the hire of camping gear, any additional equipment or clothing you might need and transport to Marangu. Transport to Marangu can be arranged for TSh 6000 (shared by up to six people).

At Marangu, the Marangu Hotel (tel Marangu 11), PO Box 40, Moshi, offers five day treks for US$445 (one climber), US$430 per person (two climbers) and US$414 per person (three or more climbers). The price includes park entry fees, hut fees, rescue fees, guide and porters (two porters per climber), food, camping equipment and any additional equipment or clothing you might need. The Marangu Hotel recommends staying at the mountain huts, but these have no camping equipment for hire.

Also at Marangu, the Kibo Hotel (tel Marangu 4), PO Box 102, Marangu, offers a five day trek for US$460 (one climber), US$440 per person (two to three climbers)

and US$420 per person (four or more climbers). Extra days cost US$80 per person. These prices include all the same things as the trek organised by the Marangu Hotel. They do not include hire of camping gear or any additional equipment or clothing. Boots, clothing and sleeping bags can be rented from the Kibo Hotel for TSh 800 per item for the length of the trek.

All these organised climbs are for the Marangu Trail – the most popular route. The Kibo Hotel can also organise a six day climb via the less used Machame Trail, but it requires five days notice. The respective charges are US$930 (one climber), US$830 per person (two to three climbers) and US$760 per person (four or more climbers). Extra days cost US$130 per person.

In Moshi you will come across individuals offering supposedly a five day organised climb up Kilimanjaro at prices which appear very tempting – US$140 plus TSh 20,000 is usual (US$242 at official rates of exchange but less if using the street exchange rate). This includes a guide and porters as well as food but you will have to organise the food and transport to Marangu which will probably involve you in quite a bit of running around. Basically, whoever offers the trek will be acting as intermediaries between you and the guides/porters and taking a commission. You can do your own negotiations with these people at the park entry gate. Obviously the choice is yours but, if you do go through someone like this, make sure you know exactly what you are paying for and bear in mind that if it doesn't work out as promised the chances of any sort of refund are nil.

Organising Your Own Climb

This is doing it the hard way! It won't save much money and you'll have to do a lot of running around including buying and transporting food from Moshi and hiring equipment or extra clothing.

Before deciding on this, use the following list to work out whether or not it will be cheaper. The fees are all payable in hard currency at the park entry gate:

Park entry fee	US$15 per day
Hut fee	US$15 per day
Rescue fee	US$20 per trek
Camping fee	US$40 per trek
Park commission	US$5
(for organising own climb)	

In addition, there will be the salaries of the guide and porters (a guide is compulsory but porters are not). Their daily wages, which can be paid in local currency, are:

Guides	TSh 1200
Porters	TSh 1000
Guides/porters hut fees	TSh 200 each
Guides/porters entry fees	TSh 250 each

These salaries are for the Marangu Trail. Entry fees for guides and porters are higher on other trails.

Adding all these costs together and assuming you take one porter per climber and spend five days on the mountain, the minimum cost per person is about US$250 if you use the huts and US$215 if you camp (or a little less, as you will be sharing the cost of the guide and his hut and park entry fees). To this amount you must add the cost of food (for you and the guide/porters), the hire of any necessary equipment (camping gear, clothing) and transport to Marangu.

Clothing and the like can be hired from the park entry gate. Typical charges are:

sleeping bag	TSh 500
boots	TSh 500
sweater	TSh 400
raincoat	TSh 400
rain trousers	TSh 400
dacron jacket	TSh 400
water bottle	TSh 200
gloves	TSh 200
balaclava	TSh 400

These fees are for a five day trek and your passport will have to be left as a deposit. The gear is said to be of reasonable quality.

Vehicles owned by the national parks can be hired for TSh 60 per km (minimum charge TSh 1000) for transport from Marangu to the park entry gate. This is a luxury extra as you can walk.

Tipping
Whether you take an organised climb or organise your own, the guide and porters will expect a tip at the end of the trek. Be generous about this. Would you spend half your life endlessly taking groups of tourists up and down Kilimanjaro for what amounts to about US$5 a day?

Getting to the Trail Heads
The Marangu Trail is the trail most taken by tourists, being the easiest way up the mountain. At the head of the trail is Marangu village, set below the park entry gate.

There are minibuses all day every day until late in the afternoon between Moshi and Marangu via Himo, terminating in Marangu village at a spot below the post office. The fare is TSh 100. A taxi over the same distance will cost about TSh 6000 shared between up to four people.

Marangu Marangu has a post office, a petrol station, a small market and several shops selling a limited range of goods. There are several places to stay in the village or close by. It's an attractive place with an alpine atmosphere and a boulder-strewn stream which flows through the centre.

At the park entry gate there's a general store which stocks items such as candles, flour, beer, soft drink, whisky, *konyagi*, tinned meat and vegetables, dried soup, biscuits, fresh bread, cooking fat, margarine, chocolate, cigarettes and matches. There's no fresh fruit or vegetables available (limited quantities of these can be bought in Marangu and at various houses between there and the park entry gate).

Places to Stay The first hotel you encounter on the road into Marangu from Moshi/Himo is the *Marangu Hotel* (tel Marangu 11), PO Box 40, Moshi. It consists of a collection of self-contained cottages set in pleasant, leafy gardens and costs US$70/100 a single/double including hot water showers, breakfast and dinner. It used to be possible to camp here (for a small fee) but the man-

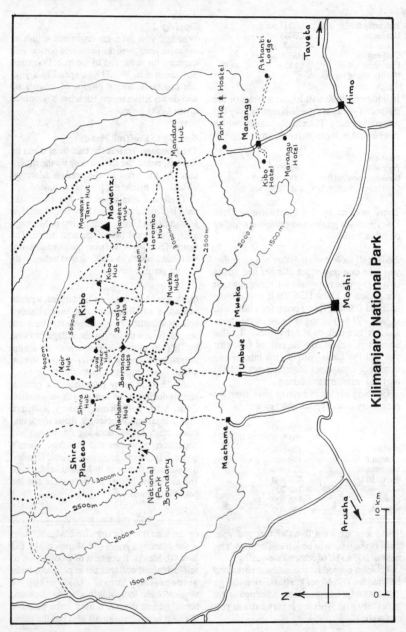

Kilimanjaro National Park

agement no longer encourage this. The hotel is seven km from the park entry gate.

By turning left over the river bridge in Marangu village and continuing on for several hundred metres you will come to the *Kibo Hotel* (tel Marangu 4), PO Box 102, Marangu. This hotel has a superb position overlooking the surrounding countryside and, like the Marandu Hotel, is set in landscaped gardens. The atmosphere is decidedly olde-worlde. B&B costs US$54/68/85 a single/double/triple and US$100 for a four-bed room, plus 5% service charge. Half-board rates are US$60/80/100/120 respectively, including taxes. All the rooms are self-contained and the parking lot is guarded. Campers are welcome and are charged TSh 1000 per person per night. The restaurant is open to nonresidents. Breakfast costs TSh 700, lunch is TSh 1300 and dinner is TSh 1500, plus 10% sales tax and 5% service charge. The Kibo is about 5½ km from the park entry gate.

On the other side of the village from the Kibo Hotel (turn right just before the river bridge) are two other places to stay. They're both considerably cheaper and both accept payment in local currency but they're quite a walk from the village. The first you arrive at is the *Babylon Bar & Restaurant*, above the road on the left-hand side (signposted). A double room costs TSh 1400 though washing facilities are primitive. The restaurant is reasonable and the beautiful beer garden, filled with exotic flowers, is popular with local people.

Much further down the track (about 3½ km from Marangu village) is the *Ashanti Lodge* (tel Arusha 2745), PO Box 6004, Arusha. Run by the very friendly Ali and his family, this is a very relaxing place to stay and has a restaurant which serves breakfast, lunch and dinner. There's a bar, a pleasant garden and a climbing gear hire service. Campers are welcome or you can rent a room for TSh 1500/2400 a single/double with breakfast. There are hot water showers. To get there from Marangu, either walk or hitch a ride with whatever is going down this gravel road – tractors, pick-ups and trucks –

though matatus are available too but are infrequent.

Up at the park entry gate (five km beyond Marangu) you can either camp for the usual fee or stay in one of the two hostels. *Hostel No 1* costs US$10 and *Hostel No 2* costs US$6 for a bunk bed in one of the rooms – four to six beds per room. A canteen offers breakfast, lunch and dinner.

The Trails
The Marangu Trail This is the trail most visitors take.

Day 1 Starting from the Marangu park entry gate at 1800 metres it's a fairly easy three to four hour walk through thick rainforest to the *Mandara Hut* (2700 metres). (This hut and the Horombo Hut (3720 metres) might be better described as lodges since they consist of a large central chalet surrounded by many smaller huts. They almost constitute villages.) There's often quite a lot of mud along this route so wear good boots. The Mandara Hut consists of a group of comfortable wooden A-frame huts with bunk beds and mattresses and has a total capacity of 60. Water is piped in from springs above the hut and there are flush toilets. There's a dining area in the main cabin.

Day 2 The route climbs steeply through giant heath forest and out across moorlands onto the slopes of Mawenzi and finally to the *Horombo Hut* (3720 metres). It's a difficult 14 km walk and you need to take it slowly. Reckon on five to seven hours. If your clothes are soaked through by the time you arrive at the Horombo Hut, don't assume you will be able to dry them there. Firewood is relatively scarce and is reserved for cooking. The Horombo Hut is similar to Mandara Hut but can accommodate 120. There are both earth and flush toilets.

Days 3 & 4 If possible, spend two nights at this hut and on the fourth day go to *Kibo Hut* (4703 metres), about six to seven hours away. Porters don't go beyond the Kibo Hut so you'll have to carry your own essential gear from here to the summit and back. Don't skimp on warm clothing. It's extremely cold on the summit and you'll freeze to death if you're not adequately clothed. Kibo Hut is a stone block house which is more like a mountain hut of the type you are likely to find on Mt Kenya. It has a small dining area and several dormitory rooms with bunk beds and mattresses (total capacity of 60). There are earth toilets but no water so you need to bring sufficient water from the stream above Horombo Hut.

Day 5 Most people find it difficult to sleep much at Kibo, so as you have to start out for the summit very early (1 or 2 am) to get to it just before sunrise, it's a good idea to stay awake the evening before. You'll feel better if you do this rather than try to grab a couple of hours of fitful sleep. The mist and cloud closes in and obscures the views by 9 am and sometimes earlier. The route over the snow to the summit is sometimes like a technicolour dream if it hasn't snowed recently due to the deposits of those who have vomited as a result of trying to get to the top too quickly! Expect to take five to six hours from Kibo Hut to Gillman's Point and a further one to two hours from there to Uhuru Peak.

On the same day you will descend from the summit to the Horombo Hut and spend the night there.

Day 6 On the last day you return to the starting point at Marangu.

The Mweka Trail Starting from Mweka village directly north of Moshi, this is the most direct, fastest and steepest route to the summit.

To get to the trailhead you will have to drive or get a lift from Moshi to Mweka village. Vehicles can usually be left safely at the College of Wildlife Management if you ask permission.

From here you follow an old logging track which is often very slippery. Two hours later the track turns into a path which follows a gully. This path will take you up above the tree line to a ridge where the *Mweka Huts*

(3000 metres) are. Expect this leg of the trek to take six to eight hours. The huts are two round metal constructions which each sleep eight people. The huts are not furnished and there are no toilets. Water can be found below the huts.

From the Mweka Huts continue up the ridge to the west until you reach the *Barafu Huts* (4600 metres). These are exactly the same as the Mweka Huts and sleep eight people each but there are no toilets and no water. The walk will take six to eight hours.

From the Barafu Huts you can ascend straight up to the rim of Kibo but the trail is very steep and will take you about six hours. Uhuru Peak is another hour away.

Umbwe Trail This is another relatively short but steep route (west of Moshi) and it's probably better to descend it from either the Mweka or Machame trails rather than attempt the ascent.

To get to the trailhead, take the main Moshi-Arusha road and turn off right to Weru Weru and Mango. Drive past Weru Weru for some 15 km along the Lyamungu road and turn right at the T-junction towards Mango. About 150 metres after crossing the Sere River turn left and you'll find the Umbwe Mission where vehicles can be left (with permission).

From the mission, follow an old forestry track up to 2100 metres and then follow the path along a narrow ridge between the Lonzo and Umbwe rivers. If it's getting late by the time you get up here then stay at *Bivouac I* (2800 metres), an all-weather rock shelter with water close by. The walk up here from Umbwe village takes four to six hours.

From Bivouac I continue up to *Bivouac II* (3780 metres) which is a rock overhang. Water is available from a spring about 15 minutes down the ravine to the west. Next go up the ridge to the end of the tree line. From here a path marked by cairns goes up to *Barranco Hut* (3900 metres). This hut, an unfurnished metal cabin with a wooden floor, sleeps up to five people. There's an earth toilet and water is available from nearby streams. The walk from Bivouac I to here takes about five hours.

From Barranco Hut head up to Lava Tower Hut and the summit via what's known as the Great Western Breach. The walk from Barranco to Lava Tower takes about three hours.

Machame Trail Some people regard this as the most scenic of the trails up Kilimanjaro. The ascent through forest is gradual until you emerge onto the moorland of Shira Plateau from which there are superb views of the Kibo peak and the Western Breach.

The turn-off on the main Moshi-Arusha road is even further west than that for Umbwe. Once you get there, head north for Machame village. If you have your own transport you can leave the vehicle at either the school or the hotel. From the village, a track leads through coffee plantations and forest to the park entry gate (about four km). From the park entry gate there's a clear track which continues up through more plantations and forest to a ridge between the Weru Weru and Makoa streams and on to the *Machame Huts* (3000 metres). These consist of two unfurnished metal huts which sleep up to six people. There are earth toilets and water is available about five minutes down the valley. From Machame village to the Machame Huts takes about nine hours so an early start is recommended.

From Machame Huts, cross the valley and continue up the steep ridge then west into a gorge and up again to the *Shira Hut* (3800 metres). This hut is an unfurnished metal cabin which sleeps up to eight people. There is no toilet but water is available in the stream about 50 metres north of the hut. The walk takes about five hours.

From the Shira Hut you have the options of continuing on to the Barranco Hut (five to six hours), the *Moir Hut* (two hours), or the *Lava Tower Hut* (4600 metres, four hours). The Lava Tower Hut is an unfinished metal cabin which sleeps up to eight people. There are no toilets but water is available close by.

Loitokitok Trail Coming in from the north,

this trail is officially closed to the public and, in any case, you're strongly advised to avoid it. Doing the rounds in Nairobi are stories of murders along this route.

ARUSHA NATIONAL PARK

Although one of Tanzania's smallest parks, Arusha is one of its most beautiful and spectacular. It's also one of the few that you're allowed to walk in (accompanied by a ranger). Yet few travellers appear to visit it, possibly because of their haste to press on to the more famous parks of Ngorongoro Crater, Serengeti and Mt Kilimanjaro. This is a profound mistake since it has all the features of those three parks, including a superb range of fauna and flora.

The park's main features are Ngurdoto Crater (often dubbed Little Ngorongoro), the Momela Lakes and rugged Mt Meru (4556 metres) which overlooks the town of Arusha to the north. Because of the differing altitudes within the park, ranging from 1500 metres to over 4500 metres, and the geological structure, there are several vegetation zones which support appropriate animal species.

The Ngurdoto Crater is surrounded by forest while the actual crater floor is a swampy area. To the west of it lies Serengeti Ndogo (Little Serengeti), an extensive area of open grassland and the only place in the park where herds of Burchell's zebra can be found.

The Momela Lakes, like many in the Rift Valley, are shallow and alkaline and attract a wide variety of waders, particularly flamingoes. The lakes are fed largely from underground streams and, because of their different mineral content, each lake supports a different type of algal growth which gives them each a different colour. As a result, the bird life varies quite distinctly from one stretch of water to another, even where they are separated by a strip of land only a few metres wide.

Mt Meru, which rivals Kilimanjaro, is a mixture of lush forest and bare rock and has on its eastern side the spectacular Meru

Crater – a sheer cliff face which rises over 1500 metres and is one of the tallest of its types in the world.

Animal life is abundant and although it's impossible to predict what you will see and exactly where you will see it, you can be fairly certain of sighting zebra, waterbuck, reedbuck, klipspringer, hippopotamus, buffalo, elephant, hyaena, mongoose, dikdik, warthog, baboon, vervet and colobus monkey. You might even catch sight of the occasional leopard, but there is no lion in this park and, sadly, no rhino due to poaching.

It's possible to see a good deal of the park in just one day – the Ngurdoto Crater, Momela Lakes and the lower slopes of Mt Meru – assuming you're in a vehicle. But this won't give you the chance to walk around, so it's much better to spend two days here, staying overnight at a camp site, the Momela Rest House or the Momela Lodge. Climbing to the top of Mt Meru at a fairly leisurely pace will take three days.

History

It's estimated that Mt Meru was formed 20 million years ago during earth movements associated with the formation of the Rift Valley. Some time later a subsidiary vent opened to the east of the volcano and Ngurdoto was born. As lava continued to spew out, the cone of Ngurdoto continued to grow over thousands of years until a violent explosion blew it apart as a result of superheated gases being trapped beneath the earth's crust. Repeated activity of this nature gradually increased the size of the crater until the molten rock withdrew to deeper levels leaving the cone without support. It then collapsed to form the caldera which you see today.

Although Ngurdoto is now extinct, Mt Meru is merely dormant having last erupted only 100 years ago. The lava flow which occurred at this time can still be seen on the north-western side of the cone. The spectacular Meru Crater was formed a quarter of a million years ago as the result of a series of violent explosions which blew away the entire eastern wall of the cone and showered the eastern side of the mountain with a mass of mud, rocks, lava and water. The Momela Lakes were formed out of depressions in the drying mud.

The first European to sight Mt Meru was the Austrian Count Teleki von Szek in 1876, at about the time of the volcano's last eruption. His comments about the prolific wildlife which he saw here suggest that it must once have rivalled Ngorongoro Crater as a sort of lost Garden of Eden. Later, in 1907, the Trappe family moved to the Momela region and set up a ranch and a game sanctuary, but when the park was gazetted in 1960 it incorporated the ranch.

Information

Before visiting Arusha National Park I strongly recommend that you buy a copy of the booklet *Arusha National Park*, edited by Deborah Snelson and published by the Tanzania National Parks in association with the African Wildlife Foundation. It contains an excellent description of the area along with descriptions of all the animals, birds and plants to be found here as well as notes on accommodation, transport, climbing Mt Meru and park management. You can find it at the bookshop in the New Arusha Hotel and elsewhere.

Places to Stay

There are three *camp sites* at Momela (close to the park headquarters) and another at Ngurdoto. All cost the usual US$10 per person per night and all have water, toilet facilities and firewood.

There's also a very pleasant self-help *Rest House* near the Momela Gate which accommodates up to five people. There are superb views from here up through Meru Crater to the peak of Mt Meru. Bookings can be made through The Warden, Arusha National Park, PO Box 3134, Arusha.

Just outside the park, north of the Momela Gate, is the *Momela Game Lodge* which can accommodate up to 40 people. It's considerably more expensive than the Rest House but it does have excellent views of both Mt Meru and Mt Kilimanjaro.

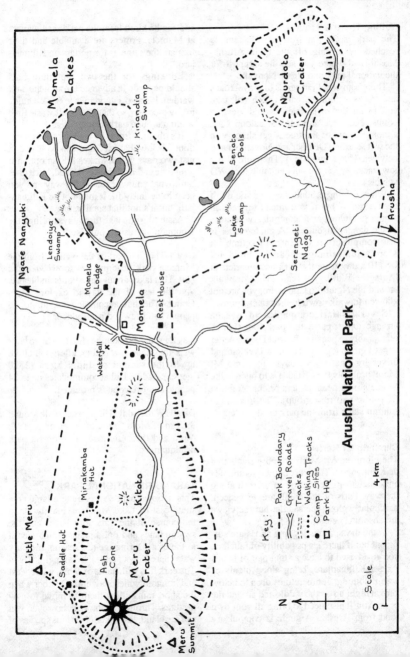

Momela Lakes

Ngurdoto Crater

Kinandia Swamp

Senato Pools

Lokie Swamp

Serengeti Ndogo

Arusha

Ngare Nanyuki

Lendoiya Swamp

Momela Lodge

Momela

Rest House

Waterfall ✕

Little Meru △

Saddle Hut

Miriakamba Hut

Kitoto

Ash Cone

Meru Crater

Meru Summit △

Key:
Park Boundary
Gravel Roads
Tracks
Walking Tracks
Camp Sites •
Park HQ ☐

Arusha National Park

N

Scale

0   4 km

Getting There & Around

The park is 21 km from Arusha and is reached by turning off the main Arusha-Moshi road where you see the signpost for the national park and Ngare Nanyuki.

There's an excellent series of gravel roads and tracks within the park which will take you to all the main features and viewing points. Most are suitable for saloon cars, although some of the tracks get slippery in the wet seasons (October and November and between March and May). There are also a few tracks which are only suitable for 4WD vehicles.

When driving around the park you don't need a guide, but if you intend to walk an armed guide/ranger is compulsory because of the danger of buffalo. A guide/ranger is also compulsory if you intend to climb Mt Meru. Guides/rangers can be hired for US$10 a day from the park headquarters at Momela. While you can drive or walk around the Ngurdoto Crater rim, you are not allowed to walk down to the crater floor.

Several safari companies in Arusha arrange day trips to the park, but they're remarkably expensive. It would be far better to get a group together and hire a vehicle and driver for one or two days. To climb Mt Meru, probably the best idea is to hitch to the Momela park headquarters or charter a taxi (if you're part of a group). The trek to the summit starts from the park headquarters.

Climbing Mt Meru

The climb up Mt Meru possibly rivals that up Kilimanjaro. There are numerous animals and changes of vegetation to be seen along the way. Parts of the climb are very steep, particularly along the saddle, but the views are absolutely stunning.

In the dry seasons jogging shoes are sufficient but if there's a possibility of rain then you're advised to have a stout pair of boots. As for Kilimanjaro, bring along plenty of warm clothing. Temperatures drop to below zero at night up on the saddle and around the peak. You'll also need to bring all your own food from Arusha. A guide is compulsory

and can be hired from the park headquarters at Momela. Porters are available and their fees are the same as for porters on Kilimanjaro.

Bookings for the two mountain huts should be made in advance through the park warden. It's also a good idea to book a guide in advance here so that you don't waste time waiting around park headquarters.

It's obvious from the walking times mentioned below that Mt Meru can be scaled in just two days which makes this an option if your time and/or money is limited, but it does limit what you will see on the way and you need to be fairly fit. It may not be Kilimanjaro, but it's not that small either.

Assuming you take three days to climb the mountain, the usual route is:

Day 1 The first part of the walk is from the Momela park headquarters to *Miriakamba Hut*. This takes about three hours and leaves you the rest of the day to explore Meru Crater. The hut accommodates up to 48 people and firewood is provided.

Day 2 From Miriakamba Hut it's a three hour walk to *Saddle Hut* and an afternoon climb up to the summit of Little Meru (3820 metres). Saddle Hut accommodates up to 24 people and firewood is provided.

Day 3 From Saddle Hut you can walk around the rim of Meru Crater to the summit of Mt Meru and then return to the Momela park headquarters.

TARANGIRE NATIONAL PARK

This national park covers quite a large area south-east of Lake Manyara, mainly along the course of the Tarangire River and the swamp lands and flood plains which feed it to the east. During the dry season, the only water here flows along the Tarangire River. The park fills with herds of zebra, wildebeest and kongoni which stay until October when the short rains allow them to move to new pastures. Throughout the year, however, you can see eland, lesser kudu, various species of gazelle, buffalo, giraffe, waterbuck, impala, elephant and the occasional rhino. The animals are very timid because there are so few visitors. For ornithologists, the best season is from October to May.

Places to Stay & Eat

There are two *public camp sites* where you can pitch a tent for the usual price (US$10 per person per night). Also, there are six so-called *special camp sites* at US$40 per person per night (US$10 for children between the ages of three and 16).

The beautifully sited *Tarangire Safari Lodge*, set on a bluff overlooking the Tarangire River, is run by Serengeti Select Safaris (tel Arusha 7182), PO Box 2703, Arusha. It consists of 35 luxury double tents shielded from the sun by makuti roofs. Each tent has comfortable beds, a solar-heated shower, a flush toilet, electricity and a verandah. The restaurant offers both Western and African dishes and there's a swimming pool. The lodge charges US$52/65 a single/ double. Lunch and dinner cost US$10 each (or the equivalent in local currency).

LAKE MANYARA NATIONAL PARK

Lake Manyara National Park is generally visited as the first stop on a safari which takes in this park and Ngorongoro and Serengeti. It's generally a bit of a letdown, apart from the hippos, since the large herds of elephant which used to inhabit the park have been decimated in recent years. Because the park is too small the elephants invade adjoining farmland for fodder during the dry season. Naturally, local farmers have been none too pleased and, of course, once outside the park boundaries the elephants are fair game (and their ivory is worth a lot of money).

Even the waterbirds which come to nest here (greater and lesser flamingoes in particular) can usually only be seen from a distance because there are no roads to the lake shore. You will certainly see wildebeest, giraffe and baboon. What you see really depends on how long you are prepared to stay and for most people (and most tours) that's just a day.

There is a reasonably interesting market in the nearby village of Mto-wa-Mbu – mainly fabrics and crafts – but they see a lot of tourists here so it's overcommercialised and devoid of bargains. Indeed, it's possibly cheaper to buy what is for sale here in Arusha.

Places to Stay & Eat

There are two *camp sites* just outside the park entrance which is just down the road from the village of Mto-wa-Mbu (River of Gnats or Mosquito Village, according to various translations, and whichever one you choose, it's true).

Camp Site No 2 is probably the best. You can either pitch a tent here or rent one of the bandas which contain two beds, blankets and sheets and have running water, a toilet and firewood. Insect repellent and/or a mosquito net would be very useful and you need to beware of thieving baboons.

Avoid camping at any sites within the park as they're all so-called *special camps* which will cost you US$40 per person per night (US$10 for children between the ages of three and 16).

There's a *youth hostel* of sorts here but it can't be recommended unless you're in love with mosquitoes. *Fig Tree Farm*, about two km from the park entrance, has been recommended by some travellers.

Budget accommodation is available in Mto-wa-Mbu village. There are several very basic hotels including the *Kudu Guest House* where doubles cost TSh 1500 per person including dinner (soup, fish, rice and beans and fruit dessert) and breakfast (chapati, rice cakes, samosas and tea).

The best place to stay, however, especially if you don't have a tent, and which I recommend without any reservation, is the *Starehe Bar & Hotel* on the escarpment up above Lake Manyara. It's about 100 metres off to the left on the turn-off for Lake Manyara Hotel (signposted) on the main road from Mto-wa-Mbu to Ngorongoro. It's not an obvious place but there is a sign. It's rustic, very clean, very comfortable and there are no bugs, mosquitoes or electricity (though candles are provided). There are only cold water showers but the staff are eager to please, very friendly and they'll cook you superb, generous meals of tasty stewed chicken, sautéed potatoes, haricot beans, mung beans, gravy and rice and great breakfasts of two eggs, bread, butter, jam and tea/coffee.

Lake Manyara Hotel (tel 3300, 3113) is the place to stay for luxury hotel accommodation. It sits right on the edge of the escarpment overlooking Lake Manyara, about three km along the same turn-off on which the Starehe Bar stands. It's part of the Tanzania Tourist Corporation chain and costs US$67/74 a single/double including breakfast, plus 22.5% taxes and service charge. From Easter Monday to 30 June there's a 50% discount on these prices. The hotel has flower gardens, a swimming pool and a curio shop.

NGORONGORO CONSERVATION AREA

There can be few people who have not heard, read or seen film or TV footage of this incredible 20 km wide volcanic crater with its 600 metre walls packed with just about every species of wildlife to be found in East Africa. The views from the crater rim are incredible and, although the wildlife might not look too impressive from up there, when you get to the bottom you'll very quickly change your mind. It's been compared to Noah's Ark and the Garden of Eden and though this is a little fanciful, it might have been about right at the turn of the century before wildlife in East Africa was decimated by the 'great White hunters' armed with the latest guns and a total lack of respect and foresight. It doesn't quite come up to expectations these days but you definitely see lion, elephant, rhino, buffalo and many of the plains herbivores such as wildebeest, Thomson's gazelle, zebra and reedbuck as well as thousands of flamingoes wading in the shallows of Lake Magadi – the soda lake on the floor of the crater.

Despite the steep walls of the crater,

there's a considerable movement of animals in and out – mostly to the Serengeti since the land between the crater and Lake Manyara is intensively farmed. Yet it remains a favoured spot for wildlife since there's permanent water and pasture on the crater floor. The animals don't have the crater entirely to themselves. Local Maasai tribespeople have grazing rights and you may well come across some of them tending their cattle. In the days when Tanzania was a German colony there was also a settler's farm there but that has long since gone.

You can visit Ngorongoro at any time of year but during the months of April and May it can be extremely wet and the roads extremely difficult to negotiate. Access to the crater floor may be restricted at this time too.

History

Ngorongoro and the other nearby craters and volcanoes are fairly recent additions to the landscape, geologically speaking. Though there has been a considerable amount of volcanic activity in the area for about 15 million years, Ngorongoro is thought to date back only 2½ million years and may at one time have rivalled Mt Kilimanjaro in size. Its vents filled with solid rock, however, and the molten material was forced elsewhere. As the lava subsided, circular fractures developed and the cone collapsed inwards to form the caldera. Nevertheless, minor volcanic activity continued as lava found cracks on the caldera floor and in the flanks of the mountain, creating small cones and hillocks which you can see on the floor of the crater today.

Only in the 1930s was a road constructed through Ngorongoro and a lodge built on the rim, but even before WW II the crater had acquired international fame as a wildlife area. In 1951 it was included in the newly created Serengeti National Park. It was hived off five years later due to conflict between the park authorities and the local Maasai who felt that being excluded from the Serengeti was bad enough but that to have their grazing rights to Ngorongoro also withdrawn was going too far. As a result it became a conservation area for the benefit of pastoralists and wildlife alike. In recognition of its importance and beauty it was declared a World Heritage site in 1978.

Places to Stay & Eat

On the crater rim there is a choice of four places to stay and a camp site. The cheapest place is the *Usiwara Guest House* (often known as the Drivers' Lodge) where you can get a bed for TSh 200, but only one sheet is provided and there are no blankets so you need a sleeping bag. You'll also need a padlock. The guest house is near the post office in Crater Village. You can buy cheap, simple food here. Otherwise you can eat at the *Ushirika Co-op Restaurant* which also offers good, cheap food.

Of the three lodges, the *Rhino Lodge* is the first one you come to, off to the left. Tariffs, including breakfast, are US$32/48/61 a single/double/triple, plus a 5% service charge. Tanzanian residents pay TSh 3100/5200/6000 respectively. There's a 50% discount between 1 April and 30 June. Good meals are available for US$6 (breakfast) and US$10 (lunch or dinner). It's on a beautiful site but is somewhat out of the way and doesn't overlook the crater. You might be able to camp here if you have a tent. Bookings can be made in Arusha at the Ngorongoro Conservation Area Authority (tel 3339, 3466), PO Box 776. Its office is by the roundabout at the junction of Makongoro and Ngoliondoi roads.

Next is the *Ngorongoro Crater Lodge* (tel Arusha 3530, 3303), an old rustic lodge built in 1937 and overlooking the crater. It has many detached cabins all with a bath and toilet. It's a very pleasant place to stay and is managed by Abercrombie & Kent (tel 7803, 3181), PO Box 427, Sokoine Rd, Arusha, through whom you can book. B&B costs US$56/70/95 a single/double/triple, plus 22.5% taxes and service charge. Tanzanian residents pay TSh 4000/6000/7000 respectively. There's a 50% discount between Easter Monday and 30 June. Meal prices are

US$6 (breakfast), US$12 (lunch) and US$15 (dinner), plus 10% tax. Picnic lunches can be arranged for US$7. The rooms are very clean, provided with towels, soap and toilet paper and have a gas fire and nonstop hot water (gas heated). Early morning tea is delivered to your door at 6.30 am. The bar, which is stuffed with hunting trophies from the old days, is a good place to meet people in the evening and, whenever it's cold, there is a roaring log fire.

The *Ngorongoro Wildlife Lodge* (tel Arusha 3300, 3114), between the Rhino Lodge and the Crater Lodge, is a very modern building set right on the edge of the crater rim and with superb views. All rooms are centrally heated, have a bath and toilet and face the crater. It's owned by the Tanzania Tourist Corporation. B&B rates are US$67/74 a single/double, plus 22.5% taxes and service charge. There is a 50% discount between Easter Monday and 30 June. Meals are excellent and you can pay for these in local currency. The bar is a good place to meet people and, like the one at the Crater Lodge, has a log fire. Bookings can be made at the TTC office on Sokoine Rd in Arusha.

Most campers stay at the *Simba* site on the crater rim, about two km from Crater Village. The site is guarded and costs US$10 per person and has hot showers, toilets and firewood. There is also a *camp site* down in the crater but there are no facilities and you need a ranger with you to stay there. It costs US$40 per person. There's a general store at Crater Village but it only has a limited range of foodstuffs so bring supplies with you from Arusha or eat at the lodges.

At Karatu (dubbed Safari Junction by just about everyone), about halfway between Lake Manyara and Ngorongoro, is *Gibb's Farm* which is managed by Abercrombie & Kent (for address and telephone number see Crater Lodge). According to everyone who has stayed here it offers the best accommodation and meals to be found in the whole country. Accommodation and meal rates are exactly the same as for the Crater Lodge. The farm is signposted on the main road into Karatu coming from Lake Manyara.

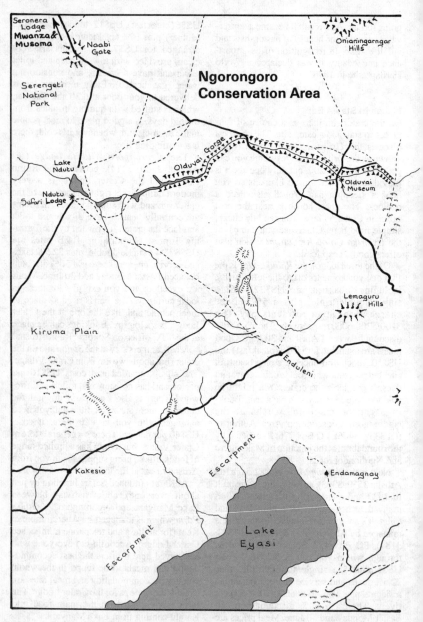

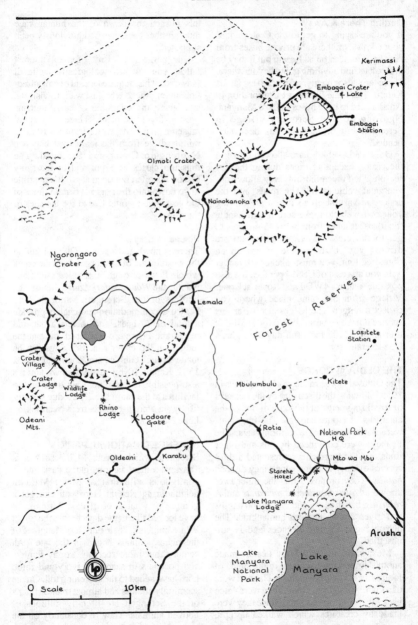

Getting There & Away

If you are trying to get to the Crater under your own steam there are private buses from Arusha at least as far as Karatu but it may be difficult to find anything going beyond there. There are also plenty of trucks as far as Karatu. The State Transport Corporation in Arusha used to have buses to Lake Manyara, Ngorongoro and Seronera village in Serengeti but the service has been suspended.

Only 4WD vehicles are allowed down in the crater, except at times during the dry season when the authorities *may* allow conventional vehicles in. The roads into the crater are very steep so if you are driving your own vehicle make sure it will handle the roads. It takes from 30 to 45 minutes to get to the crater floor. Whether you are driving your own vehicle or are on an organised tour, you must take a park ranger with you at a cost of US$15 per day. It's also possible to hire a 4WD Land Rover at Crater Village from the same place where you collect a ranger. The lodges also offer this service but they charge US$70 for a half-day tour and US$100 for a full-day tour, plus a US$15 crater service fee.

THE OLDUVAI GORGE

The Olduvai Gorge made world headlines in 1959 following the discovery by the Leakeys of fossil fragments of the skull of one of the ancestors of Homo sapiens. The fragments were dated back to 1.8 million years. The Leakeys were convinced by this and other finds that the fragments represented a third species of early humans which they dubbed *habilis*. They proposed that the other two, known as *Australopithecus africanus* and *A robustus*, had died out and that Homo habilis had given rise to modern humankind. The debate raged for two decades and is still unsettled.

Meanwhile, in 1979 Mary Leakey made another important discovery in the shape of footprints at Laetoli which she claimed were of a man, woman and child. They were dated back to 3.5 million years and, since they were made by creatures which walked upright, this pushed the dawn of the human race much further back than had previously been supposed.

The gorge itself isn't of great interest unless you are archaeologically inclined. However, it has acquired a kind of cult attraction among those who just want to visit the site where the evolution of early humans presumably took place. There is a small museum on the site, which is only a 10 to 15 minute drive from the main road between Ngorongoro Crater and Serengeti. The museum closes at 3 pm and in the rainy season it's often not open at all. It's possible to go down into the gorge at certain times of the year if you would like to see the sites of the digs.

Places to Stay

There is nowhere to stay at Olduvai but, at the western end of the gorge where the creek which flows through it empties into Lake Ndutu, the *Ndutu Safari Lodge* sits on the borders of the Serengeti National Park. Tented accommodation and chalets provide a total of 70 beds, and there's a bar and restaurant. Prices are similar to those at the lodges on the crater rim. Bookings can be made through Gibb's Farm Touring, PO Box 1501, Karatu. If you have your own tent it's also possible to camp here but there are no facilities at the camp site. The lodge is beautifully set amongst acacia trees overlooking Lake Ndutu.

SERENGETI NATIONAL PARK

Serengeti, which covers 14,763 sq km, is Tanzania's most famous game park and is contiguous with that of Masai Mara in neighbouring Kenya. Here you can get a glimpse of what a lot of East Africa must have looked like in the days before the 'great White hunters'. Their brainless slaughter of the plains animals began in the late 19th century, but more recently trophy hunters and poachers in search of ivory and rhino horn have added to the sickening toll. On the seemingly endless and almost treeless plains of the Serengeti are literally millions of hooved animals. They're constantly on the move in search of pasture and are watched and pursued by the predators which feed off them. It's one of the most incredible sights you will ever see and the numbers are simply mind boggling.

Nowhere else will you see wildebeest, gazelle, zebra and antelope in such concentrations. The wildebeest, of which there are up to two million in total, is the chief herbivore of the Serengeti and also the main prey of the large carnivores such as lion and hyaena. The wildebeest are well known for the annual migration which they undertake – a trek with many hazards not least of which is the crossing of large rivers which can leave hundreds drowned, maimed or taken by crocodile. During the rainy season the herds are widely scattered over the eastern section of the Serengeti and the Masai Mara in the north. These areas have few large rivers and streams and quickly dry out when the rains cease. When that happens the wildebeest concentrate on the few remaining green areas and gradually form huge herds which move off west in search of better pasture. At about the time when the migration starts the annual rut also begins. For a few days at a time while the herds pause, bulls establish territories which they defend against rivals and, meanwhile, try to assemble as many females as they can with which they mate. As soon as the migration resumes the female herds merge again.

The dry season is spent in the western parts of the Serengeti, at the end of which the herds move back east in anticipation of the rains. Calving begins at the start of the rainy season, but if it arrives late anything up to 80% of the new calves may die due to lack of food.

Serengeti is also famous for its lions, many of which have collars fitted with transmitters so that their movements can be studied and their location known. It's also famous for cheetah. If you want to give yourself the chance of being in on a 'kill', however, then you are going to need a pair of binoculars. Distances are so great in this park that you'll probably miss them unless they occur close to the road.

The main route from Ngorongoro to Seronera village is a good gravel road which is well maintained with the occasional kopje to one side or another. Kopjes are slight rises strewn with huge, smooth, granite boulders which generally support a few trees and are often the lookouts of cheetah. You'll see plenty of Maasai herding cattle all the way from Ngorongoro as far as the Olduvai Gorge. A census taken in 1978 put the populations of the largest mammals in the Serengeti at:

wildebeest	1,500,000
Grant's & Thomson's gazelle	1,000,000
zebra	200,000
impala	75,000
buffalo	74,000
topi	65,000
eland	18,000
giraffe	9000
elephant	5000
hyena	4000
lion	3000
cheetah	500
rhino	100

There hasn't been too much change in the numbers since then except for rhino and elephant which have suffered badly from poaching. The hard pressed but enthusiastic rangers can do little about poaching given the extremely limited resources provided them by the government. The animals are also very easy to see as the Serengeti is substantially flat grassland with bushes and trees only in clumps, particularly along river banks.

Places to Stay & Eat

Most budget travellers stay at the *camp site* (US$10 per person) close to the lodge near Seronera village. Basic meals are available in the village but the quality of the food is poor.

There are three other *public camp sites* close by and others at Nabi Hill, Kirawira and Lobo (all of which cost US$10 per person) plus some so-called *special camp sites* at Seronera, Ndutu, Nabi Hill, Hembe

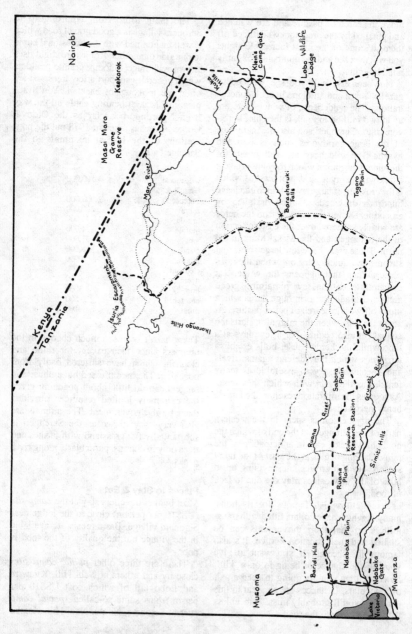

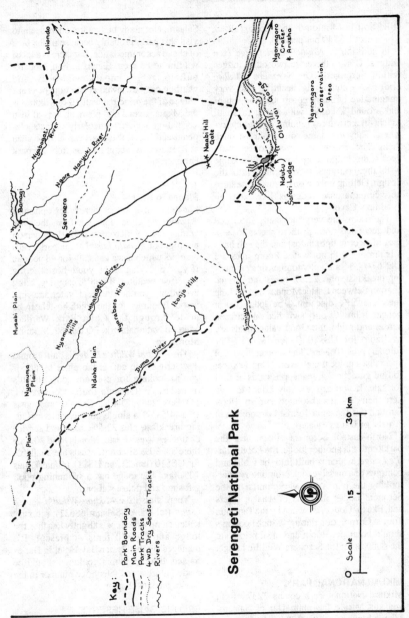

Serengeti National Park

Key:
- — — Park Boundary
- ——— Main Roads
- - - - Park Tracks
- .... 4WD Dry Season Tracks
- —— Rivers

Scale
0   15   30 km

Hill, Soit-la-Montonyi and Lobo (all of which cost US$40 per person).

In addition to *Ndutu Safari Lodge* (see Olduvai Gorge) there are two other lodges within Serengeti. The *Seronera Wildlife Lodge* is a stunningly beautiful and very imaginative building constructed on top of and around a kopje, with hyrax (a small rodent-like creature) running around everywhere. They're so tame you can almost touch them. The enormous bar and observation deck at this lodge is right on top of the kopje with the boulders incorporated into the design. Getting up to it on narrow stone steps between massive rocks is like entering Aladdin's Cave!

The rooms are very pleasantly furnished and decorated (though there seems to be a lack of electric light bulbs) and they all have a bathroom with hot water. Room rates are US$67/74/84 a single/double/triple including breakfast, plus 22.5% taxes and service charge. Between Easter Monday and 30 June there's a 50% discount. The lodge has a generator but it's only switched on between sunset and midnight. Good value meals are available for US$10 (lunch) and US$11 (dinner) plus 10% tax. The shop at the lodge specialises in local craft work. Don't expect to find guidebooks, maps, postcards or film for sale. If you can possibly afford to stay here then do – it's absolutely superb! Book through the Tanzania Tourist Corporation in Arusha or Dar es Salaam.

North-east of Seronera village near the park border is another lodge, the *Lobo Wildlife Lodge*, which is built into the faults and contours of a massive rock promontory overlooking the plains. It's very similar to the Seronera Lodge in terms of what it offers and, like that lodge, is owned by the Tanzania Tourist Corporation through which bookings should be made. Room and meal prices are the same as for the Seronera Wildlife Lodge.

MIKUMI NATIONAL PARK

Mikumi National Park covers 3237 sq km and sits astride the main Dar es Salaam-Mbeya highway, about 300 km from Dar es Salaam. Not many budget travellers seem to visit this park, probably because of the lack of cheap accommodation, but there is a lot of wildlife to be seen. Elephant, lion, leopard, buffalo, zebra, impala, wildebeest and warthog can be viewed at any time of year.

One of the principal features of Mikumi is the Mkata River flood plain, an area of lush vegetation which particularly attracts elephant and buffalo. Hippos can also be seen at Hippo Pools, about five km from the park entrance gate.

Places to Stay

For those on a budget there is the option of a *camp site* about four km from the park entrance gate which costs US$10 per person per night or a *youth hostel* at the park headquarters which has a capacity for 48 people. If you're staying at the youth hostel, bring your own bedding. If you're camping, bring everything you need except water and firewood. Bookings for the youth hostel can be made through the Chief Park Warden, Mikumi National Park, PO Box 62, Mikumi, Morogoro.

The *Mikumi Wildlife Lodge* is built around a watering hole and is the place to stay if you're looking for creature comforts. It's owned by the Tanzania Tourist Corporation, PO Box 2485, Dar es Salaam, and costs US$44/53/63 a single/double/triple including breakfast, plus 22.5% taxes and service charge. Between Easter Monday and 30 June there's a 50% discount. Meals are available for US$10 (lunch) and US$11 (dinner), plus 10% tax. The lodge has a swimming pool, gift shop and petrol station.

There's also the *Mikumi Wildlife Tented Camp* (tel Dar es Salaam 68631), a luxury tented camp which costs slightly less than the lodge and has 10 tents at present. It's managed by the Oyster Bay Hotel in Dar es Salaam through which bookings should be made (address and telephone number in the Dar es Salaam chapter).

SELOUS GAME RESERVE

The little visited, 54,600 sq km Selous is

probably the world's largest game reserve. It's the quintessential East African wilderness. Wild and largely untouched by people, it is said to contain the world's largest concentration of elephant, buffalo, crocodile, hippo and wild dog as well as plenty of lion, rhino, antelope and thousands of dazzling bird species. Poaching probably makes the estimates at wildlife populations over optimistic, but there are supposedly about 100,000 elephant in this reserve and there is a good chance of seeing a herd several hundred strong.

Established in 1922, for many years it remained largely the preserve of the trophy collectors and big game hunters, even though only the northern tip of the reserve has ever been adequately explored. Most of it is trackless wilderness and it is almost impossible to traverse during the rainy season when floods and swollen rivers block access. The best time to visit is from July to March. In any case, the lodges and camp sites are closed from April to June.

One of the main features of the reserve is the huge Rufiji River which has the largest water catchment area in East Africa. Massive amounts of silt are dumped annually during the wet season into the Indian Ocean opposite Mafia Island. For the rest of the year, when the floods subside and the water level in the river drops, extensive banks of shimmering white and golden sand are exposed.

In the northern end of the reserve, where the Great Ruaha River flows into the Rufiji, is Stiegler's Gorge, probably the best known feature of the park. On average it's 100 metres deep and 100 metres wide. A cable car spans the gorge for those who are game enough to go across. It's in the area where most of the safari camps and the lodges are. The gorge is named after the German explorer of the same name who was killed here by an elephant in 1907.

The Selous is one of the few national parks which you are allowed to explore on foot. Walking safaris are conducted by all four camps in the reserve. Boat trips up the Rufiji River are also offered by two of the camps (Rufiji River and Mbuyu Safari Camps) and

they're a very popular way of exploring the area.

Places to Stay

All park facilities are concentrated in the extreme northern end and consist of four lodges and luxury tented camps. There are no budget facilities available, including camp sites.

At the north-eastern tip of the park is the *Rufiji River Camp*, built on a high bank overlooking the Rufiji River and the plain beyond. It has 10 double tents, each with twin beds, and there are toilets and showers close by. There's also a dining room and bar as well as three boats and three Land Rovers which can be hired for safaris. Accommodation with full board and including the entry fee is US$60 per person per day (Tanzanian residents TSh 8500). Land Rover hire costs US$20 per person (Tanzanian residents TSh 2500) for each half day. Sport fishing facilities are also available. The camp is operated by Tanzania Safari Tours Ltd (tel 64177, 63546), PO Box 20058, Dar es Salaam, through which bookings should be made. Their office is on Pugu Rd, diagonally opposite the TAZARA Railway Station, and is open Monday to Friday from 8 am to 5 pm. The camp is closed during April and May (the main rainy season).

We've had a few negative reports about this place, particularly about overbooking, poor food and the inhospitable attitude of the owners, Karl and his son Igor, so don't say you were not warned.

About 30 km from the Rufiji River Camp is *Mbuyu Safari Camp* which is also built on a high bank overlooking the Rufiji River. This camp provides luxury tented accommodation with electric lights and sisal mats and the tents are sheltered from the sun by makuti roofs. Each tent has a shower, flush toilet, twin beds, mosquito netting and a verandah. Set amongst baobab trees, there's a dining room, lounge, bar and reception area. Land Rovers are available for safaris and boats are available for river trips or you can arrange a walking safari. Fishing gear can also be hired. The camp is owned by Bushtrekker hired. The camp is owned by Bushtrekker Safaris/Hotel & Tours Management Ltd (tel 31957/32671), PO Box 5350, Dar es Salaam, through which bookings should be made. There's an airstrip near to the camp.

About 40 km from the Mbuyu Camp but north of the Rufiji River is the *Selous Safari Camp* where accommodation is provided in separate units each with a shower, toilet and hand basin. The central unit contains the dining room, bar and lounge facilities.

Lastly, there is the *Stiegler's Gorge Safari Camp* which was built in 1977 for Norwegian scientists and engineers who were working in the area. The camp consists of separate, comfortable cabins each with a bathroom and hot showers, toilets and wardrobe. The reception, lounge, dining area and bar are housed in a central unit with a verandah on one side affording panoramic views of the countryside and adjacent watering hole. There's an airstrip close to the camp. Bookings can be made through Gorge Tours & Safaris Ltd (tel 21012), 30 India St, PO Box 348, Dar es Salaam.

Getting There & Away

Hitching to Selous Game Reserve is virtually out of the question. To get there you'll need to join an organised safari, have your own vehicle or go by train and arrange to have a lodge pick you up.

There are three ways to get to the Selous. The easiest but most expensive is to fly in by chartered light aircraft. All the camps have an airstrip.

Those going in by train should take the TAZARA line as far as Fuga Railway Station. From Fuga, the lodges will collect you in one of their vehicles but you must make arrangements for this before you leave Dar es Salaam. Being collected won't be cheap unless you're sharing the cost with others.

Those coming by road in their own vehicle have two options. The first is to the take the Dar es Salaam-Kibiti-Mkongo road to either the Rufiji River Camp or Mbuyu Safari Camp. The road is sealed as far as Kibiti after which it's a rough track. The last petrol station is in Kibiti and the distance from Dar es Salaam is about 250 km. The other way is to take the Dar es Salaam-Morogoro-Matombo-Kisaki road to the north and then on to Stiegler's Gorge Camp.

The companies which own the camps can arrange road transport for you if you don't have a vehicle, but it's an expensive option.

RUAHA NATIONAL PARK

Ruaha National Park was created in 1964 from half of the Rungwa Game Reserve. It covers 13,000 sq km. Like the Selous, it's a wild, undeveloped area and access is difficult, but there's a lot of wildlife here as a result. Elephant, kudu, roan and sable antelope, hippo and crocodile are particularly numerous. The Great Ruaha River, which forms the eastern boundary of the park, has spectacular gorges, though a lot of the rest of the park is undulating plateau averaging 1000 metres in height with occasional rocky outcrops.

Visiting the park is only feasible in the dry season from June to December. During the rest of the year the tracks are virtually impassable. Between February and June the grass is long, restricting game viewing.

If you're interested in helping this park to expand facilities, control poaching and fire risk and provide suitable equipment to undertake everyday maintenance, then contact the Friends of Ruaha Society (tel 20522, 26537, 37561), PO Box 60, Mufindi, or PO Box 786, Dar es Salaam. These people are doing an excellent job to help the chief park warden and his staff of 50 rangers to conserve the fauna and flora of this park (there's one ranger for every 260 sq km).

Places to Stay

Camping is permitted around the park headquarters at Msembe and at various other sites for the usual fee of US$10 per person per night. Also at the park headquarters is a permanent camp consisting of rondavels equipped with beds. Most of the essential equipment is provided but you must bring your own food and drink. This is also essenin the vicinity so bring supplies from Iringa, the nearest town. Bookings for the rondavels can be made through The Park Warden, Ruaha National Park, PO Box 369, Iringa.

The nicest place to stay if you have the money is *Ruaha River Camp* which is constructed on and around a rocky kopje overlooking the Great Ruaha River. It consists of a number of beautiful bandas which blend into their surroundings and a central dining and bar area (in the same style) on an elevated position from which there are spectacular views. The food is excellent and the owner, Chris Fox, is very gracious and helpful, as are all the staff. A double banda with full board costs US$50. It's excellent value and highly recommended. Make prior arrangements to hire 4WD vehicles or to make camp excursions to other parts of the park. Reservations should be made through Foxtreks Ltd, PO Box 84, Mufindi.

Getting There & Away
There is a good all-weather road from Iringa to the park headquarters via Mloa (112 km) which involves crossing the Ruaha River by ferry at Ibuguziwa, which is within the park. The drive should take about four hours. Hitching isn't really feasible, so you'll need to have your own vehicle or go on an organised safari.

GOMBE STREAM NATIONAL PARK
Primarily a chimpanzee sanctuary, this tiny park covering 52 sq km on the shores of Lake Tanganyika between Kigoma and the Burundi border stretches between the lake shore and the escarpment a little further inland. In recent years it has become very popular with travellers going north to or coming south from Burundi. It's well worth the effort to get here and the journey by lake taxi makes an interesting alternative to the MV *Liemba*.

The park is the site of Jane Goodall's research station which was set up in 1960. It's a beautiful place and the chimps are great fun. A group of them usually come down to the research station every day but if they

don't the rangers generally know where to find them. You must have a guide whenever you are away from the park headquarters at Kasekela on the lake shore. The guides are mellow, interesting people and you can share the fee of US$10 between however many people are with you.

Entry to the park costs US$50 per person for each 24 hour period (US$15 for children between the ages of three and 16).

Places to Stay
Camping is only permitted with special permission so, for most travellers, that means staying at the *'hostel'* which consists essentially of caged huts, each with six beds and a table and chairs. They're caged to keep the baboons out. A bed costs US$10 per night.

Bring all your own food, though eggs and fish are sometimes available at the station. If you run out of food you can get more at Mwamgongo village, about 10 km north of here on the northern extremity of the park. The village has a market twice a week (enquire at the station as to the days). Be careful when walking between the cookhouse and the huts at the station especially if you are carrying food. Baboons have jumped on quite a few people and robbed them of food. The hostel has a well-stocked library.

Getting There & Away
There are no roads to Gombe Stream so the only way in is to take one of the lake taxis – small, motorised wooden boats which service the lakeshore villages all the way from Kigoma to the Burundi border.

From Kigoma, the lake taxis leave from the small village of Kalalangabo, about three km north of town, usually between 9 and 10 am. The trips to Gombe Stream and from there to Kagunga (the last village in Tanzania) take about three hours each and the fare is TSh 250 per person for each leg of the journey. These boats are not totally reliable and do not operate on Sundays. When catching a lake taxi, if you have any choice try to get one with a cover as it gets stinking hot out on the lake in the middle of the day. The boats are often overcrowded not only with people but their produce and they offer no creature comforts whatsoever. They're good fun when the weather is fine but if there's a squall on the lake then you may be in for a rough time.

Since the boats don't operate on Sunday it's important not to arrive on a Saturday, otherwise you'll be up for two days park entry fees (US$100) and hostel fees (US$20).

MAHALE MOUNTAINS NATIONAL PARK

This national park, like Gombe Stream, is mainly a chimpanzee sanctuary but you won't find it marked on most maps since it was only created in mid-1985. It's on the knuckle-shaped area of land which protrudes into Lake Tanganyika about halfway down the lake opposite the Zaïrois port of Kalemie. The highest peak in the park, Nkungwe, at 2460 metres ensures that moist air blowing in from the lake condenses there and falls as rain. This rain supports extensive montane forests, grasslands and alpine bamboo. Numerous valleys intersect the mountains and some of these have permanent streams which flow into the lake. The eastern side of the mountains are considerably drier and support what is known as miombo woodlands. It's a very isolated area.

The animals which live in this park show closer affinities with western rather than eastern Africa. They include chimpanzee, brush-tailed porcupine, various species of colobus monkey including the Angolan black-and-white colobus, guinea fowl and mongoose. Scientists, mainly from Japan, have been studying the chimpanzees for 20 years during which time more than 100 of the animals have been habituated to human contact. The population has dramatically increased since 1975 when local people were moved to villages outside the park, thus putting a stop to poaching and field burning activities. This relocation has also led to the reappearance of leopard, lion and buffalo which were never or very rarely seen in the past.

Unlike other national parks in Tanzania, this is one which you can walk around – there are no roads in any case. Very few tourists come here because of the remoteness of the area but it's well worth it if you have the time and initiative.

The best time to visit is between May and October.

Places to Stay

Camping is allowed in specific areas if you have equipment (otherwise there may be a limited amount for hire). Camping fees are US$10 per person per day. There's also a *guest house* at Kasiha village, though the facilities are still very limited. Bring all your food requirements from Kigoma since meals are not available. It's a good idea to check with the park headquarters in Kigoma about current conditions, transport and accommodation before setting off.

Getting There & Away

The only way to get to the park is by lake steamer from Kigoma using either the MV *Liemba* or the MV *Mwongozo*. You have to get off at Lagosa (otherwise known as Mugambo), usually in the middle of the night, and take a small boat to the shore. From Lagosa you have to charter a small boat from the local fishers or merchants to go to Kasoge which should take about three hours. For the MV *Liemba* schedule, see the To/From Burundi section in the Getting There chapter. For the MV *Mwongozo* schedule, enquire in Kigoma.

Because you will be reliant on the lake steamers for getting into and out of Mahale, you may have to stay there for a whole week. This is obviously going to be expensive in terms of park entry fees and camping fees, so you need to think seriously about this before you go. It also means you'll have to bring food with you from Kigoma sufficient to last a week.

Index

554 Index

Dear traveller

Prices go up, good places go bad, bad places go bankrupt...and every guidebook is inevitably outdated in places. Fortunately, many travellers write to us about their experiences, telling us when things have changed. If we reprint a book between editions, we try to include as much of this information as possible in a Stop Press section. Most of this information has not been verified by our own writers.

We really enjoy hearing from people out on the road, and apart from guaranteeing that others will benefit from your good and bad experiences, we're prepared to bribe you with the offer of a free book for sending us substantial useful information.

Thank you to everyone who has written and, to those who haven't, I hope you do find this book useful – and that you let us know when it isn't.

Tony Wheeler

The struggle for democracy in East Africa is most evident in Kenya, but the country still has a long way to go. We keep receiving complaints from many travellers about safari companies. All we can suggest is that you follow the instructions laid out in this guide. The northern parts of Uganda and Kenya have had an increase in Sudanese refugees, and as a result are not as safe as they use to be.

The information in Stop Press was compiled from letters sent to us by the following travellers: Patrick Frewe (UK), Petrie Hottola (Fin), Jane Kahler (AUS), Herman van der Kuil (NL), Juliet Lesser (UK) & Mike Osborn (UK).

KENYA
Money & Costs
The official exchange rate is US$1 to KSh 29.05 A traveller reported that currency declaration forms are no longer needed in Kenya.

Most hotels don't as yet include the current 18% VAT which was declared on 1 January 1992

UGANDA
The border between Uganda and Rwanda is closed at the moment, because of the rebel activity in Rwanda.

Visas
British nationals now require a visa. This costs UK£20 in Nairobi, you'll require two black and white passport-sized photos and it takes 24 hours. At the land border you can get a visa for US$20.

Money & Coasts
Apparently, the black market doesn't exist anymore. All travellers should change money before they leave Kampala and only at Forex Bureaux. Banks give low rates. Once out of Kampala there are no Forex Bureaux and bank rates are even lower than in Kampala (as are the rates at hotels, shops and petrol stations). At the border town of Malaba, there is a bank with very good exchange rates. This bank will change Ugandan currency back to US dollars. They will not change Kenyan shillings. The official exchange rate is US$1 to USh 992.36.

TANZANIA
There is a new passenger ferry the *Canadian Spirit* plying the route from Mombasa (Kenya) to Zanzibar. It leaves at 10 pm on Monday evenings only, and arrives at about 1 pm the following day in Zanzibar. It stops in Pemba en route at around 7.30 am.

UTC Travel at Diamond Trust Building, near the Castle Hotel (one block away, same side), Moi Ave, seem to be the main agents. The cost is US$20 in 3rd class, US$25 in 2nd class and US$30 in 1st class.

Safari Guide

Safari Guide

ANTELOPES

The large, striped bongo antelope is rarely seen. About your only chance of sighting one is in Aberdare National Park. They live close to water in dense forest, only leaving the forest cover to graze at night in open clearings.

The bongo stands around 120 cm high at the shoulder and measures around 250 cm from head to tail. Mature males are a beautiful dark mahogany-brown colour, while the females are a much lighter reddish-brown. Both sexes have distinctive vertical white stripes on the body, never less than nine, never more than 14. Horns are sported by both males and females, and these are slightly spiralling with yellow tips, with those on the male being slightly shorter and sturdier than on the female.

The bongo grazes mainly on leaves and will often stand on its hind legs to increase its reach. It also digs for roots with its horns. They are usually found in small family herds although bulls often lead a solitary existence, meeting up with other animals only to mate.

Bongo

Scientific name: *Tragelaphus eurycerus*
Swahili name: *Bongo*

Although the small bushbuck antelope exists in fairly large numbers in most of Kenya's game parks, it is a shy solitary animal which is rarely sighted.

Standing at about 80 cm at the shoulder, the bushbuck is chestnut to dark brown in colour with a variable number of white vertical stripes on the body between the neck and rump, as well as (usually) two horizontal white stripes lower down which give the animal a 'harnessed' appearance. There are also a number of white spots on the upper thigh and a white splash on the neck. Horns are usually only grown by males but females have been known to grow them on rare occasions. They are straight with gentle spirals and average about 30 cm.

Bushbuck are rarely found in groups of more than two and prefer to stick to areas with heavy brush cover. When startled they take off and crash loudly through the undergrowth. They are nocturnal animals and browsers yet rarely move far from their chosen spot. Though shy and elusive they can be aggressive and dangerous when cornered. Their main predators are leopard and python.

Bushbuck

Scientific name: *Tragelaphus scriptus*
Swahili name: *Pongo*

Dik-dik

Full name: *Kirk's dik-dik*
Scientific name: *Rhynchotragus kirki*
Swahili name: *Dik-dik*

Kirk's dik-dik is the more common of the two dik-diks found in Kenya (the other is Gunther's dik-dik, found only in Marsabit National Reserve) and is commonly seen in Nairobi, Tsavo, Amboseli and Masai Mara reserves. Its name comes from the 'zic-zic' call it makes when alarmed.

The dik-dik is a tiny antelope, standing only around 35 cm at the shoulder. It is a reddish-brown colour on the back, with lighter flanks and white belly. Size is usually the easiest way to identify a dik-dik, but other telltale marks are the almost total lack of a tail and the tuft of dark hair on the forehead. Horns (found on the males only) are so short (around six cm) that they are often lost in the hair tuft.

Dik-diks are usually seen singly or in pairs and are often found in exceedingly dry places – it seems they don't have a great dependence on water. They are territorial creatures, each pair occupying an area of around five hectares. They are mainly nocturnal but can be seen grazing in acacia scrub in the early morning and late afternoon; like so many animals they rest in the heat of the day.

The females bear a single offspring twice a year. After six months the young dik-dik reaches sexual maturity and is then driven out of the home territory.

Duiker

Full name: *Grey (or common) duiker*
Scientific name: *Sylvicapra grimmia*
Swahili name: *Nsya*

This is the most common of the duikers, of which there are at least 10 species. Even so, they are not often sighted as they are largely nocturnal, usually only live in pairs and prefer areas with good scrub cover. They are known to exist in Marsabit, Tsavo, Nairobi, Amboseli, Meru and Masai Mara reserves.

The duiker stands only 60 cm at the shoulder, is a greyish light-brown colour with white belly and a dark brown vertical stripe on the face. The horns (males only) are very short (around 20 cm), pointed, and grow straight.

Duikers are widely distributed and can be found in a variety of habitats ranging from open bush to semidesert and up to the snow line of the highest mountains except for bamboo forest and rain forest. This ability to survive in many different habitats explains their survival in cultivated areas where other species of herbivore have been exterminated.

They are almost exclusively browsers and only rarely eat grasses though they appear to supplement their diet with insects and guinea fowl chicks. They are capable of doing without water for long periods of time but will drink it when available.

The eland looks similar to some varieties of cattle seen on the Indian subcontinent, and is found in Nairobi, Marsabit, Tsavo and Masai Mara reserves.

The biggest of the antelopes, the eland stands about 170 cm at the shoulder and a mature bull can weigh up to 1000 kg. Horns are found on both sexes and these are spiralled at the base, swept straight back and grow to about 65 cm. Males have a much hairier head than the females, and their horns are stouter and slightly shorter. They are a light greyish-brown in colour, and bear as many as 15 vertical white stripes on the body, although these are often almost indistinguishable on some animals.

The eland prefers savannah scrub to wide open spaces, but also avoids thick forest. They graze on grass and tree foliage in the early morning and late afternoon, and are also active on moonlit nights. They need to drink once a day, but can go for a month or more without water if diet includes fodder with high water content.

Eland are usually found in groups of around six to 12, but there may be as many as 50 in a herd. A small herd normally consists of several females and one male, but in larger herds there may be several males, and there is a strict hierarchy. Females reach sexual maturity at around two years and can bear up to 12 calves in a lifetime. The young are born in October-November.

Eland

Scientific name: *Taurotragus oryx*
Swahili name: *Pofu*

The gerenuk is probably the easiest of all antelopes to identify because of its inordinately long neck, which accounts for its Swahili name, meaning gazelle-giraffe. Its distribution is limited to Meru, Samburu, Tsavo and Amboseli national parks.

Growing to around 100 cm at the shoulder, the gerenuk is a dark fawn colour on the back which becomes much lighter on the sides and belly. The horns (found on the male only) curve gently backward and grow up to 40 cm long.

The gerenuk's habitat ranges from dry thorn bush country to semidesert and its food consists mainly of the tender leaves and shoots of acacia bushes. It is quite capable – in the same way as goats – of standing on its hind legs and using one of its forelegs to pull down the higher branches of bushes to get at the leaves and shoots. Also like goats, they are quite capable of doing without water.

Gerenuk

Scientific name: *Litocranius walleri*
Swahili name: *Swala twiga*

Grant's Gazelle

Scientific name: *Gazella granti*
Swahili name: *Swala granti*

This is one of the most common antelopes and exists in large numbers in Nairobi, Amboseli, Masai Mara, Tsavo and Marsabit reserves.

Grant's gazelle are most easily identified by their colouring and long horns: sandy brown on the back, clearly demarcated from a lighter colour on the flanks and white belly, and white around the tail and hind legs. They are not a large gazelle, standing around 90 cm at the shoulder. Horns are found on both sexes and are heavily ridged with around 25 rings; in the male they grow to around 60 cm (although they often appear longer because of the relatively small body) and curve gracefully and evenly up and back, usually with some outward curving as well; in the female the horns are much shorter but follow the same pattern.

You usually come across herds of Grant's gazelle in open grassy country where there is some forest cover, although they are also occasionally found in heavily wooded savannah country. Herd size is usually between 20 and 30, with one dominant male, does and young. Food consists mainly of leaves and grass. As water is obtained through dietary intake these gazelles do not need to drink.

Greater Kudu

Scientific name: *Tragelaphus strepsiceros*
Swahili name: *Tandala mkubwa*

The greater kudu is one of the largest of the antelopes but it's a rare sight and only found in any numbers in Marsabit National Reserve. Elsewhere kudu prefer hilly country with fairly dense bush cover. The kudu stands around 1.5 metres at the shoulder and weighs up to 250 kg, yet it's a very elegant creature, light grey in colour, with broad ears and a long neck. The sides of the body are marked by six to 10 vertical white stripes and there is a white chevron between the eyes. Horns are carried only by the males and are both divergent and spiralling.

Kudu live in small herds of up to four or five females with their young but these often split up during the rainy season. The males are usually solitary though occasionally they band together into small herds.

They are mainly browsers and only seldom eat grasses but are capable of eating many types of leaves which would be poisonous to other animals.

Although somewhat clumsy animals when on the move, they are capable of clearing well over two metres when jumping.

The hartebeest is a medium sized antelope and is found in Nairobi, Tsavo, Amboseli and Masai Mara parks. It is easy to recognise as it has a long, narrow face and distinctively angular short horns (on both sexes) which are heavily ridged. Colouring is generally light brown on the back, becoming paler towards the rear and under the belly. The back slopes away from the humped shoulders. They prefer grassy plains for grazing but are also found in lightly treed savannah or hills.

The hartebeest feeds exclusively on grass, and usually drinks twice daily, although it can go for months without water if necessary.

They are social beasts and often intermingle with animals such as zebra and wildebeest. Their behaviour is not unlike the wildebeest's, particularly the head tossing and shaking.

Sexual maturity is reached at around 2½ years and calving goes on throughout the year, although there are peak periods in February and August. Predators are mainly the large cats, hyaenas and hunting dogs.

Hartebeest

Scientific name:	*Alcelphus buselaphus*
Swahili name:	*Kongoni*

The graceful impala is one of the most common antelopes and is found in virtually all national parks and reserves in large numbers.

A medium sized antelope, it stands about 80 cm at the shoulder. The coat is a glossy rufous colour though paler on the flanks with the underparts, rump, throat and chin being white. A narrow black line runs along the middle of the rump to about halfway down the tail and there's also a vertical black stripe on the back of the thighs but, unlike in Grant's gazelle, this does not border the white buttocks. It's also distinguishable from Grant's gazelle by having a tuft of long black hairs above the heels of the hind legs. Only the males have horns which are long (averaging 75 cm), lyre-shaped and curve upwards as they spread.

Impala are gregarious animals with each male having a 'harem' of up to 100 females, though more usually around 15 to 20. Males without such a 'harem' form bachelor groups. There is fierce fighting between males during the rutting season but otherwise they are fairly placid animals.

One of the most noticeable characteristics of impala is their speed and prodigious ability at jumping. They are quite capable of clearing 10 metres in a single jump lengthwise or three metres in height and this they frequently do even when there are no obstacles in their path.

Impala are both browsers and grazers and are active during the day and by night. They are quite highly dependent on water but are capable of existing on just dew for fairly long periods of time.

Their main predators are leopard, cheetah and wild dog.

Impala

Scientific name:	*Aepyceros melampus*
Swahili name:	*Swala pala*

Klipspringer

Scientific name: *Oreotragus*
oreotragus
Swahili name: *Mbuzi mawe*

The distinctive klipspringers inhabit rocky outcrops in Tsavo, Amboseli, Masai Mara, Marsabit and Meru reserves.

Standing about 50 cm at the shoulder, they are easily recognised by their curious 'tip-toe' stance (the hooves are designed for balance and grip on rocky surfaces) and the greenish tinge of their speckled coarse hair. Horns (found on the male only) are short (10 cm) and widely spaced.

Klipspringers are most often seen on rocky outcrops, or in the grassland in the immediate vicinity, and when alarmed they retreat into the rocks for safety. They are amazingly agile and sure-footed creatures and can often be observed bounding up impossibly rough rock faces. These antelope can also go entirely without water if there is none around, getting all they need from the greenery they eat. They are most active just before and after midday, and single males often keep watch from a good vantage point. The klipspringer are usually found in pairs, or a male with two females, and they inhabit a clearly defined territory.

Klipspringers reach sexual maturity at around one year, and females bear one calf twice a year. Calves may stay with the adult couple for up to a year, although young males usually seek their own territory earlier than that.

Predators are mainly the leopard and the crowned eagle, but also include jackals and baboons.

Lesser Kudu

Scientific name: *Tragelaphus*
imberbis
Swahili name: *Tandala ndogo*

The lesser kudu is a smaller model of the greater kudu, the major differences being the lack of a beard, more numerous and more pronounced vertical white stripes on the body, and two white patches on the underside of the neck. As with the greater kudu, only the males have horns. The coat colour varies from brownish grey to blue grey. It stands around a metre high at the shoulder.

These kudu usually live in pairs accompanied by their fawns though females occasionally form small herds. It's a very shy animal and spends much of the day hiding in dense bush, only moving out of cover to feed in the early morning and at dusk. This makes it difficult to spot.

Kudu are browsers and feed on a mixture of leaves, young shoots and twigs and, though they drink regularly if water is available, they are capable of doing without it for relatively long periods of time – more so than the greater kudu.

The most likely places you will find them are Tsavo and Marsabit where they prefer the drier, more bushy areas.

Not unlike a duiker in appearance, the small oribi is relatively uncommon, and your best chance of spotting one is in the Masai Mara reserve.

The oribi's most distinguishing mark, although you'll need binoculars to spot it, is a circular batch of naked black skin below the ear – it is actually a scent gland. Another useful indicator is the tuft of black hair on the tip of the short tail. Otherwise the oribi is a uniform golden brown with white on the belly and insides of the legs. Short straight horns about 10 cm in length are found in the males only.

Oribi usually graze in grassy plains with good shelter. If water is available they will drink willingly but can also go without entirely. When alarmed they bolt and then make bouncing jumps with a curious action – all four legs are kept completely stiff. It is thought this helps them to orient themselves in places with poor visibility. After 100 metres or so they stop and assess the danger.

The oribi are usually found in pairs and are territorial. Sexual maturity is reached at around one year, and the females bear one calf twice a year.

Being quite small, the oribi has many predators, including the larger cats.

Oribi

Scientific name: *Ourebia ourebi*
Swahili name: *Taya*

The oryx (or beisa) is a large reddish-grey antelope which is most commonly seen in the Marsabit National Reserve and along the Tana River. The related fringe-eared oryx *(oryx callotis)* is more widespread and can be seen in Amboseli and Tsavo national parks.

Oryx are large antelopes standing around 120 cm at the shoulder. The coat is a sandy fawn with a black stripe along the spine down to the tip of the tail. The underparts are white and separated from the lower flanks by another black stripe. There are also two black rings just above the knee of the forelegs. Both types of oryx have ovate, pointed ears with the main distinguishing feature being, as the name suggests, a tuft of black hairs on the ears of the fringe-eared one. Oryx are easy to distinguish from other antelopes due to their straight, very long and heavily ridged horns which are carried almost parallel. Both the males and females have horns. These horns come into their own when the animal is forced to defend itself. Held down between the forelegs, they are formidable weapons and used to impale an enemy.

Oryx are principally grazers but will also browse on thorny shrubs. They are capable of doing without water for long periods of time but will drink daily if it is available.

Herds vary from five to 40 individuals and sometimes more though the bulls are usually solitary. Oryx are often found in association with zebra and Grant's gazelle.

Oryx

Scientific name: *Oryx beisa*
Swahili name: *Choroa*

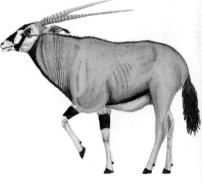

Reedbuck

Full name: *Bohor reedbuck*
Scientific name: *Redunca redunca*
Swahili name: *Tohe*

The best places to spot the dusty brown reedbuck is in Nairobi and Amboseli national parks, and they are occasionally seen in Tsavo National Park.

The reedbuck is a medium sized antelope, standing around 80 cm high at the shoulder. The most distinctive features are the forward curving horns (found on the males only) and the bushy tail. The underbelly, inside of the thighs, throat and underside of the tail are white.

The reedbuck frequent open grassy plains or hills and are never found more than around eight km from a water supply. They are very territorial and are found in small groups of up to 10 animals. The groups usually consist of an older male and accompanying females and young. Their diet consists almost exclusively of grass but does include some foliage.

At mating time males fight spiritedly. After reaching sexual maturity at around 1½ years, females bear one calf at a time.

The bohor reedbuck's main predators include the big cats, hyaena and hunting dog.

Roan Antelope

Scientific name: *Hippotragus equinus*
Swahili name: *Korongo*

The roan antelope is one of Kenya's less common species and the best place for seeing one these days is in the Shimba Hills National Reserve, where they have been translocated from other parts of the country, although there are still a few small herds in Masai Mara.

The third largest of the antelopes after eland and kudu at up to 150 cm at the shoulder, roan bear a striking resemblance to a horse – hence their name. The coat varies from reddish fawn to dark rufous with white underparts and there's a conspicuous mane of stiff, black-tipped hairs which stretches from the nape to the shoulders. Under the neck, there's another mane of sorts consisting of long dark hairs. The ears are long, narrow and pointed with a brown tassel at the tip. The face is a very distinctive black and white pattern. Both sexes have curving backswept horns which can measure up to 70 cm.

Roan are aggressive by nature and fight from a very early age – a characteristic which frequently deters predators. For most of the year they live in small herds of up to 20 and sometimes more, led by a master bull, but in the mating season, the bulls become solitary and take a female out of the herd. The pair stay together until the calf is born after which the females form a herd by themselves. They eventually return to their former herd. Herds congregate during the dry season.

Being principally grazers, roan rarely move far when food is plentiful but they are susceptible to drought and during such periods they may be constantly on the move.

Also found only in the Shimba Hills National Reserve, the sable antelope is slightly smaller than its cousin the roan, but is more solidly built. The colouring is dark brown to black, with white face markings and belly. Both sexes carry long back-swept horns which average around 80 cm, those of the male being longer and more curved.

The sable antelope is active mainly in the early morning and late afternoon, and is found in herds of up to 25 and sometimes more in the dry season. They are territorial and each group occupies a large area, although within this area individual males have demarcated territories of up to 30 hectares. Sables feed mainly off grass but leaves and foliage from trees account for around 10% of their diet.

Females start bearing calves at around three years of age, and the main calving times are January and September.

Like the roan, the sable is a fierce fighter and has been known to kill lions when attacked. Other predators include the leopard, hyaena and hunting dog.

The sitatunga is a swamp antelope with unusual elongated hooves which give it the ability to walk on marshy ground without sinking. It is restricted solely to the Saiwa Swamp National Park near Kitale, and it's well worth a visit to this small, walkers-only park.

Very similar to the bushbuck in appearance, except that the coat of the male is much darker and the hair of both sexes much longer and shaggier, the sitatunga stands something over one metre at the shoulder. The males have twisted horns up to 90 cm long. It is a fairly shy antelope and sightings are not all that common. A good swimmer, the sitatunga will often sub-merge itself almost completely when alarmed.

It feeds largely on papyrus and other reeds and is usually nocturnal though in places where it remains undisturbed it can be diurnal. Animals normally live singly or in pairs but sometimes come together in small herds numbering up to 15.

Sable Antelope
Scientific name: *Hippotragus niger*
Swahili name: *Pala hala*

Sitatunga
Scientific name: *Tragelaphus spekei*
Swahili name: *Nzohe*

Thomson's Gazelle

Scientific name: *Gazella thomsonii*
Swahili name: *Swala tomi*

The small and frisky Thomson's gazelle is instantly recognisable by the black slash across the side which separates the brown back from the white underbelly. They are very common in the plains country – Amboseli, Masai Mara and Nairobi reserves, but very rare in different habitats such as Tsavo National Park.

Standing around 60 cm at the shoulders, the 'Tommy' is one of the smaller antelopes. Horns on the male grow to about 30 cm and almost straight with just a gentle curve towards the tips; in the female the horns are straighter and much shorter. Another easy to identify characteristic is the short black tail which seems to be constantly twitching. Along with the oribi, Tommys also do the stiff legged bouncing jump when alarmed.

Group size varies: one old (largely territorial) male may be accompanied by anything from five to 50 females, or there may be herds of up to 500 young males without territory. When food is plentiful the herds tend to be smaller and more territorial. In times of drought herds of several thousand may gather and roam for food. They are often found in close proximity to other animals, including Grant's gazelles and wildebeest.

Sexual maturity is reached at around one year but males only mate after establishing their own territory, which occurs sometime after two years of age. Calving occurs throughout the year though tends to peak at the end of the rainy season.

Being a small animal, Tommys have many predators, including the big cats, hunting dog, hyaena and serval.

The topi is not unlike the hartebeest in appearance, but is a dark almost purplish colour and has black patches on the rear thighs, front legs and face. Its horns, which are found on both sexes, also differ in shape from the hartebeest in curving gently up, out and back. Although fairly widely distributed in East Africa, in Kenya it is only found in Masai Mara where it exists in large numbers.

A highly gregarious antelope which lives in herds numbering from 15 up to several hundred individuals, topi congregate at certain times of year in gatherings of up to 10,000 in preparation for a migration to fresh pastures. They are often found mingling with wildebeest, hartebeest and zebra.

In the mating season, bulls select a well defined patch of ground which is defended against rivals and this is where mating takes place. At this time females are free to wander from one patch to another. After mating, the herds split into single sex parties.

Topi are exclusively grazers and prefer flood plains which support lush pasture though they are capable of thriving on dry grasses which other antelopes will not eat. When water is available they drink frequently but they are also capable of surviving long periods without water so long as there is sufficient grass available.

Their main predator is the lion.

Topi

Scientific name: *Damaliscus topi*
Swahili name: *Nyamera*

Waterbuck

Full name: *Defassa (or common) waterbuck*
Scientific name: *Kobus ellipsiprymus*
Swahili name: *Kuru*

The defassa waterbuck is a fairly solid animal and is easily recognisable by its thick, shaggy, dark brown coat, and white inner thighs. They are fairly common and are easily seen in Nairobi and Nakuru national parks, and in Masai Mara. A second variety, the ringed waterbuck (also *kobus ellipsiprymnus*), so called because of the white ring around its rump, is also seen in Marsabit, Tsavo and Amboseli parks. Both varieties have white facial and throat markings.

Only the males have horns, and these curve gradually outwards then grow straight up to a length of about 75 cm. As you might expect from the name, waterbuck are good swimmers and readily enter the water to escape from predators. Their habitat is always close to water and males have marked territories by the water's edge. Females and younger males tend to wander at random through male territories. Herds are small and usually consist of cows, calves and one mature bull – the other bulls live in small groups apart from the herd.

The bulk of the waterbuck's diet is grass but it does eat some of the foliage of trees and bushes.

Sexual maturity is reached at just over one year, although a male will not become the dominant bull in the herd until around five years of age.

Waterbuck are usually only preyed on when other food is scarce. The reason being that when mature the flesh is tough and has a distinct odour. Predators such as lion, leopard and hunting dog go for the young calves and females.

Wildebeest are to the African savannah what the bison once were to the American prairies. Numbering in their millions in certain areas, particularly Masai Mara and over the border in Serengeti, they are unmistakable for their prehistoric appearance. Wildebeest are well known for their eccentric behaviour which includes loud snorting, tossing and shaking of the head, bucking, running around in circles and rolling in the dust (thought to be a reaction to the activity of the botfly larva which manage to find their way right up into their nostrils). They are heavily built with a massive head and wild mane, somewhat clumsy, and have been described as having the forequarters of an ox, the hind parts of an antelope and the tail of a horse.

Their sheer numbers, nevertheless, are testimony to their superb adaptation to the environment.

Almost entirely grazers, they are constantly on the move in search of good pasture and water, and their annual migration between the Serengeti and Masai Mara (and vice versa) has to be one of the world's most spectacular sights. Thousands lose their lives in this annual event, either drowned fording rivers or taken by crocodiles and other predators or just through sheer exhaustion. The migration north from Serengeti takes place in July and the return trip from Masai Mara in October.

They're very gregarious animals and are usually seen in large herds numbering up to tens of thousands in association with zebra, Thomson's gazelle and other herbivores.

During the mating season, groups of up to 150 females and their young are gathered together by one to three bulls which defend a defined territory against rivals even when on the move. There's apparently no hierarchy amongst the bulls and, at the end of the mating season, the breeding herds are reabsorbed into the main herds.

Although they graze in a scattered fashion without any apparent social organisation during the rainy season, they coalesce around water holes and remaining pasture in the dry season. Wildebeest prefer to drink daily and will walk up to 50 km to secure water but are capable of surviving for up to five days without it. They're also a noisy animal when grazing, constantly producing a series of snorts and low pitched grunts.

Their main predators are lion, cheetah and wild dog though hyaenas are also very partial to young calves.

Wildebeest (Gnu)

Full name:	*Bridled wildebeest*
Scientific name:	*Connochaetes taurinus*
Swahili name:	*Nyumbu*

BUFFALO

Scientific name: *Syncerus caffer*
Swahili name: *Mbogo*

The buffalo is another animal which appears in great numbers in all the major parks, with the exception of Nairobi National Park.

The massive animal is said to be the most dangerous (to humans) of all African animals and should be treated with caution, although for the most part they will stay out of your way. Females protecting young calves, and solitary rogue bulls, are the most aggressive, and having 800 kg of angry animal thundering towards you is no joke.

Both sexes have the distinctive curving horns which broaden and almost meet over the forehead, although those in the female are usually smaller. The buffalo's colour varies from dark reddish brown to black.

Buffalo are often found in herds of 100 or more and never stray too far from water, especially in the dry season. When food and water are plentiful the herds often disperse. They are territorial in that they have a home range of about 50 km outside of which they don't stray.

CARNIVORES

The carnivores are the animals which are most affected by the number of tourists to the game parks – you try to catch your dinner with half a dozen minibuses bringing up the rear. Although the temptation and excitement are great, keep your distance if animals are obviously hunting.

The civet is a medium sized omnivore around 40 cm high at the shoulder and 90 cm long (excluding the tail), with some canine features and short, partially retractile claws. Its coat of long coarse hair is basically grey but with a definite and variable pattern of black spots over most of the body, along with two black bands stretching from the ears to the lower neck and two black bands around the upper part of the hind legs. The tail is bushy at the base becoming thinner towards the tip, held out straight when the animal is on the move, and black except for three to four greyish bands near the base. The head is mostly greyish white and the ears are quite small, rounded and tipped with white hairs.

Civets are solitary, nocturnal animals which hide in thickets, tall grass or abandoned burrows during the day and so are rarely sighted. The most likely places to spot one are in Marsabit or Tsavo West reserves, although they are also known to inhabit Nairobi, Amboseli and the Masai Mara.

It has a very varied diet consisting of rodents, birds and their eggs, reptiles, amphibians, snails, insects (especially ants and termites) as well as berries, the young shoots of bushes and fruits.

Litters consist of up to four cubs and these have a similar colouring to the adults only slightly darker.

The other conspicuous feature of the civet is the presence of musk glands in the anal region which produce a foul smelling oily substance used to mark territory. This musk is used in the manufacture of perfumes though in Western countries it is collected from animals held in captivity.

Civet

Scientific name: *Viverra civetta*
Swahili name: *Fungo*

Cheetah

Scientific name: *Acinonyx jubatus*
Swahili name: *Duma*

The cheetah is one of the most impressive animals you can hope to come across – sleek, streamlined and menacing. They are found in small numbers in all the major game reserves – Nairobi, Amboseli, Masai Mara, Tsavo, Samburu, Buffalo Springs, Marsabit and Meru.

Similar in appearance to the leopard, the cheetah is longer and lighter in the body, has a slightly bowed back and a much smaller and rounder face. It stands around 80 cm at the shoulder, measures around 210 cm in length (including the tail) and weighs anything from 40 kg to 60 kg.

When undisturbed the cheetah hunt in early morning or late evening, although these days with the number of tourist vehicles around, they are often found hunting at midday when the rubbernecks are back in the lodges stuffing their faces and the poor animal has a chance of stalking some dinner undisturbed. This forced change in habit is particularly stressful for the cheetah as it relies on bursts of tremendous speed for catching its prey, and this speed (up to 110 km/h) is only sustainable for a very short time. Obviously as the midday heat is much greater than morning or afternoon, hunting for the cheetah becomes much more difficult. During a hunt the cheetah stalks its prey as close as possible and then sprints for 100 metres or so; if by that time it hasn't caught its victim, it will give up and try elsewhere. The prey (usually small antelope) is brought to the ground often with a flick of the paw to trip it up. Other food includes hares, jackals and young wart hogs.

Cheetah cubs reach maturity at around one year but stay with the mother much longer than that as they have to learn hunting and survival skills. Cubs are usually born in litters numbering from two to four, and the main breeding period is from March to December.

The cheetah rarely fights but predators (mainly of cubs) include lion, leopard and hyaena.

Unlike the civet, the genet distinctly resembles the domestic cat though the body is considerably more elongated and the tail longer and bushier. The coat is long and coarse with a prominent crest along the spine. The basic colour varies from grey to fawn and is patterned from the neck to the tail with roundish dark brown to blackish spots. The tail is banded with nine to 10 similarly coloured rings and has a whitish tip.

The genet lives in savannah and open country and is a very agile tree climber but not frequently sighted since it is entirely nocturnal. During the day it sleeps in abandoned burrows, rock crevices, hollow trees or up on high branches and seems to return to the same spot each day. The animals live singly or in pairs.

Its prey is generally hunted on the ground though it will climb trees to seek out nesting birds and their eggs. Like the domestic cat, it stalks prey by crouching flat on the ground. Its diet consists of a variety of small animals (mostly rodents), birds, reptiles (including snakes), insects and fruits. It is well known for being a wasteful killer, often eating only a small part of the animals which it catches.

Litters typically consist of two to three kittens.

Like the domestic cat, the genet spits and growls when angered or in danger.

Genet

Scientific name: *Genetta genetta*
Swahili name: *Kanu*

The hunting dog is the size of a large domestic dog and is of a medium build. It is found in Kenya anywhere where there is a high concentration of game animals, and so is seen in all the reserves.

The dog's unusual coloration makes it quite an ugly creature – the black and yellowish splotches are different in each animal, ranging from almost all black to almost all yellow. The only constant is the white tail tip. Prominent physical features are the large rounded ears.

Hunting dogs tend to move in packs ranging from four or five up to as many as 40. They are efficient hunters and work well together. Once the prey has been singled out and the chase is on, a couple of dogs will chase hard while the rest pace themselves; once the first two tire another two step in and so on until the quarry is exhausted. Favoured animals for lunch include gazelle, impala and other similar sized antelope. They rarely scavenge, preferring to kill their own.

Hunting dog cubs are usually born in grass lined burrows in litters averaging seven, although litters of up to 15 are not unheard of. By six months they are competent hunters and have abandoned the burrow.

The hunting dog has no predators, although unguarded cubs sometimes fall prey to hyaenas and eagles.

Hunting Dog

Scientific name: *Lycaon pictus*
Swahili name: *Mbwa mwitu*

Hyaena

Scientific name: *Crocuta crocuta*
Swahili name: *Fisi*

The spotted hyaena is a fairly common animal throughout most of Kenya and especially where game is plentiful. Bearing a distinct resemblance to dogs, it is a large, powerfully built animal with a very sloping back, broad head and large eyes but with rather weak hindquarters. The sloping back is what gives the animal its characteristic loping gait when running. Its coat is short, dull grey to buff and entirely patterned with rounded blackish spots except on the throat. Its powerful jaws and teeth enable it to crush and swallow the bones of most animals except the elephant.

Hyaenas are mainly nocturnal animals but are frequently seen during the day, especially in the vicinity of lion or cheetah kills impatiently waiting for their turn at the carcass along with vultures. Otherwise, the days are spent in long grass, abandoned aardvark holes or in large burrows which they dig out up to a metre below the surface of the soil. It's a very noisy animal and when camping out in the bush at night you'll frequently hear its characteristic and spine chilling howl which rises quickly to a high-pitched scream. This is only one of the sounds which the spotted hyaena emits. Another is the well known 'laugh', though this is generally only produced when the animal finds food or is mating.

The hyaena has highly developed senses of smell, sight and sound, all important in locating food (carrion or prey) and for mutual recognition among pack members and mating pairs.

Hyaenas are well known as scavengers and can often be seen following hunting lions and wild dogs, usually at a respectable distance, though they will occasionally force these animals to abandon their kill. On the other hand, although carrion does form an important part of their diet, hyaenas are also true predators and are more than capable of bringing down many of the larger herbivores. To do this they often form packs to run down wildebeest, zebra and gazelle, and are able to reach speeds of up to 60 km/h. They also stalk pregnant antelope and, when the female gives birth, snatch and kill the newly born foal and occasionally the mother too. Domestic stock are also preyed on.

In the mating season, hyaenas assemble in large numbers especially on moonlit nights. All hell breaks loose on these occasions and the noise is incredible. The gestation period is about 110 days and litters number up to four though usually less. The young are born in the mother's burrow. The pups are weaned at around six weeks old and become independent shortly afterwards.

The hyaena's main enemy is man, though lions and wild dogs will occasionally kill or mutilate them if they get too close to a kill. Although they are reputed to be cowardly, you're advised to keep your distance from them as they do occasionally attack humans sleeping in the open.

The black-backed jackal is a common sight in the major reserves. The black back which gives it its name is usually more silvery than black, is wide at the neck and tapers to the tail. Although the jackal is in fact a dog, the appearance is more that of a fox with its very bushy tail and long ears.

The jackal is for the most part a scavenger and so is commonly seen in the vicinity of a kill. If food is not forthcoming from that direction the jackal will hunt for itself – insects, small mammals and birds, even the occasional small antelope. They are also found on the outskirts of human settlements and will attack sheep, poultry and young calves or foals.

Jackals are territorial and a pair will guard an area of around 250 hectares. Cubs are born in litters of five to seven and, although they don't reach maturity until almost a year old, they usually leave the parents when just two months old.

Enemies of the black-backed jackal include the leopard, cheetah and eagles.

Jackal

Full name:	Black-backed jackal
Scientific name:	Canis mesomelas
Swahili name:	Bweha

The leopard is perhaps the most graceful and agile of the large cats. A powerfully built animal which uses cunning to catch its prey, it is present in all the major game reserves but is difficult to find as it is nocturnal and spends the day resting on branches of trees, often up to five metres above the ground. It is as agile as a domestic cat in climbing such trees and this is also where it carries its prey so that it's out of the way of other scavengers which might contest the kill.

The leopard's coat is usually short and dense with numerous black spots on a yellowish background, though some are black all over. The underparts are white and less densely spotted. In addition, the coats of leopards found in open country are generally lighter than those in wooded country.

Leopards are solitary animals except during the mating season when the male and female live together. The gestation period is three months and a litter usually consists of up to three cubs.

They prey on a variety of birds, reptiles and mammals including large rodents, rock hyrax, wart hogs, smaller antelopes and monkeys (especially baboon), though they occasionally take domestic animals such as goats, sheep, poultry and dogs. This wide range of prey explains why they are still able to survive even in areas of dense human settlement long after other large predators have disappeared. But their presence is generally unwelcome since they do occasionally turn human-eater. It also explains why they are found in very varied habitats ranging from semi-desert to dense forest and as high as the snow line on Mts Kenya and Kilimanjaro.

Leopard

Scientific name:	Panthera pardus
Swahili name:	Chui

Lion

Scientific name: *Panthera leo*
Swahili name: *Simba*

Lions are one of the main attractions of the game reserves and are found in all the main ones. They spend most of the day lying under bushes or in other attractive places and when you see a pride stretched out in the sun like this, they seem incredibly docile. It is possible to drive up very close to them in a vehicle – they either don't sense humans or realise that humans in vehicles are not a threat. Whatever the case, don't be tempted to get out of a vehicle at any time in the vicinity of a lion. Loud noises and sudden movement also disturb them. They're at their most active for around four hours in the late afternoon, then spend the rest of the time laying around.

Lions generally hunt in groups, with the males driving the prey towards the concealed females who do most of the actual killing. Although they cooperate well together, lions are not the most efficient hunters – as many as four out of five attacks will be unsuccessful. Their reputation as human-eaters is largely undeserved as in most circumstances they will flee on seeing a human. However, once they have the taste for human flesh, and realise how easy it is to make a meal of one, lions can become habitual killers of people. This mostly occurs among the old lions which no longer have the agility to bring down more fleet-footed animals.

Lions are territorial beasts and a pride of one to three males and accompanying females (up to 15) and young will defend an area of anything from 20 to 400 square km, depending on the type of country and the amount of game food available.

Lion cubs are born in litters averaging two or three. They become sexually mature by 1½ years and males are driven from the family group shortly after this. Lions reach full maturity at around six years of age. Unguarded cubs are preyed on by hyaenas, leopards, pythons and hunting dogs.

The banded mongoose (the one most commonly found in Kenya) is usually seen in groups in Tsavo, Amboseli and Masai Mara reserves. They are brown or grey in colour and are easily identifiable by the dark bands across the back which stretch from the shoulder to the tail. The animal is about 40 cm in length and weighs between 1.3 kg to 2.3 kg.

Mongoose are very sociable animals and live in packs of between 30 and 50 individuals which stay close to one another when foraging for prey. They are often very noisy, having a wide variety of sounds which they use to communicate with each other. When threatened they growl and spit in much the same manner as a domestic cat.

Being diurnal animals, they prefer sunny spots during the day but retire to warrens – rock crevices, hollow trees and abandoned anthills – at night. A pack frequently has several warrens within its territory.

The mongoose's most important source of food are insects, grubs and larvae but they also eat small amphibians, reptiles, birds' eggs, fruits, berries and birds. Their main predators are birds of prey though they are also taken by lion, leopard and wild dog. Snakes rarely pose a danger since these would-be predators are attacked by the entire pack and the snake is frequently killed.

Mongoose are one of the creatures which have become very habituated to humans in some places and come right up to the game lodges scavenging for scraps.

Mongoose

Full name:	*Banded mongoose*
Scientific name:	*Mungos mungo*
Swahili name:	*Kicheche*

The serval is a wild cat, about the size of a domestic cat but with much longer legs. It is found in all the major game reserves in Kenya.

The serval's colouring is a dirty yellow with large black spots which follow lines along the length of the body. Other prominent features are the large upright ears, the long neck and the relatively short tail. It stands about 50 cm high and measures 130 cm including the tail. Being a largely nocturnal animal, the serval is usually only seen in the early morning or late evening. It lives on birds, hares and rodents and is an adept hunter – it catches birds in mid-flight by leaping into the air.

Serval cat young are born in litters of up to four and although independent at one year, don't reach sexual maturity until two years of age.

Serval

Scientific name:	*Lepitailurus serval*
Swahili name:	*Mondo*

Scientific name: *Loxodonta africana*
Swahili names: *Ndovu, tembo*

ELEPHANT

Everyone knows what an elephant looks like so a description of them is unnecessary except perhaps to mention that African elephants are much larger than their Asian counterparts and that their ears are wider and flatter. A fully grown bull can weigh up to 6½ tons and sometimes more. In Kenya they are found in all the major game parks with the exception of Nairobi National Park where they would be too destructive to the environment to make their long term presence viable. They have been encountered as high as 3600 metres on the slopes of Mt Kenya.

The tusks on an old bull can weigh as much as 50 kg each, although 15 kg to 25 kg is more usual. The longest tusks ever found on an elephant in Kenya measured 3½ metres! Both the males and females grow tusks, although in the female they are usually smaller. An elephant's sense of sight is only poorly developed but its scent and hearing are excellent.

Elephants are gregarious animals and usually found in herds of between 10 and 20 individuals consisting of one mature bull, a couple of younger bulls, cows and calves, though herds of up to 50 individuals are sometimes encountered. Old bulls appear to lose the herding instinct and often lead a solitary existence, only rejoining the herd for mating. Herds are often very noisy since elephants communicate with each other by a variety of sounds, the most usual ones being various rumbles produced through the trunk or mouth. The most well known elephant sound, however, is the high-pitched trumpeting which they produce when frightened or in despair and when charging.

Herds are on the move night and day in order to secure sufficient water and fodder, both of which they consume in vast quantities – the average daily food intake of an adult is in the region of 250 kg. They are both grazers and browsers and feed on a wide variety of vegetable matter including grasses, leaves, twigs, bark, roots and fruits and they frequently break quite large trees in order to get at the leaves. Because of this destructive capacity, they can be a serious threat to a fragile environment especially in drought years and are quite capable of turning dense woodland into open grassland over a relatively short period of time. Because of Africa's rapidly increasing human population and the expansion of cultivated land, they also come into conflict with farmers when they destroy crops such as bananas, maize and sugar cane.

The other essential part of an elephant's diet are various mineral salts which they obtain from 'salt licks'. These are dug out of the earth with the aid of their tusks and swallowed in considerable quantities.

Elephants breed year-round and the period of gestation is 22 to 24 months. Expectant mothers leave the herd along with one or two other females and select a secluded spot where birth occurs. They rejoin the herd a few days later. Calves weigh around 130 kg at birth and stand just under a metre high. They're very playful and guarded carefully and fondly by their mothers until weaned at two years old. After that, they continue to grow for a further 23 years or so, reaching puberty at around 10 to 12 years. An elephant's life span is normally 60 to 70 years though some individuals reach the ripe old age of 100 and even longer.

GIRAFFE
The Masai giraffe is the more widespread of the two varieties found in Kenya. It is found in all the parks south and west of Nairobi.

The main distinguishing feature of the Masai giraffe is its irregular, often star shaped, spots, compared with the more regular design of the reticulated giraffe. The average male stands around 5½ metres; females are mere midgets at 4½ metres. Horns are found in both sexes although these are merely short projections of bone which are covered by skin and hair. These are all that's left of what would once have been antlers. Despite the fact that the giraffe has such a huge neck, it still has only seven vertebrae – the same number as humans.

Giraffes graze mainly on acacia tree foliage in the early morning and afternoon; the rest of the time they rest in the shade. At night they also rest for a couple of hours, either standing or lying down.

The reticulated giraffe differs from the Masai giraffe in both colouring and pattern. It is a deeper brown and its body has a much more intricate 'tortoiseshell' pattern. It is found in the north and north-east of the country – Meru, Marsabit and Samburu reserves. You can easily come across them at the side of the road between Isiolo and Marsabit but probably the biggest herds are to be seen in Samburu and Buffalo Springs reserves.

Masai Giraffe
Scientific name: *Giraffa camelopardalis*
Swahili name: *Twiga*

Reticulated Giraffe
Scientific name: *Giraffa reticulata*
Swahili name: *Twiga*

Scientific name: *Hippopotamus*
                   amphibius
Swahili name: *Kiboko*

HIPPOPOTAMUS

In Kenya the hippo is found in greatest numbers in Masai Mara but can also be observed at Amboseli, Nairobi and Tsavo national parks and at Lake Baringo. At Tsavo there is a submarine viewing tank but the hippos are not very cooperative and seem to have deserted the immediate area.

Hippos are too well known to need description except to note that these huge, fat animals with enormous heads and short legs vary between 1350 kg and 2600 kg when fully grown. Their ears, eyes and nostrils are so placed that they remain above water when the animal is submerged.

Hippos generally spend most of the day wallowing in shallow water, coming out to graze only at night. They are entirely herbivorous and feed on a variety of grasses in pastures up to several km away from their aquatic haunts. They are voracious feeders and can consume up to 60 kg of vegetable matter each night. They urinate and defecate in well defined areas – often in the water in which case they disperse the excreta with their tails.

Hippos are very gregarious animals and live in schools of 15 to 30 individuals though, in certain places, the schools can be much larger. Each school consists about equally of bulls and cows (with their calves) and, like other herd animals, there's an established hierarchy. Hippos may appear to be placid but they fight frequently among themselves for dominance and this is especially so among the males. The wounds inflicted in such fights are often quite horrific and virtually every hippo you see will bear the scars of such conflicts. They're not normally dangerous to humans unless cornered or frightened but you should definitely keep your distance. They may look sluggish but they are capable of running at considerable speed.

Hippos breed all year and the period of gestation is around 230 days. The cows give birth to a single calf either in the water or on land and suckle it for a period of four to six months after which it begins to graze on a regular basis. Sexual maturity is reached at about four years old and the life span is about 30 years (longer in captivity).

The only natural predators of hippos are lion and crocodile which prey on the young. Though hippos occasionally foul up fishing nets, they're considered to be beneficial since their wallowing stirs up the bottom mud and their excreta is a valuable fertiliser which encourages the growth of aquatic organisms.

PRIMATES

The yellow baboon is just one of at least seven subspecies of baboon and is the one most commonly sighted in Kenya. The other relatively common one is the olive baboon *(papio anubis)*, most often seen in Nairobi National Park. The main difference between the two is that the olive baboon has long facial hair and a mane on the shoulders, especially the males.

The baboons have a doglike snout which gives them a much more aggressive appearance than most other primates, which generally have much more humanlike facial features. They are usually found in large troops (of up to 150 animals, with a dominant male) which will have a territorial area ranging from two to 30 square km. They spend most of the time on the ground searching for insects, spiders and birds' eggs. The baboons have also found that the lodges in the game parks are easy pickings, especially when idiotic tourists throw food to them so they can get a good snap with the Instamatic.

Baboons are fierce fighters and their only real natural enemy is the leopard, although young cubs are also taken by lions and hunting dogs.

Baboon

Scientific name: *Papio cynocephalus*
Swahili name: *Nyani*

Looking more like an Australian possum, the bushbaby is in fact a small monkey and is about the size of a rabbit. It is found in all major reserves, although being a nocturnal creature it is rarely sighted by day. The head is small with large rounded ears and, as might be expected on a nocturnal animal, relatively large eyes. The thick fur is a dark brown and the bushbaby sports a thick bushy tail. Your average bushbaby measures around 80 cm in length, of which the tail is around 45 cm, and weighs less than two kg.

The lesser bushbaby *(galago senegalensis)* is about half the size of the greater bushbaby. It is a very light grey in colour and has yellowish colouring on the legs.

Bushbaby

Full name: *Thick-tailed galago*
Scientific name: *Galago crassicaudatus*
Swahili name: *Komba*

Eastern Black & White Colobus

Scientific name: *Colobus guereza caudatus*

Swahili name: *Mbega*

This forest dwelling colobus monkey is a handsome creature found only in the forest parks – Mt Kenya, Mt Elgon, Aberdare and Saiwa Swamp.

The monkey is basically black but has a white face, bushy white tail and a white 'cape' around the back which flows out behind when the monkey moves through the trees – an impressive sight. An average colobus measures about 140 cm, of which about 80 cm is tail, and weighs from 10 kg to 23 kg.

The black and white colobus spends most of its time in the forest canopy and is easily missed unless you keep a sharp eye out. It is unusual for them to leave the trees; they get most of their water from small puddles formed in the hollows of branches and trunks.

Colobus monkeys are usually found in troops of up to 12 animals, consisting of a dominant male, females and young. Newborn monkeys are initially white, gaining their adult coat at around six months.

Vervet Monkey

Scientific name: *Cercopithecus aethiops*

Swahili name: *Tumbili*

The playful vervet monkey is the most common monkey in Kenya and is seen in parks and reserves throughout the country. It is easily recognisable with its black face fringed by white hair, and yellowish-grey hair elsewhere except for the underparts which are whitish. The males have an extraordinary bright blue scrotum.

The vervet are usually found in groups of up to 30 and are extremely cheeky and inquisitive – as you may well find if camping in the game reserves; they are often very habituated to humans and will come right inside tents or minibuses in search of a handout. Normally they live in woodland and savannahs but never in rainforests or semidesert.

RHINOCEROS

One of Africa's most sought-after species by the poachers, the numbers of black rhino in Kenya has fallen dramatically in the past, although they are now once again on the increase, thanks to some determined conservation efforts. They are now thought to number around 500, compared with around 20,000 in 1970!

Rhinos are one of the more difficult animals to sight, simply because of their lack of numbers. They are seen in Amboseli quite often, and also in Masai Mara, Tsavo East (rarely), Nairobi National Park and Nakuru. Rhinos usually feed in the very early morning or late afternoon; at other times they tend to keep out of sight.

The eyesight of the rhino is extremely poor and it relies more on its keen senses of smell and hearing. Usually when alarmed they will flee from perceived danger, but if they decide to charge they need to be given a wide berth, although with their poor eyesight chances are they'll miss their target anyway. They have been known to charge trains and even the carcasses of dead elephants!

A rhino's territory depends on the type of country and the availability of food, and so can be as little as a couple of hectares or as much as 50 square km. The diet consists mainly of leaves, shoots and buds of a large variety of bushes and trees.

Rhinos reach sexual maturity by five years but females do not usually become pregnant for the first time until around seven years of age. Calves weigh around 40 kg at birth and by three months of age weigh around 140 kg. Adult animals weigh in at anything from 1000 kg to 1600 kg! They are solitary animals, only coming together for some days during mating. Calves stay with the mother for anything up to three years, although suckling generally stops after the first year.

Scientific name: *Diceros bicornis bicornis*
Swahili name: *Kifaru*

Scientific names: *Heterohyrax brucei*
                   Procavia capensis
Swahili name: *Pimbi*

HYRAX or DASSIE

The species of hyrax you're most likely to encounter (especially on Baboon Cliffs in Lake Nakuru National Park but also in Nairobi, Tsavo, Masai Mara and Marsabit reserves) is the Rock Hyrax *(Procavia capensis)*. It's a small but robust animal about the size of a large rabbit with a short and pointed snout, large ears and thick fur. The tail is either absent or reduced to a stump.

They're an extremely sociable animal and live in colonies of up to 60 individuals, usually in rocky, scrub-covered locations. A diurnal animal, they feed mostly in the morning and evening on grass, bulbs and roots, and on such insects as grasshoppers and locusts. During the rest of the day they can frequently be seen sunning themselves on rocks and chasing each other in play. Where habituated to humans, they are often quite tame but in other places, when alarmed, they dash into rock crevices uttering shrill screams. Their senses of hearing and sight are excellent.

Hyrax breed all year and the period of gestation is about seven months – a remarkably long period for animal of this size. Up to six young are born at a time and the young are cared for by the whole colony. Predators include leopard, wild dog, eagles, mongoose and python.

Despite being such a small creature, hyrax are more closely related to the elephant than any other living creature by virtue of certain common physical traits.

Scientific name: *Phacochoerus*
                  aethopicus
Swahili name: *Ngiri*

WART HOG

Although there are a number of wild pigs extant in Kenya, the one you're most likely to see is the wart hog. It is found in all the major parks – Amboseli, Masai Mara, Nairobi, Tsavo, Meru, Marsabit and Samburu.

The wart hog gets its name from the somewhat grotesque wartlike growths which grow on its face. They are usually found in family groups of a boar, a sow and three or four young. Their most (or perhaps only) endearing habit is the way they turn tail and trot away with their thin tufted tails stuck straight up in the air like some antenna.

The males are usually bigger than the females, measuring up to one metre and weighing as much as 100 kg. They grow upper and lower tusks; the upper ones curve outwards and upwards and grow as long as 60 cm; the lower ones are usually less than 15 cm.

Wart hogs live mainly on grass, but also eat fruit and bark, and, in hard times, will burrow with the snout for roots and bulbs. They rest and give birth in abandoned burrows or sometimes excavate a cavity in abandoned termite mounds. The young are born in litters of up to eight, although two to four is far more usual.

ZEBRA

Zebras are one of the most common animals in the Kenyan parks and are widely distributed. You'll find them in great numbers in Nairobi, Tsavo, Amboseli, Samburu, Buffalo Springs, Maralal and Marsabit reserves as well as Masai Mara where they are present in the thousands.

Zebras often intermingle with other animals, most commonly the wildebeest but also with topi and hartebeest.

There are two species to be seen in Kenya, the most common being Burchell's Zebra which is found in all the western and southern parks all the way up to Samburu and Maralal. In the more arid north-west and north-east, however, the most common species is the Grevy's Zebra which differs from Burchell's in having much narrower and more numerous stripes, prominent, broad, rounded ears, and a pure white underbelly.

Some taxonomists classify Burchell's zebra into various 'races' or subspecies but this is a contentious issue since it is impossible to find two zebras exactly alike even in the same herd. What is more certain is that although Burchell's and Grevy's zebra often form mixed herds over much of their range, they do not interbreed in the wild.

Zebras are grazers but will occasionally browse on leaves and scrub. They need water daily and rarely wander far from a water hole though they appear to have considerably more resistance to drought than antelope.

Reproductive rituals take the form of fierce fights between rival stallions for control of a group of mares. The gestation period is about 12 months and one foal is born at a time.

The most usual predator is the lion though hyaenas and wild dogs occasionally take them too.

Scientific name: *Equus burchelli*
                   Equus grevyi
Swahili name: *Punda milia*

Flamingo

Scientific name: *Phoeniconaias minor*
Phoenicopterus ruber

Swahili name: *Heroe*

BIRDS

Flamingos are found by the million in Kenya. They are attracted by the proliferation of algae and crustaceans which thrive in the soda lakes of Baringo, Bogoria, Nakuru and Magadi in the Rift Valley, and Lake Natron across the border in Tanzania.

There are always some birds at each lake but large concentrations seem to move capriciously from one to another over a period of years. Lake Nakuru is the current hot spot but this may well change. It is thought that the changing water levels may be one reason why they change locations. Whatever lake they are presently at, the best time of the year for flamingo viewing is in January-February when they form huge pink masses around the shores of the lakes.

Flamingos have a complicated and sophisticated system for filtering the foodstuffs out of the water. This is because the highly alkane water would be toxic if consumed in large quantities. The deep-pink lesser flamingo, *Phoeniconaias minor*, filters algae and diatoms out of the water by vigorous suction and expulsion of the water in and out of its beak several times per second. The minute particles are caught on fine hairlike protrusions which line the inside of the mandibles. This is all done with the bill upside down in the water. The suction is created by the movement of the thick and fleshy tongue which lies in a groove in the lower mandible and works to and fro like a piston. Where the *Phoeniconaias minor* obtains its food largely by sweeping its head to and fro and filtering the water, the greater flamingo, or *Phoenicopterus ruber*, is more a bottom feeder and supplements its algae diet with small molluscs, crustaceans and other organic particles from the mud. It has been estimated that one million lesser flamingos consume over 180 tons of algae and diatoms daily!

The very distinct and instantly identifiable ostrich is the largest living bird. It is widely distributed throughout the savannah plains of Kenya, and so is most widely seen in the southern parks and reserves – Masai Mara, Amboseli and Tsavo.

The adult ostrich stands around 2½ metres high and weighs as much as 150 kg. The neck and the legs are bare, and all these areas of bare skin turn bright red in breeding males. The bushy plumage on the males is dark black, with white feathers in the redundant wings and the tail. The females are a uniform greyish brown and are slightly smaller and lighter than the males. The ostrich's long and strong legs can push it along at up to 50 km/h.

Ostriches tend to be territorial and are rarely seen in groups of more than six individuals. They feed on leaves, flowers and seeds of a variety of plants. When feeding, the food is gradually accumulated in the top of the neck and then passes down to the stomach in small boluses, and it's possible to see these masses of food actually moving down the neck.

The ostrich breeds in the dry season, and the males put on quite an impressive courtship display. Having driven off any possible rival males, the male trots up to the female with tail erect, then squats down and rocks from side to side, simultaneously waving each wing in the air alternately. Just for good measure the neck also waves from side to side. The males may couple with more than one female, in which case the eggs of all the females (up to five) are laid on the same nest, and so it may contain as many as 30 eggs. The eggs are incubated by the major female (the one first mated with) by day, and by the male at night. The other female birds have nothing further to do with the eggs or offspring.

Ostrich

Scientific name: *Struthio camelus*
Swahili name: *Mbuni*

Vulture

Scientific names: *Neophron*
pernopterus
Neophron
monachus
Trigonoceps
occipitalis

Vultures are a large, eaglelike bird belonging to the Accipitridae family, of which hawks and eagles are also members. There are a whole range of different species, the most common ones in Kenya being the Egyptian *(Neophron percnopterus)*, Hooded *(Neophron monachus)* and the White-headed Vulture *(Trigonoceps occipitalis)*. They all prefer savannah country with high concentrations of game and so, like the ostrich, are mainly found in the southern parks and reserves of Amboseli, Masai Mara and Tsavo.

These large birds, with a wing span of up to three metres and weighing up to five kg, feed almost exclusively by scavenging. They are fairly inefficient fliers and so rely to a large degree on finding rising hot-air thermals on which to glide and ascend. For this reason you won't see them in the air until well into the morning when the upcurrents have started.

Vultures have no sense of smell and so depend totally on their excellent eyesight, and that of their colleagues, for locating food. Once a kill or a fallen animal has been sighted a vulture will descend rapidly and await its turn at the carcass. Of course other vultures will follow the first downwards and in this chain reaction they may come from as far afield as 50 km. They are very efficient feeders and can rapidly strip flesh from bone, although they are not good at getting a start on a completely intact carcass. A large group of vultures (and they congregate in groups, often of up to 100) can strip an antelope to the bone in half an hour. Because they are poor fliers, however, vultures often cannot fly with a belly full of food and so after gorging will retreat a short distance and digest their meal.